INSTRUCTIONS TO THE BRITISH MINISTERS
TO THE UNITED STATES
1791-1812

INSTRUCTIONS
TO THE BRITISH MINISTERS
TO THE UNITED STATES
1791-1812

Edited by Bernard Mayo

DA CAPO PRESS • NEW YORK • 1971

A Da Capo Press Reprint Edition

This Da Capo Press edition of *Instructions to the British Ministers to the United States, 1791-1812*, is an unabridged republication of the first edition published in Washington, D.C., in 1941 as Volume III of the *Annual Report of the American Historical Association for the Year 1936*.

Library of Congress Catalog Card Number 70-75280

SBN 306-71303-9

Published by Da Capo Press, Inc.
A Subsidiary of Plenum Publishing Corporation
227 West 17th Street, New York, N.Y. 10011
All Rights Reserved

Manufactured in the United States of America

INSTRUCTIONS TO THE BRITISH MINISTERS
TO THE UNITED STATES
1791-1812

INSTRUCTIONS

TO THE BRITISH MINISTERS TO THE

UNITED STATES

1791–1812

EDITED BY

BERNARD MAYO

UNITED STATES
GOVERNMENT PRINTING OFFICE
WASHINGTON : 1941

TO THE MEMORY

OF

J. FRANKLIN JAMESON

VOLUME III OF THE ANNUAL REPORT OF THE
AMERICAN HISTORICAL ASSOCIATION
FOR THE YEAR 1936

CONTENTS

PREFACE

The late J. Franklin Jameson once compared the work of those who make historical manuscripts available in printed form to the work of earthworms. It was a flattering comparison, and intended as such, for he had in mind Darwin's little book on *The Formation of Vegetable Mould through the Action of Worms*, in which the great naturalist rehabilitated the character of these humble Annelida, whose subterranean activities have done more than spectacular lightnings or terrifying storms or boastful man to give the immediate surface of the earth its present aspect.

Dr. Jameson himself will long be honored by historians for his labors upon the raw materials of American history, for discovering and quarrying the original documents that the historian must use, and printing the most important of them with such interpretative comment as they required. During his long and fruitful life he conceived many important editorial projects, and brought most of them to completion. The present volume is a by-product of his constant efforts to meet the needs of historians and to give effective aid to the progress of history.

It had long been his hope to see in print not only the instructions to the British ministers to the United States but also their dispatches, from the appointment of the first envoy in 1791 down to as late a date as possible. In the early Nineteen-twenties, under the auspices of the Carnegie Institution of Washington, he made a start toward this ambitious objective by having Miss Ruth Fisher make transcripts at the Public Record Office of the instructions from 1791 through 1806, and of the dispatches for a slightly longer period. The Carnegie Institution, however, found it impossible to carry out the project. In 1935 these transcripts were acquired by the Manuscripts Division of the Library of Congress, of which division Dr. Jameson was then the chief. The transcripts complemented the photostats of instructions and dispatches, from 1807 on, which in the meantime had been obtained by the Library. Still hopeful of getting into print at least a part of this material, Dr. Jameson turned to the American Historical Association. At his suggestion the executive committee of the Association in 1935 recommended the publication of the instructions to the British ministers from 1791 through

1812, and at the request of Dr. Jameson I assumed the task of editing them.

For copy to prepare for the printer I used the transcripts made by Miss Fisher, most of which were in longhand, and the typescripts made for Dr. Jameson from the Library photostats. In the work of editing this material many delays were encountered. On several occasions during these depression years the usual appropriations were scaled down, and it appeared that the instructions would never see printer's ink. Frequent calls were made upon Miss Fisher at London for missing instructions, for enclosures, and for enlightening information. I was seriously disturbed by the fact that the Library's photostats were of the drafts, in Foreign Office Series 5, rather than of the instructions as received by the ministers, in Foreign Office Series 115. It is a first principle of good editing, of course, to print communications actually sent, and to use file copies only when the "originals" cannot be had. If the drafts retained by the Foreign Office were printed, there would always be uncertainty as to whether they were identical with the instructions received by the ministers; as to whether the instructions were changed, material deleted or added, a sentence softened or sharpened. After some delay, caused by financial considerations, the Library of Congress arranged to have microfilms made of the instructions from 1807 through 1812, and also, if they existed, of any in the earlier period that might have been overlooked. When these arrived, after a further delay in England caused by the threat of war, I was able to collate the drafts and the instructions.

The photofilming of the instructions has given me an opportunity to put to the test my question, one which is often asked by students of diplomatic history in cases where drafts must be relied upon: Can I feel reasonably certain that there are no important differences between a draft and an instruction? My experience has been reassuring on this point. In collating, a thousand and one stylistic differences, mostly in the matter of capitalization, were noted. A very few minor textual changes were discovered, and these are pointed out in the printed documents. But there were no changes of any importance. I have also been enabled to indicate additional material written on the margin of some of the drafts for inclusion in the instructions. These are after-thoughts, and are often revealing. Dissimilar in nature are the observations (highly interesting and quoted here in editorial notes) written on the draft of Castlereagh's instruction, No. 21, of June 25, 1812, which were clearly intended as suggestions for further study by the Foreign Office. The photofilms have further enabled me to indicate discrepancies, in several cases, in the Foreign Office's numbering of drafts and instructions.

As exactly as possible, the documents printed here follow the originals both as to content and style. Each document is printed in full, and each reproduces the original even to misspelled words. They are, for the most part, the instructions received by the ministers (F. O. 115). Drafts (F. O. 4 and F. O. 5) are printed only when the instructions could not be found. All numbered instructions, and unnumbered "Separate" instructions, are printed. Some unimportant circulars, on routine matters, have been excluded; but all communications even of this general character which have pertinence to Anglo-American relations have been included. Since some of the typescripts made for Dr. Jameson had the word "and" substituted for the ampersand, I have instructed the printer to make this substitution throughout. Any other alteration is indicated by editorial brackets and notes.

In the explanatory notes I have tried to identify all persons mentioned, to indicate whether documents referred to have been published, and in general to elucidate the text. For these notes I have drawn freely upon the unpublished dispatches of the British ministers and the archives of the State Department. In some cases I have used the dispatches rather extensively when they throw light upon hitherto obscure or misunderstood topics. In doing so I have been influenced by the fact that the American Historical Association did not find it possible to publish the dispatches along with the instructions, and sees no likelihood of publishing them separately in the immediate future. I have cited relatively few studies on the period; for bibliographical references the student, of course, will consult Samuel Flagg Bemis and Grace Gardner Griffin, *Guide to the Diplomatic History of the United States, 1775–1921.*

The work of editing this volume has measurably deepened my appreciation of the men and women who for years have been engaged in such "subterranean" activities. My own annelidan efforts, lightened to be sure by the satisfaction of discovery and the increase of knowledge usual with research, have been greatly repaid by a close association of several years with the late J. Franklin Jameson. For facilitating my work I am indebted to his successor as chief of the Manuscripts Division of the Library of Congress, St. George L. Sioussat; to Grace Gardner Griffin, in charge of the division's foreign transcripts, whose aid was invaluable; to Ruth Fisher, for her work at London; to Leo F. Stock, for helpful editorial suggestions; and, a heavy debt indeed, to Barbara Mayo.

BERNARD MAYO.

UNIVERSITY OF VIRGINIA, *September 16, 1940.*

INTRODUCTION

These instructions from the British Foreign Office to the British ministers to the United States cover the twenty-two years from 1791 to 1812, a momentous period in the history of both countries, when neutral America as well as belligerent Britain was buffeted by storms unleashed by the French Revolution. They set forth the official policy towards America of the foreign country that stood foremost among the nations in her power either to accelerate or to retard the progress of the young republic, as Jefferson, Clay, and other Americans repeatedly said. Unfortunately, the earliest period of Anglo-American diplomacy, in sharp contrast with the most recent period, was marked and marred by unfriendly relations. Diplomats labored in, and sometimes accentuated, an atmosphere of suspicions and misunderstandings and conflicting views. Common bonds between Great Britain and her former colonies were loosened rather than tightened, and both peoples traveled the road leading to what Americans called their Second War for Independence.

The value of the instructions to Britain's envoys during this period is readily apparent, and it will suffice here merely to mention some of the major subjects to which the Secretaries of State for Foreign Affairs gave their attention. The documents express the official British viewpoint, and both enlarge and illuminate the area of information. They do not, of course, give a complete account even of the British side of British-American relations. Lord Grenville's negotiations with Chief Justice Jay in 1794, for example, are barely touched upon. Even were all the papers of the foreign secretaries and ministers available, both the British and the American, a knowledge of internal politics and international relations, of the economic and psychological conditions of the period, would be required for a full understanding of Anglo-American relations. Nevertheless, the documents now made available are obviously essential to such an understanding.

The first British minister to the United States was not sent until 1791, eight years after the Treaty of Peace in which Britain recognized the independence of her former colonies, and two years after the establishment of the new general government under the Constitution. The appointment of George Hammond was hastened by a threatening movement in the American Congress to apply against British commerce drastic discriminatory legislation, in imitation of Britain's navigation system. This movement had gained ground in view of Great Britain's continued disinclination to send a minister, to negotiate a commercial treaty which would remove restrictions on American goods and ships, or to evacuate her troops from frontier posts on American soil as required by the Treaty of 1783.

Hammond was instructed by Grenville to counteract the discrimination movement and to discuss principles which might serve as the basis for a commercial treaty, but he was not empowered to conclude any definite settlement either as to the frontier posts or as to commerce. The first and leading object of his mission was the execution by the United States of the provisions in the Treaty of 1783 respecting the claims of British creditors and American Loyalists. Shortly after his arrival, Hammond's discussions with Secretary Jefferson were confined to the non-execution of the Treaty of Peace by both powers, a subject which was not adjusted until Jay's Treaty of 1794. Of especial interest in the instructions to Hammond of 1791 and 1792 is the emphasis placed upon the secret *Report* of the Privy Council on Anglo-American commerce, dated January 28, 1791, and Grenville's proposal for British mediation in the Indian war which the United States was then fighting in the Ohio Valley.

The points under discussion were augmented and intensified in 1793 with the beginning of the great war between Great Britain and France. Hammond was instructed to combat the spread of "those dangerous and delusive principles of Liberty and Equality which the French Demagogues are labouring to establish in all Countries," and to counteract the unneutral activities of the French minister and of pro-French Americans, especially the outfitting in America of French privateers. He was also to explain and to defend the British orders-in-council of 1793 and 1794 which bore so heavily upon the shipping of neutral America. His labors were eased by his friendship with Secretary of the Treasury Alexander Hamilton, a confidential relationship which did much to undermine the efforts of the first two American Secretaries of State, Jefferson and Randolph. Most reassuring to Hammond in 1794, when war seemed imminent because of the frontier crisis and the wholesale seizures of American vessels, were Hamilton's statements on the British orders-in-council and on the disinclination of the United States to enter into a revived League of Armed Neutrals. Such information coming to Grenville during his negotiations with Jay could not, as he wrote Hammond, "but be very acceptable under the present circumstances."

New light is thrown on the ratification and the execution of the important treaty negotiated by Jay. Of particular interest are the instructions respecting the secret order-in-council of April 25, 1795, under which seizures were made of American ships during the period when the treaty was before the Senate. These new seizures under a secret order which was long misunderstood, together with the continuance of impressments and other grievances, perplexed and enraged even the American proponents of the treaty. In 1796 the passage of legislation necessary for the execution of the treaty was endangered by Britain's demand for an additional article to safeguard her right to trade with the Indians of the United States, and by her refusal to give up the frontier posts until the treaty was amended by such an article. Subsequently, many of the instructions dealt with the proceedings under the several claims commissions set up by Jay's Treaty.

Relations became friendlier, though not cordial, following the Grenville-Jay negotiations and during America's quasi-war with France of 1798–1800. Robert Liston, Hammond's successor, endeavored to bring about closer cooperation but he was hampered by continued impressments and other provocative activities of British naval officers. Considering the impressment evil the greatest obstacle to Anglo-American harmony, Liston suggested, and was authorized to negotiate, an additional article to Jay's Treaty enjoining the reciprocal restitution of deserters. His efforts were unavailing because of the nature of his instructions and the American repugnance to the principle of non-transferable allegiance. Especially interesting during this period are the instructions bearing on a possible concert of measures directed against France, the question of British convoys for American merchantmen, the British plan to exchange British warships for American seamen, and schemes for the conquest of Louisiana and Florida by the United States and of Santo Domingo by Great Britain. Liston countenanced the Blount conspiracy directed against the Spanish Floridas, and was most active in ferreting out Spanish and French plots directed against Canada.

These troubled waters were quieted by the Franco-American Convention of 1800 and by the Peace of Amiens. But after the brief truce in the great European war the questions of impressment and of neutral rights and duties again became paramount. In this later period Grenville's post at the Foreign Office, which he had held from 1791 to 1801, was filled by such foreign secretaries as Canning, Wellesley, and Castlereagh. The instructions reflect the negotiations at London of James Monroe and William Pinkney which led to the abortive treaty of 1806, as well as the activities of Pinkney down to his inamicable leave in 1811. Canning's instructions of 1807 to George Henry Rose, who was sent to Washington as a special envoy to adjust the *Chesapeake-Leopard* affair, are in themselves sufficient explanation why Rose's mission failed. Thereafter, to the end of the period, most of the documents bear on the warfare of British orders and French decrees, and the measures of economic coercion by which the United States endeavored to maintain neutral and national rights without resorting to war.

Of particular interest are Canning's instructions to David M. Erskine of January, 1809, setting forth proposals for an adjustment of the differences between the two countries, and his instructions of a few months later explaining his repudiation of the agreement Erskine had made with President Madison. The reader may judge for himself whether Canning's instructions to Francis James Jackson, Erskine's successor, merit the harsh evaluation made by most American historians. Canning's attitude towards America as mirrored in these documents helps to explain why Madison turned to France for a way out of the dilemma in which the United States found itself; why he accepted Napoleon's conditional revocation of the Berlin and Milan decrees, although he knew full well that it came in questionable shape and was open to serious objections; and why he revived commercial non-intercourse against Britain and pressed her to revoke her orders-in-council insofar as they affected America. The other American grievances against Great Britain were subordinated by Madison to this one issue. On this one diplomatic card he gambled for peace; a desperate gamble, yet one that all but succeeded.

During 1811 and 1812 Wellesley and Castlereagh in their instructions to Augustus J. Foster again and again explained and justified Britain's maritime policy, denied that the French decrees had been revoked, and stoutly maintained that Britain would never revoke her orders as to America until France formally and unequivocally revoked her decrees not only as to America but as to all the world. Castlereagh's instructions to Foster of April 10, 1812, are most pertinent. In them he recapitulated the British arguments and set them forth in a manner which President Madison and Secretary Monroe regarded as precluding any further discussion. On June 1, 1812, some days after these instructions became known in Washington, Madison sent to Congress his message recounting the several causes of dispute and recommending a declaration of war.

It will be noted that Castlereagh in one of his instructions of April 10, 1812, did offer a concession with respect to the notorious licensing system. Although this offer had little effect on Madison it might well be regarded as a straw in the wind. The movement in Great Britain for the revocation of the orders-in-council was making headway, and Castlereagh was soon forced to execute a sudden about-face of the uncompromising policy that Foster at Washington had stoutly maintained from his arrival in July of 1811 down to the declaration of war by the United States on June 18, 1812. Just two days before the declaration of war, on June 16, Lord Castlereagh in Parliament announced that it was the intention of the British ministry to suspend the orders-in-council. On June 23, 1812, Great Britain formally revoked the orders insofar as they affected America. The news did not reach Washington until August of 1812, and it came too late. Having reluctantly but definitely committed themselves to resistance by the sword in place of resistance by economic measures, the American government and people elected to fight on with their new weapon, to put an end to impressment and other grievances, to win if possible "reparations for the past and security for the future."

Since it is probable that war would not have been declared if Castlereagh's announcement of June 16 had been cabled that day to Washington, these events dramatically illustrate the difficulties of trans-Atlantic communication under which the diplomats of the period labored. The documents contain abundant evidence of such difficulties: sailing-ships were slow at best, and not infrequently packets conveying instructions or dispatches were captured by the French. These are but some of a multitude of subjects touched upon in these instructions. Students of the period will find many sidelights on such diverse matters as the route of packet boats, international exchange, American seafaring enterprise, British apprehension of America's pioneer manufactures and the emigration of skilled British artisans, and British resentment of the American practice of publishing current diplomatic correspondence in order to influence public opinion. The documents, for example, reveal not only the gross cruelties but the frequent frauds connected with the subject of impressment; allude to such matters as the claims of British subjects to lands in West Florida; and throw some light on the activities of such men as Joshua Barney of Baltimore and Ira Allen of Vermont, of William Augustus Bowles among the Creek Indians and John Henry among the Federalists of New England, as well as the diverting adventures of Robert Jeffery, the impressed British sailor who was marooned on a desert island for stealing his captain's spruce beer.

During the twenty-two years covered by these instructions Great Britain was represented by six ministers, one special envoy, and three chargés d'affaires. The temper of Anglo-American relations is reflected in the high mortality among the six ministers. George Hammond, who rasped Federalists as well as Republicans, was recalled by Grenville after Jay had intimated that such action would be beneficial. Anthony Merry was recalled by Charles James Fox on the bland assumption of long-continued ill health in spite of Merry's protestations that he was physically and mentally fit for the post; the real reason seems to have been the countenance Merry had given to the disunionist schemes of Aaron Burr. David Montague Erskine in his eagerness to restore amicable relations went beyond his instructions, and Canning recalled him in disgrace. Francis James Jackson managed very quickly to make himself *persona non grata* at Washington. Augustus John Foster was given his passports upon the declaration of war.

Alone of the six ministers, Robert Liston took his leave of the United States voluntarily, and alone of the ministers his conduct was the subject of a complimentary notice by the State Department. Liston was a man of good will, though not the only one. He was fortunate in representing Great Britain at a time when Jay's Treaty had paved the way for friendlier relations. Yet at the same time he possessed a sympathetic understanding of the new republic and its problems which was rare among British diplomats of his day. The leaders of America "are certainly in earnest in wishing to be well with us, and it appears to me *possible* to arrange our differences," he wrote Grenville, in a private letter of May 7, 1800 (F. O. 5:29), on the eve of his departure for England. On the other hand, he warned, "War must bring with it extensive damage to our navigation, the probable loss of Canada and the *world* behind it, the propagation of enmity and prejudices which it may be impossible to eradicate."

War did come in 1812, and with it came some of the evils Liston had prophesied. In time, however, it became possible for Britain's envoys to realize Liston's hope, as he expressed it, of being "well employed in the work of conciliation." In his letter to Grenville of 1800 he wrote that he had been pleasing his imagination "with looking forward to the distant spectacle of all the northern continent of America covered with friendly though not subject States, consuming our manufactures, speaking our language, proud of their parent State, attached to her prosperity." His successors ultimately were to harvest for Great Britain many of the advantages, "of infinite magnitude," which Liston envisioned as the fruits of sympathetic understanding and cordial Anglo-American relations.

INSTRUCTIONS OF 1791

George the Third by the Grace of God, King of Great Britain, France and Ireland, Defender of the Faith, Duke of Brunswick and Lunenburgh, Arch-Treasurer and Prince Elector of the Holy Roman Empire, etc. To the United States of America [2] sendeth Greeting. Our Good Friends: Having nothing more at Heart than to cultivate and improve the Friendship and good Understanding which happily subsist between Us; and having the fullest Confidence in the Fidelity, Prudence and other good Qualities of our Trusty and Wellbeloved George Hammond,[3] Esqr., We have thought proper to appoint him Our Minister Plenipotentiary [4] to reside with You, not doubting from the Experience We have had of His good Conduct on other Occasions, but that he will continue to merit Our Approbation, and at the

---

[1] Notes to the Department, British Legation, 1, archives of the Department of State (now in the National Archives).

[2] Although the Constitution (Art. II, Sec. 3) provides that it is the President who shall receive ambassadors and other public ministers, European sovereigns, as Secretary of State John Quincy Adams remarked in 1818 (John Bassett Moore, *A Digest of International Law*, IV, 462), have addressed their letters sometimes to the Congress, sometimes to the President and Congress, sometimes to the United States, and sometimes to the President and Senate.

[3] George Hammond (1763–1853), then twenty-eight years old, secretary to David Hartley during the peace negotiations at Paris in 1783, and chargé d'affaires at Vienna, 1788–1790, had in May of 1791 been recalled by Lord Grenville, Foreign Secretary *ad interim*, from Madrid, where for a short time he had been minister plenipotentiary under Lord St. Helens, the ambassador to Spain. Grenville to Hammond, May 24, 1791, and St. Helens to Grenville, June 15, 1791, Hist. MSS. Commission, *The Manuscripts of J. B. Fortescue, Esq., preserved at Dropmore* (hereafter cited as *Dropmore Papers*), II, 80, 99. At Philadelphia in May of 1793 Hammond married Margaret Allen, daughter of Andrew Allen, a Loyalist, formerly the Attorney General of the Province of Pennsylvania. Upon his return to England he became an under secretary for foreign affairs, 1795–1806, and 1807–1809. He was an intimate friend of George Canning (also an under secretary in the foreign department, 1796–1801), and with Canning contributed to the *Anti-Jacobin* magazine.

[4] Of the second diplomatic rank, and a relatively low one: Great Britain in 1792 maintained three ambassadors, ten envoys extraordinary and plenipotentiary, and three ministers plenipotentiary—to the court of the Austrian governor-general at Brussels, to the Diet at Ratisbon and the Elector Palatine, and to the United States. This was the rank arranged for the first French representative to the United States, Gérard, in 1778; the rank which his successor, Colonel Jean de Ternant, was then holding; and the rank which the first representative of the Dutch Republic, Pieter Johan van Berckel, had borne from his arrival in 1783 to his recall in 1788. Beginning with Robert Liston, in 1796, Great Britain's regular diplomatic representatives in the United States were accredited as envoys extraordinary and ministers plenipotentiary (also of the second rank) until 1893, when Sir Julian Pauncefote was accredited as ambassador.

1

same Time conciliate Your Friendship and good Will, by a strict Observance of the Instructions he has received from Us, to evince to You Our constant Friendship, and sincere Desire to cement and improve the Union and good Correspondence between Us. We therefore desire that You will give a favourable Reception to our said Minister Plenipotentiary, and that You will give entire Credence to whatever he may represent to You, in Our Name, especially when, in Obedience to Our Orders, he assures You of Our Esteem and Regard, and of Our hearty Wishes for Your Prosperity: And so We recommend You to the Protection of the Almighty. Given at Our Court of St. James's the Second Day of September 1791, in the 31st Year of Our Reign.

Your very good Friend

GRENVILLE [5]   GEORGE R.

GENERAL INSTRUCTIONS TO HAMMOND [6]

Instructions for Our Trusty and Wellbeloved George George R.[7] Hammond Esquire whom We have appointed Our Minister Plenipotentiary to Our Good Friends the United States of America. Given at Our Court at St. James's the second Day of September 1791 in the thirty first Year of Our Reign.

1. We reposing especial Trust and Confidence in your Fidelity, Prudence, Ability and Zeal for Our Service, have thought proper to appoint You to be Our Minister Plenipotentiary to Our Good Friends the United States of America.

As soon therefore as you shall have received these Our Instructions together with Our Letter of Credence to our said Good Friends, You are to repair with all convenient Speed to the City of Philadelphia, or such other Place where the Seat of that Government may be fixed, and where you are to reside; and being arrived there, You will deliver Our said Credential Letter, according to the Form established in like Cases, and You will add to the Assurances therein

---

[5] William Wyndham Grenville (1759–1834), Baron Grenville since Nov. 25, 1790, had been made Secretary of State for Foreign Affairs on June 8, 1791.

[6] Original in the possession (in 1921) of the Honorable Margaret Hammond. In that period a British minister received general or "public" instructions on his setting out, and particular or "private" instructions then and thereafter. The general instructions followed a common form, which in part at least had come down in British diplomatic practice for more than a hundred years. See James F. Chance, ed., *British Diplomatic Instructions, I, Sweden, 1689–1727*, pp. vi, vii. Those to Hammond are almost identical with the general instructions to David M. Erskine of July 22, 1806, and to Francis James Jackson of July 6, 1809, as ministers to the United States. These general instructions, which are not printed here, are in the Public Record Office, London, Foreign Office Records (hereafter cited as F. O.), Series 5, Volume 52, and Series 115, Volume 20, respectively.

[7] Signed here, and sealed with the royal arms.

given such further Declarations in Our Name, as may tend to evince Our sincere Esteem and Regard for the said United States, and our earnest Desire to cultivate the strictest Friendship and good Understanding with them.

2. In any Audience which may be granted to you for the abovementioned Purpose, or upon any other Occasion which may arise during the Course of your Mission, you will insist on being treated with the like Ceremonies and Distinctions as have been usually practised by that Government towards Ministers of an equal Rank with yourself; and you will be particularly careful that nothing shall pass with regard to your Reception that may in any Shape be derogatory to Our Royal Dignity.

3. You shall be very careful to support and maintain the Definitive Treaty of Peace concluded between Us and the said United States on the Third Day of September 1783, and to attend to the due Performance of the several Stipulations contained therein; and in case any attempt should be made to the Prejudice of the Interests of any Part of Our Dominions, contrary to the Tenor of the said Treaty, you shall immediately use your Endeavours to have the same remedied; but if you are unable to obtain all due Justice and Satisfaction, in consequence of your Representations, you shall report the whole Matter to Us through Our Principal Secretary of State for Foreign Affairs in order to receive Our further Instructions thereupon.

4. You shall protect and countenance on all occasions Our Subjects trading to any of the Dominions of the said United States or who may have any Suits or just pretensions depending there, and you shall endeavour to procure for them good and speedy Justice, and all the favour you are able: yet for Our Honour and your own Credit, you must not engage yourself in any Complaint without some justifiable cause, or legal Proofs, but only in such Cases as may deserve the Interposition of Our Name.

5. You will use your Endeavour to obtain for Our several Consuls residing in America [8] all such Privileges and Immunities as are enjoyed by the Consuls of any other European Power in that Country. And you will from time to time communicate to Our said Consuls such Information as you may judge proper for their Guidance in their several Districts, We having particularly enjoined them to pay the strictest Attention to all such Matters as you shall recommend to them for the Good of Our Service, and to transmit to you

---

[8] The consuls maintained by Great Britain in the United States at this time were: Sir John Temple (the consul-general), at New York; Thomas MacDonogh, at Boston, for New England; Phineas Bond, at Philadelphia, for the Middle States and Maryland; John Hamilton, at Norfolk, for Virginia; and George Miller, at Charleston, for the Carolinas and Georgia. F. O. 90 ("King's Letters") : 1, pp. 2–17.

regular Accounts of all material Occurrences within their respective Departments.

6. You are during your Residence in America to maintain a good and friendly Understanding with the Ministers of other Princes in Amity with Us, who may happen to be at the Place where you reside (and particularly with those of Our Good Brother the King of Prussia, and Our Good Friends the States General of the United Provinces,[9] who are ordered at their several Residences to live in the most perfect Friendship, and mutual Confidence with Our Ministers) as by this Means you may be able to penetrate the Designs of their Masters, and to discover their several Interests and particular Views, of all which Matters you will take care to send the most full and exact Accounts you can procure.

7. You will make it your business to discover any Overture that may be made, or any steps that may be taken for extending the Duration or altering the Terms of any Treaty or other Engagement now subsisting; for renewing former Alliances, or forming new Connexions between the said United States and any of the Courts of Europe, and you will from time to time transmit to Our principal Secretary of State for Foreign Affairs the most accurate Copies you can obtain of all such Treaties or other Engagements which have been lately or which may hereafter, during your Mission, be concluded between those States and any other Power.

8. You are likewise to inform yourself as far as you are able, of the Government of the said United States, and of the particulars of the Amount and State of their Revenues.

9. You are further to procure an Account of the Population of the Dominions of the said United States, and of the Extent and Nature of the Commerce and Manufactures carried on in the different Parts of them, and in so doing you are to pursue the Method pointed out in the circular Dispatch of Our Principal Secretary of State dated April 27th, 1773, of which a copy will be herewith delivered to you, written by Our Command, for the purpose of obtaining regular Accounts of the State of the Commerce of Our Subjects in Foreign Parts, and of the Increase and Decrease of the same.

10. You will in general be extremely attentive in obtaining the best Information you can of the Dispositions, Interests, and Inclinations of the President and leading Members of the Congress, and in making the strictest enquiries possible into the Disposition and political Sentiments of the Ministers of State, as well with regard to

---

[9] There was no minister of Prussia in the United States until 1817. The mention of Prussia and the United Provinces is a reflection of the triple alliance of 1788. At the time of Hammond's arrival the diplomatic corps at Philadelphia consisted of Colonel Jean de Ternant, minister plenipotentiary of France, Franco Petrus van Berckel, minister resident of the Netherlands, and José Ignacio de Viar, chargé d'affaires *ad interim* of Spain.

their pacific, as to their warlike Inclinations, their dispositions towards Foreign Princes, their Views, Abilities and Power, and the degree of Influence each has or is likely to have in that Country.

11. You will from time to time impart to Us all such Intelligence as you can procure on the Several Points prescribed to you in these Instructions, or on any other which may relate to Our Service of the Advantage of Our Kingdom, and you will address the same to Our Principal Secretary of State for Foreign Affairs.

12. At your return we shall expect from you, a Narrative in writing of what may have happened in America, during your Residence there, worthy of Our Notice, together with such Observations on the Situation and Views of that Government as your knowledge of it shall have enabled you to make.[10]

13. You shall at the Expiration of your Mission either deliver to your Successor or transmit to the Office of our aforesaid Secretary of State, the original of the Official Papers in your Custody and your Official Correspondence.

14. You shall follow such further Instructions and Directions as you shall from time to time receive from Us by Our Principal Secretary of State for Foreign Affairs, and in order to your corresponding with the greater Security with respect to such Matters as may require particular Caution and Secrecy, We have ordered Cyphers and Decyphers both French and English to be delivered to you.

G. R.

LORD HAWKESBURY'S DRAFT OF INSTRUCTIONS TO HAMMOND.[11]

[July 4, 1791—]

Mr. Hammond
Sir,

In the Instructions which accompany this Letter, you will find Directions for your Conduct in all the material points which are

---

[10] It does not appear that Hammond ever presented such a report, after his return to England in 1795. His going immediately into the Foreign Office as an under secretary would probably have made it seem superfluous, and indeed this requirement, though often repeated in the general instructions of envoys, seems not to have been complied with.

[11] Draft, F. O. 4 : 10. By an exceptional deviation from chronological order, drafts of Hammond's "private" instructions are, like those instructions themselves, placed after the credential and the "public" instructions. This present draft, by Lord Hawkesbury, dates from July 4, 1791, and was prepared, as shown by the note of the same date which accompanied it, at Grenville's request.

It was natural to invoke the aid of Charles Jenkinson (1727–1808), Baron Hawkesbury since 1786 (Earl of Liverpool after 1796), the president of the existing Board of Trade ever since its creation in 1786, and prominent in shaping the *Report* of January, 1791, on trade and commerce with the United States, described more particularly below. He had been a member of Parliament, 1761–86, Secretary of War under Lord North, 1778–82, one of the leaders among the "King's friends," and was an exceedingly useful man of business under Prime Minister William Pitt. He was the father of the second earl, Robert (1770–1828), who as Hawkesbury signed with Rufus King the Convention of 1802, and as Lord Liverpool was Prime Minister from 1812 to 1827.

likely to arise in the course of the Negociation with which His Majesty has thought fit to entrust you. If any Thing should occur to which these Instructions do not apply, and which may be proper for the Consideration of His Majesty's Servants, you will take the same *ad referendum*, and by the first packet transmit me an account of it.

I do not think it necessary to furnish you with any Arguments in support of such of the propositions contained in the said Instructions, as relate to Commerce and Navigation, as you will receive herewith a Copy of a Report made to His Majesty by the Lords of the Committee of Privy Council for Trade and Foreign plantations, on the Commerce and Navigation between His Majesty's Dominions and the Territories belonging to the United States of America; in which you will find a clear state of the principles on which these Instructions are founded, and all the arguments by which the Justice and policy of them are to be defended.[12] You will consider this Report as a Paper delivered to you in confidence, and on no account communicate it to any one else, as there are Matters in it, which are proper only for the Information of a person, to whom the management of so delicate and important a Business is confided, and ought not to be known by the persons concerned in the Government of the United States.[13] In your Conferences you will particularly avail Yourself of that part of the Report in which an account is given of the honourable conduct

---

[12] *A Report of the Lords of the Committee of the Privy Council, appointed for all Matters relating to Trade and Foreign Plantations, on The Commerce and Navigation between His Majesty's Dominions, and the Territories belonging to the United States of America. 28th January 1791.* (London. Pp. xli, 117.) This important, and rare, *Report* was reprinted in 1807, at London, in a volume put forth by the Society of Ship Owners, entitled *Collection of Interesting and Important Reports and Papers on the Navigation and Trade of Great Britain* etc. Mr. Worthington C. Ford, in 1888, finding among the Jefferson MSS an abstract of the *Report* in the handwriting of one of Secretary Jefferson's assistants, printed this abstract under the title, *Report of a Committee of the Lords of the Privy Council on the Trade of Great Britain with the United States. January, 1791.* (Washington, Department of State, 1888. Pp. 79.)

The *Report* had its genesis in the request of Grenville in December, 1789 (he was then Secretary of State for the Home Department), upon the Committee of the Privy Council for Trade to study and report on the effects on British commerce of the American tariff and tonnage acts of 1789. Grenville himself was an able member of the committee, but the *Report* seems to have been prepared mostly by Lord Hawkesbury, President of the Board of Trade. Gouverneur Morris, at that time informal agent of the United States in London, recorded under date of December 18, 1790 (*Diary and Letters*, ed. A. C. Morris, I, 370) that James Bland Burges, under secretary for the foreign department, told him "that sundry cabinet councils have been held on the treaty with America, and that a reference has been made of the affair to Lord Hawkesbury, whose report has not yet been received."

[13] Although it appears that only a few copies of the *Report* were printed, for members of the Privy Council, Consul Bond on October 8, 1791, informed Grenville that Secretary Jefferson knew of it, and that, at least, its "tendency" was "fully *understood* by the ministers of the United States." J. F. Jameson, ed., "Letters of Phineas Bond," *Annual Report of the American Historical Association for the Year 1897*, p. 492.

that has been held towards the people of the United States by the Legislature and Government of this Country in all matters that relate to Commerce and property, from the Time of the Definitive Treaty, by which these States were acknowledged to be independent; and you will occasionally allude, in proper Terms, to the very different Line of Conduct which many of the said States have pursued towards the Subjects and merchants of Great Britain during the same period, as it is described and contrasted in the same Report.[14] You may derive from this part of the Report, many Arguments in defence of the conduct of Great Britain, in retaining the posts and Forts on the Western Frontier of the United States. And that You may be fully apprized of all that has hitherto passed on this Subject, there will be delivered to You

[Mr. Burgess informed Lord H. that some papers on this Subject passed between the Duke of Leeds and Mr. Adams which Lord H. has never seen, but if they contain any Information they should be given to Mr. Hammond.] [15]

I have only to observe that as these posts are of great Service in securing the Fidelity and Attachment of the Indians, and as they afford to Great Britain the means of commanding the Navigation of the Great Lakes, and the communication of the said Lakes with the River St. Lawrence, they are certainly of great importance to the Security of Canada, and to the Interests of this Country, both in a commercial and political view.[16] It is to be wished therefore that they should remain in His Majesty's possession, if the Conduct of the United States should continue to justify this measure on the part of Great Britain; It is proper that you should be informed of the Regulations made by Lord Dorchester [17] and the Government of Canada for

---

[14] Pages 7 to 20 of the *Report*.

[15] The material enclosed in brackets was written on the margin of the draft. James Bland Burges (1752–1824), created baronet in 1795 but known as Sir James Lamb after 1821 by royal license, was under secretary for foreign affairs 1789 to 1795. The papers of which he informed Lord Hawkesbury presumably were the memorial of Nov. 30, 1785 presented by John Adams, minister plenipotentiary of the United States 1785–88, requesting the evacuation of the frontier posts, and the reply on Feb. 28, 1786, of the Duke of Leeds, Grenville's predecessor as Foreign Secretary (then known as the Marquis of Carmarthen), to the effect that the posts would be held until the debts owed British creditors were paid. *Diplomatic Correspondence of U. S., 1783–1789* (ed. 1833), IV, 453 ; V, 7–23.

[16] Jefferson in his note to Hammond of Dec. 15, 1791, *American State Papers, Foreign Relations* (hereafter cited as *A. S. P., F. R.*), I, 190, on British infractions of the treaty of 1783, pointed out that the British had extended their jurisdiction over the American country and American inhabitants in the vicinity of the posts, on the Great Lakes, the St. Lawrence, and Lake Champlain ; had excluded American citizens from navigating "even on our own side of the line of the middle of the rivers and lakes, established as a boundary between the two nations" under Article II of the treaty of peace ; and had by these proceedings "intercepted entirely" American commerce in furs with the Indian nations to the northward.

[17] Guy Carleton, Lord Dorchester (1724–1808), Governor-General of Canada, 1791–96. He had been Commander-in-chief of the British forces in North America, stationed at New York, 1782–83, and Governor of Quebec, 1775–77, 1786–91.

securing to His Majesty's Subjects the Navigation of the Lakes, for which purpose I enclose Copies.

[Here give Copies of the Ordinances made by the Government of Canada respecting the navigation of these Lakes.] [18]

I add an Extract of a Letter from the Lords of the Committee of Privy Council for Trade to me, which will explain to you the policy on which these Regulations appear to have been founded, and the Advantages likely to be derived from the Navigation of these Lakes, in the Intercourse between His Majesty's Subjects in Canada, and the Settlements which are now forming in the interior parts of the Continent of North America.

You will be careful to transmit to me an account, not only of every thing that may be said to you by the president and ministers of the United States concerning these posts, but of all that you can learn from any Quarter, of the policy and views of the Government and people of the United States in this respect, in order that His Majesty's Ministers may be thereby enabled to judge of their Intentions, and to send you such further Instructions on this Subject as Circumstances may appear to require.

PARTICULAR INSTRUCTIONS TO HAMMOND.[19]

Instructions to His Majesty's Minister sent to the United States of America.

Article 1. You are forthwith to repair, etc.

2. You are to assure the President and Ministers of the United States of America, that His Majesty is sincerely disposed to live on Terms of Good Correspondence and Friendship, with the Government and People of the said United States, and that He will be ready to enter into any proper Engagements for manifesting His intentions in that respect.

3. You will endeavour to convince those with whom You treat, that from the Time that the said United States were acknowledged by His Majesty to be independent, the Government of this Country has in all respects conformed to the First Article [20] of the Treaty signed at Paris, between His Majesty and the said United States, on the 3d Sept. 1783, by treating them in all Respects, particularly in commercial Matters, as Free, Sovereign and Independent States, in Peace and Amity with Great Britain (as will be shewn here after) and that the Government of this Country has even continued to them many of the Advantages, which they enjoyed before the late

---

[18] Material in brackets was written on the margin of the draft.
[19] Draft, F. O. 4: 10..
[20] The article acknowledging the independence of the thirteen states.

War, as British Colonies, and which no other independent State at present enjoys.

4. If the President or Ministers of the United States, should urge their Right to possess the Posts and Forts situated within the Boundaries, assigned to their Territories by the Second Article of the beforementioned Treaty (as they probably will) You are to say, that His Majesty would have restored these Posts and Forts immediately after the Ratification of the beforementioned Treaty, if the said States had complied with the Fourth and Fifth Articles of the said Treaty in favour of British Creditors; [21] And that His Majesty can never think of restoring the said Posts and Forts, until those Articles are fully complied with.

5. If the President and Ministers of the United States shall propose to open a Negociation for the Purpose of making a Commercial Treaty, You are to express His Majesty's Readiness to enter into such a Negociation, and to consent to a fair, liberal, and equitable System of Commerce and Navigation, founded on reciprocal Advantages.

6. You may at once declare as the Basis of such a Negociation, that His Majesty will consent to such Terms in Favour of the Subjects of the United States, as are granted by this Country to the most favoured independent Nation; provided the Government of the United States will stipulate on their Part, Terms as favourable as are, or shall be granted by them, to the Subjects of any other the most favoured Nation. [22]

7. You are to propose, that the Duties imposed on British Manufactures imported into the Territories of the United States, shall not at any Time be raised above what they are at present.

8. If this Concession can not be obtained, you may then propose, that the Duties on British Manufactures imported into the said Territories, shall not at any Time be raised above the Duties now payable

---

[21] In what sense and to what degree this was true is now well known. Professor A. C. McLaughlin in his paper on "The Western Posts and the British Debts," *Ann. Rpt. Amer. Hist. Assoc. 1894*, p. 417, revealed that Lord Sydney, Secretary of State for Home Affairs, in a letter of instructions to General Frederick Haldimand, Governor of Canada, dated April 8, 1784, *the day before* Great Britain ratified the definitive treaty of peace and enjoined her subjects to obey its articles, wrote as follows respecting the posts: "The seventh article stipulates that they should be evacuated with all convenient speed, but no time is fixed, and, as America has not, on her part, complied with even one article of the treaty, I think we may reconcile it in the present instance to delay the evacuation of these posts, at least until we are enabled to secure traders in the interior country and withdraw their property." McLaughlin's paper represents pioneer work in this period of Anglo-American relations, several aspects of which have been treated in detail by Professor Samuel Flagg Bemis in his *Jay's Treaty, A Study in Commerce and Diplomacy.*

[22] The proposals in this and the ensuing paragraphs of the present document follow, sometimes almost textually, recommendations made in the *Report of the Lords of the Privy Council* etc., of Jan. 28, 1791, described in note 12, p. 6, *supra*.

on the like Manufactures imported from Great Britain, into France or Holland, according to the Commercial Treaties with those Powers.

9. If, at last, you should find that this second Condition cannot be obtained, you may consent that these Duties shall in no Case, nor at any Time, be higher than those payable on the like Manufactures imported into the Territories of the United States, from the most favoured European Nation; and with respect to all other Merchandize, whether British or Foreign, imported from Great Britain into the Territories of the United States, you are in like manner to insist that the Duties payable thereon shall not be raised higher at any Time, than the Duties payable on the like Sorts of Merchandize imported from any other European Nation.

10. In all the foregoing Respects you may consent to a perfect Reciprocity on the part of Great Britain, by Stipulating, that any Merchandize the production or manufacture of the United States, imported from thence into Great Britain, shall not be subject to higher Duties than are payable on the like articles imported from the most favoured European Nation. You will see by the Papers which will be delivered to you, together with these Instructions, that there are several Articles which now pay less Duties when they are imported into this Country from the United States, than when they are imported from other Foreign Nations. These Distinctions in favour of the Commerce of the United States, have subsisted ever since the Conclusion of the definitive Treaty beforementioned. They may perhaps be continued for some Time longer, but his Majesty will by no means bind Himself to the continuance of them.

11. With respect to the Commercial Intercourse which still subsists, between the present British Colonies in North America or the British Islands in the West Indies, and the Countries belonging to the United States, you may consent, that it shall continue on the present Footing with respect to Merchandize exported and imported, and the Duties thereon, for a limited number of Years, unless you should find that any distinctions are now made in the duties payable in the said States on the produce of the said Colonies and Islands, to their Disadvantage; in which Case you are to insist that they shall be subject to no higher duties than the like Articles imported from the Colonies and Islands of other foreign Nations.

12. You will find in the Acts of the two last Sessions of Congress, that the said Congress has made a distinction in the Duties of Tonnage and on Goods imported in Foreign Ships, in which British Ships are included, to the Disadvantage of such Foreign Ships, and in favor of Ships built in the United States and which are wholly the property of Citizens thereof, or in Ships built in Foreign Countries, and on the 16th day of May 1789, wholly the property of Citizens of the United States, and so continuing till the time of

Importation;[23] And there is Reason to infer, from Papers which will be communicated to you, that some of the persons concerned in the Government of the said States, entertain an Intention of making further Distinctions in these Respects, in favor of their own Navigation, and to the Disadvantage of the Navigation of other Foreign Countries, particularly that of Great Britain;[24] On this head, you are to lay it down as a principle, that the Government of this Country will consent that British Ships, trading to the Ports of the United States, shall be there treated with respect to any Distinctions of the Nature before-mentioned, in like manner as Ships of the United States are treated in the Ports of Great Britain, But if the Government of the United States, in contradiction to this principle, shall proceed to make any further Distinctions to the Detriment of British Navigation, and shall refuse to consent to a fair and equitable Plan of Arrangement in this respect, You are to say that His Majesty will think Himself justified in pursuing such Measures as shall appear to Him to be sufficient and proper, for the Protection and Support of the Commerce and Navigation of His Subjects. You will acknowledge that the Commercial Intercourse which at present subsists, between Great Britain and the United States, is highly beneficial to both Countries; but You will observe that the United States have much more to apprehend from any Interruption of this Intercourse, than Great Britain has to apprehend from any restriction which the Government of the United States may put upon it. You will observe that the Ministers of this Country have Measures in View which will answer all the Purposes of just Retaliation, but that They would be very sorry to find Themselves reduced to the Necessity of making use of such Measures.

13. You will address Observations of this Nature and Arguments founded on them, particularly to the Members of Congress returned from the Southern States, who, from the Nature of the Commerce carried on by Them, are most connected in Interest with Great Britain.

---

[23] The Tonnage Act of July 20, 1789, amended July 20, 1790, levied six cents a ton on American vessels, thirty cents a ton on vessels built in the United States but owned in part by foreign subjects, and fifty cents a ton on all other foreign ships. The Tariff Act of July 4, 1789, amended Aug. 10, 1790, allowed a discount of ten per cent in imposts on all goods imported in American ships. *U. S. Statutes at Large*, I, 24, 27, 135, 180.

[24] In the debates on the tariff and tonnage acts of 1789 and 1790 Representative James Madison had advocated higher duties against Great Britain under guise of discriminating between nations having treaties with the United States and those not in "commercial alliance." With Britain's continued disinclination to negotiate a commercial treaty, open up her West Indian islands to American shippers, evacuate the frontier posts, and send a minister, the movement to discriminate against British goods and ships had gained ground. In February of 1791 a bill modeled after the British Navigation Laws, and threatening Britain's carrying trade to America, reached a second reading in the House before the subject was postponed to the reassembling of Congress in October, at which time it was expected that Secretary Jefferson would lay before Congress a report on the restrictions imposed on American commerce by foreign countries. Jefferson's report was not submitted until Dec. 16, 1793. *A. S. P., F. R.*, I, 300–304. See, also, Vernon G. Setser, *The Commercial Reciprocity Policy of the United States 1774–1829*, chap. iv.

You will address also like Arguments to all moderate Men who wish for a Connection with Great Britain, of which description there is Reason to believe that You will find great Numbers, and You will address also the like Observations and Arguments to the Members of the American Senate, who have more than once already shewn a Disposition to restrain the Impetuosity of the House of Representatives in this respect,[25] and to counteract the Endeavours of the Members of the Northern States, who of all the American States alone have any considerable Quantity of Shipping, and wish on that Account to exclude foreign Ships from the American Ports, by imposing on them as many Restrictions as possible.

14. If the Government of the United States should propose that the Ships of the said States should be allowed to enter the Ports of His Majesty's Colonies in America, and of His Islands in the West Indies, as they did before the War, when the Countries belonging to these States were British Colonies, You must give Them to understand that this Proposition cannot be admitted even as a Subject of Negociation. By the public Law of Europe every Nation has a Right to regulate the Commerce, which it carries on with it's own Colonies, in the manner that shall appear to be the most conducive to the Interest of the Mother Country. In Regulations of this Sort no foreign Government has any Right to interfere: This Branch of Freight is of the same Nature with the Freight from one American State to another: Congress has made Regulations to confine the Freight employed between different States to the Ships of the United States,[26] and Great Britain does not object to this Restriction. The United States at present enjoy all the Rights and Privileges of an independent Nation, and as such They now have no Pretence to claim the Privileges which They once enjoyed as British Colonies.

15. If in the course of this Negociation, it should be proposed to treat on maritime Regulations, you may consent to insert in a Commercial Treaty with the United States, the Articles which have usually of late been inserted in our Treaties with France and other Foreign Powers; except that any Article allowing the Ships of the United States to protect the property of the Enemies of Great Britain in Time of War, should on no account be admitted, as it would be

[25] In 1789 and again in 1790 the Senate had refused to sanction discriminations against British commerce which the House, under the leadership of Madison, had approved.

[26] Foreign ships were practically excluded from the coastwise trade by the act of July 20, 1789, amended July 20, 1790, which provided that American ships in this traffic should pay tonnage duties only once a year, while foreign ships must pay tonnage duties at every entry into an American port. *U. S. Statutes at Large*, I, 27–28, 135–36.

more dangerous to concede this privilege to the Ships of the United States, than to those of any other Foreign Country.[27]

LORD GRENVILLE TO HAMMOND [28]

[No. 1.] [29]   \   WHITEHALL, September 2, 1791.

Sir,

In addition to the general Instructions which you will receive, it is necessary that I should signify to you His Majesty's Pleasure relative to the principal points which are likely to come into Discussion upon your arrival in America. You are already apprized of the points in which the Treaty of Peace has not been carried into execution by the respective Parties and the measure adopted by His Majesty of retaining in His hands the Forts to the Southwards of the Lakes cannot certainly be considered as affording even an adequate Compensation for the Losses which this Country has sustained in consequence of the Injustice done to the Loyalists since the year 1783, and of the Obstacles which have been thrown in the way of the recovery of the Debts due to the British Merchants. Whatever Disposition may now prevail in America for removing these and other causes of complaint, it cannot be contended that the American[s] can thereby acquire a right to claim the execution of that Article of the Treaty, by which the Forts were to be ceded to them; both because it cannot be competent to one of the Parties to an Engagement to withhold for any indefinite time the performance of the Stipulations to which it has bound itself,

---

[27] At the final peace settlement of 1783 Great Britain in her treaties with enemy powers (including the United States), which were likely to be neutral in future wars, had successfully excluded from general recognition the maritime principles of the Armed Neutrality of 1780, and of the Franco-American Treaty of 1778. In her treaty with France of 1783, however, she had renewed the treaty made with France at Utrecht, April 11, 1713, which contained such principles, except as to blockade. In her commercial treaty with France of 1786 Great Britain had affirmed (Article XX) the principle of the Armed Neutrality and of the United States (as embodied in treaties with France, Holland, Prussia, and Sweden) that "free ships make free goods," and the corollary principle (Article XXIX) that "enemy ships make enemy goods," had defined (Article XXII) contraband, limiting it to military stores, and had specifically excluded (Article XXIII) foodstuffs, naval stores, and other raw materials from the contraband list. Article XX of the Anglo-French Commercial Treaty of 1786 corresponds with Article XXV [XXIII] of the Franco-American Commercial Treaty of 1778; Articles XXII and XXIII correspond with Article XXVI [XXIV]. The several treaties concluded by Great Britain and France may be found in G. F. de Martens, ed., *Recueil de Traités;* those concluded by the United States are in Hunter Miller, ed., *Treaties and other International Acts of the United States of America.* An English version of the Anglo-French Treaty of Sept. 26, 1786 is given in George Chalmers, ed., *A Collection of Treaties between Great Britain and Other Powers.*

[28] F. O. 115: 1.

[29] The draft of this instruction in F. O. 4: 11 is marked "No. 1," and is dated Sept. 1, 1791—the same date as the draft of its companion instruction, No. 2, printed here immediately following. Apparently instruction No. 1 as received by Hammond was dated a day later than the draft because of the copying of additional material (indicated below), which was written on the margin of the draft.

and afterwards, at any moment which may suit its own convenience, to perform those Stipulations and to claim a reciprocal execution of the Treaty; and also because in the present case, it is evident, that no measures that can now be taken can replace the Loyalists and British Creditors in that Situation to which they were entitled by the Articles of the Treaty of Peace. During the interval which has elapsed, many written Evidences must have been destroyed, or lost, many Witnesses must be dead, and many Families dispersed so as to be no longer able to claim that situation to which they were entitled under the Treaty. And in consequence of the non-performance of those Engagements, Individuals have suffered great and irreparable Losses, and this Country has been subjected to a heavy Expence. On these grounds therefore His Majesty would be fully justified in forming a resolution of maintaining those Posts, and in refusing to enter into any Negotiation upon the Subject: But His sincere desire to remove every occasion of misunderstanding which may arise, has induced Him to direct that you should express His readiness to enter into Negotiation on the Subject, and to consent to such Arrangements as may be found to be of mutual convenience, and not inconsistent with the just claims and Rights of His Subjects. In all your conversations upon the Subject, you will be careful to let it be clearly understood, that it must be an essential and sine quâ non condition of any such Arrangement that every practicable Measure should be adopted by the States for the execution of the Fourth, Fifth, and Sixth Articles of the Treaty of Peace [30] as far as the circumstances of the length of time which has elapsed, render it possible that effect should now be given to those Stipulations. You are to consider this as the first and leading Object of your Mission, and immediately on your arrival in America you are to procure and to transmit to me as accurate a Statement as possible of the Measures which have hitherto been adopted for that purpose since the establishment of the federal Government, and of the points in which such measures are still defective or ineffectual, in order to meet the several cases of complaint, of which you are already informed, or which may come to your knowledge in America. And you will lose no time in stating these Particulars to those with whom you may treat in America, and to the Persons of distinction and weight in the American Government, in order to learn how far they are disposed and by what means, to supply such deficiencies as may still be found

---

[30] Article IV provided that there should be no lawful impediment to the recovery of debts; Article V, that Congress should recommend to the states the restitution of the confiscated estates of the Loyalists; Article VI, that no future confiscations should be made, nor any future prosecutions commenced, against any person by reason of the part he might have taken in the late war. For the full text, see Hunter Miller, ed., *Treaties*, II, 154–155.

to exist. I am not without hopes, from the circumstances of the late Communications which have passed on this Subject, that there exists among those who have the greatest Influence in the Government of America, a real disposition to meet the just Expectations of this Country in that respect. And if you should find this Opinion confirmed by the nature of the Conversations which you will hold with these Persons on your arrival in America, you may assure them of His Majesty's disposition to contribute on His part towards removing the Grounds of future difficulties by some practicable and reasonable Arrangement on the Subject of the Posts. I am unable at the present moment to furnish you with precise Instructions with respect to the nature of such an Arrangement, or to the Ideas which you might throw out for that purpose in the course of the Negotiation, because the Expectation of Lord Dorchester's arrival in England in the course of the present Autumn has occasioned His Majesty's Servants to delay for a few Weeks longer their ultimate decision on points of so much importance to the Government which has been placed under his care, and of the Interests of which he has had so long and particular knowledge. But you are to be careful to let it be understood, that this delay has not arisen from any Disinclination to enter into discussion of this Subject, and to form a satisfactory Arrangement respecting it, and in the expectation of receiving further Instructions from hence, you will express your readiness to enter immediately into the examination of all the different points which may be necessary for the full execution of the Treaty, or at least for such an Arrangement founded upon it, as the circumstances of the present moment will admit, and to receive and transmit for consideration, any reasonable Proposals which may be made to you on those Subjects. But you will represent, that it is absolutely necessary both in point of Justice and from the regard which is due in return for the friendly line of conduct now adopted by His Majesty that no steps should be taken by the American Governments to alter the relative situation of the two Countries, such as it now exists de facto, pending the Negotiation to which your Mission will give rise. And therefore, that every degree of discouragement should be given [by] those Governments as well as [by] His Majesty's officers to any Americans who may under these circumstances attempt to settle themselves within the limits of the Country now occupied by the British. Some recent Circumstances of this nature [31] which have occurred make it particularly necessary that you should urge this point, and I am per-

---

[31] On June 14, 1791 Dorchester had reported on, and had given orders to discountenance, the penetration of American settlers into American lands in the vicinity of the posts: Vermonters had settled on the River Chazy, eight miles from the post of Pointe-au-Fer on Lake Champlain ; a customs house had been set up at Alburgh, Vermont ; Americans were coming into the country about Fort Niagara, in New York, and about Fort Erie, in Pennsylvania. Douglas Brymner, ed., *Report on Canadian Archives, 1890*, pp. 281–290.

suaded that if the American Governments are really desirous to promote a good understanding, it will not be difficult for you to convince them how repugnant it is to such an object to suffer points of so much magnitude to be brought into discussion by the Enterprises of Individuals, instead of being made the Subject of temperate and friendly negotiation between the two Governments.[32] The Subject of the Indian War [33] will naturally connect itself with every discussion relative to the Forts: the knowledge which you have of the official correspondence of the Government of Quebec will enable you to disclaim in the most unequivocal manner any Idea of Lord Dorchester's having encouraged the measures of hostility taken by the Indians. The British Government feel on the contrary that they have a strong commercial and political Interest in the restoration of Peace; and nothing would be more satisfactory to His Majesty than to find himself enabled to contribute his good Offices for that Object, thro' the medium of His Government in America. You will on all occasions endeavour to impress this Idea, and to remove the prejudices which appear to have prevailed on the Subject. The Circumstances of the War, as far as they are yet known here, have been such as will probably render the Americans sincerely desirous of Peace, and if any opportunity should occur, in which it should appear to you that your Interposition, or that of the Government of Canada could conduce to that Object in a manner not inconsistent with the security of the Indians, you are authorized to exert yourself for that purpose, taking care always to adopt no measures respecting it, except in concert with His Majesty's Government in America, under whose direction the superintendance of Indian Affairs has been placed by His Majesty.

It will not fail to be an object of your attention to inform yourself as accurately as possible of the relative Situation of the other Nations of Europe with respect to America, but particularly of France and Spain. If as appears probable the discussions with the latter of those Powers [34] should lead to serious Disputes or to measures of actual Hostility, you are to be particularly careful to use no Expressions which may in any manner commit His Majesty as a Party in those differences. His Majesty's Object in such case would be to interpose his good offices for preventing those differences from leading to an actual Rupture. But if his attempts for that purpose should be

[32] In the draft, the preceding three sentences were written on the margin.
[33] At this time General Arthur St. Clair, Governor of the Northwest Territory, was leading an army against the Indians of the Wabash tribes, who in 1790 had inflicted great slaughter upon the punitive expeditionary force of General Joseph Harmar.
[34] Since 1783 the discussions between Spain and the United States had related chiefly to the northern boundary of Spanish West Florida and, especially, to the navigation of the Mississippi through Spanish New Orleans.

ineffectual you will endevour to maintain with both the contending Parties an uninterrupted and impartial Friendship.

I am with great Truth and Regard Sir,
    Your most obedient humble Servant,

GRENVILLE.[35]

GRENVILLE TO HAMMOND [36]

No. 2.   WHITEHALL, 1st Sept: 1791.

Sir

You are already informed of the discussions which took place in the last Session of the Congress relative to the American Commerce with Great Britain, and of the intention which was then held out of resuming that subject at their next meeting. This point will form a principal object of your attention, immediately on your arrival in America. You will omit no opportunity of assuring the Members of the Government there, that His Majesty is sincerely disposed not only to maintain a good correspondence and friendship with the United States, but also to promote and facilitate the commercial intercourse between the two Countries, and that he will always be ready to enter into any proper engagements for that purpose. If therefore it should be proposed to you to open a negotiation for a commercial treaty, You are to express His Majesty's readiness to enter into such a negotiation, and to consent to stipulations for the benefit of commerce and navigation, on terms of reciprocal advantage. His Majesty is willing to adopt, as the basis of such a negotiation, the placing the commerce of each country with the other reciprocally, on the terms of the most favoured nation. You will observe from the Papers of which you are in possession, that there are several Articles which now pay less duties when imported into this Country from the United States than when imported from other foreign Nations.[37] The establishment of these distinctions in favor of the commerce of the United States, and the. circumstance of their having hitherto been continued by this Country, afford the strongest proof of the friendly disposition towards the American Commerce which is entertained here; But His Majesty cannot bind Himself to the continuance of this preference, except in return for stipulations of reciprocal benefit to His Subjects. The same prin-

---

[35] The complimentary close, with signature, is printed here, only, in order to show the customary form.

[36] Draft, F. O. 4 : 11.

[37] In addition to tobacco and beaver skins, these articles consisted chiefly of naval stores, for which the British navy was obliged to depend on foreign sources. They are listed in the *Report of the Lords of the Privy Council*, etc., of Jan. 28, 1791, pp. 8–9. See also Jefferson's report on commercial privileges and restrictions, Dec. 16, 1793, *A. S. P., F. R.*, I, 301–302.

ciple of regulating the commerce according to the terms of the most favored nation may be applied to the intercourse between His Majesty's Colonies and the United States, as well as to that which they carry on with His Majesty's European dominions.

On the subject of navigation a distinction has been made by the Congress, in favor of American Shipping by tonnage duties and duties imposed on goods imported in foreign Vessels; and there is reason to believe that some of the persons concerned in the American Government entertain an intention of increasing this distinction in favor of their own navigation. The most natural and convenient principle on this subject is evidently this; that the Vessels of the two Countries respectively should be treated in their respective Ports precisely in the same manner with respect to any distinction of this nature. This principle you will urge to the utmost, and if you should not be able to prevail upon the persons with whom you treat to give effect to it by the stipulations of the treaty You will state your persuasion that measures for that purpose will be adopted by the Parliament of Great Britain, and You will let it be understood that a plan of this nature has already been formed, tho' it will be with the greatest reluctance that His Majesty's Servants will feel themselves obliged to bring it forward.

Whatever other proposals may be brought forward in the course of the negotiation, and whatever means may be suggested for giving effect to the principles above mentioned, must be taken by you ad referendum, and transmitted home for the consideration of His Majesty's Servants, [but you are on no account to conclude anything without previous and express directions from hence.] [38] I do not thing it necessary to enter into any further detail either of the arguments to be urged in support of those principles, or of the actual state of the commerce between the two Countries, as you will receive the fullest information on those points from the Report of the Committee of Trade herewith transmitted to you, and which it is hardly necessary for me to observe, is put into your hands for your own information only, and is not to be communicated to any Person in America. You will particularly advert to that part of the Report which points out the liberal and friendly conduct which has been observed by this Country towards the Americans, and contrasts it with the restrictions and disadvantages to which the British Commerce has been subjected by the Laws of Several of the States. [39] And you will observe that even in the maintenance of the present system, Great Britain holds out advantages to America which justly entitle her to a return of reciprocal benefit. It is by no means intended that you should attempt to

---

[38] The material enclosed in brackets was written on the margin of the draft.
[39] Pages 7–11, and 11–20, of the *Report* of Jan. 28, 1791.

deny, or even to diminish in argument the advantage which this Country derives from Her commerce with America, but You will state, that this is reciprocal, [that the Commerce is highly beneficial to both Countries, and that the United States have much more to apprehend than Great Britain from any interuption or diminution of it. You will also further observe] [40] that whatever benefit is derived from it to this Country has hitherto been owing only to the enterprize and capital of our Merchants, and to the superior skill of our Manufactures, and not to any favour shewn to them by the American Government. It is His Majesty's sincere wish that a system of mutual encouragement may be adopted, and He is for that purpose ready, as I have before stated, to consent to any reasonable stipulations, which shall be compensated by reciprocal advantage, and shall be formed either on the basis which I have already stated, or in any other manner which may be proposed to you, and which shall be found equally adapted to the attainment of that object, which alone His Majesty has in view.

GRENVILLE TO HAMMOND [41]

No. 3.   WHITEHALL, Octr 5th., 1791.

Sir,

You are already acquainted with the Case of Mr. Pagan, who has suffered under a severe Prosecution at Boston, on account of the Proceeds of an American Prize, in direct Contradiction to the final Decision of the Lords of appeal, by which that Prize had been declared legal. For your further Information in this Business, I now inclose to you two Memorials which I have lately received, together with the Copy of a Letter from His Majesty's Proctor; and as, notwithstanding the Representations of His Majesty's Consul at Boston, no Redress has hitherto been obtained, I must desire that you will press this Matter in the strongest Manner, with the American Government, in order to procure the Release of Mr. Pagan, if he should be still in Confinement, and a just Compensation for the Losses he may have sustained by the Proceedings against him. [42]

---

[40] The material enclosed in brackets was written on the margin of the draft.

[41] F. O. 115 : 1.

[42] Thomas Pagan, Massachusetts Loyalist, was confined under an execution of the Massachusetts Supreme Court, which in 1789 had found judgment against him, in favor of Stephen Hooper, of some £3,000 damages arising from the seizure off Cape Ann on March 25, 1783 of Hooper's brigantine, the *Thomas,* by Pagan's privateer, the *Industry.* Hammond on Nov. 26, 1791 presented a memorial to Secretary Jefferson, who on Feb. 25, 1792 replied, that the way was open for Pagan to apply to the United States Supreme Court for a writ of error. The case of Pagan was for Hammond a subject of much correspondence, with Jefferson and with the Foreign Office. At length a compromise was reached between Pagan and Hooper, in consequence of which Pagan was released from prison. Jefferson, *Writings,* ed. H. A. Washington, III, 308–313, 335, 538–541 ; also, Grenville to Hammond, Jan. —, 1794, No. 6 ; Feb. 6, 1794, No. 8, *infra.*

INSTRUCTIONS OF 1792

No. 1.   WHITEHALL, January 3d, 1792.

Sir,

Your several Letters to No. 10 inclusive have been received, and laid before the King.

I have the Satisfaction to acquaint You that His Majesty entirely approves the Step You have taken, in presenting your Credentials, under the Circumstances mentioned in your dispatches on that Subject.[2]

Your Correspondence with Mr. Jefferson, which I received to-day with your other Letters from No. 7 to No. 10, appears to have been extremely proper and judicious.[3]

The American Mail being to be made up to-morrow, I have not time to enter into the Particulars of your other Dispatches of the same Date; but I think it highly necessary to lose no time in informing You, in Answer to what is mentioned respecting Mr. Bowles[4] in your

---

[1] F. O. 115 : 1.

[2] Hammond had presented his credentials Nov. 11, 1791, without waiting for the appointment of a minister plenipotentiary to Great Britain, after being advised by Jefferson that President Washington had offered the post to an unnamed gentleman, who Hammond thought was Edward Rutledge. Thomas Pinckney of South Carolina was appointed, to the great satisfaction (Hammond reported on Jan. 9, 1792) of Americans friendly to Great Britain. Hammond to Grenville, Nov. 16, 1791, No. 4, F. O. 4 : 11, and, to same, Nov. 1, 16, 1791, Jan. 9, 1792, *Dropmore Papers*, II, 223, 229, 250; also, Frederick J. Turner, ed., "English Policy Toward America in 1790–1791," *Amer. Hist. Review*, VII (July, 1902), 735.

[3] Pressed by Jefferson at the very beginning of their correspondence, Hammond was obliged to admit that he had no power to conclude a treaty but was merely authorized to discuss the principles which might serve as a basis for a definitive arrangement. Discussions thereafter were confined to infractions of the treaty of 1783. For the notes exchanged see *A. S. P., F. R.,* I, 188–189 ; Jefferson, *Works*, ed. P. L. Ford, VI, 341.

[4] William Augustus Bowles (1763–1805), a Loyalist of Maryland, who had settled among the Southern Indians and acquired much influence over them. In 1791 there was published in London a sketch of this young adventurer, written by Capt. Benj. Baynton, which referred to him as "Ambassador from the United Nations of the Creeks and Cherokees to the Court of London." Supported by British merchants in the West Indies, he sought to undermine the power of Alexander McGillivray, half-breed Creek chieftain, and to monopolize the profitable Indian trade of the Floridas, a trade then in the hands of William Panton, a British subject (and McGillivray's partner) who operated under Spanish license. In March of 1792 McGillivray seized and delivered Bowles to the Spanish authorities. Bowles returned in 1797 and continued his intrigues until his capture by the Spaniards in 1803. See J. W. Caughey, *McGillivray of the Creeks*; A. P. Whitaker, *The Mississippi Question 1795–1803;* and the documents printed by Turner, *Amer. Hist. Rev.,* VII, 706–735.

Letter No. 7 and its Inclosure, and also in a letter from Lieut. Colonel Beckwith,[5] which I have received from Lord Dorchester, that the Assertions said to have been made by Mr. Bowles, of his having received Powers from the British Government, to conclude a Treaty with the Creeks, of his having received Encouragement to take Measures for a Revocation of the late Treaty with the United States,[6] or of his having been furnished by this Government, with Arms, Ammunition or Cannon, are entirely without Foundation. The Particulars of his having any Sort of Commission from this Government, either as Agent or Superintendent of Indians, or in any other Character, or of his having been authorized to promise to the Creeks on the Part of this Country, the Re-establishment of their old Boundary with Georgia, or to hold out to them any Expectation of an English Reinforcement in the Spring, are also wholly groundless. From what You have mentioned in your Letter No. 7,[7] I am persuaded that You will already have availed Yourself of the Knowledge which You possess of the Sentiments of the King's Ministers with respect to America, in order to contradict Assertions which, if made in the Manner represented, can have no other effect than to raise groundless Jealousies between the two Countries, in the Room of that Harmony and good Understanding which it is so sincerely our Object to establish. But if You should not already have done this, I desire You will lose no time in giving such an Explanation on this Subject, as may effectually remove any Idea of this Country having adopted a Line of Conduct so extremely different from that which has been uniformly pursued.

GRENVILLE TO HAMMOND [8]

No. 2.   WHITEHALL, Jany. 5th, 1792.

Sir,

Lord St. Helens'[9] having communicated to me the confidential Information which His Excellency had received from Mr. Carmich-

---

[5] Lieut. Col. George Beckwith (1753–1823), an aide-de-camp of Lord Dorchester, Governor-General of Canada (upon whose staff he had served during the American Revolution). He had been employed in the United States by Dorchester as confidential agent, and later by the Foreign Office itself as Great Britain's informal representative, from 1787 to the arrival of Hammond in October of 1791.

[6] By the treaty of Aug. 7, 1790, negotiated at New York, McGillivray and other Creek chieftains had agreed to stipulated and guaranteed boundaries, accepted annuities, and placed themselves, and all of the Creek nation living within the limits of the United States, under American protection.

[7] In his dispatch No. 7 of Dec. 6, 1791, F. O. 4: 11, Hammond stated that if the charge that Bowles was countenanced by Great Britain should appear to gain credit he would contradict it in the most explicit manner.

[8] F. O. 115: 1.

[9] Alleyne Fitzherbert, Baron St. Helens (1753–1839), the British ambassador to Spain from 1791 to 1794.

ael,[10] respecting a Negotiation actually going on for a Treaty of Alliance between Spain and the United States of America, I think it necessary, in order that You may be apprized of this Circumstance, to transmit to You an Extract of his Letter on this Subject,[11] and to desire that You will be very assiduous in watching the Progress of such Negotiation and that You will acquaint me with all the Particulars You may be able to learn concerning it;[12] but You will take no public Steps to counteract any Arrangements which may be concerted between the two Countries, any further than by expressing to the American Ministers your Persuasion that they will enter into no engagement with the Court of Madrid, which may be prejudicial to the interests of Great Britain.

I take this opportunity to forward to you a List of the Debts due from the Citizens of the United States to His Majesty's Subjects, which has been transmitted to His Majesty's Secretary of State for the Home Department by the Committee of North American Merchants, together with several other Papers received from them, which will assist You in preparing your Statement upon this Subject.

GRENVILLE TO HAMMOND [13]

[No. 3.] [14]   WHITEHALL, Jan. 31st, 1792.

Sir,

Considerable Inconvenience having arisen from the Importation of Tobacco in Foreign Vessels into the Ports of His Majesty's Dominions contrary to the Act of the 12th Charles 2nd Chap. 18th Sect 3d commonly called the Navigation Act, I have it in Command from His Majesty to notify to You, for the Information of the Gov-

---

[10] William Carmichael of Maryland (d. 1795), secretary to the American mission at Paris, 1775–76; member of the Continental Congress, 1778–79; secretary to John Jay, minister plenipotentiary to Spain, 1780–82; acting chargé d'affaires at Madrid, 1782–90; chargé since 1790. In March of 1792, with William Short, American minister resident at The Hague, Carmichael was appointed joint commissioner plenipotentiary to negotiate a treaty with Spain respecting the navigation of the Mississippi and the West Florida boundary.

[11] Grenville enclosed a copy of the dispatch to him of St. Helens, Confidential, No. 44, Escurial, Nov. 25, 1791, in which St. Helens stated that Carmichael, through Anthony Merry of the British Embassy, had informed him that Count Florida Blanca had suddenly expressed a desire to accommodate differences with the United States, had admitted the American navigation and boundary claims, but had insisted upon certain articles intended to serve as the basis of a regular treaty of alliance between the United States and Spain. Carmichael told Merry that he would forward these Spanish proposals for an alliance to his government, but intended to delay sending them as long as he decently could. Carmichael said that he much preferred a connection between the United States and Great Britain, and, since Hammond's mission to America seemed to indicate that such a connection might be in view, he had thought it fitting to apprise Lord St. Helens of the state of his negotiations with Spain.

[12] Hammond reported to Grenville, on June 8, 1792, No. 20. F. O. 4: 15, his belief that the negotiations did not extend "to anything like a system of alliance upon general principles, but are confined to the avowed object of Messrs. Short and Carmichael's commission, the free and uninterrupted navigation of the river Mississippi."

[13] F. O. 115: 1.

[14] This instruction and its draft are both unnumbered. The number in brackets has been supplied by the editor.

ernment where You reside, that it has been determined strictly to inforce this Clause (a Copy of which I now inclose to You) in future,
and you will not fail immediately to communicate this Circumstance
to the American Ministers for their Information.[15]

GREENVILLE TO HAMMOND [16]

No. 4.   WHITEHALL, Jany. 31, 1792.

Sir,

I send you inclosed a Printed Copy of the most gracious Speech
with which His Majesty was pleased to open the Session of Parliament this Day,[17] and I will give Orders that the Addresses of both
Houses to the King be transmitted to you by the earliest Opportunity.

GRENVILLE TO HAMMOND [18]

No. 5.   WHITEHALL, March 17th, 1792.

Sir,

I send You herewith Duplicates of my Letters No. 1, 2, 3 and 4.
Having since they were written received from Mr. Secretary
Dundas [19] a List of the Agents to the Claimants for Debts due to
His Majesty's Subjects from the Citizens of the United States of
America, with a Letter accompanying it from the Committee of
North American Merchants, as also Copies and Extracts of several
Letters received by them from Virginia relative to this Business, I
inclose the same to you for your further Information.

---

[15] The third section of the statute forbade the importation of foreign products save in
British vessels of which the master and three-fourths at least of the crew were British
subjects. Its operation after 1783 against the United States had been offset by orders-in-
council which permitted American ships to carry to England tobacco, raw materials (with
certain specified exceptions such as oil and other whale products), unmanufactured goods,
and naval stores produced in the United States. The literal effect of the new instructions
was totally to exclude American vessels from such importations. Hammond on April 11,
1792 assured Jefferson, however, that the object, in his opinion, was merely to exclude
foreign vessels from the islands of Jersey and Guernsey because of the frauds which had
there taken place with respect to the importation of tobacco. *A. S. P., F. R.*, I, 135–36;
also Hammond to Grenville, Apr. 14, 1792, No. 17, F. O. 4: 11. Bond likewise expressed
such an opinion towards this sweeping order, which "immediately excited a very serious
alarm in the minds of the merchants and might have retarded the shipment of vast cargoes
now preparing for England." Bond to Grenville, Apr. 12, 1792, Jameson, ed., "Letters of
Phineas Bond," *Ann. Rpt. Amer. Hist. Assoc. 1897*, p. 497.

[16] F. O. 115: 1.

[17] The speech may be found in *The Parliamentary History of England* (printed by T. C.
Hansard), XXIX, 744–746.

[18] F. O. 115: 1.

[19] Henry Dundas (1742–1811), created Viscount Melville in 1802, was Grenville's successor
as Secretary for Home Affairs, a position he held from 1791 to 1794.

GRENVILLE TO HAMMOND [20]

No. 6.   WHITEHALL, March 17th, 1792.

Sir,

I send You inclosed a Copy of the Memorial of Messrs. Mures, Atkinson and Mure and Sir George Jackson, stating their Claims to certain Lands and other Property in America; purchased and acquired prior to the commencement of Hostilities between the two Countries; and I am to desire that You will give every proper Countenance and Assistance in your Power to the Agents of the Memorialists, in their Endeavours to recover and dispose of such Property, on behalf of their Principals, as they may appear to be justly entitled to.[21]

GRENVILLE TO HAMMOND [22]

No. 7.   WHITEHALL, March 17th, 1792.

Sir,

Your Dispatches to No. 13 of the last Year, and to No. 4 inclusive of the present have been received and laid before the King; and I have great Pleasure in expressing to You, that the Manner, in which you have entered on the different Discussions, which formed so material an Object of your Mission, has been entirely approved.

With respect to the two additional Points brought forward by Mr. Jefferson, concerning the Negroes, and the Boundary at the River St. Croix,[23] I have nothing to add to what You have Yourself stated; but I transmit to You herewith for your Information the Copy of a Letter, with its Inclosures, which relates to a Matter connected with the latter of those Points and which has been received by His Majesty's Principal Secretary of State for the Home Department. From the Disposition expressed to You by Mr. Hamilton,[24] as to these two Subjects, I trust that there will not ultimately be found any considerable Difficulty in arranging them satisfactorily, but it will be very material that You should obtain and transmit to me the fullest Information respecting the latter of them.

---

[20] F. O. 115 : 1.

[21] The enclosure is lacking in both F. O. 115 : 1 and F. O. 4 : 14.

[22] F. O. 115 : 1.

[23] Jefferson had opened the discussions with Hammond on the non-execution of the treaty of 1783 by his note of Dec. 15, 1791, in which he had brought forward, in addition to the failure of Great Britain to evacuate the frontier posts, the disputed Northeastern boundary and the same three thousand slaves carried off when the British forces evacuated New York. *A. S. P., F. R.*, I, 190.

[24] George Hammond, like George Beckwith before him, had entered upon an intimate relationship with Secretary of the Treasury Hamilton, the leader of "the party of the British interest" as contrasted with Secretary of State Jefferson, the leader of "the party of the French interest." His first "very long and confidential conversation" with Hamilton had "fully confirmed" his previous opinion of "that Gentleman's just and liberal

GRENVILLE TO HAMMOND [25]

No. 8.   WHITEHALL March 17th 1792.

Sir,

I have reserved to this Dispatch the Instructions which I have it in command from His Majesty to transmit to you on the important Subject of the Indian War.[26] The general Language which You have held on this Subject has been in all Respects perfectly proper, but the present Circumstances appear to be favourable for entering more directly and particularly into the Business, and for endeavouring to connect it with the Matter in Discussion between the two Countries with respect to the Frontier Posts on the Lakes, so as, if possible, to come to a satisfactory Arrangement of that long depending Business. If it should appear to you at the time of receiving this Dispatch, that the then existing circumstances continue to afford a prospect of success to such an Interposition on the Part of this Country, you are authorized to make to the American Government, in such Manner and Form as you shall judge most expedient, a Ministerial offer of the good Offices of this Country in restoring Peace between them and the Indians. The general Grounds on which it is intended that You should endeavour to negotiate such an accomodation are to be, the securing to the different Indian Nations, along the British and American Frontiers, their Lands and hunting Grounds, as an independent Country, with respect to which, both His Majesty and the United States shall withdraw all Claims or Possessions whatever, shall agree never to establish any Forts within the Boundaries to be expressed in such Agreement, and shall bind themselves to each other not to acquire or to suffer their Subjects to acquire, by purchase, or otherwise, from the Indians, any Lands or Settlements within the said Boundaries. The time and mode of bringing forward this particular Proposition, whether as part of your original Proposal, or in the course of any subsequent Discussions to which it may lead, must be left to your Discretion, guided by Circumstances on the Spot. But it should, as

---

way of thinking." Hammond to Grenville, Dec. 19, 1791, No. 13, F. O. 4 : 11. In commenting on the grievances outlined in Jefferson's note of Dec. 15, 1791, "Mr. Hamilton expressed his conviction that the surrender of the posts was the only one which could produce any lengthy or difficult investigation . . .. With respect to the Negroes Mr. Hamilton seemed partly to acquiesce in my reasoning upon this point, and added that this matter did not strike him as an object of such importance as it had appeared to other members of this government. As to the river St. Croix he acknowledged his personal belief that our statement of its position would upon inquiry be found accurate." Same to same, Jan. 9, 1792, No. 3, F. O. 4 : 14.

[25] F. O. 115 : 1.

[26] Hammond had reported to Grenville Dec. 10, 1791, No. 11, F. O. 4 : 11, on "the total defeat of the army under General St. Clair by the Indians, on the 4th November, near the Maumee (Miamis) Towns, at the distance of about ten miles from the place where Brigadier Harmar was defeated last year."

early as possible, be stated, as the Ground and Foundation of such Interference on our part, as no other Mode of terminating the Business seems to afford so fair a Prospect of a satisfactory Conclusion with a View to the permanent Interests of this Country, in that part of the World.

You are already sufficiently informed on this Subject, to render it unnecessary for me to enter into the Detail of the Arguments by which such a Proposition is to be supported and of the Advantages which it would afford by removing the Ground of difficult and hazardous Discussions between this Country and America, and by securing to the Indians, in the fullest Manner, the unmolested and independent Possession of those Countries which are necessary for their Existence and Support. And you will understand yourself to be distinctly authorized, supposing the course of the Negotiation should lead to such a Step, to offer, that His Majesty will abandon the Posts still occupied by His Troops to the Southward and Westward of the Lakes supposing that the Americans should consent, on their Part, to renounce all claims of theirs to those Posts, and to leave them, in common with the rest of that Country, in the undisturbed and independent Possession of the Indians. It will however be necessary that in that Case, a sufficient Time should be stipulated for the Merchants and others concerned in the Trade to withdraw their Effects from the Posts. This Time should, as far as I am yet informed, not be less than two Years, from the Conclusion of any such Agreement.

By the Vessel which carries out to you these Instructions, Mr. Dundas sends out Orders to Quebec corresponding with them, and His Majesty's Government there will be directed to instruct some Person more particularly versed in the detail of Indian Affairs to repair to Philadelphia, in order to assist you in the Progress of any Negotiation which may be opened on these Grounds and to concert with you the Steps to be taken by the Indian Department in the two Canadas, for disposing the Indians to agree to such Terms as may be proposed on the Ground above stated. Such Person will of course be able to give you distinct Information with respect to the Particulars of any boundary Line which may be proposed. The inclosed Description and Map [27] will shew you the suggestion made on that Subject to Lord Dorchester, by a Deputation of Indians previous to his leaving Canada, this Boundary would I apprehend be sufficient to answer the purpose which this Country has principally in View. I expect however to be able shortly to send You out more particular Information on this Point, and there appears reason to imagine,

---

[27] For a map showing the proposed boundary line of 1791, and for a detailed account of the British proposal, see Bemis, *Jay's Treaty*, p. 111, and ch. v, "The Neutral Indian Barrier State Project."

that you will receive such Intelligence soon enough for your Direction and Guidance in the future Progress of any Negotiation which may be commenced on these Grounds.

You will however bear in mind that it may be a Point of mutual Convenience, that some new Arrangement should be made respecting the Frontier on Lake Champlain to which the Indian Claims are understood not to extend and that it may also be thought right to insert in any Agreement of this Nature with the United States, an Article for securing to the British Creditors, Justice and Protection in the Recovery of their Debts to the utmost Extent which may be found practicable, after the long Delay which has taken place in this respect.

P. S.

I also send You inclosed Copy of Mr. Secretary Dundas's Letter to Lord Dorchester.

GRENVILLE TO HAMMOND [28]

No. 9.   WHITEHALL, April 25th, 1792.

Sir,

I have now to acknowledge the Receipt of your Dispatches from No. 5 to No. 13 inclusive.

The Measures you have taken on the Subject of Mr. Pagan appear to have been perfectly proper.

I observe, from what you mention in Your Letter No. 8, that you apprehend the Disposition of the Government of America, to be adverse to the Admission of any Intervention, on the Part of His Majesty, for restoring Peace with the Indians, so long as the Posts shall remain in His Majesty's Possession.[29] I cannot, however, but expect that the full and able Statement transmitted by you to Mr. Jefferson, relative to the different Infractions of Treaty on the Part of the United States,[30] must have made a very considerable Impression on the Minds of all those to whom it may have been communicated, and must have disposed them to the Acceptance of some Proposition grounded on the Basis explained in my last Dispatch to you; and combining the re-establishment of Peace with a mutual

---

[28] F. O. 115 : 1.

[29] In his No. 8 of Feb. 2, 1792, F. O. 4 : 14, Hammond had reported that he had "heard from pretty good authority" that such was "the fixed determination of this government."

[30] His answer to Jefferson's note of Dec. 15, 1791 was presented on March 5, 1792. *A. S. P., F. R.,* I, 193–200. "I flatter myself, My Lord," he wrote Grenville March 6, 1792, No. 11, F. O. 4 : 14, "that this statement will be found . . . to contain a body of proof so complete and substantial as to preclude the probability of cavil and contradiction on the part of this government." In this same dispatch Hammond paid tribute to "Mr. Bond, his Majesty's Consul at this place, who has, with great care and industry, collected, compiled, and arranged for me, not only the laws of the general government, but also the legislative acts and judicial decisions of the individual states."

Dereliction of that Territory, which this Country cannot continue to hold without exciting Jealousy on the Part of America, and which the King cannot, on the other Hand, be expected to give up to the United States, without receiving Compensation for the non-execution of the Articles of the Treaty, and for the great Expense incurred by the Public on that Account. The increasing Difficulties, which attend the Indian War, according to all the Accounts which you receive of it, will probably add a further Inducement to the Acceptance of this Mode of Arrangement, and it is for these Reasons that it has not been judged proper in any manner to vary the Instructions already transmitted to you, the Time of bringing forward which is however left to your Discretion—according to the different Circumstances which may arise.

I send you by this Packet, for your further Information and Guidance on this Subject, the Copies of a Letter from Lord Dorchester to Mr. Dundas, together with several Inclosures, which it will be very material for you to attend to in the Course of any Negotiation on the Grounds which I have stated. The Arguments to be urged, with a view to obtaining a new Frontier on Lake Champlain, according to one of the two lines suggested by Captain Mann,[31] will readily occur to you. The Object is purely and evidently defensive, and the Sacrifice, on the Part of the Americans must be allowed to be extremely small, when compared with the private Losses and public Expense which, as I have already mentioned, have been incurred by this Country, in consequence of the Infractions of Treaty by the States: It appears however, on every Account, to be infinitely more desirable to include this Object in a general Arrangement of Frontier, as now proposed, than to bring it forward separately in the more invidious Shape of a Compensation for the Losses and Expenses above stated. As such a Compensation, it would in itself be entirely inadequate, and yet would have the Appearance of being humiliating to America.

The Point relative to the River St. Croix, and to the Islands adjacent to the Coast of that Part of America, would also form a natural Part of such general Arrangements, but on these I am unable to give you any fresh Instructions, till I shall be further informed upon them.

The Boundary of the King's Possessions to the North West, as described in the Treaty of Peace, would probably be in some Degree altered, by the Adoption of any Proposition on the Basis now in question. And you will particularly bear in mind, that it will be an object of the greatest Importance, at all Events, to secure, if pos-

---

[31] Captain Gother Mann (1747–1830), was commanding officer of the Royal Engineers at Quebec 1785–91, and in command of the Royal Engineers in Canada 1794–1804.

sible, to His Majesty's Subjects in Canada, the free and uninterrupted Communication between the Lakes and the Mississippi, either by the Ouisconsing River, which I understand affords great Facility for that Purpose, or by such other Rivers, as, from such Information as you can acquire in America, shall appear more proper for the attainment of the same object.[32] You will also be careful, in every part of this Negotiation, to advert to the Necessity which is stated to you in my Letter No. 1 of last year, of including in any Agreement to be made between His Majesty and the United States, a Stipulation for the Execution of those Articles of the Treaty which relate to the Loyalists and British Creditors, as far as the Circumstances of the present Time render it practicable.

GRENVILLE TO HAMMOND [33]

No. 10.   WHITEHALL, April 25th, 1792.
Sir,
    Having referred to His Majesty's Post Master General the Representations contained in your Dispatch No. 7 on the Inconveniences arising to the American Merchants from the Packet Boats to and from this Country touching at Halifax in their Way to and from New York I find such Difficulties occur in making the Alteration desired in this respect that it is judged by no means adviseable to give Directions for that Purpose at least for the present.[34]

GRENVILLE TO HAMMOND [35]

No. 11.   WHITEHALL, June 5th, 1792.
Sir,
    I send You inclosed a printed Copy of the Proclamation, which His Majesty, by the Advice of his Privy Council, has been pleased to issue for the Purpose of discouraging wicked and seditious Publications, tending to excite Tumult and Disorder, by endeavouring to raise groundless Jealousies and Discontents in the Minds of His

---

[32] In a private letter to Grenville of Feb. 2, 1792, Dropmore Papers, II, 254, Hammond had pointed out that a boundary line drawn due west from the Lake of the Woods to the Mississippi (as provided by Article II of the Treaty of Peace) would not strike that river, the source of which appeared to be well within American territory. He trusted that the United States would not take advantage of this accidental geographical error, which, if not rectified, would not only leave the boundary undefined but also render nugatory the stipulation of Article VIII of the treaty, that the navigation of the Mississippi from its source to the ocean was to remain free and open to the subjects of Great Britain and the citizens of the United States.

[33] F. O. 115 : 1.

[34] The packets went by way of Halifax except during the winter months, and Hammond, like Bond, thought the complaints of the New York and Philadelphia merchants at the delays and inconveniences were well-grounded. Hammond to Grenville, Feb. 2, 1792, No. 7, F. O. 4 : 14 ; and, also, Bond to Hammond, Feb. 1, 1792, Ann. Rpt. Amer. Hist. Assoc. 1897, p. 495.

[35] F. O. 115 : 1.

Majesty's Subjects respecting the Laws and Constitution of this Government; together with the joint Address of both Houses of Parliament to His Majesty upon this Occasion, expressing their Indignation at such atrocious attempts, and their firm Determination to support His Majesty in his Exertions for suppressing such disorderly and dangerous Proceedings, by a due Execution of the Laws against all Offenders.[36]

GRENVILLE TO HAMMOND [37]

No. 12.   WHITEHALL, June 8th, 1792.
Sir.

I have received Your Letter No. 17, and am to signify to you His Majesty's entire Approbation of your Conduct relative to the Circular Notification which was sent to you and the Consuls in America, on the Subject of the Clause of the Navigation Act, which was at the same Time transmitted to you.[38] No Idea was entertained of altering in that Manner the System on which the Commerce between this Country and America is now carried on under the King's Proclamation, issued by virtue of an Act of Parliament; nor was anything further in Contemplation than the enforcing the Execution of the existing Laws in those Cases to which they now apply. The Effect of such a Notification transmitted to you from this Office, could indeed by Law extend no further than this; and it will be proper that you should give the most satisfactory Explanation on this Subject, if you shall judge it necessary in Addition to what you have already said.

GRENVILLE TO HAMMOND [39]

No. 13.   WHITEHALL, August 4th, 1792.
Sir,

Your Letters to No. 25 have been received and laid before the King.

As in your Dispatch No. 22 inclosing Mr. Jefferson's Answer [40] to your general Representation on the several Points of Business

---

[36] The proclamation of May 21, 1792, and the joint addresses are printed in *Parl. Hist.*, XXIX, 1476ff., and in the *Annual Register* for 1792, pp. 158–160.
[37] F. O. 115: 1.
[38] See Grenville to Hammond, Jan. 31, 1792, *supra*.
[39] F. O. 115: 1.
[40] In his No. 22 of June 8, 1792, F. O. 4: 15, Hammond had termed Jefferson's answer of May 29, 1792 to his memorial of March 5, 1792 (*A. S. P., F. R.*, I, 201–237), an acrimonious paper containing irrelevancies and unjustifiable insinuations. In a paragraph marked "Confidential," he said he had spoken very freely with Secretary Hamilton of "this extraordinary performance," and that Hamilton, "after lamenting the intemperate violence of his colleague," had assured him that Secretary Jefferson's note was very far from meeting his approbation, or from containing a faithful exposition of the administration's views.

depending between this Country and America, you mention your Intention of communicating to me some further Information relative thereto, I shall defer entering into any particular Consideration of that Paper at present; and the rather, as I have desired Mr. Bond, who is now here, to furnish me with such Observations as may occur to him on an attentive Perusal of it.[41] In the meantime, however, I cannot omit to assure you of His Majesty's gracious and entire Approbation of the prudent Conduct you have held upon this Occasion and also with respect to the discretionary Powers entrusted to you on the Subject of the Indian War and of the Frontier Posts.

Although the actual Negotiation between the Countries must necessarily be suspended till Mr. Jefferson's Paper can have been thoroughly examined, I am persuaded that in the interval, you will not relax in your Attention to the important Object of pressing forward by every means in your Power the obtaining from the States the Justice due to the British Creditors.

GRENVILLE TO HAMMOND [42]

No. 14.   WHITEHALL, August 4th, 1792.

Sir,

I send you inclosed a Memorial from Mr. George Martin, with a Case annexed, relative to certain Estates in Virginia, for which the Commissioners of American Claims only allowed a Compensation as far as his Life Interest was concerned, and did not grant any Sum for the Remainder and intailed Inheritance; but stated that Portion of the Loss under the Class of claims of "Persons who appear to have Relief provided for them under the Treaty of Peace," and praying their Compensation may be granted him for this Loss.

I also send you inclosed a Memorial from Lord Fairfax praying Compensation for the Value of the reversionary Interests in his Lordship's Estates in Virginia.

Likewise, a Memorial from Colonel Roger Morris, praying that the claim for his Four Children for their Interests in certain Estates in the Province of New York upon the Decease of their surviving Parent, may be taken into Consideration; and I am to desire you will represent these several Cases to the American Ministers, and

---

[41] Phineas Bond's observations on Jefferson's counter-memorial were transmitted to Grenville on Oct. 12, 1792, *Ann. Rpt. Amer. Hist. Assoc., 1897*, pp. 500–523. They are of particular interest, since Hammond acknowledged Bond to have been "principally instrumental in furnishing the materials" of the British memorial of March 5, 1792. Hammond to Grenville, June 8, 1792, No. 22, F. O. 4 : 15.

[42] F. O. 115 : 1.

endeavour to obtain for the Parties such Relief as they may appear entitled to under the Treaty of Peace.[43]

GRENVILLE TO HAMMOND [44]

No. 15.   WHITEHALL, August 21st, 1792.

Sir,

His Majesty having been pleased on Account of the Recent Transactions at Paris and of the present Situation of Their Most Christian Majesties to direct His Ambassador at that Court to leave the Kingdom and to return to England, I think it proper to apprize you of the Circumstance for the Information of the Government where you reside. It is not His Majesty's intention in taking this Step to depart from the line, which His Majesty has hitherto observed, of not interfering in the Internal Affairs of France or in the Settlement of the Government there, but it would neither have been consistent with the King's Dignity nor with the strong interest which His Majesty invariably takes in what regards the personal Situation of Their Most Christian Majesties, that His Ambassador should continue at Paris, where the King to whom Lord Gower [45] is accredited, is no longer in the exercise of the Executive Government but in a State of declared and avowed Captivity. Your Language on the Subject will be guided by these Principles in any Conversation which may arise respecting it between you and the Ministers of the Place where you reside.

GRENVILLE TO HAMMOND [46]

No. 16.   WHITEHALL, Nov. 5th, 1792.

Sir,

Your Letters to No. 34, inclusive, have been received, and laid before the King.

I send You inclosed the Copy of a Letter from Mr. Hopton,[47] with the Papers referred to therein, stating his Claims on the American Government, arising from the Depreciation of Paper Money in the State of South Carolina, which he was compelled to receive in Payment for Sterling Debts; and I am to desire that you will use Your Endeavours to obtain for Mr. Hopton such Relief as the Justice of his Case may appear to entitle him to.

---

[43] On the claims of George Martin (the son of Samuel Martin, whose property had been confiscated), of Robert Fairfax (1706–1793), seventh Lord Fairfax of Cameron, and of Roger Morris, see *A. S. P., F. R.*, I, 504–509. The reversionary interest of Morris's children was sold in 1809 to John Jacob Astor for £20,000. Lorenzo Sabin, *The American Loyalists*, p. 474.

[44] F. O. 115 : 1.

[45] George Granville Leveson-Gower, first Duke of Sutherland (1758–1833).

[46] F. O. 115 : 1.

[47] John Hopton, Loyalist merchant of Charleston, S. C., member of the firm of Powell, Hopton and Company. His letter and its inclosure are in F. O. 4 : 16.

INSTRUCTIONS OF 1793

GRENVILLE TO HAMMOND [1]

No. 1.   WHITEHALL, January 4th, 1793.

Sir,

Your Letters to No. — inclusive have been received and laid before the King:—but I have been prevented by the Pressure of temporary Business, from transmitting to you by this Opportunity any Instructions on the Subject of your late Dispatches.

As there is great Reason to believe in the present Situation of Affairs between this Country and France, that the Continuation of Peace is very doubtful, I think it necessary to desire, that you will be particularly attentive to discover what Negotiations may be on Foot for cultivating a more intimate Correspondence between the French Government and the United States; and it is the more necessary to recommend to You the utmost Vigilance upon this Point, as it appears by the Proceedings in the National Convention, that a new Minister to America has been lately appointed by France, who is to be charged with Instructions, by the present French Ruler, for concerting Measures with those Persons in America who favor those dangerous and delusive Principles of Liberty and Equality which the French Demagogues are labouring to establish in all Countries.[2] I am to signify to you His Majesty's Pleasure that you exert your utmost Endeavours for counteracting any such Measures, and for endeavoring to cement and improve the Harmony which now subsists between this Country and the United States.

JAMES BLAND BURGES TO HAMMOND [3]

[In cipher.]   WHITEHALL, 4th January, 1793.

Most secret private and confidential.

I mention the following circumstance to you in the utmost confidence —not that you should say or do anything in consequence of it but that you may know what the Americans are about, and be on your guard in any conversation you may have on the subject.

---

[1] F. O. 115 : 2.

[2] Edmond Charles Genêt (1763–1834), the new French minister plenipotentiary to the United States, appointed Nov. 19, 1792, was by his instructions of December, 1792 directed to take all measures comportable with his position to plant the principles of liberty and independence in Louisiana and other provinces adjacent to the United States. F. J. Turner, ed., "Correspondence of the French Ministers to the United States, 1791–1797," *Ann. Rpt. Amer. Hist. Assoc., 1903,* II, 205.

[3] F. O. 115 : 2.

Mr. Carmichael, the American Chargé d'affaires at Madrid lately received instructions to declare to that court that the United States think themselves obliged to support France in any agression she might experience in the course of her troubles and which they were apprehensive of from the march of the Spanish troops to the frontiers. Mr. Carmichael acquitted himself of the order in writing, and has received an answer from the Spanish Minister conceived in the most friendly terms, in which it is declared that the march of the troops was occasioned only by the particular circumstances of the moment and the general situation in Europe, but that there existed no motive of apprehension that the harmony and good understanding which subsist between Spain and France should by any means be interrupted.[4] [Our information is that] immediately after this the Spanish Minister at Paris delivered a note to the French Ministers proposing a neutrality.

You will see from this what are the intentions of the Americans which I think it extremely proper you ought to know, as at this moment there is every probability of our being engaged in a war with France before this letter can reach you. Let what I have observed however remain in the most perfect secrecy in your breast: As I have written the above solely for your private information.

GRENVILLE TO HAMMOND [5]

No. 2.   WHITEHALL, February 8th, 1793.
Sir,
Intelligence having been received this Day from Ostend which gives the greatest Reason to suppose that War has been declared by the French Government against Great Britain and Holland I lose no time in acquainting you with it, though I doubt not you will have received an earlier Account of it from other Quarters.

I send you inclosed Copies of His Majesty's Message to both Houses of Parliament, and of the Addresses in Answer relative to the Augmentation of His Majesty's Forces by Sea and Land.[6]

GRENVILLE TO HAMMOND [7]

No. 3.   WHITEHALL, Feby. 8th, 1793.
Sir,
Intelligence having this Day been received of the actual declaration of War against Great Britain and Holland by the National Convention at Paris, I lose no time in communicating to you this important intelligence.

---

[4] Under Secretary Burges, it appears, was misinformed. Nothing has been found to substantiate this account.
[5] F. O. 115 : 2.
[6] War was declared by France against Great Britain and Holland on Feb. 1, 1793. The King's message of Jan. 28, 1793, and the address of the Commons of Feb. 1, 1793, are in *Parl. History of England*, XXX, 238, 287.
[7] F. O. 115 : 2.

I inclose to you a Copy of His Majesty's most gracious Message to both Houses of Parliament of the 28th ultimo with a printed set of the Papers therein referred to, and also Copies of the Addresses of the two Houses thereupon. I also send you a printed Paper containing the Decree of the National Convention for commencing Hostilities against this Country and Holland. These several Papers will inform you fully of the different points which have been under discussion, and of the Line which His Majesty has uniformly pursued, and are sufficient to place in the strongest light the unjust and unprovoked Aggression of France against His Majesty and His Allies.

It is not His Majesty's intention that you should make use of these Papers for the Purpose of presenting any formal memorial on the subject, unless you should receive further directions for that purpose, but you will take every other mode to inform the minds both of the Government and of the Public in the Country where you reside as to the true nature, origin, and Grounds of the Defensive War in which the King and His Ally are now engaged in consequence of the manifest and undisguised aggression of France.

The nature of this quarrel is indeed in itself so manifest, that I conceive the French Government will hardly venture even to make any application to the United States for assistance, on the Ground of their defensive Treaty of Alliance.[8] But you will diligently watch everything that can have the smallest relation to that subject, and you will make every practicable exertion to counteract any such attempt, if it should be made on the Part of France.

The strict and incontestible justice of His Majesty's conduct towards France is so apparent that it cannot be necessary for me to detail the Arguments which you are to use on that subject. Nor will it escape you that every consideration of the Interest of the United States, must lead them to avoid an interference which is not called for by the terms of the subsisting Treaty, and which must necessarily involve them in the most serious misunderstanding with this Country.

Supposing the Neutrality of the American Government to be clearly ascertained, there would still remain the utmost occasion for your assiduity and vigilance in preventing this Neutrality from being violated by the Individual Subjects of the States. I can in the present moment only recommend this object to your most particular attention; but I may probably have occasion to write to you more at large upon it in a short time.

---

[8] In the "traité d'alliance éventuelle et défensive" of 1778 the United States by Article XI had undertaken to guarantee the French island possessions in the West Indies.

GRENVILLE TO HAMMOND [9]

No. 4.   WHITEHALL, Feb'y 12th, 1793.

Sir,

I send you inclosed a Copy of His Majesty's Message to both Houses of Parliament which was presented Yesterday on the Subject of the War declared in France against Great Britain and Holland. And I shall send you the Addresses in answer thereto by the first opportunity in order that you may communicate them at the Court where you reside.[10]

GRENVILLE TO HAMMOND [11]

No. 5.   WHITEHALL, March 8th, 1793.

Sir,

Your Letters to No. 4 inclusive have been received and laid before the King.

His Majesty having judged it for the Good of His Service to make a new Arrangement in the Districts of His Consuls in America, by appointing Sir John Temple [12] to be Consul General in the Eastern States, and Mr. Bond to be Consul General in the Southern and Middle States, I take the earliest Opportunity of acquainting You with the Alteration which has been made accordingly in these Gentlemen's Commissions.

GRENVILLE TO HAMMOND [13]

No. 6.   WHITEHALL, March 12th, 1793.

Sir,

Your several Dispatches to No. 5 inclusive have been received and laid before the King.

I avail myself of the opportunity of Mr. Bond's return to America to send you such Instructions as may enable You to regulate your Conduct under the present critical Circumstances and to take such Measures as may best conduce to the furtherance of His Majesty's Service.

---

[9] F. O. 115: 2.
[10] The King's message of Feb. 11, and the address of the Commons of Feb. 12, 1793, are printed in *Parl. History*, XXX, 344, 360.
[11] F. O. 115: 2.
[12] Sir John Temple (1732–1798), Boston-born Loyalist; in 1785 he had been made the first British consul general in the United States.
[13] F. O. 115: 2.

I have received information that a Monsieur Genet,[14] who some time acted as Chargé d'Affaires of the present French Government at Petersburgh has lately sailed from France to America, with the Character of Minister from the French Republic to the United States. There is reason to believe that this Person has been charged with several Commissions of considerable importance, and that he is instructed to prevail on the American Government to afford the present ruling Powers in France such material Assistance as may enable them to obtain Supplies of Corn, Flour and Stores and to fit out in the American Ports a number of Privateers [15] for the purpose of injuring the Trade and Navigation of this Country.

It will therefore be very necessary for you to be upon your guard, and to exert Yourself to the utmost of your Power to counteract and defeat these Views of Monsieur Genet. You will lose no Time in taking the necessary Measures to convince the American Government of the Danger as well as the Impropriety of countenancing any such Proceedings on the part of the present Rulers of France, and You will make the strongest Representations against any attempts which may appear to be making either to fit out Privateers for the Service of the French in any of the American Ports, or to afford the French any other Assistance either direct or indirect, or to suffer any Vessels to be fitted out for their Service under French Letters of Marque, of which I am informed Mons. Genet has carried great Numbers with Him. And You will lose no Opportunity of supporting as far as may be in Your Power those Persons whom you may find well disposed to maintain the present Constitution of America and those Principles of Good Government which are congenial to the Constitution of Great Britain against any Attempts which may be made to introduce into that Country Principles similar to those which have been so generally and fatally propagated in France.

I have great reason to believe, that one principal Object of Mons. Genet's Mission is to procure a Supply of Corn and Provisions from the States of America and that for this Purpose he has been instructed to open a Negotiation with the American Government for liquidating the Payment of their loan to France by transmitting to the Ports of that Country a Supply of Corn and Provisions equal

---

[14] Edmond Charles Genêt, first minister of the French Republic to the United States, had been secretary to the French minister to Russia from 1787 until his expulsion in 1792 by Catherine the Great for his revolutionary sentiments. Genêt arrived at Charleston, April 8, 1793. and was formally received by Washington, at Philadelphia, May 18, 1793.

[15] Article XVII of the Franco-American Commercial Treaty of 1778 accorded French warships and privateers, with their prizes, the exclusive privileges of reception in American ports; Article XXII prohibited the enemies of France from fitting out privateers in American ports. Genêt assumed that the treaty gave to France, by implication, the privilege of fitting out privateers in American waters. On this, and the other problems which arose, see Charles Marion Thomas, *American Neutrality in 1793*.

to the amount of the Outstanding Debt. It will therefore be proper for You to use every means in your power to ascertain whether any such Negotiation is going forward. Should you be able to discover that such a Proposal has been made it would be of the utmost Importance to inform me as early as possible, of the particulars of it.[16] If in the result of any such Negotiation, Provisions and Grain should be actually shipped on board American Vessels, on the account of the French Government, they would evidently be French Property, and, as such, liable to Capture.

It is indeed necessary to state on this occasion that the Principle of free Ships making free Goods, is one which never has been recognized by this Country and that it undoubtedly will not be allowed in the present case.

As this is a point of very great importance, it will be necessary for You to explain it so distinctly and clearly that no doubts may remain, either as to the Principle on which the Conduct of this Country is founded, or as to the Measures which it will be thought proper to take, in order to prevent any such practises as must materially affect it's Interests under the existing Circumstances. You will therefore, in any Representations which you may have occasion to make on this Subject, very strongly inforce the principle I have mentioned, that Free Ships do not make Free Goods. The Affirmative of this Proposition would in its Consequences prove extremely detrimental to the Interests of this Country, as affording to the French those Means of Subsistence, and of carrying on the War, which, from the Nature of their present Situation, and of the Forces employed against Them, They must otherwise be unable to procure.

With respect even to American Property, bonâ fide such and which is carried to French Ports, on board American Vessels, it must be observed, that the Exemption from Capture does not extend to any of the Articles comprized under the Description of Contrebande de, Guerre, and which are of such a Nature as to enable the Enemies of this Country to carry on the War against Us. This is a principle arising from the general and established Law of Nations; and the Conduct of friendly Nations under Circumstances like the present, is as much to be governed by it, as when it had been particularly agreed upon in a regular Treaty.

Another Principle to be attended to on this Occasion, is that (universally recognized) which prevents the carrying any Goods, tho'

---

[16] Such a proposal for liquidating the debt to France was made by Genêt, May 22, 1793, and rejected by the United States, which would pay only the regular installments on the debt, as they fell due. Hammond to Grenville, June 10, 1793, No. 15, F. O. 5: 1; A. S. P., F. R., I, 142. Hamilton in March had divulged to Hammond that the Cabinet had earlier refused a similar request on the part of France. Hammond to Grenville. April 2, 1793, No. 11, *Most Secret and Confidential*, F. O. 5: 1.

clearly Neutral Property and innocent in their Nature, to such Parts of an Enemy's Dominions as are besieged or blocked up. And it is the more necessary that You should explain this Point, and cause it to be generally understood, because of the very great Probability which there is, that, at no very great distance, this Mode of preventing the French from receiving Supplies of any Sort, from several of their Ports, will be resorted to. And it is therefore extremely likely that, even if such Articles should, bonâ fide, be shipped by American Merchants in Voyages of Speculation to those Ports, they may on their arrival in Europe be precluded from entering into those Ports by the Circumstances of their being blocked by His Majesty's Vessels.

These are such plain and evident Principles and have so constantly been the rule of Conduct between friendly Powers, when one of them has been engaged in War, that I should flatter myself no attempt will be made on the Part of the American Government to act in Opposition to them, whatever endeavours may be made by Mons. Genet to carry a Point so essential to the Interests of his Employers. I have however thought it right to mention these Circumstances to you, that You might distinctly know the grounds on which it is His Majesty's Intention to act, and that You might be enabled to state fully to the American Government the reasons why His Majesty expects on their Part a fair Observance of that Neutrality in the course of the present War, which is so necessary for the Success of His Arms, and on which must so greatly depend the maintenance of that Friendship and Good Understanding which it must be equally the Wish of His Majesty and of the United States to preserve. With this view, it will be proper for you to take the best Means in your power to make it generally known in the Country where You reside, what are the Principles by which the Conduct of this Country will be governed in the present instance, and what Steps will be taken in every Case of an Attempt to convey Supplies to France: that the Persons in America who might have formed any Projects of this nature may be aware of the Consequences with which they must be attended, and that discussions upon this Subject may be prevented between His Majesty and the United States, which it is so much His Majesty's wish on every occasion to avoid.

If in the course of your Inquiries on this Subject, you should discover, that any Corn or Provisions shall have been actually purchased for the Use of the French or that, in Consequence of a Compliance with the Proposal of Monsieur Genet, which I have before mentioned, such Articles should have been shipped on board of any Vessels, in the Ports of America, for the purpose of their being transported to France, You will not fail to avail Yourself of any Opportunity which may occur of giving a Notice of this Circumstance to the Commanders of any of His Majesty's Ships who may be Cruizing in those Seas, and You will also, without delay, transmit Intelligence of it to Me.

GRENVILLE TO HAMMOND [17]

No. 7.   WHITEHALL, May 2d, 1793.
Sir,
Your Letters to No. 10 inclusive have been received and laid before the King.

I inclose to You a Copy of a Letter to Mr. Dundas, with Copies of the Papers therein referred to, in order that You may be enabled the more easily to procure further Intelligence respecting the Particulars therein mentioned, and also to transmit to the Officers of any of His Majesty's Ships of War, or of any Privateers, who may be on the American Coast, the earliest Intelligence respecting the Times of sailing of the several Vessels with the Supplies purchased by M. Ternant.[18] You will endeavour to do this in such a Manner as to excite as little Alarm as possible in the Minds of the Persons concerned in this Proceeding, so as that they may not adopt Measures to render the Condemnation more difficult.

GRENVILLE TO HAMMOND [19]

No. 8.   WHITEHALL, 5th July, 1793.
Sir,
Your Dispatches to No. 14 inclusive have been received and laid before the King.

I inclose to You for Your information the copy of an additional instruction given by His Majesty's Order in Council to the Commanders of the British Armed Vessels respecting the commerce of Neutral Nations with France in the Article of Grain, and also with regard to such French Ports as may in the course of the War be

---

[17] F. O. 115: 2.
[18] Intercepted dispatches of Jean de Ternant, Genêt's predecessor, had revealed that he had been purchasing provisions with funds received in payment on the American war debt to France. Hammond reported to Grenville, July 7, 1793, No. 16, F. O. 5: 5, that "The three million livres which Mr. Ternant asserts that he had induced the Secretary of the Treasury to advance to him, were in part of payment of the installments of the French debt due on the 3rd of September and the 5th of November 1792, and the 1st of January 1793, and not an anticipation of any subsequent installments as might have been inferred from the tenor of Mr. Ternant's correspondence. I think it necessary to state this explicitly, in order to vindicate this government from the suspicion of having deviated from the determination I have uniformly attributed to it, of refusing to admit any alteration in the settled mode of discharging the debt due to France."
[19] F. O. 115: 2.

blocked by the Vessels of His Majesty or of the other Powers engaged in the War.[20]

In Your communications on this Subject You will not fail to remark that by the law of Nations as laid down by the most modern Writers, particularly by Vattel, it is expressly stated that all provisions are to be considered as Articles of contraband, and as such liable to confiscation, in the case where the depriving an Enemy of these Supplies is one of the means intended to be employed for reducing him to reasonable terms of peace. That the situation of France is notoriously such as to lead to the employing this mode of distressing Her by the joint Operations of the different Powers engaged in this War; that the reasoning which in these Authors applies to all cases of this sort is certainly much more applicable to the case where the distress results as it does in the present instance from the unusual mode of war employed by the Enemy himself in having armed almost the whole labouring class of the French Nation for the purpose of commencing and supporting hostilities against all the Governments of Europe and most of all to the circumstances of a trade which is now almost entirely carried on by the pretended Government of France itself: and which is therefore no longer to be considered as a mercantile speculation of individuals, but as an immediate operation of the very persons who have declared War, and are now carrying it on against this Country; that on these considerations therefore it would have been perfectly justifiable if the Powers at War had considered all provisions as contraband, and had directed them as such to be brought in for confiscation.

That by the present measure, so far from going to the utmost extent which the law of Nations, and the circumstances of the case would have warranted, this Government has only prevented the French from being supplied with Corn, omitting all mention of other provisions, and particularly of Rice, an article so material in the scale of the commerce of America; and that even with respect to Corn, the rule adopted is one which instead of confiscating the cargoes secures to the Proprietors, supposing them neutral, a full indemnification for any loss they may possibly sustain.

With respect to the rule about Ports blockaded, it is conformable to the general law and practice of all Nations, and the exception there

---

[20] This order-in-council, dated June 8, 1793, directed the seizure and detention of "all vessels loaded wholly or in part with corn, flour, or meal, bound for any port in France, or any port occupied by the armies of France," in order that such cargoes might be purchased on behalf of His Majesty's government, "and the ships be released after such purchase and after a due allowance for freight," or in order that the masters of such ships might, on giving due security, "be permitted to dispose of their cargoes of corn, meal, or flour, in the ports of any country in amity with His Majesty." Hammond transmitted the order to Jefferson, Sept. 12, 1793, with a letter embodying the explanations and arguments given him by Grenville. *A. S. P., F. R.,* I, 240.

mentioned as to Denmark and Sweden has reference to Our existing treaties with those Powers, and cannot therefore give any just ground of umbrage or jealousy to those Powers with whom We have no such treaties.[21]

His Majesty's Servants have seen with great satisfaction the tone and purport of the answer given to the several Memorials which You took upon You with great propriety to present relative to the Conduct of America as a Neutral Nation. You will not fail to follow up the several points therein referred to, and to use your utmost endeavours to prevail on the general Government to exert itself for the purpose of repressing such irregularities as are disgraceful to the character of a Sovereign Neutral Power, and have so manifest a tendency to involve them in disputes the most injurious to their interests.

I transmit to You for Your information copies of treaties lately entered into by His Majesty with several different Powers of Europe, and I think it right to apprize You that a similar Convention, (including the Articles respecting Neutral Commerce which You will find in that with Prussia) has been signed with the Court of Madrid, but that the ratifications are not yet known here to have been exchanged, which circumstance prevents a formal communication of that instrument.[22]

GRENVILLE TO HAMMOND [23]

No. 9.   WHITEHALL, August 12th, 1793.
Sir,

I send You inclosed Copy of a Letter from Mr. Glassford to Mr. Dundas respecting a Suit now depending in the General Court of Maryland for the Confiscation of Property formerly British, in the Possession of Mr. Robert Ferguson by Purchase; and I am to desire that You will give Mr. Ferguson all due Assistance and Support in

---

[21] The order-in-council of June 8, 1793 directed the seizure for condemnation of all vessels on their first attempt to enter a blockaded port, with the exception of Danish and Swedish vessels, which on their first attempt were to be prevented from entering, but not seized.

[22] On March 25, 1793 Great Britain and Russia agreed to stop all exports of provisions or military supplies to French ports, "to take all other measures for injuring the commerce of France," and to unite their efforts to prevent all neutral powers "from giving, on this occasion of common concern to every civilized State, any protection whatever, directly or indirectly, in consequence of their neutrality, to the commerce or property of the French on the sea, or in the ports of France." *A. S. P., F. R.,* I, 243. Similar articles were inserted in other treaties made by Great Britain in 1793, including those with Spain, on May 25, and Prussia, on July 14, 1793.

[23] F. O. 115 : 2.

the Preservation of his just Rights, if he should apply to You for that Purpose.[24]

GRENVILLE TO HAMMOND [25]

No. 10. (Circular)   WHITEHALL, Oct. 25th, 1793.

Sir,

I inclose to you by His Majesty's Command the Copy of a declaration relative to the Affairs of France which you will communicate in the King's name at the place of your residence. His Majesty intertains no doubt that the sentiments contained in this Paper will be found entirely comformable to those of the other Powers of Europe on an occasion so generally interesting to them all.[26]

---

[24] In his letter to Dundas, dated Glasgow, July 30, 1793, Henry Glassford stated that his brother-in-law, Henry Riddell, had sold the property to Robert Ferguson in 1778, and that Ferguson had taken possession of it and become an American citizen in 1779, before the enactment of the Maryland law for the confiscation of British property.

[25] F. O. 115 : 2.

[26] The declaration, published Oct. 29, 1793, is in *Parl. History*, XXX, 1057–1060. It called upon the people of France "to join the standard of an hereditary monarchy . . . to unite themselves once more under the empire of law, of morality, and of religion . . .."

INSTRUCTIONS OF 1794

GRENVILLE TO HAMMOND [1]

No. 1.   WHITEHALL, Jany. —, 1794.

Sir,

Your several Dispatches to No. 23 inclusive have been received and laid before the King.

The constant attention which you have given to His Majesty's interests in America, and the prudence and ability which have marked the whole course of the Measures you have adopted have been such as to leave no room for any instructions on my part to regulate your conduct in the different instances which have arisen and with respect to which you were in possession of the general line adopted by His Majesty.

You will have learnt before this letter reaches you, that the ruling faction in France have determined on the recall of Genet, who was connected with the party of Brissot,[2] and have sent to America a new Minister who will probably be instructed to observe a more temperate and conciliatory line of conduct. This circumstance will not fail to excite your vigilance and attention in order to counteract the Schemes with which he may be charged, and the atrocious and execrable Crimes which are now avowedly made the basis of the present system of things in France must have their effect in America as they have had in every part of Europe in opening Men's Minds as to the necessary consequences of the former principles and proceedings in France, and in exciting a detestation of the System itself and of the persons concerned in it.

With respect to the conduct of the present Government of America His Majesty's Ministers think that there appears to have prevailed in it's general tenor a desire for the maintenance of a fair Neutrality and even a disposition friendly towards this Country. This Sentiment is certainly on every account to be encouraged by you; but the persuasion of it's existence ought not to prevent friendly but urgent representations in those cases where either the acknowledged weakness of the federal Government or the evil disposition of some of the persons entrusted with provincial

---

[1] F. O. 115 : 3.

[2] Jean Pierre Brissot de Warville, a leader of the Girondists or Brissotines, whose party had been violently ousted from power by the Jacobins. In August of 1793 Washington's Cabinet had decided to send a special courier to Paris to demand the recall of Genêt. He was succeeded by Joseph Fauchet, who was presented Feb. 22, 1794. For a summary of Genêt's brief and stormy career as minister, see Jefferson to G. Morris, Aug. 16, 1793, *A. S. P., F. R.,* I, 167–172.

Authority have afforded to His Majesty or his Subjects any just ground of complaint.

One of these points is unquestionably the Acquiescence of the Governor[s?] for so long a time in what Mr. Jefferson in his Letter to you of the 9th of Septem' justly terms an Usurpation of Admiralty jurisdiction by the Consuls of France within the States.[3] Besides the gross partiality which such an Acquiescence implied and the inconvenience to which it subjected His Majesty's Subjects within the Dominions of a friendly power, it has a natural tendency to create disputes between the King's Subjects and the Inhabitants of America, as many of the latter have presumed on the sentence and condemnation passed by the Consul as sufficient proof of the legality of the prizes and have on those grounds purchased British Vessels brought into the Ports of America by the Cruizers fitted out from thence under the Authority of Mr. Genet. Some of these Vessels will, as I understand, immediately become the subject of litigation in our Courts. It does not become me to anticipate the decision but it is very important that you should prepare the American Ministers for the assertion on your part of this principle, viz, that from an act, the validity of which is not recognized, but on the contrary expressly contested by the American Government no claim can result to any of it's Subjects. It seems indeed impossible that this principle can be contested and it is therefore to be expected that in conformity to it, our Courts will consider the Vessels in question as being exactly in the same Situation in which they would have been if no such proceedings had taken place in America. With respect to such other questions as may then arise to affect the ultimate decision I have already stated that I think it improper now to anticipate the opinion of our Courts concerning Vessels under the circumstances of those likely to be the Subjects of litigation. But it must incontestably appear an object of just political representation that the very existence of these disputes is an additional motive if any such could be wanted for inducing the American Government to exert itself with effect for the prevention of such proceedings in future.

GRENVILLE TO HAMMOND [4]

No. 2.   DOWNING STREET, Jany. 1794.

Sir,

I inclose herewith the Copy of a Note which was delivered to me in the course of the last Month by Mr. Pinckney, relative to the In-

---

[3] Jefferson's letter to Hammond of Sept. 9, 1793 may be found in *A. S. P.. F. R.*, I, 176. On Sept. 7, 1793, two days before, Jefferson had sharply warned the consuls of France to desist from claiming and exercising, within the United States, a general admiralty jurisdiction. *Ibid.*, I, 175.

[4] F. O. 115 : 3.

structions to Ships of War and Privateers, dated the 18th [5] of June last.[6] It is certainly due in justice both to Mr. Pinckney and to the American Government to state that this Note is expressed in moderate and conciliatory language such as His Majesty's Ministers are desirous should always prevail in their intercourse between the Two Countries. But the Principles there laid down are such, as cannot be acknowledged or acted upon by His Majesty: and it is therefore necessary that an Answer should be given to it, refuting in the same conciliatory tone, the Arguments there contained, and stating His Majesty's Intention of adhering to the Line which He has adopted in this respect, and which he considers as more favourable to the Commerce of America, than the Principles of the Laws of Nations.

I have thought it right to transmit this Note to you, in order that you may prepare the reply and deliver it to the American Government.[7] My reason for this has been, that I well know you are perfectly in Possession of all the Reasoning upon the Subject; and that I am sure it will be stated by you with energy and precision, and at the same time with moderation and discretion. And, as it is almost certain, that this Paper will become the object of public discussion in America, you will have the additional Advantage of being able to point it in such a Manner, as may be most applicable to the State of the public opinion there, at the time when the Paper comes to be presented.

I feel it right however to direct Your attention to Three Points, though I am satisfied they would not have escaped you:

The first is,——that the doctrine of the Right of the Belligerent Power to stop and even to seize Supplies of Provisions going to the Enemy is strongly laid down in all the antient Authors, and is even recognized by Vattel, whose Writings contain, as you know, a much more modified and limited System in these respects, than that which is to be found in the Books of Authority, on which the practise and Law of Nations rest. And, in point of fact, it would, I apprehend, be found on examination that the milder usage with respect to Provisions is of recent Date.

The Second is——that the Argument alledged by Mr. Pinckney, from the Enumeration of Contreband contained in particular Treaties, is evidently fallacious, as those Treaties are not declaratory of the Law of Nations, but are restrictions and modifications of that Law by special Agreement between the Contracting Parties; and are consequently neither binding on other Powers, nor even on the

[5] Should be "8th" instead of "18th."
[6] Jefferson on Sept. 7, 1793 had instructed Pinckney to make a formal protest against the order-in-council of June 8, 1793, which Pinckney had done, in December. *A. S. P., F. R.,* I, 239–240, 449.
[7] Hammond's reply to Pinckney's memorial is printed in *A. S. P., F. R.,* I, 449–450.

Parties themselves in other Cases. But, if the Argument were just, the conclusion from it would be in our favour; for, out of the Two only existing Treaties by which His Majesty's Conduct is regulated towards Nations Neutral in the present War one (that with Sweden), expressly includes Provisions in the Enumeration of Contraband.

The Third point is——that when Mr. Pinckney urges as an Argument against this Measure, the right which it would give to France to do the same, he in effect, admits the propriety of the Conduct of this Country. It being notorious that the Conduct of France, both before and since the Instruction in question, has been such as Mr. Pinckney alledges that it might become in consequence of that Measure.

I have already said, that with respect to the general turn of the reply, and the use to be made of these Topics according to local and temporary circumstances, I rest with full Confidence on your discretion and ability, of which His Majesty's Servants have seen so many satisfactory Proofs. I have therefore nothing further to add on the Subject.

I inclose for your information a Copy of a Note, presented by Mr. Hailes [8] to the Danish Minister, when he communicated the Instruction in question.

GRENVILLE TO HAMMOND [9]

No. 3.   DOWNING STREET, 10th Jany. 1794.

Sir,

You will receive herewith inclosed the Copies of two Instructions which have been given under His Majesty's Royal Sign Manual to the Commanders of His Majesty's Ships of War and Privateers, the first dated Novem[r] 6th and the second the — of the present Month.[10]

It is possible that with respect to the former of these orders a considerable degree of dissatisfaction may have arisen in America. If anything is stated to you on the subject you will confine Yourself to

---

[8] The "declaratory memorial" presented by David Hailes, the British minister at Copenhagen, and the Danish counter-memorial, are given in the *Annual Register,* 1793, pp. 176–183.

[9] F. O. 115 : 3.

[10] The orders-in-council of Nov. 6, 1793 and Jan. 8, 1794. The first, more sweeping than the "Provision Order" of June 8, 1793, directed the seizure of "all ships laden with goods the produce of any colony belonging to France, or carrying provisions or other supplies for the use of any such colony." This order of Nov. 6, 1793 was modified by that of Jan. 8, 1794, which forbade a direct trade between the French West Indies and France yet permitted a direct trade between the islands and the United States in articles not contraband of war. *A. S. P., F. R.,* I, 430–431. Before the news of the modifying order of January reached the West Indies, under the order of November (which was not made public at London until late in December) about two hundred and fifty American vessels had been seized, most of them on direct passage between neutral ports, and one hundred and fifty of these were condemned. See Fulwar Skipwith, American consul at St. Eustatia, to the Sec. of State, March 7, 1794, *ibid.,* I, 429.

observing that this order no longer subsists—That it was occasioned by temporary Circumstances and particularly by the notoriety that by the extraordinary Events which had taken place at St. Domingo a larger and altogether unusual quantity of French Property, the produce of that Island and destined for the European Markets had been brought to America.—And that it was also known here upon indisputable evidence, that attempts would be made to bring those goods under those circumstances home to Europe in American Vessels. In this situation none of the principles by which the ordinary intercourse of Trade is or ought to be regulated, could apply, and the measure of bringing in Articles so circumstanced for *Adjudication* was grounded on a just and reasonable presumption, strengthened by the knowledge that bringing French West India Produce to the European Market from America was a Speculation wholly out of the Course of the usual Trade of the latter Country.

This measure however was in it's nature only temporary and that instruction having been now revoked, a new order has been given regulating the situation in which the Commerce of America in this respect shall be allowed to stand.

In deciding on this Subject a liberal and friendly consideration has been had of the peculiar situation in which America stands as with respect to the West Indies.

The Principle which this Country has uniformly maintained as with respect to the Colonial Commerce of it's Enemies is one which is of evident and indisputable justice. A War between two Nations ought as little as possible to prejudice the usual and accustomed Commerce of a third not engaged in the Quarrel. But the latter ought not, on the other hand, to desire or claim from the War new rights or pretentions to the prejudice of either belligerent Party. For this reason, when France, who monopolized in time of Peace the exclusive Commerce and Supply of Her West India Islands, attempted in time of War to open those branches of Trade to Neutral Nations in order to elude the naval Superiority of Great Britain; the Government of this Country has always resisted that Measure and has considered the Neutral Vessels attempting to engage in this Commerce as not entitled to carry it on.

The same principles might with justice be applied to the Case of America, but it's effect in detail would be difficult. By the System established since the Peace of 1783, France has permitted a limited Intercourse between Her Colonies and America and that even in American Vessels. But the Articles both of Import and Export which this intercourse comprized were confined, and particularly the two great Articles of Sugar on the one Side and Flour on the other were excepted from it. A Power was given to the Governors to extend the regulations in times of occasional distress; as is also the case in our Islands, but the exercise of that Power cannot be considered as constituting any case of ordinary Commerce.

It would therefore on the strictest principles of justice be perfectly just in this Government to contend, that America should not derive from the War the right of carrying the Commerce of the French Islands as to those Articles in which the Americans could not trade by the established System in time of Peace.

All the circumstances of the situation, have however been considered here, and a particular attention has been paid to the object of avoiding to give grounds of complaint which although not founded in strict principles might nevertheless assist the designs of evil disposed Persons in America against the internal Tranquillity of that Country and against the System of Neutrality which the present Government there appears sincerely disposed to maintain.

These Considerations have occasioned the Instruction which I now transmit to you. Your own knowledge of this Subject and the Principles which I have already stated will enable you to observe how favorable it is to the Commerce of America without my entering into a minute discussion of the regulations which it contains. And I have no doubt of your availing yourself in the best manner of it in order to promote His Majesty's Interests in the part of the World where you reside.

GRENVILLE TO HAMMOND [11]

No. 4.   DOWNING STREET, Jany. 1794.
Sir,

I think it right to acquaint You, that, in the conversation I had lately with Mr. Pinckney, that Gentleman made some observations on the Truce, which some time ago was concluded between the Portugueze and the Algerines. He observed that, altho' it was not a subject on which Official Representations could properly be made, he nevertheless had reason to apprehend, that it would occasion a disagreeable Sensation in America, as it might and probably would be considered there as a Measure calculated to distress the American Commerce.[12]

As it is not improbable, notwithstanding the Explanation I gave Mr. Pinckney, that this subject may become a matter of clamour and misrepresentation in America, I think it right to put you in possession of the real State of the Case, that you may be enabled to

---

[11] F. O. 115 : 3.

[12] It was so considered: after the truce arranged by Great Britain, American commerce to the Mediterranean and the Iberian peninsula was demoralized by an Algerian fleet, which had quickly appeared west of the Straits of Gilbraltar, captured vessels, and enslaved seamen. *A. S. P., F. R.,* I, 295–296, 327.

explain it satisfactorily, should circumstances render it necessary, and to do away [with] any bad impressions which may be occasioned from an imperfect or perhaps partial Statement of it.

An Application having been made, about the month of April last, to the King on the part of Her Most Faithful Majesty, that His Majesty would employ His good Offices, for the purpose of endeavouring to accomodate the difference which had arisen between the Portugueze and the Regency of Algiers, in order that the former might not be prevented from co-operating with the British Admiral for the Service of the Common Cause; His Majesty, convinced of the importance of relieving His Ally from an Embarrassment which evidently must have impeded it's operations as a Party in the War against France, did not hesitate to comply with this request. Instructions were accordingly sent to Mr. Logie, His Majesty's Consul at Algiers, directing him to make use of all the influence he might derive from the Character with which he was invested, in order to obtain this desireable object, either by means of a Truce, or by any other secure and satisfactory mode. The Application so made proved successful. In consequence of Mr. Logie's Efforts, a Truce was concluded between the Regency of Algiers and the Court of Lisbon; but the Terms of Pacification, on which the former of these Powers insists, being very unreasonable, it is probable that Hostilities will be renewed.

I have been the more particular in thus stating to you the circumstances of this very plain and natural transaction, that you might be enabled, in any conversation you may happen to have on the subject with the American Ministers, to explain it fully to them. The Transaction itself is of a nature to preclude the possibility of the American Government making any direct Representation upon it; as there cannot be a doubt that His Majesty had completely a Right to interfere, to procure Peace for His Ally from a State with which He was in Amity; especially when it is considered, that the Object of that Interference was to enable the Portugueze to act more effectually against the Common Enemy. And it is an unheard of refinement to say, that His Majesty was bound to abstain from such Interference, because the effect of a Pacification might leave the Algerines more at liberty to annoy the Trade of America.

No idea certainly existed in His Majesty's Mind of wishing to injure America by Contributing to the re-establishment of Peace between Portugal and Algiers. Even if such a Policy could have made a part of the Councils of this Country, it is evident that the Effect of a Measure of this Nature on the Supply of France must be very inconsiderable indeed, and that the property of the King's Subjects is in some Degree exposed by the risk to which American Vessels are subjected.

No. 5.   DOWNING STREET, Jany. 1794.

Sir,

I inclose to you Copy of a Letter from Mr. Secretary Dundas to Lieutenant Governor Williamson at Jamaica; by which Mr. Dundas communicates to him the information which You transmitted to me in your Dispatch No. 23 respecting the proposals made to you by the Inhabitants and Proprietors at St. Domingo, who had been driven from that Island and obliged to take refuge in America.[14] You will perceive that by this Letter Lieutenant Governor Williamson is instructed to communicate with you with respect to the mode of carying into execution the proposal made to you. I am therefore to desire, that you will pay attention to every Information on this important Subject, which the Lieutenant Governor or the Commander in Chief may from time to time transmit to you; and that you will give every assistance in your power for carrying into execution the object of arming and transporting to St. Domingo such of the French Inhabitants and Proprietors of that Island, as you may deem most deserving of confidence, and most proper to be employed on an Expedition of this nature. It is impossible for me to give you any more precise directions upon these points, the propriety and the execution of which must necessarily depend upon the circumstances of the moment, and on Considerations resulting from the actual situation of Affairs at the time when you receive this Letter: but I am convinced you will on this, as on other occasions, exert yourself to the utmost with zeal and discretion to facilitate the execution of an object which, so far as an Estimate can be formed of it at present, seems likely to be attended with the best Consequences to His Majesty's Service.

GRENVILLE TO HAMMOND [15]

No. 6.   DOWNING STREET, Jany. 1794.

Sir,

In your different Dispatches I have remarked the Steps which you have taken in Mr. Pagan's Case [16] and the decision which has taken place in America with respect thereto. It is probable that I shall by the next Packet be enabled to write to you further on that Subject, but in the meantime I think it necessary not to omit apprizing you,

---

[13] F. O. 115 : 3.
[14] Hammond in his dispatch No. 23, Nov. 10, 1793, F. O. 5 : 1 had reported that French fugitives from San Domingo, royalist in sympathy, had requested of him passports for the return of some two to three thousand men to that part of the island which had been brought under British control.
[15] F. O. 115 : 3.
[16] See Grenville to Hammond, Oct. 5, 1791, *supra.*

that persons the best qualified to judge on the subject here entertain great doubts whether there is in fact any just ground of complaint against that decision; and that it will therefore be proper for you not to take any further steps respecting it 'till you hear again from me.

GRENVILLE TO HAMMOND [17]

No. 7.   DOWNING STREET, 21 Jany. 1794.
Sir,
This Day His Majesty opened the Session of Parliament with a most Gracious Speech from the Throne, of which I send you inclosed a Printed Copy for Your information and that of the Government of the Country where you reside. The addresses of both Houses to His Majesty will be forwarded to you from my Office by the first Opportunity.[18]

GRENVILLE TO HAMMOND [19]

No. 8.   DOWNING STREET, 6th Febry. 1794.
Sir,
I have no Dispatches from you to acknowledge since the date of my last Letters which I sent by the January Packet, and of which I now send You Duplicates; Triplicates and Quadruplicates having been forwarded to you on the 13th Ult°. by the American Ships the Belvidere and Monro, under cover to Sir John Temple at New York.

It was my intention (as you will perceive from my Dispatch No. 6) to have written to you fully by this Mail on the subject of Mr. Pagan's Case,[20] with respect to which considerable doubt had been entertained by those persons here who were best qualified to form a judgement upon it. I have however recently been informed, by a letter from Consul Mr. [Mac]Donogh at Boston, that a Compromise had taken place between Mr. Pagan and Mr. Hooper in consequence of which the former had been released from his confinement. As this is the case, it will be unnecessary for me to enter into any detail of the reasons which appear to me to be evident and conclusive against any further interference on your part in favor of Mr. Pagan. I must however desire, that should any fresh application be made to you by that Gentleman to take any Steps in his behalf, you will abstain from doing so until you shall have transmitted the nature and Grounds of such Application to me, and until you shall have received further instructions upon the Subject.

---

[17] F. O. 115 : 3.
[18] These are printed in *Parl. History*, XXX, 1045, 1090.
[19] F. O. 115 : 3.
[20] See Grenville to Hammond, Oct. 5, 1791, *supra*.

GRENVILLE TO HAMMOND [21]

No. 9.   DOWNING STREET, 3d April 1794.
Sir,
I have not any Dispatches from you to acknowledge since the date of my last letter.

I send you inclosed Copy of a letter from Commodore George of His Majesty's Ship Hussar to Mr. Schoolbred the Vice Consul at Charleston, which has been transmitted by the Commodore to the Lords Commissioners of the Admiralty, and to which at appears no Answer was returned by Mr. Schoolbred. As the object which Commodore George had in view when he wrote the Letter in question namely the confinement of many of His Majesty's Subjects in a Prison Ship by the french in the Harbour of Charleston was of great importance, and as Mr. Schoolbred was bound by the duty of His Situation as a Public Officer in the Service of Government to pay attention to an Application of this nature made by one of His Majesty's Officers, I am to desire that you will forthwith call upon Mr. Schoolbred to assign the reason why no Answer was returned to Commodore George, and that you will also enquire into the fact itself, and, if you shall find it to be true, that you will make the necessary Representations upon it to the American Government.[22]

GRENVILLE TO HAMMOND [23]

No. 10.[24]   DOWNING STREET, 3d April 1794.
Sir,
I send you inclosed, for your Information, Copy of an Order made by His Majesty in Council respecting the Commercial intercourse between this Country and America.[25]

GRENVILLE TO HAMMOND [26]

No. 11.   DOWNING STREET, 10th May 1794.
Sir,
Your Dispatch No. 1 has been duly received and laid before the King.

---

[21] F. O. 115 : 3.

[22] James Schoolbred had been superseded as Vice Consul at Charleston by Benjamin Moodie within a short time after the date of Commodore George's letter. Hammond had no doubt that his failure to answer was accidental and not intentional. As to the French prison ship in Charleston harbor, Hammond had not registered a protest, since only a small number of British seamen were confined for about a month, "and since every complaint that I could have made on the occasion was anticipated by the general government with a promptitude and decision, which I should have been happy to have seen more frequently exerted." Hammond to Grenville, June 8, 1794, No. 23, F. O. 5 : 5.

[23] F. O. 115 : 3.

[24] This instruction was marked No. 8, but the proper designation is No. 10. One of the drafts in F. O. 5 : 4 was later changed from No. 8 to No. 10.

[25] The order-in-council was dated March 26, 1794, a general regulatory order respecting American trade.

[26] F. O. 115 : 3.

I send you inclosed for your information Copies of a Treaty signed at the Hague on the 19th Ulto. between His Majesty, the King of Prussia and the States General of the United Provinces; of a separate Article signed at the same time and place between His Majesty and the King of Prussia; of a Convention also signed at the same time and place between His Majesty and the States General of the United Provinces; and of a Convention between Denmark and Sweden, signed at Copenhagen the 27th of March last.[27]

GRENVILLE TO HAMMOND [28]

No. 12.   DOWNING STREET, 10th May 1794.

Sir,

A convention has been signed between Denmark and Sweden the object and tendency of which you will perceive by the copy which I inclose with my other dispatch of this date—It has just come to my knowledge that Mr. D'Engeiston [29] the Swedish minister has communicated this proposition to Mr. Pinckney that the American government should accede to this convention and that the latter having requested that this proposal should be delivered to him in writing Mr. D'Engeiston accordingly delivered to him a note containing a communication of the convention itself and an invitation from the Swedish government to the United States for their accession to it. As this is a matter too important to admit of delay, I lose no time in giving you notice of it and I must desire that you will exert yourself to the utmost to prevent the American government from acceding to the measure now proposed to them.[30] In such confidential discussions as you may have

---

[27] By the treaty of April 19, 1794 Prussia agreed to furnish 64,000 men to act with the armies of Great Britain and Holland. She was to place all conquests at their disposal on consideration of £50,000 a month, £300,000 at the beginning and £100,000 at the end of the campaign, with bread and forage money. The treaty was for the year 1794; but its renewal was stipulated in a separate article. De Martens, Traités, V, 610–616. The convention between Denmark and Sweden of March 27, 1794 reaffirmed the principles of the Armed Neutrality of 1780. James Brown Scott, ed., The Armed Neutralities of 1780 and 1800, pp. 440–443.

[28] F. O. 115 : 3. The instruction was written in cipher.

[29] Lars D'Engestrom, or von Engeström. The name was variously spelled, D'Engeiston (as above), D'Engerstroem (by Hammond in his dispatch to Grenville of Jan. 5, 1795, No. 1, F. O. 5 : 8), Engestrom, Engerstrom, Engelstroem.

[30] After deciphering this instruction Hammond called upon Hamilton and was assured by him that the United States had no intention of joining with Denmark and Sweden, because "it was the settled policy of this government in every contingency, even in that of an open contest with Great Britain, to avoid entangling itself with European connexions. ... In support of this policy Mr. Hamilton urged many of the arguments advanced in your Lordship's despatch—the dissimilitude between the political views as well as between the general interests of the United States and those of the two Baltic Powers—and the inefficiency of the latter, from their enfeebled condition, either to protect the navigation of the former in Europe, or to afford it any active assistance, if necessary, in its own territory." Hammond to Grenville, Aug. 3, 1794, No. 28, F. O. 5 : 5.

For the relation to the Jay-Grenville negotiations of this attempt to revive the Armed Neutrality of 1780, and of Hamilton's confidential assurances to Hammond, see Bemis, Jay's Treaty, chaps. xi, xii.

upon this subject with the American ministers you will not fail to observe the marked difference which subsists between the actual circumstance of America and of Denmark and Sweden and how totally the interests of the former are unconnected with those views which actuate the two Baltic powers in their late conduct. Even with relation to the pretended motives assigned by those powers for the step they have last taken it is evident that America can have no reason for being influenced by those motives supposing their application to the case of Denmark and Sweden were acknowledged instead of being so clearly to be denied. The conduct of the American ministers appears hitherto to have been uninfluenced by that scandalous partiality towards the criminal system now prevailing in France which disgraces the councils of Denmark and Sweden and the commerce and navigation of the United States have in return been so very favorably considered by this country in the late regulation—respecting the navigation of neutral flags and in all the conduct observed by his Majesty's officers. The American government must be aware of the many risks they may incur in every point of view should they suffer themselves by an acquiescence in the proposal now made by Sweden to be drawn into an eventual contest with this country in support of the collusive and fraudulent commerce which has been carried on from the ports of the Baltic, and in the encouragement of which the United States can have no interest whatever. The American ministers cannot be ignorant of the low and enfeebled state of the marine both of Denmark and Sweden and how little those powers are in a condition to carry on a naval war against the united strength of Great Britain, Holland, Spain, and Russia and less to afford any assistance to such distant Allies as the Americans. As a proof of this I send you a state of the present naval force of Sweden by which it appears that the Swedes so far from being able to assist others are totally unable to furnish the stipulated number of eight ships for completing the armament agreed to be brought forward under the recent convention, and in fact it is notorious that even for the appearance of making this armament they require a considerable subsidy from France the hope of which has been the only inducement for the signature of this convention on the part of Sweden. In addition to these arguments you will recall to the remembrance of the American government the many proofs they have had of his Majesty's cordial and friendly sentiments towards them as well as the many advantages they must derive from the continuance of the harmony and good understanding which hitherto has prevailed between the two countries and which it is his Majesty's sincere wish to maintain and improve.[31]

I think it right to acquaint you that Admiral Murray is now under orders to proceed to America with a squadron of ships of war—he is directed to take an early practicable opportunity to communicate with you respecting the state of affairs and the political situation of this country as with regard to the United States. One of the material objects of your attention will be to lose no time in obtaining from the American government a renewal of the assurance formerly given to you of permitting his Majesty's fleets to remain in the American ports in the same manner as has been allowed to the French ships of war.[32] With respect to all political points that may occur Admiral Murray will as much as possible regulate his conduct by your advice and information and I am persuaded that his appearance and continuance on the American coast cannot but be productive of advantage under these circumstances. At a proper period Admiral Murray will dispatch such convoys as he shall judge expedient to protect the British trade from America home, and as several of his Majesty's subjects may under the present circumstances be interested in the cargoes of American vessels destined for British ports or for the ports of powers in alliance or amity with his Majesty and as the present situation of America both as with respect to France and the Barbary powers renders the navigation of American ships in some degree precarious his Majesty would not disapprove of Admiral Murray's taking under his protection such American ships as have British property on board or any such as having American property shall appear to be incontestibly bound to British ports or to the ports of such other powers as above mentioned, supposing that the situation and conduct of the American government was such as to render this act of friendship on his part politically expedient and likely to be received in America with a proper sense of his Majesty's friendly disposition so manifested.[33]

---

[31] When Grenville wrote this he was not fully aware of the high indignation which prevailed in the United States against Great Britain, based on various grounds: the disinclination to continue the negotiations begun with Jefferson by Hammond or to evacuate the frontier posts, the Algerine truce, Lord Dorchester's inflammatory speech to the Indians, Lieut.-Governor Simcoe's occupation of the Miamis fort, and the sudden wholesale captures, without warning, of American vessels under the order-in-council of November 6, 1793; all of which had led to demands for commercial non-intercourse and for war with Britain, and to the enactment of the thirty-day Embargo of March 26, 1794.

[32] From Secretary of State Edmund Randolph (who had succeeded Jefferson on Jan. 2, 1792) Hammond obtained a renewal of the assurances given him by Jefferson in his letter of Sept. 9, 1793 (*A. S. P., F. R.*, I, 176). Hammond to Grenville, Aug. 3, 1794, No. 28, F. O. 5 : 5.

[33] Hammond thought it inexpedient under existing circumstances to protect such American ships by British convoy: it was by no means probable that Americans would regard it as a friendly gesture, and it was quite probable that every artifice would be employed to derive some collusive advantage from it. He was pleased to report that the squadron under Rear Admiral George Murray had arrived off the American coast, and had captured sixteen of the American vessels laden with flour and provisions on account of the French government, as they were preparing to leave the Delaware under French convoy. Hammond to Grenville, Aug. 3, 1794, No. 28, F. O. 5 : 5. Later, in 1796, Phineas Bond suggested that

You will best be able to judge of the manner of bringing forward and arranging a matter which involves points of such delicacy and that may if properly managed under favorable circumstances be made the means of establishing a system of mutual good offices and friendship and is therefore a very desirable arrangement. You must however remark that in settling this point in concert with Admiral Murray the utmost care must be taken to prevent any collusion which might otherwise be practised by ships destined for the supply of France which may avail themselves of this convoy to a certain latitude and there quit it in order to run into the French ports. I am confident of your attention to this particular point as well as of your zeal and ability in the management of the whole business and therefore feel that it may be with the greatest safety to his Majesty's interests left to your discretion aided by the concurrence and advice of Admiral Murray with whom you will communicate without reserve on all points in any manner connected with the objects of this dispatch or any other of his instructions.[34]

GRENVILLE TO HAMMOND [35]

No. 13.   DOWNING STREET, 5th June 1794.

Sir,

I have no Dispatches from You to acknowledge since the Date of my last letter.

An account has been received here from Amsterdam through a New York newspaper of a general embargo having been laid on the 26th of March on all vessels in the ports of North America.[36] This account however has not been accompanied with information of the circumstances which attended this measure or any of those which induced the American government to adopt it.

A measure of this nature so important in itself and the consequences by which it may be attended cannot fail to make a considerable impression here and to engage the serious attention of his Majesty's government. Destitute as we have been for some time past of authentic advices from America there are no means of ascertaining satisfactorily either the reality of the information itself or the motives

---

it might be well to force American ships to accept British convoys. He cited the case of the *New Jersey*, bound from Philadelphia with flour ostensibly for English ports, the supercargo of which had contracted to land the flour in France, if possible, in return for a ten per cent commission. Bond to Grenville, Mar. 18, 1796, No. 15, F. O. 5 : 13.

[34] This cipher instruction of May 10, 1794, No. 12, was deciphered only to this point, although eighteen lines of numbers follow. The draft in F. O. 5 : 4 does not contain these extra eighteen lines.

[35] F. O. 115 : 3. In cipher.

[36] The Embargo enacted March 26, 1794 was for thirty days; on April 18, 1794 it was extended for another period of thirty days.

which may have led to its adoption.[37] The great zeal and attention
which you have constantly manifested during your residence in America and the punctuality which you have shewn in your transmission
of everything which related to the important objects of your mission
convince me that though so very considerable an interval has elapsed
since I have any letters from you, this interruption is to be attributed
to unforeseen accidents which have retarded the arrival of your
late dispatches or to circumstances which may have occurred in America of which we have not been informed here. At a moment like the
present however it is so extremely important that his Majesty's government should frequently and punctually receive every information
which you may have it in your power to give, that I must desire that
you will exert yourself to the utmost for this purpose and embrace
every opportunity whether by public or private conveyance of sending
me over regular and detailed accounts of what passes in the country
where you reside. By using the cypher which you have in your possession you will avoid the risk of any discovery being made of the information transmitted to me and you may farther insure the arrival
of your letters by intrusting duplicates and triplicates of them so
cyphered by different conveyances. Since I wrote my dispatch No. 12
I have had reason to believe that the communication I there mentioned
to have been made by the Swedish minister to Mr. Pinckney of the
desire of his court that America should accede to the convention lately
signed between Denmark and Sweden has not been approved of by the
former of those courts, and that no measures have hitherto been
taken by the Danish government to procure the accession of any other
power to its late engagements with the court of Stockholm, but the
future course of this business as it may concern America will require your most serious and constant attention.[38]

GRENVILLE TO HAMMOND [39]

No. 14.   DOWNING STREET, 15th July 1794.

Sir,

Your several Dispatches, to No. 26 inclusive, have been duly received and laid before the King.

---

[37] Hammond's dispatches from Feb. 22 to April 17, 1794, Nos. 2 to 16 inclusive, were not
received at London until June 10, 1794. In them he had reported on the "universal
fermentation" in the United States against Great Britain, Madison's proposal for commercial retaliation, the Embargo, and other suggested measures of a much more hostile
nature, which, if carried, would lead to war.
The difficulties of communication at this time of crisis in Anglo-American relations are
further revealed by Hammond's dispatch of Nov. 12, 1794, No. 34, F. O. 5 : 5. In it he
stated that while he had received Grenville's instruction of Sept. 4, 1794, No. 18, he had
received neither the originals nor the duplicates of Grenville's Nos. 15, 16, and 17, all of
which were dated Aug. 8, 1794. The August mail had been in His Majesty's packet
Antelope, which had been captured by a French squadron from Brest.
[38] Although five lines of numbers follow this sentence in both the instruction above and
its draft in F. O. 5 : 5, in both instruction and draft these last five lines were not deciphered.
[39] F. O. 115 : 3.

The shortness of the time, which I understand to be allotted for the Sailing of the American Ship which carries this Dispatch, and the uncertainty of the Conveyance, do not allow me to enter into the particulars of what has passed here since the arrival of Mr. Jay,[40] on the subject of the important Commission with which he is charged. I shall therefore confine myself to the informing you, that the general Language and Conduct of that Gentleman has hitherto been satisfactory to this Government, and that, in consequence of a Conversation which we have had relative to the supposed intention of His Majesty's Officers in Canada to establish a Fort on the little Miamis River,[41] the motives and Apprehensions in which that Measure may probably have originated and the Consequences to which it may have led. He gave me the most explicit assurances, that General Wayne [42] had no orders, which could authorize his attacking any of the Posts held by His Majesty since the Peace; and it was agreed between us, that, during the present Negotiation, and until the Conclusion of it, all things ought to remain and be preserved in Statu Quo; that, therefore, both Parties should continue to hold their Possessions, and that all Encroachments on either side should be done away; that all Hostile Measures (if any such should have taken place) shall cease; and that, in case it should unfortunately have happened that Prisoners or Property should have been taken, the Prisoners shall be releásed, and the Property restored; and' that Both Governments should immediately give Orders and Instructions accordingly.

---

[40] John Jay (1745–1829), Chief Justice of the United States Supreme Court from 1789 to 1795, had been commissioned Envoy Extraordinary to Great Britain on April 19, and had arrived in England on June 8, 1794. Upon Jay's nomination Hammond had sounded out Secretary Hamilton as to the purpose of the mission. Hamilton, he reported, was prepared to accept the principles of the British orders of June 8, 1793 and Jan. 8, 1794. While Hamilton did not expressly deny the legality of the British order of Nov. 6, 1793, he condemned the extreme interpretations of it by the vice-admiralty courts in the West Indies, and he expected compensation for cargoes seized under this order except in cases where the property could be proved to be French. Hammond to Grenville, April 17, No. 15, also, March 23, No. 8, F. O. 5: 4. To aid Grenville in the negotiations, Hammond transmitted a summary of his correspondence with the American government since 1791. *Dropmore Papers*, III, 520–528.

[41] Convinced that war with the United States was imminent, and that the British posts, particularly Detroit, were endangered by the American army then operating against the Northwestern Indians, Lieut. Gov. Simcoe in April of 1794 had fortified the old Miamis post at the rapids of the Maumee River, some twenty miles south of Lake Erie and well within the territory of the United States. Lord Dorchester had sanctioned this action on February 17, just a week after his inflammatory speech to the Indians, in which he told them that the Americans had refused British offers of mediation and would soon be at war with the British, and that the Indians and the British could then draw a boundary line to suit themselves. The aggressive actions of the Canadian officials led to an acrimonious correspondence between Hammond and Randolph, *A. S. P., F. R.*, I, 461, 464.

[42] Anthony Wayne of Pennsylvania (1745–1796), appointed major general of the western army in 1792, succeeding St. Clair, in the late autumn of 1793 had begun his campaigning against the hostile Northwestern tribes.

Orders to this effect will accordingly be sent to Lord Dorchester and Colonel Simcoe,[43] by the first direct Conveyance to Quebec; and I inclose you a Duplicate, in order that you may forward it to Upper Canada.[44]

GRENVILLE TO HAMMOND [45]

No. 15.   DOWNING STREET, 8th August 1794.
Sir,

Your several Dispatches to No. 27 Inclusive, have been duly received and laid before The King.

It affords me much satisfaction to be enabled to express to you His Majesty's most gracious approbation of your conduct, under the trying circumstances in which you have lately been placed, and in which you have manifested great judgment and discretion, while you maintained with a proper degree of spirit the Rights of this Country, and of those British Subjects in whose favor you had occasion to interfere.

I now proceed to reply to such parts of your late Dispatches as require an Answer, and to send you Instructions on those points on which it may be necessary that you should receive fresh information for the regulation of your future conduct, in consequence of the recent events which have taken place in America.

The circumstance which you mention in your Dispatch No. 4, of the Publication in the Common Newspapers of some Letters which passed between yourself and Mr. Randolph, appears to have been extremely improper and injustifiable.[46] A practice of that nature is undoubtedly contrary not only to the established usage under every regular Government, but it is replete with inconveniences, and must be attended with bad consequences, which are sufficiently obvious to

---

[43] John Graves Simcoe (1752–1806), colonel of the Queen's Rangers, a regiment of Loyalists, during the Revolution, was Lieutenant Governor of Canada (and Governor of Upper Canada) 1791 to 1796.

[44] Hammond duly forwarded the duplicate order, and to Grenville expressed the hope "that these dispatches will arrive in time, if not to prevent the commencement at least to arrest the progress of hostilities between his Majesty's forces in the garrison of Upper Canada, and those of the United States, under the command of General Wayne." Hammond to Grenville, Sept. 28, 1794, No. 32, F. O. 5: 5. The status quo agreement between Jay and Grenville (*Corres. of Jay,* ed. H. P. Johnston, IV, 33–34) was construed by the Canadian officials as permitting them to retain the Miamis fort, contrary to Jay's understanding of the agreement. It was not evacuated until the other posts on American soil were given up in June of 1796, in execution of Jay's Treaty.

[44] F. O. 115: 3.

[46] In his dispatch No. 4, March 7, 1794, F. O. 5: 4, Hammond had criticized the American practice of making diplomatic notes public, and had referred particularly to the notes which had passed between himself and Secretary Randolph on Feb. 21, 1794. On that date Hammond had been obliged to admit to Randolph that he had not as yet received instructions from London respecting the negotiations begun with Jefferson over the non-execution of the treaty of 1783, which by this time had been suspended for more than a year and a half. *A. S. P., F. R.,* I, 328.

strike every one who reflects upon it. Nor indeed can any fair reason be assigned for such a conduct; as no Government, however feebly constituted, can be under a necessity of thus prematurely appealing to the public, much less of appealing to it in the manner you represent to have happened, by publishing only such part of the Correspondence as appeared most likely to produce the Effect of creating jealousies and prejudices to which there was already too great a disposition. You have done very properly in taking notice of such a practice, and you will not fail to avail yourself of such opportunities as may present themselves of stating to the American Ministers the Inconveniences which must necessarily result from it. It may be proper for me to add, that Mr. Jay, to whom I have in the course of our conversations mentioned this circumstance, has appeared sensible of it's impropriety; but it will not be proper for you, in any discussions you may have on the subject, to commit his name.

As the Case of Capt. Barney,[47] which you mention in your Dispatch No. 15, is now decided, I have only on this occasion to lament the violence to which it has given rise, which cannot but be considered as a proof of that spirit which appears unfortunately to prevail too strongly in America, and which has been so much increased by the successful efforts of the French Agents in that Country.

What you mention in your Dispatch No. 16, of the Encroachments on the British Territory by the Citizens of Vermont,[48] is connected with the Subject of the Posts now under discussion with Mr. Jay. Upon this point therefore it does not appear necessary that I should give you any Instructions at present.

In your Dispatches Nos. 17, 18 and 19, you acquaint me with some proceedings of the American Legislature, tending either to interrupt the intercourse between that Country and Great Britain, or to throw impediments in the way of the Commerce carried on by the latter. Of this nature, are the Bill for suspending Commercial Intercourse with Great Britain after the 1st of next November, the proposal of imposing a Duty of 25 Cents per Ton on Foreign Shipping—and the

---

[47] Joshua Barney of Baltimore (1759–1818), Revolutionary naval hero, master of an American merchant vessel that had been captured and brought into Jamaica. There Barney had stood trial for having on a previous voyage, when captured by a British privateer, retrieved his ship from the prizemaster, and in the scuffle dangerously wounded two of his captors. His detention had caused great excitement in Baltimore, where retaliatory threats were made against the life of Edward Thornton, the British consul. Secretary Randolph had requested Hammond's interposition in Barney's case, and Hammond had presented the matter to Grenville in such a way as to show how politic it would be if Barney were released. Eventually Barney obtained his freedom and escaped being hanged for "piracy." Hammond to Grenville, April 17, 1794, No. 15, F. O. 5 : 4. See, also, Bond to Grenville, April 17, 1794, *Ann. Rpt. Amer. Hist. Assoc., 1897*, p. 546.

[48] Hammond on March 10, 1794 had complained to Randolph of "the encroachments by the citizens of Vermont on the territory occupied by his Majesty's arms," and had returned to the subject in his note of May 22, 1794. Hammond to Grenville, April 17, 1794, No. 16, F. O. 5 : 4 ; *A. S. P., F. R.*, I, 462.

Motion for laying an Extra Duty of Ten per Cent on Articles the produce or manufacture of Great Britain. As neither the Bill nor the Motions in question were finally adopted, nothing is now necessary to be said on the subject, except that it will be proper for you on all occasions to shew to those with whom you may converse on the subject how injurious the effect of such Measures would be to America. However the people of that Country may be influenced by the insidious Representations which have been made to them, or however they may [be] hurried into violent measures by an ill-founded jealousy, they cannot be ignorant that the consequences of measures of this nature must very seriously affect themselves, tho' they may be proposed as the means of injuring the interests of Great Britain. And indeed the recent experience shews how much they are impressed with this truth; for, tho' the obvious intention of the late Embargo on all Foreign Vessels in the American Ports was to distress this Country, a short trial was sufficient to prove that it's immediate effect was to injure themselves, and that it's continuance would have been productive of very fatal consequences to their own Interests. It was therefore withdrawn before the unfriendly purposes for which it had been calculated were effected, and it was withdrawn by the very party by whom it had originally been brought forward.

With respect to the Case of Captains Oakes and Manning,[49] mentioned in your Dispatch No. 18, proper Representations will be made tho' [through] Mr. Jay on this Subject, and some satisfactory Explanation will be expected with regard to it, as what has hitherto passed cannot be considered in that light.

With regard to the Correspondence on the Subject of Lord Dorchester's speech, and Col. Simcoe's intentions of taking Post at the foot of the Miami's Rapids, your language has been extremely proper. I am however to inform you that those Measures have not been approved by His Majesty; and with respect to the latter, I must refer you to my last Dispatch No. — duplicate of which is herewith sent which will shew you the resolution which has been taken upon it by His Majesty's Government.

---

[49] Captains Oakes and Manning of the British navy were prisoners of war recently released on parole by the French squadron in the Chesapeake. While at Philadelphia, waiting for Hammond to get them passports so that they could get through the Embargo and back to England in a schooner expressly engaged for the purpose, they were assaulted by a mob and their vessel was stripped of its sails and rigging. Hammond got little satisfaction from Secretary Randolph, who refused to issue passports for Oakes and Manning. He was much concerned about this and other incidents indicative of "the prevailing hostility to Great Britain which pervades the whole continent, and which has increased most rapidly in the course of the last two weeks." Hammond to Grenville, May 8, 1794, No. 18, F. O. 5: 8. See, also, same to same, March 7, 1794, No. 5, F. O. 5: 4. Article XXIII of Jay's Treaty, it might be noted, provided that naval officers were to be treated with the respect due to their commissions.

In your Dispatch No. 27, you mention your apprehension that British Officers may possibly, under the circumstances of the present temper prevailing in America, be arrested for the value of American Prizes they may have taken in the West Indies, and you desire to have precise Instructions for your conduct in case of any event of that nature taking place. Should any British Officer, actually on the King's Service, be arrested in the Manner you suppose probable, you will not fail to represent to the American Government, in the most pointed terms, against such a Measure, as a Violation of the Laws of Nations, and you will demand his instant release, nothing being more absurd than the idea of making a foreign officer amenable to the civil jurisdiction of America for acts done by him in a distant Country and by virtue of his Commission from his own Sovereign. It will also be proper for any Officer so arrested to bring the question in a legal form under the immediate view of the Court from which the process of arrest shall have issued, and if there is any regard paid to the clearest principles of Justice and Universal Law such application must be attended with success; if however this should not be the case, you will then facilitate to such Officer the means of procuring Bail; and you will at the same time deliver to Mr. Randolph a Ministerial Note containing a formal and express protest against the Measure reserving it for the decision of your Court, as an instance in which the most unquestionable principles of Justice and of the Laws of Nations are openly violated.

GRENVILLE TO HAMMOND [50]

No. 16.   DOWNING STREET, 8th August 1794.

Sir,

By your Dispatch No. 27, of the 27th June last, received here since the date of my last Letters to you, I was informed of the steps which you had been induced to take in consequence of the Notification made to you by Mr. Randolph of a new Regulation fixing the interval to be allowed between the sailing from the American Ports of Vessels belonging to the Powers at War with each other.[51]   The very extraor-

---

[50] F. O. 115 : 3.

[51] In his dispatch No. 27 of June 27, 1794, F. O. 5 : 5, Hammond reported that it was not until the news had come of the arrival off the American coast of a strong British squadron that Secretary Randolph had announced the intention of the United States to put into effect the principle that twenty-four hours must elapse between the sailing from the same port of vessels belonging to powers at war with each other. "Determined not to be the dupe of so shallow an artifice," since "the adoption of this principle at this *precise moment* could only be intended to operate in a manner, prejudicial to the interests of Great Britain, and favorable to those of France," Hammond had refused to recommend to British naval commanders conformity with the rule until he could hear from Grenville.

Secretary Randolph, in reply to Hammond's note of June 18, 1794, repelled the insinuation that the rule had been adopted because of the arrival of the British squadron, and pointed out that it had been approved on June 16, two days before such news had reached Philadelphia, and that it had been brought into discussion on June 13 not by the French but by the Dutch Minister. Randolph to Hammond, June 19, 1794, Domestic Letters, 6.

dinary determination taken by the American Government as signified to you in that Notification to enforce under circumstances favorable to the interests of the French Navy in the American Seas, a Regulation which had been so long delayed to be established when it might have operated advantageously to the British Interests in the same Quarter, can be imputed only to the Bias towards the cause of the French Convention or to the weakness on the part of the American Government, the effects of which have already too frequently appeared. As the French Ships from whatever cause were so long allowed to avail themselves of their superiority without any attempt on the part of the American Government to subject them to the observance of a rule usually enforced in Neutral Ports it is certainly just that this Rule should not have been made to operate as against the British Interests precisely at the moment when the continuance of the former practise would have been advantageous to us. The King therefore entirely approves of your conduct, in not recommending to the Commanders of His Majesty's Ships of War on the American Station that immediate compliance with the regulation in question, on which the American Government, after having neglected to attend to your requisition on the Subject suddenly thought proper to insist. It is however to be considered that the former Neglect to enforce the Regulation in Question rather than the subsequent determination to have it executed is the real and proper ground of Complaint which His Majesty might make on this Subject; and that the determination notified by them to you, cannot ultimately be resisted by His Majesty consistently with that strict attention which The King has uniformly shewn to the Clear and acknowledged rights of Neutral Powers. And as the interval which will have elapsed before you receive this Dispatch appears to have allowed sufficient time for giving to His Majesty's Ships being now superior in those Seas the means of availing themselves of that superiority without being controuled by the effect of the New Regulation in the same manner as the French did before it was issued, it is the King's Pleasure that you should not any longer delay to recommend to the Commanders of His Majesty's Ships of War, to pay due regard to a regulation reasonable in itself and the impartial execution of which would never have been disputed by His Majesty.

GRENVILLE TO HAMMOND [52]

No. 17.　　　　　　　　　　　　DOWNING STREET, 8th August 1794.

Sir,

The arrival of Mr. Jay has led to discussions of much length and importance with that Minister respecting all the different points

---

[52] F. O. 115: 3.

which have been in dispute between this Country and the United States of America since the Peace. It appears unnecessary for me now to enter into the details of those Discussions; especially as there is, I trust, a considerable probability of their being terminated in a manner satisfactory to both Countries, and tending to conciliation and friendship.

Under these Circumstances, it gives me much concern to find that the tone of Mr. Randolph's Letters to you is so unfriendly, and that the late Events have led to a Correspondence between you and that Gentleman, the effect of which may be to increase the prevailing animosities, at a time when there seems reason to hope that all points of differences, really subsisting between the Two Governments, may be amicably adjusted. I am far from wishing that you should collect from what I now state any Disapprobation of the Language held by you on these occasions, which, on the contrary, I feel to have been such as was called for by the tone of Mr. Randolph's Letters, but I think it right now to intimate to you, that it will be desireable that you should abstain, as far as possible from further communications of this nature; and, if any new point of difference should arise, that you should content yourself with referring it to the issue of such discussions as may take place here, between His Majesty's Government and Mr. Jay.

One of the points which appears to have created the greatest uneasiness in America has been that of the condemnation of American Vessels at Martinique. On that subject I think it right to apprize you, that I have received no other information than what is contained in a Paper, (Copy of which is inclosed) which was delivered to me by Mr. Jay, and is entitled "A general Statement by the Captains of American Vessels seized at Martinique." This being an Ex Parte Statement of Facts, it is impossible for His Majesty's Government to proceed upon it, as affording conclusive information of the Transactions in question. But I have not hesitated to inform Mr. Jay, that, if the Allegations there made are true, the Proceedings therein mentioned are wholly Informal and void, there being no Vice Admiralty Court at Martinique constituted by His Majesty's Authority, nor any Power in His Majesty's Officers to erect such a Jurisdiction, so that the owners of all such Vessels will be entitled to their remedy in due course of Law, against all persons who may have acted under the sentences of a Tribunal not competent to hear or decide on those Causes, or indeed on any other.[53]

---

[53] The advantages of the Martinique captures early in 1794, and the condemnations by a prize court illegally set up for the purpose, chiefly enured to Admiral Sir John Jervis, later the Earl of St. Vincent, and General Sir Charles Grey, by whose forces Martinique was captured. For the history of these cases, and their adjudication, see J. B. Moore, *International Adjudications, Modern Series*, IV, 48–62.

You will find in the inclosed Notes the result of what has passed between Mr. Jay and myself on the general subject of the Capture and Condemnation of American Vessels,[54] and I trust, if no unforeseen Impediment arises, that by the September packet I shall be enabled to transmit to you the account of an amicable Adjustment of all the points which could create disunion between the Two Countries.

His Majesty's Ministers are however by no means unaware, that the maintaining the Rights of His Majesty in America, and the insuring of His Subjects of every description such Treatment as they are entitled to claim there, does not depend merely on the Terms of any Treaty, nor even on the Disposition of those who are ostensibly intrusted with the Powers of Government there. But considerable hope is entertained that, when all public grounds of dissatisfaction are removed, and the well: intentioned Party in America are relieved from the difficulties in which they have lately stood in that respect, they may be induced to come forward with more energy and vigour, to maintain those principles of public order, which it is the interest of this Country to support in every quarter of the Globe. The Measures taken for increasing the public forces of America (tho' adopted perhaps under the prevalence of different ideas) may afford facilities in that respect to the American Government which they did not before possess; and it should be the object of the King's Representative in America to give encouragement and support, as far as it can be done with propriety to those who are willing to resist the Torrent of Jacobin Principles, which seem to have made so much progress in the United States.[55]

GRENVILLE TO HAMMOND [56]

No. 18.   DOWNING STREET, 4th Sept. 1794.

Sir,

I have no Dispatches from you to acknowledge since the Date of my last Letter.

---

[54] See Jay to Grenville, July 30, Grenville's answer, Aug. 1, and the order-in-council of Aug. 6, 1794, admitting West India cases to appeal, in *A. S. P., F. R.*, I, 481–482. On Aug. 6, 1794, also, so much of the order-in-council of June 8, 1793, as directed the capture and preemption of neutral grain ships bound for France was revoked. The revoking order of August 6, 1794 is printed in Josiah T. Newcomb, "New Light on Jay's Treaty," *American Journal of International Law*, XXVIII (Oct. 1934), 686.

[55] In the spring of 1794 Congress had authorized the building of six naval vessels for the protection of American commerce, especially against the Dey of Algiers; had passed bills for the defense of American harbors; and had augmented the army. The zeal of the Federalists for energetic measures was construed by the Republicans as designed to hamper the policy of commercial retaliation pressed by Madison, and to increase the power of the general government and of the ruling party at the expense of the states and of the opposition party. The Federalists had resorted to "the old trick of turning every contingency into a resource for accumulating force in the Government," wrote Madison to Jefferson, March 14, 1794, Madison, *Writings* (Phila., 1865), II, 7.

[56] F. O. 115 : 3.

I am now to acquaint you that projets have been prepared and delivered to Mr. Jay relative to a final arrangement between this Country and America.[57] From the shortness of the Period which has since elapsed, it cannot yet be known what turn the business will take. I shall however continue to send you from time to time such information respecting it, as may be necessary for your guidance in the discharge of the important trust committed to your care.

GRENVILLE TO HAMMOND [58]

No. 19.   DOWNING STREET, 2nd Oct. 1794.

Sir,

Your several Dispatches to No. 29 Inclusive have been duly received and laid before The King.

The Information which you sent me in your Letter No. 28 relative to the actual disinclination of the American Government to the formation of a Connection with Sweden or Denmark, cannot but be very acceptable under the present circumstances.[59] From the weight and influence of Mr. Hamilton, and from the opportunities which he undoubtedly has of knowing the views and plans of his Government; there is great reason to suppose that his opinion on this subject must be well founded; and indeed the present situation of the United States, and the obvious inconveniences which would result to them from such a Connection, should the course of events in Europe lead to any serious misunderstanding between this Country and the Two Baltic Powers tend very much to strengthen such a supposition. It will however be necessary that you should still attend to this subject, and that you should renew it from time to time in conversation with those whom you may have reason to think well disposed; as there is strong ground to believe that the Project is not wholly dropped by Sweden.[60]

With respect to the Insults which you mention to have been offered to His Majesty's Officers in different American Ports, altho' the conduct of the Americans appears to have been, in the several instances which you have stated, extremely violent and unjustifiable, yet, under

---

[57] See *A. S. P., F. R.,* I, 486–487, and ff. Bemis, *Jay's Treaty,* Appendix II, gives Grenville's "Project of Heads of Proposals to be made to Mr. Jay."

[58] F. O. 115 : 3.

[59] On Hammond's dispatch No. 28 of Aug. 3, 1794, F. O. 5 : 5, see note 30, p. 54, *supra.*

[60] Upon receipt of this instruction Hammond renewed his inquiries, and from Secretary Hamilton learned that the Cabinet were of the opinion "that, in no political situation of this country, would such a measure be expedient, as it would involve it in engagements with powers, with which it can have no common interest, and from which, in the moment of difficulty or danger it would derive no benefit or assistance. Exclusively of these obvious considerations, which dictates this policy, this country is generally in too unsettled a state, to admit of its entangling itself in connexions, which might eventually have a tendency to add a participation in the disputes of Europe to the internal causes of agitation." Hammond to Grenville, Jan. 5, 1795, No. 1, F. O. 5 : 8.

the existing circumstance of a depending Negotiation between the Two Countries, it may be sufficient for me at present to observe that, should the Negotiation now carrying on with Mr. Jay terminate in a satisfactory manner, there will probably be some Stipulation agreed to on this subject. In the mean time it will be proper for you to continue to state to the American Government, as matters of Complaint, but in moderate and friendly terms, every fresh instance of this sort which may occur. The Disposition, which is so evidently prevalent in America towards the principles of French Anarchy, makes it certainly very difficult for such a Government as the American to prevent these transactions; but it is on that account the more incumbent upon that Government to apologize for them, and to endeavour to bring the Offenders to punishment.

With respect to the particular Case of Captain Cochrane, I shall probably soon have occasion to write to you more particularly upon it.[61]

I feel much satisfaction in acquainting you that your conduct in regard to the Seamen on board of His Majesty's Ships who have been claimed as Americans, is entirely approved.[62]

I acquainted you in my last Dispatch that a Projet of a Treaty has been delivered to Mr. Jay. I have since received from him a Contreprojet, but as there has not been time to submit it to the Consideration of His Majesty's Confidential Servants I am not enabled to do more by this opportunity than to express to you my hope that the business may terminate in a satisfactory manner.

GRENVILLE TO HAMMOND [63]

No. 20.   DOWNING STREET, 20th Nov. 1794.

Sir,

Your several Dispatches to No. 32 Inclusive have been duly received and laid before The King.

I feel great pleasure in being able to inform you that the Negotiation which has been for some time carried on here for the con-

---

[61] Capt. Alexander F. Cochrane of the frigate *Thetis* had impressed seamen from American vessels and, at New York, had violated harbor regulations and insulted the port officials. Randolph to Hammond, July 24, Sept. 3, 1794, Domestic Letters, 7. Hammond, transmitting Randolph's complaints, reported that Cochrane and other British officers had been insulted by the people of New York and other seaports, that Cochrane had been threatened with arrest on account of an American vessel captured by the *Thetis*, and that any British officer who stayed on shore any length of time was likely to be arrested on some pretext or other. Hammond to Grenville, Aug. 3, 16, Sept. 5, 28, 1794, Nos. 28, 29, 31, 32, F. O. 5: 5.

[62] Relative to Randolph's complaints about impressments by Admiral Murray's squadron. Hammond had reported that "as it is extremely necessary to obviate the inconvenience which would arise from the indiscriminate demand and release of all persons stiling themselves American citizens, I have thought it the most eligible mode, to impose upon this government the necessity of *previously* producing satisfactory proof of the persons demanded being really American citizens. . . ." Hammond to Grenville, Aug. 3, 1794, No. 28, F. O. 5: 5.

[63] Draft, F. O. 5: 5.

clusion of a Treaty of Amity, Commerce, and Navigation between This Country and America has at length been terminated in a very satisfactory manner. I now send you inclosed Copy of the Treaty which was signed by Mr. Jay and myself on the 19th Instant.[64] Triplicates of this Treaty will be forwarded by Mr. Jay to the American Government; and as soon as the Ratification of it shall be sent over to Mr. Jay, it will be exchanged in the usual manner with His Majesty's Ratification.

The whole Conduct of Mr. Jay in the course of this arduous and intricate Negotiation has been entirely Satisfactory; and I trust that the issue of the business will prove equally so to the American Government; as the Stipulations of this Treaty appear to be in every respect calculated to remove those difficulties and embarassments which, by whatever cause occasioned, tended to keep alive a spirit of disunion and discontent. A foundation is I trust now laid for permanent harmony and good understanding between the Two Countries in future.

It has unavoidably happened, from the complicated nature of the discussion between Mr. Jay and myself, that some points have remained unadjusted. With respect to these that Gentleman proposes to write by This Mail to Mr. Randolph; and it were much to be wished that, in the consideration of these Several points in America, the same Candour and conciliatory Spirit should prevail which I have had occasion to remark with much satisfaction in the course of the late Negotiation. If on the perusal of the Treaty any point should occur to you from your local observation and knowledge, or should be suggested to you by others, as requiring explanation or further regulation you will not fail to apprize me of it.

You will observe that in the [sixth] and [seventh] Articles certain Regulations have been established respecting The Appointment of Commissioners for the purpose of ascertaining and determining the Claims of British Subjects, who, from various causes may now be unable to obtain by the ordinary course of judicial proceedings full compensation for the losses they have sustained by the operation of the lawful impediments which have obstructed the due execution in America of the 6th Article of the Treaty of Peace—And also for the purpose of ascertaining in like manner the claims of Americans who may be unable to obtain by course of Law compensation for any Losses sustained by them from the Capture and Detention of their Vessels and Cargoes or from the undue condemnation thereof. In

---

[64] For the treaty see Miller, *Treaties*, II, 245–267.

those Articles a general provision [65] has been made for the payment of the Salaries and expences of the Commissioners; but no specific sums for that purpose have been named, as it was necessary previously to have been informed of the wishes of the American Government in that respect. You will therefore take an early opportunity of conversing with Mr. Randolph on That Subject; and you will state to him that the idea of His Majesty's Government is to allow the Sum of £1,500 per Annum to each of the Commissioners to be appointed for Those purposes from hence, together with an Extra Allowance of all the expences of Their voyage to those of them who will be [required?] to cross The Sea; as it does not appear probable that proper and sufficient persons for The execution of the important trusts to be committed to them can be engaged here for a smaller Salary to undertake a business which must be attended with considerable trouble and interruption of all other business, and which will require great ability and information. If this allowance should appear to the American Government to be too large to be made to their Commissioners, there does not appear any absolute necessity for an uniformity in the Salaries of the Commissioners of the two Countries. This however is left entirely to the Decision of the American Government, and you will only press that Mr. Jay may be fully instructed and authorized to settle it when the Ratifications are exchanged in order that there may be no further delay in the business than such as may be unavoidably necessary. It is probable that His Majesty's Government may judge it adviseable to appoint to each Commission on the part of this Country, One Merchant and one Lawyer or Civilian; but no nomination has as yet taken place. As however it is to be wished that as little delay as possible should occur in the execution of these provisions, you will not fail to represent to Mr. Randolph that it is extremely desireable that the nomination of the Commissioners on the part of the American Government should take place as immediately as may be, so that a Similar appointment may take place here as soon as The American Ratification shall be received.

There is also a similar provision in the Treaty for The Appointment of Commissioners to ascertain The course of the river St. Croix.[66] As this is a Service of less importance and difficulty and which will probably be attended with an inferior degree of trouble, it is conceived here that an Appointment of £1,000 per Annum with an Allowance for expences of voyage as above will be an adequate Compensation to the persons to be employed upon it.

---

[65] Article VIII.
[66] Article V.

GRENVILLE TO HAMMOND [67]

Separate.
No. 21.   DOWNING STREET, 20th Nov. 1794.
Sir,

In the Course of my late Negotiation with Mr. Jay, much Discussion took place between us with respect to the Indian War,[68] now subsisting on the North West Frontier of the United States. It was extremely evident that nothing could be more desirable under the present Circumstances, and with a view to the realization of those Advantages which may be reciprocally expected from the Treaty now concluded, than that this War should be brought to a Termination, and the arrangement of some of the Points which may still lead to animosity and hostility was impeded by it's continuation. In conformity therefore both with these Sentiments and with the uniform Line of Conduct which His Majesty has pursued on this Subject, I did not hesitate to propose to Mr. Jay the Mediation of His Majesty for the purpose of bringing those Differences to a conclusion, and I referred in general terms to the fact of your having been before authorized to consent to this measure if a favourable Opening had been afforded you for it. Mr. Jay appeared to be by no Means disinclined to adopt this Proposal; but no Step of that Nature was concluded upon, as he did not think himself sufficiently authorized by his Instructions and as he conceived that, in the present State of Acrimony and Warmth which prevails in America with respect to this Country, and particularly on the Subject of the Indian War, it might not perhaps be attended with the Success which might be looked for under more favourable Circumstances.

The success of a Plan of this nature is however a matter of such Importance with a view both to the maintenance of the Harmony and Union which this Government is desirous of cultivating with that of the United States and also to the particular and local Interests of Canada that I must desire you will take an early Opportunity of conferring upon it confidentially with Mr. Hamilton,[69] and of suggesting

---

[67] F. O. 115 : 3.

[68] On Aug. 20, 1794, a few miles from the British post on the Maumee River recently fortified by Simcoe, Wayne had won a smashing victory over the Northwestern Indians at the battle of Fallen Timbers. His victory, and his Treaty of Greenville of Aug. 3, 1795, terminated the Indian wars which had persisted since the Revolution. *A. S. P., Indian Affairs*, I, 491, 562.

[69] Hammond did not receive this instruction until July 22, 1795, the instructions of November and December having been thrown overboard when the packet *Tankerville* was captured by the *Lovely Lass* privateer. Since he was then about to sail for England and would probably arrive as soon as any letter, he thought it expedient to make his communications on the subject orally, "especially as I have desired Mr. Jay and Mr. Hamilton to meet me at New York," and from these gentlemen "I shall receive more accurate and substantial information on several points than from any other quarter." Hammond to Grenville, Aug. 14, 1795, No. 32, F. O. 5 : 9. It is not known whether the neutral Indian barrier state was discussed at New York. In the meantime Wayne's decisive victory of August, 1794, and his Treaty of Greenville of August, 1795, had dampened, though not entirely extinguished, British hopes of that project.

to him the advantages with which it is likely to be attended to both Parties, not only by the Termination of the present Hostilities in which the United States are engaged, but by affording immediate facilities for the Operation of the recent Treaty, and for the Adjustment of several Points connected with it, which as Mr. Jay will probably have informed his Government, we had discussed, but were obliged to postpone from the Impossibility of bringing them to any satisfactory Issue during the continuance of the Indian War.   Should you find from your Inter-course with Mr. Hamilton that the American Government is disposed to adopt such a Proposal, the proper Steps for carrying it into Execution may be immediately taken; and even should he express any Disinclination on their Part to enter into any public Stipulation to that effect, such an Arrangement might be settled between him and yourself by a secret Understanding or Agreement to be communicated to Lord Dorchester and Lieut. Governor Simcoe.   It is particularly desirable for Reasons with which you are not unacquainted that this Matter should be adjusted in the Manner I have mentioned before the Evacuation of the Posts takes place.[70]   If therefore any favourable Opening is given for the Execution of such a Plan you will communicate it without delay to Lieut. Governor Simcoe and you will take his Opinion as to the Terms on which it is probable that any such Arrangement could be concluded with the Indians, and as to the Mode of carrying it into Effect, and whatever may be done as the Result of your Joint Opinions on this Subject will be approved by His Majesty's Government.   There are many Reasons for wishing that the Discussion of this important Business may, if possible, pass between you and Mr. Hamilton without any Communication of it being made to Mr. Randolph at least 'till it shall have been brought to a State in which it may be rendered public, as the whole Conduct of that Gentleman since his first Appointment to the Official Situation he now holds has given the greatest Dissatisfaction here, and particularly as with respect to the Indian War, and to the unfounded Assertions on that Subject which he has thought proper to bring forward in his Correspondence with you and to circulate through the whole of the Country by the publication of that Correspondence.   I have not failed to express to Mr. Jay the Sentiments of His Majesty's Government on this Conduct of the American Secretary of State; and I think it is not improbable that Mr. Jay will represent it in a proper Point of view to his Government; but, in order to put the business on a proper footing and to remove any Impressions which may have been made in America by such false Representations it has been agreed between Mr. Jay and me, that he shall write me a Letter on this Subject, in answer to which I shall have the Opportunity of disclaiming the Fact of any Instruc-

---

[70] Article II of Jay's Treaty provided for the evacuation of the British posts on American soil on or before June 1, 1796.

tions having ever been given from hence to stir up the Indians against the United States.

You will observe that what I have hitherto stated applies with equal force to almost any Mode by which the Indian War may be terminated, but it is much to be desired that this Object should be accomplished by the Assistance and through the Mediation of this Country. You will therefore not fail to exert yourself to the utmost to bring forward this Point which must however be done with Caution and Delicacy as too great an Eagerness on our Part may give room to unfounded Jealousies on that of the American Government. The strongest inducement to be held out to that Government will be the shewing them that if the Indian War should be satisfactorily concluded by the Interference of His Majesty's Government in America, it would naturally follow that His Majesty and the United States might then enter into a mutual Guaranty of such Arrangements.

GRENVILLE TO HAMMOND [71]

No. 22.   DOWNING STREET, 20th Nov. 1794.

Sir,

Having in my Letter marked *Separate* of this Date had occasion to advert to a Part of Mr. Randolph's late Conduct, I think it proper in this Dispatch to speak more particularly on that Subject.

Nothing can on every Account be more perfectly improper than the regular Publication from Time to Time of an Official Correspondence between the Public Ministers of two Governments on Matters which are still in Discussion and the Subject of amicable Negotiation. Such a Proceeding is altogether unusual, and the Inconveniences resulting from it are obvious, as it tends to destroy that Confidence with which the reciprocal Communications of two friendly Governments are understood to be carried on, and to produce and increase irritation and Animosity in the Minds of the People at large in both Countries, and thereby frequently to preclude those Modes of amicable Accomodation which might otherwise have been resorted to. The late conduct of Mr. Randolph in this respect is doubly blameable when the relative situation of the Two Countries is considered and particularly the Circumstance of a Negotiation actually pending here for a compleat Arrangement of all existing Differences. Nor are the Stile and Tenour of Mr. Randolph's Letters less objectionable than the constant Publication of the Correspondence between You. Those Letters uniformly breathe a Spirit of Hostility towards Great Britain and a desire of turning to that Object every Event which has occurred. The same observation applies still more strongly to the Letter ad-

[71] F. O. 115 : 3.

dressed by him to the French Convention and read in that Assembly by the New Envoy Mr. Monroe [72] the expressions of which go far beyond the Resolutions of Congress on which they are grounded, and are indeed such as to be not only altogether inconsistent with the Assurances of friendly disposition conveyed to this Government through Mr. Jay (and in conformity to which the whole of his Conduct since his Arrival here has been directed) but are also perfectly at variance with every Principle of fair Neutrality, at the Time when Neutrality has so repeatedly been professed by the Government of the United States.

It is impossible not to attribute to the same unfriendly Motives Mr. Randolph's Publication of the List of American Shipping supposed to have been taken by Great Britain, a Step, which was in itself highly improper and inflammatory, by which is aggravated in the highest degree by what you have remarked in your last Dispatch of the gross Inaccuracy of that Publication, not to speak of it in any harsher Terms.[73] It is hardly possible to suppose such an Error to have been voluntary and intentional on his part, but the Charge of Precipitation and Negligence on so very important an Occasion is by no Means a slight one, when his Official Situation and the relative State of Our two Countries at that Period are considered.

I have in my separate Dispatch taken notice of the Indecency of Mr. Randolph's repeated and public Insinuations that the Indian War had been promoted or encouraged by this Country.[74] In addition to what I have there said, I have to observe that even if the Facts mentioned in one of his Letters on that subject had been

---

[72] James Monroe (1758–1831), appointed minister to France on May 28, 1794, had been most cordially received by the National Convention of France on Aug. 26, 1794. His instructions of June 10, the resolutions of Congress of April 24 and 25, Randolph's letters of June 10 transmitting the congressional resolutions, together with Randolph's letter of December 2 reproving Monroe for his speech before the Convention, are printed in *A. S. P., F. R.,* I, 668, 674, 690. In his dispatch No. 22 of May 27, 1794, F. O. 5 : 4, Hammond had described Monroe as "a man of moderate abilities and of embarrassed circumstances . . . long distinguished by his hostility to Great Britain and his admiration of the principles of the French revolution."

[73] On Sept. 5, 1794 Hammond had transmitted a list issued by the Department of State of "American vessels carried into British ports," the correctness of which he had questioned. Subsequently he had reported it to be a list of "*all* the vessels, on the subjects of which complaints were intended to be waged by this government to *different* foreign powers, and that, by some oversight of Mr. Randolph (as I imagine) it was published in its present form, as referring to complaints against the conduct of Great Britain *alone*." Hammond to Grenville, Sept. 5, 28, 1794, Nos. 31 and 32, F. O. 5 : 5.

[74] The correspondence on this subject was most acrimonious from May through November of 1794. *A. S. P., F. R.,* I, 461–464, 474–484 ; Domestic Letters, 6, 7 ; and see Wayne's report of July 7, 1794 on the "white and red savages" he was encountering in Ohio, *A. S. P., Indian Affairs,* I, 477–478. Secretary Randolph had but reflected the general American opinion. President Washington on August 30, 1794 wrote Jay that "there does not remain a doubt . . . that all the difficulties we encounter with the Indians, their hostilities, the murders of helpless women and innocent children along our frontiers, result from the conduct of the agents of Great Britain in this country. In vain, is it, then, for its administration, in *Britain,* to disavow having given orders which will warrant such conduct, while their agents go unpunished. . . ." *Corres. of Jay,* IV, 55–56.

true in the manner in which they are there stated, the Conduct of a few unauthorized Individuals joining the Indians cannot be considered as affording any Evidence of the Intentions or Instructions of the King's Government here or in America any more than the numerous Acts of Hostility committed by Americans against this Country during the present War would prove the Conduct or Views of the American Government to be hostile towards Us. In both Instances the Dispositions of the Two Governments may be friendly and yet the Acts of their Subjects may frequently be at variance with those Dispositions. The Case is common between friendly Nations, and the remedy is no less so.—The usual course followed on these occasions is well known and established by all Treaties.

A State in such Cases may either call upon the Government of a friendly Nation to punish Individuals if the Crime can be proved against them, or may take the Punishment into it's own Hands when the Individuals are actually found in the Commission of such Acts. But it requires the strongest Evidence to authorize the imputing those Acts to the Government of another Country and in this instance no such Evidence existed or could exist.

I have detailed these Points because they must become the subject of serious but friendly Representation where such Representation can be useful. Whatever stipulations may be made by public Treaties it is impossible that Friendship and Harmony should be maintained between the two Countries so long as a System of this Sort is followed by those who conduct the Official Intercourse between them. Many Opportunities will continually occur which may be thus inflamed into Bickerings and Quarrels. It will therefore be absolutely necessary that without making any Ministerial Remonstrances on what is passed, you should converse confidentially on this Subject with those Persons in America who are Friends to a System of amicable Intercourse between the two Countries, in the view that some Step may be taken in respect to the Affair so as either to convince Mr. Randolph of the necessity of his adopting a different Language and Conduct, or at least, to place him in a Situation where his personal Sentiments may not endanger the Peace of Two Countries between whom I trust a permanent Union is now established. You will readily see that this is to be done with prudence and delicacy on Your Part, and that you are to take effectual care to let it be understood that we have no other wish on the Subject than the contributing to the Maintenance of Good Understanding between the Governments by providing for an amicable Correspondence between their Ministers and Agents and that in all other respects the Person of Mr. Randolph or any other public Minister in America must be totally indifferent to Us.

GRENVILLE TO HAMMOND [75]

No. 23.   DOWNING STREET, Dec. 10th, 1794.

Sir,

Your several Dispatches to No. 33 inclusive have been received and laid before the King.

I send you inclosed Quadruplicates of my Dispatches Nos. 15, 16 and 17 which had been forwarded to you by the Antelope Packet and by private Ships in August last. I also send you inclosed Duplicates of my Dispatches Nos. 20, 21 and 22, with Copy of the Treaty of Amity, Commerce and Navigation signed by myself and Mr. Jay on the 19th of last Month which were forwarded to you by the November Packet.

I am sorry to find from your last letter that the same hostile Spirit appears to prevail among certain descriptions of Persons in America which you have had occasion several times lately to notice, and that attempts have again been made to arrest the King's Officers on account of Vessels captured and retaken.[76] I trust however that when the result of Mr. Jay's Negotiation shall be known in America and when the Provisions of the late Treaty shall have been made public there, the people of that Country will be no longer liable to be misled by false and interested representations into the perpetration of excesses which cannot be justified and in which it is impossible they can be supported by the Executive Government.

Your Correspondence with Mr. Randolph on the Subject of the Privatee[r] Experiment, was perfectly proper and has been entirely approved of. As I wrote to you at large the last Packet on the Subject of this Gentleman's Conduct it will be unnecessary for me now to add any thing to what I then said; but I must observe that, in the case of the Americans taken in French Ships concerning which Mr. Randolph wrote to you on the 23d of October,[77] the Doctrine which he states cannot be admitted as grounded on any principle of the Law of Nations,

---

[75] F. O. 115 : 3.

[76] Writing from New York, and reporting an interview with Admiral Murray on the *Cleopatra* frigate, off Staten Island, Hammond had stated that it was fortunate that Murray had not landed in New York, since it had been planned to arrest the admiral on account of a small sloop which one of his ships had captured, and which had been later recaptured by its American master. "The employment of so frivolous a pretext, as this, is another incontrovertible evidence of the existence of the settled plan, to which I have before adverted . . . of arresting the commanders of any of his Majesty's ships, who may land in American ports." Hammond to Grenville, Nov. 5, 1794, No. 33, F. O. 5 : 5,

[77] Referring to a letter from Captain Cochrane of the frigate *Thetis* to John Hamilton, British consul at Norfolk, Randolph on Oct. 23, 1794 wrote Hammond that he had been "compelled with pain to learn that all the captains of his Britannic Majesty's ships are particularly ordered, to convey to Halifax every person, not being a French Citizen, but belonging to any nation at peace with Great Britain, who may be found on board of French privateers, there to be tried as a *pirate*." Randolph argued that this British order conflicted with settled principles of international law. Domestic Letters, 7 ; and see J. B. Moore, *Digest Int. Law,* II, 974.

however the humanity and forbearence of the King's Officers may induce them in individual Cases sometimes to relax that Severity which they would be justified in exercising.

GRENVILLE TO HAMMOND [78]

No. 24.   DOWNING STREET, 10th Dec. 1794.

Sir,

As it has been judged that, in the present situation of Affairs between this Country and America, your presence here may be advantageous to His Majesty's Service, I have the pleasure of acquainting you that the King has been graciously pleased to allow you a Leave of Absence, that you may be enabled to give His Majesty's Servants information concerning the State of Affairs in the Country where you now reside. When you avail yourself of His Majesty's gracious permission to return to England, you will deliver over the Cyphers and other papers belonging to your Mission to Mr. Bond, His Majesty's Consul General at Philadelphia, and you will communicate to that Gentleman every information which may be necessary in order to enable him to conduct His Majesty's Affairs in America during Your Absence from that Country.[79]

---

[78] F. O. 115 : 3.

[79] In an exchange of private notes, Nov. 21, 22, 1794, Jay had suggested to Grenville the recall of Hammond. *Corres. of Jay*, IV, 145–146. In a private letter of Dec. 9, 1794 Grenville assured Hammond that his conduct had been "such as to merit, under very trying circumstances, the most complete approbation . . . ." *Dropmore Papers*, II, 651. Hammond did not take formal leave until August 14, 1795.

INSTRUCTIONS OF 1795

No. 1.   DOWNING STREET, Jan. 7, 1795.

Sir,

I have not any Dispatches from you to acknowledge since the date of my last Letter, which was forwarded by the December Mail. I send you inclosed Copy of a Memorial, which I have received from Mr. Elmslie, a Merchant of this City relative to the capture and Confiscation of a Vessel belonging to him in America; and I am to desire that you will take such measures thereupon as you may judge most adviseable and most adapted to the circumstances of the Case.[2]

GRENVILLE TO HAMMOND [3]

No. 2.   DOWNING STREET, 7th March 1795.

Sir,

Your several Dispatches to No. 3 inclusive have been duly received and laid before The King.

The steps which you have taken with respect to the British Vessels captured by French Privateers and brought into American Ports were very proper.[4] I should have hoped, after what passed on this subject between yourself and the American Government that the King's Subjects would not have continued to be exposed to the griev-

---

[1] F. O. 115 : 4.

[2] The *Sans Pareille* privateer, "illegally fitted out at Charleston," in April of 1794 had captured and carried Mr. Elmslie's brig, the *Savannah*, into Charleston, where the ship and cargo valued at £12,358 sterling had been sold for £160 sterling. Hammond to Grenville, April 28, 1795, No. 9, F. O. 5 : 9.

[3] F. O. 115 : 4.

[4] Hammond had reported that of seventy-five British prizes brought into American ports since the beginning of hostilities to August 1, 1794, forty-six had been taken by privateers fitted out in the United States; that the depredations of such privateers had of late increased; and that he had been zealous in investigating accounts that vessels were being fitted out as privateers in American ports contrary to the American Neutrality Act of June 5, 1794. At the request of Edward Thornton, British vice consul at Baltimore, the Federal authorities had seized the *Lovely Lass* (a prize of a French privateer which had been fitted out at Philadelphia) on suspicion that the *Lovely Lass* was being armed as a privateer. Hammond had attempted, in vain, to stop the sale at Baltimore of the British vessel *Hope*, the prize of another French privateer which had been fitted out in the United States. Hammond to Grenville, Nov. 5, Dec. 1, 1794, Nos. 33 and 35, F. O. 5 : 5; Jan. 1, 1795, No. 1, F. O. 5 : 8; also, Randolph to Hammond, Dec. 24, 1794, Jan. 24, 1795, Domestic Letters, 8.

ances under which they appear still to labour, or at least that, if the fitting out of French Privateers in the American Ports and the bringing in English captured Vessels had been suffered to continue, an adequate satisfaction would have been made on the part of America to the British Sufferers. In the correspondence you had in the year 1793 with Mr. Jefferson on this Subject, that Gentleman seems to have compleatly recognized the Principles of Compensation being incumbent on the United States for Vessels and Effects captured on the Seas near the American Shores, or even on the High Seas, and brought into their Ports, if done by Vessels which had been armed within them. For altho' he avoided in his Letter to you of the 5th Sept. 1793 [5] to make any absolute Engagement to this effect with respect to Vessels so captured and brought in after the 5th of the preceding June, as he had engaged should be done with regard to the Vessels under those circumstances before that period; yet he expressly said that, if any Cases should arise subsequent to that date, the circumstances of which should place them on similar ground with those before it, the President would think Compensation equally incumbent on the United States.

This Principle forms the Basis of the Stipulation for mutual Compensation contained in the Seventh Article of the Treaty lately signed by Mr. Jay and myself, of which a Copy has been transmitted to you. Conformably with that regulation, all Losses and Damages which may have been sustained by His Majesty's Subjects by reason of the Capture of their Vessels and Merchandize, taken within the limits and jurisdictions of the States, and brought into their Ports, or taken by Vessels originally armed in Ports of the said States, and where restitution shall not have been made agreably to the tenor of Mr. Jefferson's Letter, shall be compensated by the United States, and the Amount of the ascertained loss or damage shall be awarded to the Claimants in Specie without deduction.

The Case of the Brig William Tell [6] appears to come directly within the Principle thus laid down, and the fair interpretation of that Principle would also extend it to the case of the Ship Hope. the circumstances attending it amounting to so strong a presumption of the French Privateer having been a British Captured Vessel fitted out by His Majesty's Enemies in an American Port. It cannot therefore but be matter of surprize, that Mr. Randolph should have declined to comply with your request of at least suspending the Sale of the Vessel and Cargo until those circumstances could be

---

[5] Jefferson's letter to Hammond of Sept. 5, 1793 (*A. S. P., F. R.,* I., 175) had been made a part of Jay's Treaty under Article VII. For the adjudications by the mixed commission under that article see J. B. Moore, *Int. Adjudications,* IV.

[6] The British brig *William Tell* in 1793 had been captured by a French armed vessel off the American coast and carried into New York. See Jefferson to Genêt, Sept. 9, 1793, *A. S. P., F. R.,* I, 175.

ascertained, especially as he grounds his denial on such an Acquiescense being inconsistent with the Rules of Impartiality which the American Government has prescribed to itself. I will not however say more on this Subject at present, because I trust that, before you receive this Dispatch, the Treaty concluded with Mr. Jay will have been ratified in America, and that in consequence the Principle to which I have alluded will have been established as a rule of Conduct in all matters of this nature. In that case, there will be no difficulty in procuring for such of His Majesty's Subjects as may have been injured by such Captures the Satisfaction to which they are so fully entitled. But it will be proper for you, at all events, to continue your exertions in their behalf, and to take every measure in your power to inforce upon the American Government the necessity of preventing the continuance of a practice so unjustifiable and injurious to the interests of His Majesty's Subjects, and which so evidently tends to interrupt the harmony and good understanding, which on every account is so desirable to maintain between the two Countries.

GRENVILLE TO HAMMOND [7]

No. 3.   DOWNING STREET, 15th April 1795.
Sir,
I have no Dispatches from you to acknowledge since the Date of my last letter.

Nearly five Months having elapsed since I transmitted to you a Copy of the Treaty of Amity Commerce and Navigation signed here by Mr. Jay and myself I cannot but feel a great degree of uneasiness at not having received any account of it's having reached Philadelphia. At the same time that I sent it to you by the November Packet, Mr. Jay transmitted two other Copies, one by the Packet, addressed to Mr. Randolph under cover to yourself, and another to the same Gentleman by a Private Ship; and I sent you another Copy by the December Packet. As it is very unlikely that all these Conveyances should have miscarried, I feel anxious to receive the Assurance of the Treaty having arrived in America [8] and I must desire that you will avail yourself of every opportunity which may occur of letting me know whether it has been received, as well as what Steps have been taken respecting it on the part of the American Government.

---

[7] F. O. 115 : 4.
[8] The packet *Tankerville* with the November and December mails had been captured. See Grenville to Hammond, May 9, 1795, No. 7, *infra*. The copy of the treaty sent by Mr. Jay arrived in Philadelphia March 7, 1795. Hammond to Grenville, March 7, 1795, No. 6, F. O. 5 : 9.

GRENVILLE TO HAMMOND [9]

No. 4.   DOWNING STREET, 15th April 1795.

Sir,

I send you inclosed Draft of a Note containing a Representation to
the American Government on the Subject of Two Memorials which
I have received from the acting Governor of the British Colony of
Sierra Leone on the Coast of Africa and from the Agent of Messrs.
John and Alexander Anderson, Proprietors of Bame Island on the
same Coast (Copies of which are also inclosed) complaining of the
violent and illegal Conduct of certain American Subjects and stating
their respective Claims to Satisfaction and Compensation for the
Injuries they have thereby sustained. I am to desire that you will
immediately present this Note with its Inclosures to the American
Secretary of State, and transmit to me by the first Opportunity the
Answer which you may receive from that Gentleman. The Note
which you are instructed to deliver enters so fully into this Subject
that I do not feel it necessary to add any Thing further to what is
there contained.[10]

GRENVILLE TO HAMMOND [11]

No. 5.   DOWNING STREET, 15th April 1795.

Sir,

I send you inclosed for your Information Copy of an Order in
Council of the 8th Instant, containing regulations to prevent Artificers, Manufacturers Seamen and Seafaring Men, His Majesty's Subjects, from embarking on Board Foreign Ships or Vessels for the
purpose of quitting this Kingdom and going into Parts beyond the
Seas contrary to the Laws and Statutes of the Realm.[12]

---

[9] F. O. 115 : 4.

[10] Hammond's note stating that certain American citizens, notably David Newell, commanding the schooner *Massachusetts* of Boston, and Peter Williams, commanding a
schooner from New York, in the fall of 1794 had aided the French force which had at-
tacked Sierra Leone, and had plundered British subjects, was referred by Randolph to the
Attorney General. Hammond to Randolph, June 25, 1795, Notes from British Legation,
1a; Randolph to Hammond, July 6, 1795, Domestic Letters, 8; Hammond to Grenville,
June 28, July 18, 1795, Nos. 18 and 24, F. O. 5 : 9.

[11] F. O. 115 : 4.

[12] Hammond, and Bond also, had frequently reported on the development of manu-
facturing in the United States, and had urged a greater vigilance in Great Britain "to
prevent the emigration of artists and the exportation of the machines necessary for the
different branches of manufactures." Hammond to Grenville, Dec. 6, 1791, No. 9, F. O.
4 : 11 ; Feb. 2, 1792, No. 9, F. O. 4 : 14 ; Oct. 3, 1792, No. 37, F. O. 4 : 16 ; Jameson, ed.,
"Letters of Phineas Bond," *Ann. Rpt. Amer. Hist. Assoc.*, 1897, p. 486 and ff. See, also,
Grenville to Hammond, Aug. 29, 1795, No. 18, *infra.*

No. 6.   DOWNING STREET, 18th April 1795.

Sir,

I send you inclosed Extract of a Letter from General Sir John Vaughan [14] to Mr. Secretary Dundas, with the Copy of a Proclamation issued by him for the purpose of preventing the Enemy from receiving Supplies in the Islands of Guadaloupe, Marie Galante and Desiada, together with a Copy of Mr. Dundas's Letter to the Lords Commissioners of the Admiralty; and I am to desire that you will without delay make a proper notification on this subject to the American Government. [15]

GRENVILLE TO HAMMOND [16]

No. 7.   DOWNING STREET, 9th May 1795.

Sir,

Your several Dispatches to No. 6 inclusive have been duly received and laid before the King.

In consequence of the notice you give me in your Dispatch No. 6 that the Senate cannot be assembled for the purpose of taking into consideration the Treaty of Commerce Amity and Navigation signed by Mr. Jay and myself 'till the 8th of June, I am to desire that you will take the first opportunity of explaining to the American Minister that, as the Ratifications cannot arrive here 'till the end of July at soonest, it will be impossible to keep Parliament sitting, or to take any steps to execute the Treaty in the mean while, as far as Parliamentary Provisions are necessary for that purpose.

Advice having been received here of the Capture of the Tankerville Packet with the November and December Mails on board, by a French Armed Vessel, I now send you inclosed Duplicates of my Dispatches Nos. 3, 4, 5 and 6, Triplicates of my Dispatches Nos. 20, 21, 22, 23 and 24, Quintuplicates of my Dispatches Nos. 15, 16 and 17, and Quadruplicate of the Treaty signed by Mr. Jay and myself on the 19th of Nov. and which had been sent to you by that Conveyance.

---

[13] F. O. 115 : 4.

[14] General Sir John Vaughan (1748?–1795), commander of the Leeward Islands and of the British troops then investing the French West Indies in conjunction with naval forces under Vice Admiral Caldwell.

[15] The blockade proclamation of Jan. 29, 1795 had already been made public by Consul General Bond, on April 10. Hammond transmitted a copy of it on June 25, and was informed on June 30 by Randolph that, being uncertain whether its operation would require the United States to controvert its propriety, he would only observe that his government held itself free to contest, if need be, its effect on American shipping. Domestic Letters, 8. During May of 1795 French Minister Fauchet complained bitterly to Randolph against the yielding of the United States to this "illegal" blockade. *A S. P., F. R.,* I, 609, 613–614.

[16] F. O. 115 : 4.

GRENVILLE TO HAMMOND [17]

No. 8.   DOWNING STREET, 9th May 1795.

Sir,

I send you inclosed for your information a Précis of certain Dispatches from the different Ministers and Agents of the French Convention in America, which were found on board the Jean Bart, a French Vessel, captured by His Majesty's Cruizers on it's passage from America to France. It is probable that by a future Conveyance I may be enabled to send you the Original Dispatches the Communication of some of which to well disposed Persons in America may possibly be usefull to the King's Service.[18]

GRENVILLE TO HAMMOND [19]

Confidential.
No. 9.   DOWNING STREET, 14th May 1795.

Sir,

I send you inclosed Extract of a Letter from Lieut. Governor Simcoe to His Grace The Duke of Portland,[20] containing his reasons for wishing that Col¹ Pickering [21] may not be employed on the part of the United States as an Agent to carry into effect any Stipulations contained in the Treaty lately signed by Mr. Jay and myself, and mentioning Gen Hull [22] as a Gentleman whose being employed for that purpose would be very satisfactory. As Mr. Jay will probably have

---

[17] F. O. 115 : 4.
[18] Among the captured dispatches was Fauchet's No. 10 which placed Randolph's relations with the French Minister in a questionable light, and forced Randolph's resignation on Aug. 19, 1795. Fauchet's dispatches, No. 10 of Oct. 31, 1794, and those to which allusions were made, No. 3 of June 4, and No. 6 of Sept. 5, 1794, are printed in Turner, ed., "Correspondence of the French Ministers to the United States, 1791–1797," *Ann. Rpt. Amer. Hist. Assoc., 1903*, pp. 444, 372, 411. In April, Hammond, in a cipher letter marked "Secret and Confidential," had reported Randolph to be openly pro-French and given to talking "in terms of arrogance and menace," threatening that the United States in face of continued British aggressions would not ratify Jay's Treaty. He suspected Randolph of being improperly influenced by the French agents at Philadelphia, "a circumstance . . . which the pecuniary embarrassments and general character of Mr. Randolph render far from improbable." Hammond to Grenville, April 28, 1795, No. 8, F. O. 5 : 9.
[20] William Henry Cavendish Bentinck, third Duke of Portland (1738–1809), on Aug. 7, 1794 had succeeded Henry Dundas as Home Secretary.
[21] Timothy Pickering of Massachusetts (1745–1829), Postmaster General from 1791 to 1795, Secretary of War since Jan. 2, 1795. Later, on Aug. 20, 1795, he became Secretary of State *ad interim*, and on Dec. 10, 1795 was formally commissioned to that office. As one of the three commissioners sent in 1793 to negotiate a treaty with the Six Nations, he had become acquainted with Simcoe, who informed the Duke of Portland on Dec. 22, 1794 that Pickering was "in principle a Jacobin." E. A. Cruikshank, ed., *Corres. of Lieut. Gov. John Graves Simcoe*, III, 239. Hammond, also, at this time regarded Pickering as possessing a "most blind and undistinguishing hatred of Great Britain." Hammond to Grenville, Jan. 5, 1795, F. O. 5 : 8, and July 27, 1795, No. 25, F. O. 5 : 9.
[22] General William Hull of Massachusetts (1753–1825), who in 1784 had been sent to Canada to arrange for the evacuation of the British posts on American soil.

arrived in America before this Letter reaches you, I wish you to communicate confidentially on this Subject with that Gentleman, and such other Persons as he shall judge most proper to assist in furthering the Attainment of the Object stated in General Simcoe's Letter.

GRENVILLE TO HAMMOND [23]

No. 10.   DOWNING STREET, 14th May 1795.

Sir,

Since I wrote to you on the 9th Ins^t I have received your Dispatch No. 7, which has been laid before the King.

Having received from the King's Advocate a Report on the Subject of the Apprehensions you had entertained that some individuals in America had the intention of arresting such English Officers as might have been concerned in capturing American Ships laden with property for the Use of the King's Enemies, and learning from your last Letter that Captn Cochrane has actually been arrested at the suit of an individual at New York on such a pretence,[24] I lose no time in forwarding to you a Copy of the King's Advocate's opinion on this Subject, by which you may be enabled to regulate your Conduct in the further progress of this or any similar matter which may arise.[25] I have only to add, that the Steps which you inform me you had already taken, for supporting Captn Cochrane and bringing the Suit to a full and public decision, appear to have been very proper, and have been approved of here.

GRENVILLE TO HAMMOND [26]

No. 11.   DOWNING STREET, 14th May 1795.

Sir,

I send you inclosed Extract of a Letter from Governor Craufurd to His Grace the Duke of Portland, together with it's inclosure, re-

---

[23] F. O. 115 : 4.

[24] In his No. 7 of April 3, 1795, F. O. 5 : 9, Hammond had reported that a suit had been instituted at New York against Captain Cochrane of the *Thetis* for the recovery of the value of a sloop captured by Cochrane, even though the Court of Admiralty at Nova Scotia had condemned the sloop as a legal prize.

[25] Sir William Scott, the King's Advocate, stated: "supposing that the Arrests had actually taken place at the suit of private Individuals and without any Communication with the Governments, I do not think that the Government would have been responsible for these ill-advised Acts of Individuals unless the Courts of Justice had rejected the defensive Plea . . . that the Ships had been taken *Jure Belli*, and condemned by a Sentence of a Court of Admiralty. To these Sentences full Faith is to be given by the Law of Nations in all Courts in all other Countries, and the Refusal of such Faith wou'd be a denial of Justice which the Government of the Country wou'd be bound to repair. But I am not aware that the improper attempts of Individuals to convert a Question of Prize into a Question of Civil Debt can be deemed violations of the Law of Nations by the Country to which such Individuals belong unless it shall appear that the Government countenanced the Attempts, And that the Courts of Justice did not immediately dismiss the Proceedings (and with Costs) as soon as ever the real nature of them was fairly disclosed." Enclosure, with above instruction, "Extracts of a Report from Sir William Scott to Lord Grenville, Dec. 23rd 1794."

[26] F. O. 115 : 4.

specting the Capture of a Vessel belonging to the Bermudas; and I am to desire that you will afford to the parties concerned any assistance which the circumstances may admit of.[27]

GRENVILLE TO HAMMOND [28]

No. 12.   DOWNING STREET, 5th June 1795.
Sir,
I have no dispatches to acknowledge from you since the Date of my last Letters.

I send you inclosed Copy of a Letter, which was taken on board of a Ship carried into Halifax and transmitted hither by Governor Wentworth; and I am to desire that you will communicate it's contents confidentially to Mr. Jay and to such other Persons as he or yourself may be of Opinion should be made acquainted with them.[29]

I also send you inclosed the Original of the Dispatches from the different Ministers and Agents of the French Convention in America which were found on board the French Vessel, Jean Bart, captured by His Majesty's Cruizers on its Passage from America to France, of which I sent you a Précis in my Dispatch No. 8, with the view that you should communicate such Parts of them as you may deem expedient to well disposed Persons in America.[30]

GRENVILLE TO HAMMOND [31]

No. 13.   DOWNING STREET, 1st July 1795.
Sir,
Your Several Dispatches to No. 11 Inclusive, were received yesterday and have been laid before the King.

---

[27] The letter of James Craufurd (the name was variously spelled: Craufurd, Crauford, Crawford), Governor of Bermuda from 1794 to 1796, referred to the sloop *Jolly Bacchus*, which had been captured and brought into Charleston. Hammond did not believe that there was any prospect of procuring redress for the owners, except under the provisions made for such captures in Jay's Treaty. Hammond to Grenville, July 27, 1795, No. 27, F. O. 5 : 9.

[28] F. O. 115 : 4.

[29] The intercepted letter was from Joshua Barney (see note 47, p. 61, *supra*) to his brother, written at Bordeaux Dec. 21, 1794, in which Barney described the reception of Monroe (whom he had accompanied) by the French National Convention, and said he was most desirous to hear what Jay had done in England, "for we cannot learn any thing about him in this Country. . . ." In this connection it might be noted that Randolph on May 21, 1795 complained to Hammond of the interception of three of Monroe's dispatches. Moore, *Digest of Int. Law*, IV, 710. On May 27, 1795 Sir John Wentworth sent to Hammond from Halifax copies of Monroe's letters: to Madison, Oct. 16, 1794; to Secretary Randolph, Nov. 20, No. 6, Dec. 2, No. 7, and Dec. 9, private, 1794. These are in F. O. 95 ; 502.

[30] Hammond acknowledged this instruction with its enclosures in his No. 28 of July 27, 1795, F. O. 5 : 9, and promptly made use of Fauchet's dispatch No. 10 in forcing the resignation of Secretary Randolph. George Gibbs, *Administrations of Washington and Adams*, I, 232–233 ; Moncure D. Conway, *Edmund Randolph*, pp. 270–289.

[31] F. O. 115 : 4.

As it has been judged inconvenient to delay the sailing of the Packet, it will be impossible for me at present to enter fully into the different matters which form the Subject of your Dispatches; and I shall therefore confine myself to the noticing those points in them which are most immediately pressing, and on which it appears to be necessary that you should receive Instructions.

You will perceive by my Dispatches forwarded by the May Packet Duplicates of which were sent by the Packet which sailed last Month that intelligence had been received here of the Capture of His Majesty's Packet Tankerville, with the Mails of November and December by the Lovely Lass Privateer. Without entering into any discussion of the circumstances which you state to have accompanied the fitting out and arming of this Vessel, which undoubtedly tends very greatly to aggravate the case,[32] I shall observe that this, and all other similar cases, fall under the Seventh Article of the Treaty signed here by Mr. Jay and myself, which Article extends as you will have observed to all Cases existing at the time of exchanging the Ratifications of the Treaty. It will therefore be proper that you should be very attentive to collect every kind of evidence that may be material with respect to all such Cases.

With respect also to the Citizens of America, fitting out or serving in Privateers, exercising Acts of Hostility against His Majesty's Subjects or accepting Commissions or Instructions so to act from a State at enmity with His Majesty, I must also refer you to the Twenty First Article of the Treaty, which not only provides that the Laws against such Offences shall be punctually executed by the Neutral Government but declares that it is lawful for the Belligerent Power to treat such offenders, when taken in the Act, as Pirates. You will therefore exert yourself to procure the most ample information on this Subject as it may become necessary to make some striking example agreably to the declaration contained in the above Article in order to deter others from a practise which is now carried to so great an extent.

As the obligation of this Article is reciprocal and equally binding upon His Majesty's Subjects as on those of the United States, the King will undoubtedly in every instance not only prohibit the Commission of any such enormities as those which Mr. Randolph in his Letter to you states to have been committed by the inhabitants of the

---

[32] Although the *Lovely Lass* had been seized at Baltimore, at the request of the British consul, the Federal authorities had released her when they found that she had been divested of warlike equipment. In January of 1795 the vessel had sailed from Baltimore, after taking on board "either in that port or in Chesapeake Bay, fourteen cannon, and proceeded on a cruise, in the course of which she captured the Tankerville. . . . " The number of privateers, "fitted out in the ports of the United States, continue to increase in number to a most alarming extent," Hammond to Grenville, April 28, 1795, No. 8, F. O. 5 : 9.

Bermudas, but will cause those who may have been guilty of them to suffer the penalties provided against such Offenders. His Majesty therefore has been pleased entirely to approve of the line which you adopted in consequence of Mr. Randolph's Representation, and of the Letter which you wrote to Governor Craufurd, and it is to be hoped, that the Measures already taken, and the Exertions of His Majesty's Officers in that quarter, will prove successfull in putting a Stop to practises, whatever may be their Extent, must meet with the King's entire disapprobation and displeasure.[33]

With respect to Mr. Randolph's Notification on the Subject of the King's Ships taking a Station in the Ports of the United States for the purpose of cruising from thence, that point is also clearly regulated by the 23rd Article of the Treaty, which gives to the King's Ships an unlimited right of admission into the Ports of the United States, as well as the most compleat protection to the Officers on board of them. Tho' the Article in question is decisive as to this point, it does not however appear to go to the length of warranting the Commander of the King's Ships in the American Station bringing their Prizes into American Ports; and in this respect the first of The Two Constructions mentioned in Mr. Randolph's letter to you—namely—that the clause in their Treaty with France forbids British Ships to come in *with* their Prizes seems to be the true one; it will therefore be right that you should, whenever this matter should come into discussion, consider it in that light, and it would be desireable that this point should be properly understood by the King's Officers stationed in the American Seas; for tho' those acting contrary to that Stipulation may justly be argued on the grounds stated by you not to be guilty of an offence against the Sovereignty of the United States, it will be right for them to abstain from the practise; as it places the Government of America under the necessity of inforcing Regulations apparently injurious to the British interests and leads to promote and increase mutual animosity.[34]

---

[33] Randolph had protested to Hammond against the activities of the Bermuda privateers, notorious for bringing into the Bermuda prize courts every American vessel they met regardless of destination of cargo; and against the indiscriminate condemnations by the judge of the Admiralty Court at that place. Though Hammond thought the charges "not a little exaggerated" he was "induced to believe that they were not altogether destitute of foundation," and he had taken up the matter with Admiral Murray and with Governor Crauford of Bermuda. Hammond to Grenville, April 28, 1795, No. 8, F. O. 5 : 9.

[34] Secretary Randolph had protested against the capture of an American ship in home waters by the *Lynx* sloop of war; the conduct of Captain Beresford of the *Lynx* in firing upon, and taking temporary possession of, an American revenue cutter; the bringing into Norfolk by the *Argonaut* of her prize, the French national corvette *Esperance;* and the commissioning of the *Esperance* into the British service. Hammond to Grenville, April 28, 1795, No. 8, F. O. 5 : 9.

GRENVILLE TO HAMMOND [35]

No. 14.   DOWNING STREET, 1st July 1795.

Sir,

I send you inclosed Copies of Two Notes which I have lately received from Mr. Deas,[36] who now officiates in the Absence of Mr. Pinckney as the Chargé d'Affaires of the American Government at this Court together with a Copy of my Answer to the Same.

Nothing can be more evident than the impropriety of a Representation of this Nature,[37] especially when couched in such terms as Mr. Deas has thought proper to use on a point which has already been settled between the two Countries by the Treaty signed by Mr. Jay and myself,[38] of which it was impossible he could be ignorant. Neither was Mr. Deas entitled to receive any Answer on a point, on which it was impossible in point of time that he could have received the Orders of his Employers.

I have however omitted to notice these Circumstances as the matter in question will be finally settled by the Ratification of the Treaty,[39] and as it is the wish of His Majesty's Government to manifest on

---

[35] F. O. 115 : 4.

[36] William Allen Deas of South Carolina, secretary of legation under Thomas Pinckney, who had been left in charge upon the latter's departure as special envoy to negotiate a treaty with Spain. The enclosed copies of his notes to Grenville were dated June 5, 18, 1795.

[37] Deas had inquired about the continued seizures of American provision vessels. Fresh seizures were then being made under a secret order-in-council of April 25, 1795, directing the detention of ships bound for French ports with grain or provisions suspected of having been purchased by agents of the French government. This order-in-council (which is printed on p. 97, *infra*) was not published ; as late as October 28, 1795 Deas reported that he had not seen it. The order was rescinded in September of 1795, yet seizures continued because of the length of time necessary to communicate with British ships of war. Deas assumed, and all Americans assumed, that this secret order (for the seizure of enemy provisions in neutral ships) was a renewal of, or was similar to, the general provision order of June 8, 1793, which called for the seizure of all ships conveying grain or other provisions to an enemy port and the preemption of their cargoes. Deas to the Secretary of State, Oct. 13, 23, 28, 1795, Dispatches, Great Britain, 3 ; Moore, *Int. Adjud.*, IV, 28–29, 121–123. On the serious and prolonged misunderstanding as to the nature of the unpublished order of April 25, 1795, see Josiah T. Newcomb, "New Light on Jay's Treaty," *Amer. Jour. International Law,* XXVIII (Oct. 1934), 685–692.

[38] By Article XVII of Jay's Treaty it was agreed that enemy property in neutral bottoms was lawful prize. Grenville, however, did not make clear to Deas or to the American government that the secret order of April 25, 1795, under which seizures were being made, was based on this article, rather than on the arguments that had been used to justify the provision order of June 8, 1793.

[39] The Senate debated the treaty from June 8 to June 24, 1795, then, after amending it so as to make inoperative so much of Article XII as related to the West Indian trade, consented to its ratification by the President by the bare two-thirds vote required. While the treaty was being considered, news arrived of British seizures under the new, secret, and misunderstood order-in-council. These fresh seizures, together with accounts of impressments and of the activities of Capt. Rodham Home (see note 77, p. 99, *infra*), augmented the general opposition to the treaty, perplexed and enraged proponents of an amicable understanding with England, and caused both Washington and Hamilton to agree with Secretary Randolph, temporarily at least, that the treaty should be ratified only on condition that the offensive order was revoked. See Washington to Hamilton, Aug. 31 ; to Jay, Aug. 31, 1795, Washington, *Writings,* ed. W. C. Ford, XIII, 96–97, 99 ; and Hamilton to Wolcott, Aug. 10, 1795, Hamilton, *Works,* ed. H. C. Lodge, X, 113–114.

every occasion the disposition to maintain that system of harmony and good understanding which the Treaty was calculated to produce and not to suffer it to be interrupted by the effects of these ill judged or intemperate Representations especially from a Subordinate Agent.[40] You will not fail to state the matter in this point of view to the American Government, and you will express the hope that a similar Spirit may in future be adopted by those employed to speak in Their Name.

GRENVILLE TO HAMMOND [41]

No. 15.   DOWNING STREET, 1st July 1795.

Sir,

I send you inclosed, for your information, a Precis of certain Letters from the House of Cheriot and Richard Sun who reside at New York to their Correspondents in France, respecting the extensive Trade now carrying on between America and France, which were found in the possession of a Frenchman on board of the Isis, an American Schooner, stopt in her passage to France, by Capt. Robinson of His Majesty's Ship Arethusa; and I am to desire that you will make such Communication of the Same to well disposed persons in America and to the King's Officers employed on that station, as you may judge most usefull for His Majesty's Service.[42]

GRENVILLE TO HAMMOND [43]

No. 16.   DOWNING STREET, August 25, 1795.

Sir,

Your several Dispatches to No. 22 have been duly received and laid before the King.

In my Dispatch No. 14 which was forwarded by the July Packet, I sent you Two Notes which I have received from Mr. Deas, who now officiates in the absence of Mr. Pinckney as the Chargé d'Affaires of the American Government at this Court, together with a Copy of my Answer to the same. I now send You Duplicates of them, together

---

[40] In his instruction to Deas of Sept. 15, 1795, Secretary Pickering, referring to the two notes dated June 16 and July 2, 1795, which the chargé d'affaires had sent Grenville, stated that the first note "was certainly well judged, as a protest against the instructions for capturing American vessels laden with provisions and bound to France; although a revocation of the instructions was not expected as a consequence of your representation." U. S. Ministers, Instructions, 3.

[41] F. O. 115 : 4.

[42] This instruction was acknowledged on Sept. 29, 1795, F. O. 5 : 10, by Phineas Bond, the Consul General at Philadelphia, who had become chargé d'affaires upon Hammond's departure from Philadelphia on August 14, 1795. Bond said he would try "to unravel all the Mysteries of this Commerce; which tho' disguised with so much Art, is plainly calculated to furnish supplies to the present Rulers of France under the Shape of Neutral Property."

[43] Draft, F. O. 5 : 9.

with Copies of several Notes which I have since received from the same Gentleman, and of a Letter which I wrote to him. The Impropriety of the language which Mr. Deas has thought proper to hold in the course of this Correspondence is sufficiently obvious, and it must be matter of sincere regret to every person who wishes well to the maintenance of harmony and good understanding between the Two Countries to observe that a person employed in a situation like that of Mr. Deas shou'd conduct himself in a manner so little calculated to promote that object.

As however Mr. Deas has in some of his subsequent communications adopted a stile of correspondence more suited to what is usual between friendly Governments it will not be necessary for you to make any formal complaint on that subject, but to take whatever you may judge the most proper mode of conveying to the President the desire of this Government that either Mr. Deas may be instructed to communicate with His Majesty's servants in a manner calculated to promote the objects of conciliation, or if this cannot be done, that, during Mr. Pinckney's absence, the American Affairs will be intrusted to some person whose principles and disposition will be likely to produce the same effect.[44]

GRENVILLE TO HAMMOND [45]

No. 17.   DOWNING STREET, 26th Aug. 1795.

Sir,

Having referred to the Lords Commissioners of the Admiralty the Suggestions contained in your last Letters respecting the propriety of Instructions being sent to the Commanders of His Majesty's Ships in the West Indies, directing them to transmit details of the Privateers captured by them, and also as to the propriety of forwarding fresh Instructions to the Bermudas, respecting the Revocation of the Order in Council of the 6th Nov. 1793, I now send you inclosed the Answers on these several points which I have received from their Lordships by which you will perceive that such Instructions have been forwarded.[46]

---

[44] On July 27, and again on August 22, 1795, Under Secretary Burges complained to Gouverneur Morris of Deas' "very improper" protests against the order-in-council directing the seizure of American provision vessels. Morris, *Diary*, II, 93, 113. Secretary Pickering admitted to Bond that Deas' note of July 27, 1795 was evidently "couched in the Style of a young and inexperienced person." Bond to Grenville, Nov. 15, 1795, No. 13, F. O. 5 : 10. Referring to Deas' letters to Grenville (of July 6, 14, 19, 27, and Aug. 4, 1795), Pickering informed Deas on November 10, 1795 that "some sentiments *and particularly the manner of expressing them* were noticed as exceptionable," and stated that when the instructions of the Secretary of State were expressed in warm and indignant terms it by no means followed that such language should be used in addressing foreign courts. U. S. Ministers, Instructions, 3. See, also, Grenville to Bond, Jan. 7, 1796, No. 4, *infra.*

[45] Draft, F. O. 5 : 9.

[46] Hammond had suggested that such information be obtained, especially in regard to British ships taken by French privateers fitted out in the United States, in preparation for the adjudication of such cases by the mixed commission provided under Article VII of Jay's Treaty. Hammond to Grenville, May 28, 1795, No. 12, F. O. 5 : 9.

No. 18.   DOWNING STREET, 29th August 1795.
Sir,

Having referred to the King's Advocate General the Statement which you sent me of the Complaint which had been made to you by Mr. Randolph respecting indented Servants and Redemptioners having been taken out of an American Vessel by the King's Officers,[48] I now send you inclosed Two Reports which I have received from that Gentleman on the subject; and I am to desire that you will make your Conduct and Language on this Subject conformable to what is stated in these Papers and that the purport of them may be communicated to the Officers commanding His Majesty's Ships of War on the American Station. You will however not fail to observe that the Opinion of the King's Advocate on the Question of taking British Artificers out of Neutral Ships rests only on a deficiency in the Provisions of the present Laws on that Subject, and that if Parliament should think proper to make any new Provisions in that behalf, it does not appear, that the Execution of such Laws could be obstructed by any privilege belonging to American Vessels either as Neutral, or Foreign Ships.

No. 19.   DOWNING STREET, 31st Aug. 1795.
Sir,

Since the date of my Letter No. 17 your several Dispatches to No. 24 inclusive have been duly received and laid before the King.

With respect to these, I have at present only to express the great satisfaction which I have received from the Statement you transmitted to me of Admiral Murray's conduct respecting the Complaints which had been made of the Conduct of the Officers acting under his Command; and I trust that this must have convinced the American Government of the constant attention shewn by that Officer, to

---

[47] Draft, F. O. 5 : 9.
[48] Thirty-two Irish emigrants had been seized from the American brig *Harmony* on the pretext that the signature of the Mayor of Cork to the indentures they held had been forged. Randolph had inquired whether British laws and instructions on the seizure of British subjects out of neutral bottoms on the high seas applied generally or only to "artists and seamen." Randolph to Hammond, June 1, 1795, Domestic Letters, 8. See, also, Grenville to Hammond, April 15, 1795, No. 5, *supra*. Hammond hoped the British officers had acted upon sufficient grounds, since nothing could be devised more capable of checking "the rapid and increasing progress of the immigration from Ireland to this country" than an apprehension of similar seizures. Hammond to Grenville, June 4, 1795, No. 14 ; and May 29, No. 12, June 28, No. 20, 1795, F. O. 5 : 9. Bond, acknowledging this instruction, suggested various indirect ways of discouraging and eventually stopping "this Ruinous Trade." Jameson, ed., "Letters of Phineas Bond," *Ann. Rpt. Amer. Hist. Assoc. 1896*, p. 581 ff.
[49] Draft, F. O. 5 : 9.

observe that part of his Instructions which enjoined an attention to keep up an amicable intercourse with the United States of America.[50]

GRENVILLE TO HAMMOND [51]

Separate.

No. 20.   DOWNING STREET, 31st August 1795.

Sir,

I have reserved to this separate Dispatch to make some Observations on the present Situation of Affairs as between this Country and the United States to which I am the rather induced from the Contents of your Dispatch No. 25 [52] which was received here on the 24th Instant. I cannot however enter so particularly as I should wish into this Subject 'till I shall have received from you the Memorial which it was Mr. Randolph's Intention to deliver to you.[53]

On the general Subject of the Treaty it is not necessary for me to enter into much detail. You are acquainted with the Stipulations which it contains. You will have learnt the Nature of the Objections made to it, and the Answers to those Objections will readily occur to you. It was not difficult to foresee that whenever that Instrument became known in America, the French and Democratical Party there would exert all the Means in their Power to excite a Prejudice against any Agreement which should do away the Grounds of existing differences between Great Britain and America and lay the foundation of future Harmony and Friendship. But it was conceived here that if the Government of America had Strength and Firmness enough in the first Instance to resist these Clamours the beneficial Effects of the Treaty itself would gradually operate to strengthen the System so established, and at the same time to give additional Weight to the Government itself by whose means it had been established.

I am sorry to see any Appearances of Wavering, or Hesitation on this Subject: and it is much to be wished that some proper mode

---

[50] In his No. 21 of June 28, 1795, F. O. 5 : 9, Hammond had enclosed a copy of a letter he had received from Admiral Murray, dated June 2, 1795 (Admiralty, I, 493), justifying the conduct of his officers against the complaints of Secretary Randolph (see note 34, p. 87, *supra*)—Captain Beresford had fired upon the American revenue cutter because, with no colors flying, he suspected her of being one of the "piratical privateers" fitted out at Charleston ; Captain Ball had brought the captured *Esperance* into Lynnhaven Bay for water and provisions, and had not at that place formally commissioned her into the British service.

[51] Draft, F. O. 5 : 9.

[52] Reference is doubtless made to Hammond's dispatch No. 23 of July 18, 1795, F. O. 5 : 9, which was endorsed as received on August 24, 1795. Hammond's No. 25 of July 27, referring to Grenville's No. 9, *supra*, was not received until September 8, 1795.

[53] While Randolph had informed Hammond that the President intended to ratify the treaty as amended by the Senate, he had also stated that the President would require more time to determine his course if, as reported, Great Britain had issued a new order-in-council for the seizure of provision vessels bound for France. Randolph had promised to give Hammond in a few days a memorial in which the motives of the President's decision on this subject would be amply detailed. Hammond to Grenville, July 18, 1795, No. 23, F. O. 5 : 9.

could be found of bringing before the Consideration of those who are to decide this Question the great Inconvenience and Hazard of further discussion and delay. Supposing it were true that the popular Objections against the Treaty in America were well grounded, it must be remembered that this like every other Negotiation has proceeded on a mutual disposition to Accomodation and Agreement:—that Advantages on One Side are compensated by Sacrifices on the Other and that the Treaty is to be considered as a general result of many separate discussions and difficulties. If therefore a new Negotiation is opened, it cannot be expected that the Difficulties which exist in America can be done away without withdrawing from the Treaty other Points some of them materially advantageous to that Country, in order to maintain a just Balance of Reciprocity. In this form therefore, after long discussion and much difference and dispute the Treaty must again be submitted to the public decision in America,—and in this Form it will unquestionably afford fresh Matter for exciting Opposition to the Government and Animosity against this Country.—So that no Advantage will be gained by a present Appearance of Weakness on the Part of the American Government.

With respect to the Points mentioned to you by Mr. Randolph, that of the detention of Vessels laden with Provisions bound to the Enemy's Ports, it seems hardly necessary to re: capitulate all that appears in my Correspondence with you on this Subject for the last three Years. But these Points may be considered as incontestable and as amply sufficient to justify the Conduct of this Government in that Respect.

1. That by the Law of Nations as laid down by all Writers without exception, and particularly by Vattel, the most recent and the most moderate on these Points, a Belligerent Power has the right to prevent the Supplies of Provisions to an Enemy whose distress in that respect affords a Means of War and Hope of Peace. And that this might accordingly be done in such a Case by the usual Course of Seizure and Confiscation.

2. That the Case of France is by her own Confession and by a Notoriety quite indisputable such in this respect as to justify the Application of that Principle.

3. That in proceeding by the Way of Detention and Purchase instead of that of Seizure and Confiscation, this Government has therefore adopted a line much more favourable to Neutral Commerce than the Law of Nations would require in a Case where no Treaty existed.

4. That this principle is expressly recognized, and this Mode of Conduct stipulated, in the Treaty concluded last Year.[54]

---

[54] The language of Article XVIII of Jay's Treaty implies acceptance of the British principle that foodstuffs could be treated as contraband when there existed a well-founded expectation of reducing the enemy by the want thereof, and that in such cases foodstuffs were to be preempted, purchased not confiscated, with a grant of freight and demurrage.

5. That so far therefore from affording to the American Government any just ground of Complaint by the adoption of that Line of Conduct, this Country has given a Proof of it's amicable disposition towards the United States by acting upon the Treaty previous to it's Ratification, precisely as it would have been bound to do if that Instrument had been in full force.

6. That if the Treaty should not be ratified, the United States so far from having any ground for demanding to be treated more favourably in this Respect, could have no just ground to expect a continuance of the same Modification which has now been adopted, of a principle which is in distinct and express Terms recognized by all the Writers on the Law of Nations, and the Application of which to the Case in Question no Man can contest.[55]

I have thought it right to state these Points thus distinctly to you, in order to enable you to regulate your Communications and Language by them; but I earnestly hope that the Necessity for these discussions will not exist.

I think it further right to acquaint you on the subject of the Proceedings in the Island of Bermuda that I find on reference to the Admiralty that His Majesty's Instructions dated 8th January 1794 by which the Instruction dated 6th November 1793 was revoked in so far as related to the Point therein mentioned was transmitted to the Island of Bermuda on the 16th January 1794; but that as there appears reason to doubt whether the said Revocation has been received there, the Lords Commissioners of the Admiralty have given Directions for a fresh Transmission thereof.[56]

If when this Dispatch is received the Treaty should not have been ratified, you will find some proper mode of communicating as directly as possible with the President on these several Points— And His Majesty is pleased to leave it to your Discretion under all the then existing Circumstances to avail yourself or not, as you shall judge best for His Service, of the leave of Absence which I transmitted to you in November last, and a Triplicate of which is herewith inclosed.[57]

---

[55] From the phrasing of paragraphs 5 and 6 it would appear that Grenville was unaware that the text of the order-in-council of April 25, 1795 was not known in the United States. See his instruction to Bond, Nov. 4, 1795, No. 4, *infra*.

[56] Since Pickering, like Randolph before him, frequently brought up the subject of Bermuda captures, "a Source of endless Complaints," Bond was particularly pleased to be able to inform the Secretary of State that fresh instructions had been sent to Bermuda relative to the order of Nov. 6, 1793. Bond to Grenville, Nov. 15, 1795, No. 13, F. O. 5 : 10.

[57] Hammond took leave of the President August 14, 1795, and left Philadelphia on the following day for New York, whence he expected to embark for Halifax on the frigate *Thisbe*. He landed in England Sept. 28, 1795. Bond to Grenville, Aug. 16, No. 1, Nov. 15, No. 13, Nov. 25, No. 15, 1795, F. O. 5 : 10.

No. 1.   DOWNING STREET, 10th Oct. 1795.

Sir,

I deem it proper to inform you that from the turn which Affairs have recently taken in Europe, it is by no means improbable that this Country may be involved in a War with Spain. Under this impression it would be very desireable to learn the part which the United States might be inclined to take in such an event. More especially as a Treaty is now pending between them and the Court of Spain, and as there is a reasonable ground of Suspicion either that Mr. Pinckney conceives himself authorized to comprehend other objects in his negotiation than that which has hitherto Appeared to be the most essential if not the sole point of discussion between his Government and that of Spain (the opening of the Navigation of the river Mississippi[)] or that the latter power is sollicitous in any arrangement which it may form with the United States, of rendering them a party with itself to a System of defensive Alliance with France and Prussia.[59]

I have therefore to desire that you will exert yourself to the utmost to endeavour to discover whether Mr. Pinckney be invested with powers to proceed to the extent of entering into a System of the nature above specified or whether if a proposition to that effect should be made by the Court of Spain, the United States would be disposed to accede to it. Though it is scarcely presumable that any Considerations can be so weighty as to draw the American Government from its present beneficial Neutrality into a State of hostility with any European Power, you will nevertheless not fail, upon all proper occasions to endeavour to impress upon the minds of persons of influence in America a Sense of the mischievous Consequences which would result from too close a Connection with Spain, and a Conviction that if it should ever be expedient for the United States to become a party in a War which may take place between Great Britain and Spain every motive of local advantage and of Commercial policy would prescribe the participation in a Common cause with the former rather than with the latter

---

[58] F. O. 115: 4. Bond had become chargé d'affaires when Hámmond took his formal leave, on Aug. 14, 1795.

[59] Thomas Pinckney, sent from London as special envoy to Spain, had been given no additional instructions but had been referred to those already given Carmichael and Short on March 18, 1792. Randolph to Pinckney, Nov. 28, 1794, *A. S. P., F. R.*, I, 534. During his negotiations proposals were made by Godoy as to an alliance with mutual guarantee of territories, and as to a triple alliance between the United States, Spain, and France. Pinckney had treated these proposals in the spirit of Pickering's statement to Short of Aug. 31, 1795: "In your letter of March 3rd you intimate that Spain wants an alliance with us; but rightly conclude that the United States will on no consideration which Spain can offer, entangle themselves with European politics by connections of this kind." U. S. Ministers, Instructions. ?.

power. Indeed the American Ministers cannot have been unmindful of the conduct which the Spanish Cabinet has uniformly observed with respect to the Navigation of the Mississippi professing a desire to grant it, whenever the pressure of its political relations has rendered it expedient for it to attempt to conciliate the inhabitants of America, and constantly receding as soon as that pressure has been removed. While on the other hand Great Britain having itself a permanent interest in obtaining the freedom of that navigation offers an unquestionable security for the sincerity of it's endeavors both in obtaining the Object, and in ensuring the undisturbed possession of it, to it's own Subjects and to the Citizens of the United States. The General Commercial faculties of Spain are so unimportant, and it's particular relations with America are so contracted that it is absolutely unnecessary to draw any sort of Comparison between the trivial inconvenience which would arise from a temporary suspension of the Commerce carried on with that power and the extent of the evil which the inhabitants of America would suffer from any interruption of their Commerce with Great Britain, the most important consumer of the productions of the Country and the principal Source of it's revenue.

In addition to Mr. Walcot[60] from whom you will naturally endeavour to acquire information on the points I have mentioned, I cannot avoid suggesting the probability that Mr. de [Treire],[61] from his connection with the Spanish Agents may be able to communicate to you intelligence that may be useful.

GEORGE HAMMOND TO BOND[62]

No. 2.[63]   DOWNING STREET, 27 Oct. 1795.

Sir,

Herewith I transmit to you a Dispatch from the Duke of Portland to Lieutenant Governor Simcoe which you will forward to Upper Canada as expeditiously as possible, by some confidential person.[63a]

---

[60] Oliver Wolcott had succeeded Hamilton not only as Secretary of the Treasury but also as Hammond's confidential informant. He had revealed to Hammond the secret debates of the Senate on Jay's Treaty. Hammond to Grenville, June 25, 1795, No. 15, cipher, F. O. 5 : 9. Nevertheless Wolcott, in common with such Federalists as Fisher Ames, during the war crisis of the spring of 1794 had resented Hammond's conduct, which he considered to be as extreme and as harmful as that of the Jeffersonians. "The British Minister," wrote Wolcott, "is a weak, vain and imprudent character, very much in the company and under the influence of sour and prejudiced tories, who wish to see the country disgraced." Wolcott to Oliver Wolcott, Sr., April 14, 1794, Gibbs, *Adms. of Washington and Adams*, I, 133.

[61] In the draft, in F. O. 5 : 10, the name given is Monsieur de Treire.

[62] F. O. 115 : 4. Hammond upon his return to England had become an under secretary in the foreign department.

[63] The draft in F. O. 5 : 10 is designated No. 2, but the instruction is not numbered.

[63a] There are no enclosures in either F. O. 115 : 4 or F. O. 5 : 10. Bond reported to Grenville on April 6, 1796, No. 23, F. O. 5 : 13, that neither the original nor the duplicate of the above instruction had as yet been received.

GRENVILLE TO BOND [64]

No. 3.   DOWNING STREET, 4th Nov. 1795.

Sir,

As I perceive from the concluding Part of Mr. Randolph's Memorial to Mr. Hammond of the 14th of August last [65] and from the language held to me by Mr. Deas,[66] that a mistaken Opinion has been entertained in America with respect to the real nature and tenor of the Instruction given on the 25th of April last to the Commanders of His Majesty's Ships of War, respecting Vessels bound to the Enemy's Ports, and laden with Corn and other Provisions, I now transmit to you a Copy of the Instruction in question. In communicating this Paper to the American Ministers [67] you will observe that it was

[64] F. O. 115 : 4.

[65] In his memorial of Aug. 14, 1795, announcing that the President would ratify Jay's Treaty conformable to the advice and consent of the Senate, Secretary Randolph stated that the sensibility of the President had been greatly excited by the capture of provision vessels under a recent order-in-council said to have been issued by Great Britain, and that Mr. John Quincy Adams had been instructed to inquire into the existence of such an order. Randolph to Hammond, Aug. 14, 1795, Domestic Letters, 8. Adams in his dispatch from London of Dec. 5, 1795 reported his discussion with Grenville, on the preceding day, relative to the order of April 25, 1795, and noted that the order had been revoked. J. Q. Adams, *Memoirs*, I, 150–161.

[66] See notes 36–38, p. 88 ; note 44, p. 90 ; note 55, p. 94, *supra*.

[67] Upon receipt of Grenville's No. 3, above, with its copy of "the secret Instruction" of April 25, 1795, Bond, so he reported "immediately communicated to the Secretary of State, the observations contained in that Dispatch. . . ." Bond to Grenville, Jan. 19, 1796, No. 2, F. O. 5 : 13. Bond, it would seem, did not transmit a copy of the secret Instruction to Pickering (there is no copy of it in the State Department archives) ; Americans generally continued to regard the order of April 25, 1795 as having been similar to or identical with the order of June 8, 1793, not only in effect but in legal basis ; and the mystery surrounding it was not cleared up until the twentieth century. The copy of the order in F. O. 115 : 4 is here printed :

Secret Instruction to the Commanders of all Our Ships of War, Given at Our Court at St. James's the Twenty-fifth day of April, 1795, in the Thirty-fifth Year of Our Reign.

George R
[L. S.]

Whereas Information has been received that the Persons exercising the Powers of Government in France have made large Purchases of Corn and other Provisions, for the Purpose of being imported into France, under feigned Names and Destinations, in order to supply the Want of Corn and Provisions now existing in that Country, and to enable them to provide for the Support of their Military and Naval Forces in the Prosecution of the unjust War which they are carrying on against Us and Our Allies ;

We, judging it necessary to counteract the said Purposes, and to provide for the Interests of Our People in this Respect, have thought fit to direct that the Commanders of Our Ships of War should, 'till Our further Order herein, detain all Ships loaden with Corn, or other Provisions, that shall be bound to France, or to the Ports occupied by the Armies of France, or which they shall have reason to believe are proceeding to France, or to the Ports occupied by the Armies of France, and which they shall also have reason to believe are laden on Account of the said Persons or of any other His Majesty's Enemies ; and that they should bring all such Ships into such Ports of Great Britain as shall be prescribed to them by Instruction from the Lords Commissioners of the Admiralty, in order to be there dealt with as the Case shall appear to require.

By His Majesty's Command,

PORTLAND.

A Copy.
Evan Nepean.

founded on indisputable Information (of the Accuracy of which the
American Government especially can have no doubt) that Cargoes of
Provisions had in a very great number of instances and to a very large
extent been actually purchased by French Agents in Foreign Countries,
and shipped for France under fictitious names. [68] And as by the
established Law of Nations as expressly recognized by the American
Government itself cargoes of this description would have been liable
to Seizure and Confiscation if no such Instruction had existed, the
issuing of it cannot by any construction be said to afford any reasonable ground of complaint or even of dissatisfaction.   Much less when
it is considered that all the Vessels detained under this order have been
dealt with according to the precise terms of the Article contained in
the late Treaty,[69] by which it is expressly provided that the conduct
of the Two Nations shall for the present be governed by the Rules
there laid down.

GRENVILLE TO BOND [70]

No. 4.   DOWNING STREET, Nov. 4, 1795.
Sir,
    I have the satisfaction of informing you that on Wednesday last
the 28th Ulti.mo the ratifications of the Treaty concluded on the
19 Nov[r]. between His Majesty and the United States, were exchanged
between myself and Mr. Deas,[71] who will I understand transmit to his
Government by this conveyance his Majesty's ratification.
    The President having expressed a desire to enter into new negocia-
tions respecting the twelfth article of the treaty, of which the operation
is suspended by the additional Article inserted in the instrument of
ratification, You will inform the American Ministers that on Mr.
Adams's [72] arrival in this Country, I shall be ready to receive any

---

[68] From June of 1794 to April of 1795 Hammond had reported on the activities of
French agents in purchasing and forwarding, "on account of the French government,"
quantities of flour, salted provisions, military and naval stores.   Hammond to Grenville,
June 27, 1794, No. 27, Aug. 3, 1794, No. 28, Sept. 5, 1794, No. 31, Nov. 5, 1794 (postscript
of Nov. 8), No. 33, F. O. 5 : 5; Feb. 24, 1795, No. 5, April 3, 1795, No. 7, F. O. 5 : 9.

[69] Article XVII of Jay's Treaty.

[70] F. O. 115 : 4.

[71] Pickering had transmitted the ratified treaty to Deas on Aug. 25, 1795, and had instructed him to exchange ratifications if John Quincy Adams had not arrived in London
from The Hague by Oct. 20, 1795, and to govern himself according to the instructions
given Adams.   Pickering to Deas, Aug. 25, 1795, U. S. Ministers, Instructions, 3.

[72] John Quincy Adams (1767–1848), minister resident at The Hague from 1794 to 1797.
He had been instructed by Pickering on Aug. 25, 1795, to repair to London for the purpose
of exchanging ratifications of the Jay Treaty : he was to urge the revocation of the new
provision order (of April 25, 1795), if still existing ; to assert that ratification must not
be construed into an admission of the legality of that order ; but he was not to delay the
exchange of ratifications should Great Britain refuse to revoke it.   Pickering and Upham,
The Life of Timothy Pickering, III, 243–245.

communications which that Gentleman may be instructed to make upon this subject.[73]

No. 5.   DOWNING STREET, Novem. 4th 1795.

Sir,

The King having been pleased to destine Mr. Liston [75] at present his Majesty's Ambassador at the Porte, to succeed Mr. Hammond, I have to desire that you will communicate this circumstance to the members of the American Government, and will at the same time express His Majesty's confidence that this appointment will not fail to be agreeable to that Government.

Mr. Liston is presumed to be now on his return from Constantinople, and will shortly after his arrival in this Country prepare to embark for America by the earliest conveyance.

No. 6.   DOWNING STREET, 4th Nov. 1795.

Sir,

Your several Dispatches to No. 6 Inclusive have been received and laid before the King.

His Majesty's Ministers have seen with Concern that the Conduct of Capt. Home,[77] as well in the Detention of the Packet Boat bound

---

[73] Adams had not been empowered to negotiate respecting the additional article inserted by the Senate which excluded Article XII of Jay's Treaty. Particular instructions for further negotiations were to be sent later, but as late as Feb. 26, 1796 Pinckney, who had returned to London from Spain, reported that these particular instructions had not yet arrived. Pinckney to Pickering, Feb. 26, 1796, Dispatches, Great Britain, 3.

[74] F. O. 115 : 4.

[75] Robert Liston (1742–1836), a Scot, personable, well-educated, and experienced, had been minister plenipotentiary at Madrid from 1783 to 1788, envoy extraordinary at Stockholm from 1788 to 1793, ambassador extraordinary and plenipotentiary at Constantinople from 1793 to February of 1796. Liston presented his credentials as envoy extraordinary and minister plenipotentiary (Hammond had held the rank of minister plenipotentiary only) to President Washington, at Philadelphia, on May 16, 1796. Liston to Grenville, May 28, 1796, No. 2, F. O. 5 : 14. To Federalists, who had found young Mr. Hammond somewhat trying, Liston appeared to be "an amiable and worthy man." Gibbs, *Adms. of Washington and Adams,* I, 340. Thomas Pinckney was pleased with Liston's appointment, and thought he would "do what is in his power to soften down the Asperities which have so long prevailed between the two Countries." Pinckney to the Secretary of State, March 7, 1796, Dispatches, Great Britain, 3.

[76] F. O. 115 : 4.

[77] Capt. Rodham Home of H. M. S. *Africa.* While watching the French frigate *Medusa* in the harbor at Newport, Rhode Island, Home had impressed several seamen from American vessels. On July 31, 1795 he had sent an insolent letter to Governor Fenner of Rhode Island demanding aid in reclaiming all British sailors at liberty on shore, "and that without loss of time." The next day, August 1, he had stopped, within American territorial waters, the packet boat *Peggy* on which Fauchet had embarked from New York to Newport, ransacked the sloop, searched the French Minister's baggage, but failed to capture Fauchet, who, forewarned, had got off at Stonington and made his way by land to Newport and to the *Medusa.* On September 1, when the *Medusa* with Fauchet aboard

from New York to Newport, as in the Letter which through Mr. Moore [78] he addressed to the Governor of Rhode Island appears at the first View to have afforded to the American Government just cause of Complaint and Dissatisfaction. But as no Counter Statement of Facts on his Part has hitherto been received, and as the Governor of Rhode Island appears in this Case and in the former Instance of the Nautilus [79] to be actuated by a Spirit of peculiar indisposition and even Injustice towards the Officers employed in His Majesty's Service, no other Measure can for the present be adopted 'till Captain Home shall, in compliance with the direction which he will receive from the Lords of the Admiralty, explain the Circumstances of the Two Transactions which have been alleged as Matters of Complaint against him.

In regard to the Measures adopted by the President towards Mr. Moore, in consequence of his Communication to the Governor of Rhode Island of Capt. Home's Letter; though I am willing to believe that this unguarded Proceeding of Mr. Moore was dictated solely by the deference which he conceived due from him to an Officer of Capt. Home's Situation and Rank in His Majesty's Service, yet, as by the 16th Article of the Treaty concluded with the United States His Majesty and the American Government have expressly reserved to themselves the right of dismissing the Consuls appointed by either of the Parties in the Dominion of the Other, for any Reasons which they may think sufficient, and as the Conduct of Mr. Moore in this Instance was certainly liable to just exception on the Part of the American Government, it would not be proper for His Majesty's Ministers to advise His Majesty to request that Government to reverse the Measures which it has pursued respecting Mr. Moore and still less to restore that Gentleman to his Consular Functions which can in any Country be executed only under the Recognition of the Sovereign Power of that Country.

---

put out to sea (and by means of a dense fog managed to get to France in safety), Home had given chase before the expiration of the twenty-four hour interval required in such cases.

Pickering made strong representations to London on Home's conduct; attempted to mollify Adet, the new French Minister; and, ordering all intercourse to cease between American citizens and the Africa, demanded of Home that he liberate the impressed seamen and remove himself from American waters. A. S. P., F. R., I, 633, 665–667; Pickering and Upham, Pickering, III, 231–239; Domestic Letters, 8; and U. S. Ministers, Instructions, 3, August–September, 1795.

[78] Thomas William Moore, British vice consul at Newport. For transmitting to the Governor of Rhode Island Captain Home's "indecent and unjustifiable" stand-and-deliver letter of July 31, 1795, and for cooperating in "grossly insulting" the government by whose authority he had exercised his consular functions, Pickering on Sept. 5, 1795 had sent Moore the President's revocation of his exequatur. Domestic Letters, 8.

[79] In May of 1794 the Rhode Island authorities had forced the release from H. M. S. Nautilus of six American citizens who had been impressed. Randolph to Hammond, June 4, 1794, with enclosures, A. S. P., F. R., I, 464–468; and same to same, July 23, 1794, Domestic Letters, 7.

INSTRUCTIONS OF 1796

GRENVILLE TO BOND [1]

No. 1.   DOWNING STREET, January, 1796.

Sir,

Your several Dispatches to No. 15 inclusive have been received and laid before the King.

Your Correspondence with Mr. Pickering respecting the Privateer les Jumeaux and the Practise of American Citizens engaging in the Service of the Enemy (inclosed in your Dispatch No. 11) has been so proper that it is unnecessary for me to give you any other Instructions on the former of those Subjects than to desire you upon every future similar occasion to pursue the same Conduct as that which you have observed in the present Instance.[2]

With regard to the Reluctance manifested by Colonel Pickering to prosecute the American Citizen commanding les Jumeaux, it may be easily imagined that the Government of the United States will be unwilling *to originate* any Measures of this Nature, which may have a tendency in the present moment to increase the existing Discontents. As however this Consideration cannot in the same Degree influence the Government of this Country, and as Depredations on the Commerce of His Majesty's Subjects continue to be committed by American Citizens, to an alarming extent, it cannot be expected that the Officers in His Majesty's Service should persevere in the lenient System which has hitherto been observed towards American Citizens taken in Arms and in the employ of the Enemy; and you will therefore on any future occasion of this nature give it to be understood that Individuals taken under this

---

[1] F. O. 115 : 5.

[2] Under the name of *Les Jumeaux* the French armed corvette *Le Cassius* had been illegally fitted out at Philadelphia in December of 1794. After forcibly resisting arrest, she had escaped to the open sea, where an American, Samuel B. Davis, had assumed command. Upon the ship's return to Philadelphia in August of 1795 it was libelled by the owner of a captured Philadelphia schooner, and Davis was arrested. After prolonged and involved litigation, and much correspondence between Pickering and French Minister Adet, both suits were defeated. *A. S. P., F. R.,* I, 629–639; II, 193. To Bond's representations Pickering on Sept. 3, 1795 replied that the case of the ship and its American master had been referred for action to the District Attorney of Pennsylvania. Domestic Letters, 8.

Predicament in the Commission of an Offence, equally injurious to the respect which they owe to their own Government and to the maintenance of Peace and Harmony between the Two Nations, must expect to experience that degree of Rigor which is justified by the Law of Nations in similar Cases as recognized in the Treaty lately concluded between His Majesty and the United States.[3]

GRENVILLE TO BOND [4]

No. 2.   DOWNING STREET, Jany. 1796.

Sir,

The Proposition mentioned in your Dispatches Nos. 10 and 12, as having been made to you by the American Government, for the purpose of obtaining the benefit of your Assistance in facilitating the Payment of the American Loans to Individuals in Holland,[5] is of a Nature so novel and peculiar, that any sort of Acquiescence in it, on the Part of His Majesty's Government must be considered as an Act of extreme Accomodation and Indulgence to the American Government; going considerably beyond those Measures of Attention which the Principles or Practice of the Law of Nations require in the Conduct of Belligerant States towards the Commercial Interests of those which are Neutral. To guaranty from enquiry, and from detention for the purpose of enquiry, Ships and Cargoes sailing from the Neutral Ports by Certificates given on the Part of the Belligerant State, through it's Representative residing in the Neutral Country is certainly a practise to be adopted with considerable Caution; because in ordinary Cases it is impossible for such a Representative to certify upon the Ground of his own immediate and direct knowledge, or on any other Ground, than that of the Representations which may be made to him, without any Opportunity on his part of ascertaining their exact Truth.

---

[3] Article XXI of Jay's Treaty prohibited subjects or citizens of one party from accepting commissions from a foreign state at war with the other party. "And if any subject or citizen of the said parties respectively shall accept any foreign commission or letters of marque for arming any vessel to act as a privateer against the other party, and be taken by the other party, it is hereby declared to be lawful for the said party to treat and punish the said subject or citizen having such commission or letters of marque as a pirate."

[4] F. O. 115: 5.

[5] Because of the difficulties in the way of making the usual remittances, payment of the interest charges on the Dutch loans was to be made by the American government in the form of non-contraband merchandise and provisions. Articles such as coffee, sugar, and cotton to the value of about $200,000 were to be sent to meet payments due in January of 1796. In requesting Bond's aid in obtaining their immunity from capture, Secretary Wolcott had pointed out that remitting by means of bills of exchange through Hamburg was not only very uncertain and irregular but also subject to a loss of 12 to 14 per cent. Bond to Grenville, Oct. 13, 1795, No. 10, F. O. 5: 10. Bond issued passports for three ships destined for Amsterdam, the *Ariel*, the *Maria*, and the *Active*, laden with sugar and coffee to satisfy the interest due on the Dutch loans. Same to same, Oct. 30, Dec. 9, 1795, Nos. 12 and 18, F. O. 5: 10.

But altho' a compliance with the request made by the Government of the United States must for these Reasons be considered as a relaxation of that undoubted right which every Belligerent Nation possesses of examining by the Process of it's own Tribunals the Property of Cargoes bound to an Enemy's Ports, His Majesty, from an anxiety to evince His good disposition towards the Government of the United States and from a persuasion that the present measure originates in circumstances of necessity which may be permitted to create a distinction between this and other Cases, has been pleased to consent that you should continue to grant on the Solicitation of the American Ministers Certificates similar to those which are inclosed in your Dispatch No. 12. Great Caution will however be necessary on your Part to obviate the possibility of those Certificates being applied to any other purpose than that specified by Mr. Wolcott and to avoid giving the Appearance of your Sanction to exempt from Capture any Articles which may be considered as Contraband according to the Sense of that Term entertained by His Majesty.

I think it farther proper to remark, in order to prevent any misconception on the part of the American Government on this Point, that these Certificates can not *legally* restrain the King's Cruizers or Privateers from bringing in Ships that are possessed of them; As they are not Documents which according to the Law of this Country an Acquiescence is legally or necessarily due. They are however more likely to be generally submitted to from Considerations of Prudence, and from Motives of respect to the Station of the King's Representative.[6]

GRENVILLE TO BOND [7]

No. 3.   DOWNING STREET, Jany. 7th 1796.

Sir,

The Government of the United States having expressed a desire that some summary mode might be adopted of determining certain Cases of American Captures, which, from the smallness of their value and other Circumstances, it might not be advisable to refer to the ordinary course of judicial Proceedings, I transmit to you for your Information a Proposal upon the subject which was drawn up in consequence of a

---

[6] Acknowledging this instruction in his No. 18 of April 5, 1796, F. O. 5 : 13, Bond reported that Secretary Wolcott had well understood that the certificates were not to be considered "as an absolute Security against every proper Scrutiny and Search : His chief object was to secure the vessels from the Detention of Privateers, in those Seas, being under no Sort of Apprehension from the Examination to be made by His Majesty's Ships of War, whose Commanders would not, upon frivolous Pretexts, arrest Cargoes engaged in a lawful Trade. And even if such Arrests should happen, if the Vessels should be brought into England, the Delay would not only be small, but the means of satisfying the Persons interested in Holland, would be so accessible, that every Censure upon the Credit of this Government and its Intention to evade its Contracts must vanish."

[7] F. O. 115 : 5.

Conversation between myself and Mr. Adams.[8] As that Gentleman is however of Opinion, that the Powers with which he is invested in this Country do not authorize him to take any Measures conformable to this Proposition, it's Operation must be suspended until Mr. Pinckney shall have returned to England and expressed his Concurrence in it. It is matter of some regret to His Majesty's Ministers that there was not in this Country any Person possessing on the Part of the American Government sufficient Power to consent to a Proposal the Object and effect of which are manifestly and exclusively advantageous to the United States. It is however satisfactory to them to reflect that this Step must be considered as an unequivocal Proof of the sincerity of their desire to facilitate the Prosecution of the Claims of American Citizens, and to ensure to them the most expeditious mode of obtaining any redress to which they may be found entitled.

[Feby. 9th 1796.

Since the Original of this Dispatch was written Mr. Pinckney (who is returned to this Country) has informed me that Orders have been received from his Government to suspend any Agreement on the Subject here spoken of. It is difficult to conceive from what Motive those Orders have originated, but in all Events it is necessary that you should remark to the American Secretary of State that the Inconvenience (if any) resulting to the American Merchants from this Delay does not arise from any change of that disposition which had been expressed here to give every practicable Accomodation on this subject

G.][9]

GRENVILLE TO BOND [10]

No. 4.   DOWNING STREET, Jan. 7, 1796.

Sir,

I send you inclosed the copy of a Letter which I have received from Mr. Deas and upon which I think it right to observe to you, for the information of the American Ministers, that His Majesty's Govern-

---

[8] According to the enclosed proposal, Samuel Bayard, the American agent, could bring cases of this description before two arbitrators, one being the King's Advocate, the other to be named by Bayard or by John Quincy Adams, for a decision "both on the question of the amount of any compensation . . . and also on that of the probability of adequate compensation in the ordinary course of judicial proceeding. . . ." The decision of the two arbitrators would be binding only if it were acquiesced in by both the King's Proctor and the American agent.

[9] The postscript of Feb. 9, 1796, enclosed in brackets above, appears in the draft, in F. O. 5: 13. A duplicate No. 3 with postscript added was also sent to Bond. In acknowledging it Bond stated that "Col. Pickering assured me He did not recollect any Instructions originating with Him; or indeed with his Predecessor in Office, that could bear the Construction which Mr. Pinckney had taken up." Bond to Grenville, April 6, 1796, No. 19, F. O. 5 : 13. Bond later reported that the American government in instructions sent its representatives at London had confirmed the propriety of acceding to the proposal. Same to same, May 3, 1796, No. 29, F. O. 5 : 13.

[10] F. O. 115 : 5.

ment will at all times receive with attention, and with the utmost desire to render the most rigid justice, every specific complaint which may be exhibited by the Government of the United States or by the individuals of that Country against any person acting under His Majesty's Authority; but that it would be as improper as it must be useless to enter into the discussion of accusations so indefinite, and so entirely unsubstantiated by any sort of proof as are those which are contained in Mr. Deas's Letter. The American Minister must be sensible that if loose and general complaints of the partiality of inferior tribunals, or the misconduct of subordinate officers were admitted as fit matter for official communications between the two Governments, what has passed in America for the last two years would afford ample ground for such representations on the part of this Country. But this Government has always abstained from that species of communication, and has deemed it more proper to confine it's complaints on those subjects to the individual cases in which there appeared just reason for dissatisfaction, confiding in the general disposition expressed by the Government of the United States to cause impartial justice to be done and to observe a conduct consistent with Neutrality and Peace, and by no means imputing to any failure in that disposition, the occasional and frequent violation of those principles on the part of inferior Tribunals or individual Officers.[11]

GRENVILLE TO BOND [12]

No. 5.   DOWNING STREET, Jany. 1796.

Sir,

Mr. Adams and Mr. Deas having expressed to me the solicitude of the American Government to learn His Majesty's Determination respecting the Appointment of Commissioners for the several Pur-

---

[11] Deas' notes to Grenville, including that of Dec. 22, 1795, of which a copy was enclosed, had reflected the indignant tone of his instructions from Secretary Pickering. In September Pickering had instructed him to ask not only for the restoration of impressed seamen but for reparations and the exemplary punishment of British naval officers, whose "ignorance, caprice or malice" made sport of American rights. Particular attention was called to the conduct of Captain Rodham Home (see note 77, p. 99, *supra*) and to the "cruelty and brutality" of the captain of the British frigate *Hermione*, "who on the 4th of July 1795, came down from Port au Prince to Jeremie, in the Island of Hispaniola, and there stripped upwards of twenty American vessels of their crews; impressing all the men, excepting the Captains and Mates." On Oct. 22, 1795, aroused by fresh captures of "the Privateering Gentlemen of Bermuda," Pickering had informed Deas that it was "the President's express direction and earnest desire that you make . . . a pointed memorial on the subject. . . . If this nest of plunderers cannot be broken up, if their privateering cannot be absolutely stopped, at least it may be restrained within the limits of the laws of nations. But an adherence to those just rules, we can hardly expect, unless the British Government go to the root of the evil, by removing the present Judge [Judge John Green of Bermuda, formerly a Loyalist of Philadelphia] and appointing a man who has some pretentions to character—some regard to Justice, and some concern for his own and his nations honor." Pickering to Deas, Sept. 12, 14, Oct. 22, 1795, U. S. Ministers, Instructions, 3.

[12] F. O. 115 : 5.

poses specified in the Treaty lately concluded with the United States, and the Salaries to be allowed to them.—I think it merely necessary to refer you to my Dispatch to Mr. Hammond No. 20 of the Year 1794, and to signify to you His Majesty's Pleasure, that as no Circumstances have arisen to render any Alteration expedient in the Opinions therein stated, you make a formal Communication of them to the American Ministers, as the result of the Opinion of His Majesty's Government upon the Subject.

No Commissioners have as yet been appointed by His Majesty, but as little delay will occur in the Appointment of them as may be consistent with the time requisite for obtaining a proper knowledge of the Persons who may be the best qualified for the important Office in which they are to be employed.

GRENVILLE TO BOND [13]

No. 6.   DOWNING STREET, Jany. 7, 1796.

Sir,

It is with great Satisfaction and pleasure I inform You that between Nine and Ten o'clock this Morning Her Royal Highness The Princess of Wales was safely delivered of a Princess,[14] and that Her Royal Highness and the young princess are in as perfect Health as can be expected.

GRENVILLE TO BOND [15]

No. 7.   DOWNING STREET, 18th Jany. 1796.

Sir,

As the period is now approaching in which His Majesty has stipulated that His forces should evacuate the Posts on the American side of the Boundary line assigned to the United States by the Treaty of Peace, instructions have been sent to His Majesty's Governor General in America to concert the necessary measures for this purpose with any person duly authorized by the Government of the United States agreably to the 2d Article of the Treaty signed there in November 1794.[16]

It is however indispensably necessary on every principle of justice and good faith that previously to the actual execution of this part of the Treaty, His Majesty's Government should be assured that the Stipulations entered into by the United States will be equally fulfilled by their Government. Interesting as this consideration would have

---

[13] F. O. 115 : 5.
[14] Princess Charlotte.
[15] F. O. 115 : 5.
[16] These instructions, Portland to Dorchester, Jan. 15, 1796, are printed in Cruikshank, ed., *Corres. of Simcoe,* IV, 170–171.

been at all times it is rendered peculiarly so, at the present moment, by circumstances which have recently occurred in America apparently inconsistent with some of the stipulations so recently entered into, and also the possible contingency of events arising in that Country subversive of the whole principle and effect of those Engagements and of the very existence of the Treaty. It is necessary to bring these matters to a precise point in order that His Majesty's Officers of Canada may if a satisfactory explanation is received, surrender the Posts conformably to the Treaty or may still retain them if a Conduct should be adopted in America on this Subject, different from that which it is the earnest desire of His Majesty to pursue.

In your Dispatch No. 8, of last Year, and in a subsequent Communication from Lord Dorchester were transmitted Copies of a Treaty concluded on the 3d of August last between the United States and the Chiefs of the respective Western Tribes of Indians with which the former have so long been engaged in War.[17] Some doubts might arise on several of the Articles of this Treaty, when compared with the stipulations by which the United States are bound to His Majesty: But these are of small importance in comparison with that which results from the Eighth Article of the Indian treaty. It is there stipulated that no persons shall be allowed to reside among or to trade with these Indian Tribes, unless they be furnished with a License from the Government of the United States, and that any person so trading without such a License shall be delivered up by the Indians to an American Superintendant to be dealt with according to Law, meaning evidently by this phrase the Law of the United States. If this Article is to be understood in it's obvious and literal sense it is manifestly inconsistent with the third Article of the Treaty of Amity, Commerce and Navigation with His Majesty by which it is agreed that "it shall at all times be free to His Majesty's Subjects "and the Citizens of the United States, and also to the Indians "dwelling on either side of the Boundary Line, freely *to pass and* "*repass* by land or inland *Navigation* into *the respective territories* "*and Countries of the two parties on the Continent of America* (the "Country within the limits of the Hudson's Bay Company only "excepted) and to *navigate all the Lakes, Rivers and Waters thereof,* "*and freely to carry on trade and Commerce with each other.*" His Majesty's Confidential Servants have therefore seen with great surprize the insertion of such an Article in a treaty concluded so long after the period when the British Treaty had arrived in America. If they were inclined to entertain doubts of the sincerity and good faith of the Government of the United States, strong arguments in support of such a suspicion might be drawn from observing that

---

[17] The Treaty of Greenville, Aug. 3, 1795, concluded by General Anthony Wayne. The text is given in *A. S. P., Indian Affairs*, 1, 562–563.

that Treaty reached America on the 8th of March 1795 was approved
by the Senate on the 24th of June following and that subsequently
to that period there was ample time for it's being communicated to
General Wayne long before his treaty with the Indians. His Majesty's Ministers are nevertheless unwilling to admit such a Suspicion,
and are therefore very desirous to be assured either that General
Wayne concluded that Treaty in consequence of Instructions laid
down for his conduct previously to the Ratification of the treaty
entered into with His Majesty and which by inadvertence had not
been explained or revoked, or that notwithstanding the exceptionable
form in which the Indian treaty is worded it was clearly understood
by both the contracting parties at the time of its conclusion to relate
only to the people of the United States who might have occasion to
come into the Country there described, and that no idea then existed
or now exists of imposing on His Majesty's Subjects restraints so
inconsistent with the general Spirit and express Stipulations of the
late Treaty. In either case however it is absolutely necessary that all
misconstruction or doubt on this most important point should be
clearly and unequivocally removed, and if the Government of the
United States mean fairly and honourably towards this Country no
hesitation can arise on their part in complying with the just expectations of the King on this Subject. It is not enough that we should
be assured that the Government of the United States disclaim the intention of violating by so solemn and public an Act the Engagements
which had been so recently contracted with this Country or that they
affix to the Indian Treaty a sense not incompatible with those engagements, which the obvious and natural interpretation of the words
used is in manifest contradiction to their engagements with Great
Britain. No doubt ought to remain on the Subject, no possible misconstruction ought to be suffered upon a point on which the maintenance of the harmony between the two Countries must so much
depend. In order therefore to do away any misconception on this
important point, on the part either of His Majesty's Subjects or of the
Citizens of the United States, and (more especially) of the Indians
themselves, it is indisputably necessary that an explanation should
take place between His Majesty and the United States. And that
this should be done by an Act equally public and solemn with the
two treaties which now appear at variance. The form of such explanation is already pointed out in the last Article of the treaty
signed here which engages that explanatory or additional articles
may be added to the treaty so as to form a part of it. I have therefore to signify to you His Majesty's pleasure that you deliver to
the American Minister the Note herein inclosed, which you are to
support by the most conciliatory and temperate language, but at the

same time by such arguments as may shew the absolute impossibility of the King's consenting to leave this most important matter on it's present equivocal and precarious footing. You will urge the American Minister as much as possible, to return you an early and explicit Answer to the proposal therein contained, and if, as His Majesty trusts, the Government of the United States is willing to enter into such explanation as good faith and justice require on this occasion you will proceed to negotiate and arrange with them the form of an explanatory Article: for the conclusion of which (subject to His Majesty's ratification) the necessary full powers are herewith transmitted to you. With respect to the precise wording of the Article, the King is pleased to leave it to your discretion to settle it with the American Ministers, directing only that it shall be so clear and distinct as to leave no room for doubt or misrepresentation on the subject.

Whenever you shall have brought this matter to it's issue (which I trust will be such as to correspond with the King's sincere desire to maintain Peace and Friendship with the United States) you are to transmit the earliest information of it, and by the most expeditious mode of conveyance to His Majesty's Governor General and to the Lt. Governor of Upper Canada who are instructed to act accordingly. But as these officers are expressly restricted by their instructions (copy of which is herewith inclosed for your information) from delivering up the Posts unless information shall have been received from you that the point above mentioned has been satisfactorily explained agreably to His Majesty's expectation, you will be very particular on this point so that the King's Officers in Canada may not be at a loss as to the duty required from them according to the circumstances which may exist.

His Majesty's Ministers have sufficient confidence in the Sincerity and good faith of the individuals who compose the American Government to believe that this equitable proposition will experience no opposition from them, there are however other Contingencies which unhappily they may perhaps be unable to guide or controul but to which it is right that I should direct your attention, as being equally connected with the Line of conduct which the King's Officers in Canada are instructed to pursue.

From the most recent information received from America, there is but too much reason to apprehend that a considerable party exists in the House of Representatives of the United States, which is desirous of disclaiming the validity and binding force of the late treaty concluded between His Majesty and the United States either by a Declaration that the President and Senate exceeded the Power delegated to them by the Constitution in concluding and ratifying that treaty and consequently that it is not binding on the United States, or by a refusal on the part of the House of Representatives to establish any legal provisions which may be requisite to carry into effect the stipulations of it. If either of these Cases should arise it is His Majesty's pleasure that you should transmit the most early intelligence thereof to His Majesty's Governors of Canada in order that they may suspend the execution of the Treaty on the part of His Majesty until you shall be able to ascertain the precise effects which may result from either of the Contingencies that I have specified: and at all events you will not fail to apprize His Majesty's Governors of Canada of the measures consequent on the delivery of this Note or on the progress of any discussion connected with the treaty.[18]

GRENVILLE TO BOND [19]

Separate.   DOWNING STREET, 18 Jany. 1796.
Sir,

Although I have thought it right to address my Dispatches to you on the Subject of the Treaty lately concluded between General Wayne and the Indians; yet as I have reason to believe that Mr. Liston (who is daily expected in England) will be able to proceed shortly to America and as it is probable that a Negotiation of this nature may be conducted with a greater prospect of success by a Minister immediately arriving from this Country I have to desire that under the expectation of Mr. Liston's Arrival you will defer acting upon the instructions contained in my Dispatch No. 7 as long as a delay may be practicable, and not likely from it's duration to defeat the important object to which those instructions refer. Your Conduct in this respect must also be regulated by the necessity of finally arranging this matter previously to the adjournment of the Senate whose Approbation will be requisite for the Article which may be signed.

---

[18] Upon receipt of this instruction, Bond was induced by attacks on the treaty in the House to submit the enclosed note. He presented it to Pickering on March 26, 1796, at a critical period in the treaty deliberations, two days after the House had called upon President Washington for the papers relating to Jay's negotiations, and four days before Washington refused the request. Not receiving an answer, he pressed the matter in conversations with Pickering and in a note on April 9, making it plain that until the explanatory article was acceded to the orders given for evacuating the frontier posts must be considered as only provisional in nature. Bond to Grenville, March 31, April 17, 1796, Nos. 17 and 25, F. O. 5: 13. The note sent by Grenville, and presented by Bond on March 26, 1796, is in A. S. P., F. R., I, 551–552.

Bond's demands for an additional explanatory article, in conjunction with British impressments and seizures, were regarded by the Federalists as most impolitic, as endangering the passage in the Republican House of necessary legislation appropriating money to execute the much criticized treaty, just as British captures under the unpublished provision order of April 25, 1795 had endangered the conditional ratification of the treaty in August of 1795. "The British ministry are as great fools or as great rascals as our Jacobins," wrote Hamilton, "else our commerce would not continue to be distressed as it is by their cruisers; nor would the Executive be embarrassed as it now is by the new propositions" made by Bond. Hamilton to Wolcott, April 20, 1796, Hamilton, Works, ed. Lodge, X, 161–162.

[19] F. O. 115: 5.

GRENVILLE TO BOND [20]

Separate.   DOWNING STREET, 18 Jany. 1796.
Sir,

As I think it by no means improbable that the American Ministers, in the discussions which you may have with them on the
Treaty concluded between General Wayne and the Indians, may
explain the Eighth Article of it as being intended to restrain the
Citizens of the United States alone in their intercourse with the
Indians, and in no manner to infringe the just rights of His Majesty's Subjects, it is proper for me to signify to you His Majesty's
pleasure that, in that Event you should express the most complete
Satisfaction on His Majesty's part in this interpretation of the
Article in question, and His willingness to consider it as entirely
removing all objection and difficulty which may have arisen on
that Account. But you will not fail to represent in this Case the
absolute and indispensable necessity that this interpretation should
be clearly defined and ascertained by some public agreement (of
the nature specified in my Dispatch No. 7) to be entered into by
His Majesty and the United States. The particular circumstances
and situation of the Indian Nations (so liable to be imposed upon
by false representations) will afford you unanswerable arguments
in support of this proposal, and it is not conceived that there can
exist on the part of the American Government any reasonable
ground to decline it provided that their intentions are as fair and
liberal as His Majesty is willing and desirous to believe.

GRENVILLE TO BOND [20a]

No. 8.   DOWNING STREET, Feby. 1796.
Sir,

Your several Dispatches to No. 21 inclusive have been received
and laid before the King.

The Attestation of the American Consul at Bordeaux of the fictitious bill of lading inclosed in your last Dispatch is a Circumstance
so extraordinary that it is His Majesty's Pleasure that you make a
formal Complaint upon the Subject to the American Ministers and
that you represent not only the extreme impropriety of Mr. Fenwick's
Conduct upon this and other similar Occasions, but also the necessity
which the knowledge of such a deception imposes on the Commanders
of His Majesty's Ships of War to examine with the most scrupulous

---

[20] F. O. 115 : 5.
[20a] F. O. 115 : 5.

diligence any American Ships that may be furnished with Official Documents by the American Consul at Bordeaux.[21]

GRENVILLE TO BOND [22]

No. 9.   DOWNING STREET, Feby. 1796.

Sir,

I think it right to inform you that Mr. Liston who arrived here last Week will embark for America in the Course of three or four Weeks. You will therefore in pursuance of my separate Letter which accompanied the Instructions transmitted by the last Packet, authorizing you to negotiate with the American Ministers an additional Article to the Treaty, defer acting upon those Instructions so long as delay may be practicable and as any reasonable expectation can be formed of Mr. Liston's arriving in time to conduct the Negotiation antecedently to the Adjournment of the Senate or to the Period assigned for the Evacuation of the Posts in Canada.

GRENVILLE TO BOND [23]

No. 10.   DOWNING STREET, March 1796.

Sir,

This Letter will be delivered to you by Mr. Liston, whom His Majesty has been pleased to appoint His Envoy Extraordinary and Minister Plenipotentiary to the United States. You will give up to Mr. Liston the Cyphers and Official Correspondence belonging to the Mission, and you will communicate to him every information of which You may be possessed that may be necessary or useful to Him in the situation to which he is appointed.

GRENVILLE TO ROBERT LISTON [24]

No. 1.   DOWNING STREET, MARCH 18, 1796.

Sir,

The two principal objects to which I think it right to direct your attention immediately on your arrival at Philadelphia are the measures which may have been adopted by the House of Representatives,

---

[21] Bond had transmitted a bill of lading attested by Consul Joseph Fenwick at Bordeaux for the cargo of an American vessel which, when the vessel was captured and sent into Halifax, had been condemned as French property. Bond to Grenville, Dec. 27, 1795, No. 21, F. O. 5: 10. At London in November of 1795 John Quincy Adams was present when the case of the *Molly* was heard, in which the counsel for the defendant admitted that the cargo, attested as being entirely American by Consul Fenwick at Bordeaux, was in truth altogether French. Adams, *Memoirs*, I, 136.

[22] F. O. 115: 5.

[23] F. O. 115: 5.

[24] Draft, F. O. 5: 14.

in order to give validity to the treaty concluded between His Majesty and the United States on the 19th of November 1794 and a Negotiation, which in the event of your not arriving in America, at a period sufficiently early for conducting it Yourself, Mr. Bond was instructed by my Dispatch to Him (No. 7 of this Year) to enter into with the American Government, for the purpose of removing, by a formal agreement on the subject, any doubts or misconstructions, which might arise from the apparent contrariety that subsists between the stipulations of the Treaty concluded with His Majesty, and those of a subsequent Treaty concluded between the United States and the Indian Confederacy with which they have been so long engaged in War.

As the sentiments of His Majesty's Ministers upon these points, and the Measures which they think should be pursued respecting them are so amply detailed in the dispatch to Mr. Bond to which I have alluded, and as no further intelligence has been since received from America on this point, it seems merely necessary to refer You to Mr. Bond's instructions as the rule of Your Conduct.[25]

In regard to the language by which it may be proper for You to support the arguments contained in that dispatch it must depend upon circumstances as they may appear to You at the time of your arrival in America. You will however give the most unequivocal assurances of the sincere desire of His Majesty to carry into effect, on his part, every stipulation of the Treaty, and of the concern which he would feel, if any measures on the part of the United States should place him under the disagreeable necessity of withholding even for the shortest time the full execution of an arrangement calculated as His Majesty trusts to lay the foundation of permanent union and harmony between the two Countries.

GRENVILLE TO LISTON [26]

Secret.
No. 2.   DOWNING STREET, 18 March 1796.

Sir,

I have received intelligence from a very respectable quarter that it is the present intention of the French Government immediately to

---

[25] In the meantime, on the eve of Liston's arrival at Philadelphia, Bond had acted under the instructions given in Grenville's No. 7 of Jan. 18, 1796 (see note 18, p. 110, *supra*), and had obtained the desired explanatory article. "The Negotiation of this Matter had been protracted . . . particularly from an Apprehension that if the Negotiation should be discovered by the Party opposed to the Treaty, it might afford them an opportunity of defeating it. . . . As soon as the Question of making an Appropriation was carried . . . Col. Pickering became extremely solicitous to have the explanatory Article concluded, knowing that the provisional Instructions transmitted to His Majesty's officers in Respect to the Delivery of the Posts, now probably rested upon the Completion of this Article." The article was drawn up on May 4, and approved by the Senate for ratification on May 9, 1796. Bond to Grenville, May 6, 9, 1796, Nos. 31 and 32, F. O. 5 : 13. The additional explanatory article is printed in *A. S. P., F. R.,* I, 552–553 ; Miller, *Treaties,* II, 346–347.
[26] Draft, F. O. 5 : 14.

Dispatch M. Fontaine (the person appointed to succeed M. Adet [27] as Minister Plenipotentiary to the United States) to America with instructions to declare to the Government of the United States that the engagements which Subsisted between France and America under a former Treaty are considered by the French Directory as annulled by the late Treaty concluded between His Majesty and the United States. It is further stated to me that M. Fontaine is charged to demand within the space of fifteen days a Categorical Answer to his Complaints upon this Subject and that in order to give weight to his representations they are to be accompanied or followed by the appearance of a French Naval Force on the Coasts of America.[28] I think it right to communicate this information to you, altho' it is impossible not to entertain some doubt whether an intention so contrary to the most evident interests of the French Government has in fact existed, and still more whether such a design if ever entertained must not have been abandoned since the distresses and difficulties of France have been found to press upon Her to so extraordinary a degree.

If however M. Fontaine on his arrival in America should adopt such a Line of Conduct as I have here mentioned, you will consider yourself as distinctly authorized by His Majesty to assure the American Government that, if France should commence Hostilities against it, in consequence of the Treaty concluded with this Country, His Majesty will be ready to enter into such engagements with the United States as may appear best calculated to repel an aggression of this nature and to make common Cause against an Attack which can be dictated by no other motive than by a desire, to prevent the Establishment of a good understanding between Great Britain and the United States and grounded on no other hope than that of exciting internal discontents in the latter Country. And you will adopt such a Conduct and Language as you shall judge best calculated to give encouragement to the Govt. and well disposed party in the United States.

---

[27] Pierre Auguste Adet (1763–c. 1832), who had succeeded Fauchet on June 15, 1795, was not replaced by M. Fontaine or any of the other persons then under consideration as his successor. Adet announced the suspension of his ministerial functions on Nov. 15, 1796, but he remained in the United States to influence the presidential electors in favor of Jefferson. He did not depart until May of 1797, at which time he left Létombe, the French consul general, in charge.

[28] Similar information was transmitted from London to Washington and Hamilton on March 4, 1796 by Gouverneur Morris. Morris, *Diary*, II, 158–159. Such a plan leading to a rupture with the United States was contemplated by the French Directory, but Monroe urged against it, and hinted that the American people if left to themselves would (by electing Jefferson in November of 1796) bring about the restoration of cordial relations. Monroe's dispatches of Feb. 16, 20, March 10, 1796, *A. S. P., F. R.*, I, 730–731 ; and S. F. Bemis, "Washington's Farewell Address : A Foreign Policy of Independence," *Amer. Hist. Rev.*, XXXIX, 250–268. .

GRENVILLE TO LISTON [29]

No. 3.   DOWNING STREET, March 18, 1796.
Sir,

As I understand from the most recent accounts received from America that no authentic Copy of the ratified Treaty of Amity, Commerce and Navigation concluded between His Majesty and the United States, and exchanged between me and Mr. Deas on the 28th of October last had been received in America and, as it appears that some difficulties and delays have arisen there, in consequence of this circumstance, I send You an authenticated duplicate of that instrument ratified by His Majesty in the usual forms, which in case no similar copy should have been received from Mr. Pinckney at the period of Your arrival in America, You will deliver to the Secretary of State, and taking a receipt for it in the usual form You will express to him your hope that the American Government will perceive in this mark of attention the anxiety of His Majesty to obviate any delay which might tend to retard the operation of the Treaty.[30]

GRENVILLE TO LISTON [31]

No. 4.   DOWNING STREET, March 18, 1796.
Sir,

I send you herewith Copies of the Commission and Instructions which the King has been pleased to direct to be given to Thomas Barclay, Esq.,[32] whom His Majesty has appointed to be the Commissioner on his part for the purposes specified in the fifth Article of the Treaty of Amity, Commerce and Navigation concluded between His Majesty and the United States, you will communicate these Copies to the American Ministers in order that if they approve of them, they may give similar commissions and Instructions to the Commissioner who may be appointed to act with Mr. Barclay.

---

[29] Draft, F. O. 5 : 14.
[30] Deas on Oct. 28, 1795 had transmitted an unauthenticated copy of the British instrument of ratification, which was received on Dec. 28, 1795. The original instrument, sent by Pinckney, did not arrive until April 22, 1796. Washington, however, proclaimed the ratification of the treaty on Feb. 29, 1796. See Bond to Grenville, March 4, 1796, No. 11, F. O. 5 : 13 ; and Miller, *Treaties*, II, 273.
[31] Draft, F. O. 5 : 14.
[32] Thomas Barclay (1731–1830), of Annapolis, Nova Scotia, an American Loyalist during the Revolution. In 1799 he succeeded Sir John Temple, deceased, as consul general at New York. Barclay served as a British commissioner in a series of arbitrations relative to the Northeastern boundary.

GRENVILLE TO LISTON [33]

No. 5.   DOWNING STREET, March 18, 1796.

Sir,

From several parts of my correspondence with Mr. Bond You will perceive that the conduct of Mr. Deas, who officiated as Chargé d' Affaires of the United States, during the continuance of Mr. Pinckney's mission in Spain, was such as to give just cause of dissatisfaction to His Majesty's Governt. Although Mr. Pinckney's return to this country renders it unnecessary for You to address any formal complaint upon the subject at present, I have nevertheless to signify to You His Majesty's pleasure that You should mention confidentially to the Secretary of State of the United States that in the event of any future absence of Mr. Pinckney it would be by no means agreable to this Government that Mr. .Deas should again be authorized to act as Chargé d' Affaires of the United States. The maintenance of harmony and good understanding between the two Countries evidently requiring that their official communications in this country should pass thro' the medium of persons more inclined to observe such a course of conduct as the dignity of the Two Governments requires.[34]

GRENVILLE TO LISTON [35]

No. 6.   DOWNING STREET, March 18, 1796.

Sir,

I herewith transmit to You His Majesty's Commission, granting to You full powers for the general purposes therein mentioned. Although this instrument be intended principally to apply to the negociation alluded to in my dispatch, No. 1, yet You will perceive that you are empowered by it to treat of and conclude other articles or conventions, upon which You may receive His Majesty's directions at any future period, or which being proposed to You by the American Government, the urgency of the case may render it in your opinion advisable to conclude *sub sperati*, without waiting for any positive in-

---

[33] Draft, F. O. 5 : 14.

[34] At London in December of 1795 Under Secretary George Hammond (whom John Quincy Adams termed an intriguer of none too subtle methods, who affected to believe that American resentment of injuries from Britain was confined exclusively to "the French party") complained that Deas' letters were "too violent and fractious." Adams, however, said of Deas that "if the language of his memorial [see note 11, p. 105, *supra*] was warm, it was such as the occasion naturally suggested." Adams, *Memoirs*, I, 140–146, 160. Some light is thrown on the state of mind of young Deas, and of young Adams, by Gouverneur Morris, who recorded on Feb. 22, 1796: "Mr. Adams . . . in his wrath and indignation at the conduct of the British Government, seemed absolutely mad. He breathed nothing but war, and was content to run into it at the hazard of our finances and even of our Constitution." Morris, *Diary*, II, 157.

[35] Draft, F. O. 5 : 14.

structions from His Majesty upon the subject. It is hardly necessary for me to remark to You that the latter power is not to be used by You but in cases of the most extreme and urgent necessity, and where from the general tenor of your Instructions You shall have reason to believe that the agreement to be concluded is perfectly conformable to the sentiments of H. M. Government.

GRENVILLE TO BOND [36]

No. 11.   DOWNING STREET, 19 May 1796.

Sir,

Your Several Dispatches to No. 25 inclusive have been received and laid before the King.

With regard to the Acts of Outrage committed at Norfolk in detaining the Vessels bound for the British West Indies with Horses on board,[37] I have to signify to you His Majesty's pleasure that you direct His Majesty's Consul at Norfolk or the persons employed by him in the purchase of those Horses, or in the hiring of the Vessels for their Conveyance, to commence prosecutions in the federal Courts against the different individuals acting under the Authority of the Governor of Virginia upon this Occasion for Demeurrage and any other expenses that may have been incurred in consequence of these unwarrantable proceedings. For although nothing may perhaps be recovered from them yet, as the general Government has declined interfering in this and in former instances, it seems proper for His Majesty's Gov. to resort to the Courts of Law in hopes that the result of these proceedings may operate in some Respects as a punishment of the persons concerned in this disgraceful transaction (and who I perceive are the same that have been active upon other Occasions) and may likewise prevent a repetition of such vexatious proceedings in that part of the United States, which has been so peculiarly distinguished by it's hostility to Great Britain.

---

[36] Draft, F. O. 5 : 13.

[37] Bond on Feb. 8, 1796 had complained of the persons at Norfolk who had damaged and detained the sloop *Diana*, and of the order of the Governor of Virginia, issued at the instance of the French vice consul, detaining all vessels conveying horses to the British armed forces in the West Indies. He was informed by Pickering that the President had made known to the French Minister and to the Governor of Virginia that he "deemed such shipments not repugnant either to the laws of nations, to the laws of the United States or to our treaty with France." The outrage upon the *Diana* was regretted and disapproved, but redress was within the ordinary reach of the law. Pickering to Bond, Feb. 16, 1796, Domestic Letters, 9 ; see, also, the correspondence with Adet, *A. S. P., F. R.,* I, 646.

GRENVILLE TO BOND [38]

No. 12.   DOWNING STREET, May 19 1796.

Sir,

The Report of the House of Representatives inclosed in Your Dispatch No. 11, and the Act that has since passed,[39] in conformity to it relative to the impressment of American seamen, having naturally attracted the attention of His Majesty's Ministers, I think it right to put you in possession of their sentiments upon it, which, although it is not intended that You should make any formal communication of them to the American Government, may nevertheless serve as the rule of your conduct in any conversations upon the subject which you may have with persons of influence in the United States.

With respect to the facts upon which this report is founded no doubt can be entertained of their being greatly exaggerated; for, altho' it is probable that American seamen may have been at different times impressed into His Majesty's Service, the number of native American mariners is so small, and the part of the navigation of the United States carried on by British Seamen is so considerable, that instances of such impressments of American Citizens can have but rarely occurred, and certainly cannot be compared in number with the attempts that are daily made by the owners and masters of American Vessels to protect natives of this country under the denomination of Citizens of the United States.

This Part of the Report therefore, however it may be credited in America, will necessarily be admitted in this country with some degree of caution: and indeed, if the examples of the detention of American seamen in His Majesty's Service had been no numerous and notorious as they are there represented Mr. Pinckney's applications for redress would have been more frequent and, when made, better substantiated than they have hitherto been.[40]

---

[38] Draft, F. O. 5 : 13.

[39] In his dispatch No. 11 of March 4, 1796, F. O. 5 : 13, Bond had transmitted the report of a committee of the House on legislation necessary for the relief of impressed American seamen. The act of May 28, 1796 provided for the issuance of certificates of citizenship to seamen, and for the appointment of agents (at Halifax and in the West Indies) to inquire into cases of impressment. *U. S. Stat. at Large,* I, 477–478.

[40] At the time the above instruction was written Pickering was complaining to Bond of "the outrages daily committing in the West Indies on American seamen." Admitting that many seamen went without written proofs of citizenship, he declared that "in all such cases common justice requires that such reasonable proofs as can be obtained on the spot should be admitted." Pickering to Bond, May 19, 25, 1796, Domestic Letters, 9. On April 13, 1797 Rufus King, minister to London, reported that since July of 1796 he had applied to the British government in 271 cases of impressment : of these he had obtained the discharge of 86 ; his claims had been rejected in 37 cases ; while the remaining 148 were still pending because the seamen were on board British ships on active duty. *A. S. P., F. R.,* II, 146. David Lennox, agent for impressed seamen in Great Britain, listed on Jan. 1, 1799 a total of 651 cases, of which 173 had been discharged, and 99 had been ordered discharged. *Ibid.,* II, 270.

Every specific instance of complaint brought forward by the American Minister has been without delay investigated, to those applications the fullest and most immediate attention has invariably been paid, and those individuals alleged by him to be American Seamen have uniformly been liberated where the presumption appeared to be reasonably in favour of their being American.[41]

It has however happened that in a very great proportion of cases of this nature the persons claimed as Citizens of the United States have proved on enquiry to be British Subjects.

After a conduct so liberal on the part of His Majesty's Government, the necessity of the measures adopted by the American legislature does not appear very obvious, and the two modes of remedying the supposed evil are liable to just grounds of exception, and will be inadequate to the purpose which they are designed to effect. For it cannot be expected that His Majesty's Government will so far depart from the policy which it has invariably observed with regard to it's foreign dependencies, as to tolerate the residence in them of Official agents appointed by the American Government,[42] or that the certificate of Citizenship granted by the United States will be considered here as evidence of the fact so conclusive as to supersede the necessity of any farther enquiry.

GRENVILLE TO BOND [43]

No. 13.   DOWNING STREET, May, 1796.

Sir,

I send you inclosed the Copy of a Memorial which I have received from Mr. Taggart and I have to desire that you will afford to that person or his Agent any assistance which the nature of his Application may appear to you to require in the Prosecution of his Claims.[44]

---

[41] Grenville's statement may be contrasted with that of Captain H. Mowat, Senior Officer of His Majesty's Navy, who in 1796 succeeded Admiral Murray in command of British warships on the American station. In reply to Liston's representations in behalf of impressed American seamen, Mowat, after complaining that the American people invariably befriended and aided deserting British seamen, stated that until the American government effectually prevented such actions of its people "all the orders and Instructions that can be given by the Government of Great Britain, never can heal the evil, that you so much recommend to be avoided :—because it is my duty to keep my Ship manned, and I will do so wherever I find men, that speak the same language with me, and not a small part of them British Subjects, and that too producing Certificates as being American Citizens : at the same time I tell you, Sir, that I have not got an American Subject on board, but I will not say how long it will be so." Mowat to Liston, from H. M. S. *Assistance,* Hampton Roads, March 27, 1797, Admiralty, I, 494.

[42] See note 56, p. 122 ; note 57, p. 123, *infra.*

[43] Draft, F. O. 5 : 13.

[44] There is no copy of the memorial either in F. O. 5 : 13 or F. O. 115 : 5.

GRENVILLE TO LISTON [45]

No. 7.   DOWNING STREET, July 8 1796.

Sir,

Your dispatch No. 1 and Mr. Bond's dispatches to No. 32 inclusive have been received and laid before the King.

I transmit to you by this packet His Majesty's ratification of the explanatory article signed by Mr. Bond and Mr. Pickering on the 4th of May last, which ratification You will deliver to the American Secretary of State, and receive from him in return an acknowledgement agreeably to the draft inclosed. At the same time you will also deliver a similar acknowledgement signed by Mr. Bond in return for the ratified Copy of the article delivered to him by Mr. Pickering.

GRENVILLE TO LISTON [46]

No. 8.   DOWNING STREET, July 8, 1796.

Sir,

I send You inclosed the Copy of a memorial which I have received from Mess[rs]. John and Alexander Anderson Merchants of this City, and I have to desire that you take such measures as may appear to You best calculated to obtain for Mess[rs]. Anderson, the redress which they solicit.[47]

GRENVILLE TO LISTON [48]

No. 9.   DOWNING STREET, July 1796.

Sir,

As I perceive by Mr. Bond's dispatch No. 27 that some difficulty exists with respect to the manner of paying to Mr. Breese his salary, as His Majesty's Vice Consul for the State of Rhode Island, I have to desire that You will advance to him quarte[r]ly such sums as may be equal to the payment of his salary, which is settled at the rate of £300 per Annum free of all deductions. For your reimbursement You will draw upon Mr. Bidewell of my office at two months after sight.[49]

---

[45] Draft, F. O. 5 : 14.
[46] Draft, F. O. 5 : 14.
[47] The Andersons wanted reparations for the loss of their trading sloop, *Martha's Goodwill*, which had been captured off the coast of Africa on Jan. 29, 1796 by the armed schooner *Industry*. According to John Johnston, master of the sloop, whose affidavit supported the memorial, the *Industry* was American owned and manned, said to be under the direction of Mr. Patterson of Baltimore, and without any regular commission from the French Republic.
[48] Draft, F. O. 5 : 14.
[49] Breese, successor of Thomas W. Moore, had not been informed of the manner in which his salary would be paid. Bond had advised him to appoint an agent in London to receive it, in his behalf, as the quarterly payments fell due. Bond to Grenville, May 1, 1796, No. 27, F. O. 5 : 13.

GRENVILLE TO LISTON [50]

No. 10.   DOWNING STREET, July 8, 1796.

Sir,

I send you inclosed several copies of an extract of an Act of Parliament passed last session, which You will transmit to all His Majesty's Consuls, and direct them to publish it, in any manner that may be thought most adviseable for the information of the Merchants and Traders of the United States.[51]

GRENVILLE TO LISTON [52]

No. 11.   DOWNING STREET, Augt. 12th 1796.

Sir,

As the execution of the 4th Article of the Treaty of Amity, Commerce and Navigation respecting the Survey to be made of the boundaries between His Majesty's dominions in America, and those of the United States is a matter that will require considerable attention—You will take an early opportunity to ascertain by conversing with the Members of the American Government upon the Subject at what time and in what manner it is their wish that this Article should be carried into execution.

You will at the same time enter into correspondence upon this subject with the Governor of the Canadas: and will report to me the result of these several communications in order that His Majesty may proceed in due time to appoint proper persons conjointly with such as may be nominated for that purpose by the American Government. An officer now resident in Canada has been recommended to me as a person properly qualified to undertake this commission on the part of His Majesty [53] but no step will be taken here for the appointment of him or of any other person, until I shall have heard from You that the American Government is prepared to take it's measures with respect to that article of the Treaty, and till I am informed of the description of and rank of the person whom it may be wished to entrust with the execution of it on the part of the United States.

---

[50] Draft, F. O. 5 : 14.

[51] From Liston's dispatch to Grenville of Oct. 14, 1796, No. 20, F. O. 5 : 14, it appears that the act related to the admission of certain articles into Great Britain in neutral ships, and that news of the act had already been published in the American press. The enclosure is lacking in F. O. 5 : 14 and F. O. 115 : 5; no copy was found in the British consular correspondence or in the Notes from British Legation, archives of the State Department; and it has not been possible to identify with certainty this act, one of several relating to America passed during the 6th session of the 717th Parliament, from the British *Statutes at Large* or from the American press.

[52] Draft, F. O. 5 : 14.

[53] Lieut. Gov. Simcoe had recommended Lieut. Robert Pilkington of the Royal Engineers. Cruikshank, ed., *Corres. of Simcoe*, IV, 335. Pilkington had built the fort on the Maumee, in April of 1794, under orders from Simcoe.

No. 12.   DOWNING STREET, Oct. 7, 1796.

Sir,

Your several Dispatches to No. 8 inclusive have been received and laid before the King.

His Majesty has learnt from them with great pleasure that the surrender of the Posts occupied by His Troops within the American Territory has been arranged in so satisfactory a manner, and has been accompanied by Acts of mutual civility and attention so highly creditable to His Majesty's Government of Canada and that of the United States.

On the subject of Dr. Fraser [55] I think it proper to inform you that, however desirable a circumstance it might have been, if the State of South Carolina had observed a more liberal conduct towards that Gentleman, it is far from being the wish of His Majesty's Government to bring on discussions upon questions of this nature which do not appear to come exactly within the purview of the Treaty, and which may probably produce the effect of reviving distinctions that are gradually dying away.

As to the conduct imputed to Captain Pigot in the complaint of Mr. William Jessup,[56] His Majesty has been pleased to direct the Lords of the Admiralty to institute an immediate and scrupulous inquiry into the circumstances of this transaction: And you may assure the American Ministers that neither in this, nor in any other instance which may occur will His Majesty's Government justify any of His Majesty's Officers in the Commission of similar aggressions if properly verified on due enquiry, nor screen them from the consequences to which such Conduct may expose them.

---

[54] Draft. F. O. 5 : 14.

[55] Dr. James Fraser, a Loyalist, had been imprisoned in South Carolina upon his return to that state for having deliberately violated the act of banishment of 1782. To Liston's representations Pickering replied that Jay's Treaty, while providing in general terms a free intercourse between the two countries, could not fairly be interpreted as repealing the laws which South Carolina and other states had enacted against Loyalists. Liston to Grenville, July 3, 1796, No. 4, F. O. 5 : 14 ; Pickering to Liston, Oct. 8, 1796, Domestic Letters, 9.

[56] Captain Pigot of H. M. frigate *Success* had flogged Capt. William Jessup of the American ship *Mercury* and impressed half a dozen seamen. His conduct was such, reported Liston, as to merit "the most serious attention" since it had augmented the increasing "complaints of acts of injustice and insult committed by our Naval Officers against American Citizens." So strong was popular indignation that Liston did not think it advisable to withhold any longer letters of recommendation requested of him by Pickering, on June 25, for Col. Silas Talbot, the American agent to be sent to the West Indies to inquire into the grievances of impressed American seamen. Liston to Grenville, Aug. 13, 1796, No. 7, F. O. 5 : 14. On Sept. 10, 1796, Pickering instructed King to make at London "a solemn remonstrance on the tyrannical and inhuman conduct of Captain Pigot. . . . I am only astonished at the quiet submission of Captain Jessup and other American citizens, victims of the frequent tyranny and cruelty of British officers, and that some of them do not take instant vengeance on the ruffians who thus put them to the torture." Pickering and Upham, *Pickering*, III, 338–339 ; also, *Life and Corres. of Rufus King*, ed. Charles R. King, II, 115–116.

Having in my Dispatch No. 12 to Mr. Bond stated so fully the sentiments of His Majesty's Servants respecting the measures pursued by the American Government for the protection of the Seamen navigating American Vessels, it is unnecessary for me to give you any farther instructions upon that point than to refer you to the dispatch above mentioned.[57]

GRENVILLE TO LISTON [58]

No. 13.   DOWNING STREET, Dec. 8 1796.

Sir,

As I understand from Mr. Barclay, His Majesty's Commissioner appointed to carry into effect the fifth Article of the Treaty of Amity, Commerce and Navigation concluded between His Majesty and the United States, that upon a comparison of His Majesty's commission to Him, with that which Mr. Howell [59] had received from the President of the United States, there exists a difference between them in point of expression—Inasmuch as in the Commission to Mr. Howell the President of the United States uses this form of expression; "and thereupon with the other Commissioners duly sworn to proceed to decide the said Question, and exactly perform all the duties enjoined and necessary to be done to carry the said Fifth Article into complete execution:" While in His Majesty's Commission to Mr. Barclay it is declared "We will give and cause to be given full force and effect to "such final decision in the premises, as by Our said Commissioners "together with the other two Commissioners above mentioned, or by "the Major part of the said three Commissioners shall be duly made "according to the Provisions of the said Treaty." I have to signify to you His Majesty's pleasure that you deliver a Note to the American Ministers, in which you will represent the circumstances above mentioned, and propose to them that they should interchange declarations with you stating the agreement of His Majesty and the United States to consider as final and conclusive the decision of the three Commis-

---

[57] Liston received Grenville's No. 12 to Bond, of May 19, 1796, in August, shortly after he had assured Pickering that he would facilitate Talbot's mission to the West Indies. Much chagrined, he was forced to tell Pickering that Talbot should return immediately. According to Pickering, Liston told him that while he had felt that Grenville might possibly disapprove of his action, "he thought the object a just one, and the step he had taken conciliatory ; and he would trust to the rectitude of his views for his justification. He added, I have long been in this line of public business without meeting a reproof, and I am too old to receive one now. But my instructions corresponded with my wishes,—*where the former were not too explicit, to be directed by a spirit of conciliation ; and in this spirit I acted.*" Pickering's memo, Substance of a Conversation with Liston, Aug. 24, 1796, Domestic Letters, 9. See also, Pickering to Talbot, Aug. 31, 1796, Pickering and Upham, *Pickering*, III, 334.

[58] Draft, F. O. 5 : 14.

[59] David Howell (1747–1824), of Providence, Rhode Island; a lawyer, judge, and onetime professor of mathematics and natural philosophy at Brown University. For the organization of the commission and its work, see Moore, *Int. Adjud.* I, II.

sioners or of a majority of them as to the river which was the river St Croix intended by the definitive Treaty of Peace between His Majesty and the United States.[60]

It must however be observed that in order to render the proceedings under this Commission conformable to the principle established for the other two Commissions no such decision (nor indeed any other proceeding) can take place but in the presence of the three Commissioners.

GRENVILLE TO LISTON [61]

No. 14.   DOWNING STREET, Dec. 12 1796.

Sir,

Your several dispatches to No. 21 inclusive have been received and laid before the King.

The state of uncertainty which has so long existed with respect to the probability of a rupture between this Country and Spain being at length terminated by a declaration of War on the part of that power,[62] it becomes necessary that you should enter into some immediate explanation with the American Government on two points which relate to the treaties concluded by the United States with His Majesty and with the King of Spain.

The first refers to the navigation of the River Mississippi. Although the right of His Majesty's subjects and of the Citizens of the United States freely to navigate that river from it's source to the Ocean forms a distinct stipulation of the definitive treaty of Peace between His Majesty and the United States and is again expressly recognized in the Treaty of Amity Commerce and Navigation, yet it is possible that some doubts may arise on the subject in consequence of the fourth Article of the treaty concluded between His Catholic Majesty and the United States on the 20th Oct. 1795.[63] It is therefore His Majesty's pleasure that you should deliver to the American Ministers a note, in which you will specify these circum-

---

[60] In answer to Liston's note on the subject Pickering wrote that Howell's commission was deemed adequate, and that "the award of the Commissioners will derive its binding force from the treaty itself, which being by our Constitution a supreme law of the land, the President is of course *to take care that it be faithfully executed.*" Nevertheless, Pickering assured Liston in express terms that the United States would consider the decision of the commissioners as final and conclusive. Pickering to Liston, April 3, 1797, Domestic Letters, 10. Liston in his No. 12 of April 3, 1797, F. O. 5 : 18, enclosing the above note, stated that it was evident that Secretary Pickering "was a little hurt as well at the imputation of inaccuracy or insufficiency thus cast on an instrument which had been carefully drawn up by himself, as at the surmise that appeared to be started respecting the sincerity and good faith of the Government of the United States."

[61] F. O. 5 : 14.

[62] Spain had declared war against Great Britain on Oct. 5, 1796.

[63] The treaty of friendship, limits, and navigation with Spain, negotiated by Thomas Pinckney, was signed at San Lorenzo el Real on Oct. 27, 1795. The text is given in Miller, *Treaties*, II, 318–345.

stances and propose to them that they should give you a formal declaration stating that the right of His Majesty's subjects to the free navigation of the River Mississippi from it's source to the Ocean is not to be regarded as being in any manner affected or impaired by the treaty concluded between the Catholic King and the United States on the 20 of Oct. 1795.[64] Should the American Government object to this proceeding you will observe that as the consideration which induced the United States to acquiesce in His Majesty's proposal of concluding an article explanatory of the difference which appeared to subsist between their treaty with His Majesty and that concluded with the North Western Indians, apply equally to the present case, His Majesty can entertain no doubt of the readiness of the American Government to deliver to you a declaration to the effect which I have before mentioned.

The second point relates to the twenty fourth and twenty fifth Articles of the Treaty of Amity, Commerce and Navigation between His Majesty and the United States. Upon this subject you will take an early opportunity of expressing to the American Ministers His Majesty's expectation that the same conduct, inasmuch as Spain is concerned, will be pursued towards British Ships of War and privateers, as has been adopted by the Government of the United States with regard to those of France, the stipulations in the Treaty with His Majesty being precisely similar to the provisions upon this head which are contained in the Treaty between the United States and France. If the American Ministers should in their conversations with you start any doubts or difficulties as to their compliance with His Majesty's desires, you will immediately deliver a Ministerial Note requiring a due execution of these Articles of the Treaty on the part of the United States.[65] As soon as you shall have obtained a satisfactory answer on this point from the American Government you will instruct His Majesty's Consuls in the different ports of the United States, to pursue the most effectual measures in their power for excluding from them all Spanish privateers, and for preventing the admission into them of any Spanish Ships of War which may attempt to bring in with them any British Prizes. And you will also inform the Commanders of His Majesty's Ships

[64] Such a declaration was obtained from Pickering, who pointed out that Article VIII of the Treaty of Paris of 1783 had been confirmed by Article III of Jay's Treaty. "I add, Sir, and with pride as well as pleasure . . . that when the Prince of Peace, on the part of Spain, proposed to Mr. Pinckney . . . a stipulation to restrict the navigation of the Mississippi 'solely and exclusively' to the contracting parties, the latter rejected the idea, remarking that Spain could hardly rely on the good faith of the United States, or on the treaty about to be concluded, if they agreed to an article which would be an infraction of a treaty before concluded." Pickering to Liston, April 3, 1797, Domestic Letters, 10.

[65] The American government "did not make the smallest objection to the full effect and execution" of Articles XXIV and XXV of Jay's Treaty. Liston to Grenville, April 4, 1797, No. 13, F. O. 5 : 18.

of War that they are authorized under the Treaty (whenever it may be convenient to them to do so) to bring into any of the Ports of the United States the Spanish Vessels which they may happen to capture.

GRENVILLE TO LISTON [66]

No. 15.   DOWNING STREET, Dec. 14th 1796.

Sir,

This Dispatch will be delivered to You by Mr. Macdonald and Mr. Rich [67] whom the King has been pleased to appoint to be the Commissioners on the Part of His Majesty for carrying into Effect the Sixth Article of the Treaty of Amity, Commerce and Navigation concluded between His Majesty and the United States.

As the good Effects expected from the Mission of these Gentlemen may in a great Measure depend on the Choice of the Fifth Commissioner, I have it in Command from His Majesty to recommend this Matter to Your particular Attention. By the Article of the Treaty under which this Commission is appointed You will perceive that the Fifth Commissioner is to be appointed by the unanimous Voice of the other Four—or in the Event of their not agreeing in such a Choice then the Commissioners named by the Two Parties shall respectively propose one Person and of the Two Names so proposed one shall be drawn by Lot in the presence of the Four original Commissioners. Upon the First of these Points, I think it right to inform You that as the Two American Commissioners in this Country [68] refused to acquiesce in any joint Nomination of any Person who was not an American Citizen it will be proper for the British Commissioners in America to express a Resolution on their Part not to concur in the joint Nomination of any Person who is not a British Subject. The Mode of Proceeding on the other Point, which was adopted by the Commissioners here, was that the Commissioners of the Two Parties, on each Side, proposed a List containing three Names of which one was selected by the other respectively, the Two Names so selected were considered as the Nomination of both Parties to be balloted for, and the one which was first drawn was appointed the Fifth Commissioner. I have thought

---

[66] Draft, F. O. 5 : 14.

[67] Thomas MacDonald and Henry Pye Rich. The commissioners on the part of the United States under Article VI of Jay's Treaty (pre-war debts) were Thomas Fitzsimmons of Philadelphia and James Innes of Virginia.

[68] The American commissioners under Article VII of Jay's Treaty (neutral rights and neutral duties) were Christopher Gore of Massachusetts and William Pinkney of Maryland. The two British commissioners were Dr. John Nicholl and John Anstey. The fifth commissioner, selected by lot, was Col. John Trumbull of Connecticut, who had been secretary to John Jay in 1794–1795. Moore, *Int. Adjud.*, IV, 72.

it right to inform You of the Mode of proceeding in both these Cases, which was pursued by the Commissioners in this Country, in order that You may recommend a similar Course to Messrs. Macdonald and Rich, who are instructed to act conformably to any Recommendations, which they may receive from You, both as to the Mode of proceeding and to the Selection of Persons to be proposed as the Fifth Commissioner.[69]

I have also to signify to You the King's Pleasure that You should nominate a proper Person to act as a *general Agent* in assisting the individual Agents of the British Creditors in the Prosecution of their respective Claims before the Commissioners.

With respect to the Appointment of a Secretary to the Commission, it is His Majesty's Pleasure that it should be left to the American Government to nominate to that Station any proper Person agreeably to the Manner in which that Point was arranged by the Commission that meets at London, and of which Mr. Macdonald and Mr. Rich are informed.

---

[69] The fifth commissioner under Article VI, chosen by lot, was John Guillemard, a British subject residing in Philadelphia. The American agent was John Read, Jr., and the British agent, William M. Smith. Griffith Evans was secretary of the commission. Moore, *Int. Adjud.*, III, 22 ; and Liston to Grenville, June 27, 1797, No. 29, F. O. 5 : 18.

INSTRUCTIONS OF 1797

No. 1.   DOWNING STREET, Jan. 27, 1797.

Sir,

Your several Dispatches to No. 31 inclusive have been received and laid before the King.

As You are probably apprized that some doubts which had arisen respecting the nature of their powers has delayed the proceedings of the Commissioners appointed to carry into effect the seventh Article of the Treaty with the United States, I think it right to inform You that there appears now the greatest reason to believe that the proceedings will go on satisfactorily and without further delay, and this by the exercise on the part of the Commissioners of their own judgment and discretion in the discharge of the trust which they have undertaken, rather than by any attempt to open fresh discussions between the Governments for the purpose of prescribing any rule of Conduct to Them in this respect.[2]

As it is not impossible that these differences or the decision on them may be mistated in America, I have thus far explained to You the turn which the business has taken—not that You should make any communication upon it to the American Government but that You may be prepared to hold this general language in case anything is said to You upon it.[3]

No. 2.   DOWNING STREET, Jany. 27th 1797.

Sir,

The Result of the Dispatches which have for some Time subsisted between the American Government and that of France, is still so un-

---

[1] F. O. 115 : 5.

[2] The two British members had withdrawn from the Spoliations Commission in order to prevent a decision by the three American members as to the commission's jurisdiction. A compromise was arranged, however, which enabled the commission to proceed. Rufus King to Pickering, Feb. 26, 1797, *Corres. of Rufus King*, II, 620–633 ; Moore, *Int. Adjud.*, IV, 82–87.

[3] Nothing had been said to Liston about it, and he had not mentioned it because he had no doubt that Rufus King, the American Minister at London, reported fully on all subjects "with perfect candour and a constant view to conciliation." Liston to Grenville, April 18, 1797, No. 15, F. O. 5 : 18.

[4] F. O. 115 : 5.

certain, that notwithstanding the Interest which this Country must take in it, it is impossible for me to give you any other Instructions at present, than that you should persevere in that prudent and cautious Line of Conduct which you have hitherto observed upon this Subject. If however a Rupture should actually take place between the Two Countries or should appear highly probable, it is the King's Pleasure that you should express His Majesty's Willingness to afford a naval Protection to the Commerce of the United States against the Attacks of the Common Enemy. For Your Guidance, as well in this Contingency, as in the present Moment, if the Measure should appear to you adviseable, I refer you to a Dispatch of mine to Mr. Hammond (No. 12 of 1794) in which he was instructed to offer to the American Government Convoys for their Vessels bound from Ports of the United States to Great Britain, provided that such a Proceeding should appear to him to be advantageous to His Majesty's Service, and likely to be met with a suitable Return of Gratitude on the Part of the United States. For Reasons which Mr. Hammond stated at that Time, the Offer was not then made, and you are to understand that you are not now instructed to revive it, unless it's Expediency should appear to you unquestionable according to the Circumstances which may have arisen in America.⁵

His Majesty has entirely approved your forbearing to take any Measure in Consequence of Monsʳ. Adet's Note ⁶ which might have indicated a Wish to add to the Embarrassments of the American Government on that Occasion. But His Majesty relies on your Zeal and Vigilance that in the final Settlement of the Business, You will not suffer His Majesty's Interests and those of His Subjects, to be placed on a Footing of less relative Advantage, as compared with those of France, than that in which they now stand. If France is suffered to consider the Treaty as null on her Part, and to withdraw from America, the Advantages secured by it to that Power, there can be no Doubt, that the Treaty must equally be considered as null on the Part of

---

⁵ In April of 1797 Liston reported that while a rupture between the United States and France seemed still at some distance, as a friendly gesture he had directed Captain Hardy of the frigate *Squirrel*, then in the Delaware, to convoy the merchant ships of Americans "who were known with certainty to be our friends and who carry on trade to the British possessions." When he afterwards mentioned this to Pickering, the Secretary "seemed much pleased. . . . Indeed his late contestations with Mr. Adet appear to have operated a complete conversion on Mr. Pickering, who is become one of the most Antigallicans I ever met with." Liston to Grenville, April 18, 1797, No. 16, F. O. 5: 18.

⁶ With his note of Oct. 27, 1796 (presented Oct. 28, 1796), Adet had transmitted the French decree of July 2, 1796 that all neutral vessels would be treated in the same manner they suffered the British to treat them. *A. S. P., F. R.*, I, 577–578. Liston reported that Adet's memorials of Oct. 27, and of Nov. 15, 1796 (*ibid.*, I, 583, in which he announced the suspension of his ministerial functions) were actually manifestoes to the American people, published in the Philadelphia *Aurora* about the same time they were presented to Pickering, and designed to aid in the election, in 1796, of a president favorable to France. Liston to Grenville, Oct. 31, No. 23 ; also, Nov. 15, No. 24, 1796, F. O. 5: 14.

America, and that both the general Principles of impartial Neutrality and the express Letter of the Treaty with Great Britain require, that the Advantages which France enjoyed under her Treaty, in Preference to all other Powers, and particularly to Great Britain, should in like Manner cease.[7]

GRENVILLE TO LISTON [8]

No. 3.   DOWNING STREET, Jan. 27th 1797.

Sir,

In one of my most recent Conversations with Mr. King,[9] that Gentleman informed me that he was instructed by his Government to express to me the favorable Opinion, which it entertained of your Conduct during Your Residence in America.[10] You may be assured that this Communication afforded me considerable Satisfaction, not only on account of my personal Regard for You, but also of the Benefit, which must arise to His Majesty's Service from the Continuance of Confidence and good Understanding between You and the American Ministers.

As Mr. King's Conduct has been equally satisfactory to His Majesty's Government, it is His Majesty's Pleasure, that You should take an early Opportunity of representing to the American Secretary of State the favorable Impressions, which are entertained respecting Mr. King's Conduct, since he has resided in this Country.

GRENVILLE TO LISTON [11]

No. 4.   DOWNING STREET, January 27th 1797.

Sir,

A Committee having been appointed by the Merchants and Underwriters of London interested in Vessels and Cargoes captured and carried into the Ports of the United States, during the present War, I have to signify to You the King's Pleasure, that you instruct the several Consuls of His Majesty, resident in America, to answer such Enquiries respecting this Business as may be made by the Committee above-mentioned, and generally to give the Parties interested, every

---

[7] "There seems to be no risk that either he [Pickering] or any of his Brother Ministers, whatever may be the issue of their quarrel with the Directory, will be inclined to allow to France the enjoyment of any advantages that may be denied to Great Britain." Liston to Grenville, April 18, 1797, No. 16, F. O. 5: 18.

[8] Draft, F. O. 5: 18.

[9] Rufus King (1755–1827), an influential Federalist senator and friend of Hamilton, was minister plenipotentiary to Great Britain from 1796 to 1803. King was handsome, eloquent, well-informed, and tactful ; an effective man.

[10] A Federalist comment was that of William Smith, to Rufus King, April 3, 1797 : "Mr. and Mrs. Liston are much liked, so much so as to be, in the eyes of the Jacobins, *dangerous* people." *Corres. of King*, II, 165.

[11] F. O. 115: 5.

Assistance and Information which may be of Use in the Prosecution of their respective Claims, before the Commissioners appointed to investigate them. It is also His Majesty's Pleasure, that you should transmit to me a List of all British Vessels and Cargoes carried into the Ports of the United States between the Months of August 1794 and November 1795 as far as you can procure Information thereof.

GRENVILLE TO LISTON [12]

No. 5.   DOWNING STREET, April 8, 1797.

Sir,

Your several dispatches to No. 7 inclusive have been received and laid before the King.

The intelligence contained in your dispatch No. 1 relative to the designs of the French upon Canada,[13] has since been corroborated by direct information from General Prescott,[14] but there is reason to hope that those designs will be frustrated by the measures of precaution taken within the province and by the fortunate interruption of the American Vessel (the Olive Branch) laden with Arms on the pretended Account of General Ira Allen,[15] which was captured by one of His Majesty's Ships of War, and is now detained at Portsmouth.

Notwithstanding these circumstances it is His Majesty's pleasure that you should continue to watch the proceedings of the French emissaries in the United States with the most unremitting Attention, and that you should communicate every particular which you may learn respecting their operations to General Prescott, who (as you will perceive by the inclosed Copy of a Dispatch to him from the Duke of Portland) is instructed to transmit to you any information which he may obtain in Canada, and which may be of use to you

---

[12] F. O. 115 : 5.

[13] In his dispatch No. 1 of Jan. 25, 1797, cipher, F. O. 5 : 18, Liston had reported a French plan for an invasion of Canada in the spring of 1797 by a force of twelve to fifteen thousand men, and an insurrection among the French Canadians incited by the agents of Adet, who had hopes of support by American sympathizers. Liston had informed the American government, and was confident that measures would be taken to prevent the assembling or arming of troops on American soil. This confirmed accounts Liston had transmitted in his No. 26 of Nov. 18, 1796, cipher, F. O. 5 : 14. See abstract of correspondence on "French Republican Designs on Canada," 1793–1801, *Rpt. on Canadian Archives, 1891,* ed. D. Brymner, pp. 57–84 ; also, pp. 145–160.

[14] Major General Robert Prescott (1725–1816), acting Governor-General of Canada. In 1797 he succeeded Lord Dorchester in that office, and held it until 1799.

[15] Ira Allen (1751–1814) in 1795 purchased arms from the French government to sell to the Vermont militia of which he was ranking general. In November of 1796 he and his vessel, the *Olive Branch,* were seized off the west coast of Ireland on the ground that the arms were intended for Irish or Canadian revolutionists. Allen returned home in 1801, but the cargo was not awarded to him until 1804, when the arms were rusted and the market for them was gone—as Allen bitterly set forth in his *"Olive Branch* pamphlets." Liston, after talks with Pickering, reported that it appeared that the arms were really destined for Vermont. Liston to Grenville, June 17, 1797, No. 25, F. O. 5 : 18. See also *Corres. of Rufus King,* II, 163, 187 ; and *Rpt. on Canadian Archives, 1891,* pp. 63–64.

in prosecuting your enquiries on this head. I have farther to signify to you His Majesty's pleasure that you should, upon every occasion, which may justify your interference, repeat to the American Government those Representations which you have already, with so much propriety made to it upon this interesting Subject.

GRENVILLE TO LISTON [16]

No. 6.   DOWNING STREET, April 8th, 1797.

Sir,

In answer to your Dispatches Nos. 2 and 3, I have to inform you that the proposal which has been made to you by Mr. Chisholm [17] (as mentioned in those Dispatches) for endeavouring to wrest the two Floridas from Spain, has been taken into consideration by His Majesty's confidential Servants, but it has not been thought expedient to accede to it, or to adopt any measures for carrying it into execution.

Without entering into a detail of the various Considerations that have led to this decision, I think it merely necessary to observe that, exclusively of the inadequacy of the means to the end proposed, the two Objections which have occurred to yourself—the necessity of employing the Indians—and the impropriety of originating within the United States any hostile expedition against a Nation with which they are at peace—are of sufficient magnitude to counter-balance the advantages which are likely to result from the execution of such a plan.

I have therefore to signify to you the King's pleasure that you take an early opportunity of informing Mr. Chisholm that you have submitted His design to His Majesty's Government, but that it has not been thought adviseable to afford any Assistance from this Country towards carrying it into effect. [18]

---

[16] F. O. 115 : 5.
[17] In his dispatch No. 2, in cipher, of Jan. 25, 1797, F. O. 5 : 18, Liston had reported the overtures made to him by Capt. John Chisholm respecting British aid for a filibustering expedition against the Spanish Floridas, and had asked for instructions. His dispatch is printed in F. J. Turner, ed., "Documents on the Blount Conspiracy, 1795–1797," *Amer. Hist. Rev.*, X (April, 1905), 576–577. In his No. 3 of Feb. 13, 1797, draft in F. O. 115 : 5, Liston went into various details of the scheme, and stated that Chisholm had countered his objections by asserting that the Indian warriors to be employed would be under the strict control of the white leaders and that all hostile preparations would be made not on American soil but across the boundary on Spanish territory.

[18] Before receiving this instruction Liston had yielded to Chisholm's view that the project should be pressed at London, and had paid Chisholm's passage to England. Expressing his concern, he now urged Grenville to send Chisholm back to America immediately, "both for the sake of appearances, and that he may have no pretence for making claims on me for considerable sums of money." Liston to Grenville, March 16, No. 8, in cipher ; June 24, No. 22 ; and same to Hammond, private, March 16, 1797, F. O. 5 : 18. All three letters are printed by Turner, *Amer. Hist. Rev.*, X, 582–584, 589–590.

GRENVILLE TO LISTON [19]

No. 7.   DOWNING STREET, April 8th 1797.

Sir,

As I understand from your Dispatch No. 7 that there is reason to apprehend that Joseph Brandt [20] conceives himself to have been ill treated by the Governors of Canada with regard to a Grant of Land from the Crown, I think it right to transmit to you an Extract of a Letter from His Grace the Duke of Portland to Mr. President Russel [21] from which you will perceive the liberal policy that has been and is intended to be observed in this Respect by His Majesty's Government towards the Mohawks, and the little ground which there is for any complaint on their part. With regard to Brandt himself there is indeed reason to suspect that he has been for some time past disaffected to the Government of Canada, in consequence of it's neutrality in the late War between the North Western Indians and the United States. It will be therefore proper for you carefully to observe him, and to communicate to General Prescott any information which you may obtain relative to his Conduct during his Residence in Philadelphia. [22]

GRENVILLE TO LISTON [23]

No. 8.   DOWNING STREET, April 8th 1797.

Sir,

I send you inclosed for your information a translation of the Decree of the French executive Directory, as published in France, relative to the conduct intended to be pursued by that Country towards the vessels of neutral powers. [24]

---

[19] F. O. 115 : 5.

[20] Joseph Brant, "Thayendanegea," (1742–1807), the famous Mohawk chieftain. Liston had reported his arrival in Philadelphia, and his threats that unless he obtained immediate redress of grievances respecting lands in Canada assigned to him after the Revolution he would "offer his services to the French Minister here and march his Mohawks to assist in a Revolution and overturning of the British Government in that Province." Liston to Grenville, Feb. 24, 1797, No. 7, part cipher, F. O. 5 : 18.

[21] Peter Russell (1733–1808), president of the Executive Council of Upper Canada, and administrator of that province from Simcoe's departure in 1796 until the arrival of Lieut. Gov. Peter Hunter in 1799.

[22] Upon receipt of the above instruction Liston reported that Brant during his short stay in Philadelphia had seen no foreign minister except himself. Nevertheless, the threats of the Mohawk chieftain, a man of great vanity, "equally determined, able and artful," had made it expedient for Liston to play the rôle of mediator between Brant and the British government. Liston to Grenville, March 18, 1797, No. 9, F. O. 5 : 18.

[23] F. O. 115 : 5.

[24] The French decree of March 2, 1797, expanding the decree of July 2, 1796. See note 6, p. 129, *supra.* The new decree abandoned the "free ships make free goods" provision of the Franco-American treaty of 1778; declared that all neutrals serving on board an enemy ship of war were to be treated as pirates (making no distinction for impressed seamen), and subjected to seizure American vessels that did not have on board the precise form of crew's list prescribed in the Franco-American treaty of 1778. The decree is printed in *A. S. P., F. R.,* II, 30–32.

This Decree is, as you will perceive, founded on the pretended right of France to modify her Treaty with the United States according to the Treaty subsequently concluded by them with Great Britain— and it professes to follow up and apply to France, the stipulations which have been agreed upon between Great Britain and the United States.

The first of these positions has been so ably combated by Mr. Pickering in his Letters to Mr. Adet and Mr. Pinckney,[25] that it is unnecessary for me to add any observations to those of that Gentleman upon it. But even admitting that this position was better founded than it really is, the manner in which the French Directory has thought proper to interpret some of the Articles of the Treaty concluded between His Majesty and the United States, is so evidently false that it cannot be accounted for on any other principle than that of the most decided resolution to observe no bounds in the measures of rigour to be practised on the property and persons of American Citizens in the hopes of terrifying that Country into a compliance with all their Demands.

The two Articles to which I particularly advert are the seventeenth and twenty first of the Treaty between this Country and the United States. The first of these Articles stipulates that the property of the enemy *only*, found on board of the vessels of either party shall be made prize: But the interpretation of it by the French Directory adds that not only all merchandise of the enemy, but also "*all merchandise not sufficiently ascertained to be neutral conveyed under American flags shall be confiscated.*" It is needless to enlarge on the mischievous tendency of this clause, or to the vexation and injustice to which the operation of it will expose the whole commerce of America. With regard to the twenty first Article, you will remark that the penalties authorized by it attach on such individuals only of either country, as shall *accept any commission* for fitting out any armed Vessel to act as a privateer against the other party, and to this extent the stipulation is conformable to the provisions of many Treaties between Maritime Powers. But the French interpretation of it extends the same penalties also to every American Seaman who shall be a part of the Crew of the Ships and Vessels of the Enemies of France, without allowing the party to establish that the Act was the consequence of threats or violence. The insidious tendency of this clause is easily seen thro'— But as it may perhaps be made in America the foundation of injust

---

[25] Pickering's famous answer to Adet, actually a counter-manifesto, reviewed Franco-American relations from the beginning, and took up *seriatim* the complaints made by Genêt, Fauchet, and Adet as to American neutrality and as to Jay's Treaty. It was put in the form of instructions (dated Jan. 16, 1797, laid before Congress Jan. 19, and published by congressional order in the Philadelphia *Aurora*, Jan. 24–Feb. 3, 1797) to Charles Cotesworth Pinckney of South Carolina, Monroe's successor as minister to France. *A. S. P., F. R.,* I, 559–576.

clamour against this Country it seems very material that the manner in which France has perverted the stipulations of the British Treaty should be publickly exposed to notice and the attention of the well disposed in America particularly called to it. You will best be able to judge of the propriety of Official representations on these points. I have therefore only to leave this to your own discretion, observing to you that if you should make any such representation you must be very careful not to admit into it any phrase which should convey even an implied admission of the doctrine by which France claims the right to modify her Treaty by the stipulations of that concluded with this Country.—But it may be material to shew that even supposing that pretence to be as just and wellfounded as it is manifestly otherwise, still the Acts done and authorized by France far exceed the bounds to which even the admission of that principle would limit them. And altho' it is not desireable to distress the American Government on this Subject, or to have the appearance of wishing to drive them into a War with France, yet it is absolutely necessary in some early period of this business to lay in the claim which I mentioned in a former letter that the Question shall not be ultimately adjusted except on grounds of complete justice toward this Country by placing us on that footing to which we should on fair reasoning be entitled if the pretensions of France are given way to in the present instance.

GRENVILLE TO LISTON [26]

No. 9.   DOWNING STREET, 5th July 1797.

Sir,

Your several Dispatches to No. 23 inclusive have been received and laid before the King.

In Conformity to the Suggestion in Your Dispatch No. 22 [27] I enclose to You the Draft of an Article stipulating the reciprocal Restitution of all Deserters from the Naval or Land Service of Great Britain or the United States who may take refuge in the Territories of either Country; and I have to signify to You His Majesty's Pleasure that You submit it to the Consideration of the American Ministers, and inform them that You are authorized by His Majesty to conclude with them an Article of this Nature either in this form or in

---

[26] F. O. 115 : 5.

[27] In suggesting an additional article to Jay's Treaty enjoining the reciprocal restitution of deserters Liston stated that since his arrival in America the greatest obstacle to "a perfect good understanding" had been the increasing complaints over impressment. These, "though frequently false and always exaggerated, had made an impression on the publick mind which could not be removed but by a grant of redress and a change of conduct." In this detailed and frank dispatch on impressment Liston gave prophetic warning : "If the progress of this evil is alarming, the consequences that may possibly arise from it . . . appear to be no less dangerous." Liston to Grenville, May 12, 1797, No. 22, F. O. 5 : 18.

any other which may be equally applicable to the Objects that His Majesty's Government has in view,

The Policy of some Measure of this kind, and the good effects that are likely to result from it both to Great Britain and the United States, are so obvious, that it is unnecessary for Me to suggest to You any Arguments by which this Proposition to the Government of the United States is to be supported.

You will observe that the Article is grounded on that contained in the Treaty between the United States and France, but that Two Additions are made.—The first seeems absolutely necessary in order to prevent the American Consuls from claiming as Deserters from American Ships, all Seamen being the King's Subjects and who may have entered into His Service or been impressed under due Authority for that purpose.[28]

The second is inserted with a view to the Cases mentioned in Your Dispatch and to the local Situation and Circumstances of the respective Territories of the Two Parties in the Northern Part of the Continent.[29]

The General full Powers with which You are already furnished are sufficient to authorize You to sign an Article to this Effect with any Plenipotentiary who may be appointed by the United States to treat with You.

GRENVILLE TO LISTON [30]

No. 10.   DOWNING STREET, July 5, 1797.

Sir,

I send you inclosed the copy of a Letter from Captain Dobson of His Majesty's Navy to Sir Hyde Parker [31] together with the paper referred to in it; and it is His Majesty's pleasure that you should communicate these papers to the American Ministers; in order that they

---

[28] According to the proposed additional article, paragraph 5, the consuls in demanding the custody of deserters were to exhibit the registers or crew's list of those vessels from which the seamen had deserted. According to paragraph 7, they were not to demand the delivery "of any sailors, subjects, or citizens belonging to the other party . . . who have in time of war or threatened hostility, voluntarily entered into the service of their own sovereign or nation, or have been compelled to enter therein according to the laws and practice prevailing in the two countries respectively." Liston's project, wrote Secretary Pickering to President Adams, "appears . . . utterly inadmissible, unless it would put an end to impressment, which Mr. Liston seemed to imagine, while the seventh paragraph of his project expressly recognizes the right of impressing British subjects, and consequently American citizens, as at present." The proposed additional article, formally submitted by Liston on Feb. 4, 1800, together with the comments of members of the Cabinet, are printed in A. S. P., F. R., III, 576-581.

[29] In his No. 22 of May 12, 1797, F. O. 5: 18, Liston had noted a few instances in which deserting American soldiers had found refuge on board British warships. The proposed article, paragraph 8, provided that no refuge or protection was to be given deserting soldiers but that the most effectual measures were to be taken for their restitution.

[30] F. O. 115: 5.

[31] Admiral Sir Hyde Parker (1739–1807), commanding British naval forces on the Jamaica station from 1796 to 1800.

may perceive how impossible it is for His Majesty's Government possessed of such evidence of deception in this and in many other similar instances, to give that credit to certificates of this kind which the American Government appears to require.

As you will observe that Sir John Temple has affixed his Consular attestation to this Certificate it is further His Majesty's pleasure that you should instruct Sir John Temple and His Majesty's other Consuls in America, to abstain in future from attesting any certificates of this nature.[32]

GRENVILLE TO LISTON [33]

No. 11.   DOWNING STREET, Sept. 9th 1797.

Sir,

Your several Dispatches to No. 35 inclusive, have been received and laid before the King.

I have the satisfaction to inform you that His Majesty has been graciously pleased to approve of your Conduct, (as stated in Your Dispatch No. 27) with respect to the Appointment of a fifth Commissioner, to carry into Effect the Provisions of the Sixth Article of the Treaty with the United States. The Instruction to which you refer that the Commissioners named by His Majesty, should decline consenting to the Election (otherwise than by Lot) of any Person who was not a natural born Subject of the King, originated solely in the Desire of pursuing the same Course relative to the Commission under the Sixth Article, as that which had been adopted in the Appointment of the fifth Commissioner of the Board established in this Country.[34]

GRENVILLE TO LISTON [35]

No. 12.   DOWNING STREET, Sept. 9, 1797.

Sir,

Notwithstanding the repeated Representations which have been made to the American Government, through you and Mr. King, of

---

[32] Liston before the receipt of the above instruction had already mentioned the instance stated by Captain Dobson to Admiral Parker (of a British seaman, Cyril Bailey, who obtained from Mr. Keefe, a New York notary public, a certificate of American citizenship, which had later been attested by Sir John Temple), and other cases as well, wherein certificates of American citizenship had been obtained by collusion. Liston had represented "the necessary tendency of frauds of this nature to destroy the credit of every paper bearing the title of a protection or certificate produced by an American Seaman," but he much doubted whether any good would come from a further discussion of the matter. Early in 1797 Liston had sent a circular letter to British consuls in America "urging them to decline legalizing any Certificate except in cases where the person making the application was to their certain knowledge a native of the United States or settled in this country prior to the recognition of independence." Liston to Grenville, Oct. 4, 1797, No. 44, duplicate, F. O. 5 : 18; Liston to Pickering, Aug. 30, 1797 (enclosing copy of letter from Capt. Dobson of H. M. S. Queen to Sir Hyde Parker, April 18, 1797), Notes from British Legation, 2.
[33] F. O. 115 : 5.
[34] See note 69, page 127, supra.
[35] F. O. 115 : 5.

the improper Conduct of the Consuls of the United States, in granting to British Seamen, Certificates representing them to be American Citizens,[36] I am again under the Necessity of transmitting to you an original Certificate under the Seal of the American Vice Consul at Lisbon, which was given by him to a British Seaman, and also the Copy of a similar Document given by the American Consul at the same Port to another Subject of His Majesty.

I likewise inclose an Affidavit of this last mentioned Seaman from which it appears that there is the greatest Reason to believe, that the Consuls of the United States are accustomed to grant Certificates of this Nature without Enquiry, and in the View of obtaining a Gratuity from the Persons applying to them for such fraudulent Protections.

In order to put an End to a Practice so injurious to the Commercial and Naval Interests of this Kingdom I have to signify to You His Majesty's Pleasure that you present a Ministerial Note to the Government of the United States, complaining of the Conduct of the two Officers in it's Service above mentioned, and requiring that their Conduct should be examined into, and that they should, unless they can sufficiently justify themselves, undergo such Censure and Punishment as the Law of Nations requires in the Case of so high an Offence against the Rights of His Majesty.[37]

GRENVILLE TO LISTON [38]

No. 13.   DOWNING STREET, Sept. 9th, 1797.

Sir,

The King having been pleased to appoint George Leonard Esq., to be Superintendent of the Trade and Fisheries carried on on the Coasts of His Majesty's North American Colonies, and Mr. Leonard having represented that the Execution of his Commission (one material Object of which is to restrain the illicit Trade between the United States and the Coast above mentioned) would be greatly facilitated by the Co-operation of His Majesty's Consuls in the United States, I have to

---

[36] Grenville had made objections to King against the issuance of certificates of citizenship by American consuls in Great Britain. *A. S. P., F. R.,* II, 145–150.

[37] Pickering had already begun an investigation into charges that William Porter Eastman (a young Englishman), American vice consul at Lisbon, had given protections as American seamen to known British subjects. Pickering to David Humphreys, Dec. 7, 1796, U. S. Ministers, Instructions, 3. Upon Liston's representations, Pickering expressed marked disapprobation and stated that both Eastman and Edward Church, the consul at Lisbon, had been discharged. Liston doubted whether this would be much of a deterrent to other American consuls, since these officers were frequently not native Americans, were ill-paid or not paid at all, and a dismissal was to them not a very serious matter. Liston to Grenville, March 20, 1798, No. 8, F. O. 5 : 18. See also Edward Thornton to same, Dec. 3, 1797, No. 53, F. O. 5 : 18; and Liston to Pickering, Dec. 16, 1797, Notes from British Legation, 2.

[38] F. O. 115 : 5.

signify to you the King's Pleasure that you instruct His Majesty's Consuls (particularly in the Eastern States) to inform the Superintendant, as well as the respective Governors of His Majesty's North American Colonies, of all Cases coming to their Knowledge wherein the Vessels of the United States, carrying on their Fisheries on the Coasts of those Colonies, pursuant to the Right ceded by the Definitive Treaty of Peace between Great Britain and the United States, take on board Contraband Articles for the Purpose of importing them into His Majesty's Colonies, and of thereby defrauding His Majesty's Revenue.

GRENVILLE TO LISTON [39]

No. 14.   DOWNING STREET, Sept. 9th, 1797.

Sir,

I am entirely unacquainted with the particulars of the case of Messrs. Mallebay and Durand, to which you refer in your dispatch No. 31—but whatever may have been the proceedings of the Court of Admiralty at Tortola, as the Case is now brought before the Lords of Appeal, it will certainly be decided by that Tribunal conformably to the Principles of Justice, and the Law of Nations. This is indeed so obvious that I should not have thought it necessary to advert to it, if the American Minister had not sollicited the good Offices of His Majesty's Government on a Subject in which any intervention would in its present State be evidently improper.[40]

GRENVILLE TO LISTON [41]

No. 15.   DOWNING STREET, Sept. 9th, 1797.

Sir,

I have the satisfaction to inform You that from a consideration of all the circumstances stated in your dispatch No. 33 His Majesty has been graciously pleased to approve of your conduct in refraining from presenting any memorial to the American Government, on the subject of the interests of this country, as they may be affected by the result

---

[39] F. O. 115 : 5.

[40] Liston had requested the good offices of Grenville upon application of Secretary Pickering in favor of Mallebay and Durand, merchants of New York, whose brigantine *Fortitude* and her cargo had been condemned by the admiralty court at Tortola. Liston said he had no intention of interfering with British justice but he wished to point out that Mallebay and Durand, although natives of France, were enemies of the existing French regime, men of a very respectable character, who from their arrival in America as exiles had almost entirely confined their trade to the British possessions. Liston to Grenville, July 11, 1797, No. 31, F. O. 5 : 18.

[41] F. O. 115 : 5.

of the present dispute between the United States and France.[42] It is at the same time however His Majesty's pleasure that you should watch with the utmost vigilance the progress of the negotiation which seems now likely to be entered into between the Government of the United States and that of France and that You should employ every exertion in your power to prevail on the American Government to resist any attempt which may be made by France, to infringe or render nugatory any part of the treaty concluded between His Majesty and the United States in the year 1794, or to impose any conditions injurious to the rights and interests of His Majesty's subjects as with respect to the United States, whether political or commercial.

GRENVILLE TO LISTON [43]

No. 16.   DOWNING STREET, Sep. 9th, 1797.

Sir,

In my dispatch No. 7 I inclosed You the Copy of a dispatch from the Duke of Portland to Mr. President Russell containing instructions to that Gentleman for the purpose of adjusting the points that are now in a state of litigation between the Government of Upper Canada, and the Mohawks. Those Instructions have been communicated to Lieutenant Governor Simcoe (since his return from St. Domingo [)],[44] who I understand considers them to be calculated to promote the tranquility of the Province of Upper Canada as well as to secure the just rights of the Indians residing within it's limits. You will therefore in any future communications which you may have with Joseph Brandt, (altho' I am far from wishing you to discourage the continuance of the Correspondence which he has opened with You, as a knowledge of his Sentiments may be extremely useful to the Government of Canada) carefully avoid throwing out anything which can incline that Chief to believe that any efforts, or intrigues on his part, can induce his Majesty's Government to deviate from the system which it has formed respecting any territorial

---

[42] Reporting on the appointment of commissioners to France (C. C. Pinckney, John Marshall, and Elbridge Gerry), Liston stated that he had not thought it politic to present a memorial expressing his hope and trust that there would be no arrangement entered into but such as would place Great Britain on a footing of fair and impartial equality. Being sensible "that if the present practice of printing every paper that has a relation to the political affairs of the country should continue to prevail, a memorial of the tenour alluded to might easily be misinterpreted, and urged as an additional evidence of what is asserted with equal insolence and perseverance in the opposition newspapers of every day—that neither the Secretary of State nor the President ever do anything without the previous opinion and advice of the British Minister, I determined to content myself with the verbal representations I had already made." Liston to Grenville, July 13, 1797, No. 33, F. O. 5 : 18.

[43] F. O. 115 : 5.

[44] Simcoe, on leave from his Canadian post, was in command of the British part of San Domingo from December of 1796 to July of 1797.

Rights, or immunities, within the Province of Upper Canada, which may be claimed by him, and the Indians under his direction.[45]

GRENVILLE TO LISTON [46]

No. 17.   DOWNING STREET, Sept. 9th, 1797.

Sir,

As the Communications which you have made to the Government of the United States [47] on the Subject of the Plan in which Mr. Blount [48] appears to have been concerned, have been abundantly sufficient to remove any doubt that could be thrown by his Majesty's enemies on the good faith of His Majesty's Government, and on the friendly dispositions manifested by his Majesty towards the tranquility and peace of the United States, it does not appear necessary for me to say anything further to you on that Subject at present: It is perhaps on the whole not unfavorable to his Majesty's Interests in that Quarter of the World that by the discovery of Mr. Blount's Correspondence so fair an opportunity has been afforded to you, of placing in its true light the correctness of those Principles by which the King's Conduct is always actuated in every thing that concerns the rights of neutral states, and of contrasting them with the conduct of his Majesty's enemies.[49]   And certainly the Government of the United States must be sensible, that in the extent and openness of

[45] Liston was able to report in October that President Russell, by the unanimous advice of the Council of Upper Canada, had confirmed by the King's Letter Patent the sales of land on the Grand River already contracted for by the Five Nations, and to the selling of which by the Indians objections had previously been made by Joseph Brant. In view of the activities of French and Spanish agents in attempting to employ the Indians of the back country against Canada, Liston considered the disposition of the matter "highly prudent, not to say essential to His Majesty's interest." Liston to Grenville, Oct. 3, 1797, No. 42, duplicate, F. O. 5 : 18 ; also, same to same, July 19, 1797, No. 35, F. O. 5 : 18.

[46] F. O. 115 : 5.

[47] Liston's statements of June 29 and July 2, 1797, both in reply to inquiries by Pickering, the first denying that a British expedition was preparing in Canada to attack Spanish Louisiana, and the second giving an account of Chisholm's overtures and their rejection by Grenville, are printed in *A. S. P., F. R.*, II, 69, 71.

[48] William Blount (1749–1800), senator from Tennessee from Aug. 2, 1796 to July 8, 1797. Implicated in the filibustering project against the Spanish possessions, he was expelled from the Senate by a vote of 25 to 1 for "a high misdemeanor entirely inconsistent with his public trust and duty as a Senator."

[49] In August Liston reported that after Blount's connection with the filibustering project became known, "finding the extreme Aversion of the country in general to any measure that might risk involving the United States in a quarrel with Spain (while that power was connected with France) ;—and observing the malignant use which the democratick faction were already endeavouring to make of the disclosure, to the disadvantage of the American Ministry (who were falsely accused of being privy to the business), and to the detriment of the British interest in this country ;—I conceived it to be essential to remove every doubt with regard to the intentions of England, by producing your Lordship's original dispatch on the subject, addressed to me [April 8, 1797, No. 6, *supra*]. This I put into the hands of the Secretary of State, with leave to shew it to the President, and to make such other use of it as he might in his discretion deem expedient. The effect of this communication has fully answered my expectation, and has stopped the mouths of our most formidable adversaries." Liston to Grenville, Aug. 30, 1797, No. 36, F. O. 5 : 18. See, also, same to same, July 8, 1797, No. 30, F. O. 5 : 18, printed (with the exception of a paragraph on the impeachment of Blount) by Turner, *Amer. Hist. Rev.*, X, 592–594.

your communications to them on this point, you have gone far beyond what they could have the smallest right to require from a public Minister, representing a foreign Government, and even to the very utmost Limits of what a proper Attention to the rights, and duties of that Situation could in any case authorise. The question put to you by Colonel Pickering was one to which in the Common course of Public Business a foreign Minister would have wholly declined making any answer, and in any future discussions, if any such there should be, on this Subject, it will be necessary that you should take care that this principle is not lost sight of and that the frankness and liberality of the communications voluntarily made on this Occasion, should not in future be drawn into precedent for a similar course of proceeding in other Cases.[50]

GRENVILLE TO LISTON [51]

No. 18.   DOWNING STREET, Nov. 17th, 1797.

Sir,

Your several Dispatches to No. 39 inclusive have been received and laid before the King.

The point on which it appears most immediately necessary for me to make some observations is that of the discussions between you and Colonel Pickering relative to the respective conduct of Sir Hyde Parker and Mr. Talbot.[52]

The behaviour of the latter has, in the instance which you state been so unbecoming and so inconsistent with the situation in which he was placed, that, if other means had not been found to counteract the effect of such proceedings it would have been absolutely necessary for His Majesty's Government to have taken the resolution of directing that he should no longer be suffered to execute a function, to which he was

---

[50] Upon receipt of the above instruction Liston stated that regard for justice made it necessary to record that his communications had not been "indiscreetly required" by the American government; that Pickering's requests for information had been written with his foreknowledge and consent, and with the express view of giving him an opportunity to be the first to disclose, with advantage to Great Britain, what could not possibly be concealed; and that under the circumstances he trusted that there was no danger of a precedent being drawn in the future from what had occurred. Liston to Grenville, Feb. 6, 1798, No. 3, F. O. 5: 22. See also Grenville to King, Aug. 30, 1797, *Corres. of Rufus King,* II, 218–219.

[51] F. O. 115: 5.

[52] Pickering on Aug. 11, 1797 had transmitted to Liston a copy of a letter dated July 4, 1797 from Silas Talbot, agent in the West Indies for procuring the release of impressed American seamen. Talbot set forth the obstacles placed in his way by Admiral Sir Hyde Parker, and reported (what Pickering called *"past enduring"*) that Captain Otway of the frigate *Ceres,* on board of which were some twenty impressed sailors, had all those men who attempted to write to Talbot brought to the gangway and whipped. Domestic Letters, 8; also, for Talbot's letter, *A. S. P., F. R.,* II, 144. Liston did not believe that his representations to Pickering had much effect: "The ill treatment of American Seamen is the only subject upon which I have never been able to bring him to speak with moderation." Liston to Grenville, Aug. 30, 1797, No. 37, F. O. 5: 18.

named, without any previous sanction from His Majesty's Government, and which he exercised for purposes so injurious to the rights and interests of these Kingdoms.

The inclosed Copies of a Letter written by Mr. King to me on this subject on the 28 of January last, and of my answer to it,[53] will put you fully in possession of the sentiments of His Majesty's Government on the subject of the pretended certificates of Citizenship so frequently exhibited by British Seamen as protections against the lawful claim which His Majesty has upon their Service in time of War. You will strictly conform yourself to the language of that paper in all future discussions on the subject. I hardly need remark to you how much the arguments there stated are strengthened by the facts which I have had occasion to communicate to You subsequent to it's date, for the purpose of your making proper representations and complaints upon them.

I cannot conclude this dispatch without observing on an expression in your letter to Colonel Pickering which contains an admission which I could have wished not to have seen in a paper so likely to become public. The practice of the impressment of Sailors is not as you seem to imagine contrary either to the Letter or Spirit of the English Statutes, but has on the contrary frequently been recognized as legal, both by the terms of our Statutes and by the decisions of Our Courts of Law.[54]

---

[53] These letters, King's of Jan. 28, and Grenville's of March 27, 1797, are printed in *A. S. P., F. R.*, II, 147–150.

[54] In his note to Pickering of August 30, 1797 (the original is not in the State Department files, but a copy was enclosed with Liston's No. 37 to Grenville of August 30, 1797, F. O. 5: 18) Liston had discussed fraudulent certificates of citizenship. With reference to Talbot's attempt to obtain the release of impressed sailors by an application to the British civil authorities, Liston had stated: "The practice of enrolling sailors by force, though contrary perhaps to the letter and to the spirit of the English Statutes, is established by ancient custom; it is sanctioned by high authority; and it is in the present state of things essential to the support of our naval power. So that every endeavour to suppress it by means of legal proofs must be looked upon as a dangerous precedent, and may be eagerly opposed by a patriotic officer, even when he is sensible of the justice of the particular case to which it is applied."

INSTRUCTIONS OF 1798

No. 1.   DOWNING STREET, Jan. 9th, 1798.

Sir,

Your several dispatches to No. 49 and Mr. Thornton's [2] to No. 56 inclusive have been received and laid before the King.

Although His Majesty's Government is by no means convinced by the arguments used by the American ministers (as stated in your dispatches Nos. 43 and 45 that the United States could receive any injury from the agreeing to the additional article, respecting Deserters, in the form in which it was transmitted to you, yet His Majesty would be extremely unwilling to urge any measure which might, at this crisis, afford to the disaffected party in America a pretext of exciting discontent against this government.[3] At the same time however His Majesty cannot consistently with a sense of what he owes to the interests of His people, consent to a formal stipulation of so partial a tendency as that would be, which while it insured to the United States the return of their military deserters, should provide no means of recovering for Great Britain those Seamen (even avowedly British) who may occasionally desert from His Majesty's Ships of War employed on the coast of the United States.

For these reasons it is His Majesty's pleasure that you should for the present suspend altogether any farther proceedings respecting the

---

[1] F. O. 115 : 6.

[2] Edward Thornton (1766–1852), secretary of legation since March of 1796. A protégé of James Bland Burges, he had come to the United States as Hammond's secretary, and from 1793 to 1796 had been vice consul at Baltimore. While Liston was on a tour to the southward, Thornton was in charge of the legation.

[3] See note 28, p. 136, *supra*. While members of the administration, reported Liston, favored in general terms an additional article on deserters, American public opinion made it impossible for them to accept the principle of non-transferable allegiance. "Indeed so long as America remains in her present half-peopled and half-cultivated condition, her natural policy must be to encourage the immigration of inhabitants from other quarters of the world : and although the law of nations gives no countenance to the idea that absence from home, or residence in any foreign country, can dissolve the ties of natural allegiance . . . general opinion is different. . . . This being the case—whatever the private sentiments of the American ministry may be, (and I must confirm what I have already done them the justice to state that they have in no instance that has come to my knowledge made a peremptory demand of the release of any seaman, who was not either a native of America or a resident . . . before the peace of 1783)—it is not to be expected that watched and harassed as they are . . . they should formally give up a point which is regarded as of so great importance. . . ." Liston to Grenville, Oct. 28, 1797, No. 45, F. O. 5 : 18.

additional Article in question—more especially as there is the greatest reason to believe that in a very short time the disputes between France and the United States will terminate in actual hostility; in which event the latter would soon perceive it to be for their interest to enter into some engagement with His Majesty, for the purpose of retaining the respective Seamen in the Service of the Country to which they belong.

With regard to the delivering up of such military deserters as may take refuge in the respective territories of His Majesty and the United States, it is not necessary that your suspending the additional article should defeat any measure of that nature if it should appear advisable: Since it may be carried into effect, by an agreement between His Majesty's Governor General or other Commanding officer in America and the Commanders of any of the Military Posts or Garrisons of the United States, as satisfactorily as by any public arrangement between the two countries to the same effect.   You will communicate this last suggestion to the American Ministers, and will inform them that orders will be sent to His Majesty's officers and Governors in America author-izing them to give their sanction to any local and provisional arrange-ment for the purposes above-mentioned, which may from time to time be concluded between officers acting under their authority, and the Commanding officers of any of the Military Posts or Garrisons of the United States.

GRENVILLE TO LISTON [4]

No. 2.   DOWNING STREET, Jan. 9th, 1798.
Sir,
I send You inclosed Copies of a dispatch to the Duke of Portland from Lieut-Governor Carleton [5] and of two letters from Mr. Chipman [6] therein referred to.

With regard to the article which the last mentioned Gentleman and the Agent of the United States recommend to be added to the Treaty of Amity, Commerce and Navigation, as explanatory of the fifth Article, it does not appear advisable to conclude it exactly on the principles which the Agents have suggested.

---

[4] F. O. 115 : 6.
[5] Thomas Carleton, Lieutenant Governor and Commander-in-chief of the Province of New Brunswick.   Carleton informed Portland, Sept. 20, 1797, that the commissioners under Article V of Jay's Treaty had suggested an application to their respective govern-ments to dispense with that part of the treaty which required them to ascertain the latitude and longitude of the source of the river St. Croix. D. Brymner, ed., *Rpt. on Canadian Archives, 1895,* New Brunswick, p. 46.
[6] Ward Chipman, British agent of the commission set up under Article V of Jay's Treaty. A Massachusetts Loyalist, he had taken refuge after the Revolution in New Brunswick, and at the time of his appointment was the Solicitor General of that province.

Those Gentlemen, and the Commissioners themselves do not seem to have fully adverted to the extreme importance of ascertaining with the utmost accuracy the precise point which is to be called the source of that river which shall be determined to be the River St. Croix intended by the Treaty of Peace—with a view to obviate the difficulties and disputes which might hereafter arise from the common case of many forks or branches nearly of equal magnitude which are usually found near the source, or head of considerable rivers; and this is more particularly deserving of attention because by the second Article of the Treaty of 1783 the North-Eastern boundary of the United States is described as commencing from the North-Western Angle of Nova Scotia viz. "that Angle which is formed by a line drawn due North from the Source of St. Croix River to the Highlands etc." Any doubt or uncertainty therefore as to the precise spot of that particular spring or river-head which is to be considered as the real source of the River would affect this important boundary not less essentially than the Eastern one which alone appears to have been in the contemplation of the Agents at the period of their making the recommendation in question.

Those Gentlemen and the Commissioners being upon the Spot are unquestionably best able to decide on the degree of accuracy which it is practicable to attain in a matter of this nature, but its great importance cannot be too strongly stated. The difficulties alleged by them as to the ascertainment of the latitude and longitude of the source by astronomical observations are of considerable weight particularly as any inaccuracy in the astronomical observations such as are perhaps to be expected when made in a Country so difficult of access and where there are no ascertained points to refer to would create instead of removing uncertainty and disputes.

It seems therefore right that the Commissioners should be released from the obligation imposed upon them by the fifth Article of the Treaty if the possibility of future doubt and disputes can be as effectually guarded against by any other mode of proceeding as by that which is prescribed in the Article.

The course of proceeding which appears the least liable to objection and the most conformable to the spirit of the treaty would be—that the latitude and longitude of the *mouth* of the rivers which form the subject of the present controversy should be ascertained with the utmost practicable accuracy and by actual observation—that the surveys of the rivers should be prosecuted by the persons employed in them until they shall have ascertained the respective sources of the various springs and small branches in which the principal branch of each River terminates, and that these surveys shall be laid down on maps to be delivered to the Commissioners—that the map of the river determined to be the real St. Croix should be annexed to the declaration of the Commissioners, and that such declaration shall specify the longitude and latitude of the mouth, and shall describe which of the several spring-heads marked on the map is to be considered as the source of the true River St. Croix—and that such declaration shall be considered as conclusive and shall release the Commissioners from the necessity of particularizing the longitude and latitude of the source of the river—In order however to avoid any dispute hereafter, the two governments should further agree to proceed without delay to erect at their joint expence, at the place designated as the source of the true River St. Croix a durable monument (which from the facility of finding the rough materials for such a building in those regions it is presumed could be easily executed) and in order to prevent its being defaced or destroyed proper Surveyors should be appointed by the two Governments to visit it together once in the course of every three Years, and should direct the necessary repairs to be made at the joint expence of the two Governments.

It is His Majesty's pleasure that you should submit these suggestions to the American ministers and to Lieut-Governor Carleton (to whom a Copy of this dispatch will be forwarded by the first opportunity) and if no objections to them are offered, You will consider Yourself authorized to conclude, in virtue of your general full Powers, an additional Article on these principles which shall embrace the two objects of exonerating the Commissioners from the necessity of a strict compliance with the letter of the Article, and of providing a permanent and definitive boundary between His Majesty's possessions and those of the United States. The mode of expressing this article and the regulation of any details not inconsistent with the general objects herein before stated to You are left to Yourself and to the American Ministers, but it will certainly be desirable that nothing shall be finally concluded until after You shall have consulted Lieut. Governor Carleton, and the . . .[7] Commissioners and agents appointed under the fifth article of the Treaty of Amity, Commerce and Navigation, who being most conversant with the subject, are the best qualified to point out the most certain modes of precluding any future ambiguity.

P. S.[8]   Feb. 8th, 1798.

Since the above was written Mr. King has received full Powers to treat of this Subject here, and as he appears anxious to proceed without Delay in this Negotiation, for the Reasons assigned in his Letter

---

[7] Omission in original.
[8] This postscript of Feb. 8, 1798 is taken from the draft of the duplicate instruction to Liston, Jan. 9, 1798, No. 1, F. O. 5 : 22.

of Yesterday's Date of which a Copy is inclosed,[9] I shall forthwith receive His Majesty's Commands for that Purpose, and You may expect to receive the Article with it's Ratification by the next Packet— You will therefore suspend any further Steps which you may have had in Contemplation for the Execution of the Orders conveyed to You by the original of the above Dispatch.

GRENVILLE TO LISTON [10]

No. 3.   DOWNING STREET, Jan. 15th, 1798.

Sir,

I send You inclosed a Translation of a Message from the French Directory to the two Legislative Councils [11] which was received on Saturday last from France; and as there seems little Reason to doubt that in the present State of the French Convention a Decree will immediately be passed there in conformity to the Principles contained in the Message, I have to signify to You His Majesty's Pleasure that You lose no Time in communicating Copies of this Paper to His Majesty's Consuls in the United States, and in directing them to recommend to the British Merchants or Agents in America to take such Precautions as may appear to them the best calculated to guard against any Injury which this desperate Project of the Enemy might produce to the established Commerce between Great Britain and the United States.

It is almost unnecessary to point out to You the unexampled Extent of the Principles on which this Message proceeds, respecting the Navigation of Neutral Powers, when it declares that the single Fact of a Vessel's having any English Produce, or Manufactures on board, shall be held sufficient to justify her Capture and Condemnation, and that although both the Vessel and the Cargo shall be neutral Property the whole shall be considered as lawful Prize [12]—a rule directly contrary to every Principle of the Law of Nations which tho' it establishes the Right of taking the Property of an Enemy in the Vessel of a Friend, so far from making *that* a reason for condemning the rest of the Cargo or the Vessel requires that the Captor should indemnify

---

[9] The enclosed copy of the letter from King is dated Feb. 5, 1798. It is partially printed in *Corres. of Rufus King*, II, 277.

[10] F. O. 115 : 6.

[11] A copy of this message of the Directory, of Jan. 4, 1798, urging the enactment of a law for the seizure of neutral vessels carrying goods from British possessions, and the shutting out from French ports of neutral vessels that touched at British ports, was sent to the Secretary of State on Jan. 8, 1798 by the American mission to France (C. C. Pinckney, John Marshall, and Elbridge Gerry). It is printed in *A. S. P., F. R.*, II, 151.

[12] This was the substance of the French law enacted on January 18, 1798. The character of a vessel was to be determined by its cargo: all neutral vessels laden in whole or in part with goods coming from Great Britain or from British possessions were declared lawful prize, together with their cargoes. Further, every vessel which touched at a British port was forbidden to enter a French port. The law of Jan. 18, 1798 (29th Nivose, 6th year) is printed in *A. S. P., F. R.*, III, 288.

the Neutral Owner of the Vessel by the Payment, not only of the Freight of the Part of the Cargo taken, but also of any other incidental Loss which he might sustain by the Detention of the Vessel.

Mr. King writes on this Subject to his Government by the present Opportunity.[13] There is every reason to believe that such a Measure as this, cannot have been adopted by the Directory, but under the fixed Determination to proceed to Hostilities against the United States, since it is perfectly evident, that the Rule now laid down could not be inforced without a Total Interruption of all Commerce between the United States and the rest of the World. There being very few Cases in which a Merchant trading from the United States, could so frame an Assortment of Goods for American Importation as wholly to exclude from it all British Articles, even if it were possible for an independant Nation to submit to such a Rule.

I expect therefore that we shall in a very few Days receive the Account of the Dismissal of the American Ministers in France.[14] And in that Event, as an early Knowledge of the Fact may be of the utmost Importance to the Interests of the American Government, and to those of Great Britain, as connected with them, the most effective Measures will be taken for the speediest Conveyance of the Intelligence.

By that opportunity I shall write to You again, but I shall of course be particularly anxious to learn Your Opinion on all the various Points of Policy to which this new Situation of Affairs will lead. It will be the Object of His Majesty's Government to improve it by every Means which can best tend to unite the two Governments, and to prove to the People of America, that their Interest when independant, no less than their former Bonds of Connection, leads them to look to Great Britain, as their Most Natural Friend and Support.

GRENVILLE TO LISTON [15]

No. 4.   DOWNING STREET, Febr. 8, 1798.
Sir,

Mr. Thornton's Letters to No. 1 inclusive have been received and laid before the King.

Ever since the Date of my last Dispatch we have been in constant Expectation here, of receiving Information of the Dismissal of the

---

[13] See Grenville to King, Jan. 13, King to Pickering, Jan. 14, and King to Grenville, Jan. 15, 1798, *Corres. of Rufus King*, II, 270–273.

[14] The correspondence of the commissioners (C. C. Pinckney, Marshall, and Gerry) sent to France by President Adams is printed in *A. S. P., F. R.*, II, 153–201. Pinckney and Marshall departed from Paris in April of 1798, after their unsuccessful negotiations; Gerry stayed on until August of 1798. See A. J. Beveridge, *John Marshall*, II, chaps. vi-ix, and E. Wilson Lyon, "The Directory and the United States," *Amer. Hist. Rev.*, XLIII (April, 1938), 514–532.

[15] F. O. 115: 6.

American Ministers from Paris; but no account of that Event having actually taken place has as yet reached this Country. From various Sources of Information, however, little Doubt can be entertained that their Mission will very shortly be closed in that Manner.

The Decree which I inclosed in my last Dispatch had not, at the Date of our latest Advises from Paris, passed the Council of Elders, but although there is no Cause assigned for the Delay which has occurred, there is every Reason to believe that it will not meet any Opposition on the Part of that Body.[16]

We are as yet without Information, as to the Effect which the last mentioned Measure has produced on the Northern Powers of Europe; but I trust that, by the Packet of next Month, I shall be able to acquaint You with the Steps which they are likely to take either separately or in concert with His Majesty, for the Protection of their Commerce and Navigation from the Dangers with which they are menaced.

I wait with much Impatience for an Account of Your Return to Philadelphia,[17] where Your Presence at this critical Period, must evidently be of such extreme Importance to the Interests of His Majesty's Service and to the Objects of Your Mission.

GRENVILLE TO LISTON [18]

No. 5.   DOWNING STREET, March 16th, 1798.

Sir,

Conformably to the intimation in the Postscript to my dispatch No. 2, I herewith transmit to you an explanatory Article which was yesterday signed by Mr. King and myself, to be added to the Treaty of Amity, Commerce and Navigation between His Majesty and the United States, together with the King's ratification thereof.[19] And I have to signify to you His Majesty's pleasure that you take the earliest opportunity to inform the American Ministers that you are in possession of this instrument and of His Majesty's ratification of it, and that you are authorized to exchange this ratification with the American Ministers for a similar ratification on the part of the President of the United States. In order to avoid accidents you will desire the American Ministers to furnish you with two original rati-

---

[16] See note 12, p. 148, *supra.*
[17] See note 2, p. 144, *supra.*
[18] F. O. 115 : 6.
[19] The additional explanatory article relative to the St. Croix boundary, signed at London, March 15, 1798, with correspondence pertaining thereto, is printed in *A. S. P., F. R.,* II, 183–185. See also Miller, *Treaties,* II, 427–428. Ratifications were exchanged at Philadelphia, June 9, 1798, Liston to Grenville, June 11. 1798, No. 31, F. O. 5 : 22.

fications of this article by the President of the United States, which, after you shall have exchanged them for His Majesty's ratification of this Article, you will transmit to me by two separate occasions.

GRENVILLE TO LISTON [20]

Separate.   DOWNING STREET, April 7, 1798.
Sir,

I have not received any public Dispatches from you, since the Date of my last Letter, and after so long an Interval, I still wait with the greatest Anxiety, to be informed of the many Particulars, the Knowledge of which, in the present State of Affairs betweeen France and the United States, must necessarily be interesting to His Majesty's Government.

No Measure has yet been proposed to Parliament, on the Subject of Convoys for neutral Ships, nor are, as I believe, the Details of the new Regulations respecting British Convoys finally adjusted: As soon as I can write to you with any Certainty on the Subject, I shall not fail to do so.

No Modification has yet appeared of the French Decree nor is it probable, that in the present Circumstances, any such will be adopted.

In Answer to your private Letter of the 7th of February, in which you express your Wish to make an Excursion during the Summer Months to the Northern Parts of the United States, and possibly to Canada, I can only say, that as there does not appear to me to be the smallest Probability, that the State of public Affairs, in the Course of next Summer, can be such, as to admit of your absenting yourself for any considerable Length of Time, from the Seat of Government, without great Prejudice to His Majesty's Service, and much less of your going beyond the Limits of the United States, I have not thought myself at Liberty to solicit on your Behalf from His Majesty the Permission you have desired.

GRENVILLE TO LISTON [21]

No. 6.   DOWNING STREET, June 8, 1798.
Sir,

Your several dispatches to No. 19 inclusive have been received, and laid before the King.

I have the Satisfaction to inform you, that His Majesty has been pleased to approve of your conduct in regard to the Circumstances of Mr. Sinclair's detention, (as stated in your dispatch No. 2) and of

---

[20] F. O. 115 : 6.
[21] F. O. 115 : 6.

the directions which you gave for the purpose of extricating that Officer from the unpleasant situation in which he was placed.[22]

No. 7.   DOWNING STREET, June 8, 1798.

Sir,

It has afforded me much satisfaction to learn from your dispatch No. 5 that the causes of the delays which have occurred on the part of the British Creditors in submitting their Cases to the Commissioners appointed under the Sixth Article of the Treaty of Amity, Commerce and Navigation between His Majesty and the United States, are removed, and that the decisions of those Gentlemen are likely to be favorable to the Claims of the King's Subjects.[24] His Majesty has in consequence of your representation of the diligence, labor, and ability of Mr. Smith, the Agent for the British Creditors, been graciously pleased to approve of your Suggestions on the Subject of the Allowances to be made to that Gentleman, and to the Clerks appointed under him, and has accordingly directed that an Allowance at the rate of £1000 per Annum should be made to Mr. Smith, together with an additional annual sum of £250 for the payment of his two clerks and that this allowance should take place from the date of Mr. Smith's appointment, and together with the other Sum above mentioned be paid in the same manner and at the same periods, as the allowances granted to Mr. Macdonald and Mr. Rich. This mode of Remuneration has been preferred to that of allowing the Agent to receive Fees for his trouble, as that course of proceeding would, under many points of view, be considered as justly liable to several weighty objections.

With respect to the proposal which has been made to you by the American Government relative to the payment of the Salaries of

---

[22] Capt. Henry Sinclair, commanding the British armed brigantine *Swinger*, at Alexandria, Virginia, early in 1798 had been arrested at the suit of David Stewart and Sons and John Pannell of Baltimore for having on the high seas robbed the captain of a ship belonging to them of considerable property, and for having afterwards unjustly seized the ship and carried her into a British port. Sinclair was admitted to bail, and later, after Liston's representations to Pickering as to the legality of his seizure of the American ship, was released. Liston had also directed the British vice consul at Alexandria to assist Sinclair in bringing suit for false imprisonment, but, since Sinclair himself was aware of irregularity in his carrying off certain articles from the American ship, the matter was compromised. Liston to Grenville, Feb. 6, 1798, No. 2, F. O. 5 : 22.

[23] F. O. 115 : 6.

[24] Liston had endeavored to have the British creditors make their applications to the commission without further delay. They had procrastinated because they wished first to learn from the commission's decisions what general principles would be applied, and consequently what the prospect of their success would be, and also because they had believed that the commission would remove from Philadelphia and take up cases in various parts of the country. Liston to Grenville, Feb. 22, 1797, No. 5, F. O. 5 : 22.

Mr. Guillemard and Mr. Trumbull,[25] there can be no difficulty on the part of His Majesty's Government in acceding to it, as the Salary of each of those Gentlemen is of the same amount, and as the expenses attendant on the several Commissions established under the Treaty between His Majesty and the United States, are defrayed not out of the Civil List, but by a vote of Parliament. It will however be proper before any definite arrangement is made on this Subject, that the date of Mr. Guillemard's nomination should be ascertained, as that must be regarded as the proper period, from which his allowances ought to commence.

GRENVILLE TO LISTON [26]

No. 8.   DOWNING STREET, June 8th, 1798.

Sir,

The offer which has been made to you, under the Authority of the American Government, of a Lot of Ground for the purpose of erecting a house upon it for the future residence of His Majesty's Ministers to the United States, appears to have been attended with so many expressions of personal civility to Yourself, and of general good Will to this Country, that His Majesty is graciously pleased to authorise you to accept it, and to accompany your acceptance with a declaration to the effect which you mention in your dispatch upon this Subject.[27] At the same time however you will give it clearly to be understood that whatever may be the King's future intentions in this respect, it is by no means judged expedient in the present moment to incur the expense which would necessarily arise from immediately appropriating the Ground to the purpose for which it has been reserved.

GRENVILLE TO LISTON [28]

No. 9.   DOWNING STREET, June 8th, 1798.

Sir,

The Intelligence contained in your Dispatch No. 11 respecting the Projects of the French in Canada, is corroborated by so many cir-

---

[25] Since the expenses were to be defrayed jointly, and since the salaries of John Guillemard, at Philadelphia, the fifth commissioner under Article VI, and John Trumbull, at London, the fifth commissioner under Article VII, were the same, Pickering had proposed that Guillemard's salary should be paid by the American government and Trumbull's by the British.

[26] F. O. 115 : 6.

[27] The commissioners superintending the building of the new city of Washington had made similar offers to the Spanish and Portuguese envoys and to the agents of the French and Dutch republics. Liston in the fall of 1797 on passing through Washington on his tour to the southward had selected a likely site, a square of two hundred feet "on the North Side of the Park, about midway between the President's House and what is termed the *Capitol*," but because of the expense involved he had thought it expedient to await instructions. Liston to Grenville, March 20, 1798, No. 9, F. O. 5 : 22. Nothing came of these offers, in view of the failure of Congress to authorize such grants of land by the commissioners. Same to same, Nov. 28, 1800, No. 46, F. O. 5 : 29.

[28] F. O. 115 : 6.

cumstances, that I cannot too earnestly recommend this Matter to your most serious Attention. You will therefore watch it with the utmost Vigilance, and continue to transmit to General Prescott, as well as to me, every information which you can obtain on this interesting Subject.[29]

GRENVILLE TO LISTON [30]

No. 10.   DOWNING STREET, June 8th, 1798.

Sir,

With respect to the Applications, which, as you mention in your dispatch No. 13, are frequently made to you by distressed British Subjects for a passage to England, free from expence, on board of His Majesty's Packets, I can only observe to you, that as no general rule can be prescribed for your government, You must be left to the exercise of your own discretion, on the Subject, but that there certinly can be no objection to your granting such an indulgence to any Individuals who may appear to you deserving of it.[31]

GRENVILLE TO LISTON [32]

No. 11.   DOWNING STREET, June 8th, 1798.

Sir,

I send you inclosed the Copy of a Dispatch of this date from me to Sir John Temple, respecting the Affair in which Capt[n]. Tucker was concerned; [33] and I have to signify to You His Majesty's pleasure, that You transmit to me all the Documents relative to this transaction, which you can procure, as all the Statements of it which I have

---

[29] Liston was certain, from the letters and proclamations sent by Adet from Paris to French partisans and agents in the United States, that France by no means had abandoned the project of a Canadian insurrection. He had suggested to Prescott the countering of French propaganda in Lower Canada by the distribution of anti-Jacobin literature, "such as the *Bloody Buoy*, written by a person who assumes the name of Peter Porcupine" (i. e., William Cobbett, British immigrant, Federalist editor and pamphleteer at Philadelphia). Liston to Grenville, April 2, 1798, No. 11, F. O. 5 : 22.

[30] F. O. 115 : 6.

[31] Liston received frequent requests for such aid not only from distressed sailors, and an occasional soldier who had served in the West Indian campaigns, but from British artisans and mechanics who had been disappointed in their dreams of rapidly acquiring fame and fortune in America. He wished to be assured that the matter was within his discretion. Liston to Grenville, April 5, 1798, No. 13, F. O. 5 : 22.

[32] F. O. 115 : 6.

[33] Writs had been issued at New York against Captain Tucker for his detention of two American seamen on board the sloop-of-war *Hunter*. He had been threatened with arrest unless he gave bail to a large amount. Unable to procure bail, he was at length permitted to go to sea after he had released the two sailors and given up his commission as security for his personal appearance. Liston had endeavored, in vain, to persuade Sir John Temple, consul general at New York, that he should have interposed his good offices in Tucker's case (as the civil officers at New York had requested of him), and in any similar case. Liston to Grenville, April 11, 1798, No. 16, F. O. 5 : 22. Temple's conduct was so exceptionable that Grenville instructed him to submit a detailed account of the incident. Enclosure with above instruction, Grenville to Temple, June —, 1798, F. O. 115 : 6.

hitherto received, have been too incomplete to enable me to form a definitive opinion on the Subject, altho' at first view there appears to have been neglect of duty on the part of His Majesty's Consul at New York.[34]

GRENVILLE TO LISTON [35]

No. 12.   DOWNING STREET, June 8th, 1798.
Sir,

The Events which have occurred in America since the Date of my last Dispatches to you, and the Departure of the American Ministers from Paris, seem no longer to leave any Doubt as to the Question of Peace or War between the United States and France; For although the Formality of a Declaration of War on either Part, may not take place, the Perseverance of the French Directory in it's Aggressions on the American Commerce, and the Permission which has been granted by the Government of the United States to their Citizens to arm their Vessels for their own Defence will necessarily give rise to individual Acts of Hostility between the respective Citizens of the two Countries, which must ultimately lead to a state of general and open War.

The American Government indeed seems prepared for this Result, and accordingly Mr. King has been instructed to solicit a Permission (which will not be refused him, provided that it be compatible with the Exigencies of the public Service of this Country) to procure a certain Quantity of Naval and warlike Stores here, of which the United States are represented to be in Want. He has also thrown out some Suggestions on the Possibility of establishing a naval Co-operation between His Majesty and the United States.[36]

As it is highly probable that the American Ministers will endeavour to enter into some Discussion with you on this last mentioned Point, and as the present relative Situation of Great Britain and the United

---

[34] Upon receipt of this instruction Liston transmitted the affidavit of the sheriff at New York which established the fact that Temple had declined to interfere in the case of Captain Tucker, a fact which Temple did not deny. Liston said the American government had promised to reprimand severely the commander of the garrison on Governor's Island, for having threatened to fire upon the *Hunter* should Tucker attempt to escape to sea and evade the action brought against him by the civil authorities. Liston to Grenville, Sept. 1, 1798, No. 51, F. O. 5: 22.

[35] F. O. 115: 6.

[36] On June 7, 1798, the day before the above instruction was written, King had reported to Pickering (the italicized parts in cipher) that he had *"always carefully avoided,* particularly upon the Subject *of Convoys, to ask anything which could be considered as a mere favor solicited by us and gratuitously conferred by them."* Alluding to disputes over the jurisdiction of the Spoliation Commission set up at London under Article VII of Jay's Treaty, King further stated: "I have hitherto forborne . . . *to express to you the dissatisfaction and even disgust that I often experience in* our intercourse and connection with this Government. *The indifference, the procrastination and in short the exclusive principles by which they consider almost every question* that is brought before them, *should admonish us, as it has done every* other Nation, *to depend upon ourselves as much, and upon others as little as possible."* *Corres. of Rufus King,* II, 339.

States, affords a Prospect of making some Arrangements which may be reciprocally beneficial to both Countries, inasmuch as His Majesty has several Officers of Reputation who are not actually serving, and has also a considerable Number of Ships, which He is incapable of employing, from the Want of Seamen to man them, while, on the contrary, the United States possesses Seamen without Officers of Experience or Vessels, I have to signify to you His Majesty's Pleasure that in the Event of the American Ministers requiring any Explanations on this Subject, you should assume the Principle of Reciprocity here stated as the Basis of your reasoning. You will observe that if His Majesty should be induced to lend or sell any Ships of War to the United States or should allow any of His officers to enter into their Service, or should appropriate any Part of His Fleet to the joint Protection of the British and American Commerce, His Majesty would expect in Return for these Favours, some Aid and Advantage from the United States, and particularly that the American Government would furnish Him with a certain Number of Seamen; since it could not be expected that the King should divert to the Service of another Power any Portion of those Seamen who are now in His Service, and who are scarcely adequate in Point of Number to the various Services to which they are applied.

With respect to the Apprehension stated in your private Letter of the 27th of April that some Misunderstanding may arise between the Commanders of His Majesty's Ships of War, and those of any American Ships having Merchant-Vessels under their Convoy, with respect to the Right of visiting the latter, I can only remark, that though His Majesty would lament any Circumstance of that Kind which might lead to unfavorable Impressions in America, His Majesty cannot authorize any Departure from the Usages which have been long established on this Subject.[37]

At the Moment of closing this Dispatch I have received Your Letters No. 20–21 and 22.[38] The first and last of these do not require any

---

[37] Although the convoying of American merchantmen by American naval vessels "must almost infallibly lead to hostilities with France, it is at the same time but too likely to give rise to serious difficulties between the commanders of the convoys in question and the captains of His Majesty's Ships of war." Liston to Grenville, Apr. 27, 1798, private, F. O. 5 : 22. In view of the opinion widely entertained in America that vessels under convoy were exempt from being stopped and searched, Liston had stated to members of the Cabinet that "exemption from search is a privilege which has never been, and will not probably ever be, recognized by Great Britain." He had strongly urged them to take care in selecting prudent naval officers for convoy duty in order to prevent "any attempt to bring the question to an issue by acts of violence," and he proposed to write to British commanders in American waters, urging upon them "the exercise of every possible degree of forbearance and civility, to avert any collision that might impair the harmony now subsisting between the two countries." Same to same, May 2, 1798, No. 21, F. O. 5 : 22.

[38] In his dispatch No. 20 Liston had reported on the submission to Congress of the "X, Y, Z," correspondence, and the warlike measures enacted; in his No. 21 he had remarked on American policy; and in his No. 22 he had reported on Spanish-American relations. All three are dated May 2, 1798 and are in F. O. 5 : 22.

particular Answer, but I shall be desirous of learning from you the Nature and Provisions of the Alien and Naturalization Bills, whenever the Measures are brought forward.

With respect to the Contents of No. 21, you will probably have been informed of the very great Impression that has been produced here by the Publication of the American Correspondence, and it is likely that the Sentiments of the Public here may in some Degree contribute to strengthen and maintain those which you represent to be prevalent in America. It appears that as late as the End of last Month, the Directory had not ventured to publish any Thing on the Subject, though these Papers must long before that Time have been known to them; and all the Papers published at Paris have hitherto been obliged to abstain from any Mention of that Business.

I think it probable that the French Government apprized of the Nature of the American Government, and sensible of the Embarrassment which the present State of Affairs throws in the Way of Negotiations for Cooperation and Concert with this Country, will persevere in the Line which they have hitherto adopted, and while they continue to act with the most decided Hostility towards America, will, nevertheless abstain from any positive Declaration of War. It will therefore be for the Government of the United States to consider whether after a certain Period of Forbearance they must not of Necessity put an End to this Difficulty, by proposing to the Congress to declare that War does in fact, actually subsist between them and France.

The Apprehension which you mention as prevailing in America respecting the Conclusion of Peace between Great Britain and France is certainly solid and well-founded. If the Directory shall either be foiled in it's Projects of Invasion in these Kingdoms, or shall finally abandon the Scheme from a Conviction of it's Impracticability, it is by no Means improbable that some Offer of Peace may suddenly be made, and although it certainly would be very difficult for His Majesty's Servants to place any Reliance on the Reality of any sincere Disposition for Peace on the Part of the Directory, yet the Conditions offered, might be such, as they would not think themselves at Liberty to advise His Majesty to reject, if His Majesty continued free from all Engagements to other Powers. And in this Manner, the United States might be left, though against the Wishes and Interests of this Country, yet still unavoidably, exposed to the Resentment of France—Whereas if mutual Engagements of any Sort had previously been contracted between the Two Governments, those would unquestionably be fulfilled with that scrupulous good Faith which has distinguished all the Measures of His Majesty during the whole Course of this Contest, and in the midst of the most disgracefull Conduct on the Part of other Powers.

You may with the fullest Confidence assure the President that any Proposals for Concert and Cooperation will be cordially received here and this, not more on Account of the direct Advantage whatever it may be, which this Country may derive from them, than from the Interest which we feel in contributing to enable the United States to defend themselves against the Prevalence of the Principles of Anarchy which would inevitably follow any Submission on their Part to the Insolence of France; and you may add that if more distinct Proposals are not made from hence, it is owing only to our being unapprized of the Nature and Extent of the mutual Engagements into which the United States would be disposed to enter. But that it is much wished that Mr. King (with whose Conduct His Majesty has every Reason to be satisfied) should be fully instructed on the Subject: And you will further remark that by opening themselves at the same Time to you upon it, the American Ministers will still more facilitate the Conclusion of any Agreement which it may be found expedient to conclude either in America or here.[39]

The Conquest of Louisiana and Florida by the United States, instead of any Cause of Jealousy, would certainly be Matter of Satisfaction to this Government, and in that State of Affairs, it is also easy to see the Advantage which America would derive from seeing Saint Domingo in the Hands of His Majesty rather than of any other European Power.[40]

But independently of these Views of Acquisition, there may be very usefully contracted mutual Engagements of Support in War distinct from every such Consideration. It may perhaps be difficult for either of the Two Governments constituted as they are, to enter into positive Engagements, not, in any Case to make Peace without the Consent of each other. But without going to this Extent, it might be very practicable and the History of Nations affords more

[39] While Liston believed that the greatest object of anxiety at Philadelphia was the possibility that a treaty of peace might be concluded between Britain and France, he had informed Grenville that the American officials "do not think the public sentiments of America yet ripe for a close connection with us." He had held several conversations with President Adams, who "conceived it probable (he says) that the Americans may be 'obliged to battle it with the French for a year or two alone (in which he does not think there would be much harm) and that then Great Britain will help them out of the scrape.'" Liston to Grenville, May 2, 1798, No. 21, F. O. 5 : 22.

[40] In May Liston had reported "that the American Ministers have their views fixed on the conquest of the Floridas and Louisiana for themselves and the acquisition of St. Domingo (if not of the other French Islands) by Great Britain." Liston to Grenville, May 2, 1798, No. 21, F. O. 5 : 22. By June 12, however, Liston noted a change in American opinion : the independence of Santo Domingo and of the larger West Indian islands was now regarded as inevitable, and, by many Americans, as desirable, because of the prospect of eventual American dominion and of immediate commercial intercourse unhampered by the exclusive colonial systems of the European powers. Liston to Grenville, June 12, 1798, No. 33, *Confidential;* Sept. 27, 1798, No. 56, F. O. 5 : 22.

than one Example of it, to engage, that in the Event of Peace being made by the one Party, it shall nevertheless continue to furnish as an Ally to the other, certain limited Advantages and reciprocal Succours so long as such Confederate shall find itself obliged to continue the War.

The Assistance to be derived to this Country from America, must, as I have already stated, consist principally in Seamen, that which Great Britain could give to the United States, might probably extend in such Case, to the Service of a Squadron of Ships more or less numerous in Proportion to the reciprocal Stipulation.

These are the general Grounds on which you will converse with the American Government.[41] With respect to Subjects of Complaint, all that can be done here to avoid them will be carefully attended to, but to do so wholly is hardly possible.

You have judged very right in giving the earliest Intimation to the American Ministers of the Principle uniformly maintained here, as to the Right of visiting Ships, notwithstanding any Convoy, and you will particularly observe to them, that this Right was acknowledged about a Year before the Commencement of the present War, even by France herself.

One of His Majesty's Frigates in the East Indies visited a Ship suspected of carrying Military Stores to Tippo Sultan,[42] though under Convoy of a French Frigate. This being resisted by the latter, an Action ensued, in which the French Captain was, I think, killed and his Ship being wholly disabled struck her Colours; Intelligence being received of this Affair in Europe, Complaint was by the King's Direction immediately made at Paris of the Conduct of the French Officer, as an Act of Hostility against Great Britain, and in the Discussions on this Subject, the Principle on which the British Officer had acted was not only justified and maintained on His Majesty's Part, but was in the End completely acquiesced in by the French Government.

---

[41] In September Liston reported that he had held conversations with President Adams, who had "little or no reserve in talking of political subjects." Adams thought it best for both countries "to enter into mutual engagements, and to concert plans of operation," against France. Yet he was apprehensive that Britain might make peace with France and leave America to carry on the struggle alone. "He said that, for his part . . . he would enter into the engagements in question without scruple and without loss of time," but the nature of the American Constitution made it proper to wait for the approbation of the people. Liston thought that within a few months public opinion would be sufficiently ripened for the laying before the Senate by the President of a convention providing for cooperation with Great Britain. In the meantime, while the President did not wish to go into the details of any stipulation, he was willing to listen to any proposal Britain might make. Liston to Grenville, Sept. 27, 1798, No. 55, F. O. 5 : 22.

[42] Tippoo, Sultan of Mysore. He was later defeated by Richard Wellesley, Governor-General of India from 1797 to 1805.

Immediate Enquiry shall be made respecting the Court of Vice Admiralty at Cape Nicola Mole.[43] I have no Knowledge that any such Court exists there, under any competent Authority. If, as I apprehend will be found to be the Case, it has been irregularly established, Directions will without Delay be given for it's being discontinued, and in that Case, the Government of the United States will be aware that all it's Proceedings will be considered here as Nullities.

GRENVILLE TO LISTON [44]

No. 13.   DOWNING STREET, June 8th, 1798.

Sir,

As I perceive by your Dispatch No. 21 that one of the Grounds of Complaint in America against this Country, is the Act, by which certain countervailing Duties have been imposed upon American Ships, I think it right to inform you that Mr. King attended to the whole progress and to the details of that Act, during the time in which it was under discussion, with the most scrupulous assiduity, and he appeared finally satisfied, that in the form in which it passed, it contained not only a just, but also a liberal Execution of the provisions of the Treaty of Amity, Commerce, and Navigation between His Majesty and the United States.[45]

As I doubt not, that the American Government is fully possessed of Mr. King's opinion on this point, and of the reasoning on which it is founded, it appears unnecessary to give you instructions on this Subject, which could not indeed be fully explained without knowing in detail the objections made in America to the Act.

GRENVILLE TO LISTON [46]

No. 14.   DOWNING STREET, June 8th, 1798.

Sir,

I send you inclosed the Copies of a Letter from Mr. Nepean [47] to Mr. Hammond, and of the dispatch from Earl St. Vincents [48] therein

---

[43] In May Liston had reported that the Adams administration "receive with much concern perpetual complaints" of the unjust seizure of American property by British warships and privateers, and of the harsh sentences pronounced by the British Vice Admiralty Court recently established at Môle Saint Nicholas, Santo Domingo. "I know that these complaints are in general ill founded . . . but the astonishing frequency and scandalous nature of the charges brought against the Judge of Vice Admiralty at the Mole, seems to demand some enquiry." According to reports widely circulated and believed, "no vessel can with certainty escape condemnation at the Mole except by means of downright corruption." Liston to Grenville, May 2, 1798, No. 21, F. O. 5: 22. See also *Corres. of Rufus King*, II. 375, 395.

[44] F. O. 115 : 6.

[45] The act of Parliament of July 4, 1797, as well as the act of July 19, 1797 respecting trade with the British possessions in India, and King's correspondence with Grenville, which were submitted to Congress on Feb. 3, 1798, are printed in *A. S. P., F. R.*, II, 103–115.

[46] F. O. 115 : 6.

[47] Evan Nepean (1751–1822), secretary to the Admiralty from 1795 to 1804.

[48] Formerly Sir John Jervis (1735–1823), created Earl St. Vincent (spelled "St. Vincents" above, and in the enclosures) after his notable victory over the Spanish fleet, Feb. 14, 1797, off Cape St. Vincent.

referred to: I have to signify to you His Majesty's pleasure, that you take the earliest opportunity to represent these particulars to the American Ministers, and to express His Majesty's just Expectation that Mr. Pintard [49] will be immediately removed from a Situation the Privileges of which he so much abuses, and that he may undergo such further censure and punishment, as by the Laws of the United States may be inflicted on a Person guilty of so manifest a violation of his duty, and so gross a Breach of the Laws of Nations.

GRENVILLE TO LISTON [50]

No. 15.   DOWNING STREET, June 8, 1798.

Sir,

I send You inclosed, for Your Information, the Copy of a Dispatch from the Duke of Portland to Mr. President Russell, and I have to signify to You His Majesty's Pleasure that You make Your Language conformable to the Suggestions therein contained, in any future Communications which You may have with Captain Brandt.[51]

GRENVILLE TO LISTON [52]

No. 16.   DOWNING STREET, Aug^st. 6, 1798.

Sir,

Your several Dispatches to No. 35 inclusive have been received and laid before the King.

Since the Date of my last Dispatches to You some Difference of Opinion has arisen between His Majesty's Commissioners and those appointed by the American Government under the 7th Article of the Treaty between His Majesty and the United States with respect to the Competency of their Board to decide Cases that were pending in the Court of Appeals, and to pass awards binding on His Majesty's Government in such Cases without waiting for the Sentence of the

---

[49] Liston made representations, based upon the enclosures (St. Vincent to Nepean, May 18, 1798, and Nepean to Grenville, June 8, 1798), to the effect that Mr. Pintard, the American consul for the Island of Madeira, "had made a most improper use of the advantages of his situation, to convey the property of the King's enemies in safety to Old Spain, under the sanction of the American Flag." Liston to Pickering, Oct. 6, 1798, Notes from British Legation, 2. The American government was apparently disposed to dismiss Pintard, reported Liston to Grenville, from Kingston, N. J., Nov. 7, 1798, F. O. 5 : 22.

[50] F. O. 115 : 6.

[51] An abstract of Portland's instruction to Russell of June 7, 1798, urging him to be vigilant in respect to Joseph Brant and his Indians, is printed in Brymner, ed., *Rpt. on Canadian Archives, 1891*, Upper Canada, p. 96. Reporting in August on French and Spanish schemes to conquer Canada and to incite hostility among the Indians against the United States, Liston stated that while of late he had not heard directly from Brant, accounts in the American press made it appear that he was continuing his intrigues. It was possible, however, that Brant had inspired such reports in order to enhance his consequence in British eyes. Liston to Grenville, Aug. 12, 1798, No. 45, F. O. 5 : 22.

[52] F. O. 115 : 6.

Court.—Although the Discussions which took place between His Majesty's Commissioners and those of the United States with regard to this Difference were conducted with Moderation on both Sides; yet as during their Continuance, the Proceedings of the Board were necessarily suspended, His Majesty was pleased on the 27th of last Month to transmit an Instruction to His Commissioners of which I inclose a Copy for Your Information and which I have the Satisfaction to inform You has produced the desired Effect of preventing any further Difficulties upon this Subject.

It is material that I should remark to You for Your Information and Guidance in Case any similar Discussion should arise in the Execution of the 6th Article that the Construction of the Treaty contended for by the King's Government was: that the Commissioners were precluded from entering on the Consideration of any Cases pending in the ordinary *Course* of Justice—but that neither the Principle nor the particular Points urged, would go to the Extent of excluding them from the Consideration of such Cases when any extraordinary, and still more where any proposed Delay, could be shewn to be interposed with the View of obstructing the Claimant in obtaining Redress in the ordinary Course of Justice.[53]

GRENVILLE TO LISTON [54]

No. 17.   DOWNING STREET, Oct. 20, 1798.
Sir,

Since the date of my last dispatch, Your dispatches No. 40, 41, 42, 43 have been received, and laid before the King, but those from No. 36 to No. 39 both inclusive, are yet missing.

I have the Satisfaction to inform You that, in consequence of the proposition that was made to you by Mr. Pickering (as stated in your dispatch No. 35) on the subject of purchasing or borrowing, for the use of the United States, certain Iron Guns, now lying in the Kings Stores at Halifax,[55] and of an application to the same effect which I have since received from Mr. King, His Majesty has been graciously pleased to consent to this request of the American Government, on condition that the Cannon shall be returned into His Majesty's Stores at Halifax, whenever His Majesty shall think proper to require them.

---

[53] For this dispute and for the arrangement as to judicial remedies see Moore, *Int. Adjud.,* IV, 95–102.

[54] F. O. 115 : 6.

[55] Liston had reported a singular request made of him by Secretary Pickering respecting certain cannons taken from the French man-of-war *Foudroyant* during the French and Indian War and given to the Province of South Carolina by George II, which had been carried off to Halifax when the British evacuated Charleston during the Revolution. "Mr. Pickering proposed, in the present perilous state of the coasts of the United States, and in the present correspondence of interests between Great Britain and America, either to *beg* or *borrow* or *buy* these guns, to be once more transported to Charleston." Liston to Grenville, June 12, 1798, No. 35, F. O. 5 : 22.

I inclose to you the Copies of a letter which I have received from the Duke of Portland upon this subject, and of the Instructions that have been sent by His Majesty's Command to the Lieutenant Governor of Nova Scotia, which it is His Majesty's pleasure that you should communicate to the American Ministers: not doubting that they will perceive in the Alacrity with which His Majesty has Complied with the request of their Government an additional proof of His Majesty's desire to cement the good understanding which so happily subsists between the two Countries, and of his Sollicitude to assist the United States in the great contest in which they appear likely to be engaged against the Enemy, not only of Great Britain, and the United States, but of all Civilized Society.

You will perceive from the Duke of Portland's dispatch to Lieutenant Governor Wentworth, that that Gentleman is instructed to deliver the Cannon to any person who may be properly authorized by the American Government to receive them.[56]

GRENVILLE TO LISTON [57]

No. 18.   DOWNING STREET, Oct. 20, 1798.
Sir,

I send you inclosed the Copy of a Letter from Mr. Nepean to Mr. Hammond relative to an American Vessel which is supposed to be on its Voyage from La Guaira with fictitious documents: and I have to signify to you His Majesty's pleasure that in the Event of the Arrival of this Vessel in an American Port, You should take such Measures as may appear to you best adapted to defeat the Success of a Fraud of this Nature, which must in its Consequences, if frequently repeated, be so injurious to the Interests of His Majesty's Subjects, and to the Commerce of the Fair Traders in the United States.[58]

GRENVILLE TO LISTON [59]

No. 19.   DOWNING STREET, Nov. 13th, 1798.
Sir,

I send you inclosed the Copy of a letter which I have received from His Royal Highness the Commander in Chief of His Majesty's Forces, on the Subject of the Application that was made to you, as

---

[56] In November of 1798 twenty-five pieces of cannon and eighteen hundred and seventy shot were delivered at Halifax to an agent for the United States by Lieut. Gov. Sir John Wentworth. Wentworth to Liston, Nov. 23, 1798, Nova Scotia Archives, vol. 52.
[57] F. O. 115 : 6.
[58] According to the enclosure, Nepean to Hammond, Sept. 19, 1798, it appeared from "some Spanish Papers lately intercepted, that a Vessel called the *Roanoke*, Ebenezer Payne Master, has been freighted at La Guaira with a cargo of Merchandise, Spanish Property, for Cadiz, but furnished nevertheless at the former Port with fictitious documents describing the Vessel and Cargo as belonging to him the said Ebenezer Payne, in order more effectually to elude the Scrutiny of the British Cruissers. . . ."
[59] F. O. 115 : 6.

stated in your dispatch No. 50, by some Officers on the British Half Pay, residing within the United States, and I have to signify to you His Majesty's Pleasure, that You take an early opportunity of Communicating the Substance of His Royal Highness's letter to the Officers in Question.[60]

GRENVILLE TO LISTON [61]

No. 20.   DOWNING STREET, Dec. 8th, 1798.

Sir,

Your several Dispatches to No. 65 inclusive have been received and laid before the King.

I had entertained Hopes that long before the Date of those Dispatches the Course of the Disputes between America and France would have led to a State of open Hostility between them, and that the People of the United States would have perceived in the temporizing Policy, which has been recently observed toward them by France, nothing more than an Attempt to promote Dissentions between them and their own Government, and a Desire to procrastinate a Rupture until France should be relieved from the Apprehension of a Renewal of Hostilities against Her by the Powers on the Continent. It was therefore with much Concern that I learnt from your last Dispatches, that the same Doubts and Hesitation, which have existed on this Point, still continue, and that the Members of the American Government have been unable to communicate to their Citizens a due Portion of their own Energy and Decision.[62]

In this State of Uncertainty His Majesty has not thought it necessary that I should add any other Instructions to those contained in my Dispatch No. 12 (which were transmitted at a Moment when the great Question of Peace or War seemed as likely to be speedily determined as it does at present) than to desire You to persevere in the Language which You have held upon them, and which has been perfectly proper, and to assure the American Government, that in the Event of a War with France, His Majesty will be at all Times disposed to enter into any Concert of Measures for mutual Defense and

---

[60] In his dispatch No. 50 of Aug. 31, 1798, F. O. 5 : 22, Liston had reported that a number of retired British officers resident in the United States wished to offer their services to the American government in the quasi war against France. In his letter to Grenville of Oct. 26, 1798, copy enclosed, Frederick, Duke of York, stated that he could see no objection to such officers "entering into the service of that Government against the Common Enemy, at the same time considering themselves liable, as they would have been before, to be called upon whenever His Majesty may have occasion for their Services."

[61] F. O. 115 : 6.

[62] Liston had reported that the administration was disappointed at the failure of France to force the issue of war ; apprehensive of the difficulties in effectuating the "natural and reasonable" proposal by which the services of American seamen would be exchanged for the aid of British warships ; chagrined at the success of the Jeffersonians in swinging public opinion to the view that the administration, if it so desired, could easily procure peace with France. Liston to Grenville, Nov. 7, 1798, Nos. 63 and 64, F. O. 5 : 22.

Security, which may be founded either on those Instructions, or on any other Principles that may be equally beneficial to both Countries. But you will of course not enter into any specific or direct Engagements on those Subjects without more particular Instructions from His Majesty.

Although the unfounded Jealousy, which appears to have prevailed in America, of a Desire on the part of this Government to bind her in a permanent System of Alliance for general Purposes, has been confuted by Mr. Adams; it is nevertheless the King's Pleasure that in order to prevent any farther Misconstructions, You should, whenever it may be necessary, expressly disclaim any such Intention in this Government as that which has been imputed to it, or any other Motive for the Concert of Measures which You are authorized to propose, than a Sense of the reciprocal Benefit which would arise from Co-operation to both Countries, in the Case of their being engaged in War with a common Enemy.

GRENVILLE TO LISTON [63]

No. 21.   DOWNING STREET, Dec. 8th, 1798.
Sir,

No other Account of the Decision which has been given by the Commissioners appointed to determine the River St. Croix intended by the Treaty of Peace having been received in this Country, than that which is contained in Your Dispatch No. 61, it is as yet impossible for His Majesty's Government to form any Opinion with respect to the Benefits or Disadvantages resulting to this Country from that Decision. In the meantime, I have the Satisfaction to inform you that His Majesty is fully persuaded that the Advice which you gave to Mr. Chipman, was dictated by a Persuasion that the Interests of this Country would be best promoted by acceding to the Proposal of the Agent for the United States.[64]

His Majesty is pleased to authorize You to draw Bills on the Treasury for the Sums necessary for paying to Judge Benson,[65] the Moiety of his Salary as third Commissioner. You will draw these Bills payable at not less than Sixty Days after Sight and send Advice thereof both to the Lords Commissioners of the Treasury and to me by the first Opportunity.

---

[63] F. O. 115 : 6.

[64] Liston had advised Chipman, the British agent, to accept the Chiputnaticook as the upper St. Croix River. Liston to Grenville, Nov. 6, 1798, No. 61, F. O. 5 : 22. See also Moore, *Int. Adjud.*, II, 368–374; and the declaration of the commissioners, signed at Providence, Oct. 25, 1798, as to the course of the St. Croix river, in Miller, *Treaties*, II, 430–431.

[65] Egbert Benson (1746–1833), a justice of the Supreme Court of New York from 1794 to 1801. His salary as commissioner was paid in equal parts by the United States and Great Britain.

GRENVILLE TO LISTON [66]

No. 22.   DOWNING STREET, Dec. 8th, 1798.

Sir,

I have the Satisfaction to inform You that His Majesty has been graciously pleased entirely to approve of the Vigilance which you have manifested on the Subject of the Views and Proceedings of France in regard to the Canadas, and of the Measures, (which as stated in Your Dispatch No. 45,) you had taken for counteracting them.[67]

As there is no Doubt that the Success of these Proceedings on the Part of the Enemy, and the Attempts of his Emissaries to prevail on the Indians to take a part in them must be ultimately injurious to the United States; I have to signify to You His Majesty's Pleasure that you propose to the American Ministers to concert such Measures with you and the Governor General of His Majesty's Provinces in North America as may tend by mutual Assistance and Information to facilitate the Endeavours of both Governments to discover any French Spies or Emissaries who may be employed either in the Canadas or in the United States;—and to engage the Indians residing on both Sides of the Treaty Line to detain and give up any such Spies or Emissaries who may appear among them with a Design to seduce and to make them Parties to any Proceedings injurious to the Interests of His Majesty's Canadian Provinces or to those of the United States. Such a System of vigilant Cooperation on the Part of both Governments could not fail to produce the happiest Effects in frustrating the Designs of the French against their respective Tranquillity and Security.

GRENVILLE TO LISTON [68]

No. 23.   DOWNING STREET, December 11th, 1798.

Sir,

As it is possible that some Misconstruction may be entertained in America respecting the Circumstances which attended the Evacuation of St Domingo by His Majesty's Forces under the Command of General Maitland [69] and the Agreement entered into by that Officer with

---

[66] F. O. 115 : 6.

[67] Liston had reported that the French plans, though suspended, had not been given up; that in conjunction with Secretary Pickering he had attempted to gain information from the French Consul and the Spanish Minister at Philadelphia through Silas Hathaway of Vermont, who posed as a pro-French conspirator; and that he had employed a French royalist to win the confidence of the French agents and their American sympathizers on the northern frontier and in Canada. Liston to Grenville, Aug. 12, 1798, No. 45, F. O. 5 : 22.

[68] F. O. 115 : 6.

[69] Colonel Thomas Maitland (1759?-1824), second son of James Maitland, the seventh Earl of Lauderdale; he was at this time Brigadier General in command of the British forces in Santo Domingo.

the Negro Chief Toussaint,[70] I send you inclosed Copies of that Agreement and of a Letter from Mr. Dundas to Mr. King relative to the Causes which gave Rise to it:[71] And I have to signify to you His Majesty's Pleasure that in any Conversations which you may have on the Subject of the Transactions in Question you confine yourself strictly to the Explanations of them that is contained in these Papers which you will remark are both of them to be considered as being of a very secret Nature.

GRENVILLE TO LISTON [72]

No. 24.   DOWNING STREET, Dec. 15, 1798.

Sir,

I send you inclosed for your information, Copy of a dispatch which by His Majesty's command I have transmitted to Sir John Temple, respecting his conduct on the subject of the arrest of Captain Tucker of His Majesty's Ship Hunter.[73]

---

[70] François Dominique Toussaint, "Louverture" (c. 1743–1803), the most influential Negro general in Santo Domingo.

[71] On April 30, 1798 Maitland had entered into an armistice with Toussaint, out of which had come the secret treaty of August 31, 1798. By it both parties agreed to a policy of non-interference, political and military, in their respective territories, and Maitland promised to send Toussaint certain supplies which were to be paid for in colonial produce. Rufus King was apprehensive that the secret convention gave Great Britain exclusive trade advantages, and that privateers from Toussaint's dominions might attack American commerce. He was assured by Dundas, who outlined the Maitland-Toussaint treaty, that every consideration would be given to American wishes and suggestions. For a detailed and scholarly account of these proceedings, see Charles Callan Tansill, *The United States and Santo Domingo, 1798–1873*, pp. 26–29, 36–37.

[72] F. O. 115 : 6.

[73] See Grenville to Liston, June 8, 1798, No. 11, *supra*. In his instruction to Temple of Dec. —, 1798, copy enclosed, Grenville reprimanded him for not having gone to the aid of Captain Tucker, and for the tone of his correspondence with Liston. In the meantime, Temple had died at New York on Nov. 17, 1798. Liston to Grenville, Nov. 18, 1798, No. 67, F. O. 5 : 22.

INSTRUCTIONS OF 1799

GRENVILLE TO LISTON [1]

No. 1.   DOWNING STREET, Jan. 19th, 1799.

Sir,

Since the date of my last dispatches your No. 67 has been received and laid before the King.

From information received from Lieutenant Governor Wentworth, it appears that the Cannon and Shot which the American Government has requested to be furnished from His Majesty's Magazines at Halifax by way of Loan to the United States, had been delivered by Brigadier General Murray to the American Officers appointed to receive them: and that the Secretary of War of the United States had transmitted to you an Engagement to return the Cannon and Shot abovementioned to any of His Majesty's American Possessions whenever they might be redemanded.

Although the presenting and accepting of the Conditions contained in that Engagement were perfectly proper and necessary, in order to place the transaction unequivocally on its true Principle, and to prevent the possibility of any misconstruction, or misinterpretation of it hereafter: Yet, as that End has been completely answered by the form of the Paper which has been delivered to you, His Majesty has been pleased as a Testimony of Friendship towards the United States, to direct that you should return that Engagement to the American Government, accompanied by a letter in which you will state that you have been authorised by His Majesty to desire that the same may be cancelled.[2]

GRENVILLE TO LISTON [3]

No. 2.   DOWNING STREET, Jan. 19th, 1799.

Sir,

Since the date of my dispatch No. 21 of last year, I have received from Mr. Barclay a copy of the decision of the Commissioners appointed to ascertain the true River St. Croix, intended by the Treaty

---

[1] F. O. 115 : 7.
[2] See Grenville to Liston, Oct. 20, 1798, No. 17, *supra;* and *Corres. of Rufus King,* III, 10–11.
[3] F. O. 115 : 7.

of Peace: but as this cannot be considered as an official communication, it will be proper to defer, until the receipt of the Instrument itself, any direction to you to make a formal notification to the American Government of the King's acceptance of this decision as an act final and conclusive according to the terms of the 5th Article of the Treaty of Amity, Commerce, and navigation between His Majesty and the United States.[4]

You are already apprised by my letter No. 20, that it is the King's intention so to consider it, whenever it shall be regularly received here.

GRENVILLE TO LISTON [5]

No. 3.   DOWNING STREET, Jan. 19th, 1799.
Sir,

Since the Date of my last Dispatch to you I have had repeated Communications with Mr. King, on the Subject of the Arrangements to be made respecting St. Domingo.[6] Much and, as I think, not unreasonable apprehension was expressed by him of the Effect which might be produced in the United States, if there appeared on the Part of this Government an Intention to monopolize the Intercourse and Supply of that Island in its present Situation: and also as to the Inconvenience which might arise to both Countries from contending and clashing Interests betwen them in this respect.

In the course of these Discussions the most unquestionable Proofs have been given to that Gentleman of the Liberality of Sentiment with which this great Subject is viewed by His Majesty: as one which in every Point of Consideration involves Interests of infinitely higher Importance than those of a mere commercial Monopoly.

But those Sentiments, liberal as they are, and favourable to the commercial Interests of the United States (as connected with those of Great Britain) must in this Instance be made subordinate to Considerations of a higher nature. In looking at the present State of St. Domingo, and at the Shape which, it may probably assume under the Direction of an internal military Force commanded by a Person of Toussaint's Description, the first of all Objects of Attention is the Security both of our West India Colonies, and of the Southern States of America, from the Effect which such circumstances may produce on the Slaves, who form the great Mass of Population there. To hope that this Evil should be wholly guarded against would be a very vain Delusion, but it's Influence will at least be greatly checked if it

---

[4] See Barclay to Grenville, Nov. 10, 1798, in G. L. Rives, ed., *Selections from the Correspondence of Thomas Barclay*, pp. 90–94.
[5] F. O. 115 : 7.
[6] See *Corres. of Rufus King*, II, 499–505, 511–512, 524–525, and ff. ; and Tansill, *U. S. and Santo Domingo*, pp. 40–42.

shall be found possible effectually to prevent Emissaries being sent to St. Domingo into those Colonies and Provinces. So long as any Channel is open thro' which this may be done, France will unquestionably avail herself of it, and she cannot be at a Loss to find in St. Domingo Instruments but too well adapted for that Purpose. An unrestrained Freedom of Commercial Intercourse from St. Domingo, either with our Colonies or with the United States, and still more with both, would infallibly open this Source of Ruin, the Course of which would rapidly extend from the one to the other. The Mode of restraining the Intercourse, the Checks to be interposed and the Regulations to be applied in order to make those Checks effectual, are however Points of very great Difficulty and the more so as we are not now to give Laws to a Country over which we can exercise either jointly or separately any authority, but must endeavour to establish by Negotiation those Points which we think essential to our Security.

The inclosed Minute contains a Sketch of such a Plan [7] as appears to His Majesty's Servants the best calculated for that Purpose,—supposing that it's Execution should be found on Trial not to be attended with insurmountable Difficulties. And there are it is conceived Grounds of very evident and pressing Interest which may be urged to Toussaint as Motives for obtaining his Consent.

But as the necessity of some present arrangement with him does not admit of the delay attending the Discussion and Establishment of such a System, His Majesty has been pleased to direct that Col. Harcourt shall proceed immediately to St. Domingo to ratify and carry into Execution the Article concluded with Col! Maitland as a temporary System only, and with an express Reserve of such Measures as shall be taken in Concert respecting the Commerce of the United States. And Col! Maitland will without Delay proceed in a Frigate to the United States in order to convey to You such detailed Information as may enable You, with his Assistance, to discuss this Matter, under all it's bearings and to conclude with the American Government such Arrangement respecting it as may be practicable and as much as possible conformable to the Principles of the inclosed Minute.

From the United States, Col! Maitland will proceed to St. Domingo and will I conclude be accompanied by some Person authorized by the American Government to carry into execution the agreement

---

[7] According to this plan, an outline of which was sent to Rufus King (see note immediately preceding), all trade with territory under Toussaint's control was to be confined to a single port of entry, Port-au-Prince, and was to be carried on by a joint British-American company, to be formed by the governments of Great Britain and the United States. This company was to be required to furnish no manufactures but from British territories, and no produce or live stock but from the United States.

that may be formed there, either in conformity to the Stipulations of the inclosed Minute, or of any other arrangement by which the object of Gen¹ Maitland's Instructions may be equally accomplished. I shall write to you more particularly by Col¹ Maitland.

GRENVILLE TO LISTON [8]

No. 4.   DOWNING STREET, Jan. 19, 1799.
Sir,

The King having been pleased to appoint Thomas Barclay Esq. to be His Majesty's Consul General for the Eastern States of America, I have to signify to you His Majesty's pleasure that you communicate Mr. Barclay's Appointment to the American Government, and that you procure for him the usual Exequatur to enable him to enter upon the Duties of his Office. You will also forward to Mr. Barclay the inclosed letter, announcing to him his Appointment, by the first opportunity that may occur of sending it to Nova Scotia.

GRENVILLE TO LISTON [9]

No. 5.   DOWNING STREET, Jan. 25th, 1799.
Sir,

In pursuance of the intimation contained in my dispatch No. 3, Colonel Maitland (who will deliver to You this letter) has been directed to proceed to Philadelphia for the purpose of forming with the Government of the United States, some arrangement as to the mode of carrying on the commercial intercourse of Great Britain and the United States with the parts of St. Domingo which are under the authority of General Toüssaint.

Colonel Maitland's instructions,[10] which he will communicate to you, are so ample and detailed, that it is unnecessary for me to give you any other directions respecting them than to signify to You His Majesty's pleasure that you are to consider those instructions as the rule of your conduct in the negotiations on the subject of them, into which, in conjunction with Colonel Maitland you are authorized to enter with the American Ministers.

---

[8] F. O. 115 : 7.

[9] F. O. 115 : 7.

[10] The instructions to Col. Thomas Maitland, of Jan. 26, 1799; the negotiations of Maitland and Liston with Secretary Pickering respecting regulations to be proposed to Toussaint; and the negotiations with Toussaint of Maitland and of Edward Stevens, the American Consul General in Santo Domingo, which resulted in agreements (May 22, June 13, 1799) favorable to British and American commerce, are exhaustively treated in Tansill, *U. S. and Santo Domingo*, chap. ii, "The Maitland Mission," pp. 43–69.

GRENVILLE TO LISTON [11]

No. 6.   DOWNING STREET, March 23ᵈ. 1799.

Sir,

Your several dispatches to No. 10 inclusive have been received and laid before the King. The only point contained in them on which the King has thought it necessary that I should send you instructions by this mail, is the Complaint which has been made by the American Government (as stated in your dispatch No. 3) of the conduct of Captⁿ. Loring of His Majesty's Ship Carnatic. The inclosed Copy of a note which I have presented to Mr. King, will explain to you the Sentiments of His Majesty's Government upon this subject: and the assurances which Mr. King has received that a strict enquiry will be instituted respecting Captain Loring's conduct on the occasion in question will, it is presumable, be satisfactory to the American Ministers.[12]

I have the satisfaction to inform you that his Majesty has been graciously pleased entirely to approve of the manner in which you have availed yourself of this circumstance, to bring forward the Additional Article relative to the mutual delivery of deserters from the Military [and] Naval Service[s] of the two Countries, which you were instructed in the year 1797 to propose to the government of the United States:[13] And I have to signify to you his Majesty's pleasure that you should use your utmost endeavours to prevail upon the American Secretary of State to accede to this Stipulation, as being not only equitable in itself, but also as affording the greatest probability of preventing any future Collision on a subject which has been, and seems likely to be, the cause of much inconvenience and misunderstanding both in Great Britain and the United States.[14]

By the next Mail I shall transmit to you some observations respecting the present state of the Islands in the Bay of Fundy, mentioned in one of your dispatches last received.[15]

---

[11] F. O. 115 : 7.

[12] On Nov. 17, 1798, H. M. S. *Carnatic*, commanded by Capt. John Loring (an American Loyalist during the Revolution), in company with two other British ships of the line and two frigates had stopped on the high seas the American sloop of war *Baltimore*, Capt. Phillips, which was convoying several American merchantmen to Havana, and had impressed fifty-five seamen, of which number fifty were afterwards given up. For his "pusilanimous conduct, so disgraceful to himself and unworthy an officer in the American Navy" (as Pickering termed it), Capt. Phillips of the *Baltimore* was dismissed from the service. Grenville's note, of March 21, 1799, was in reply to King's representations to him of March 11, 1799 ; both notes are printed in *Corres. of Rufus King*, II, 553–554, 585–586. See also Liston to Grenville, Jan. 16, 1799, No. 3, F. O. 5 : 22.

[13] See note 28, p. 136, note 3, p. 144, *supra.*

[14] At the express order of President Adams, Rufus King at London had also renewed the discussions relative to an additional article. His letter to Grenville of Oct. 7, 1799 summarized the situation, and pointed out how vitally important to a good understanding between the two countries was an arrangement in regard to impressment. *Corres. of Rufus King*, III, 115–121. King's negotiations were unsuccessful.

[15] The St. Croix commission had defined the true St. Croix River from mouth to source, but yet to be determined was the boundary line eastward from the mouth of the river through the islands in the Bay of Fundy. See Liston to Grenville, Dec. 31, 1798, No. 71, F. O. 5 : 22.

GRENVILLE TO LISTON [16]

No. 7.   DOWNING STREET, March 23ᵈ, 1799.

Sir,

I send You inclosed for Your Information the Copy of a Letter with its Inclosure from Mr. Nepean to Mr. Hammond, which as it relates to a Transaction that has been misrepresented in the Newspapers of this Country, it is desirable it should be stated fairly in America.[17]

GRENVILLE TO LISTON [18]

No. 8.   DOWNING STREET, March 23ᵈ, 1799.

Sir,

In Answer to Your Dispatch No. 1 relative to the Payment of Mr. Benson's Salary as the Third Commissioner for deciding the true Position of the River St. Croix, I think it right to refer You to my Dispatch No. 21 of last Year, and to signify to You His Majesty's Pleasure that You pay the whole Sum due to Mr. Benson in the Manner therein prescribed.

GRENVILLE TO LISTON [19]

No. 9.   DOWNING STREET, April 19th, 1799.

Sir,

I have no dispatches from you to acknowledge since the date of my last.

In addition to what I have stated to you in my dispatch No. 6 respecting the complaint made by the American Government of the conduct of Captain Loring of His Majesty's Ship Carnatic, I now transmit to you the Copy of a letter from Mr. Nepean to Mr. Hammond with its inclosure upon the same subject. You will however observe that you are not to make any official use of these papers, as they are sent to you solely for your own information.[20]

---

[16] F. O. 115 : 7.

[17] The enclosures, Nepean to Hammond, Feb. 12, 1799, and Captain Southeron of H. M. S. *Latona* to Nepean, Feb. 8, 1799, concerned the accidental attack by the *Latona* (which was flying Spanish colors) upon the American ship *Aurora*, which had at first flown the French flag and then (too late to avoid a cannonading from the *Latona*) the American flag.

[18] F. O. 115 : 6.

[19] F. O. 115 : 7.

[20] In his letter to Under Secretary Hammond of April 2, 1799 Nepean stated that the practice of impressing British subjects from foreign ships of war "has not recently prevailed." Nepean enclosed a copy of his letter to Admiral Sir Hyde Parker of April 2, 1799 in which Parker was instructed to make a minute inquiry into the impressments from the U. S. S. *Baltimore* by Captain Loring of the *Carnatic*, and, should he find Loring's actions to have been as represented by the American Minister, Mr. King, to send Loring to England and to reprimand severely the petty officers of the *Carnatic* for their improper behavior.

GRENVILLE TO LISTON [21]

No. 10.   DOWNING STREET, April 19th, 1799.

Sir,

It was my Intention as I stated to you in my Dispatch No. 6, to have transmitted to you by this Mail some Observations on the State of the Islands in the Bay of Fundy to which the President of the United States adverted in his Speech at the Opening of the last session of Congress; [22] but as the Duke of Portland has, by the King's Command, written very fully to the Lieutenant Governors of Nova Scotia and New Brunswick on this Point, it is merely necessary for me at present to signify to You His Majesty's Pleasure, that in any incidental Conversation which You may have with the American Ministers respecting it, You will untill You receive farther Instructions from me upon the subject, regulate Your Language by such Communications as you may receive from Sir John Wentworth and General Carleton.

GRENVILLE TO LISTON [23]

No. 11.   DOWNING STREET, July 22, 1799.

Sir,

Your several Dispatches to No. 35 inclusive, have been received and laid before the King.

Ever since the receipt of your Dispatch No. 18 I have been in constant expectation of learning some further details relative to the proceedings of the Commissioners appointed under the sixth Article of the Treaty with the United States, and to the representations which you will doubtless have thought it your duty to make to that Government on the Subject, if the resolution of the seceding Commissioners shall have been persisted in, but to my great disappointment and surprize I have not received from you any information whatever subsequent to the Date of the Dispatch above mentioned on this most interesting and important Subject.[24]

---

[21] F. O. 115 : 7.

[22] In his message of Dec. 8, 1798 President Adams announced the settlement of the controversy as to the source and mouth of the St. Croix River, and noted that a subordinate question, the boundary from the mouth of the river to the open sea, was yet to be settled. Although Adams thought that this was not a difficult matter, the differences as to the boundary channel proved to be as irritating and as embittering as those pertaining to the river St. Croix. James D. Richardson, ed., *Messages and Papers of the Presidents*, I, 264.

[23] F. O. 115 : 7.

[24] In his dispatch No. 18 Liston had reported that much wrangling had taken place between the two American and the three British commissioners over such questions as the payment of British debts in depreciated currency, interest on debts during the war, and, especially, the claims of Loyalists against whom acts of attainder had been passed. After

In this state of doubt and uncertainty as to any favourable turn which since the date of your Dispatch this business has taken or may be likely to take in America, it is not in my power to recive the King's pleasure on the Instructions necessary to be given for the regulation of your conduct and that of the Commissioners appointed by His Majesty. Indeed I cannot but hope that notwithstanding the disposition which the American Commissioners have manifested to defeat by their absence the object of any award being made in favour of British Subjects, some description at least of claims may have been found in which they may have been willing to concur with the majority of the Board in a favourable decision. If however the American Commissioners should, contrary to my expectation, persist in seceding on every question of which the result may be favourable to the British Claimant, it will then be necessary that the whole matter should again be brought under the review of His Majesty's Government, in order to secure to His Subjects by an arrangement with that of the United States, that justice which it was the object of the article in question to obtain for them.

With a view to this last contingency, and as a measure of precaution, the King has been pleased to direct that the Commissioners appointed by His Majesty for the purposes specified in the seventh article, should suspend their attendance at the Board until the impediments which have obstructed the progress of the Commission in America shall be removed. I inclose a Copy of this Instruction for your information: and I have to signify to you His Majesty's pleasure that in any conversation respecting it which you may have with the American Ministers, you will express in the strongest Terms His Majesty's determination to fulfill on His part with punctuality and good faith the Engagements which He has contracted, but that His Majesty in Justice to His own Subjects cannot, in addition to the very large Sums which have been already paid to American claimants in virtue of Awards made by the Board of Commissioners sitting in this Country continue to sanction any farther Awards of this nature until the British Claimants soliciting redress under the sixth Article of the Treaty shall experience a similarly equitable treatment in the United States.

It was my intention to have adverted in this Dispatch to the Instructions to Dr. Stevens the American Agent and Consul General

having on occasion frustrated the attempts of the British majority to lay down certain ruling principles, the American minority had now expressed a determination to secede from the board permanently. Liston later reported that the American commissioners had absented themselves and brought about a total cessation of the commission's functions. Liston to Grenville, March 9, 1799, No. 18, Aug. 4, 1799, No. 50, Sept. 30, 1799, No. 53, F. O. 5 : 25. For the issues involved, and for the correspondence and negotiations leading to the convention of Jan. 8, 1802, by which the vexatious British Debts question was settled by the payment of a lump sum of £600,000, see *A. S. P., F. R.*, II, 382–428 ; Moore, *Int. Adjud.*, III ; *Corres. of Rufus King*, III, IV.

at St. Domingo,[25] which were inclosed in your No. 32 and which appear liable to some objections.[26]   But as I understand that Gen.[1] Maitland is daily expected, I shall defer until his return transmitting to you any observations upon the Subject.

GRENVILLE TO LISTON [27]

No. 12.   DOWNING STREET, August 13th, 1799.

Sir,

I send you inclosed for your information the Copy of a Letter which I have received from His Grace the Duke of Portland, and I have to signify to you His Majesty's Pleasure that you take such Measures as may appear to you the most expedient for procuring the Block Houses therein mentioned on the most reasonable Terms, and for conveying to Jamaica in the most secure and expeditious Manner.[28]

GRENVILLE TO LISTON [29]

No. 13.   DOWNING STREET, Oct[r] 21th, 1799.

Sir,

No Dispatches from you having reached me of a later date than the 2d of Aug., I have been induced to detain the Mail of the present Month until this Day, under the Expectation of receiving from you some farther details on the subject of the important question which has arisen in America respecting the proceedings of the Board of Commissioners appointed under the sixth article of the Treaty of 1794. But as the Packet which has been daily expected from America has not yet arrived, and more especially as Mr. King has informed me that he expects to receive by that conveyance some communication to be made here from His Government respecting the Points in dispute: I must defer until the arrival of the

---

[25] Little is known of Dr. Edward Stevens' early life, other than that he was closely related to Alexander Hamilton, and, like Hamilton, was born in the West Indies. See J. Franklin Jameson, ed., "Letters of Toussaint Louverture and of Edward Stevens, 1798–1800," *Amer. Hist. Rev.,* XVI (Oct., 1910), 64–101.

[26] Before the arrival of Colonel Maitland at Philadelphia on April 2, 1799, Stevens, the American Consul General in Santo Domingo, had left for his post with instructions to obtain commercial concessions from General Toussaint, and a pledge that attacks upon American shipping in waters adjacent to ports controlled by Toussaint should cease. When Maitland embarked for Santo Domingo on April 23, 1799, he carried with him fresh instructions to Stevens from Secretary Pickering, in which Pickering explained the purport of the agreement he had reached with Maitland and Liston for joint negotiations with Toussaint. See note 10, p. 171, *supra.* A copy of these instructions to Stevens was enclosed by Liston in his No. 32 of May 9, 1799, F. O. 5: 22.

[27] F. O. 115: 7.

[28] Eight blockhouses were to be constructed for the defense of the windward quarter of the Island of Jamaica. The materials, which with the labor came to a cost of £6,500, were shipped from New York in March of 1800. Listen to Grenville. Nov. 4. 1799. No. 58, F. O. 5: 25; April 5, 1800, No. 14, F. O. 5: 29.

[29] F. O. 115: 7.

next Packet transmitting to you any instructions for the regulation of your conduct on this most interesting subject.[30] In the meantime I cannot forbear expressing to you my great regret that you should contrary to the expectation which I had confidently entertained on the subject, have suffered the business to proceed to the length of an open breach between the Commissioners, and even to a suspension of all their proceedings without any official intervention on your part, such as might have induced the American Government to interpose it's authority and to moderate the intemperance of it's Commissioners: you must I am sure feel how striking the contrast is between this conduct and the satisfactory arrangement of a similar point in this Country by the immediate and conciliatory intervention of Mr. King and myself.[31] The unfortunate situation in which the Commission in America is now placed, might surely in like manner, and with equal facility, have been obviated if the American Ministers had been induced by your application to enter with you into an early and friendly discussion of the several objects which have now led to a state of affairs so injurious to the subsisting friendship between the two Countries.

I have already apprized you that at the point to which matters are now brought it has been judged best to wait for further information from America and to take no other steps than that of the suspension of the proceedings of the Board of Commissioners constituted here. But it is proper that you should be informed that unless (contrary to what can now be hoped) the proposal of the American Government shall be found to be of a nature to remove the present difficulties, the idea now entertained by His Majesty's Government is that of instructing you to consider the declaration of the American Commissioners of their intention not to attend the board, as a formal resignation of their Trust, and consequently to

---

[30] On Oct. 11, 1799, from London, King reported that there was manifest ever since the news arrived of a fresh American mission to France a coldness toward the United States, an indifference to American affairs, and a disposition to give unfavorable interpretations to American conduct. In his conferences with Grenville respecting the dispute at Philadelphia King had repelled the latter's imputations of want of sincerity and integrity on the part of the American government in regard to the payment of the British Debts. *Corres. of Rufus King*, III, 122–131.

[31] Upon receipt of this instruction in December, Liston pointed out that there was a marked distinction between the disputes arising under Article VII and Article VI. In his opinion the secession of the American commissioners at Philadelphia could not have been prevented by any powers with which he had been invested or by any exertions he might have made, because the American commissioners were supported by American public opinion, by the most eminent American lawyers, and by the Adams administration. Earlier Liston had reported that he had not intervened because he had believed that Grenville was well informed of the proceedings of the commission; that it would be better to have the commission proceed to causes in which a unanimous decision was possible, thus avoiding a formal rupture; that he had hoped to see the administration exert a conciliatory influence upon the American commissioners; and that he had expected Mr. King at London to negotiate with Grenville if negotiations became necessary. Liston to Grenville, Dec. 30, No. 66, Aug. 4, No. 50, Sept. 30, No. 53, 1799, F. O. 5 : 25.

claim that a fresh nomination should forthwith be made by the American Government under the express engagements of the Treaty to that effect. It is evident that this suggestion will afford to them an opening which may, if a conciliatory disposition prevails, be very advantageously employed to remove the present evil, nor indeed can that demand be refused without it's being justly considered here as an open and manifest breach of the Treaty.

It appears necessary that I should make a remark to you on what you say of the opinion of Mr. Jay,[32] tho' the observation is so obvious that I conceive it to be impossible it should have escaped you. The difficulty of agreeing as to the general principles which ought to govern this subject and still more as to the application of those principles to each particular case, was the very reason which lead the two Negotiators of the American Treaty to adopt, after much discussion, the mode of referring the decision of those points to arbitration. The separate opinion therefore of one of those Negotiators on any of those points is not entitled to the smallest weight in determining the true construction of the Treaty. If it were otherwise I should have been very culpable in suffering the Commission here to proceed so far as it has done. For I could without the least difficulty affirm on oath, that several of those decisions which have been acquiesced in and acted upon here, are as far as I understand the subject contrary to judgement which I should have given on the true and just construction of the Treaty, had I been placed in a situation to pronounce upon it in reference to those cases.

The principle of construing any Treaty by the personal understanding of the Individual who negotiated it, is totally inadmissible as between independant Governments but it is above all so in any instance where the very nature of the Treaty itself implies a difference of opinion between the Negotiators: Mr. Jay's personal talents and probity are entitled to every respect, and I am persuaded that at the outset of this dispute his intervention might have been most usefully employed in preventing what has since happened. But if the execution of the decision of the arbitrators in America is to be suspended because that decision is contrary to his opinion, much of the money already paid here to American Claimants must in justice be refunded, as having been most certainly granted by the arbitra-

---

[32] According to Liston's dispatch of Aug. 4, 1799 (received Sept. 13, 1799), the opinion that the British majority of the commission had laid down principles which went beyond the intention of the treaty was held not only by the administration and prominent Federalists but also by Mr. John Jay. In December, upon receipt of the above instruction, Liston stated that "in regard to the opinion of Mr. Jay, I only meant to express that he agreed with the majority of the friends of good government in this country in holding (contrary to the decision of the Board of Commissioners) that American Loyalists are not by the Treaty of Amity entitled to recover those of their debts which were confiscated during the war." Liston to Grenville, Aug. 4, No. 50, Dec. 30, No. 66, 1799, F. O. 5 : 25.

tors here on Grounds in which the other Negotiator of the Treaty does not concur.

GRENVILLE TO LISTON [33]

No. 14.   •   DOWNING STREET, Oct. 21st., 1799.

Sir,

I send you inclosed the Copy of a Letter which I have received from the Lords Commissioners of the Admiralty together with the Papers to which it refers, and I have to signify to you His Majesty's Pleasure that if the Vessel mentioned in them (the Brig Experience) should be brought into any Port of the United States, you should make a formal Demand that she may be delivered up to you together with the Deserters and Seamen who rescued her out of the Possession of the Prize Master, in order that they may be sent to Jamaica or to some other of His Majesty's Colonies, to be there dealt with agreeably to the Law of Nations.[34]

GRENVILLE TO LISTON [35]

No. 15.   DOWNING STREET, Oct. 22nd, 1799.

Sir,

I transmit to you inclosed the Copy of a letter with its inclosures from Lord Hugh Seymour to Mr. Secretary Dundas relating to the Capture of the French Corvette the Hussar, in order that if any question should arise upon the Subject there stated, you may be furnished with such an authentic detail of the Events, as it may be necessary for you to produce in Opposition to the Claims which will

---

[33] F. O. 115 : 7.

[34] The brigantine *Experience*, detained by Captain Poyntz of H. M. S. *Solebay* on suspicion of carrying enemy property in logwood, had been retaken by its American master and supercargo, aided by members of the British prize crew. Liston said he would demand its restitution, but doubted of success in view of the case of the *Eliza*, an American vessel taken by Captain Cochrane of the *Thetis* and retaken by Americans left on board. Pickering had advised recourse to the District Court of New York in this case, but the evidence respecting the cargo was such that both Liston and Alexander Hamilton, Cochrane's attorney, thought it advisable not to bring suit. A special act of Congress covering such cases was suggested by Secretary of the Navy Stoddert, yet Liston doubted whether it could be passed because American opinion was all too general that "no possible evidence of the neutrality of the property can protect an American Merchantman from seizure by British cruizers, and that seizure and condemnation are synnonimous terms." Liston to Grenville, Dec. 31, 1799, No. 67, F. O. 5 : 25.

When Liston made representations on Feb. 2, 1800 in the case of the *Experience*, and of two other American merchantmen, the *Lucy* and the *Fair Columbian,* that by force and guile had similarly been recovered from their British captors, Pickering, reenforced by opinions of members of the Cabinet, advised recourse to the American courts. *A. S. P., F. R.,* III, 576–581.

[35] F. O. 115 : 7.

probably be asserted by the pretended Captors of the Vessel in question.[36]

GRENVILLE TO LISTON [37]

Circular.   DOWNING STREET, Dec. 19, 1799.

Sir,

As it appears from examinations taken before the Lords of His Majesty's Privy Council that grain may probably be procured from foreign Countries, I have to signify to You His Majesty's Pleasure that you use your utmost endeavours to obtain from the government of the Country in which you reside permission for the exportation from thence of all sorts of grain, meal and flour to be brought into this Country.

---

[36] Captain MacNeil of the American Navy, after some months spent in preventing the French corvette *Hussar* from escaping to sea, had taken that vessel when the British captured Surinam. He had protested the ruling of Vice Admiral Lord Hugh Seymour that all French ships at Surinam at the time of capture were to be considered British property. Benjamin Stoddert, Secretary of the Navy, assured Liston "that if he could obtain proofs of what he violently suspected,—that Macneil had made a pecuniary arrangement with the Commander of the French Ship—he should be immediately dismissed from the service of the United States." Liston to Grenville, Feb. 2, 1800, No. 4, F. O. 5 : 29.

[37] Draft, F. O. 5 : 25.

INSTRUCTIONS OF 1800

GRENVILLE TO LISTON [1]

Circular.   DOWNING STREET, Jan. 7, 1800.

Sir,

I send you inclosed the Copies of a letter which I have received from M. Talleyrand and of a letter addressed to The King by Genl Bonaparte that was inclosed in it, together with a Copy of the Answer, which by His Majesty's Command I have returned to M. Talleyrand's letter; and I have to signify to you His Majesty's Pleasure that you lose no time in communicating these Papers to the Ministers of the United States for their Information.[2]

I inclose to you for your Convenience in making this Communication a French Translation of my letter, and of the official note annexed to it. But you are to observe that the English Copies are the Originals, and are to be communicated as such.

GRENVILLE TO LISTON [3]

No. 1.   DOWNING STREET, Jan. 25th, 1800.

Sir,

Your several Dispatches to No. 62 inclusive have been received and laid before the King.

His Majesty's Government is waiting with considerable Impatience for the Instructions which, according to your Dispatches, and to Mr. King's own Information, that Minister may be in Expectation of receiving with respect to the Difficulties that have arisen in the Proceedings of the Commissioners appointed under the 6th Article of the Treaty with the United States.[4] Whenever those Instructions

---

[1] F. O. 115: 8.

[2] First Consul Bonaparte on Christmas Day, 1799, had made peace overtures which Grenville, in his letter to Talleyrand of Jan. 4, 1800, had rejected.

[3] F. O. 115: 8.

[4] Grenville's impatience was manifested to Rufus King in no uncertain terms. The latter was compelled to use emphatic language in ascribing the delay in receiving instructions from Philadelphia to the unavoidable interruption of public business caused by the contagious fever at that place, and in repelling Grenville's view that the object of the American government was to delay a settlement until it ascertained the issue of the negotiations President Adams had renewed with France. *Corres. of Rufus King*, III, 175–181, 184–185.

shall arrive, His Majesty's Ministers will be ready to enter with Mr. King into the most amicable and ample Discussion of them, and to adopt in concert with the United States, such Measures as may be best calculated to procure for the British Creditors that Justice to which they are entitled and which has been so long delayed.

GRENVILLE TO LISTON [5]

No. 2.   DOWNING STREET, Feb. 28th, 1800.
Sir,
Your several Dispatches to No. 2 of the present year inclusive have been received and laid before the King.

By the last Packet Mr. King received from his Government the Instructions of which he has been so long in Expectation relative to the Proceedings of the Commissioners appointed under the 6th Article of the Treaty with the United States. He has transmitted to me a Proposal founded upon those Instructions [6] which is now under the consideration of His Majesty's confidential Servants; and as soon as any Decision is taken upon the Subject I shall not fail to acquaint you with it for your Information.

Mr. Sitgreaves [7] is not yet arrived. His Majesty's Government would have no objection to Mr. Macdonald's availing himself of the present suspension in the proceedings of the Commission of which he is a Member to return to this Country on leave of absence; but in the present moment it would not be possible to appropriate a Ship of War to the particular service of conveying him hither.

GRENVILLE TO LISTON [8]

No. 3.   DOWNING STREET, Feb. 28th, 1800.
Sir,
I herewith transmit to you for your Information the Copy of a Letter from Mr. Nepean to Mr. Hammond, inclosing a Deposition of Richard Thomas, relative to the mode in which he obtained a Certificate of his being an American Citizen, although he was in fact a Subject of Great Britain. It is His Majesty's Pleasure that You should communicate this Paper to the American Ministers, as an additional Evidence of the Carelessness and facility with which these important Documents are granted in the United States, and as

---

[5] F. O. 115 : 8.

[6] See *Corres. of Rufus King*, III, 194–197 ; and *A. S. P., F. R.*, II, 384–385.

[7] Samuel Sitgreaves (1764–1824), distinguished Pennsylvania lawyer, the successor of James Innes, deceased, as one of the two American commissioners under Article VI of Jay's Treaty, had been ordered to London to assist King in negotiating a settlement of the dispute.

[8] F. O. 115 : 8.

a Justification of the Suspicions which are necessarily excited in this Country with regard to such Persons as are furnished with similar Protection.[9]

The Publication of this Paper may perhaps be advantageous, but of that You will judge.

GRENVILLE TO LISTON [10]

No. 4.   DOWNING STREET, Febr., 28, 1800.

Sir,

Having had the honour to lay before the King the representations which you have made of the state of your health,[11] His Majesty has been graciously pleased, on that account, to grant you permission to return to this country: But His Majesty relies on your discretion that you will not avail yourself of this permission, if at the time of your receiving this dispatch, any circumtsances should have occurred which could, in your opinion, render your absence from the United States inexpedient or in any manner likely to be disadvantageous to His Majesty's service.[12]

GRENVILLE TO LISTON [13]

No. 5.   DOWNING STREET, March 6th, 1800.

Sir,

A Representation having been made to His Majesty's Government by several Merchants of this City, trading to the Bay of Honduras, that the Citizens of the United States have opened, and are carrying

---

[9] The deposition of Richard Thomas was enclosed by Liston in his note to Pickering of May 2, 1800, Notes from British Legation, 2. Thomas, a native of Penzance, Cornwall, together with several other British seamen had deserted from the packet *Jane* at New York in October of 1799. With the aid of persons who falsely swore that the deserters had been born in America, they had obtained affidavits of American citizenship from a New York notary public, and with these had been able to get protections from the Collector of Customs at New York. Pickering, "disappointed and mortified to find that the Notaries Public continued to be guilty of the same malpractices as formerly," assured Liston that all possible punitive measures would be taken. Liston to Grenville, May 5, 1800, No. 17, F. O. 5 : 29.

[10] F. O. 115 : 8.

[11] Liston had looked forward to a leave of absence not so much because of "the epidemical distemper" which continue to prevail in the coast towns but because of the generally unfavorable effect of the American climate upon his health. Liston to Grenville, Oct. 7, 1799, No. 57, from Greenwich, near New York, F. O. 5 : 25.

[12] In acknowledging the above instruction Liston stated that he intended to put off his departure until the fall or winter in "the hope of being possibly well employed in the work of conciliation." Mindful of the turn public opinion had taken toward Great Britain, and convinced that the advantages to be ultimately reaped from a policy of conciliation were "of infinite magnitude," he said he would greatly deprecate a rupture or even an alteration of system. "The Rulers are certainly in earnest in wishing to be well with us, and it appears to me *possible* to arrange our differences. We might I think make a composition on every article but that of the Loyalist claims," and even if these claims came as high as half a million sterling "we perhaps had better consent to indemnify them ourselves, than resolve on war." Liston to Grenville, May 7, 1800, private, F. O. 5 : 29.

[13] F. O. 115 : 8.

on a very exclusive commerce in the British Settlements there, I
have to signify to you His Majesty's Pleasure that you communicate
this Circumstance to the American Ministers, and inform them that
a commerce of this Nature being contrary to the Laws of this Country, all but British Subjects, in British Ships, navigated according
to Law, will in future be excluded from cutting Logwood in, and
trading in and to His Majesty's Settlements in the Bay of Honduras.[14]

GRENVILLE TO LISTON [15]

No. 6.   DOWNING STREET, April 24, 1800.

Sir,

Your several Dispatches to No. 8 inclusive have been received and
laid before the King.

I send you inclosed for your Information, the copy of a communication which I have received from Mr. King, containing proposals of
the Government of the United States, relative to the difficulties that
have occurred in the proceedings of the Commissioners appointed
under the 6th Article of the Treaty of 1794, and also the copy of the
answer which I have returned to it by His Majesty's command.[16]

The principles stated in the answer appear to me so clear and
equitable as to require no additional observations on my part to
enforce them; and I have therefore only to signify to you His Majesty's pleasure that you make your language strictly conformable to
it, in any discussions which may take place between you and the
American Ministers on this most important subject.

In consquence however of a conversation which I have had with Mr.
King subsequent to the date of my answer, I expect shortly to transmit
to you His Majesty's commands to transmit to you farther instructions
on this point, but I am unwilling any longer to detain the American
Mail of this month for that purpose.

---

[14] Secretary Pickering did not see the necessity of the communication, since the British
had it in their power to drive away all those who attempted to carry on a prohibited trade
in British Honduras.   Liston explained that his government thought it proper to give
warning before it took vigorous suppressive measures.   "The matter has been viewed in
this light, and since Mr. Lee came into the office [Charles Lee of Virginia, the Attorney
General, had succeeded Pickering upon the latter's dismissal, and was Secretary of State
ad interim, May 13–June 5, 1800], a formal notification on the subject has been published
in the newspapers by orders of the Department of State."   Liston to Grenville, May 30,
1800, No. 25, F. O. 5 : 29.

[15] F. O. 115 : 8.

[16] In his answer of April 19, 1800, Grenville rejected the proposals for an explanatory
article delivered to him by King on Feb. 18, 1800, but stated that Great Britain was willing
to have a new board of commissioners appointed "to execute the same duty and to be
invested with the same discretion, which the Treaty has given to the present Commissioners."
Thereafter the discussions centered upon the proposal of a gross sum to be paid by the
United States to satisfy the claims of the British creditors.   *A. S. P., F. R.,* II, 394–399.

GRENVILLE TO LISTON [17]

No. 7.   DOWNING STREET, April 24, 1800.

Sir,

In the event of your availing yourself of the conditional leave of absence which (as stated in my Dispatch No. 4) The King has been pleased to grant you,[18] I have to signify to you His Majesty's Pleasure that you leave the Cyphers and Official Correspondence in your Possession with Mr. Thornton [19] whom you will present to the American Ministers as His Majesty's Chargé d' Affaires during your Absence.

GRENVILLE TO LISTON [20]

No. 8.   DOWNING STREET, May 9, 1800.

Sir,

Your several Dispatches to No. 12 inclusive have been received and laid before the King.

As I perceive from your Dispatch No. 9 that, notwithstanding the satisfactory Explanations which you had given (as stated in that Dispatch and in your No. 64 of last year) the American Ministers seem still to entertain some suspicions respecting the conduct and situation of Mr. Bowles,[21] I have to signify to you Mis Majesty's Pleasure that in any future Discussion between you and the American Ministers on this Subject, you should state in the most unequivocal manner that His Majesty's Ministers are entirely unacquainted with any hostile Designs which Mr. Bowles may meditate in the Indian Territory, and that he has no authority, commission, Instruction, nor Promise of Support from His Majesty's Government. You will farther add, that the King's Ministers have had no farther Knowledge of his Proceedings than that he solicited and received permission to proceed to the West-Indies, for the purpose of endeavoring to procure a safe passage from thence to his Native Country ; that during his residence in Barbadoes, Jamaica

---

[17] Draft, F. O. 5 : 29.

[18] In February Liston had renewed his application for leave, mainly on the ground of ill health but also because his property in Scotland had been much injured during his absence, and he had not been able to save anything from his salary during his stay at Philadelphia. Liston to Grenville, Feb. 6, 1800, private, F. O. 5 : 29.

[19] Edward Thornton, secretary of legation (see note 2, p. 144, *supra*). He became chargé d'affaires Dec. 2, 1800.

[20] F. O. 115 : 8.

[21] William Augustus Bowles (see note 4, p. 20, *supra*). Since this adventurer had returned from Jamaica in the British naval schooner, *Fox*, with presents for the Indians and with warlike equipment, the Secretary of State had informed Liston that it might be presumed that his enterprise was countenanced by Great Britain. By his bellicose vauntings, Bowles, who had proclaimed himself "Director General" of the Creeks, for a while caused grave apprehensions of an Indian war. Even the Secretary of State seemed to hold the prevailing opinion, wrote Liston in March, "that the British Government intended to bring about that calamity upon the United States, in indignation at the recent overtures made by this country for a renewal of a friendly connection with the ruling power in France." Liston to Grenville, Dec. 13, 1799, No. 64, F. O. 5 : 25, March 7, 1800, No. 9, F. O. 5 : 29.

and at the Bahamas he obtained from the Governors of those respective Islands some small pecuniary assistance in order to supply his immediate Wants; that, no other convenient opportunity occuring he was allowed to take his passage on board of one of His Majesty's Ships of War to the Continent of America. And in conversing upon this subject you will not fail to express the just surprize of His Majesty's Government at the ready credit which seems to be given in America to every groundless report of hostile measures or designs on the part of this country.

If the Conduct of His Majesty's Government has not been such as to establish in the minds of those who are employed in public stations in America a stronger confidence in the Dispositions which are entertained here towards the United States, I know not what future hope can be entertained of creating such a belief by any measures hereafter to be pursued.

GRENVILLE TO LISTON [22]

Separate.   DOWNING STREET, June 6, 1800.
Sir,

I have the satisfaction to inform you that the Postmasters-General have appointed Mr. Moore [23] the Gentleman recommended by you in your Dispatch No. 15 for this Situation, to be the Agent for His Majesty's Packets at New-York.

GRENVILLE TO LISTON [24]

No. 9.   DOWNING STREET, Sept. 30, 1800.
Sir,

Your several Dispatches to No. 34 inclusive have been received and laid before the King.

I shall take an opportunity to advert fully to the several Subjects of them by Mr. Merry, who will most probably sail for America by the Packet of next Month, and who has been directed by His Majesty to proceed thither for the purpose of discussing and endeavouring to adjust the differences which have arisen between His Majesty's Government and that of the United States, with respect to the proceedings of the Commission appointed under the sixth Article of the Treaty of 1794. [25]

---

[22] F. O. 115 : 8.
[23] Thomas William Moore, the son of the late British vice consul at Newport, Rhode Island.
[24] F. O. 115 : 8.
[25] On the same day, Sept. 30, 1800, King reported that it was the intention of the British government to send out Anthony Merry (who was Minister at Washington from 1803 to 1806) "as the successor of Mr. Liston, who has leave of absence and will not return to America after he leaves it. Mr. Merry was several years in Spain, and I think as Consul General is said to have acted with ability in the affairs of Nootka, and has lately returned from Denmark, where he has served in a diplomatic character." *Corres. of Rufus King*, III, 315.

GRENVILLE TO LISTON [26]

No. 10. DOWNING STREET, Sept. 30th, 1800.

Sir,

The complaint contained in Your Dispatch No. 29 against the Conduct of Captain Raper of His Majesty's Frigate, the Amiable, in converting an American Ship into a Privateer, having been transmitted to the Lords Commissioners of the Admiralty, their Lordships have directed the Commander in Chief of His Majesty's Ships at Jamaica to make a very particular enquiry into the Circumstances stated in Your Dispatch. As soon as the report upon this Subject shall be received here I shall not fail to communicate it to you for the information of the American Government.[27]

GRENVILLE TO LISTON [28]

No. 11. DOWNING STREET, Nov. 28th, 1800.

Sir,

Your several Dispatches to No. 38 inclusive (with the exception of No. 35) have been received and laid before the King.

Since the date of my last Dispatches to you, I have learnt from Mr. King that he has received Instructions to enter into some fresh discussion with the King's Ministers on the subject of the suspension of the Commission appointed under the sixth Article of the Treaty of 1794. In consequence of this circumstance, Mr. Merry's departure must necessarily be postponed, until it can be ascertained, whether the propositions which Mr. King may be instructed to offer are of such a Nature as that His Majesty's Government can accede to them, consistently with the justice due to those Classes of His Majesty's subjects to which the sixth Article refers.[29]

---

[26] F. O. 115 : 8.

[27] The American ship *Crocodile* had been taken by Captain Raper with a view to adjudication in Jamaica, but before the case was tried he had armed the vessel and employed it in cruising against American merchantmen. The complaint was made to Liston by John Marshall, whose nomination as Secretary of State had been confirmed by the Senate on May 14, and who had entered upon his duties on June 6, 1800. Liston to Grenville, July 4, 1800, No. 29, F. O. 5 : 29.

[28] F. O 115 : 8.

[29] See *Corres. of Rufus King*, III, 325, 332.

INSTRUCTIONS OF 1801

No. 1.   DOWNING STREET, Jany. 1st, 1801.

Sir.

The King having in consequence of the Union of His Kingdoms of Great Britain and Ireland thought proper to make an alteration in the Royal Stile and Titles, I have received The King's Commands to inform you that the Stile and Title appertaining to the Imperial Crown of the United Kingdom of Great Britain and Ireland, will henceforward be expressed,

In the Latin Language by the Words,

Georgius Tertius, Dei Gratia Britanniarum Rex Fidei Defensor; And in the English Language by the Words,

George the Third, by the Grace of God, of the United Kingdom of Great Britain and Ireland King and Defender of the Faith.

It is His Majesty's Pleasure that you should communicate this alteration to the Government of the United States in order that they may be apprized of the form in which all letters to His Majesty are hereafter to be addressed.

No. 1.   DOWNING STREET, 13th Ap[rl], 1801.

Sir,

Your Dispatches to No. 11 inclusive have been duly received.

I send you inclosed for your Information, Copies of a Note which I have received from Mr. King, the American Minister at this Court, and of my Answer to it—and I am to desire that in any Conversations which you may have upon this Subject with the American Ministers, you will make your Language conformable to that contained in my Note.[3]

---

[1] F. O. 115 : 9.

[2] Draft, F. O. 5 : 32. Robert Banks Jenkinson, Lord Hawkesbury, on Feb. 20, 1801 had succeeded Grenville as Foreign Secretary. The latter had resigned with Pitt (who had been succeeded as premier by Henry Addington) because of the King's opposition to Catholic Emancipation. Edward Thornton (see note 2, p. 144, *supra*), secretary of legation, had become chargé d'affaires Dec. 2, 1800. upon Liston's departure from Philadelphia. Thornton to Grenville, Dec. 6, 1800. No. 1, F. O. 5 : 29.

[3] King on March 13. 1801 had protested against British interference with the indirect trade between Spain and the Spanish West Indies, via the United States. His protest had been upheld by the King's Advocate. Hawkesbury to King, April 11, 1801, with enclosures, *Corres. of Rufus King*, III, 427–429 ; *A. S. P., F. R.*, II, 490–491.

GEORGE HAMMOND TO THORNTON [4]

No. 2.   DOWNING STREET, June 6th, 1801.

Sir,

I send you inclosed by Lord Hawkesbury's Direction for Your Information the Copy of a Letter from His Lordship to Mr. King, the American Minister, together with the Inclosures therein referred to, which have been transmitted to me by Mr. King the Under Secretary of State for the Home Department, in consequence of Lord Hawkesbury's having communicated to his Grace the Duke of Portland, an Extract of Your Dispatch No. 14 relative to the Capture of American Ships trading to the Spanish Settlements in the West. Indies.[5]

HAWKESBURY TO THORNTON [6]

No. 2.[7]   DOWNING STREET, July 3d, 1801.

Sir,

Your several Dispatches to No. 25 inclusive have been received and laid before the King.

I herewith transmit to You the Copy of a Letter from Mr. Addington to Mr. Hammond, together with a representation inclosed in it from the Commissioners of the Customs to the Lords Commissioners of the Treasury, and I have to desire that You will take all the proper means in Your power to give publicity to the intimation contained in the last mentioned of those Papers.[8]

---

[4] F. O. 115 : 9.

[5] Hawkesbury had obtained from the King's Advocate a statement to the effect that the Rule of 1756 had been relaxed, and that the indirect or re-export trade was clearly permitted. *Corres. of Rufus King*, III, 468–472; *A. S. P., F. R.*, II, 496–497. In his No. 14 of Feb. 28, 1801, F. O. 5 : 32, Thornton had reported to Grenville the indignation of American merchants at the great number of captures, and at the principles and practices of the British vice admiralty courts in the West Indies. See also Barclay to Grenville, March 12, 1801, *Corres. of Thomas Barclay*, pp. 118–120.

[6] Draft, F. O. 5 : 32.

[7] This bears the same number as the Instruction from Under Secretary George Hammond, of June 6, 1801, F. O. 115 : 9.

[8] On Sept. 4, 1801 Thornton transmitted to Secretary of State James Madison a copy of the report of the Commissioners of the Customs dated June 19, 1801 (which had been requested of them on May 22, 1801 by John Hiley Addington, to whom Rufus King had complained about the seizures of American tobacco), concerning the importation of tobacco "in mutilated and other illegal packages." Notes from British Legation, 2. See also Thornton to Hawkesbury, Sept. 10, 1801, No. 44, F. O. 5 : 32.

HAMMOND TO THORNTON [9]

DOWNING STREET, 10th Oct., 1801.

Sir,

I am directed by Lord Hawkesbury to inform you that Preliminaries of Peace between His Majesty and the French Republick were signed on the 1st Inst. by Lord Hawkesbury on the part of His Majesty and M. Otto [10] on the part of the French Government.

---

[9] F. O. 115 : 9.
[10] Louis Guillaume Otto, afterwards Count de Mosloy.

INSTRUCTIONS OF 1802

No. 1.   DOWNING STREET, Jan. 12, 1802.

Sir,

Your several Dispatches to No. 50 inclusive have been received and laid before the King.

I herewith transmit to You for Your Information, the Copy of a Convention, signed by me and Mr. King, on the 8th of this Month, and which I trust will satisfactorily arrange the Differences that have so long subsisted between His Majesty's Government and that of the United States on the Subject of the sixth Article of the Treaty of Amity Commerce and Navigation concluded in the year 1794.[2]

DOWNING STREET, February 13, 1802.

Sir,

I transmit to you herewith, Copy of a Letter and of it's Inclosures from the Commissioners of Transports, respecting the Transport Windsor, which was taken forcible possession of by the French Prisoners that were on board, on her Voyage from the West Indies, and carried into Boston; and I am to desire that you will make a proper Representation to the American Government on this subject, in order that the Vessel may be restored to her proper Owners, or a due Compensation given for the same.[4]

---

[1] Draft, F. O. 5 : 35.

[2] Under Article I of the convention of Jan. 8, 1802, which cancelled Article VI of Jay's Treaty, the United States engaged to pay Great Britain £600,000 sterling, in three annual installments, in satisfaction of the claims of British creditors. Article II reconfirmed Article IV of the treaty of peace : creditors of either power were to meet with no lawful impediment to the collection of their debts. Article III provided that the commissioners under Article VII of Jay's Treaty should reassemble and proceed with the execution of their duties. Miller, *Treaties*, II, 488–490 ; *A. S. P., F. R.,* II, 382–383.

[3] F. O. 115 : 10.

[4] The *Windsor*, captured early in July of 1801, had put in at Boston for repairs, where the authorities had refused the request of the British Consul for the vessel's expulsion as a prize of war in conformity with Jay's Treaty. The ship was sold, and later departed from Boston. Thornton carried on much correspondence with Madison about the incident until September of 1802, when he reported : "I was unwilling to lay further stress upon the culpable negligence, if not the intentional misconduct of the officers of the Customs at Boston in this transaction, as they belong to the party called federal, and as the President [Jefferson] might avail himself with alacrity of an accusation coming from such a quarter to increase the number of removals from office, which have already sufficiently depressed that party." Thornton to Hawkesbury, Sept. 27, 1802, No. 41, F. O. 5 : 35.

HAWKESBURY TO THORNTON [5]

DOWNING STREET, March 30, 1802.

Sir,

I have the Satisfaction to inform You that the definitive Treaty of Peace, was signed at Amiens, on the 27 Inst: by His Majesty's Plenipotentiary and the French, Spanish and Batavian Plenipotentiaries. I sincerely congratulate You on this important Event.

HAWKESBURY TO THORNTON [6]

DOWNING STREET, April 8, 1802.

Sir,

I inclose to you herewith a Memorial from Isaac Du Bois Esq., and I am to desire that you will use every proper Endeavour to obtain from the American Government the Redress to which he may appear to be entitled.[7]

HAWKESBURY TO THORNTON [8]

No. 2.   DOWNING STREET, May 6, 1802.

Sir,

I send you inclosed the Copy of a Confidential Letter which I have received from Mr. King, together with the Answer which I have returned to it by His Majesty's Command—and I am to desire that in any Conversation you may have with the American Ministers on the subject, you will make Your Language conformable to that contained in my Answer.[9]

HAWKESBURY TO THORNTON [10]

Circular.   DOWNING STREET, Sept. 27th, 1802.

Sir,

I send you inclosed for your information and guidance, the Copy of a Letter from Mr. Fawkener to Mr. Hammond and of the docu-

---

[5] F. O. 115 : 10.

[6] F. O. 115 : 10.

[7] Du Bois, a native of Wilmington, North Carolina, was an American Loyalist whose property had been confiscated. In 1784 he had been imprisoned for ten months in North Carolina. Thornton forbore making any representations to Secretary Madison respecting the personal injury he might have suffered by imprisonment, eighteen years before. Thornton to Hawkesbury, June 14, 1802, No. 27, F. O. 5 : 35.

[8] F. O 115 : 10.

[9] King's letter of April 21, 1802, and Hawkesbury's reply of May 7, 1802, respecting the views of the British government on the cession of Louisiana by Spain to France, are given in *Corres. of Rufus King*, IV, 108, 123 ; *A. S. P., F. R.*, II, 516–517. Hawkesbury stated that Great Britain had not acquiesced in or sanctioned the cession. Thornton's dispatch No. 29 of July 3, 1802, F. O. 5 : 35, reporting his conversations with President Jefferson, is partially printed in Henry Adams, *History of the United States*, II, 348.

[10] F. O. 115 : 10.

ments therein referred to, relative to Goods coming into His Majesty's United Kingdom from any foreign Port, at which there is not a regular Establishment for the performance of Quarantine—and I have to signify to you the King's commands, that you pay strict Attention to the Rules and Regulations therein prescribed.[11]

HAWKESBURY TO THORNTON [12]

No. 3.   DOWNING STREET, October 25, 1802.

Sir,

Your several dispatches to No. 39 inclusive have been received and laid before The King.

Having received information from Mr. Macdonald that the Claims presented by the British Creditors to the Board of Commissioners appointed under the 6th Article of the Treaty of 1794–5, and other documents have been delivered to you by Mr. Smith, late Secretary to that Board, I have to signify to you His Majesty's Pleasure, that you transmit to me without delay, all papers of that description which may be in your possession.

HAWKESBURY TO THORNTON [13]

DOWNING STREET, 16: Dec^r., 1802.

Sir,

I transmit to you herewith the Copy of a Letter from Mr. Sullivan to Mr. Hammond on the subject of your dispatch No. 40, and I have to desire, that you will give assurances to the extent specified in the other inclosure which also accompanied this, to any of His Majesty's Subjects who may have experienced disappointment in the views which have led them to emigrate to the United States, and who are well disposed and willing to remove to Trinidad; where the necessary instructions will be given for their reception by His Majesty's Secretary of State for the Colonial Department.[14]

---

[11] These rules and regulations respecting quarantine, which William Fawkener, Clerk of the Privy Council, had transmitted to Hammond on Sept. 25, 1802, were printed in the American newspapers at the request of Consul General Barclay. See Philadelphia *Aurora*, June 15. 1803.

[12] F. O. 115 : 10.

[13] F. O. 115 : 10.

[14] In his dispatch No. 40 of Sept. 27, 1802, F. O. 5 : 35, Thornton had reported that certain disappointed British emigrants to the United States had requested assistance in migrating to British possessions, especially to the recently ceded island of Trinidad. He himself favored giving them aid, and stated that they "will not make less faithful subjects of His Majesty for having been seduced to this country and disappointed in their views of advantage from it." Upon receipt of the above instruction from Hawkesbury, with its enclosures, including the letter of Nov. 29, 1802 of John Sullivan, under secretary for the war and colonial departments, under Lord Hobart, Thornton stated that he would in a discreet manner bring to the notice of British emigrants in America the liberal offers of His Majesty's government for the encouragement of emigration to Trinidad. Thornton to Hawkesbury, March 7, 1803, No. 12, F. O. 5 : 38.

INSTRUCTIONS OF 1803

Separate.   DOWNING STREET, June 28th, 1803.

Sir,

I herewith transmit to You for Your Information the Copy of a Note which, by His Majesty's Command I have this day delivered to the Ministers of the Powers most immediately interested in the navigation of the River Elbe. In communicating this Note to the American Government you will express to them the deep concern which His Majesty has felt in being under the necessity of having recourse to a Measure of this Nature. But the Conduct of His Majesty's business has imposed upon Him this Necessity, which it has not been in His Power to avoid consistently with a sense of what is due to His own Dignity and to the Interests of His Subjects. His Majesty will however, conformably to what is stated in the note be ready to discontinue the Blockade whenever the Government of France shall, in consequence of the interposition of other powers, or of any other motive, withdraw their Troops now stationed on the Banks of the Elbe, to such a distance from them, as to leave the course of the River secure and open to the Navigation of His Subjects.[2]

DOWNING STREET, 2nd August, 1803.

Sir,

General Martin, having represented to me, that Dr. Macky, as Executor to his Brother, Colonel Martin, who died in Virginia about four years ago, is engaged in a Law Suit on behalf of that Gentleman's Heirs, in which he experiences great Difficulties on the Part of the Government of Virginia, and having been advised to request him to have Recourse to Your Support; I have to desire that in that Event, you will afford Dr. Macky every proper Assistance in Your Power in prosecuting the Claims of the Heirs of Colonel Martin.

---

[1] F. O. 115 : 11.

[2] Thornton informed Madison of the blockade of the mouth of the Elbe in his note of Aug. 30, 1803, with enclosure, Notes from British Legation, 2. War between Great Britain and France had been renewed in May of 1803.

[3] F. O. 115 : 11.

HAWKESBURY TO THORNTON [4]

DOWNING STREET, Aug. 12th, 1803.

Sir,

I herewith transmit to you for your information, the copy of a Note which I have this day, by His Majesty's command delivered to the Ministers of Foreign Powers resident at this Court, notifying the Blockade of the Ports of Genoa and Spezzia.

I also enclose to you a printed copy of the most gracious speech with which His Majesty was this day pleased to prorogue the Parliament of His United Kingdom until the 6th October next.[5]

HAWKESBURY TO THORNTON [6]

DOWNING STREET, Sept. 6: 1803.

Sir,

I herewith transmit to you, for your information, the Copy of a Note which I have this day, by His Majesty's Command, delivered to the Ministers of Neutral Powers resident at this Court, notifying the Blockade of the Entrance of the Port of Havre de Grace, and the other ports of the Seine.

HAWKESBURY TO THORNTON [7]

No. 1.   DOWNING STREET, Sept. 8, 1803.

Sir,

Your several dispatches to No. 33 inclusive with the Exception of No. 25, 26 and 27 (neither in original nor duplicate) have been duly received and laid before the King.

With respect to the first installment of two hundred thousand Pounds agreed to be paid by the United States in pursuance of the Convention of January 8th, 1802, and which became due on the 15th of July last, I think it right to inform you that Mr. Merry,[8] who will proceed to his destination in the course of a few days, will be authorized to receive this Sum in *Specie*, and to ship it partly on

---

[4] F. O. 115 : 11.
[5] With a few exceptions, communications such as the above, and the one immediately following (which are usually marked "Circular"), have been excluded from this volume.
[6] F. O. 115 : 11.
[7] F. O. 115 : 11.
[8] There had been a possibility that Francis James Jackson, whom Rufus King reported to be "positive, vain, and intolerant," would be sent out as minister to the United States instead of Anthony Merry, whom King considered to be "in almost every point of character the reverse of Mr. Jackson." King to Madison, April 10, 1802, Henry Adams, *Hist. of U. S.*, II, 360–361.

board of the frigate which will convey him to America, and partly on board of another armed Vessel which will be appointed for the purpose.

In consequence of this arrangement it will be extremely desirable that the eight hundred and eighty eight thousand dollars should be deposited at New York whither the frigate, which is to convey Mr. Merry, will proceed after having landed that Gentleman at Norfolk, and as I infer from Mr. Gallatin's letter to you inclosed in your No. 32, that the Government of the United States will have no objection to this measure, I have therefore to desire that you will lose no time in proposing to the American Ministers that they take immediately the necessary Steps for collecting and depositing the dollars above mentioned at New York at which place they may remain until the arrival at that port of the frigate and armed Vessel above-mentioned.[9]

HAWKESBURY TO THORNTON [10]

No. 2.   DOWNING STREET, Sept. 16, 1803.

Sir,

Your several Dispatches to No. — inclusive have been received and laid before the King, and I have the Satisfaction to inform you that His Majesty has been graciously pleased entirely to approve of your Conduct during the Period of your acting as His Majesty's Chargé d'Affaires to the United States.

This Letter will be delivered to you by Mr. Merry, whom His Majesty has been pleased to appoint his Envoy Extraordinary and Minister Plenipotentiary to the United States, and to whom you will deliver the Cyphers and Official Correspondence in your Possession. His Majesty has been graciously pleased to grant you the Permission which you have solicited to return to England, but he relies on your not availing yourself of this Permission so long as, in the Judgement of Mr. Merry, your Continuance in America may be useful to His Majesty's Service.[11]

---

[9] Thornton in several dispatches, including his No. 32 of July 6, 1803, F. O. 5 : 38, had requested instructions as to the method of payment. He enclosed with his No. 32 Secretary Gallatin's letter of June 21, 1803, asking whether it would be agreeable to pay the first installment at a seaport town rather than at Washington. Article I of the Convention of Jan. 8. 1802, specified that the payments were to be made at Washington.

[10] F. O. 115 : 11.

[11] Merry arrived at Norfolk on H. M. S. *Phaeton* on Nov. 4, 1803, but on account of unfavorable winds in the Chesapeake did not reach Washington until Nov. 26, 1803. Thornton in May of 1804 was appointed secretary of legation at Berlin. He sailed from Philadelphia for England on July 21, 1804.

No. 1.   DOWNING STREET, Sept. 16: 1803.

Sir,

Herewith you will receive His Majesty's Letter of Credence (together with it's Copy) appointing you to be His Majesty's Envoy Extraordinary and Minister Plenipotentiary to the United States.

On your arrival at Washington you will desire an Audience of the President of the United States, in which you will deliver to him His Majesty's Letter, accompanying it with the strongest Assurances of His Majesty's sincere anxiety to promote and improve the Harmony and good Understanding which so happily subsist between His Majesty's Government and that of the United States.

I likewise inclose to you the general instructions with which His Majesty has directed that you should be furnished on your proceeding to your mission.

All the points in Dispute between His Majesty's Government and the United States which arose shortly after the Treaty of Peace, having been amicably arranged by the Treaty of Amity, Commerce and Navigation of 1794, and by the explanatory and additional Conventions which have been subsequently concluded, it is not probable that any new Circumstances should occur of a nature to create any serious Discussion between You and the American Ministers. I have therefore no particular Instructions to give you for the Regulation of your Conduct towards the American Government except that you endeavour to cultivate a good Understanding with the several Individuals who compose it.

The Principal object to which I have to direct your attention is the obtaining a due enforcement, on the part of the American Government, of the Stipulations of the Treaty of Amity, Commerce and Navigation.—The Treaties which existed between France and the United States having been formally annulled, in consequence of the differences which took place between the two Governments towards the Close of the last War,[18] the preeminence which France enjoyed under it's Treaties as the most favoured Nation is now transferred in

---

[12] F. O. 115 : 11. Anthony Merry, the son of a London merchant dealing in Spanish wines, had spent some twenty years in Spain, as consul general, and as chargé d'affaires. During the negotiations of the treaty of Amiens he had been secretary of legation to Lord Cornwallis. A man of mediocre talents (he is the only British minister to the United States during this period not listed in the British *Dictionary of National Biography*), whose gravity of deportment belied the Merry motto, "Toujours Gai," he is chiefly remembered, apart from his connection with Burr's Conspiracy, for his resentment of the social slights put upon him and Mrs. Merry (formerly Elizabeth Death) as he conceived by President Jefferson. Merry served as minister "in pompous unhappiness" (as Dr. J. Franklin Jameson once phrased it) from November 1803 to November 1806. See note 25, p. 186, and note 8, p. 195, *supra.*

[18] On July 7, 1798 Congress had declared the treaties abrogated. This was confirmed by the Convention of September 30, 1800 with France, as approved by the Senate on Dec. 18, 1801.

a great Degree to His Majesty's Subjects by the Treaty of 1794; the Provisions of which can be neither suspended nor invalidated by any subsequent Treaties which the United States may conclude with France or with any other Power. You will therefore most carefully guard against any attempts which may be made to infringe the just Rights that His Majesty's Subjects enjoy under the Treaty of 1794, and you will avail yourself of all the proper means in your power to render them abortive.

As in the present reduced State of the marine of France, it is not improbable that Individuals of that Country may attempt to fit out Privateers in the Ports of the United States, you will employ your utmost Exertions to defeat any Projects of this Nature, which are not only repugnant to the general Principles of Neutrality, but are also prohibited under very severe Penalties by an especial Provision (vide Article 21st in the Treaty with His Majesty[ )].

I have farther to observe to you that by the 25th Article of the above-mentioned Treaty it is stipulated that no Vessels shall be allowed to enter the Ports of one of the Parties which had made Prize of the Property or Vessels of the other. A similar Stipulation was inserted in the former Treaties between the United States and France; and the Sense in which it was interpreted by the American Government during the last War, as applicable to British Vessels, was, not that the Vessels themselves under those Circumstances should be excluded from the American Ports, but that they should not be allowed to bring into them any Prizes which they had taken. As this Construction has been formerly acted upon, and as it appears to be equitable, His Majesty's Government are willing that it should be adopted with respect to French Vessels bringing any Prizes into the American Ports, instead of insisting on a literal Compliance with the Terms of the Article.

From the 24th Article of the same Treaty you will perceive that no refuge shall be allowed in the Ports of one of the Parties to Privateers fitted out to cruize against the Vessels or Property of the other, and if any such Privateer should be driven into any of the Ports by Stress of Weather only such a Supply of Provisions shall be granted to them as will enable them to navigate to the nearest Port of the Country to which they belong. This is an object peculiarly deserving of your attention, as if this Prohibition be vigorously enforced, it will tend most effectually to discourage any French Privateers from cruizing on the coasts of the United States.

I have thought it right to direct your Attention more particularly to these three Stipulations of the Treaty of 1794, as in consequence of the War between Great Britain and France there is reason to apprehend that the Cases to which they have reference may not unfrequently occur.

No. 2.   DOWNING STREET, September 16: 1803.

Sir,

I herewith inclose to you, for your Information, the Extract of an American Newspaper which has been transmitted to me by Mr. Thornton; and which is stated to be a Memorial presented by Mr. Livingston the American Minister at Paris, on the subject of the Negotiation for the Cession of Louisiana to the United States. The Passages in this Memorial with respect to Great Britain are of so hostile and offensive a tendency as to render it impossible for His Majesty's Government to pass it over in Silence.[15] I have therefore to signify to you His Majesty's Pleasure, that you take an early opportunity to express to the American Ministers the hope entertained by His Majesty's Government that this publication is not authentic; as it is scarcely to be credited that Mr. Livingston should have so far degraded himself as to have rendered his written Communications with the French Government the instruments of casting unwarrantable and unmerited Aspersions on a Power with which his Country was at Peace, and which had not the remotest Connexion with the object of his Negotiation.[16] If however the American Ministers should confirm the Authenticity of the Memorial in question, you will then state to them the sense which is entertained in this Country of the Passages to which I have alluded, and the Conviction of His Majesty's Government that Mr. Livingston could not have been justified by his official Superiors in America in the injurious imputations which he has thought proper to cast upon the Government of Great Britain:—Indeed a different proceeding on the part of the American Government would be wholly irreconcileable with those Assurances of their anxious desire to maintain the most friendly and cordial Connexion with this Country, which Mr. King was formerly instructed to make, and which have been repeated by Mr. Monroe [17] since his arrival in England.

---

[14] F. O. 115 : 11.

[15] Robert R. Livingston in August of 1802 had presented a memorial to the French government on the retrocession of Louisiana in which he had alluded to the common interest which both France and the United States had in opposing the maritime "tyranny" of Great Britain. The memorial appeared in the American newspapers in July of 1803 (Philadelphia *Aurora,* July 7, 1803; an expurgated version is given in *A. S. P., F. R.,* II, 520–524). For its effect in London. see *Corres. of Rufus King,* IV. 299.

[16] Madison assured Merry that Livingston's allusion to Great Britain was unauthorized, and highly disapproved, and that the memorial had been published without the authority or even the cognizance of the government. Merry to Hawkesbury, Dec. 6, 1803, No. 2, F. O. 5 : 41.

[17] James Monroe had arrived in London in July of 1803 and on Aug. 17 had been presented as the successor of Rufus King, who had resigned and sailed for New York in May of 1803.

No. 3.   DOWNING STREET, September 16, 1803.

Sir,

I inclose to you for your information, the Copy of a Convention which was signed by Mr. King and myself on the 12th of May last, and which will I presume have been ratified by the Government of the United States previously to your arrival in America.

In any conversation which you may have with the American Ministers on the subject of this Convention you will state to them, that His Majesty's Government will be ready to appoint the Commissioners for the purposes specified in the 2d and 5th Article whenever it may be agreeable and convenient to the Government of the United States to nominate Commissioners on their part.[19]

No. 4.   DOWNING STREET, Sept. 16th, 1803.

Sir,

I inclose to You, for Your Information, the Copy of a Convention signed by Mr. King and myself, for the purpose of arranging the differences which had taken place between His Majesty's Government and that of the United States, relative to the Proceedings of the Commissioners appointed under the sixth and Seventh Articles of the Treaty of Amity, Commerce and Navigation.

From the first Article of this Convention You will perceive that the American Government have agreed to pay, and His Majesty has consented to accept, the Sum of Six Hundred Thousand Pounds Sterling, payable in three annual Instalments, as an equivalent for any Sums which the United States might have been rendered liable to pay, by the Awards of the Commissioners appointed under the sixth Article of the Treaty of 1794.

The first Instalment of eight Hundred and eighty eight Thousand Dollars (a Sum equal to two hundred thousand Pounds St.) became due on the 13th of July last, and has been represented by the American Ministers to be deposited in Specie in the Bank of the United States at Philadelphia and to remain there at the disposal of His Majesty's Government. They have also stated that it would be more convenient to themselves that this Sum, instead of being paid in the City of Washington conformably to the Terms of the Convention should be delivered to such Person as His Majesty should

---

[18] F. O. 115 : 11.
[19] The Convention of May 12, 1803 pertained to the Northeastern and Northwestern boundaries. It received the assent of the Senate but on condition that Article V (relating to the Northwestern boundary, and considered as a possible source of embarrassment because of the new territorial claims acquired by the Louisiana Purchase) should be cancelled. Ratifications were not exchanged. *A. S. P., F. R., II,* 584–591, III 89, 97–98.
[20] F O. 115 : 11.

think proper to appoint for that purpose, either at Philadelphia or New York. As this Arrangement appears to be no less advantageous to His Majesty's Government than to that of the United States, I have to signify to You His Majesty's Pleasure that You take the earliest Opportunity after Your Arrival at Washington to inform the American Ministers that You are authorized to give a Receipt in such form as may be agreed upon between You and them, for the Eight Hundred and eighty-eight Thousand Dollars above-mentioned on your learning from Mr. Barclay, His Majesty's Consul General at New York (to whom you will write upon the Subject) that this Sum has been deposited in the Bank of that City and will be delivered to him or any other Person duly authorized by You, whenever he may make a Requisition to that Effect.[21]

With respect to the future disposal of this Sum, I have to inform You that with a view to guard against any risque or loss which might result from its being remitted to this Country by Bills of Exchange, His Majesty's Government have agreed to assign the Eight Hundred and eighty-eight Thousand Dollars in Specie to the East India Company, on condition of the latter paying in London the Sum of Two Hundred Thousand Pounds Sterling. And in order to insure the Removal of the Dollars in safety from New York, the Commander of His Majesty's Ship Phaeton will be directed, after having landed You at Norfolk to proceed to New York, and there to await the Arrival of a Ship belonging to the East India Company, which will be dispatched to that Port, for the purpose of receiving on board one half of the eight Hundred and eighty-eight Thousand Dollars, the other half being destined to be shipped on board of the Phaeton.

You will lose no time in apprizing Mr. Barclay of this Arrangement and in directing him as soon as he shall be informed by the Commanders of the Phaeton and of the East India Ship before mentioned, that they are in readiness to receive the Dollars, to concert with those Officers the most secure mode of conveying them on board of the respective Ships. You will also instruct Mr. Barclay to take Receipts in triplicate from the two Commanders for the Quantity of Dollars which they may have received on board of their respective Ships, which Receipts Mr. Barclay will transmit to You in order that You may send them to me by separate Conveyances, as vouchers of the delivery of the Dollars on Account of the East India Company.

---

[21] Although Merry, given a Treasury draft by Gallatin, had some difficulty in finding such a large amount of specie, the money was obtained by Consul General Barclay at New York, and by Consul Hamilton at Norfolk, and shipped to England in January of 1804. Of the total sum of $888,000 ($400,000 of which in Spanish dollars was sent from Norfolk) only $885,295 was sent to England, for Barclay withheld $265 for the expense of counting and packing, and $2,440 for himself as commission for his trouble. Merry to Hawkesbury, Dec. 6, 1803, Jan. 2, 31, March 1, 1804, Nos. 4, 9, 17, 18, F. O. 5: 41. In a private letter to Hammond of Jan. 30, 1804, F. O. 5: 41, Merry noted that Barclay as a general rule exacted fees although paid a salary, and complained of Barclay's "love of gain."

INSTRUCTIONS OF 1804

HAWKESBURY TO THORNTON [1]

No. 1.   DOWNING STREET, 6: January, 1804.

Sir,

Your several dispatches to No. 52, have been received and laid before the King. Having directed your Dispatch No. 50 with its several inclosures [2] to be transmitted to the Lords of the Admiralty, I now inclose to you the Copy of a letter from Sir Evan Nepean to Mr. Hammond upon the subject of that dispatch, and specifying the nature of the instructions which have been sent to Commodore Hood and to the Judges of the Vice Admiralty Courts in the West Indies.[3] You will take the earliest opportunity to communicate this letter to the American Ministers, who will I doubt not consider the promptitude that has been manifested in redressing the grievance of which they had complained as an additional evidence of His Majesty's constant and sincere desire to remove any ground of misunderstanding that could have a tendency to interrupt the Harmony which so happily subsists between His Government and that of the United States.

---

[1] F. O. 115 : 13.

[2] In his dispatch No. 50 of Oct. 28, 1803, F. O. 5 : 38, Thornton reported that on October 18 he had received a letter from Commodore Hood requesting him to apprise the American government that the islands of Martinique and Guadaloupe had been placed under blockade. Because of the extent of Hood's blockade, because of its being declared effective from June 17, although Hood's notice of it was not written until July 25, and not received until October 18, and because Hood meanwhile had sailed away to attack the Dutch settlements on the mainland, Thornton had refused to make it public. It was published, however, at New York and Philadelphia by Consul Generals Barclay and Bond. Thornton said he agreed with the justice of Madison's observations in regard to "permitting in almost any case an officer at a distance from his government to take upon himself so great an act as the proclamation of a *general* blockade ; and that it were much to be desired, that officers should be totally restrained from acts, on which so much of the tranquillity of other countries depended, or should at least refer them to persons the best capable of judging of their general effect." For Madison's note to Thornton on this subject, of Oct. 27, 1803, see Carlton Savage, ed., *Policy of the United States toward Maritime Commerce in War,* I, 241–242.

[3] In his letter to Hammond of Jan. 5, 1804, Nepean stated that Hood and the vice admiralty judges in the West Indies had been ordered to consider a blockade as valid only when specified ports were actually invested by a naval force, and that vessels bound for such ports could be captured only when they had been previously warned not to enter them. A copy was transmitted to Madison by Merry on April 12, 1804, and is printed in *A. S. P., F. R.,* III, 265–266.

HAWKESBURY TO MERRY [4]

Separate.   DOWNING STREET, Feb. 3, 1804.

Sir,

I herewith transmit to you for your information the Copy of a Letter from Mr. Sullivan to Mr. Hammond, together with the inclosure therein referred to; and I have to signify to You His Majesty's Pleasure that, conformably to Lord Hobart's Opinion as stated in Mr. Sullivan's Letter, you afford Colonel Williamson [5] every Assistance in your power that may tend to facilitate the Business with which he is interested.[5a]

HAWKESBURY TO MERRY [6]

Separate.   DOWNING STREET, 9 Feb., 1804.

Sir,

I send You inclosed, for Your Information, the Copy of a Memorial which I have received from several Proprietors of Land in His Majesty's late Province of West Florida, complaining of the Injury, which they are likely to sustain from the Provisions of an Act of the American Congress, which passed in the Course of their last Session; and I have to signify to You His Majesty's Pleasure that You lose no Time in representing the Circumstances of this Case to the American Government; and that You use every Exertion in Your Power for the Purpose of obtaining for these Persons that Redress to which they are so manifestly entitled.[7]

---

[4] F. O. 115 : 13.

[5] Col. Charles Williamson (1757–1808), formerly of the British army, land speculator in New York State, friend of Lord Melville, and associate of Aaron Burr, from 1803 on was interested in recruiting men for filibustering against the French and Spanish colonies in America. His "levy" scheme of recruiting appears to have been set aside in 1805 by the British government. See Thomas Robson Hay, "Charles Williamson and the Burr Conspiracy," *Journal of Southern History,* II (May, 1936), 175–210; and I. J. Cox, "Hispanic-American Phases of the 'Burr Conspiracy,'" *Hispanic-American Hist. Rev.,* XII (May, 1932), 145–175.

[5a] Under Secretary John Sullivan in his letter to Hammond of Aug. 31, 1803, *"Secret,"* enclosed a copy of a letter received from Williamson, dated July 20, 1803, in which Williamson stated that there were many British emigrants in the United States who would, if given aid, migrate to British possessions and return to their British allegiance. It was the opinion of Lord Hobart, wrote Sullivan, that British officials in the United States should assist Williamson, and that Merry should be authorized to advance such sums of money as might be necessary, not exceeding £5 for each returning emigrant.

[6] F. O. 115 : 13.

[7] The act of Congress in question was that of March 3, 1803, for regulating grants of land, and providing for the disposal of Federal lands, south of Tennessee. Merry reported that the supplementary act of March 27, 1804, by prolonging the period for the filing of claims, and by allowing the admission as evidence of transcripts of record from His Majesty's late province of West Florida, should be the means of affording the petitioners complete redress. Merry to Hawkesbury, March 31, 1804, separate, F. O. 5 : 41.

LORD HARROWBY TO MERRY [8]

No. 1.   DOWNING STREET, August 3rd, 1804.

Sir,

The second annual Installment of two Hundred Thousand Pounds Sterling, equal in value to Eight Hundred and Eighty Eight Thousand Dollars of the Sum stipulated, to be paid to His Majesty by the United States in the Convention concluded between Lord Hawkesbury and Mr. King, (a Copy of which was transmitted to You in his Lordship's Dispatch No. 4 of last Year,) having become due on the 15th of last Month, I have to signify to You His Majesty's Pleasure, that You make without Delay the necessary Application to the American Government, for the purpose of receiving from them the Eight Hundred and Eighty Eight Thousand Dollars mentioned, and of remitting them to this Country. As this Sum is vested in His Majesty in order that it may be distributed among a very considerable Body of His Subjects, who are Claimants under the Convention, it is extremely desirable, that it should be received in this Country if it be possible, without any Defalcation whatsoever. It cannot be doubted, that if so considerable a Sum were to be remitted in Bills of Exchange, however respectable might be the mercantile House from which they might be purchased and however favorable the Course of Exchange might be for the Moment, the risk which would attend such a Proceeding would not be inconsiderable and it might, and most probably would, eventually affect for a Time the Rate of Exchange between Great Britain and the United States.

With a View to obviate these Inconveniences, it has therefore been thought most advisable that the Sum in question should be sent to this Country in either Spanish or American Dollars supposing them to be, as they are represented, of the same intrinsic Value; [9] as the present high Price of Silver in this Country would, it is conceived, be sufficient to cover the Expenses of Freight and Insurance of the Dollars, and leave a *Nett* Sum of at least Two Hundred Thousand Pounds Sterling applicable to the Uses specified in the Convention.

As it is presumable, that the same Causes will continue to exist, which rendered it inconvenient to the American Government, that

---

[8] F. O. 115: 13. Dudley Ryder, Lord Harrowby (1762–1847), in May of 1804, when Pitt succeeded Henry Addington as prime minister, had taken Hawkesbury's place as foreign secretary. Harrowby had served the Duke of Leeds as under secretary for foreign affairs, been paymaster of the forces, and vice president of the Board of Trade.

[9] Upon receipt of this instruction Merry reported that there was a difference of one per cent in the value of American and Spanish silver dollars. He reported a more than usual scarcity of specie, especially of Spanish dollars; a three per cent premium was actually being paid for Spanish dollars because of the immense exportation in the course of the year. Merry to Harrowby, Oct. 24, 1804, No. 55, F. O. 5: 42.

the Amount of the first Installment should be paid in the City of Washington conformably to the terms of the Convention and that it must be indifferent to them from what Port the Dollars may be shipped, I have to inform You, that one of His Majesty's Frigates will be dispatched in the Course of three or four Weeks to Norfolk in Virginia, for the Purpose of receiving on board the Eight Hundred and Eighty Eight Thousand Dollars, and of conveying them hither, in order that they may be deposited in the Bank of England.[10]

You will therefore lose no Time in apprizing the American Ministers of this Arrangement, and in informing them, that You are authorized to give a Receipt similar to that which You gave on the Payment of the first Installment, for the present Installment of Eight Hundred and Eighty Eight Thousand Dollars, on Your learning from His Majesty's Consul at Norfolk, that this Sum has been deposited in the Bank of that Town, and is ready to be delivered to him or any other Person duly authorized by You, whenever a Requisition may be made to that Effect.

You will also send without Delay to His Majesty's Consul at Norfolk, such Instructions as You may judge necessary, in order that he may be enabled to receive the Dollars, when they are deposited in the Bank, and to concert with the Commander of the Frigate destined to receive them, the Mode of their being conveyed to the Frigate.

You will further instruct His Majesty's Consul at Norfolk, to receive from the Commander of the Frigate Triplicate Receipts for the Amount of the Dollars shipped, which You will transmit to me by separate Conveyance. You will likewise inform the Consul, that he is not to expect any other Remuneration for his Trouble, than Reimbursement of the Expenses which he may actually incur in providing the necessary Packages for the Dollars, and in conveying them on board of the Frigate.

If it should be an Object of Convenience to the American Government, that one part of the Dollars in Question should be shipped at Norfolk and the other at New York You are authorized to consent to this Deviation from the Arrangement before proposed; and You will send to His Majesty's Consul General at New York, Instructions similar to those which You are here directed to give upon the Subject to His Majesty's Consul at Norfolk; and You will in that Case leave to the Captain of the Frigate his Option with respect to the Port

---

[10] It was utterly impossible to make the payment in the manner of his instructions, wrote Merry in November, for, despite the willingness of the American government, there was in the bank at New York but $25,000 in silver coins of all description, of which the proportion of Spanish dollars did not amount to $6,000. It was possible to get only $588,000 in specie, in both American and Spanish dollars, at the three ports of Norfolk, Baltimore, and Charleston. The remaining $300,000 must be paid in gold coins of various description. Merry to Harrowby, Nov. 10, 1804, No. 57, F. O. 5 : 42.

which he would prefer for the purpose of receiving the first Portion of the Dollars to be shipped on board of the Frigate under his Command.

I send You inclosed under flying Seal a Dispatch which I have thought it expedient to write to His Majesty's Consul General at New York, on the Subject of his Conduct with respect to the Shipment of the Amount of the first Installment,[11] and which You will forward to him by some private Conveyance.

HARROWBY TO MERRY [12]

No. 2.   DOWNING STREET, August 4th, 1804.
Sir,
Your several Dispatches to No. 35 inclusive, have been received and laid before the King.

I think it necessary, that You should be apprized of the Substance of a Conversation which I had yesterday with Mr. Monro, and which I desired him to report to his Government.[13]

Some doubt had been entertained in this Country, respecting the Period at which the temporary part of the Treaty of 1794 expired[14] and it had not been remarked, that the Act by which the Provisions of that Treaty were enforced, expired with it.

The Sessions of Parliament being closed, without any Law having been passed either to continue that Act, or to entrust to the King in Council that Power which had been given Him by the annual American Intercourse Bills, the Trade between the two Countries would fall into the same cramped and doubtful State in which it was left after the Peace of 1783.—In order to prevent the Inconvenience which must result both to Great Britain and America, His Majesty has decided to act in all Points to which his Prerogative reaches, in the same Manner as if the Treaty of 1794 were still in Force, and to give

---

[11] Consul General Barclay was reprimanded for withholding without authority $2,440 as his "commission" from the first installment paid in 1803. See note 21, p. 201, *supra.* Barclay remitted this to Merry, and it was included in the total sum sent to England of $890,-440, as follows: $140,440 (including Barclay's remittance) from Norfolk in silver coin, and $750,000 from New York in gold coins, British, Portuguese, Spanish, and French. Merry to Harrowby, Dec. 3, 1804, No. 60, F. O. 5: 42; Jan. 25, 1805, No. 1, F. O. 5: 45.

[12] F. O. 115: 13.

[13] See Monroe to Madison, Aug. 7, 1804, Monroe, *Writings,* ed. S. M. Hamilton, IV, 228–236; *A. S. P., F. R.,* III, 94–95.

[14] Article XXVIII of Jay's Treaty provided that the first ten articles were to be permanent, and that the subsequent articles, except the twelfth, were to be limited to twelve years from the exchange of ratifications. A conditioning factor, however, was Article XII, relating to the West India trade, which was to expire by limitation at the end of two years from the signing of the preliminary or other articles of peace terminating the war in which Britain was then engaged. During that two years' period, according to Article XXVIII, the two governments were to agree on some new arrangements on the subject of Article XII; if that proved impossible all the articles of the treaty except the first ten were to cease and expire together. Article XII, however, had been suspended by the amendment of the Senate, in its resolution advising ratification, June 24, 1795.

Orders to the Boards of Revenue and Customs, to continue to regulate their Conduct by the Act of 1795, until Parliament should meet. In apprizing Mr. Monro of this Determination of His Majesty, I informed him, that His Perseverance in it must depend upon the Conduct pursued by the American Government. He said, that he was not aware of their having hitherto taken any Measure contrary to the Treaty, and he did not doubt, that they would continue to act in the same Manner, till some Arrangement could be formed.

I asked him, whether he had any Instructions upon that Subject; and I understood from him in reply, that his Powers were of a very general and extensive Nature—but that the American Government had not conceived, that a time of War was favourable to the Conclusion of any Treaty, which might settle the relative Situation of the two Countries upon a permanent Basis; that such a Basis was the Object of their Wishes; and that as the Interests of America and Great Britain grew to be better understood by Experience, than they were at the Time when the Treaty of 1794. was concluded, he did not doubt, but much might be changed, and much added, whenever a permanent Settlement was made. As he repeated again, that this did not seem a favourable Moment for adjusting such complicated Concerns, — I took Occasion to observe, that it had evidently been the Opinion of both Governments in 1794., that a Period of Peace was best calculated for that Purpose; that, although in Strictness, the Treaty was certainly expired, yet in Equity, it might be considered as still in Force, since the Period of two Years of Peace, which was supposed to be necessary for accomplishing such a Work, had never taken Place; and therefore the Contingency, by which the Duration of the Treaty was limited, had never happened. That, under these Circumstances, it appeared to me to be perfectly easy to meet what he conceived to be the Wish of the American Government; that I concurred with him, both in this Wish, and in the Reasons which he assigned for it; and that I was ready to propose, that the Treaty should be revived, and it's Duration extended, at least to the full Period originally designed, i : e : Twelve Years from the Ratification.—I added, that I did not make this Proposal, from the Idea that any particular Advantages were to be derived from it to Great-Britain; and that I was perfectly aware of the great Interest felt by America in continuing for a further Period upon the same Footing the Trade with India, which had made so great a Progress since the Treaty of 1794., but so much at least was clear, that during the continuance of that Treaty, the Intercourse between the two countries had been greatly extended, and their Harmony uninterrupted; and if we were both of Opinion, that it was not advisable, in the present State of Things, to attempt the Formation of a permanent

Settlement we could not do better than take for our Guide in the mean time a Rule of which the general beneficial Tendency had received the Sanction of Nine Years Experience.

I desired Mr. Monro to communicate this Proposal to his Government, in order that he might receive Instructions upon the Subject without Loss of time, and that something might be settled, if possible, before the Meeting of Parliament.

He said, that he did not doubt, that the Determination of His Majesty's Government, to continue to act as if the Treaty were in Force, and the Proposal to prolong its Duration, for the Reasons I had assigned, would be received in America, as Proofs of the Desire entertained in this Country, to preserve a friendly and cordial Intercourse; but having no particular Instructions, he could not give me any further Answer.

I had some conversation with him on the subject of the additional ad Valorem Duties,[15] which, I stated, as contrary to the Letter, if not to the Spirit of the Treaty; for although the Proportion between the Duties on Goods brought in British and American Bottoms is not altered, yet the positive Difference is increased; and I recalled to his Recollection that in the Act of Parliament passed for the Execution of the Treaty of 1794., it was expressly provided, that the Ten per Cent, imposed on Goods brought in American Ships, should not be extended to the Duties of Ten and Five per Cent, granted by an Act passed subsequent to the Treaty.[16]

As Mr. Monro stated, that he had not yet received the Acts of the last Session of Congress, and had no Information upon the Subject, I did not press this Topic any further.

HARROWBY TO MERRY [17]

No. 3.   DOWNING STREET, Nov. 7th, 1804.

Sir,

Your several Dispatches to No. 49 inclusive, have been received, and laid before the King.

As I presume that the Congress will be assembled, and the Members of the American Administration be returned to Washington at the

---

[15] By the act of March 26, 1804, an additional ad valorem duty of 2½% was imposed for the purpose of building up a "Mediterranean Fund" to carry on the war with the Barbary Powers. *U. S. Statutes at Large*, II, 291–292.

[16] By Article XV of Jay's Treaty the United States agreed to treat for the more exact equalization of duties. "The arrangements for this purpose shall be made at the same time with those mentioned at the conclusion of the twelfth article of this treaty, and are to be considered as a part thereof. In the interval it is agreed that the United States will not impose any new or additional tonnage duties on British vessels, nor increase the now-subsisting differences between the duties payable on the importation of any articles in British or American vessels."

The act of Parliament of July 4, 1797, for the execution of the treaty is printed in *A. S. P., F. R.*, II, 103–107.

[17] F. O. 115: 13.

time of your receiving this Dispatch, I think it right to put You in Possession of the Sentiments of His Majesty's Government on the several Points which are likely to become Subjects of Discussion between them and the United States.

His Majesty's Government have perceived with considerable Concern from some of your most recent Dispatches the increasing Acrimony which appears to pervade the Representations that have been made to You by the American Secretary of State on the Subject of the Impressment of Seamen from on board of American Ships. The Pretension advanced by Mr. Madison that the American Flag should protect every Individual sailing under it on board of a Merchant Ship is too extravagant to require any serious Refutation. In the Exercise of the Right, which has been asserted by His Majesty and His Predecessors for Ages, of reclaiming from a Foreign Service the Subjects of Great Britain, whether they are found on the High Seas, or in the Ports of His own Dominions, Irregularities must undoubtedly frequently occur, but the utmost Solicitude has been uniformly manifested by His Majesty's Government to prevent them in as far as may be possible, and to redress them, whenever they have actually taken place. In the recent Instance of the Proceedings of Captain Bradley of the Cambrian Frigate, with respect to the Ship Pitt,[18] which appears to have excited so much Animosity in America, His Majesty's Government did not wait for any Representation on the Subject, but conceiving from Mr. Barclay's Statement of the occurrence, that Captain Bradley's Conduct had been extremely irregular, they lost no time in removing him from the Command of the Frigate, and in directing him to return to this Country to account for his Proceedings.[19] If any similar Instance should occur the same prompt and vigorous Measures will be employed, and strictest Orders will be given without delay to the Commanders of His Majesty's Ships of War to observe the utmost Lenity in visiting Ships on the High Seas, and to abstain from Impressments in the Ports of the United States.

In my Dispatch No. 2 I apprized You that I had desired Mr. Monroe to inform the Government of the United States, that His Majesty

---

[18] In June of 1804 the British frigate *Cambrian*, Captain Bradley, had impressed fourteen seamen from the British merchant vessel *Pitt* in New York harbor, within American jurisdiction. The press gang had insulted and prevented from coming on board the *Pitt* revenue and quarantine officers of the United States. Madison had demanded an apology from the commander of the *Cambrian* (which was given) and the deliverance to the American authorities of Lieut. Pigot, who had been in charge of the impressment party. Later, in July of 1804, Madison made a fresh complaint against the *Cambrian*, when that frigate impressed six British passengers out of the American ship *Diana* two and a half leagues from the lighthouse at Sandy Hook. Merry to Hawkesbury, July 2, 18, Aug. 6, Sept. 4, 1804, Nos. 36, 40, 42, 45, F. O. 5 : 42 ; *Corres. of Thomas Barclay*, p. 165 ff.

[19] Captain Bradley was recalled, but within a year he was promoted to the command of a ship of the line. *A. S. P., F. R.*, III, 96, 106 ; Merry to Mulgrave, June 30, 1805, No. 26, F. O. 5 : 45.

would be willing to agree with them in considering the Articles of the Treaty of 1794. as being in force, until some new Arrangement could be formed. No account has as yet been received of the Light in which this Proposition has been viewed by the American Government, but until their Decision respecting it can be known, it is intended to propose to Parliament to lodge the Power of regulating the Commerce with America in the King in Council, in the same Manner as before the Treaty of 1794. The Offer of considering that Treaty as being in Force until the Year 1807, (the Period at which the temporary Articles would have expired, if a Peace had not been previously concluded,) must be regarded as a Boon to America: and it was made, merely under the Persuasion that if accepted, it would be accepted with a view to maintain a friendly Relation between the two Countries, and to avoid in the Interval every thing which could lead to interrupt it. If this System is followed in America, it will be followed here in every respect with an anxious Desire for the Continuance of Harmony and Cordiality. The Hopes entertained by His Majesty's Government that this would be the System adopted in America, were confirmed by the Circumstance of the two Bills which were proposed in Congress at the Beginning of this Year, and inclosed in Your Dispatch No. 12 not having been passed into Laws.[20] It is to be presumed that the same right Judgement, by which the American Government was induced to postpone these offensive Bills will be exerted to prevent their Revival; but if, contrary to the just Expectations of His Majesty's Government these Bills should be passed, it is right that You should be apprized, that the Offer made to Mr. Monroe will in that case be considered as set aside; and His Majesty's Power in the regulation of the Trade with America, will undoubtedly be so exercised as to manifest the Sense entertained here of a Conduct so little compatible with amicable Intercourse. I have farther to observe upon this Subject that if these Bills, or any Bills similar to them should be passed in the ensuing Session of Congress, and if any Steps should be taken by the American Government in consequence of the Provisions contained in them, it would be impossible for His Majesty to refrain from adopting such measures of Retaliation as circumstances may appear to require. Such a System of Retaliation, if His Majesty should be compelled by the conduct of the American Government to persevere in it, might unquestionably be injurious to both Countries; but I believe that it would require little reasoning to prove, that it's Effects would be much more severely felt by the Citizens of the United States than by His Majesty's Subjects.

---

[20] The two bills intreduced in January of 1804, one in the House and one in the Senate, were for the further protection of American seamen. Both were postponed to the following session. *Annals of Congress*, 8th Cong., 1st sess., pp. 232, 264, 876, 1237.

The only remaining Point on which I think it expedient to make any Observations at present is the refusal of the American Government to ratify the Convention concluded between Lord Hawkesbury and Mr. King, unless the first Article should be omitted.[21] His Majesty's Government would at all times be ready to enter into a Discussion of all the Articles of that Convention, with the most sincere Desire to form a satisfactory Arrangement with respect to the Objects to which they refer, but they can never acquiesce in the Precedent, which in this as well as in a former Instance, the American Government has endeavoured to establish of agreeing to ratify such Parts of a Convention as they may select, and of rejecting other Stipulations of it, formally agreed upon by a Minister invested with Full Power for the Purpose.

I have, as stated in the beginning of this Dispatch, thought it right to put you in Possession of the Sentiments of His Majesty's Government on these several Points; but it is not intended that You should make them the Subject of an official Note. You will urge them as Circumstances may render it necessary, in any Conferences with the American Government; but you will, as far as possible, avoid any Language which might be conceived to be of a menacing or hostile Tendency or which might be construed into an Indication of a Desire on the Part of His Majesty's Government to decline any Discussion of the several Points now pending between the two Countries. This Discussion as you will perceive from another Dispatch of this date, is only suspended, and will be received [revived] on Mr. Monroe's return from Spain.[22]

HARROWBY TO MERRY [23]

Separate.   DOWNING STREET, November 7th, 1804.
Sir,
As it is very probable that some Observations may be made to You by the American Government on the little Progress which has taken place in a Negotiation into which Mr. Monroe was instructed to enter with His Majesty's Government, I think it necessary to acquaint You, that upon a Reference to Dates, no intentional delay can be ascribed to His Majesty's Government. On the 29th of November, Mr. Monroe delivered a Note to Lord Hawkesbury, complaining of the Impressment of American Seamen. This Note was sent without Delay to the Admiralty, but as some of the Facts to

---

[21] The article in question, of the Hawkesbury-King Convention of May 12, 1803, was the fifth, not the first. See note 19, p. 200, *supra;* also, *A. S. P., F. R.* III, 92–93.
[22] Monroe left for Madrid Oct 8, 1804, and after unsuccessful negotiations respecting West Florida and spoliation claims, returned to London, July 23, 1805.
[23] F. O. 115 : 13.

which it related, had occurred at a distance, no immediate Decision can be taken upon it. Very shortly after the Change of the Administration, Mr. Monroe acquainted me, in a Conversation which I had with him, that he was authorized to open a Negotiation with His Majesty's Ministers on some Subjects of considerable Interest to the United States. It was not however till the first of September in a Conference which I had with Mr. Monroe that he delivered to me the Projet of a Convention relative to the Regulation of the Impressment of American or pretended American Seamen and to some proposals of a Commercial Nature. On the 5th of September Mr. Monroe transmitted to me some farther papers on the same Subjects. Within a few days afterwards I sent a Note to Mr. Monroe, signifying that I was under the Necessity of attending His Majesty at Weymouth, but that on my return from that place, I should be ready to enter into a Discussion of the several points contained in his Projet, which he had delivered to me. On the 29th I received a Note from Mr. Monroe, of which, and of my Answer returned upon the same day, I inclose Copies. Here this matter rests for the present, but on Mr. Monroe's Return from Spain, I shall be able, as I have stated in my Note, to enter with him into a full discussion of the Propositions which I have received from him.[24]

HARROWBY TO MERRY [25]

Separate.   DOWNING STREET, November 7th, 1804.

Sir,

In order that You may be acquainted with the Opinions entertained, upon the Question of the Impressment of Seamen from on board of American Ships, by Persons the most competent to decide upon it;—I inclose to You the Copies of a Statement which I have received from the Lords of the Admiralty, and of a Communication from Sir William Scott.[26] You will however observe, that these Papers are intended solely for Your private Information, and for the purpose of availing Yourself in Conversation of the Facts and Opinions which they contain, but You will on no account refer to them in any Correspondence which You may have with the American Ministers.

---

[24] In his note to Harrowby of Sept. 29, 1804, informing him of his intention to proceed to Spain, Monroe placed responsibility for the delay in negotiations upon the British government. For Monroe's instructions and dispatches, January to October, 1804, and for the American project of a convention, see *A. S. P., F. R.*, III, 81–99.

[25] F. O. 115: 13.

[26] Both Sir William Scott (Judge of the High Court of Admiralty from 1798 to 1828), in his letter to Harrowby of Sept. 20, 1804, and the Lords of the Admiralty, in their statement upon American complaints respecting British maritime practices, declared that the right claimed by Great Britain of impressing British seamen out of foreign vessels must not be surrendered, but that all unnecessary inconvenience and all unnecessary violence in exercising the right should be avoided or repressed.

INSTRUCTIONS OF 1805

GEORGE HAMMOND TO MERRY [1]

DOWNING STREET, January 2: 1805.

Sir,

In the absence of Lord Harrowby I am directed to transmit to you the Copy of a leter from Sir Stephen Cottrell [2] to me, expressing the desire of the Lords of the Committee of Privy Council for Trade to be furnished with the account of the several Imports and Exports into, and from the United States; and I am to request that you will instruct His Majesty's Consuls General to transmit to you the same, in order that you may forward them to this Office accordingly.

HAMMOND TO MERRY [3]

Circular.   DOWNING STREET, Jan. 8th, 1805.

Sir,

In the Absence of Lord Harrowby I am directed to acquaint You, that War was declared on the Part of His Catholic Majesty against Great Britain on the 12th of December last. [4]

LORD MULGRAVE TO MERRY [5]

DOWNING STREET, February 17th, 1805.

Sir,

I transmit to you, for your information, Copies of a letter, and of it's inclosures from Mr. Cooke to Mr. Hammond, respecting the Fishery carried on by the Subjects of the United States of America,

---

[1] F. O. 115: 13.

[2] Sir Stephen Cottrell was for many years the Clerk of the Privy Council and the Keeper of the Privy Council Records.

[3] F. O. 115: 13.

[4] On Oct. 5, 1804, a British squadron under orders had seized three Spanish treasure ships off Ferrol, en route from South America to Spain. The British justified the action on the ground that Spain was the actual, if secret, ally of France. The declaration of war by Spain followed.

[5] F. O. 115: 13. Henry Phipps, Lord Mulgrave (1755–1831), chancellor of the Duchy of Lancaster in Pitt's second ministry (May 1804–Feb. 1806), and Pitt's chief spokesman in the House of Lords. He had succeeded Harrowby as foreign secretary in January of 1805, when the latter resigned because of injuries resulting from a fall downstairs at the Foreign Office late in 1804.

213

on the Coast of Labrador, and the Interruption given by them to the British Fishermen.[6]

MULGRAVE TO MERRY [7]

No. 1.   DOWNING STREET, March 8, 1805.

Sir,

In consequence of the representation in your dispatch No. 2 of the Sensation produced in America by the indiscreet notification published by Mr. Barclay with respect to the Proclamation of the Lieutenant Governor and Council of Jamaica,[8] and in compliance with the urgent representation of the West India Planters, it appears expedient that you should be authorised to state to the American Government at such time, and in such manner as you shall deem most expedient, that no orders have been sent by His Majesty to the Governors of His Colonies in the West Indies, by which they are deprived of the discretion formerly entrusted to them of relaxing, under certain circumstances, the rigid provisions of the Navigation Laws: you will however at the same time take care to have it distinctly understood that no Foreign Nation can be admitted to advance any Claim to such relaxation of the Navigation Laws of Great Britain, and that the exercise of this discretion by His Majesty's Governors will be regulated alone, by a due consideration of circumstances connected with the interest and Convenience of His Majesty's Colonies.

You will without delay give the necessary instructions to His Majesty's Consuls in the different Ports of America, to take such steps and make such Communications on this subject, as you shall deem most expedient for the Advantage of His Majesty's Colonies, and for securing to them the necessary Supply of Provisions and Lumber, so long as it shall be thought advisable by His Majesty's Government to keep the Ports of those Colonies open to the admission of American Vessels.

Inclosed you will receive, for your better information, Copies of the Instructions sent out by the Earl Camden[9] to Lieut. Governor

---

[6] In his letter to George Hammond of Jan. 12, 1805, Edward Cooke, Under Secretary for war and colonies, enclosed papers relative to the recent seizure of two American vessels that had dried and cured their fish on the shores of Newfoundland, contrary to Article III of the treaty of 1783.

[7] F. O. 115: 13.

[8] In his No. 2 of Jan. 25, 1805, F. O. 5: 45, Merry had reported the "very disagreeable Sensation" caused by the proclamation issued Nov. 21, 1804, by Lieut. Gov. Nugent of Jamaica, and published in the United States by Consul General Barclay without notice being given to Merry, to the effect that, after a period of six months, the importation into that island of lumber and provisions in American vessels would no longer be permitted. It was generally supposed that Nugent's action was based upon instructions from London, and that the prohibition would extend to the other British West Indian islands.

[9] Sir John Jeffreys Pratt, second Earl of Camden (1759–1840), Secretary for war and colonies 1804–05.

Nugent, together with a Copy of the letter of Mr. Lyon, Agent for the Island of Jamaica, addressed to his Lordship,[10] which came enclosed in one from Mr. Cooke to Mr. Hammond, of which I send you also a Copy.

I have expressed to Mr. Barclay His Majesty's disapprobation of his taking upon himself to make any declaration upon matters of great and public Concern without previous Communication with you.[11]

MULGRAVE TO MERRY [12]

No. 2.[13]   DOWNING STREET, March 5, 1805.

Sir,

I herewith transmit to you a Commission signed by The King appointing Andrew Allen Junr. Esqr.[14] to be His Majesty's Consul to the States of Massachusetts, Connecticut, Rhode Island and New Hampshire, and I have to signify to you His Majesty's pleasure that, previously to your delivering this Commission to Mr. Allen, you exhibit it to the American Government and obtain from them the necessary Exaquatur to enable Mr. Allen to discharge the duties of his office.

MULGRAVE TO MERRY [15]

No. 3.   DOWNING STREET, April 3: 180[

Sir,

Your several dispatches to No. 7 of the present Year inclusive, have been received and laid before The King.

As the period is now approaching, at which the Third Instalment of the Sum agreed to be paid by the United States, under the Convention concluded by Lord Hawkesbury and Mr. King, will become due, I have to signify to you His Majesty's Pleasure that, in order

---

[10] In his letter to the Earl of Camden of March 7, 1805, Edmond P. Lyon expressed the alarm felt by the planters of Jamaica at Nugent's proclamation prohibiting all commercial intercourse between the island and the United States, and noted that a deputation from the Jamaica Assembly had in vain warned Nugent of "the certain and immediate destruction that will impend over their lives and properties, whenever the regulation which they deprecate shall be adopted."

[11] A copy of Mulgrave's letter to Barclay to this effect, dated March 8, 1805, was transmitted to Merry by Hammond in a separate dispatch of this same date, F. O. 115 : 13. Earlier, on Jan. 6, 1804, Hawkesbury had reprimanded Barclay for having made public, without authorization from Thornton, the chargé d'affaires, Commodore Hood's proclamation of the blockade of Martinique and Guadalupe. See note 2, page 202, *supra*. In a private dispatch to Merry of March 7, 1805, F. O. 115 : 13, Hammond stated : "Mr. Barclay's conduct . . . has *really* excited considerable disapprobation, and I have reason to believe that his next offence of this kind will be followed by immediate dismission."

[12] F. O. 115 : 13.

[13] It will be noted that instruction "No. 2" antedates instruction "No. 1."

[14] Andrew Allen, Jr., was George Hammond's brother-in-law, and the son of Andrew Allen, Philadelphia Loyalist and former Attorney General of the Province of Pennsylvania. He succeeded Thomas MacDonogh, deceased, at Boston.

[15] F. O. 115 : 13.

to prevent a recurrence of the delays which took place with respect to the payment of the First and Second Installments,[16] you enter into some arrangements with the Government of the United States, for the purpose of facilitating the payment of the Third at the time of it's being due, and of holding the amount of it in Specie (in either Silver or Gold Coin) in readiness to be conveyed to this Country in such manner as His Majesty may hereafter be pleased to direct.

MULGRAVE TO MERRY [17]

No. 4.   DOWNING [STREET], May 4th, 1805.
Sir,
    Your several Dispatches to No. 11 inclusive have been received and laid before The King.
    The early departure of the Packet with the Mail of this Month prevents me from sending your Instructions on any other of the Subjects to which they relate than on the Proposition made to you by the Secretary of the Treasury for the Payment in London of the Third Instalment of the Sum due by the United States under the Convention concluded between Lord Hawkesbury and Mr. King. Upon this Point I have to signify to you The King's Pleasure that you inform the American Secretary of the Treasury that His Majesty's Government will be ready to accede to this Proposition provided the Payment be made on the 15th of September next in London, either in Specie or in Notes of the Bank of England. You will in the first Instance use every proper exertion in your power to prevail upon the American Government to direct the Sum of Two Hundred Thousand Pounds to be paid in Specie, but if they appear decidedly adverse to this Measure you will then propose to them the other Alternative of the Notes of the Bank of England. You will at the same time acquaint them that His Majesty's Government cannot acquiesce in this deviation from the Terms of the Convention unless the Payment in London be made in one of the two Modes prescribed in this Dispatch.[18]

MULGRAVE TO MERRY [19]

No. 5.   DOWNING STREET, June 6th, 1805.
Sir,
    I inclose to you for your information, Copies of a letter which I have received from Mr. Erving, and of the Answer which I returned

---

[16] See note 21, p. 201; note 10, p. 205; note 11, p. 206, supra.
[17] F. O. 115: 13.
[18] Gallatin, so Merry reported in July, was willing to engage to make payment at London either in specie or in notes on the Bank of England. Merry to Mulgrave, July 1, 1805, No. 29, F. O. 5: 45.
[19] F. O. 115: 13.

to it; from which You will perceive that His Majesty's Government have acquiesced in the Arrangement that Mr. Erving was instructed to propose, and that the Amount of the third Instalment will be paid in London on the 15 of next Month.[20]

MULGRAVE TO MERRY [21]

No. 6.[22]   DOWNING STREET, June 5th, 1805.

Sir,

I transmit to you herewith, the Copy of a letter and of it's inclosures, from Mr. Marsden to Mr. Hammond, and, as it is important that no opportunity should be omitted of securing a supply of Ship Timber for His Majesty's Dock-Yards, I am to signify to you The King's Pleasure, that you lose no time in taking such Steps as you may judge proper, in order to ascertain whether the timber in question can now be procured, — and how far the quantity and quality may correspond with the description contained in these papers.[23]

MULGRAVE TO MERRY [24]

No. 7.   DOWNING STREET, July 2d, 1805.

Sir,

I inclose to you herewith, for your information, the Copy of a letter from Mr. Fawkener to Mr. Hammond, relative to the British-built Ship *Belfast* which had been captured by the Enemies of this Country, and afterwards bought and freighted for Liverpool by American Citizens. In conformity to the suggestion of the Lords of His Majesty's Most Honorable Privy Council, I have to desire that you will take the proper means for notifying to the Merchants concerned in the Trade from the United States to this Kingdom, that Vessels under the circumstances of the one above-mentioned, cannot

---

[20] In his letter to Mulgrave of May 7, 1805, George William Erving, American consul at London, had proposed, under instructions from Madison, that the third and final installment under the Convention of Jan. 8, 1802, should be paid at London, rather than at Washington, thus avoiding the exportation of specie. In his answer of May 17, 1805, Mulgrave had acquiesced in this arrangement.

[21] F. O. 115 : 13.

[22] It will be noted that instruction "No. 6" antedates instruction "No. 5."

[23] In his letter to George Hammond of May 23, 1805, William Marsden, first secretary to the Admiralty, asked that inquiries be made respecting live oak ship-timber "growing on a sea Island on the Coast of Carolina." Upon the advice of Consul Moodie at Charleston and Consul Hamilton at Norfolk, Merry reported that such timber was believed to be unsuitable. Merry to Mulgrave, Sept. 30, 1805, No. 39, F. O. 5 : 45. Nevertheless, from 1805 on there was a lively trade in southern timber for the British navy. See R. G. Albion, *Forests and Sea Power, The Timber Problem of the Royal Navy 1652–1862*, p. 358 ff.

[24] F. O. 115 : 13.

be admitted to Entry as American Vessels, according to the Terms of the Act of the 37 of His Majesty C. 97.[25]

MULGRAVE TO MERRY [26]

No. 8.   DOWNING STREET, 4 July, 1805.

Sir,

I have no dispatches from you to acknowledge of a later date than the 5th of March last. This circumstance is I presume to be attributed to the Capture of the Queen Charlotte Packet, and to the non arrival of the Packet with the Mail of the Month of May.

Authentic intelligence has been received here, that Mr. Monroe has entirely failed in the Negociation in which he was engaged with the Spanish Government,[27] and at the date of the latest accounts received from Lisbon was preparing to quit Madrid for the purpose of returning to this Country. I have thought it right to inform you of this Event, as it may materially affect the Political and Commercial relations subsisting between Spain and the United States.

MULGRAVE TO MERRY [28]

No. 9.[29]   DOWNING STREET, 3 July, 1805.

Sir,

I herewith enclose to you the Copy of a letter which I have this day written to Mr. Barclay on the subject of an application which he has made for permission to receive fees on certificates or other documents attested by him.

You will communicate to His Majesty's other Consuls in the United States the determination of His Majesty's Government not only with respect to their not receiving fees but also to the necessity of their using the utmost circumspection in adding their authentication to any certificates or other documents of a similar nature. So many abuses have arisen and are likely to arise for the indiscriminate and incautious manner in which in some instances some of the Consuls in the United States have been accustomed to attest papers of this description, as

---

[25] The act of 37 George III c. 97, dated July 4, 1797, provided for the execution of the Jay Treaty of 1794. An exception was made in the case of the *Belfast,* which was allowed to discharge her cargo of provisions and naval stores, for British consumption, on the ground that there was no fraudulent intention. W. Fawkener to George Hammond, June 18, 1805, copy enclosed with above.

[26] F. O. 115 : 13.

[27] See note 22, p. 211, *supra.*

[28] F. O. 115 : 13.

[29] It will be noted that instruction "No. 9" antedates instruction "No. 8."

to render it indispensably requisite to repress practises of so injurious a tendency.[30]

MULGRAVE TO MERRY [31]

No. 10.   DOWNING ST., August 8th, 1805.

Sir,

I transmit to you herewith the Copy of a letter from Sir S. Cottrell to Mr. Hammond referring to a letter from Mr. Fawkener of the 17th June, of which I inclosed to you a Copy in my No. 7 of the 3 July; and I am to desire that you will take proper means for acquainting the Merchants in America of the Sentiments of the Lords of His Majesty's Most Honorable Privy Council, with respect to Vessels arriving in British Ports of the Description of those mentioned in the accompanying Paper, and the one to which it refers.[32]

MULGRAVE TO MERRY [33]

No. 11.   DOWNING STREET, September 5, 1805.

Sir,

I herewith transmit to you the Copy of a letter from Sir Stephen Cottrell to Mr. Hammond, together with the Extract of a Minute of Council therein referred to; and I am to desire you will take such measures as you may think best adapted for communicating generally and without delay to the Merchants residing in the United States, the determination of His Majesty's Government as expressed in the Minute of Council above mentioned.[34]

MULGRAVE TO MERRY [35]

No. 12.   DOWNING STREET, October 3rd, 1805.

Sir,

I transmit to you herewith the Copy of a letter and its Inclosure from Mr. Thomas of the Pay Office to Mr. Hammond, relative to the Form of Certificates required from Officers on Half Pay—and I am to desire that you will take the proper steps for making these Regulations generally known to all Officers on the British Half Pay Establishment, residing in the United States.

---

[30] Merry reported that he had already advised Barclay to suspend asking for fees and giving authentication to documents purporting to show the neutral quality of vessels and merchandise. Merry to Mulgrave, Sept. 2, 1805, No. 36, F. O. 5 : 45.

[31] F. O. 115 : 13.

[32] In his letter to Hammond of August 1, 1805, Sir Stephen Cottrell stated that the American-owned ships *Louisiana* and *Nancy* had been permitted to discharge their cargoes despite the act of 37 George III c. 97. Although these were British ships which had been captured and sold by France, they had been admitted on the ground that no fraud was intended, as in the case of the *Belfast* set forth in Fawkener's letter to Hammond of June 18, 1805 (cited in above instruction as of June 17, 1805).

[33] F. O. 115 : 13.

[34] The "Extract of Council Minute of the 3rd August 1805," sent by Cottrell to Hammond, stated, with reference to the act of 44 George III, c. 80, that their Lordships, upon representations by American merchants, would allow the entry of neutral ships laden with produce of enemy colonies, provided such ships had been cleared before Nov. 1, 1805.

[35] F. O. 115 : 13.

INSTRUCTIONS OF 1806

No. 1.   DOWNING STREET, March 7th, 1806.

Sir,

In consequence of your long continued ill State of Health, His Majesty is graciously pleased to grant you Leave of Absence to return to this Country: and as there are various important Matters which now remain for Discussion between the Two Governments, His Majesty has judged it expedient to lose no time in nominating the Earl of Selkirk [2] to be your Successor as His Envoy Extraordinary and Minister Plenipotentiary to the United States. You will notify to the American Government in the usual Manner this Appointment, which it is not doubted will be perfectly agreeable to them from the Character and Talents of the Earl of Selkirk and the intimate knowledge which he possesses of the reciprocal Interest of the Two Countries.

It is very gratifying to me to convey to you upon this Occasion His Majesty's entire Approbation of the whole of your Conduct.[3]

FOX TO MERRY [4]

No. 2.   DOWNING STREET, April 2nd, 1806.

Sir,

It having been represented to the Lords of His Majesty's most Honorable Privy Council, that, from the Situation of the West Indies

---

[1] F. O. 115 : 13. Upon Pitt's death, Jan. 23, 1806, the ministry of "All the Talents" was formed, with Grenville as prime minister and Charles James Fox (1749–Sept. 13, 1806) as foreign secretary.

[2] Thomas Douglas, fifth Earl of Selkirk (1771–1820) ; in 1803 he had settled eight hundred Scottish emigrants on Prince Edward's Island, in 1803–04 had made a tour of Canada and the United States, and in 1805 had published his *Observations of the Highlands of Scotland, with a View of the Causes of Emigration*, in defense of his colonization schemes. Later, from 1810 on, he exercised a controlling influence in the Hudson's Bay Company.

[3] This was accompanied by a private letter in which Fox designated Merry's health as the reason for his recall. He said nothing about Merry's connection with the schemes of Aaron Burr. Merry, in reply, expressed his chagrin : he had not solicited a change, and he did not believe that his health, his age, and his record of twenty-three years in the foreign service, precluded him from that activity and responsibility in which Fox had "insinuated" he might be deficient. He was pleased to note that the whole of his conduct had been approved, and he suggested that a mark of that approbation might be given him by means of the usual pecuniary reward. Merry to Fox, June 1, 1806, private, F. O. 5 : 49.

[4] F. O. 115 : 13.

and of other Parts of the World, the introduction of Pestilential Diseases into the Territories of the United States was to be apprehended, and that Vessels are permitted to depart for Europe from the Lazarette Ground, long before they have remained there the period competent to justify their Admission into the Port of Philadelphia, I have to signify to you His Majesty's special Commands, to collect and transmit the best intelligence which you can procure, respecting the departure of Ships (whether bound to the Ports of the United Kingdom or elsewhere) from any place in America where any contagious Disease is known, or suspected, to prevail: and more especially respecting the dangerous Practice above stated.[5]

FOX TO MERRY [6]

No. 3.   DOWNING STREET, 7th April, 1806.

Sir,

Notwithstanding the Impatience manifested here for an Answer to Mr. Monroe's Complaints,[7] and the Heat which appears to be rising in America on the important subject of them, the Extent of Inquiry which the Business requires, and the pressure of other Affairs, have hitherto prevented His Majesty's Confidential Servants form preparing a proper final answer to be submitted for His Majesty's Consideration.

In the meantime I am commanded by His Majesty to instruct you to assure the Ministers of the United States, of His Majesty's good Will towards the said States, and of his earnest wish so to arrange all Matters liable to cause Dispute, that a ground may be laid for permanent Friendship and good Understanding between the Two Nations.

You may further assure the above mentioned Ministers, that His Majesty's Confidential Servants will very shortly be enabled to enter into Treaty with Mr. Monroe, and will not suffer the Business to be delayed one Day beyond what is absolutely necessary.

---

[5] From information received from the British consuls, Merry reported that Philadelphia appeared to be the only port where the practice prevailed, and that the Philadelphia Board of Health, after Mr. Bond's representations, had given orders to prevent ships and passengers from leaving the lazaretto grounds for Europe until a sufficient time had elapsed to remove all suspicion of danger. Merry to Fox, June 29, 1806, No. 32, F. O. 5 : 49

[6] F. O. 115 : 13.

[7] Upon Fox's accession to office Monroe had related to him his unsuccessful attempts to negotiate a treaty with Hawkesbury, Harrowby, and Mulgrave, relative to neutral rights, impressment, and boundaries, subjects to which the blockades and seizures and impressments by British cruisers in American waters, and the wholesale captures of American ships (engaged in the indirect West Indian trade) under the *Essex* decision of 1805, had given a pressing importance. *A. S. P., F. R.,* III, 113 ff.

FOX TO MERRY [8]

No. 4.   DOWNING STREET, April 8, 1806.
Sir,

I herewith transmit to you, for your Information, the Copy of a Note which, by His Majesty's Command, I have this day delivered to the Ministers of the Powers most immediately interested in the Navigation of the Rivers Ems, Weser, Elbe and Trave.[9] In communicating this Note to the American Ministers, you will express to them the deep concern which His Majesty has felt in being under the necessity of having recourse to a Measure of this nature; but the Conduct of His Majesty the King of Prussia has imposed upon him this Necessity which it has not been in His Power to avoid, consistently with a Sense of what is due to His own Dignity and to the Interests of His Subjects.[10]

FOX TO MERRY [11]

Circular.   DOWNING STREET, May 16: 1806.
Sir,

I herewith transmit to you for your information the Copy of a Note which, by His Majesty's Command, I have this day addressed to the Ministers of Foreign Powers resident at this Court, notifying the Blockade of the Coast, Rivers and Ports, from the River Elbe to the Port of Brest.[12]

FOX TO MERRY [13]

Circular.   DOWNING STREET, May 20th, 1806.
Sir,

I inclose to you, for your information, the Copy of a Note which I have this day addressed to the Ministers of Friendly and Neutral

---

[8] F. O. 115 : 13.

[9] Fox's note of April 8, 1806, to Monroe is printed in *A. S. P., F. R.*, III, 267. The blockade was in consequence of the forcible seizure of parts of the Electorate of Hanover by Prussia, and the exclusion of British ships from the ports of the Prussian dominions, and from certain other ports in the north of Europe.

[10] Madison informed Merry that the American government could only regard the notification as a mark of friendly intention; that the notification itself imposed no legal restraint on neutrals, since a blockade to be legal must be effective. He said he was the more disposed to view the communication in this light because of the explanation which Merry (under Lord Hawkesbury's instruction of Jan. 6, 1804) had given him in April of 1804, in respect to Hood's blockade of Martinique and Guadalupe. See note 3, p. 202, *supra*.

The news of the blockade order, reported Merry, "has produced all that Sensation throughout this Country which is manifested immediately whenever any Thing occurs to impede the Inhabitants from enjoying their full Scope of Commercial Gain . . . it is represented as a fresh Instance of what is termed that intolerable Tyranny over the Seas which is constantly exercised by the British." Merry to Fox, June 29, 1806, No. 33, F. O. 5 : 49.

[11] F. O. 115 : 13.

[12] Fox's note to Monroe of May 16, 1806, and Monroe's comments to Madison of May 17 and May 20, 1806, are printed in *A. S. P., F. R.*, III, 124–126.

[13] F. O. 115 : 13.

Powers resident at this Court, by which you will perceive it is not His Majesty's intention that the blockade announced in my Circular Note of the 8th Ultimo to those Ministers, shall extend to the River Trave.

FOX TO MERRY [14]

No. 5.   DOWNING STREET, June 6: 1806.

Sir,
    Your Dispatches to No. 19 inclusive, have been received and laid before The King.

Accounts have reached this Country of the very unfortunate event of an American Seaman having been killed in the Harbour of New York, by a Shot from His Majesty's Ship Leander, and of the strong Spirit of Resentment and Hostility excited by it in that City.[15]

Having received no official account of the Circumstance, it is impossible to give any opinion upon it, or to send you any positive Instructions how to act. If however any Application on the subject is made to you, you will state, in General Terms, that His Majesty's Government, tho' perfectly unacquainted with the Merits of the case, cannot but sincerely deplore the Result; and that they will not fail to cause all proper Investigation into all the circumstances which led to the Melancholy Transaction, to take place, with a view to remove any Sensation of Enmity or Distrust to which it may have given rise.

SIR FRANCIS VINCENT TO MERRY [16]

DOWNING STREET, 31 July, 1806.

Sir,
    I have received Mr. Secretary Fox's directions to transmit to you the inclosed Letter [17] from Messrs. Hoare Hill Barnetts Roan and Hill, and I am to acquaint you that it is His Majesty's Pleasure that you should lose no time in applying to the American Government for permission to have Thomas Bateman and Lydia Wilson apprehended and brought back to this Country in order that such steps as the Law directs may be taken to recover the property belonging to the above mentioned Bankers of which they have been defrauded by Thos. Bateman, and to bring the offenders to Justice.

---

[14] F. O. 115 : 13.

[15] The *Leander,* which with the *Cambrian* and the *Driver* had for some time been active off New York in searching, seizing, and impressing, on April 25, 1806, had by one of her warning shots killed John Pierce, helmsman of the American coasting sloop *Richard.* On May 3, 1806, Jefferson ordered the ports of the United States forever closed to the three British frigates and to their commanders, and ordered the arrest of Captain Whitby of the *Leander* should he ever be found within American jurisdiction.

[16] Draft, F. O. 5 : 49. Sir Francis Vincent was first under secretary in the foreign department. Fox was in ill health in May ; by the end of June, 1806, he was incapable of attending to his duties.

[17] The enclosure is lacking.

Separate.   DOWNING STREET, August 8: 1806.
Sir,

Your Dispatches to No. 34 inclusive have been received and laid before The King.

Messieurs Pinckney [19] and Monroe had on the 21st ultimo the Honour of presenting their Joint Credentials to His Majesty. It is understood that when the present subsisting discussions are gone through, Mr. Monroe will return to America, and Mr. Pinckney remain here as Minister of the United States—It is rumoured that Mr. Monroe is destined by his Party as a Candidate for the Presidency.—It would be desirable to ascertain what foundation there is for this Report, and what Probability of Success would attend that Gentleman's offering himself for that high Situation. [20]

Nothing has yet transpired here on the subject of Mr. Skipwith's Mission to Paris [21]—and Mr. Erskine, [22] who has been appointed by His Majesty to succeed you, is making every preparation for his immediate Departure, which will take place certainly in the course of the present Month.

You will on his Arrival deliver to him the official Correspondence and the Cyphers and Decyphers entrusted to your care, and give him all the Information in your power on the State of Public Affairs in America.

It is in consequence of Mr. Fox's Indisposition (which, although he is very considerably better, renders it proper not to intrude upon him any business that can be avoided without Inconvenience to the

---

[18] F. O. 115: 13.

[19] William Pinkney of Maryland (1764–1822), a commissioner at London under Article VII of Jay's Treaty from 1796 to 1804, in April of 1806 had been appointed a joint commissioner extraordinary and plenipotentiary, with James Monroe, to negotiate a treaty with Great Britain. Pinkney (often misspelled "Pinckney") had arrived in London on June 24, 1806.

[20] Merry reported that Madison and Monroe were considered to be the only two prospective candidates of the Republican party to succeed Jefferson. Of the two, Madison was regarded as having the stronger support, especially since John Randolph's attempts at the last session of Congress to lower Madison's reputation, and, thereby, to elevate Monroe's. Merry to Fox, Nov. 2, 1806, No. 49, F. O. 5: 49.

[21] Fulwar Skipwith, for some years past American consul at Paris, had sailed from New York on March 29, 1806 with remittances to the sum of two million dollars, to be used as a boon to induce Napoleon, so Merry reported, to exert his influence upon Spain, and bring about the sale of the Floridas to the United States. If successful, the acquisition would be paid for thereafter in a separate transaction. Merry to Fox, April 6, May 14, 1806, Nos. 18 and 22, F. O. 5: 48.

[22] David Montague Erskine (1776–1855), eldest son of Thomas Erskine, first Baron Erskine. In 1799 he had married the daughter of General John Cadwallader of Philadelphia. Lord Erskine wrote Grenville on May 22, 1806, that he had asked Fox three months before to appoint his son as envoy to America: "He is 32 years of age, has been four years in America, is acquainted intimately with all the considerable persons there, and his wife's family are most extensively connected, and I can venture to be quite sure that it would be a most popular appointment." *Dropmore Papers*, VIII, 152. Erskine was presented to President Jefferson on Nov. 3, 1806.

Public Service) that I have the Honour of addressing you—an irregularity which I trust you will have the goodness to excuse.

VINCENT TO DAVID M. ERSKINE [23]

No. 1.   DOWNING STREET, 18th Aug., 1806.

Sir,

I transmit to you herewith His My's general Instructions [24] for the regulation of your conduct during your residence in America, as His Majesty's Envoy Extraordinary and Minister Plenipotentiary to the United States. Such further Instructions as circumstances may from time to time render expedient, will be regularly transmitted to you from this office.

I also inclose to you His Majesty's Credential Letter, (with a Copy) which you will deliver in the usual form, accompanied by suitable Expression in His Majesty's Name.

You will avail yourself of the earliest opportunity to acquaint the American Government, that His Majesty has been pleased to appoint Lord Holland and Lord Auckland Joint Commissioners,[25] and to invest their Lordships with Full Powers to treat with Mr. Monroe and Mr. Pinckney, upon all such matters as these Commissioners may be instructed by their Governm. to bring into discussion and finally to conclude, and sign such an arrangement, as shall establish on a permanent Basis, the political and Commercial Relation of the Two Countries, and be reciprocally advantageous to both.

As His Majesty has nothing more at heart than the immediate Establishment between His Majesty's Government and that of the United States, His Majesty directs you to express His earnest Hope that no premature or hasty proceedings will be adopted on their part, but that every thing will be referred for adjustment to the Commissioners now appointed on the part of the Two Governments.

It is owing to Mr. Fox's indisposition that I have the Honour of addressing you, an irregularity which I trust you will excuse.

EARL SPENCER TO ERSKINE [26]

No. 2.   DOWNING STREET, September 17th, 1806.

Sir,

The first meeting between Lord Auckland and Lord Holland, His Majesty's Commissioners for arranging the Differences subsisting be-

---

[23] Draft, F. O. 5 : 52. On Erskine, see note immediately preceding.

[24] Erskine's general instructions, dated July 22, 1806, F. O. 5 : 52, are not printed here. since they are almost identical, paragraph for paragraph, with the general instructions given Hammond in 1791, pp. 2–5, supra.

[25] William Eden, first Baron Auckland (1744–1814), distinguished diplomat, president of the Board of Trade 1806–07; and Henry Richard Vassal Fox, third Baron Holland (1773–1840), nephew of Charles James Fox and prominent Whig politician.

[26] F. O. 115 : 13. George John Spencer, second Earl Spencer (1758–1834), home secretary in the Grenville ministry, Feb. 1806—March 1807, had become foreign secretary ad interim, following the death of Fox on Sept. 13, 1806.

tween His Government and that of the United States, and Mr. Pinckney and Mr. Monroe the Commissioners appointed by the President and Congress for the same purpose, was held on the 23d ultimo, since which time several Conferences have taken place between them.

The particulars of what passed at these Conferences, will be transmitted to you more at large at a future opportunity—At present I have to inform you that to an urgent Request on the part of His Majesty's Commissioners for a Repeal of the Prohibitory Act [27] passed in the last Session of Congress the American Commissioners returned a very Civil and Conciliatory Answer. It is expected that they will make representations to their Government in favour of the Repeal, or at least of the Suspension of the Effects of this Act. You will take every opportunity of adding Weight to these Representations by your Language on the subject—observing how contrary the hasty passing this Act appears to that Spirit of Moderation which His Majesty is so anxious should ever characterise all transactions between the two Countries, and how ill calculated such premature proceedings ever must be to procure Redress for real, or explanation for supposed Injuries.

LORD HOWICK TO ERSKINE [28]

Circular. DOWNING STREET, 24th Sept., 1806.
Sir,

I transmit to you herewith for your Information a Gazette containing an Order of His Majesty in Council, authorizing the Governors and Lieutenant Governors of the British West India Islands, (in which Description the Bahama Islands and the Bermuda or Somer Islands are included) and of the Lands and Territories belonging to His Majesty on the Continent of South America, to permit, for a limited Time, the Importation of Staves and Lumber in any Ships belonging to the Subjects of any State in Amity with His Majesty, and of every kind of provision (Beef, Pork, and Butter excepted) being the produce of the Country to which such Ships shall belong; and also to permit the Exportation, in such Ships, of Rum, Molasses, and other Articles, except as therein excepted.

You will also find in the same Gazette an Order of His Majesty in Council relative to the Communication now established with Buenos Ayres.[29]

---

[27] The Non-Importation Act of April 18, 1806, prohibited the importation after Nov. 15, 1806, of certain enumerated articles of British manufacture. The time limit was extended, and the act did not go into effect until December of 1807.

[28] F. O. 115 : 13. Charles Grey, Lord Howick (1764–1845), a Whig associated with Fox in opposition to Pitt, first lord of the Admiralty in the ministry of "All the Talents," in September of 1806, upon the death of Fox, had become foreign secretary. Later, as Earl Grey, he was to sponsor and carry the Reform Bill of 1832.

[29] Buenos Aires had been taken in June of 1806 by a British force under General Beresford—only to be re-taken by the Spaniards in August.

HOWICK TO ERSKINE [30]

DOWNING STREET, September 25, 1806.

Sir,

I transmit to you herewith for your information, and for that of the Court where you reside, the Copy of a Note which by His Majesty's Command, I have this day addressed to the Ministers of Friendly and Neutral Powers resident here notifying the Cessation of the Blockade from the River Elbe to the River Ems both inclusive.[31]

HOWICK TO ERSKINE [32]

DOWNING STREET, October 7, 1806.

Sir,

I transmit to you for your information an Order of His Majesty in Council directing that Horses, Mules, and Asses, Neat Cattle, Sheep, Hogs, Poultry, and every other Species of Live Stock and live provisions be added to the articles which His Majesty by His Order in Council of the 17 of last Month, has authorized the Governors and Lieutenant Governors of His Majesty's Islands and Colonies in the West Indies,· and of any Lands or Territories on the Continent of South America to His Majesty belonging, to permit to be imported into the said Islands, Colonies Lands and Territories respectively.[33]

HOWICK TO ERSKINE [34]

Separate.   DOWNING STREET, November 6: 1806.

Sir,

I transmit to you the Copy of a letter from Mr. Marsden in date of the 14th of October together with its Inclosure, stating that Thomas Woods (then under Sentence of Death and since executed) having been convicted as concerned in the Mutiny on board the Hermione, and in the Murder of the Officers of that Frigate, had deposed, that the Surgeon's Mate was the principal Adviser of the Mutiny, and that he left him not long since at the Town of Providence in America in Trade with a Mr. Powell Druggist, and that he goes by the Name of Evans. I am to desire that you will take measures for ascertaining the Truth of this Statement, and that if it appears to be correct, you will make application to the Government of the United States, that means may be taken for securing the said

---

[30] F. O. 115: 13.
[31] Howick's note to Monroe of Sept. 25, 1806, is in *A. S. P., F. R.*, III, 267. Prussia and France were enemies again.
[32] F. O. 115: 13.
[33] See Howick to Erskine, Sept. 24, 1806, *supra.*
[34] F. O. 115: 13.

Person called Evans, that he may be sent Home to take his Trial in England.[35]

HOWICK TO ERSKINE [36]

Separate.   DOWNING STREET, November 6: 1806.

Sir,

It having been represented to me by Commissioners of Bankrupt in Liverpool, that one Blayney who has committed different Acts of Felony under the Bankrupt Laws, has taken Refuge in the Territories of the United States, and his Creditors having taken measures for procuring his Arrest, I have to desire that you will give them every facility in your power.

HOWICK TO ERSKINE [37]

No. 3.   DOWNING STREET, December 4: 1806.

Sir,

Mr. Merry's Dispatches to No. 48 inclusive, have been duly received and laid before The King.

There appears to be nothing in them which requires any particular Answer.

The Representations which the American Government will probably make upon the subject of the supposed Violation of their Neutrality by His Majesty's Naval Forces in the Capture of the Impetueux,[38] will probably be received through the Channel of their Minister here. The subject will however certainly be mentioned to you by Mr. Madison. You will decline entering upon the Discussion of it without precise Instructions, and engage only to transmit to your Court such Communications as may be made to you, but you will express your Conviction, that any transaction which seems to give any cause of Complaint to the United States, will undergo a careful Investigation here, and that the Decisions of His Majesty's Government will be equally guided by the Considerations which He owes to the Dignity of His Crown, the Interests of His Subjects, and the Rights of other Nations.

---

[35] Erskine in his No. 4 of Feb. 1, 1807, F. O. 5: 52, reported that his inquiries had not been fruitful respecting the Surgeon's Mate on the *Hermione,* the principal adviser of the mutiny on that frigate in September of 1797, according to the affidavit procured by William Marsden of the Admiralty Office. He further stated that Secretary Madison did not consider the American government justified in surrendering any fugitive, since Article XVII of Jay's Treaty had expired, and the Executive, however well disposed, could not exercise such authority without the sanction of a law upon the subject.

[36] F. O. 115: 13.

[37] F. O. 115: 13.

[38] On Sept. 14, 1806, the British ships *Belleisle, Bellona,* and *Melampus* fell in with the French ship *L'Impetueux* about ten leagues south of Cape Henry, and gave chase. The French ship made for the shore, ran aground, and was burned. When members of the crew were brought to Norfolk, the French consul refused to recognize them as prisoners of war on the ground that the ship had been captured within the limits of the United States. Merry to Fox, Sept. 28, 29, Nos. 47, 48, F. O. 5: 49. Madison preferred to make representations at London on the illegality of the capture. Erskine to Howick, March 1, 1807, No. 6, F. O. 5: 52.

INSTRUCTIONS OF 1807

No. 1.   DOWNING STREET, Jan'y 8: 1807.

Sir,

Your Dispatch No. 1, announcing your Arrival at Annapolis [2] on board the Avon Sloop of War was received here on the 6th of December, and together with Mr. Merry's Dispatches, which were received at the same time has been laid before The King.

It is with great satisfaction that I inform you that the Treaty of Amity, Navigation and Commerce between this Country and the United States, was signed on the 31st Ulto by Lords Holland and Auckland on the part of His Majesty, and by Messieurs Monroe and Pinckney on the part of their Government.[3]

Mr. Purviance, Secretary to the American Legation here, who leaves London today, is the Bearer of the Treaty for Ratification. I have the Honour herewith to transmit a Copy of this Treaty for your Information, together with the Copy of a Note delivered previous to the Signature by the Lords Holland and Auckland relative to the Complaints of the Canada Merchants, on the Subject of the Estimation of the Duties on the Inland Trade, in certain parts of the United States.[4] These Complaints which were communicated by Mr. Merry in the early part of last Year, but from various circumstances postponed for Consideration, certainly must not be lost sight of, by His Majesty's Government, and every means will be taken to obtain Redress for the Removal of the Inconveniences complained of.

I transmit to you also, the Copy of another Note presented by their Lordships to the American Commissioners previously to the Signature of the Treaty, on the subject of the Extraordinary Declarations and Orders of the French Government issued at Berlin on the 16th of

---

[1] F. O. 115: 16.

[2] Erskine arrived at Annapolis on Oct. 29, and was presented to President Jefferson in Washington on Nov. 3, 1806. Erskine to Fox, Nov. 4, 1806, No. 1, F. O. 5: 52.

[3] The treaty of Dec. 31, 1806, and the explanatory letter of Monroe and Pinkney of Jan. 3, 1807, are printed in *A. S. P., F. R.* III, 142–152.

[4] The complaints of the Canadian merchants were under three heads: their exclusion from Louisiana, the higher duties imposed on imports into the United States from Canada as compared with the importation of the same goods in American vessels, and minor grievances respecting alleged violations of Article III of Jay's Treaty. *A. S. P., F. R.* III, 152–153; and see Merry to Madison, Jan. 7, 8, 1806, Notes from British Legation, 3.

November last.[5] This Note I must recommend to your particular attention. You will state to the American Government that H. M. relies with Confidence on their Good Sense and Firmness in resisting pretensions which, if suffered to take effect, must prove so destructive to the Commerce of all Neutral Nations.

His Majesty has learnt that the measures announced in this Decree have already, in some instances, been carried into execution by the Privateers of the Enemy, and there could be no doubt that His Majesty would have an indisputable right to exercise a just retaliation. Neutral Nations cannot indeed expect that The King should suffer the Commerce of his Enemies to be carried on thro' them, whilst they submit to the prohibitions which France has decreed against the Commerce of His Majesty's Subjects.

But tho' this Right of Retaliation would unquestionably accrue to His Majesty, yet His Majesty is unwilling, except in the last extremity, to have recourse to measures which must prove so distressing to all Nations not engaged in the War against France.

His Majesty therefore with that forbearance and Moderation, which have at all times distinguished his Conduct, has determined for the present to confine Himself to the Exercise of the Power given him by his decided Naval Superiority, in such manner only as is authorized by the acknowledged principles of the Law of Nations, and has issued an Order [5] for preventing all Commerce from Port to Port of his Enemies, comprehending in this Order not only the Ports of France, but those of such Nations, as either in alliance with France or subject to her Dominion, have by measures of active Offence, or by the exclusion of British Ships, taken a part in the present War.

His Majesty feels an entire Confidence that the Moderation and Justice of this Conduct will be duly appreciated by the United States, and you will express to that Government, in the strongest Terms, the Regret His Majesty has experienced in being thus compelled in His own Defence, to act in a manner which must prove in some degree embarrassing to the Commerce of Neutral Nations, and His Majesty's sincere desire to avoid any stronger Measures, to which however, if the Injustice and Aggression of His Enemies should not be resisted by those Nations whose Rights and Interest are invaded by so flagrant a Violation of all public Law, it may be ultimately necessary for The King to have recourse.[6]

---

[5] The note presented by Lords Holland and Auckland on Dec. 31, 1806, in consequence of Napoleon's Berlin Decree declaring the British Isles to be in a state of blockade, was to the effect that Great Britain would ratify the treaty only in case the United States refused to submit to French "innovations on the established system of maritime law." *A. S. P., F. R.* III, 151–152. Because of this British reservation, and of the omission of the subject of impressment, Jefferson did not submit the treaty to the Senate.

[5] The order-in-council of Jan. 7, 1807. It is printed in *A. S. P., F. R.,* III, 267–268.

[6] Erskine's note to Madison on the order of Jan. 7, 1807, dated March 12, 1807, and Madison's replies, dated March 20, 29, 1807, are printed in *A. S. P., F. R.,* III, 158–159.

HOWICK TO ERSKINE [7]

No. 2.   DOWNING STREET, January 8, 1807.

Sir,

I inclose to you under a flying-seal for your Information, a letter for Mr. Foster [8] communicating to that Gentleman His Majesty's Gracious Permission to return to England on his Private Affairs, as soon as you can conveniently spare him from the Duties of the Mission.

HOWICK TO ERSKINE [9]

Circular.   DOWNING STREET, January 10, 1807.

Sir,

I transmit to you herewith for your information and for that of the American Government, the Copy of a Note [10] which by His Majesty's Command I have this day delivered to the Ministers of Friendly and Neutral Powers resident at this Court, relative to the new Measures which His Majesty has found it necessary to adopt in the just defence of the Commerce of His Subjects.

In presenting this Note, you will accompany it with such observations as the case naturally suggests. You will state that it is the unavoidable consequence of the unprecedented attempts of the Enemy—that in limiting this measure according to the acknowledged Principles of the Law of Nations, His Majesty has given an unequivocal proof of His forebearance and of the desire which he has always manifested of not unnecessarily restraining the Commerce of Neutral Powers, and that The King looks with a just confidence to the firmness of those Powers in resisting the first Introduction of a system by the Enemy which must so much aggravate all the Calamities of War.

Nothing will be so painful to His Majesty as to see Himself compelled to have recourse to measures of a more severe retaliation; but it must be distinctly undestood, and you will explain to the American Government, that if the Enemy should presevere in this system of violence and injustice, His Majesty must reserve to himself the indisputable right of enforcing against the commerce of France, whenever for the just Defence of the Rights and Interests of His People it may become necessary to do so, the same measures which Neutral

---

[7] F. O. 115 : 16.

[8] Augustus John Foster (1780–1848), son of the Duchess of Devonshire, had been in Washington since Dec. 23, 1804, as secretary of legation. He had succeeded Edward Thornton in that position. Foster did not take advantage of this leave of absence until March of 1808.

[9] F. O. 115 : 16.

[10] The note stated that since France had violated international law by prohibiting the commerce of neutrals with Great Britain, declaring Britain to be blockaded although France possessed no naval force on the sea, Great Britain therefore prohibited vessels from trading from one enemy port to another, or to ports from which British vessels were excluded.

Nations shall suffer to be executed by France against the Commerce of His Majesty's Dominions.

HOWICK TO ERSKINE [11]

No. 3.   DOWNING STREET, February 5, 1807.

Sir,

Your Dispatches to No. 3 inclusive, have been received and laid before The King.

I transmit to you herewith several Papers relative to an extraordinary Outrage committed by the Commander of the American Schooner Enterprize, by ordering Thomas Grant, a British Seaman employed in His Majesty's Transport Service in the Mediterranean, to be tied to the Gangway and to receive Twelve Lashes on the bare Back; and I am to signify to you His Majesty's Pleasure, that you make an immediate Representation to the American Government on this violent proceeding.

His Majesty feels confident that that Government will at once see the necessity of giving His Majesty the satisfaction which The King has a Right to expect for the Commission of so flagrant an Outrage, and that such steps will be taken with respect to the offender as, by the example they will afford, may prevent the recurrence of a similar circumstance.[12]

GEORGE CANNING TO ERSKINE [13]

No. 1.   FOREIGN OFFICE, April 16, 1807.

Sir,

I transmit to you herewith the Copy of a letter from Mr. Liston— and I am to desire that you will select the Documents therein described from the Records of His Majesty's Mission in North America, and transmit them to this office without loss of time.[14]

---

[11] F. O. 115 : 16.

[12] Thomas Grant, seaman on the British transport *Arethusa*, at Malta had visited the American Navy's armed schooner *Enterprise* and, for having been insolent to one of her officers, had been ordered flogged by Capt. David Porter of that vessel. Upon Erskine's representations, Secretary Madison promised an investigation, but stated as to Porter, whose reputation was excellent, that possibly "the authority assumed by him was an error of Judgment, resulting from the Practice of other naval Commanders." Enclosures with above instruction, and Erskine to Howick, June 3, 1807, No. 15, F. O. 5 : 52, enclosing Madison's note to Erskine of May 19, 1807.

[13] F. O. 115 : 16. George Canning (1770–1827), under secretary for foreign affairs from 1796 to 1801, and treasurer of the navy from 1804 to 1806, had succeeded Howick as Foreign Secretary on March 25, 1807. The Grenville ministry had fallen, in March of 1807, because of the opposition of George III to the opening of all commissions in the army and navy to Roman Catholics. Grenville was succeeded by the Duke of Portland.

[14] Robert Liston wanted accounts and vouchers relative to the blockhouses procured by him in the United States, in 1799–1800, for the island of Jamaica. See Grenville to Liston, Aug. 13, 1799, No. 12, *supra.*

CANNING TO ERSKINE [15]

No. 2.   FOREIGN OFFICE, 8th May, 1807.

Sir,

I transmit to you herewith for your information, the Copy of a Memorial from George Clarke Esq. of Charlton Lodge in Oxfordshire; and I am to desire that you will afford that Gentleman all proper Assistance in your power, with a view to obtain for him such compensation for his losses, as upon investigation he may appear to be justly entitled to.[16]

CANNING TO ERSKINE [17]

No. 3.   FOREIGN OFFICE, July 6, 1807.

Sir,

I transmit to you herewith the Copy of an Order of His Majesty in Council [18] authorizing the Governors and Lieutenant Governors of the British West India Islands (in which description the Bahama Islands and the Bermuda or Summer Islands are included) and of the Lands and Territories belonging to His Majesty on the Continent of South America, to permit for a limited time, the importation of Staves and lumber, in any Ships belonging to the Subjects of any State in amity with His Majesty, and of every kind of provisions [and] other articles except as therein excepted.

CANNING TO ERSKINE [19]

No. 4.   FOREIGN OFFICE, August 3rd, 1807.

Sir,

I transmit to you herewith a Memorial from Mr. John Hurst, late Merchant of the City of London—and I am to desire that you will make a suitable representation on this subject to the American Government, and use your best Endeavours to obtain for the Memorialist some Compensation for the losses he has sustained in consequence of the Negligence of the Post Master at Charlestown.[20]

---

[15] F. O. 115: 16.
[16] There is no copy of the memorial either in F. O. 5: 52 or F. O. 115: 16. Erskine reported that he would try to obtain the compensation desired by Clarke from the State of New York, although the chances of success were slight, since similar applications had been rejected by both New York and Vermont. Erskine to Canning, July 1, 1807, No. 16, F. O. 5: 52.
[17] F. O. 115: 16.
[18] Dated July 1, 1807.
[19] F. O. 115: 16.
[20] John Hurst charged neglect to the postmaster at Charleston, S. C., for failing to forward a letter, relative to Hurst's claims as a British creditor under Article VI of Jay's Treaty, addressed to his attorney, Moore Smith, at Charleston or elsewhere. After remaining in the postoffice at Charleston for about seventeen months, the letter was sent to Smith at Philadelphia, but too late for Hurst's claim in the sum of £6,233 to be filed. Upon representations by Erskine, Madison advised that Hurst seek redress through the courts, pointing out that he should anticipate the plea that the superscription "elsewhere" was too vague. Erskine to Canning, Jan. 18, 1808, No. 1, F. O. 5: 57, enclosing Erskine's note to Madison of Dec. 9, 1807, and Madison's reply of Dec. 16, 1807.

No. 5.   FOREIGN OFFICE, August 3rd, 1807.
Sir,
      I transmit to you herewith Copies of a letter from Mr.
Monroe and of my Answer thereto, relative to the Conduct of the Commander
of His Majesty's Ship Leopard in attacking an American Frigate
off the Coast of the United States and I have to desire that in any
Conversations which you may have with the American Government
on this subject, you will make your Language conformable to the
Sentiments contained in my answer to Mr. Monroe.[22]

No. 6.   FOREIGN OFFICE, September 4, 1807.
Sir,
      I transmit to you herewith the Copy of a Memorial from Messrs.
Ritchie and Co., owners of the Brigantine Ceres of Saltcoats, which
Vessel is stated to have been captured off Cape Henry by a Schooner
under Spanish Colours, in violation of the territorial Jurisdiction of
the United States; and I am to desire that you will make a suitable
Representation on this Case to the American Government, and endeavour to obtain for the Memorialists that Redress, to which they
may appear to be entitled.[24]

No. 7.   FOREIGN OFFICE, 8th October, 1807.
Sir,
      I send you inclosed herewith for your Information, Copies of the
Correspondence which has taken place between Mr. Monroe and my-
self subsequent to that which I transmitted to you in my Dispatch
No. 5 of the 3d. of August; and I have to desire that in any Con-

---

[21] F. O. 115 : 16.
[22] Monroe's note of July 29, and Canning's reply of August 2 (printed as August 3),
1807, relative to the attack of the Leopard upon the Chesapeake on June 22, 1807, in
which three members of the Chesapeake's crew were killed, eighteen wounded, and four
impressed as alleged British deserters, are printed in A. S. P., F. R., III, 187–188. See,
also, for notes exchanged by Canning and Pinkney in 1807–08, Papers Relating to America,
Presented to the House of Commons, 1809 (London, printed by A. Strahan, 1810).
[23] F. O. 115 : 16.
[24] Upon Erskine's representations, Madison had the Collector of the port of Norfolk
inquire into the character and conduct of the capturing vessel, and particularly whether
the vessel had been unlawfully fitted out in the United States. The inquiry revealed, so
Madison reported to Erskine, that the vessel had been fitted out at St. Mary's, in Spanish
East Florida ; that it was manned, with a single exception, by Frenchmen and Spaniards ;
and that it did not appear "that any unlawful Equipment or other unlawful Circumstance
occurred within the United States." Erskine to Canning, Dec. 3, 1807, No. 30, F. O. 5 : 52,
enclosing Madison's note to Erskine of Nov. 23, 1807.
[25] F. O. 115 : 16.

versations you may have with the American Ministers on the subjects to which they relate, you will make your Language conformable to the sentiments expressed in my letters to Mr. Monroe.[26]

CANNING TO ERSKINE [27]

No. 8.   FOREIGN OFFICE, 30th Octr., 1807.
Sir,

I transmit to you herewith for your information, Copies of the Correspondence which has taken place between Mr. Monroe and myself since that which I inclosed to you in my Dispatch No. 7 of the 8th of October, and I have to desire that you will continue to conform your language, in any conversations you may have with the American Ministers, to the sentiments expressed in my Letters to Mr. Monroe.[28]

CANNING TO ERSKINE [29]

No. 9.   FOREIGN OFFICE, October 25., 1807.
Sir,

This Dispatch will be delivered to you by Mr. Rose,[30] whom His Majesty has appointed to proceed to America on a Special Mission, the Nature of which he will explain to you. And I have to signify to you His Majesty's Pleasure that you afford Mr. Rose every assistance in your power for procuring an audience of the President, and (generally) in facilitating the object of his Mission.

INSTRUCTIONS TO GEORGE HENRY ROSE [31]

No. 1.   October 24th; 1807.
Sir,

His Majesty having been graciously pleased to appoint you to proceed on a Special Mission to the Government of the United States of America, for the purpose of adjusting the differences which have

---

[26] The enclosures consisted of copies of notes exchanged since August 6, 1807; see *A. S. P., F. R.,* III, 188–202. Canning had refused to link the *Chesapeake* outrage with the general subject of impressment; he would treat with Monroe upon the former subject but not, at present, upon the latter.

[27] F. O. 115: 16.

[28] The enclosures consisted of Monroe's note to Canning of Oct. 6, and Canning's reply of Oct. 9, 1807, respecting Monroe's replacement as minister by William Pinkney; and the following notes which are printed in *A. S. P., F. R.,* III, 192, 197–199, 202–203: Monroe to Canning, Oct. 9, Canning's reply of Oct. 10, and Canning's notes of Oct. 17, 22, 1807

[29] F. O. 115: 16.

[30] George Henry Rose (1771–1855), eldest son of George Rose, who at this time was vice president of the Board of Trade. George Henry Rose had been secretary of legation at The Hague, 1792–93, chargé d'affaires at Berlin, 1793–94, deputy paymaster of the forces, 1805, and member of Parliament for Southampton since 1794.

[31] Draft, F. O. 5: 56.

arisen with that Government from the Encounter between H. My's: Ship the Leopard and the Frigate of the United States, the Cheasapeake; I inclose to you, by the King's Command, a Letter from H: My: to the President of the United States; together with a Full Power, enabling you to negotiate and conclude any Instrument conformable to the tenour of these Instructions.

Immediately upon your arrival off any port of the United States, you will concert with the Commander of H: My's: Ship of War, destined for your Conveyance, or with the Commander of any Squadron of H: My: lying off Norfolk or it's vicinity, the means of making known to the American Government your arrival, charged with a Special Mission from His Majesty.

The most positive assurances have been given by the Minister of the United States in London, not only that every facility will be afforded to your admission into any of the American Ports, but that you will be received therein with the respect due to the Character with which you are invested.[32]

But should the Proclamation issued by the President of the United States on the 2nd of July [33] be still in force at the time of your arrival off the Coast of America; and should any attempt be made to apply the Prohibitions contained in that Proclamation to the Frigate in which you arrive, you will give it to be distinctly understood, that you are expressly precluded from acquiescing in any Condition or Restriction whatever, either upon the mode of your own landing, or upon the reception and treatment of H: My's: Frigate, which should differ, in the slightest degree, from the established usages, in cases of this nature, between independant and friendly nations.

And should the municipal officers of the place, or the commandant of any fortress or garrison to whom you may, in the first instance, have applied for the purpose of announcing your arrival, persist in enforcing any Regulations inconsistent with those established usages, (such as the proposing to you to land under a Flag of Truce—the denying the rights of Hospitality to the Frigate on board which you are embarked,—or the interposing any obstacle to your free Communication with H: My's: Minister at the Seat of the American Government, or with His Consul at the Port at which you may arrive) you will protest against any such measure, will declare that the perseverance in it will prevent you from executing the object of your Mission, and will require that such declaration shall be immediately reported to the Government of the United States, and if the answer of the Government should be unsatisfactory, or should be delayed beyond a reasonable time, you will forthwith return to England.

---

[32] See *A. S. P., F. R.*, III, 199.
[33] The proclamation of President Jefferson of July 2, 1807, excluding British warships from American waters, is printed in *A. S. P., F. R.*, III, 23–24.

Presuming that no such impediments will be thrown in the way of your arrival at the Seat of Government, I am commanded to Signify to you H: My's: Pleasure that immediately upon your arrival at Washington, you shall announce to the Secretary of State of the United States, that you are charged with a special Mission from H: My: and that you are desirous of obtaining an audience of the President for the purpose of delivering to Him H: My's: Letter.

Upon your obtaining that Audience you will present H: My's: Letter in the usual form; accompanying it with the Assurances of H: My's: disposition to bring to an amicable termination the discussion relating to the Encounter of the Leopard and the Cheasapeake: and stating that you are furnished with Full Powers to enter into negotiation upon that Subject.

Immediately after your audience of the President, you will take an opportunity of expressing the Same Sentiments to the Secretary of State, and of explaining to him more particularly the nature and extent of the Powers with which you are furnished.

You will inform the Secretary of State, that Mr. Monroe having been precluded, by his Instructions, from entering into any Separate discussion on this Affair; and having been directed to bring forward at the same time, and blend inseparably in the same discussion the question so frequently agitated between the Two Governments; and always hitherto ineffectually, respecting the search of neutral merchant Vessels for British Seamen; H: My: had determined to send a Minister to America, for the express purpose of relieving the present question from the embarrassment of a complicated discussion and of accelerating, as much as possible, the Settlement of a dispute so interesting to both Nations.

With this view, you will represent yourself as not only not empowered to enter into any discussion respecting the question of Impressment from Merchant Vessels; but as being absolutely prohibited by your Instructions from entertaining any proposition upon that Subject, or upon any other unconnected with the Specific object which you are authorized to discuss.

With respect to that object, you will express your Conviction that the Instructions under which you act would enable you to terminate your negotiation amicably and Satisfactorily.

But you will state that you are distinctly instructed, previously to entering into any negotiation, to require the Recall of the Proclamation of the President of the United States, and the discontinuance of the Measures which have been adopted under it.

The ground upon which the American Minister here has defended the issuing of that Proclamation, namely; that of an apprehension that the conduct of the British Commander in Chief of H: My's:

Squadron in North America was indicative of a hostile intention on the part of the British Government, having been completely done away by the early, unequivocal and unsolicited disavowal of the unauthorized Act of the British Officer, the Proclamation can no longer be maintained on that Ground.

It is obviously impossible that H: My: should consent that His accredited Minister, in actual negotiation for the adjustment of a difference between Himself and a friendly Power, should be subjected to Restrictions and Interdictions, in the course of his correspondence, which would neither have been inforced nor submitted in negotiation with an Enemy.

Neither can His Majesty be satisfied with a partial Suspension of the effects of the Proclamation, so far as concerns your Mission alone—A Modification which may possibly be proposed: but which, if acquiesced in, would imply that the Correspóndence of H: My's resident Minister in America was justly to be subjected to such restrictions.

H: My:, however, at the same time that He commands me to provide, by these Instructions, for the case of the Proclamation being still in force when you arrive in America; yet can hardly conceive it possible that it should not have been recalled immediately upon the Knowledge of H: My's: disavowal of the Attack upon the Cheaspeake—But is it fit that you should declare without reserve that H: My: would, on no account, suffer any negotiation to be carried on, on His behalf, under an interdict, which, even if justifiable in the first moments of Irritation and Misapprehension, cannot be continued, after the declaration of H: My's: Sentiments upon the transaction which gave rise to the Proclamation, except in a Spirit of Hostility; and can be considered, under such Circumstances, in no other light than as an Act of Aggression.

I inclose to you my notes to Mr. Monroe of the 8th: of August and of the 23d: of September and his replies of the 9th: of August and of the 29th: of Sept'r:[34] for the topicks with which you will enforce this Proposition: and I am to direct you to State distinctly to the Secretary of State, that you cannot proceed to execute the object of your Mission until the Proclamation shall be recalled—and the Freedom of Correspondence between all H: My's: Agents in America restored.

And upon a Refusal of this demand, you will declare your Mission at an end.

Supposing these preliminary Points to be settled satisfactorily, and that the Secretary of State or some other person shall have been duly invested with the necessary Full-Powers for treating with

---

[34] These notes are printed in *A. S. P., F. R.,* III, 188, 199–201, 189, 201–202.

you on the part of the American Government, you will proceed without delay to the Execution of the Object of your Mission.

You are, without waiting for any demand on the part of the American Commissioner, to state at once, that H: My: disavows the forcible attack upon the Cheasapeake; you will refer to my Correspondence with Mr. Monroe, and to H: My's: Proclamation, in proof of the Promptitude with which this Disavowal has been made, and of the Publicity which has been given to it.

You will state further, that Admiral Berkeley [35] has been recalled from his command for having acted, in an affair of such Importance, without authority. You will add that H: My: is prepared to discharge those men who were taken by this Unauthorized Act out of the American Frigate; reserving to Himself the Right of reclaiming such of them as shall be proved to have been deserters from H: My's Service, or natural born Subjects of His Majesty; and further that, in order to repair, as far as possible, the consequences of an act which H: My: dis-avows, H: My: is ready to secure to the widows and orphans, (if such there be) of such of the men who were unfortunately killed on board the Cheasapeake, as shall be proved not to have been British Subjects, or Deserters from His Majesty's Service, a Provision adequate to their respective Situation and Condition in Life.

All this His Majesty is willing to engage to do, as a Reparation due for a hostile act committed against a neutral State by an Officer of His Majesty without authority.

The Causes from which this dispute arose are not considered as having invalidated the Claim of the American Government to some Reparation for an unauthorized act of Hostility, but They cannot be over-looked in proportioning the extent of that reparation.

The Correspondence of Admiral Berkeley and of His Majesty's Consuls in the United States will have put you in possession of the many gross and unjustifiable instances of insult towards the Officers of H: My's: Ships, and of Seduction of the Crews, which had preceeded and provoked the Attack upon the Cheasapeake; and which had too much the appearance of a hostile disposition not to make a deep impression upon the Minds of those of H: My's: Commanders who were most immediately affected by them: H: My: at the Same time that He feels it right, on the Principles already stated, not to continue Adm'l Berkeley in a Command, in which he has acted hostilely without authority, against a Government with which H: My: was at Peace does however consider these Circumstances as greatly extenuating that Officer's procedure; and H: My: therefore commands me

---

[35] Vice Admiral George Cranfield Berkeley, seventeenth Baron Berkeley (1753-1818). His order to search the *Chesapeake* for deserters is printed in *A. S. P., F. R.*, III, 12.

to instruct you peremptorily to reject any Suggestion for any farther mark of H: My's: displeasure towards Adm'l Berkeley.

In like manner, the Conduct of the American Government, and of It's Agents, subsequently to the transaction of the Cheasapeake, the outrage and violence offered in Some instances to the persons of H: My's: Subjects, and the menacing Language and hostile Preparations directed avowedly against this Country, might justify the Supposition that the Government of the United. States had determined to take Reparation entirely into their own Hands: and might therefore have been considered as releasing H: My: from the obligation of tendering it.

H: My:, however, actuated by those Sentiments of Justice and Moderation by which His conduct towards Foreign Nations is uniformly governed, has not hesitated to make this Offer of Reparation.

You will next proceed to state, that after this voluntary Offer of Reparation, on H: My's: part, H: My: expects that the Government of the United States will be equally ready to remove those causes of just Complaint, which have led to this unfortunate Transaction.

H: My: requires this, not only as a due Return for the Reparation which He has thus voluntarily tendered: but as indispensable to any well founded expectation of the Restoration and continuance of that Harmony and good understanding between the Two Governments, which it is equally the interest of Both to cultivate and improve.

However much H: My: may regret the summary mode of redress which has been resorted to in the present instance, it cannot be supposed that His Majesty is prepared to acquiesce in an Injury, so grievous to H: My: as the Encouragement of Desertion from His Naval Service.

The Extent to which this practice has been carried is too notorious to require illustration. But the Instance of the Cheasapeake itself is sufficient to justify the Demand of adequate Satisfaction.

The Protestation of Commodore Barron is contradicted, in the face of the World, by the Conviction and Confession of one of those unhappy men who had been seduced from his allegiance to H: My: and to whom Commodore Barron had promised his Protection.[36]

H: My: however does not require any Proceeding of Severity against Commodore Barron. But He requires a formal disavowal of that Officer's conduct, in encouraging deserters from H: My's Service, in retaining them on board his Ship, and in denying the fact of their being there: and He requires that this disavowal shall be such as

---

[36] Commodore James Barron (1769–1851), who had commanded the *Chesapeake*, stated that he had given orders against the enlisting of British deserters. Jenkin Ratford, one of the four seamen impressed from the *Chesapeake* (on which vessel he had enlisted under the name of Wilson), proved to be a genuine British deserter, and was hanged. The other three seamen were native-born Americans, previously impressed into the British service, who had escaped from the British frigate *Melampus*.

plainly to show that the American Government did not countenance such proceedings, and to deter any Officer in their Service from similar mis-conduct in future.

He requires a disavowal of other flagrant proceedings, (detailed in the papers which have been communicated to you) unauthorized H: My, has no doubt; but with respect to which it ought to be known to the World that the American Government did not authorize and does not approve them.

You will state that such disavowals, solemnly expressed, would afford to His Majesty a satisfactory Pledge, on the part of the American Government, that the recurrence of Similar Causes of complaint will not, on any Occasion, impose on His Majesty the necessity of authorizing those means of Force to which Admiral Berkeley has resorted without authority; but which the continued Repetition of such Provocations, as unfortunately led to the attack upon the Cheasapeake, might render necessary as a just Reprisal on the part of His Majesty.

And you will observe therefore, that if the American Government is animated by an equally sincere desire with that which H: My: entertains to preserve the relations of Peace between the Two Countries from being violated by the Repetition of such Transactions, they can have no difficulty in consenting to make these disavowals.[37]

This Consent is to be the express and indispensable condition of your agreeing to reduce into an authentic and official form the particulars of the Reparation which you are, instructed to offer.

The precise form to which such mutual Stipulations shall be reduced—whether of declaratory notes to be reciprocally exchanged at the same time—or of a Convention to be signed on both parts,—is left to your dis-cretion.

But upon the Refusal, on the part of the Government of the United States, to give this reciprocal Satisfaction to H: My:, you will declare your Mission to [be] at an end: and will forthwith demand your Passports and return home.[38]

DRAFT OF CONVENTION FOR MR. ROSE [39]

Octr: 25th: 1807.

His Britannick Majesty, and the United States of America, equally animated by a sincere desire to terminate the differences which have unhappily arisen between them, in consequence of the Encounter be-

---

[37] In this draft there is a space of three lines between the end of this paragraph and the beginning of the next.

[38] Rose was received by President Jefferson on January 16 and took leave of him on March 21, 1808. For his unsuccessful mission are Henry Adams, *History of the United States*, IV. ch. viii, and the Madison-Rose correspondence in *A. S. P., F. R.*, III, 213–220.

[39] Draft, F. O. 5 : 56.

tween H. B. My's: Ship Leopard and the Frigate of the United States the Cheasapeake; have agreed to nominate Commissioners, duly authorized by them, to treat for the adjustment of these differences; and They have, for this purpose, nominated and appointed,— that is to say,—H: My: the King of the United Kingdom of Great Britain and Ireland, George Henry Rose Esquire, Member of the Parliament of the United Kingdom, and the United States,—, who having mutually communicated to each other their respective Full Powers have agreed upon the following Articles.

Article I.

H: B: My: disavows the Act of Admiral Berkeley in directing the hostile attack upon the United States Frigate the Cheasapeake: and His Majesty, in consideration of the Irregularity of that Proceeding, consents to discharge the men taken by that Act of Force out of the American Frigate. And His Majesty, from the same Consideration, is willing to direct a pecuniary Provision to be made for the widows and orphans (if such there be) of such of the men killed on board the Cheasapeake in the Encounter with H: My's: Ship Leopard, as shall be proved not to have been H: My's: Subjects, or Deserters from H: My's Service, suitable to their Situation and Condition in Life.

Article II.

The United States dis-avow the conduct of their agents in encouraging Desertion from H: My's: Service. They dis-avow the Conduct of Commodore Barron, in engaging to protect such Deserters, though natural-born Subjects of H: My:, in harbouring such Deserters on board of his Ship, and in refusing to discharge them upon demand. They dis-avow also all Acts of Violence and Outrage committed upon the Persons and Property of His Majesty's Subjects etc. etc. etc.

Article III:

This Convention shall be ratified, and the Ratifications exchanged in London, within three months of the date thereof, or sooner if it can be done.

In Witness whereof etc.

CANNING TO ERSKINE [39a]

No. 10.   FOREIGN OFFICE, December 1, 1807
Sir,

I herewith transmit to you the Copies of certain Orders of Council which His Majesty has thought proper to issue in consequence of

---
[39a] F. O. 115 : 16.

the hostile Conduct of France towards the Navigation and Commerce of Great Britain and of Neutral States.[40]

His Majesty has been induced hitherto to forbear recurring to measures of this Nature, by the Expectation that the Governments of the Neutral States, who have been the objects of the French Decrees, would have been awakened to a just Sense of what they owe to their Interests and Own Rights, and would have interposed with effect, either to prevent the Execution of the French Decrees, or to procure their Abrogation.

But His Majesty, having been disappointed in this just expectation, and perceiving that the Neutral Nations, so far from opposing any effectual Resistance, have submitted to whatever Regulations France may have prescribed for giving effect to her Decrees, can no longer refrain from having recourse to such Measures as, by retorting on the Enemy the Inconveniences and Evils produced by his Injustice and Violence, may afford the only remaining chance of putting an End to a System, the Perseverance in which is not more Injurious to His Majesty's Dominions, than to Nations not Parties to the War between Great Britain and France.

It is unnecessary to point out to you that the Principle upon which His Majesty finds Himself compelled to proceed, would justify a complete and unqualified Retaliation on His part of the System announced and acted upon by France, in respect to His Majesty's Dominions: and that His Majesty might therefore have declared in a State of rigorous and unmitigated Blockade all the Coasts and Colonies of France and Her Allies. Such a Measure the Maritime Power of this Country would have enabled His Majesty to inforce: Nor would those Nations which have acquiesced, without effectual Remonstrance, in the French Decree of Blockade, have derived any Right from the more perfect Execution of a corresponding determination on the part of His Majesty to complain of His Majesty's enforcing that Measure which the Enemy has executed imperfectly only from want of the Means of Execution.

His Majesty however, actuated by the same Sentiments of Moderation by which His Majesty's Conduct has been uniformly governed, is desirous of alleviating, as much as possible, the Inconveniences necessarily brought upon Neutral Nations by a State of Things so unfavorable to the Commercial Intercourse of the World; and has therefore anxiously considered what Modifications it would be practicable to apply to the Principle upon which He is compelled to act, which would not, at the same time that they might afford Relief from the Pressure of that Principle upon Neutral or Friendly Nations, impede or enfeeble its operation upon the Enemy.

---

[40] The enclosures are lacking, but presumably they were copies of the orders of Nov. 11, and those of Nov. 25, 1807. These orders are printed in *A. S. P., F. R.*, III, 269–273.

In pursuance of this Desire, the Order in Council,[41] which, if it had ended with the Sixth Paragraph, would have been no more than a strict and justifiable Retaliation for the French Decree of November 1806, proceeds, as you will observe, to provide many material Exceptions, which are calculated to qualify the Operation of the Order upon Neutral Nations in General; but which must be considered as most peculiarly favorable to the particular Interests of the United States.

The Paper which I herewith inclose to you, and which has been drawn up by a Committee of American Merchants, after Communication with the Board of Trade, will explain to you correctly the practical Effect which the Order in Council will have upon the Commerce of the United States, after the Regulations mentioned in it shall have received the Sanction of Parliament.[42]

It will not escape you, that by this Order in Council, thus modified and regulated, the direct Intercourse of the United States with the Colonies of the Enemy, is unrestrained: an Indulgence which, when it is considered to be (as it really is) not only a Mitigation of that Principle of just Reprisal upon which the Order itself is framed, but a Deviation, in favour of the United States, from that ancient and established Principle of Maritime Law by which the Intercourse with the Colonies of an Enemy, in time of War, is limited to the extent which that Enemy was accustomed in time of Peace to prescribe for it—and which, by reference to the Conduct of France in a time of Peace, would amount to a complete Interdiction, cannot fail to afford to the American Government a Proof of the amicable Disposition of His Majesty towards the United States.

You will observe also that the Transportation of the Colonial Produce of the Enemy from the United States to Europe, instead of being altogether prohibited (which would have been the Natural Retaliation for the rigorous and universal Prohibition of British Produce and Manufactures by France) is freely permitted to the Ports of this Country; with the power of subsequently re-exporting it to any part of Europe, under certain Regulations.

The object of these Regulations will be the Establishment of such a protecting Duty, as shall prevent the Enemy from obtaining the Produce of his own Colonies at a cheaper rate than that of the Colonies of Great Britain. In this duty it is evident that America is no otherwise concerned than as being to make an Advance to that Amount for which it is in Her own power amply to indemnify Herself at the Expence of the Foreign Consumer.

---

[41] The first of the three orders of Nov. 11, 1807, A. S. P., F. R., III, 269.
[42] This statement, is dated City of London Tavern, Nov. 21, 1807, and signed by John Gray, secretary.

I have thought it right to point your particular attention to these Two Provisions, as most prominent among those which are peculiarly favourable to America—and as those upon which it is most probable that you would immediately be required to give some Explanation. Another most important Relaxation of the Principles upon which His Majesty's Orders proceed, which will be particularly adverted to by you, is that which licences the Importation of all Flour and Meal, and all Grain, Tobacco, and other Articles, the Produce of the Soil of America, with the exception of Cotton, through the Ports of His Majesty's Dominions, into those of His Enemies, without the Payment of any Duty on the Transit—This cannot fail to be represented by you as an Instance in which His Majesty has deprived His Measure of its most Efficacious and Hurtful Operation against the Enemy, through Motives of Consideration for the Interests of America— And you should be prepared to state the Reason why His Majesty could not feel Himself at liberty, consistent with what was necessary for the Execution of His purpose, in any tolerable degree, to allow this Relaxation to apply to Cotton. That reason is to be found in the great extent to which France has pushed the Manufacture of that Article, and the consequent Embarrassment upon her Trade which a heavy Impost upon Cotton, as it passes thro' this Country to France, must necessarily produce.

In all your Communications you will not fail so to exhibit the State in which the Trade of America will be left after this Order, as to make it Evident, that a State of War with this Country would deprive her of very great Advantages.

Of course you will be cautious not to bring this Idea forward in any manner in which it could, by possibility, be received by America, in the insulting and odious Light of a Threat.

It will be right also that you should contrast the different Modes in which His Majesty's Orders and those of France are carried into execution. By His Majesty's, the utmost Consideration is manifested for the Interests of those Nations whose Commerce He is reluctantly compelled to impede, and ample time allowed for their becoming acquainted with the New Regulations and conforming to them. Whereas France, without any previous notice, and without any Interval, applies Her Orders to Trade already entered upon in ignorance of any such Orders, and subjects to Condemnation Ships whose Voyages, when commenced, were in strict conformity to all the Regulations at that time promulgated by France.

Even with these and other Modifications, His Majesty is not unaware that a measure extorted from Him by the Injustice of the Enemy, must inevitably produce Inconveniences to the Neutral Parties who are affected by its Operation.

The Right of His Majesty to resort to Retaliation cannot be questioned. The Suffering occasioned to Neutral Parties is incidental and not of His Majesty's Seeking.

In the Exercise of this undoubted Right, His Majesty has studiously endeavoured to avoid aggravating unnecessarily the Inconveniences suffered by the Neutral.

And I am commanded by His Majesty especially to instruct you, in all your Conversations with the American Secretary of State, to represent the earnest Desire of His Majesty to see the Commerce of the World restored once more to that Freedom which is necessary for Its Prosperity—His Readiness to abandon the System which has been forced upon Him, whenever the Enemy shall retract the Principles which have rendered it necessary—and the Conviction which His Majesty entertains, and upon which alone His present Measures are founded, that it would be vain to hope for such a Retraction, until the Enemy shall himself have been made to feel a Portion of the Evils which he has endeavored to inflict upon others.

CANNING TO ERSKINE [43]

No. 11.   FOREIGN OFFICE, 3d Decr., 1807.
Sir,

I transmit to you herewith, for your Information, the Copy of a letter and of its Inclosures from Mr. Barrow, Secretary to the Admiralty, containing additional proofs of the extent to which the Practice of granting American Protections to British Seamen continues to be carried on in that Country.[44]

[43] F. O. 115 : 16.
[44] John Barrow of the Admiralty on Nov. 30, 1807 had transmitted a complaint of Captain Sir Robert Laurie respecting desertions from H. M. S. *Milan* and enclosing three American protections furnished deserters by the collectors or deputy collectors of the ports of Alexandria, Va., Philadelphia, and Newburyport. When Erskine made these facts known, Madison acknowledged the imperfections of the system and stated that in the future no protections in the manner hitherto granted would be issued. Erskine to Canning, April 4, 1808, No. 14, F. O. 5 : 57.

INSTRUCTIONS OF 1808

CANNING TO ERSKINE [1]

No. 1.　　　　　　　FOREIGN OFFICE, 6th January, 1808.

Sir,

I transmit to you herewith, the Copy of a Letter from Mr. Shaw, accompanied by a Memorial from several other British Subjects, Proprietors of Land in His Majesty's late Province of West Florida. As a Memorial from the same Body was transmitted from this Office to Mr. Merry on the 9th February 1804, by referring to the Correspondence of the Mission, you will be apprized of the measures that were then taken in America, in consequence of the representations which, in pursuance of his instructions, that Minister made to the American Government on the subject.[2]

From the assurances contained in Mr. Madison's letter to Mr. Merry of the 27th March 1804, His Majesty's Government doubt not, that on your making a suitable Representation of the difficulties arising from the Provisions of the Act of the American Congress of 1805, as pointed out in the inclosed Papers, the American Government will take the necessary steps for removing them, and for affording to the Memorialists that justice, to which that Government acknowledged them to be entitled at the period above mentioned.[3]

---

[1] F. O. 115: 18.

[2] See note 7, p. 203, *supra*.

[3] Upon Erskine's representations, based upon the letter of Charles Shaw and the memorial of other claimants, dated Dec. 15, 1807, Madison reviewed the whole vexatious subject. He noted that the act of March 3, 1803 gave the claimants until March 31, 1804 to exhibit proofs of ownership; that the act of March 27, 1804 extended the time limit to Nov. 30, 1804, and allowed the claimants to submit transcripts of the original records; that the act of March 2, 1805 extended the period for fixing claims to Dec. 1, 1805, and in fact to Jan. 1, 1807, when the sales might begin. Since the British claimants during all this time had taken no steps toward specifying their titles, it seemed evident to Madison that they were speculators, whose object was to make profit out of the patronage of their government. Nevertheless, the date for the sale of lands had now been put off until Jan. 1, 1809. If any of the British memorialists filed their claims before that day, the Executive was empowered to suspend the sale of any particular parcel of land until the proper authority could decide upon the title. Erskine to Canning, May 4, 1808, No. 19, F. O. 5: 57.

Separate.   DOWNING STREET, February 27, 1808.

Sir,

This letter will be delivered to you by Archibald Mc Neill Esqr. whom His Majesty has been pleased to appoint His Consul in the Province of Louisiana; and I am to desire that you will present Mr. Mc Neill to the President of the United States as His Majesty's Consul aforesaid, and take the necessary steps for obtaining the Exsequatur [Exequatur] to enable him to discharge the Functions of his Office. You will also give to Mr. Mc Neill such Instructions for the regulation of his Conduct as your knowledge of the actual Situation of the District in which he is appointed to reside will enable you to supply.[5]

Separate.   FOREIGN OFFICE, March 4, 1808.

Sir,

Mr. Pinkney having expressed to me in a conversation which I had with him some time ago, his opinion that it would be more satisfactory to the feelings of his Government, and of the Citizens of the United States generally, if the re-exportation of Cotton found on board of Vessels brought into this Country under the Orders of Council of the 11th of November, should be wholly prohibited, rather than that it should be liable to a duty on it's being re-exported; I addressed to Mr. Pinkney a letter upon this subject, of which I herewith transmit to you a Copy for your information.[7]

No. 2.   FOREIGN OFFICE, April 7: 1808.

Sir,

Your several Dispatches to those of the 17th of February inclusive, have been received and laid before The King.

I herewith transmit to you the Copy of a Letter with it's several Inclosures, which I have received from Mr. Pinckney.

---

[4] F. O. 115 : 18.
[5] Mr. McNeil, apparently, never reached his post. He died, not far from Albany, New York, in October of 1808. Erskine to Canning, Nov. 3, 1808, No. 40, F. O. 5 : 58.
[6] F. O. 115 : 18.
[7] Pinkney on Jan. 26, 1808, had remonstrated against the duty imposed on American cotton intended for re-exportation to the continent. When Canning asked whether an absolute interdict would be preferred to a prohibitory duty, Pinkney stated that he did not consider himself authorized to say whether the United States would give a preference to either; whatever the object or the means, the United States could only consider the whole system of regulation inadmissible. On Feb. 22, 1808, Canning informed Pinkney (a copy of the letter was sent to Erskine with the above instruction) that the British government intended to prohibit all cotton brought into England from being exported to the territories of the enemy. *A. S. P., F. R.,* III, 207–209. In April of 1808 the export of cotton, except by license, was prohibited.
[8] F. O. 115 : 18.

The Lieutenant Governor of Gibraltar acted upon a Mistaken Opinion with respect to the Orders in Council; and no Time was lost by His Majesty's Government, in stating to that Officer the true Explanation of these Orders, and in desiring him in conformity thereto, to give immediate Relief in the Cases of which Mr. Pinckney has complained.[9]

I also inclose to you the Copy of the Act which has been passed for the purpose of carrying into Effect the Orders in Council, so far as the same required legislative provisions.[10]

CANNING TO ERSKINE [11]

No. 3.   FOREIGN OFFICE, April 7th, 1808.

Sir,

I transmit to you herewith, for your Information, the Duplicate of a Copy (inclosed to you in my Dispatch by the last Mail) of a letter from me to Mr. Pinkney, relative to an Alteration of the Regulations respecting Cotton brought into this Country under the Orders of Council; which alteration was made at the Suggestion of Mr. Pinkney.[12]

CANNING TO ERSKINE [13]

No. 4.[14]   FOREIGN OFFICE, 6th: April, 1808.

Sir,

I transmit to you herewith for your Information, the Copy of a Letter from Mr. Pole, with its several Inclosures, respecting certain Stores supplied to Ships in the Service of the Government of the United States which have not yet been paid for: and I am to desire that you will make the necessary application to the American Government for payment of the same.[15]

---

[9] Pinkney on March 7, 1808 had complained that Sir Hugh Dalrymple at Gibraltar had given notice that no neutral vessels bearing the produce of enemy colonies should be cleared for any port whatsoever except for a port in Great Britain.

[10] Presumably, the act of March 28, 1808 (48 Geo. III c. 26) ; printed in *A. S. P., F. R.,* III, 274–280.

[11] F. O. 115 : 18.

[12] The letter to Pinkney was dated Feb. 22, 1808. See Canning's separate instruction of March 4, 1808, *supra,* and the explanatory note. It will be observed that Canning, contrary to Pinkney's account, again states that the change was made at Pinkney's suggestion.

[13] F. O. 115 : 18.

[14] It will be noted that this instruction, although marked "No. 4," is dated a day earlier than instruction No. 3.

[15] William Wellesley-Pole of the Admiralty in the enclosed letter of March 7, 1808 referred to stores supplied American naval vessels, when in distress, at Malta and Gibraltar from 1801 to 1808. Upon Erskine's representations, Robert Smith, Secretary of the Navy, in November of 1808 empowered James Mackensie and A. Glennie, Navy Agents at London, to make payment. Erskine to Canning, Nov. 3, 1808, No. 41, F. O. 5 : 58.

CANNING TO ERSKINE [16]

No. 5.   FOREIGN OFFICE, May 6th, 1808.

Sir,

Your several Dispatches to No. 10 inclusive have been received and laid before The King.

I have to acquaint you that Mr. Pinkney waited upon me this morning, and I now inclose to you the substance of what he stated to me in the course of our Conversation. I have thought it right to put you in possession of this Information, in order that you may be apprized of the Extent of the Communication which Mr. Pinkney has made to His Majesty's Government.[17]

CANNING TO ERSKINE [18]

No. 6.   FOREIGN OFFICE, May 6th, 1808.

Sir,

The American newspapers which have lately arrived in this Country contain a Statement of the Contents of the Dispatch from Mr. Pinckney to his Government, mentioned in Mr. Rose's Dispatches as having been communicated to the Congress.

From this Statement it would appear that in a formal Conference held between Mr. Pinckney and myself for the express Purpose of discussing the merits of the Orders in Council issued by His Majesty on the 11th of Novr. 1807, Mr. Pinckney had stated at great Length, and with considerable Force of reasoning, the several Objections felt by him, and likely to be felt by His Government against the principles of this Measure of just and necessary retaliation on His Majesty's Part; and that I heard him throughout without offering any thing either in answer to his Arguments, or in extenuation of the injustice and violence imputed to the Acts of the British Government.

I do not say that this is precisely and verbally the Substance of the Statement in the American Newspapers—but it is it's Effect and Impression.

As nothing could be less respectful to any independant Government than the Conduct imputed by this Statement to a British Minister, I am particularly anxious to put you in possession of the Fact as it really took place; and to enable you to vindicate the British Government from the Imputation of having listened to Complaints against It's Conduct, without taking any pains to answer them.

[16] F. O. 115 : 18.
[17] An extract of Pinkney's report of this interview, to Madison, May 9, 1808, is given in *A. S. P., F. R.,* III, 223. Canning, it appeared to him, had expected a communication or a proposal from the American government respecting the subjects at issue between the two countries. See Canning to Erskine, May 6, 1808, No. 6, and Nov. 25, 1808, No. 15, *infra.*
[18] F. O. 115 : 18.

I requested to see Mr. Pinckney a few days after the Orders in Council had been issued, not for the purpose of discussing generally the Policy, the Wisdom, or the Justice of that Measure, but simply for that of explaining to him any part of them upon which he might require Explanation.

Even if I had intended on that Occasion to enter into discussion with him, I should have been led at the very Outset of our Conversation to forego that intention, by Mr. Pinckney's immediately informing me that he was preparing an Official Note on the Subject; in which he proposed to state the whole of his own Feelings and Opinions and of what he imagined would be those of His Government upon the Subject. I answered that I should be most happy to receive his Objections in that shape; conceiving that a written discussion best suited the Nature and Magnitude of the Question. That I should of course reserve what I might have to say in answer to those objections, until they were thus formally stated to me:—but that in the mean Time I should willingly reply to any Questions which he might wish to put to me, not in the Spirit of Controversy, but for the purpose of clearing up any doubtfull Points, previously to our Official Discussion.

Nothing passed on my part in the Conference, which had any other Object, or was conceived in any other Sense than that here stated.

Mr. Pinckney did undoubtedly expatiate upon the general Character of the Measure: but always in reference to the Note which he was to send, and uniformly with the Understanding that my answer was to be deferred 'till that Note had been received by me. And the Conference ended with no other apprehension on my part, and I believe none on that of Mr. Pinckney, than that the discussion was yet to come.

The promised Note, however, of Mr. Pinckney I never received. What might be the Considerations which induced him to alter his intention of sending it, I presume he explained to his Government— and probably in the same Dispatches of which so partial and (in that case) so unfair an Extract has been given to the American Public.

It certainly was Matter of extreme regret and disappointment to me to be thus deprived of the fair and expected Opportunity of recording in a regular and permanent Form the Justification of the British Government upon a measure in which I conceive the rectitude and Equity of It's conduct to be as unquestionable as it's Forbearance had been exemplary.

I have only to add that Mr. Pinckney called upon me, within a few days after the arrival here of the American Newspapers containing the Statement in question, for the express Purpose of disclaiming the partial Account which he is therein made to give of his Conversation with me; that his recollection of what had passed between us perfectly agreed with mine; and that he has this day read to me an extract from that very Dispatch which is represented to have been communicated to Congress in which he appears to have reported the Conference, it's occasion, and it's purport, precisely as I have now described them to you.

You will make use of the matter of this Dispatch in any Conference which you may have with Mr. Maddison, to set right a Misrepresentation, not intentional I am persuaded nor in any Degree imputable to the Government of the United States—but not therefore the less mischievous in it's Tendency; and to satisfy the American Minister that whatever may be the Subject, or the Issue of any Discussions between the two Countries, there is at least every disposition on the part of the British Government to conduct every such Discussion, with mutual respect, Liberality, and Candour.[19]

CANNING TO ERSKINE [20]

No. 7.   FOREIGN OFFICE, July 9, 1808.
Sir,
Your several Dispatches to No. 16 inclusive have been received and laid before The King.

I herewith transmit to you the Copy of a Dispatch from Sir George Prevost [21] to Lord Castlereagh, Secretary of State for the War Department, relative to the Military Occupation, by the United States, of Moose Island in Passamaquoddy Bay, and the Violent Seizure of a Boat laden with Flour, after it had touched at Deer Island, a Dependency of the Province of New Brunswick.[22]

These Transactions are of so hostile a Tendency as to render it indispensably necessary for His Majesty to receive some Explanation respecting them from the Government of the United States.

I have therefore to signify to you His Majesty's Pleasure, that you present a written Note to the American Secretary of State on the

---

[19] Erskine was assured by Madison that no credit was given to the unfounded and regrettable newspaper accounts, and that Pinkney "had uniformly represented that he had always experienced the most candid and liberal reception." Nevertheless, Erskine felt certain that Pinkney's dispatches were of a different tenor, and that these had materially aided in winning Republican votes in the Senate for Pinkney's confirmation as minister to London. Erskine himself wrote an anonymous statement contradicting the reports that Canning, unlike Bonaparte, had contemptuously rejected communications from the United States, and this statement, so he reported in August, appeared "in all the Federal Papers." Erskine to Canning, July 15, Nos. 25, 26, and Aug. 2, 1808, separate, F. O. 5: 58.

[20] F. O. 115: 18.

[21] Sir George Prevost, first baronet (1767–1816), was appointed Lieut. Governor of Nova Scotia in 1808, and Governor General of Canada in 1811.

[22] Prevost's dispatch to Castlereagh, dated May 28, 1808, with its enclosures, not only referred to the occupation of Moose Island but also to the seizure of boats at Niagara by American revenue officers, which is the subject of the instruction immediately following.

subject of both these Transactions. With respect to the first of them you will observe, that The King's Right to the Sovereignty of Moose Island, was clearly defined by the Treaty of Peace of 1783; and that by no subsequent Act has His Majesty divested Himself of that Right; and that therefore the Government of the United States, cannot be justified in occupying this Island, and much less in converting it into a Military Post. You will therefore require a distinct Explanation of the Views and Intentions of the American Government respecting the future Possession of this Island. The violent seizure of the Boat being an Act of more direct Hostility, His Majesty is willing to believe that the American Officer must have acted in this Instance without Instructions, and to entertain the fullest persuasion that upon a Representation being made upon the subject of it, the Government of the United States will not only disavow the Aggression, but take effectual Measures to prevent its Recurrence.[23]

CANNING TO ERSKINE [24]

No. 8.   FOREIGN OFFICE, August 4th: 1808.
Sir,
Your several Dispatches to No. 22 inclusive have been received and laid before the King.

I herewith inclose to you the Extract of a Letter from Montreal, which has been transmitted to Lord Castlereagh, His Majesty's Secretary of State for the War and Colonies, by a respectable Mercantile House in London. The Shape in which this Information comes does not give it official Authenticity: but supposing the Facts to be true as stated, it appears that several Boats belonging to the Michellimackenack Company were fired at by the American Garrison at Niagara, as they were passing along the Shore of Lake Ontario in their Way to Michellimackennack, were compelled to bring to, and were seized by that Garrison.

Notwithstanding the hostile Character of this Transaction (as it appears upon the Face of the Information), His Majesty is still de-

---

[23] Moose Island (Eastport) had long been claimed by the United States, and by Article 1 of the uncompleted Hawkesbury-King Convention of May 12, 1803 (*A. S. P., F. R.,* II, 584) was to be ceded to the United States. To Erskine, Madison dwelt much upon the fact that the island had been occupied by the United States since the Declaration of Independence and declared that the American government intended to keep it regardless of British protests. As to the seizure of the flour-laden boat after it had touched at Deer Island, within British jurisdiction, he would make inquiries. Meanwhile, it was reasonable to assume that the seizure resulted from the pursuit of known transgressors of the Embargo Act, and from a mistake as to the boundary. Erskine to Canning, Nov. 2, 1808. No. 39, enclosing copies of Erskine's note to Madison of Sept. 11, and Madison's reply of Oct. 1, 1808, F. O. 5: 58. In a separate dispatch of Nov. 6, 1808, F. O. 5: 58, Erskine enclosed a letter he had received from Consul General Barclay, dated Oct. 28, 1808, in which Barclay, formerly British commissioner to settle the northeastern boundary, declared that Great Britain could not justify taking possession of Moose Island. See also *Corres. of Barclay,* pp. 278, 285–288.
[24] F. O. 115: 18.

sirous not to consider it as indicative of any System of Hostility against Great Britain, on the part of the American Government; but to impute it to individual officers acting without any Authority.

Coupling, however, this Aggression with the Transactions in Passamaquoddy Bay which formed the Subject of my last Dispatch, it is impossible for His Majesty to pass over in Silence acts of such a Description, following so closely upon each other, and so injurious to the Interests of His Subjects, as well as derogatory to the Dignity of His Crown. I have therefore to signify to you His Majesty's Pleasure that you do take every possible Step for ascertaining the Truth of the Statement contained in the inclosed Letter; and that if you shall find reason to believe that Statement well founded, you should lose no Time in representing the Circumstances of the Transaction to the American Government, and requiring from them a distinct avowal of their Sentiments respecting it; and if (as is presumed to be the Case) the Act here complained of shall appear to be the unauthorized Act of any individual officer, you are to express His Majesty's confident Expectation, that not only due Punishment will be inflicted on such Officer, but also that a pecuniary Indemnification will be made by the American Government for any Losses which may have been sustained by Subjects of His Majesty on this occasion.[25]

CANNING TO ERSKINE [26]

No. 9.   FOREIGN OFFICE, August 4, 1808.

Sir,

I transmit to you herewith the Copy of a Note which I have received from Mr. Pinkney, and of the answer which, by His Majesty's Command, I have returned to it.[27]

---

[25] In his No. 23 of July 5, 1808, F. O. 5: 57, Erskine had informed Canning of the seizure by the Collector of the port of Niagara, aided by 100 American troops, of eight Canadian boats engaged in the Indian trade, and the retention of the cargoes, which were later released upon security. The ground for the seizure was the failure of the boats to report at Niagara: Erskine contended that they were not required to report. In his No. 42 of Nov. 3, 1808, F. O. 5: 58, Erskine reported that Madison had referred him to Gallatin, who told him that he was still trying to get a full and accurate account of the incident.

[26] F. O. 115: 18.

[27] On August 2, 1808 Pinkney informed Canning that five seamen, all with American protections, had deserted from the American dispatch vessel St. Michael. Four of them had shipped on an English transport, while the fifth was then at Falmouth, which appeared to be his native town. In his reply of August 3, Canning reminded Pinkney of the facility with which American protections were obtained by British deserters, and of "the repeated instances in which the Government of the United States have declined interfering in any manner, for preventing desertion from British Ships in the Ports of America."

CANNING TO ERSKINE [28]

No. 9.[29]   FOREIGN OFFICE, Sep'r 7th. 1808.
Sir,
Your several dispatches to No. 24 inclusive have been received
and laid before the King.

I herewith transmit to you the Copy of a letter from Capn. Skene
of His Majesty's Ship Guerrière relative to a French Privateer which
had been refitted in the Port of Charleston, and furnished with stores
and Provisions for three Months.   I have to signify to you His
Majesty's Pleasure that you make the strongest Representations on
the Circumstances of this Case to the American Government, and that
you express to them the Kings just expectation, that while His
Majesty's Ships of War are denied the common Rights of Hospitality
in the Harbours of the United States, the armed Ships of His Enemies should not be allowed to be furnished in those Harbours with
the additional Means of annoying the Commerce of His Majesty's
Vessels.[30]

CANNING TO ERSKINE [31]

No. 10.   FOREIGN OFFICE, October 8th., 1808.
Sir,
Your Dispatches Nos. 27 and 28, have been received and laid before
The King.

I transmit to you herewith the Copy of a Note which I have received from Mr. Pinkney, and of the Answers which, by His Majesty's Command, I have returned to it—and I have to signify to
you His Majesty's Pleasure, that, in any Conversations which you may
have with the American Ministers upon this subject, you make your
Language conformable to that contained in my Note to Mr. Pinkney.[32]

---

[28] F. O. 115 : 18.
[29] This and the preceding instruction are both marked "No. 9."
[30] Capt. Ar. Skene's letter of July 20, 1808 referred to the French privateer *Peraty* of
Guadaloupe (formerly His Majesty's cutter *Barbara*), which had been captured on July 17,
1808.   Upon Erskine's representations, Madison promised to make an inquiry and to take
punitive measures if any improper or unlawful aid had been afforded the *Peraty* at Charleston.   Mr. Madison "added that the Reasons for the difference of reception which His
Majesty's Ships met with from that which the French had found lately in the Ports and
Harbours of the United States, were too obvious to make it necessary for him to mention—
by which he meant the President's Proclamation" excluding British warships.   Erskine
to Canning, Nov. 3, 1808, No. 40, F. O. 5 : 58.
[31] Draft, F. O. 5 : 58.
[32] Pinkney's note of August 23, and Canning's two notes of Sept. 23, 1808, are printed
in *A. S. P., F. R.*, III, 228, 230–232. See Canning to Erskine, Nov. 25, 1808, No. 15, *infra*.

CANNING TO ERSKINE [33]

No. 11. FOREIGN OFFICE, November 22d., 1808.

Sir,

Your Dispatches to No. 38 inclusive, have been received and laid before The King.

Your Dispatch No. 29 containing a Letter with its Inclosures, which Mr. Maddison had addressed to you, complaining of the Conduct of William Reeve, Master's mate of His Majesty's Ship Hebe, was referred by my direction to the Admiralty, in order that that Board might take the proper Steps for duly investigating this Transaction.

Previously however to the Receipt of that Dispatch, some Communications on this subject had been transmitted to my Office by the Admiralty, Copies of which I now inclose to you for your Information, and I shall apprize you of the Result of the Investigation which the Admiralty has directed to be instituted into the Conduct of Mr. Reeve, as soon as it shall be concluded.[34]

CANNING TO ERSKINE [35]

No. 12. FOREIGN OFFICE, November 25, 1808.

Sir,

I transmit to you for your information, Copies of a letter and it's inclosures which have been received from the War Department upon the subject of the proceeding of the Americans at Moose Island, and the pretension set forth with respect to Boundaries between His Majesty's Territories in North America, and those of the United States, and I am to desire that you will repeat to the American Government the Representations which in my Dispatch No. 7 you were instructed to make upon this subject.[36]

CANNING TO ERSKINE [37]

No. 13.[37a] FOREIGN OFFICE, November 21, 1808.

Sir,

Having referred to The King's Advocate, for his Investigation, the Correspondence between you and Mr. Maddison, respecting cer-

---

[33] Draft, F. O. 5 : 58.
[34] Madison on Sept. 1, 1808 had complained of the insulting letter sent by Reeve on June 4 to Governor Claiborne at New Orleans relative to the (temporary) detention of the prize ship, the Spanish schooner *Candelaria*, of which Reeve was the master. Erskine to Canning, Sept. 3, 1808, No. 29, Oct. 1, 1808, No. 34, F. O. 5 : 58.
[35] Draft, F. O. 5 : 58.
[36] The papers transmitted by the War Department, Nov. 3, 1808, consisted of two letters. with enclosures, from Lt. Genl. Sir George Prevost to Lord Castlereagh, dated Halifax August 24 and Sept. 7, 1808. See note 23, p. 253, *supra*.
[37] Draft, F. O. 5 : 58.
[37a] It will be noted that "No. 13" is dated earlier than both "No. 11" and "No. 12."

tain Dispatches addressed to the Government of the United States which, having been taken in the Ship Thalia by a British Cruizer, were stated to have been, some broken open, and one detained, I transmit to you, for your Information, the Copy of a detailed Report which I have received from The King's Advocate on this subject; by which you will perceive, that there are just grounds for doubting the Accuracy of the Information which Mr. Maddison had received respecting this Transaction.

You acted very properly, in your answer to Mr. Maddison, in recalling to his Recollection the unjustifiable seizure and Detention, by an American Citizen, of some Dispatches addressed to you. Mr. Maddison's attempt to defend that most unwarrantable Act, by assimilating it to the Conduct of the Commanders of His Majesty's Ships of War and of the British Courts of Admiralty in opening Letters found on board of Vessels captured or detained, is evidently fallacious—as the Seizure of your Dispatches was the Act of an unauthorized Individual, and as the Proceeding to which he compared it, is directed by a competent Authority, and is justified upon the principles which The King's Advocate has stated in his Report.[38]

CANNING TO ERSKINE [39]

No. 14.   FOREIGN OFFICE, Nov'r 25, 1808.

Sir,

I herewith inclose to you, for your Information The Copies of a Letter from Sir John Warren inclosing a Report from the Commander of His Majesty's Packet the Lord Hobart relative to the Boarding and Detention of that Vessel, by the Direction of the Commanding Officer of the American Frigate the Chesapeak.

Although I have no Doubt, that, in compliance with Sir John Warren's Suggestion, You have brought this Transaction before the American Government, I have nevertheless, to signify to you His Majesty's Pleasure, that you make the strongest Representations upon it to the American Government.

You will observe to Them that the Packet being a Royal Vessel. is not liable to the Regulations to which Merchant Vessels are sub-

---

[38] In his No. 29 of Sept. 3, 1808, F. O. 5 : 58, Erskine had enclosed Madison's complaint, of August 9, respecting the seizure of the dispatches of John Armstrong, American minister to France, and his reply to Madison of August 23 in which he recalled to the Secretary of State the seizure "by a Citizen of the United States, William Duane (now Lieut. Col. Duane) of certain Dispatches addressed to me by His Majesty's Admiral on the Halifax Station." The King's Advocate General, Sir John Nicholl, in his report of Nov. 14, 1808 (enclosure in F. O. 115 : 18) stated that all papers found on the *Thalia* had been restored to the master of the vessel. No official dispatches had been on board, and the master, who now asserted that he had carried a packet from General Armstrong, had not listed such dispatches in his deposition before the Admiralty Court.

[39] Draft, F. O. 5 : 58.

jected; and that the Demand of the American Officer to see the Commission of it's Commander was a wanton Insult; as the Packet had been lying for some Weeks in the Harbour of New York, most probably in sight of the Chesapeak; that it's Flag designated the Nation to which it belonged, and the Service on which it was employed.[40]

CANNING TO ERSKINE [41]

No. 15.   FOREIGN OFFICE, Nov. 25th., 1808.
Sir,

I inclose to you, for your information, the Copies of a Letter from Mr. Pinkney, in reply to that which I addressed to him on the 23d. of September last, and of the answer which I have returned to Mr. Pinkney's Letter.[42]

From one part of this answer you will perceive that I have adverted to a Mis-representation which appeared in an American Newspaper transmitted by you of my assertion in Parliament, that subsequently to the termination of Mr. Rose's Mission, the American Government had not made any communication here in the Shape of a Remonstrance or in the tone of irritation. In what I stated upon that Occasion, I certainly had no reference to Mr. Maddison's Letter to you of the 25th of March, which I had considered as closing in America that discussion of the Subject which you had commenced in your letter to Mr. Maddison which discussion I the rather understood to be closed because I had every reason to believe that the Vessel the Osage, whose departure with Messengers for England and France was so ostentatiously announced in America, and whose arrival in this Country was expected with so much impatience by the American Minister here, would certainly bring to Mr. Pinkney instructions for making some direct communication on the Subject of the Orders in Council, of the Affair of the Chesapeake, or of both. In this expectation I was however disappointed, and Mr. Pinkney declared to me, in answer to an Inquiry of mine, that he had nothing to communicate to me, in consequence of the instructions which he had received by the Osage.

<hr>

[40] In his report of Oct. 24, 1808 (transmitted by Admiral Sir John Borlase Warren on Oct. 26, 1808; both in F. O. 115: 18), Alex. Hamilton, master of the dispatch vessel Lord Hobart, stated that an officer of the Chesapeake had boarded the vessel off Staten Island on Oct. 10 and demanded first that he show a clearance from the Custom House and then that he show his commission as a British officer. After representations by Consul General Barclay, and after Hamilton had denied that he had on board "a large quantity of specie . . . which the laws of the United States prohibited being exported," the Lord Hobart was allowed to proceed to Halifax.
[41] F. O. 115: 18.
[42] Pinkney's notes to Canning of Sept. 24, and Oct. 10, and Canning's answer of Nov. 22, 1808, are printed in A. S. P., F. R., III, 232–239. See Canning to Erskine, May 6, 1808, Nos. 5 and 6, supra.

The impression of the Osage was strong upon my mind when I made the Assertion which has been referred to; and I am confident that the arrival of the Osage was the Circumstance which induced the Inquiry to which my Assertion was an answer.

Since the Receipt of your Dispatch, I have looked back to Mr. Maddison's Letter and find that it was dated on the 25th of March, a very few days after Mr. Rose had quitted Washington, but previously to his Departure from the territory of the United States. I certainly do not pretend to have had these precise dates accurately present to my recollection when I stated, the "termination of Mr. Rose's Mission" as the Period since which the American Government had made no communication of the sort which I described.

Nor do I conceive the Circumstance of your Dispatch which contained the Copy of Mr. Maddison's Letter having arrived (as it undoubtedly did) here a few weeks later than Mr. Rose, though dated within a day or two of his Departure from America, at all varies the Character of that Letter, or can be supposed to make it, in a fair sense, a Transaction subsequent to the termination of Mr. Rose's Mission. I am however not anxious to lay any great stress upon this point: Mr. Maddison's Letter which, as I have before said, appeared to me to have closed the Discussion in America, not having been at all in my Contemplation when I used in Parliament the Expressions which have been so much misrepresented.

INSTRUCTIONS OF 1809

CANNING TO ERSKINE [1]

No. 1.　　　　　　　　　　FOREIGN OFFICE, January 5, 1809.

Sir,

Your several Dispatches to No. 45 inclusive, have been received and laid before The King.

I herewith inclose to you the Copy of a Letter which I addressed to Mr. Pinkney on the 24th of last Month, accompanying the Copy of an Order which His Majesty in Council was pleased to issue on the Wednesday preceding. I also inclose to you the Copy of Mr. Pinkney's Answer.

It is needless for me to make any observations upon this Correspondence, [other] than that the Tone of Mr. Pinkney's letter, and the manner in which he has received this spontaneous Communication, are not calculated to induce me to address any other future Communications to him in future than such as are indispensably necessary.[2]

CANNING TO ERSKINE [3]

No. 2.　　　　　　　　　　FOREIGN OFFICE, 5th January, 1809.

Sir,

I inclose to you herewith for your information, the Copy of a letter from Lieut. General Sir James Craig [4] to Lord Castlereagh, transmitting a Memorial addressed to that Officer by the Merchants of Montreal concerned in the Trade with the Indians within the Territory of the United States.

As you have already been made so fully acquainted, as well by the Merchants as by Sir James Craig, with all the particulars of the outrage committed by the American Officers on His Majesty's Subjects,[5] I have no doubt that you will have made such representations

---

[1] F. O. 115 : 20.

[2] Canning's note of Dec. 24, 1808. and its enclosure, and Pinkney's reply of Dec. 28, 1808, are printed in *A. S. P., F. R.,* III, 239–240. In his reply Pinkney acknowledged receipt of the order modifying the British system and curtly reiterated that what his government wanted was not the modification but the repeal of the orders.

[3] F. O. 115 : 20.

[4] Sir James Henry Craig (1748–1812), Lieut. Gov. of Canada 1807–1811. His letter to Castlereagh is dated Oct. 29, 1808 ; a copy of the memorial is lacking in both F. O. 115 : 20 and F. O. 5 : 62.

[5] See note 25, p. 254, *supra.*

260

to the American Government on these proceedings, as the occasion required.

It appears therefore only necessary to signify to you His Majesty's Pleasure, that you make such further Representations on this subject, in the sense of Sir James Craig's letter to you, as circumstances may render expedient, in order to obtain due satisfaction for the insult offered to His Majesty, and the restitution of the Vessels and Property belonging to the Merchants, together with indemnification for the losses which they have sustained; and an assurance that the necessary steps will be taken by the American Government to prevent a recurrence of the like proceedings.

CANNING TO ERSKINE [6]

No. 1.[7]   FOREIGN OFFICE, 23d January, 1809.

Sir,

Your Dispatches from No. 46 to No. 49 both inclusive, have been received and laid before the King.

The most serious Attention of His Majesty's Government has been directed to the important Matters treated in those Dispatches; and especially to those confidential Communications, which you represent yourself to have received from different Individuals of Weight and Influence in the American Government,[8] respecting the political relations of Great Britain and the United States.

It must be confessed, that the conciliatory disposition which these Individuals describe to you as existing on the part of the American Administration, does not appear either in the Acts of the Government, or in the debates of Congress. But the intimations which have been given to you of the difference between the personal Sentiments of Mr. Jefferson, and those of his probable Successor in the Presidency, with respect to this Country, and the hopes which you have been led to entertain, that the beginning of the new Presidency may be favourable to a change of Policy in America, if opportunity and encouragement for such a change shall be afforded by this Country, have induced His Majesty's Government to review and reconsider the most important points of disagreement between the two Governments; and I have received His Majesty's Commands to send you such Instructions on those subjects, as must, if the Government of the

---

[6] F. O. 115: 20.

[7] This is the second instruction to Erskine of 1809 marked "No. 1." The draft of this in F. O. 5: 62 is marked "No. 3."

[8] The Cabinet members referred to were Secretary of State (and President-elect) Madison, Secretary of the Treasury Gallatin, and Secretary of the Navy Robert Smith. Erskine to Canning, Dec. 3, 4, 1808, Nos. 46 and 47, F. O. 5: 62. These two dispatches, together with Canning's instructions Nos. 1, 2, and 3 (above) of Jan. 23, 1809, are printed in *Correspondence Relating to America, Presented to Parliament in 1810* (London, printed by A. Strahan, 1811), pp. 5–14, 26–38.

United States be seriously disposed to accomodation, lead to their immediate and satisfactory adjustment.

The first of these points is the Affair of the Cheasapeake.

Nothing prevented an amicable conclusion of this discussion by Mr. Rose, except the refusal of the American Government to withdraw the Proclamation issued on the 2d. July 1807, by which the Ships of War of Great Britain were interdicted from the Harbours of the United States, while those of France continued to be allowed a free resort to them.

The construction given by Mr. Madison, to the resolution of the Committee to whom the consideration of the Foreign Relations of the United States was referred at the opening of the present Session of Congress, undoubtedly goes a considerable way to remove the objection to which the Proclamation was liable. .

Of the exclusion of the Ships of War of both belligerents from the Ports of a Neutral State neither Belligerent has a right to complain: the partiality of that Regulation alone gave to it a character of hostility.

If therefore the Ships of War of France shall in point of fact have been excluded from the Ports of the United States, and such Ships of that description as were in those Ports at the time of passing the Resolution, shall have been warned to depart, His Majesty would no longer insist upon the formal recall of the Proclamation, as a Preliminary to the adjustment of the difference arising from the affair of the Cheasapeake.

It is still necessary, however, that either the Proclamation should be withdrawn, or it's operation formally declared to be at an end; but it will be sufficient if that withdrawal, or Declaration, is recorded (according to the arrangement which Mr. Madison professed himself ready to adopt) in the same instrument, or at the same time, with the terms of Reparation which His Majesty is now willing to offer.

The terms of reparation, which Mr. Rose was authorized to propose, were, in substance:

1st: A formal disavowal by His Majesty of the act of Admiral Berkeley.

2dly: The restoration of the men forcibly taken from on board the Cheasapeake; reserving to His Majesty the right of claiming in a regular way from the American Government the discharge of such of them as might prove upon investigation to be either natural born Subjects of His Majesty, or Deserters from His Majesty's Service.

3dly: A pecuniary provision, suitable to their respective situations in Life, for the Widows or Orphans of such Men (not being natural born Subjects of His Majesty, nor deserters from His Majesty's Service) as may have been unfortunately killed on board the Cheasapeake.

In return for these concessions, His Majesty required:

1st: A disavowal on the part of the American Government of the detention, by Commodore Barron, of deserters from His Majesty's Service; of his denial of his having such persons on board of the Ship under his Command, and his refusal to deliver them upon demand. 2dly: A like disavowal of the Outrages committed on the Persons or Property of His Majesty's Subjects at Norfolk, or elsewhere, in consequence of this Affair.

An Engagement was also to be required that the American Government should not, in future, countenance any of It's Agents, civil or military, in encouraging desertion from His Majesty's Service.

This last point being, according to the Statement in your No. 47, to be provided for by a Special Act of Congress, it is not necessary to obtain any specific engagement or declaration respecting it. And as it is above all things desireable to simplify as much as possible the conclusion of an arrangement which has been so long pending; as a recurrence to the details of the Affair of the Cheasapeake, of the causes which led to it, and of the discussions immediately arising out of it, might lead to complicated and fruitless controversy, His Majesty on His part, would be contented at present to wave any demand for retrospective disavowals on the part of the Government of the United States; that Government being, on the other hand, contented to receive back the Men forcibly taken out of the Cheasapeake, as the single and sufficient Act of reparation. To which, however, His Majesty would still be willing to add the provision for the Widows and Orphans of the Men killed in the action: but as an Act of His Majesty's Spontaneous Generosity.

This arrangement I have every reason to believe, both from what Mr. Pinckney has stated to me,[8a] and what Mr. Rose reports of Mr. Madison's unofficial Conversations, would be satisfactory to the American Government upon this Subject.

Whether this arrangement shall be settled by a formal Convention or by the exchange of Ministerial Notes dated on the same day, and reciprocally delivered at the same time, is left to the decision of yourself and of the American Minister.

I have only to add (though I see no ground to apprehend that such a demand is likely to be brought forward) that you are steadily and peremptorily to refuse any demand for any further Mark of His Majesty's displeasure to Adml. Berkeley, than that, which was in the first instance manifested, by that Officer's immediate recall.[9]

[8a] Pinkney's account of his conversations with Canning on Jan. 18 and 22, 1809, is printed in *A. S. P., F. R.*, III, 299–300.

[9] Towards the close of his conversation with Canning on Jan. 22, 1809, about the revoking of commercial restrictions by Great Britain and the United States respectively, Pinkney alluded to the recent "unfortunate" appointment of Admiral Berkeley to the Lisbon station but did not enter into a discussion of it.

You are to open the Subject of the Cheasapeake separately and distinctly. The Manner, in which the proposal for the adjustment of that difference may be received, will be the best test of the general disposition of the American Government, and will naturally indicate the course to be pursued in respect to the further Instructions which I shall proceed to communicate to you in another Dispatch.

CANNING TO ERSKINE [10]

No. 2.[11]   FOREIGN OFFICE, January 23rd, 1809.
Sir,

If there really exists in those Individuals who are to have a leading Share in the new Administration of the United States, that disposition to come to a complete and cordial understanding with Great Britain, of which you have received from them such positive Assurances, in meeting that disposition, it would be useless and unprofitable to recur to a Recapitulation of the Causes from which the differences between the two Governments have arisen, or of the Arguments, already so often repeated, in support of that System of Retaliation to which His Majesty has unwillingly had recourse.

That System His Majesty must unquestionably continue to maintain, unless the Object of it can be otherwise accomplished.

But after a profession, on the part of so many of the leading Members of the Government of The United States, of a sincere desire to contribute to that object, in a manner which should render the continuance of the System adopted by the British Government unnecessary, it is thought right that a fair opportunity should be afforded to the American Government to explain It's Meaning, and to give proof of It's Sincerity.

The Extension of the interdiction of the American Harbours to the Ships of War of France as well as of Great Britain is, as stated in my other Dispatch, an acceptable Symptom of a System of Impartiality towards both Belligerents—the first that has been publicly manifested by the American Government.

The like Extension of the Non-Importation Act to other Belligerents, is equally proper in this View. These Measures remove those preliminary objections which must otherwise have precluded any useful or amicable discussion.

In this State of things it is possible for Great Britain to entertain Propositions which, while such manifest partiality was shewn to her Enemies, were not consistent either with her Dignity or her interest.

---

[10] F. O. 115: 20.
[11] This is the second instruction to Erskine of 1809 marked "No. 2." The draft of this in F. O. 5: 62 is marked "No. 4."

From the Report of your Conversations [12] with Mr. Maddison, Mr. Galatin, and Mr. Smith it appears:

1st. That the American Government is prepared, in the Event of His Majesty's consenting to withdraw the Orders in Council of January and November 1807, to withdraw, contemporaneously, on It's Part, the Interdiction of it's Harbours to Ships of War, and all Non-Intercourse and Non-Importation Acts so far as respects Great Britain; leaving them in force with respect to France, and the Powers which adopt or act under her Decrees.

2ndly. What is of the utmost importance, as precluding a new Source of Misunderstanding which might arise after the adjustment of the other Questions, that America is willing to renounce, during the present War, the pretension of carrying on, in time of War, all Trade with the Enemies Colonies, from which she was excluded during Peace.

3rdly. That Great Britain, for the purpose of securing the operation of the Embargo, and of the *bonâ fide* intention of America to prevent her Citizens from trading with France, and the Powers adopting and acting under the French Decrees, is to be considered as being at Liberty to capture all such American Vessels, as may be found attempting to Trade with the Ports of any of those Powers; without which Security for the Observance of the Embargo, the raising it nominally, with respect to Great Britain alone, would in fact raise it with respect to all the World.

On these Conditions His Majesty would consent to withdraw the Orders in Council of January and November 1807—so far as respects America.

As the first and second of these Conditions are the Suggestions of the persons in Authority in America, to you, and as Mr. Pinckney [13] has recently (but for the first time) expressed to me his Opinion that there will be no indisposition on the part of His Government to the Enforcement, by the Naval Power of Great Britain, of the Regulations of America with respect to France, and the Countries to which those Regulations continue to apply; but that his Government was itself aware, that, without such Enforcement, those Regulations must be altogether nugatory; I flatter myself that there will be no difficulty in obtaining a distinct and official Recognition of these Conditions from the American Government.

For this purpose, you are at liberty to communicate this Dispatch, *in extenso*, to the American Secretary of State.

---

[12] Later in 1809, after this instruction had been laid before Parliament by Canning and published, Smith and Gallatin exchanged notes with Erskine respecting the subject matter of these conversations. *A. S. P., F. R.*, III, 304–308.

[13] For Pinkney's comment on the use to which Canning had put his informal remarks of January 22, 1809, see *A. S. P., F. R.*, III, 303.

Upon receiving through you, on the part of the American Government, a distinct and official Recognition of the three above-mentioned Conditions, His Majesty will lose no time in sending to America a Minister fully empowered to consign them to a formal and regular Treaty.

As however it is possible, that the delay which must intervene before the actual Conclusion of a Treaty, may appear to the American Government to deprive this arrangement of Part of its benefits; I am to authorize you, if the American Government should be desirous of acting upon the Agreement before it is reduced into a regular form, either by the immediate repeal of the Embargo, and the other Acts in question, or by engaging to repeal them on a particular day, to assure the American Government of His Majesty's Readiness to meet such a Disposition in the Manner best calculated to give it immediate Effect. Upon the receipt here of an official Note, containing an Engagement, for the adoption by the American Government of the three conditions above-specified, His Majesty will be prepared, on the Faith of such Engagement, either immediately (if the Repeal shall have been immediate in America) or on any day specified by the American Government for that repeal, reciprocally to recall the Orders in Council, without waiting for the Conclusion of a Treaty.

And you are authorized, in the Circumstances herein-described, to take such reciprocal Engagement on His Majesty's Behalf.

CANNING TO ERSKINE [14]

No. 3.[15]   FOREIGN OFFICE, January 23, 1809.
Sir,

In addition to what I have stated in my preceding dispatch of this date, I think it right to assure you, that the intention of sending a Minister to America, as therein announced, for the purpose of concluding a Treaty with the United States, has not arisen from any doubt of your executing the Commission, if it had been entrusted to you, with zeal and with ability; but it is presumed, that after the long suspension of friendly Intercourse with the United States, a Minister sent for this single and special purpose, and fully apprized of all the Sentiments on this Subject of the Government by which he is employed, would have a better prospect of removing any difficulties which might occur, than if the Negotiation were to be conducted by the resident Minister.

---

[14] F. O. 115 : 20.
[15] The draft in F. O. 5 : 62 is marked "No. 5."

No. 4.[17]   FOREIGN OFFICE, January 23, 1809.

Sir,

In your Dispatch No. 47,[18] among the other important suggestions which you state yourself to have received from Mr. Galatin, is one the purport of which is, that, supposing all the existing differences between the two Countries to be done away, the System of their commercial Intercourse might be better regulated by the short and simple agreement, either to admit each other's productions on equal and reciprocal duties, or reciprocally to place each on the footing of the most favoured Nation, than by any more minute and complicated Provisions.

The Sentiments upon which this Suggestion appears to be founded, are so much in unison with those entertained here, that I am to direct you, in the Event of the Subjects mentioned in my other Dispatches being put in a train of adjustment, to endeavour to obtain from the American Government some more precise and authentic Exposition of their Views upon this Subject, to be transmitted here for consideration, if possible, at the same time with their answers upon the Subjects of those other Dispatches.

It will not however be desireable that those answers should be delayed for this purpose.

But you are authorized to assure the American Government of the Readiness with which we shall be prepared to enter into the amicable discussion of the commercial Relations of the two Countries, on the basis of the latter of the two Principles proposed by Mr. Galatin, whenever those obstacles which stand in the Way of the renewal of their intercourse, shall have been happily removed.

In this case as in respect to the Subjects of my Dispatches, you will see that the Sincerity of the good disposition professed by the persons composing the new American Administration, is the point the most important in the View of the British Government.

If such a disposition really exists, all Difficulties will (as Mr. Galatin has expressed himself) be easily smoothed away.

If unfortunately this hope should be disappointed, Great Britain has only to continue the System of Self-Defence and Retaliation upon her Enemies, to which she has been compelled to have recourse, with the consciousness of having eagerly seized the first opportunity that appeared to be offered to her, of attaining, through an amicable arrangement with America, the Object for which that System was established.

---

[16] F. O. 115 : 20.
[17] The draft in F. O. 5 : 62 is marked "No. 6."
[18] Dated Dec. 4, 1808, F. O. 5 : 58. See note 8, p. 261, and note 12, p. 265, *supra*.

CANNING TO ERSKINE [19]

Separate.   FOREIGN OFFICE, 2d February, 1809.

Sir,

I transmit to you herewith for your information the Copy of a Letter and of it's Inclosures which have been received at this Office from the Admiralty, containing a correspondence between Lieut. Ramsay of His Majesty's Ship Eurydice, and the Commanding Officer of the United States Gun Boat No. 42., relative to the temporary detention by that Vessel of a British Merchant Ship called the Eliza and I am to desire that you will lose no time in making a suitable representation on the subject to the American Government.[20]

CANNING TO ERSKINE [21]

No. 5.[22]   FOREIGN OFFICE, Feb'y 6th, 1809.

Sir,

My Dispatches of last Month have been detained for the purpose of their being conveyed to you by Mr. Oakeley,[23] whom His Majesty has been pleased to appoint to be Secretary of Legation to the United States.

Since they were written, your Dispatches Nos. 1, 2, and 3 have been received. Although the Contents of these Dispatches exhibit a more hostile disposition on the Part of the American Government, than might have been expected from the tenour of your preceding Reports, the important Suggestions which have been thrown out to you by persons of Authority in America, nevertheless appear to be so highly deserving of Attention, that His Majesty has not been pleased to direct that any Alteration should be made in the Instructions which were prepared for you previously to the Receipt of your last Dispatches.

CANNING TO ERSKINE [24]

No. 8.[25]   FOREIGN OFFICE, April 6, 1809.

Sir,

Your several Dispatches to No. 13 inclusive have been received and laid before The King.

The measures which have been adopted by the American Government and the conversations which you have had with the different

---

[19] Draft, F. O. 5 : 62.
[20] In Passamaquoddy Bay, October, 1808, the *Eliza* had been forced by adverse conditions to anchor in American waters. Seized on suspicion of having violated the Embargo, she had been released after three days' detention.
[21] F. O. 115 : 20.
[22] The draft in F. O. 5 : 62 is marked "No. 7."
[23] Charles Oakeley.
[24] F. O. 115 : 20.
[25] In F. O. 115 : 20 there are no instructions to Erskine marked "No. 6" and "No. 7."

Members of it, as stated in your last Dispatches do not render any alterations necessary in the instructions which were transmitted by Mr. Oakeley; and I shall therefore have nothing to add on the subject of those instructions, untill I shall hear from you the manner in which the overtures contained in them, have been received by the American Government.

I herewith inclose to you, for your information, the Copies of several statements which have been communicated to me by the Board of Trade, and which will enable you to form a judgment how little the effects, that have been produced on the Commerce of these Kingdoms by the restrictions imposed by the Legislature of the United States have corresponded with the expectation entertained in America on that subject.[26]

CANNING TO ERSKINE [27]

No. 9.[28]   FOREIGN OFFICE, 6th. April, 1809.

Sir,

I inclose to you herewith several Documents which have been transmitted to this Office by direction of the Lords Commissioners of the Admiralty, relative to the Treatment experienced by Lieutenant Foley, Commanding His Majesty's Ship Sandwich, on his arrival at Savannah.

I perceive by your Dispatch No. 55 [No. 5] that you have already made a representation on this subject to the American Government; but as these Papers contain a more detailed account of that Transaction, than that of which you appear to have been then in possession; I am to signify to you His Majesty's Pleasure that you renew your application, in order to obtain due redress for this outrage.[29]

---

[26] The statements, dated March 6 and April 6, 1809, showed that the decrease in the value of exports (from England alone) to the United States in 1808, which was £5,790,000 below the average for 1806 and 1807, had been balanced by the increase in the value of exports to other parts of the Western Hemisphere in 1808, which was £4,230,000 above the average for 1806 and 1807.

[27] F. O. 115 : 20.

[28] The draft in F. O. 5 : 63 is unnumbered, and marked "Separate."

[29] Lieut. Foley had put in at Savannah for the purpose of conveying to Nassau a Spanish felucca, prize of His Majesty's brig *Firefly* (which had been brought into Savannah, in distress, in August of 1808). Although his purpose had been explained to the Collector of the port, Captain Armistead of the United States Artillery (basing his action apparently upon the proclamation of 1807 excluding British warships from American waters) had peremptorily, in "the most illiberal and insulting" fashion, ordered Lieut. Foley and the *Sandwich* to depart immediately. Foley had been compelled to return to his vessel in such haste that his pilot was left on shore. Erskine to Canning, Jan. 18, 1809, No. 5, F. O. 5 : 62. The Admiralty account, accompanying the above instruction, was sent to George Hammond by John Barrow, March 31, 1809.

CANNING TO ERSKINE [30]

No. 9.[31]   FOREIGN FFFICE, May 2d, 1809.

Sir,

I herewith inclose to you the Copy of a letter which I have written to Mr. Pinkney, inclosing a new Order of Council which was passed on Wednesday last, and by which the former Orders of Council are in part revoked.[32]

The System which His Majesty has determined to pursue with respect to the Commerce and Navigation of His Enemies, is so simplified by the Provisions of the New Orders of Council, as to render it unnecessary for me to state to you any explanatory observations upon them, or to make any alteration in the Instructions which I transmitted to you by Mr. Oakeley.

You will not fail however to observe that the Substitution of a simple Blockade of the Countries, an Intercourse with which remains interdicted to Neutrals, for the circuitous Voyage touching and paying Duty in the Ports of England, entirely relieves the Retaliatory System from that Objection which appears to have been most sensibly felt in America, as a Grievance and an Injury.

CANNING TO ERSKINE [33]

No. 10.   FOREIGN OFFICE, May 22, 1809.

Sir,

Your Dispatches Nos. 19 and 20, of the 19th and 20th of April, have been received here this day, and laid before The King.

I have lost no time in receiving His Majesty's Commands to signify to you His Majesty's Sentiments, on the Manner in which you have executed the Instructions conveyed to you in my Dispatches by Mr. Oakeley.

It is much to be regretted, that, in the Execution of Instructions upon points of so much delicacy and importance, you should have thought yourself authorized to depart so widely not only from their Letter but from their Spirit.[34]

With respect to the Instructions relating to the Chesapeake, which form the Subject of my Dispatch No. 1 [of Jan. 23, 1809], I have to remark—first—the total omission by you of a preliminary of the most

---

[30] Draft. F. O. 5 : 63.

[31] It will be noted that the preceding instruction, F. O. 115 : 20, is also marked "No. 9."

[32] Canning's note of April 30, and the order-in-council of April 26, 1809, are printed in *A. S. P., F. R.,* III, 241.

[33] F. O. 115 : 20.

[34] For the negotiations leading to the Erskine Agreement of April 19, 1809, see Charles C. Tansill's account of Robert Smith in *American Secretaries of State,* ed. S. F. Bemis, III, 157–164; Henry Adams, *Hist. U. S.,* V, 66–108; and Erskine's dispatches printed in *Correspondence Relating to America, Presented to Parliament in 1810.*

material importance. Secondly—a Departure from the Forms of your Instructions in the manner of conducting the Negotiation, and Thirdly—the admission by you, and, so far as appears, without Remonstrance or observation, of a Note containing Expressions offensive to His Majesty's dignity, such as no Minister of His Majesty ought to have submitted to receive, and to transmit to his Government.

First:—It is distinctly stated by me, as the Condition of His Majesty's "no longer insisting upon the Recall of the Proclamation of July 1807 as a Preliminary to the adjustment of the difference arising from the affair of the Chesapeake—that the Ships of War of France shall in point of fact have been excluded from the Ports of the United States, and such Ships of that description as were in those Ports, shall have been warned to depart."

Of this Condition you appear to have taken no notice whatever. The Non-Intercourse Bill operated only to the prospective exclusion: but as to the warning to be given to any Ships of War of France (if any such there were) in the Ports of the United States, it nowhere appears that even a question was put by you on this subject; much less that you received any satisfactory Assurance upon it.

Secondly:—But if this preliminary Condition had been fulfilled, your Instructions proceed to state that even then "it would still be necessary that either the Proclamation should be withdrawn or it's operation formally declared to be at an End—though it would be sufficient that such Withdrawal or Declaration should be recorded in the same Instrument, or at the same time with the terms of Reparation."

So far from this indispensable Condition having been obtained by you, Mr. Smith,[35] in the answer returned by him to your Note, studiously avoids any thing like a recognition of the principle on which alone the demand of the formal recall of the Proclamation was to be waved. Neither is the Proclamation itself withdrawn, nor it's operation declared to be at an End.

The obvious consequence of this omission is, that if the non-intercourse Act, which is a temporary Act, were to be suffered to expire, the Proclamation might revive, and the inequality between the two Belligerents be thereby restored.

It was obviously your duty, before you committed His Majesty's Name by a written offer of reparation, to ascertain in what manner that offer would be received and answered; and if you found that the express Condition either of withdrawing the Proclamation, or declaring it's Operation to be at an end, would not be complied with,

---

[35] Robert Smith of Maryland (1757–1842), formerly Secretary of the Navy under Jefferson, Secretary of State under Madison from March 4, 1809 to April 1, 1811. Erskine's note to Smith of April 17, 1809, and Smith's reply of the same date, to which allusion is made above, are printed in *A. S. P., F. R.*, III, 295–296.

to abstain from proceeding one single Step in the Negotiation until you had referred home for further Instructions.

That Part of your Instructions which directed that this Arrangement, if not made the Subject of a Convention, should be settled "by the Exchange of Ministerial Notes dated on the same day, and reciprocally delivered at the same time," was expressly intended to guard against the possibility of your committing yourself by a written proposal, in the uncertainty of what might be the nature of the answer to be returned to it.

His Majesty will not suppose it possible that Mr. Smith's intended answer can have been communicated to you previously and have obtained your approbation.

In the proposal for restoring the Men taken from on board of the Chesapeake, it was not intended that the Condition of His Majesty's Right to reclaim them in a regular way from the American Government, if either natural born Subjects of His Majesty, or deserters from His Majesty's Service, should have been omitted. I dwell, however, the less on this point, as His Majesty's Right in this Respect is founded on Publick Law, and does not require to be justified by the recognition of any other Government.

But I cannot forbear observing with regret that the Bounty of His Majesty, in the intended provision for the relations of the Men killed on board of the Chesapeake, is not only stated by you without a similar restriction, but is brought forward at once as a part of the Reparation originally offered; and thus converted, by you, from an Act of spontaneous generosity, into one of positive obligation.

Thirdly:—In addition to the Substance of Mr. Smith's Note, which I have already mentioned, it remains for me to notice the expressions so full of disrespect to His Majesty with which that Note concludes.[36] And I am to signify to you the displeasure which His Majesty feels, that any Minister of His Majesty should have shown himself so far insensible of what is due to the dignity of His Sovereign, as to have consented to receive and transmit, to be laid before His Majesty, a Note in which such expressions were contained.[37]

---

[36] In the concluding paragraph of Secretary Smith's note to Erskine of April 17, 1809, it was stated that while the President did not insist upon further punishment of Admiral Berkeley he was "not the less sensible of the justice and utility of such an example, nor the less persuaded that it would best comport with what is due from His Britannic Majesty to his own honor." *A. S. P., F. R.*, III, 295–296.

[37] Erskine's reply to Canning's criticisms, dated Aug. 3, 1809, explaining and justifying his negotiations respecting the *Chesapeake* affair, is printed in *Correspondence Relating to America, Presented to Parliament in 1810*, pp. 60–66.

CANNING TO ERSKINE [38]

No. 11.   FOREIGN OFFICE, May 23d: 1809.

Sir,

I proceed in this Dispatch to point out to you those deviations from the Instructions conveyed to you in my Dispatch No. 3 [No. 1, of Jan. 23, 1809, *supra*], which you have unfortunately thought yourself at liberty to adopt, and of which I am to express to you His Majesty's entire disapprobation.

I do not dwell upon the singular and offensive Step taken by the American Government in publishing the whole of the Correspondence which had taken place between you and the American Secretary of State: because His Majesty is willing to believe that you cannot have been a Party to this Publication: His Majesty conceives it impossible that you should have given your consent to such a proceeding, especially in respect to a transaction which you profess yourself to consider as merely "conditional." But as the publication appears to have taken place on the 19th of April,[39] the day of the date of your Dispatches, it seems difficult to understand how it happens that your Dispatches should not contain any notification of your intention to remonstrate against a proceeding so extraordinary as that of the publication of the Correspondence of a Minister, without his concurrence, and previously to the transmission of it to his Court.

I am, in the first place, to observe to you, that the Instructions which I transmitted to you, by His Majesty's Command, in my Dispatch No. 1, expressly stated that "the manner in which the proposal for the adjustment of that difference may be received, would be the best test of the general disposition of the American Government and would naturally indicate the course to be pursued in respect to the further Instructions," which I proceeded to communicate to you in another Dispatch—and I am to express His Majesty's Surprise and Regret that such a Note as that which you received from Mr. Smith, in answer to your offer of reparation for the affair of the Chesapeake, can have been received by you as a proof of the acceptance, by the Government of the United States, of the honourable reparation tendered by His Majesty "in the same Spirit of conciliation in which it was proposed." That Note itself being an offence against His Majesty's dignity, such as no Minister of His Majesty ought to have passed by unresented.

---

[38] F. O. 115 : 20.
[39] The notes exchanged between Erskine and Smith on April 17, 18, and 19, six in all, together with Madison's proclamation of April 19, 1809, were published in the *National Intelligencer* on April 21, 1809.

I am at a loss to conceive on what ground you thought yourself authorized to open your Correspondence, on the Subject of the Orders in Council, with the intimation of His Majesty's determination to send to the United States an Envoy Extraordinary "invested with Full Powers to conclude a Treaty on all the points of the relations between the two Countries."

Your Instructions do not authorize you to hold out the expectation of any such Mission, until His Majesty should have received, on the part of the Government of the United States, an authentick and official Recognition of the Conditions which you were directed to require.

The Instructions which I was commanded by His Majesty to transmit to you, on the subject of the Orders in Council, were framed on the Basis of three Conditions:—the agreement to which, on the part of the American Government, was stated to be indispensable to His Majesty's consenting to withdraw His Orders in Council.

The first of these conditions was—That the Interdiction of the Harbours of America to the Ships of War of Great Britain and all non-intercourse or non-importation Acts should be withdrawn so far as respects Great Britain, leaving them "in force with respect to France and the Powers which adopt or act under her decrees."

The Second. That America should renounce during the present War, the pretension of carrying on in time of War all Trade with the Enemies Colonies from which She was excluded during Peace.

The Third. That it should be understood and agreed between the Two Powers, that Great Britain should be at liberty to capture all American Vessels that should be found attempting to trade with France, or any Powers which adopted or acted under Her decrees.

I was commanded to state to you that "upon receiving on the part of the American Government, a distinct and official recognition of these three Conditions," His Majesty would lose no time in sending a Minister to America fully empowered to consign *them* (these three Conditions) to a formal and regular Treaty. His Majesty, on His Part, withdrawing His Orders in Council of January and November 1807, or, if the delay were thought to be inconvenient, you were authorized to engage for His Majesty that "upon the Receipt here of an official Note containing an engagement for the adoption by the American Government of these three Conditions, His Majesty would be prepared on the faith of such engagement to recall the Orders in Council without waiting for the conclusion of a Treaty."

The Recall therefore, on His Majesty's part, of the Orders in Council, was to depend entirely and exclusively on the acceptance, by the American Government, of the three Conditions so precisely described and so repeatedly referred to.

In this respect the Instructions were peremptory; and admitted of no discretion.

The only discretion left to you was, in the event of the American Government expressing a wish to that effect, to anticipate the operation of the Treaty by engaging, in His Majesty's Name, that His Majesty would withdraw the Orders in Council on the Receipt here of an official Note containing the formal Engagement of the American Government to adopt these three Conditions.

Nothing can be more clear than that not one of these three Conditions has been adopted by the American Government—nor any Engagement taken for their adoption.

The Second and Third Condition you appear to have given up altogether. No mention whatever is made of them in your written Communications to Mr. Smith: and in respect to them therefore you have acted in direct contradiction to your Instructions.

But even of the first Condition, of which alone you appear to have attempted to obtain the fulfilment, the most material part has either been overlooked or conceded by you.

This Condition did not require solely the repeal of the offensive Acts with respect to Great Britain—but that repeal coupled with the continuance of those Acts in Force with respect to "France and the Powers which adopt and act under Her Decrees."

Upon this Clause, the most important part of the Condition— you do not appear to have insisted in any part, not only of your Correspondence, but of your verbal Communications with the American Government.

This Clause, above all others, it was necessary to consign to a formal and written agreement. As the matter at present stands before the World, in your official Correspondence with Mr. Smith, the American Government would be at liberty tomorrow to repeal the Non-intercourse Act altogether, without infringing the Agreement which you have thought proper to enter into on behalf of His Majesty: and if such a Clause was thought necessary to this Condition at the time when my Instructions were written, it was obviously become much more so, when the Non-intercourse Act was passed for a limited time. You must also have been aware, at the time of making the Agreement, that the American Government had in fact formally exempted Holland,[40] a Power which has unquestionably "adopted and acted under the Decrees of France," from the operation of the Non-intercourse Act; an Exemption in direct contravention of the Condition prescribed to you and which, of itself, ought to have prevented you from coming to any agreement whatever.

---

[40] On this point, see Henry Adams, *Hist. U. S.*, V, 91.

Without therefore obtaining even one of those Conditions, on the obtaining of all of which the concession of His Majesty was to depend, you have pledged His Majesty to the full extent of that concession; and have placed His Majesty in the painful Alternative, of having either to refuse to abide by an Engagement taken in His Majesty's Name by an accredited Minister of His Majesty, or to acquiesce in a measure which has been adopted, not only not in conformity to His Majesty's views, but in contradiction to His positive directions.[41]

CANNING TO ERSKINE [42]

No. 12.   FOREIGN OFFICE, May 30, 1809.

Sir,

I herewith inclose to you the Copies of an Order which was passed by The King in Council on Wednesday the 24th Instant; [43] and I have to signify to you His Majesty's Pleasure, that you deliver one Copy of this Order to the American Secretary of State, and that you use your utmost Exertions to render it as public as may be possible, among the Merchants of the United States.

This Order in Council contains, as you will perceive, His Majesty's disavowal of the Agreement which you have concluded with the American Government.

I am directed by His Majesty to state to you, that His Majesty entertains no doubt of the good Intentions and Zeal for His Majesty's Service by which you have been led to depart from your Instructions.

But you must be sensible that the Consequences of such a Step, and the Publicity which has been given to it by the American Government, render it impossible that you should continue in the Exercise of your Functions, either with Satisfaction to Yourself, or with Advantage to His Majesty's Service.

I have therefore received His Majesty's Commands to inform you, that His Majesty has been graciously pleased to appoint Mr. Jackson [44] to replace you, by whom I shall transmit to you your Letter of Recall.

---

[41] Erskine's reply to Canning's criticisms, dated Aug. 7, 1809, explaining and justifying his negotiations respecting the revocation of the orders-in-council, is printed in *Correspondence Relating to America, Presented to Parliament in 1810*, pp. 67–70.

[42] F. O. 115 : 20.

[43] The order of May 24, 1809, is printed in *A. S. P., F. R.*, III, 302.

[44] Francis James Jackson (1770–1814) ; he had been secretary of legation at Berlin and Milan, ambassador at Constantinople, plenipotentiary to France and Prussia, and, in 1807, envoy to Denmark. See note 8, p. 195, *supra*.

No. 13.   FOREIGN OFFICE, July 5, 1809.
Sir,
I transmit to you herewith His Majesty's Letter to the United States of America, recalling You from that Mission; and I am to desire that You will deliver it in the usual Form accompanied by suitable Compliments in His Majesty's Name.
I have it also in Command from His Majesty to desire that You will deliver to Mr. Jackson, who will be the Bearer of this Dispatch, all the Cyphers and Official Correspondence of the Mission; after which You will be at Liberty to set out on Your return to England, as soon as it may suit Your Convenience.

No. 1.   FOREIGN OFFICE, July 1st, 1809.
Sir,
His Majesty having been Graciously pleased to appoint you to be His Majesty's Envoy Extraordinary and Minister Plenipotentiary to the United States of America, I herewith transmit to you His Majesty's General Instructions signed by His Majesty, together with His Majesty's Letter of Credence to The President of The United States; the delivery of which Credential Letter I am to direct you to accompany with the Expression of His Majesty's Sincere desire to maintain a perfect and cordial Understanding with the United States, and to bring to a complete and satisfactory adjustment all the points of Difference which have arisen between the two Governments.
I am further commanded by His Majesty to furnish you with such Instructions with respect to the points which have been recently and are now, in discussion; as, if there exists on the part of the American Government the same disposition which is entertained by His Majesty, can hardly fail to effect the object which His Majesty has in view.
The Correspondence of Mr. Erskine with this office having been submitted to your perusal, you are aware of the degree to which that Minister was induced to deviate from the Instructions which had been given to him for the settlement of the points in dispute between the two Governments; and of the embarrassment to which His Majesty's Government has been subjected by such deviation.
There was no other option with respect to Mr. Erskine's Arrangement, after the publicity so unwarrantably given to it in America, but either to sanction an unequivocal and uncompensated surrender of all the Principles upon which this Government had acted for the

---

[45] F. O. 115 : 20.
[46] F. O. 115 : 20.   On Jackson, see note 44, p. 276, *supra.*

last two Years, and to submit, henceforward, without resistance or retaliation, to the operation of the Decrees of France against the Commerce of this Country; or to disavow that Arrangement in the face of the World.

The premature publication of the Correspondence by the American Government, so effectually precluded any middle course of Explanation and accommodation, that it is hardly possible to suppose that it must not have been resorted to in a great measure with that View.

The American Government cannot have believed, that such an Arrangement as Mr. Erskine consented to accept, was conformable to his Instructions. If Mr. Erskine availed himself of the liberty allowed to him of communicating those Instructions on the affair of the Orders in Council, they must have known that it was not so. But, even without such communication, they cannot, by possibility, have believed, that, without any new motive, and without any apparent change in the dispositions of the Enemy, the British Government could have been disposed at once and unconditionally to give up the System on which they had been acting; and which they had so recently refused to relinquish, even in return for Considerations which though far from being satisfactory, were yet infinitely more so than any thing which can be supposed to have been gained by Mr. Erskine's Arrangement.

But it is by no means impossible that the American Government may have thought that, by precipitating the publication of this Unauthorized Arrangement,—and thus contriving that the first knowledge of it's having been concluded, should reach this Country, accompanied by the simultaneous Renewal of extensive Commercial Speculations between America and England, such would be the difficulty created here, and such the unwillingness to destroy Expectations so confidently cherished, and to check an intercourse actually begun, that the British Government would feel Itself compelled, however reluctantly, to sanction even what it had not previously authorised.

If such were the Motives of the publication in America; the American Government have only Themselves to blame for whatever of public Disappointment or of Detriment to individuals may have been produced by the Rejection, on the part of the British Government, of an Arrangement which no man who had either any knowledge of the policy by which they had been guided, or of the declarations which they had uniformly made upon these Subjects, or who had formed any just Estimate, either of the Interests or the Honour of Great Britain, could reasonably expect to see confirmed.

So far therefore from the American Government having any reason to complain of the Non-Ratification of Mr. Erskine's unauthorized Agreement, His Majesty has, on His part, just Ground of Complaint, for that share of the Inconvenience from the Publication, which may have fallen upon His Majesty's Subjects, so far as their interests may have been involved in the renewed Speculations of their American Correspondents:—and His Majesty cannot but think any Complaint, if any should be made on this occasion in America, the more unreasonable, as the Government of the United States is that Government, which perhaps of all others has most freely exercised the Right of withholding it's Ratification from even the authorized Acts of it's own Diplomatic Agents.

I have thought it right to state His Majesty's Sentiments thus distinctly upon this point—as it is one upon which, in all probability, some preliminary Discussion may arise, before you are enabled to proceed to the more detailed objects of Negotiation.

Of the manner in which this Negotiation has been conducted by Mr. Erskine, and the objections to which his management of it is liable, it is unnecessary for me to say any thing. I content myself with referring you, on that Subject, to my last Dispatches to that Minister: Copies of which, as well as of those Dispatches of his in answer to which mine were written, I herewith inclose—in order that you may have them present to your Consideration during your Passage to America. The remainder of the Correspondence will be delivered over to you by Mr. Erskine, on your arrival at the Seat of the American Government.

I shall proceed, in other Dispatches, to prescribe to you the Course which His Majesty is pleased to direct to be taken by you, for the purpose of extricating the Two Governments from the State of Embarrassment in which they are involved, by the results of Mr. Erskine's Negotiation, upon the two important Objects which he was instructed to bring to a Conclusion.

CANNING TO JACKSON [47]

No. 2.   FOREIGN OFFICE, July 1st, 1809.
Sir,

According to the Order in which Mr. Erskine was directed to bring forward the two Objects of his Negotiation, I proceed to state to you His Majesty's Pleasure as to the Mode in which you should now open your discussion respecting The Affair of the Chesapeake.

You will observe to the American Minister that if His Majesty were capable of being actuated by any desire to retract an Offer of Reparation which He had once made, His Majesty might be well warranted in doing so, both by the Form in which His Majesty's

---

[47] F. O. 115 : 20.

accredited Minister has tendered that Reparation, and by the Manner in which that Tender has been received.

Mr. Erskine has acted in several Points (as you will have learnt by the Correspondence of which you are in Possession) in Contradiction to his Instructions upon this Subject; and the tone of Asperity and of Disrespect to His Majesty which marks the Correspondence of the Secretary of State Mr. Smith, is such, as renders it more difficult for His Majesty's Confidential Servants to advise His Majesty to pass over that Cause of Offence in Silence, than it would be to justify on that Ground alone the complete disavowal and Abandonment of an Attempt at Conciliation, which has been met with a temper so little corresponding with the Spirit in which it was made.

Upon a full Consideration, however, of all the Circumstances of this Case, but especially of this leading fact, that an Act was done by an Officer of His Majesty for which Reparation has been admitted to be due, His Majesty has commanded me to direct you to renew the Offers which Mr. Erskine was instructed to make with the Modifications hereinafter described, notwithstanding the ungracious manner in which they have been received.

Upon Mr. Smith's Note, offensive as it is, His Majesty is pleased to direct that you should confine yourself to this single Observation; that, if there had been no other Grounds for the Recall of Mr. Erskine, he would unquestionably have been recalled not merely for having acted upon that Note as satisfactory, but for having accepted it without Remonstrance.

His Majesty is further contented not to take exception to the Manner in which Mr. Erskine has blended in his original Offer of Reparation, His Majesty's proposal to provide for the Widows and Children of the Men slain in the Action with the Chesapeake, with that which was intended by His Majesty and described by me to Mr. Erskine as "the single and sufficient Act of Reparation," namely the Restoration of the Men taken out of that Frigate. But it must be distinctly understood that this gratuitous Bounty of His Majesty cannot be extended to the family of any Person who shall not be satisfactorily shewn to have been "neither a natural Born Subject of His Majesty, nor a Deserter from His Majesty's Service."

There is another Point, however, upon which it is necessary to insist. His Majesty was willing to consider the Proclamation of July 2d 1807 as virtually recalled by the Provisions of the Non Intercourse Act. Upon this Ground the demand of it's distinct recall was to be waved. But Mr. Erskine was instructed, in waving this demand, to require a distinct Acknowledgement on the Part of the American Government that such also was their view of the effect of the Non Intercourse Act upon the Proclamation.

This Acknowledgement is given (if it can be considered as given) by Mr. Smith, in such a Form as to render it wholly nugatory. He admits that a State of Equality as with respect to the Two Belligerents is in Effect produced by the Non Intercourse Act: but he ascribes this Effect to "distinct Considerations;" [48]—to Considerations, that is to say, growing out of the Relations of the United States, not with Great Britain only, but with France; Considerations therefore liable to be varied by Circumstances independent of Great Britain; and which might, in the Event of the Adjustment of the Differences between the United States and France, and the Consequent repeal of the Non Intercourse Act as with respect to France, lead to the Revival of the Proclamation against the Ships of Great Britain. Nay further, as there is no Security obtained by Mr. Erskine that the Non Intercourse Act shall not be repealed as with respect to France, even without any Adjustment of the Differences between that Power and America; and as the Non Intercourse Act is a temporary Act and liable to expire or probably may have expired before the present Moment; it is possible that the Repeal or the discontinuance of that Act might have revived the Proclamation against Great Britain—even while France continues in a State not only of Hostility with Great Britain, but of Agression against America; and after the differences between Great Britain and America had ceased.

To the Possibility of a State of Things so inequitable and so irrational His Majesty can never consent.

The formal Repeal of the Proclamation is not now required. But it is necessary, and you are hereby instructed, to require an Acknowledgement or distinct Declaration in writing from the American Government, that the Operation of the Proclamation is considered by them not as suspended, but as at an end; not as merely merged for a Time, in the Provision of a Law liable to be repealed, or to expire, if not specially renewed, but as actually, though not formally, annulled.

A Declaration or Acknowledgement to this Effect is a sine quâ non Condition of your proceeding to execute any Part of Mr. Erskine's Agreement.

So far from the demand of this Acknowledgement or declaration being made in a hostile Temper; so far from the Compliance with it being likely to lead to any unfriendly Results—the very view and purpose of insisting upon it are to preclude the Chance of future Hostility.

The Case which I have above imagined, of the Revival of the Operation of this Proclamation either by the Repeal or by the Expiration of the Non: Intercourse Act (which alone suspends it)—after the

---

[48] Reference is made to the note of Secretary Smith to Erskine, April 17, 1809, printed in *A. S. P., F. R.*, III, 295–296.

Adjustment of that difference between Great Britain and The United States which was the principal (if it is not admitted to have been the only) cause of issuing it—and the exclusion thereby of British Ships of War from the Harbours of America, while those of Her Enemy should be admitted into them, could, after all that has passed upon the Subject, be considered in no other Light than as an Act of Hostility.

If the Views of the American Administration are the same as those of The British Government, there can be no hesitation on their Part, in providing, by so slight a Concession as the Acknowledgement required, against even the Possibility, however remote, of an Issue so earnestly to be deprecated.

It remains for me to state, as to the form of the Agreement to be concluded on this point, that the Acknowledgement or Declaration required from the American Government must be consigned to an Official Note to be exchanged by the American Secretary of State against a Note to be delivered at the same time by You, in which You shall specify the Terms of Reparation which His Majesty offers and is ready to fulfill.

These Terms are:—1st. The Restoration of the Men taken out of The Chesapeake, which you will accompany with an express Reserve of His Majesty's Right to claim in a regular way by Application to The American Government the discharge of such of them (if any) as shall be proved to be, either natural born Subjects of His Majesty, or Deserters from His Majesty's Service.

2d. A Provision, the Amount of which is to depend absolutely upon His Majesty's spontaneous Generosity for the Families of such Men as were slain on board The Chesapeake, in consequence of the unauthorized Attack upon that Frigate.

Which You will accompany in a like Manner with an express Reserve, that such Bounty is not to extend to the family of any Man, who shall have been either a natural born Subject of His Majesty or a Deserter from His Majesty's Service.

So soon as Notes to the Effect herein described shall have been exchanged between You and The American Secretary of State, You are authorized to write to the Officer commanding His Majesty's Vessels off the American Coast, directing him, in pursuance of such Agreement, to discharge those of the Men in question who are on board of the Ships under his Command, by landing them at the nearest Port in the Territory of the United States, giving Notice of the time of his so doing to such Officer of The American Government as may be appointed for that purpose.

I have only to add that if either previously to your Arrival in America, or previously to the Commencement, or during the Course, of your Negotiation any Measure shall have been or shall be adopted such as may be in it's effect, clearly equivalent to the Acknowledgement or Declaration required:—should for instance, the Proclamation itself have been specifically recalled, or the Act enabling The President to enforce it repealed—it will then be unnecessary for you to demand any new Step on the part of the American Government; and you will proceed to the Execution of His Majesty's Part of the Agreement, reciting in the Note which you deliver to The American Secretary of State, the Circumstance which thus enables you to dispense with any further mention of the Proclamation.

CANNING TO JACKSON [49]

No. 3.   FOREIGN OFFICE, July 1st: 1809.
Sir.

I have reserved for this Dispatch the Instructions with which I have received His Majesty's Commands to furnish You on that part of Mr. Erskine's Arrangement which relates to the withdrawing His Majesty's Orders in Council of January and November 1807.

Mr. Erskine's Arrangement not only does not secure the fulfillment of the three Conditions, the fulfillment of which he was directed to obtain before he should consider himself authorized to conclude any Agreement whatever: but of the Material Condition, of which alone he attempts to obtain the fulfillment, the essential part is omitted.

No Engagement is taken on the part of America to continue in force the Provisions of the Non-Intercourse Act, or any Regulations equivalent to them, with respect to France and the Powers adopting and acting under her Decrees.—On the contrary, Holland, one of those Powers, had been publickly withdrawn from their Operation: And the Act itself might have been repealed, or have expired, without His Majesty's deriving any Right from the Agreement concluded by Mr. Erskine, (even if His Majesty had ratified it,) to remonstrate against such a Concession to His Enemies.

There appears in the whole of this Transaction a fundamental Mistake of the Object to which it was directed.

Mr. Erskine reasons throughout as if His Majesty had proposed to make Sacrifices to propitiate the Government of the United States, in order to induce it to consent to the Renewal of Commercial Intercourse between the two Countries; as if such had been the Relation between Great Britain and America, as that the Advantages of Commercial Intercourse were wholly on the Side of Great Britain; and as if in any Arrangement, whether commercial or political, His Majesty could condescend to barter Objects of National Policy and Dignity, for permission to trade with another Country.

---

[49] F. O. 115 : 20.

The Character, even more than the Stipulations, of such a Compact, must, under any Circumstances, have put out of the Question the Possibility of His Majesty's consenting to confirm it.

The Orders in Council were framed for the purpose of making the Enemy himself feel those Evils which he endeavoured by his Decrees, to inflict upon Great Britain; but which the Enemy had so endeavoured to inflict, not for Commercial Purposes, but with the view to impair the resources, and to break down the Strength of this Country.

It was felt and acknowledged that this Object of defensive Retaliation could not be accomplished without incidental Inconvenience to Neutral Nations: as through the Medium of their Trade, France aimed her Blow at Great Britain,—and as through that same Medium the Blow must necessarily be returned.

The Complaint of America against the Orders in Council was not so much that their Purpose was illegitimate, as that the Means taken to effect it were, on the one hand, prejudicial, to the Rights and Interests of Neutral Nations; and on the other hand, unnecessary; in so far as it ought to have been presumed that those Neutral Nations themselves would have been willing and able to resist the French Decrees.

On the Question of Prejudice to the Rights and Interests of Neutral Nations, it has always been stated on His Majesty's part, that that Complaint should be made to France, the Original Aggressor, and redress sought at her Hands.

As to the Willingness and Ability of Neutral Nations to resist the Decrees of France, and to resist them effectually, His Majesty has always professed a Desire to be convinced by proof; and a disposition to relax or modify His Measures of Retaliation and self-Defence, in proportion as those of Neutral Nations should come in aid of them and take their Place.

On this principle alone, and not merely with the view to the Restoration of Commercial Intercourse between Great Britain and America, the whole of this Negotiation was intended to be carried on.

The Restoration of Commercial Intercourse would necessarily follow the Cessation of all Causes of Difference: but the Difference to be adjusted was one, not of Commerce, but of Policy. In the Arrangement agreed to by Mr. Erskine the incidental Consequence is mistaken for the Object of the Negotiation.

His Majesty is made by His Minister to concede the whole Point in dispute, by the total and unconditional Recall of the Orders in Council: and nothing is done by the United States in return, except to permit their Citizens to renew their Commercial Intercourse with Great Britain:—Whereas before His Majesty's Consent to withdraw or even to modify the Orders in Council was declared, the United States should have taken upon themselves to execute, in substance, the objects of the Orders in Council, by effectually prohibiting all Trade between their Citizens and France, or the Powers acting under her Decrees; and by engaging for the Continuance and Enforcement of that Prohibition, so long as those Decrees should continue unrepealed.

This was the professed principle of the Offer which Mr. Pinckney was instructed to make in the Summer of last Year. This was the principle of that Arrangement which after the Apparent Restoration of a System of Equality and Impartiality on the part of the United States, towards both Belligerents, Mr. Erskine was instructed to propose; accompanying that Proposal with the Suggestion of such collateral and subsidiary Regulations as should ensure the operation of the Principle to it's full Extent.

Had the Arrangement been at that Time concluded in conformity to the Instructions which Mr. Erskine had received, His Majesty would unquestionably have ratified it. But the circumstances under which the same Proposal would now be to be renewed are so far varied from those under which Mr. Erskine was directed to bring it forward; the Sentiments of the American Government, upon two of the three Conditions which Mr. Erskine was instructed to propose, have proved to be so different from what they were then understood to be; and there is therefore so much less probability of this Proposal being accepted than it was hoped there might be at that Time, that I am not commanded to instruct You to renew directly and officially Mr. Erskine's Proposal.

You are to inform the American Secretary of State that in the Event of the Government of the United States being desirous now to adopt that Proposal, You are authorized to renew the Negotiation, and to conclude it on the Terms of my Instructions to Mr. Erskine. But that you are not instructed to press upon the acceptance of the American Government, an Arrangement which they have so recently declined: especially as the Arrangement itself is become less important, and the Terms of it less applicable to the State of Things now existing.

You will remark to the American Minister that Considerations which were first intimated in my official Letter to Mr. Pinckney of, the 23d September 1808, and which in the Process of the following six Months acquired greater Weight and Influence, induced His Majesty before the Result of Mr. Erskine's Negotiation was known, to modify the Orders in Council of November 1807, by that of the 26th. of April 1809.[50]

---

[50] The order of April 26, 1809, and Canning's letter of Sept. 23, 1808, are printed in A. S. P., F. R., III, 241, 231–232.

The Effect of this new Order is to relieve the System, under which the former Orders were issued, from that which has always been represented in America as the most objectionable and offensive part of it, the Option given to Neutrals to Trade with the Enemies of this Country through the Ports of this Country on payment of a transit Duty.

This was originally devized and intended as a Mitigation of what is certainly more correct, but more rigid in principle: the total and unqualified Interdiction of all Trade with the Enemy.

If however this Mitigation was felt as an Aggravation, and, as has been sometimes warmly asserted, as an Insult; that Cause of Complaint is now entirely removed. By the Order in Council of April the 26th. 1809, all Trade with France and Holland, and the Ports of Italy comprehended under the denomination of the Kingdom of Italy, is simply prohibited altogether. No Option is afforded; and consequently no transit duty is required to be paid.

In another respect the Order in Council of the 26th. of April must be admitted to be more restrictive than those of November 1807.

The Trade with Enemies Colonies which was opened to Neutrals at the Commencement of the present War by the Order in Council of the 24th. of June 1803,—was continued to be left open by those of November 1807. The Order in Council of April the 26th. retracts this Indulgence.

But it is to be observed, that since the Period when the Orders in Council of November 1807 were issued, the opening of the Ports of Spain; of Portugal; of the South of Italy and of Turkey has afforded a more ample Scope to Neutral Commerce; and that, by the Capture of Martinique, in addition to that of almost all the Colonies of the Enemies of Great Britain, together with the Blockade of Guadaloupe, the Extent to which the Liberty of Commerce with Enemies Colonies applied, has been so far narrowed, that there is little of practical hardship in recurring to the Rule, which however occasionally mitigated in it's Application, this Country can never cease in principle to maintain.

It is further to be observed, that the Order of April 26th. has this Operation, highly favorable to Neutrals; that, restricting the Regulations of Blockade to France, Holland and their Colonies, and to the territories denominated the Kingdom of Italy, it lays open to the direct Trade of Neutrals the Ports of the North of Europe.

Under the Order of the 26th. of April therefore, while there are, on the one hand, fewer points of difference to stand in the way of a Satisfactory Arrangement between Great Britain and the United States; it must be confessed that there is, on the other hand, less Temptation to America to enter into such Arrangement: as the

Extent of her Commerce may be, if She pleases, nearly as great, under the Order in Council of April the 26th., as it would be under any Arrangement which should effect the indispensable Objects to which that Order applies; or as it would be even without any such Order, so long as France and the Powers subservient to France continue to enforce their Decrees. It is, in the same proportion, Matter of Indifference to this Country whether the Order in Council is continued, or an Arrangement by mutual Consent substituted in it's Room.

I am therefore not to direct You to propose to the American Government any formal Agreement to be substituted for that which His Majesty has been under the Necessity of disavowing.

You are, however, at Liberty to receive for reference home any Proposal which the American Government may tender to you. But it is only in the Case of that Proposal comprehending all the three Conditions which Mr. Erskine was instructed to require viz:

1st. An Engagement to maintain her Interdictions against the Commerce of France, and of the Powers acting under the French Decrees (including Holland) so long as those Decrees remain unrepealed.

2dly. A Renunciation, during the present War, of the Pretension to trade with the Colonies of the Enemies of Great Britain, who did not permit such Trade in Time of Peace.

3dly. A Specifick Agreement that Great Britain should capture American Ships violating the Principles of the Interdictions, before described:—It is only in this Case that You are authorized to promise, in His Majesty's Name, the Recall of the Orders in Council, now subsisting, namely those of January and November 1807, and of April 1809.

CANNING TO JACKSON [51]

No. 4.   FOREIGN OFFICE, July 1st. 1809:
Sir,

As it is only in the case last supposed in my preceding Dispatch of this Date, that of the American Government consenting to all the Three Conditions which Mr. Erskine was instructed to propose to them, that His Majesty can now consent to withdraw the existing Orders in Council, it is in that case only that any formal Agreement will be to be entered into between you and the American Secretary of State on this subject.

Should such an Agreement take place, it will be right that it should be recorded, as in the case of the Chesapeake, in Ministerial Notes to be interchanged, at the same time, between you and the American Secretary of State.

---

[51] F. O. 115 : 20.

In executing this Arrangement, as in that of the Chesapeake, you will be particularly careful to avoid the Error into which Mr. Erskine has fallen, of engaging for any thing in His Majesty's Behalf previously to the enunciation of the reciprocal Engagement on the part of the United States. You will, with equal care, avoid and reject any expression implying that His Majesty's Consent to this Arrangement is in any degree obtained by the Consideration of the Renewal of the Commercial Intercourse with Great Britain. The Consideration to be obtained from the United States is their effectual Execution of the objects of the Orders in Council, and no other.

You are also specially to require that, in order to avoid the possibility of any Misunderstanding, the Terms of the Agreement now concluded shall not be made publick in America, sooner than Six Weeks after Its Conclusion; before which time it may be reasonably supposed, that the Intelligence of it will have been received by this Government.

If the American Government should wish to prolong this period, you are at liberty to agree to do so.

CANNING TO JACKSON [52]

No. 5.   FOREIGN OFFICE, 1st: July, 1809.

Sir,

It is not improbable, that when you state to the American Minister the Authority which you have to conclude an Agreement on the Terms originally proposed (or intended to be proposed) by Mr. Erskine, you may be pressed to acquiesce in the Modifications suggested by the American Government to that Minister—and to accept an unofficial Understanding as to the two last of the Three Conditions which he was instructed to obtain. The Understanding with which he was induced to be satisfied in respect to the first of these Two Conditions, "the Renunciation by America, during the present War, of the Pretension to trade with Enemies' Colonies, from which Her Trade was excluded in Peace"—was that such a Stipulation might be taken into Consideration hereafter, with a view to its making part of a Treaty regulating the general System of Commercial Intercourse between the two Countries.

The Understanding with respect to the second, which relates to the "Agreement that the Ships of War of this Country should capture American Ships breaking the Non Intercourse Regulations with respect to France, or the Powers acting under Her Decrees," was, that the United States would not countenance or support any Complaints

<hr>

[52] F. O. 115 : 20.

from the Owners of Ships so captured—but that they would not make the right to capture them the subject of a formal Recognition.

These Suggestions of the American Government are not, in effect, Equivalents for the Orders in Council—and therefore cannot be accepted as the Price of their Recall.

Nothing could be fairer than the Offer to consider the question of Renunciation proposed in the first of these Two Conditions, if the pretension there in question were an acknowledged Right of Neutral Nations—which the British Government admitted in Principle, but of which they were anxious to purchase the Surrender or Suspension.

But the fact being otherwise—the Pretension being one of which Great Britain denies the Validity; of which She has permitted the Exercise only by indulgence; the Question is not "whether The United States shall concede to us a valuable Right, of which they are in the undisturbed and undisputed Enjoyment, in return for some valuable Concession on Our part"—but, the Indulgence which was granted for peculiar and temporary Reasons, being now withdrawn, the question is merely, "whether the Rule, from which such Indulgence was a Deviation, shall be established by the Admission of America, or enforced, as heretofore, by the Naval Power of Great Britain?"

It was felt to be Matter of Courtesy to give America this Option, after the Disposition which was understood, from Mr. Erskine's Report of his Extra-official Conversations with the Leading Persons in the American Government, to have been expressed on this subject. But, by giving this Option, it was not intended to admit a doubt upon the Principle of the Rule itself, or to consent that its Establishment (in one way or other) should become Matter of new Negotiation or of Conventional Settlement.

As to the Second Point, the Objection to the proposed Understanding is still more palpable. An Understanding could in no degree effect the object in View. The Capture of Ships must be followed by their Release or Condemnation. That Condemnation must be the Act of the competent Tribunal,—which Tribunal can found its Decisions only on one of two Grounds:—viz't. either on a written Compact between State and State, or upon the established Law of Nations, and the declared and authorized Application of the Principles of that Law to the peculiar Circumstances of the time.

Here again therefore it was not the thing to be done, but the Mode of doing it, that was referred to the option of the American Government.

If the Government of The United States had preferred, that the Capture of the Ships of their Citizens, violating at once the Rights of His Majesty and the Municipal Regulations of their Own Country, should be sanctioned by their express Concurrence, there was no objection, on His Majesty's Part, to allowing the Judgment upon the Legality of Captures so to be made, to pass under the Authority of a Treaty, instead of under that of an Order of His Majesty in Council, applying the Principles of the Law of Nations to the Circumstances of the particular Case. But either Authority is sufficient. No Offence is taken at the Refusal of The United States to make this matter subject of Compact. The Result is, that it must be the Subject of an Order in Council.

CANNING TO JACKSON [53]

No. 6. *Secret.*	FOREIGN OFFICE, July 1, 1809.

Sir,

There is one point, which, though I have not to direct you to bring forward any observation upon it, nor to enter into any discussion upon it, unless absolutely obliged to do so, it is yet right that you should keep in mind, and should be aware of all it's importance.

In the correspondence of the American Minister at Paris, (Mr. Armstrong) with his government, which was published last year (Copy of which publication I inclose to You) You will perceive, that he suggests to the French Government the expedient of repealing such part of their decrees as go to sanction the capture on the high Seas of vessels laden with British Produce or manufactures, or destined to, or coming from British Ports; retaining in force that part which condemns such vessels on entering the ports of France: Mr. Armstrong even intimates, that, if the decrees were so far modified, neutral nations would willingly acquiesce in them.[54]

The distinction taken is, that the latter is a mere municipal regulation, of which other nations have no right to complain:—while the seizure on the high seas is a general violation of neutral rights.

This distinction has been often hinted at in conversation by Mr. Pinkney—and it appears to be not obscurely pointed out in that part of the new President Mr. Madison's Message to Congress, on the opening of the last Session which I have marked in the inclosed Copy.[55]

The little disposition which France has shewn to modify, any more than to repeal, her decrees, affords ground to hope, that this distinction may not become matter of practical discussion:—and it is highly desirable to avoid discussing prematurely and hypothetically a point upon which, by possibility, it may never be necessary to enter;—but upon which, if the question between the two governments

[53] F. O. 115 : 20.
[54] See John Armstrong to Champagny, Aug. 6, 1808, quoted in part, *A. S. P., F. R.*, III, 255.
[55] See sixth paragraph of Madison's message of May 23, 1809, Richardson, *Messages and Papers of the Presidents*, I, 454.

should ever come to turn upon it, there would but too probably be found an irreconcilable difference of opinion.

But I think it necessary to put You upon your guard against any admission either in your correspondence with the American Government, or in extra-official conversations, which could lead to the supposition, that this distinction would be acquiesced in by His Majesty;—that He would consider such partial modification of the decrees of France, as releasing neutral nations from the obligation to resist them, and entitling them to claim, at His Majesty's hands, the recall of His measures of defensive retaliation.

The regulations of a State with a view to the protection and improvement of it's own commerce, or to a preference to be given to that of favoured Nations are unquestionably matters of it's own municipal competency with the incidental effect of which upon themselves, or upon other Countries, no Nations, whether hostile, or neutral, or friendly, have a right to quarrel.

But regulations made by a Government, not with the fair intention of commercial benefit to it's own Subjects, or of commercial favour to other Nations, but with the direct and avowed view of national hostility, are in effect measures of war; and the neutral nation, which, by acquiescing in, and furthering such measures, makes itself an instrument of hostility in the hands of one of the belligerent Parties against the other, must expect correspondent measures to be adopted by that other Belligerent, of which, in like manner, the neutral may be made the instrument, or the medium.

This is the principle upon which all such modification would be considered as nugatory and all compromise, which should leave so much of the French decrees in force, as is substantially a proscription of British Commerce, to be executed through Neutrals, would be wholly rejected.

The case in which the principle can be brought into discussion can only arise, if France should so modify her decrees as Mr. Madison and Mr. Armstrong have suggested. Even if that case should occur, and a proposition should be made to you upon it, You will only take such proposition (as in my other dispatch You are directed to receive every new proposition submitted to you on the subject of the Orders in Council) for reference home :—without entering into any direct Statement of His Majesty's sentiments upon it;—carefully avoiding, however, to hold out any encouragement, or expectation that it will be accepted, and keeping the principle which I have stated constantly in mind, lest You should be betrayed into any admission inconsistent with it.

CANNING TO JACKSON [56]

No. 7. *Secret.*   FOREIGN OFFICE, July 1. 1809:

Sir,

I herewith inclose to You the Extract of a Note which I have received from Admiral Apodaca,[57] containing Information of certain hostile Movements on the Part of the Government of the United States, which appear to indicate the intention of an Attack upon some of The Spanish Settlements in North America.

I have to signify to You His Majesty's Pleasure that You lose no time, after your arrival in America, in making the most diligent Enquiries into the Circumstances stated in Admiral Apodaca's Note; and that, in the Event of your learning that these hostile Demonstrations are continued, you make the strongest Representations respecting them to the American Government; and use Your utmost Endeavours to dissuade them from an Enterprize, which cannot be justified by any conduct of the Present Government of Spain, and even the successful Issue of which could not counterbalance the inevitable Evils of a War with Spain in which such an unprovoked Aggression would necessarily involve the United States.

You will, in the first Instance, confine your Representations to these topicks exclusively, and will take care, at all times, that there is nothing of Asperity or Unfriendliness in the Tone of your Remonstrance.

But, you will not disguise the deep and lively Interest which His Majesty takes in every thing that relates to Spain; and while you profess His Majesty's Willingness to mediate between Spain and The United States on any point of Controversy which may exist between them with the most entire Impartiality and Good-will towards both Parties, You will let it be understood that such are the ties by which His Majesty is bound to Spain that He could not see with Indifference any Attack upon Her Interests in America.

CANNING TO JACKSON [58]

No. 8.   FOREIGN OFFICE, 6th. July, 1809.

Sir,

I enclose to you, together with the Copy of the Order in Council issued on the 24th. of May, for preventing the inconveniences likely

---

[56] F. O. 115 : 20.

[57] Admiral Juan Ruíz de Apodaca, the Spanish ambassador at London. In his note to Canning of May 18, 1809 (copy enclosed), he expressed fears that the United States was preparing some hostile plan against the possessions of Spain, since General James Wilkinson with 4,000 troops was to embark at Norfolk for New Orleans, and Congress was discussing the raising of 50,000 volunteers. The Spanish Junta, he said, was alarmed, suspected French intrigue, and wished Great Britain to ask the United States for an explanation. Jackson, soon after his arrival in Washington, obtained from Secretary of State Smith a disavowal of hostile intentions against Spain. See J. F. Rippy, *Rivalry of the United States and Great Britain over Latin America (1808–1830)*, pp. 32–34.

[58] F. O. 115 : 20.

to arise from the renewal of commercial speculations in America under Mr. Erskine's unauthorized agreement, the copy of an instruction since issued for the purpose of obviating a misapprehension to which the original order was supposed to be liable.[59]

This instruction has been framed in consequence of a suggestion from Mr. Pinkney, that, without it, doubts might be entertained as to the trade with Batavia, to which Colony Mr. Pinkney represented that it was probable that trade to a very great extent might have been undertaken by the Merchants of the United States, under the impression that the permission to trade with Holland, which Mr. Erskine's agreement had sanctioned, must include permission to trade with the Dutch Colonies.

There was another representation made by Mr. Pinkney at the same time, with which it was not thought by any means necessary or right to comply.

He complained, as of a hardship, that the provision in the order of the 24th. of May, for permitting American vessels to export return cargoes from the ports of Holland, is not co: extensive with that for admitting their entry into those ports.

This omission was not an oversight.

It was intended to prevent, as far as was practicable, the inconveniences likely to be created by Mr. Erskine's unauthorized agreement: but it neither was, nor could be intended to obviate all possible inconveniences;—even such as might have arisen if Mr. Erskine's agreement had never been made.

If an American vessel had sailed from America for Holland in time of profound peace, or in time of ordinary war, the ports of Holland not being, at the date of sailing, under blockade, it might yet have happened, that, in the period between the commencement of such voyage, and the arrival of the vessel at the port of destination, a blockade might have been established before that port. The vessel arriving would, in that case, have been warned not to enter the port, and would have been turned away with the loss of the whole object of the voyage. This would be no extraordinary hardship, and would afford no legitimate ground of complaint.

The order in Council is far less strict than such a blockade would be; forasmuch as it provides for [the completion of] [60] the original voyage, commenced in expectation of being admitted to the port of destination, by permitting the entry into the ports of Holland: and it is no just ground of complaint, that it does not superadd to that permission, the liberty to re: export a cargo of the enemy's goods or produce.

---

[59] The order of May 24, 1809, is printed in A. S. P., F. R., III, 302. The enclosures consisted of a printed copy of Instructions to Naval Officers, May 31, 1809, and a copy of Additional Instructions to British Naval Commanders, July —, 1809.

[60] The draft, F. O. 5 : 68, has the words enclosed in brackets.

CANNING TO JACKSON [61]

No. 9.   FOREIGN OFFICE, July 8th. 1809.
Sir,

Mr. Erskine appears to have excited an expectation that an Envoy was to be sent out from England fully empowered and instructed to proceed immediately to the conclusion of a Treaty upon all the Subjects that have been in discussion between Great Britain and the United States; and you will perhaps be expected to come provided with such Powers and Instructions.

From what part of my instructions to Mr. Erskine he thought himself warranted in drawing such an inference, I am at a loss to imagine. True it is that if he had obtained all the conditions that he was instructed to obtain, he was authorized to say that a Special Mission would be sent to "consign to a regular Treaty *those conditions,*" and His Majesty's consequent agreement to withdraw the Orders in Council;—and that supposing that done, there would be a disposition to enter into a discussion of the general Commercial Interests of the two Countries upon the Principles suggested to Mr. Erskine by Mr. Gallatin as the fit grounds of such a Treaty. But the whole of this Authority to Mr. Erskine was conditional, and depended upon his succeeding in his Negotiation upon the Terms precisely prescribed to him.

Still however there exists the same disposition on the part of His Majesty: and should what you are instructed to propose in respect to the points immediately in discussion lead to the result which is confidently anticipated, His Majesty will then be willing to authorize you to receive, or to propose, an Arrangement of all other points in the most amicable and satisfactory manner, upon the first intimation of a readiness on the part of the American Government to open, or to entertain, such a Negotiation.

In order that there may be no doubt as to your full and sufficient Authority to bring to a conclusion the points which you are specially instructed to settle, I transmit to you herewith a regular Full Power under the Great Seal:—which will also be applicable to any further Negotiations in which you may hereafter be engaged with The American Government.

CANNING TO JACKSON [62]

No. 10.   FOREIGN OFFICE, July 10, 1809.
Sir,

I transmit to you herewith the Copy of a letter from Mr. Charles Shaw, Chairman of a General Meeting of British Claimants of Land

[61] F. O. 115 : 20.
[62] F. O. 115 : 20.

in West Florida, together with the Memorial therein referred to from that body; and I am to desire that you will take an early opportunity of submitting this subject to the American Government, and use your best endeavours to obtain for the Memorialists the redress which they solicit.[63]

GEORGE HAMMOND TO JACKSON [64]

FOREIGN OFFICE, October 11th, 1809.

Sir,

I have the honour to inclose to you, by Mr. Secretary Canning's direction, the Copy of an order which was passed by His Majesty in Council on the 16th of August last; and which I am farther directed to desire, you will make publick within the Territories of the United States.[65]

EARL BATHURST TO JACKSON [66]

No. 1.   FOREIGN OFFICE, November 8, 1809.

Sir,

Your Dispatches Nos. 1–2–3 and 4 have been received, and laid before the King.

I have the satisfaction to inform you, that His Majesty approves, of your having declined to deliver your Credentials, to the President of the United States, at his Private Residence in the Country, and to commence an un-official negociation, before his return. The continued absence of the President, from the Seat of Government, after the notification of your arrival, may have been occasioned only, by the cause assigned, and may not have proceeded from a wish, to mark his indifference, to an amicable adjustment with Great Britain: but your following him into his retirement, would have been an instance on your part, of unbecoming impatience to begin your Mission;—and it would have given the President a great advantage, if he had become acquainted with the nature of your Instructions, before he began to negociate.

The right, of insisting on the Committment in the United States of British Seamen, for desertion, is under any circumstances very

---

[63] See note 3, p. 247, *supra.* Shaw's letter and the memorial are dated July 10, 1809. Canning was urged to press the United States for a repeal of restrictive acts pertaining to the memorialists, or for a compromise settlement of their claims.

[64] F. O. 115 : 20.

[65] This order, transmitted to Jackson by Under Secretary Hammond, empowered British governors in the West Indies to increase import duties, as set forth in the order-in-council of April 12, 1809, when such duties were paid in depreciated colonial currency.

[66] F. O. 115 : 20. After Canning's resignation in September of 1809, Henry Bathurst, third Earl Bathurst (1762–1834), president of the Board of Trade since 1807, with a seat in the cabinet, had taken over the seals of the foreign office, pending the arrival from Spain of Lord Wellesley. He filled the post temporarily, from Oct. 11 to Dec. 6, 1809.

questionable, and as it does not appear, under what authority, a British Consul, can have committed to Jail, any person in the Territories of the United States, I trust that you will not make any official complaint, against the conduct of the Magistrate, who released the persons, you state were committed by Mr. Wood His Majesty's Consul at Baltimore.[67]

By Mr. Champagny's letter to General Armstrong, written from Altenburgh on the 22d of August,[68] you will see, that there did not then exist, any disposition on the part of France, to withdraw, what is stated to be, the obnoxious part of her Decrees.

It is therefore only necessary to repeat the Instructions you have already received on that head, not to compromise His Majesty's Government by any intimation, that a partial repeal of the French Decrees, would be satisfactory: nor to give it to be understood, what conduct his Majesty's Government, might under such circumstances, think it proper to adopt: and you will not engage to write home for further Instructions in this particular, although pressed so to do, unless the precise case has actually arrived, and a Copy of the Instrument is in your possession, by which this Repeal has been effected.

It is hoped that the state of Irritation, which you describe to exist, in many parts of the United States, will gradually subside. These disturbances were probably encouraged on your arrival, by the Partizans of France, who may wish to avail themselves of any advantage, which they might derive, from your being induced to depart from that conciliatory, but firm conduct, to which it is not to be doubted you will carefully adhere.

BATHURST TO JACKSON [69]

No. 2.   FOREIGN OFFICE, Novem'r 8th 1809.
Sir,

In conformity with my other Dispatch of this date, I proceed to state to you the Grounds upon which His Majesty's Government disclaim the acknowledgement made by Mr. Erskine, that "the Right to carry on the Trade, from the Colonies of Belligerents to the United States, had never been called in question, and had been recognised by his Majesty's Supreme Court of Admiralty."

Whatever Trade has been exercised by the United States with the Colonies of Belligerents, either during the last War, except so far as

---

[67] Reporting the hostile temper of the American people, Jackson stated that some deserting seamen of H. M. Frigate *Africaine*, which had carried him to America, "were apprehended and committed to Jail by Mr. Wood, His Majesty's Consul at Baltimore, and immediately released by a Magistrate of the Town on the avowed Alledgment of an illegal Committment, but probably under the Intimidation of the Mob who threatened to pull down the Prison." Jackson to Canning, Sept. 12, 1809, No. 1, F. O. 5 : 64.

[68] Champagny's note to Armstrong of Aug. 22, 1809, is printed in *A. S. P., F. R.*, III, 325–326.

[69] F. O. 115 : 20.

it could be shewn to have existed during the Peace immediately preceding the last War; or during the present War, has been considered by the British Government, as concessions conveyed from time to time in his Majesty's Instructions.

At the Commencement of the last War, by the Instructions of the 6th November 1793, the Capture was generally directed, of all Ships laden with Goods, the produce of any Colony belonging to France.

On the 8th January 1794, this Instruction to capture, was restricted to Vessels coming direct from the Colonies of France, to any Port in Europe, or to any port whatever, if the Goods were the Property of the Enemy.

By the Instruction of the 25th of January, 1798, a further relaxation took place in favor of Neutral Commerce, by allowing a Trade from the Colonies of Belligerents, to the Ports of this Country, and to the Ports of such Countries in Europe, to which the Ships, being Neutral Ships, respectively belonged.

It was always considered by the British Government, that, whatever Trade was carried on by the United States with the Colonies of Belligerents during the last War, was under the two last Instructions: and Neutral Ships, whether belonging to the United States, or to any other Neutral Country, were condemned or released by his Majesty's Supreme Court of Admiralty (if engaged in a Trade with the Enemy's Colonies) as they did or did not fall, within the Instructions above-mentioned.

When The King's Advocate stated, in his Letter of the 16th of March 1801, "that it was now distinctly understood, and has been repeatedly so decided by the High Court of Appeal, that the Produce of the Colonies of the Enemy, may be imported by a Neutral into his own Country, and may be re-exported from thence, even to the Mother Country of such Colony," he had reference to the Trade allowed to be carried on under the instructions then in force, and not to any general Right claimed by Neutrals and acknowledged by us.

This is clear, both from the Substance of the opinion delivered, and from the occasion on which it was written. No distinction, you will observe, is here made between the Neutrals in Europe, and in the other Quarters of the World:—if therefore it was hereby intended to admit, that Neutrals had, independent of any temporary concessions made by this Country, a right to trade direct with the Colonies of the Enemy, such an opinion would have been irreconcileable with the Instruction of the 8th of January 1794, and with the practice of the Courts thereupon: For it was not until the Instructions of the 25th of January 1798, that Neutral European States were allowed this direct Trade to their own Ports, from the Colonies of the Enemy;

and, until that period, such Vessels were, under the Instructions of the 8th of January 1794, captured and condemned. The declaration of The King's Advocate above recited, could only have had reference therefore, to this last Instruction, and to the practice of the Court upon it.

By the order of the 8th January 1794, the direct Trade from the Colonies of Belligerents to the Ports of the United States, was allowed; but a Trade between such Colonies to any Port, except of Countries to which the Neutral Vessels belonged, was equally prohibited by the Instruction of the 8th of January 1794, and that of the 25th of January 1798.

In observance of this prohibition, the Court of Admiralty held, that an importation of such produce into the ports of Neutrals, with a direct purpose of re-exporting it to Ports prohibited by these Instructions, could only be considered as a colourable importation, and that the Voyage must take it's Character in that case; not from the last Port of Clearance, but from the Port of original Shipment. Thus the bona fides of these Importations into Neutral States, became a Subject of Discussion in the Court of Admiralty. The letter of The King's Advocate was written to state what at that time, was considered by the Court as Evidence of a *bonâ fide* Importation: that this however was not to be considered as conclusive Evidence, in bar of any other which might prove a contrary Intent, appears from several cases, where all the Evidence stated in this letter to be requisite, was produced, and yet, on doubts arising of the true Intent of the Importation, further proof was ordered by the Court.

Where the Question is, what is the Intent of an Act?—what is done to conceal the Intent cannot be stated to be conclusive Evidence to disprove it: for this would be to substitute, for the observance of the Law, the means taken to cover the breach of it.

A luminous Judgement delivered by the High Court of Appeal, on the 11th March 1806, sets this part of the question beyond all doubt. It is also worthy of remark, as explaining the Sense in which the eleventh Article of the Treaty of Commerce hereafter to be referred to, was understood by the British Government; that one of his Majesty's Plenipotentiaries for that Treaty, was a Member of the High Court of Appeal, present, when that judgement was delivered.

With respect to the present War, the direct Trade which has been carried on between the United States and the Colonies of Belligerents, has been always considered by the British Government to have been carried on by His Majesty's Permission, conveyed in an Order of Council of the 24th June 1803. In this Order His Majesty was pleased to direct, that the Commanders of his Ships, should not seize any Neutral Vessel which should be carrying on Trade directly, between the Colonies of the Enemy, and the Neutral Country to which the Vessel belonged. In all cases, having any reference to a Trade by Neutrals, with the Colonies of the Enemy, the proceedings of the Court of Admiralty have been regulated by this Order, and by so much of the Order of the 11th November 1807, as renewed the order abovementioned: and it is to be observed, that the order of January 24th 1803 was not published, as the rule by which this Trade was to be regulated, even during the present War, but in the Preamble it is stated to be "in consideration of the present state of Commerce."

As for the Treaty of 1806, the American Government cannot surely claim any right under an Article of a Treaty, which they refused to ratify.

The Article referred to in Mr. Erskine's Notes, is the eleventh,[70] which arranged the conditions, under which [the] Enemy's Colonial Produce should be re-exported from the Ports of the United States. This Article left the direct trade, between the United States and the Colonies of the Enemy, on the footing on which it had been placed by the Order of January 24th 1803, and would in effect have conceded during the present War the circuitous Trade, under the Conditions therein stipulated, between the Ports of the Enemy's Colonies, not only to Neutral Ports in Europe, but to the Ports of Belligerents in Europe, unless such Ports were under strict and rigorous Blockade.

But then it must be remembered, that this Article established no Right beyond the term for which it was to last. That which is matter of right is not matter of agreement: and what is conceded by Agreement, is not obtained, if the agreement is not concluded. If the right claimed had been acknowledged in the Treaty, the acknowledgement would not have been valid as the Treaty was not ratified.

So far, however, from any acknowledgement of this Right, claimed by the United States, being to be discovered in this Article, there is an express Reservation that "this Article was not to operate to the Prejudice of any right, belonging to either party: but that, after the Expiration of the time limited by the Article, the Rights on both sides shall revive, and be in full force."

In this detail of what has passed relating to this Subject, from the commencement of Hostilities in 1793, you will not fail to remark the great caution which the British Government has observed, under all the Successive Administrations, not to make any admission, or to enter into any agreement, by which the direct Trade between the Ports of the United States, and the Ports of the Enemy's Colonies should be considered as acknowledged to be exercised as a Right.

When therefore in Mr. Erskine's Dispatch No. 34, it was represented that a Member of the American Government had said that he

---

[70] Article XI, of the abortive Monroe-Pinkney Treaty; see *A. S. P.*, *F. R.*, III, 149.

knew "that it was intended by the American Government to abandon the attempt to carry on a Trade with the Colonies of Belligerents in time of War, which was not allowed in time of Peace, and to trust to the being permitted by the French to carry on such Trade, in time of Peace, so as to continue it in time of War;" [71] it was not to be imagined, that so unqualified a declaration had a limited Interpretation.

Had such a Declaration been made by an American Minister to the British Government, it would hardly have been considered as a fair proceeding, if, meaning it in a limited Sense, he had delivered it without any Explanation. But when a British Minister transmits home so unqualified a declaration, without a single Line of Explanation, it was impossible for His Majesty's Government to have imagined, that he could be aware of the exception stated, or that any other Construction could have been put upon it, than that which the Words obviously convey, and which is contained in the Letter of Mr. Secretary Canning.

BATHURST TO JACKSON [72]

Separate. FOREIGN OFFICE, November 8, 1809.

Sir,

Mr. Erskine in his Dispatch No. 34, inclosed several Notes, which had passed between him, and some members of the American Government, relating to unofficial communications, between him and these members. As Mr. Erskine will be on his return home, before this Dispatch arrives, the contents of Mr. Erskine's Notes, would not have required any comment, if they had been confined to a Vindication of his own conduct.

He has however in the course of his Correspondence, stated, that, "The Right to carry on the Trade from the Colonies of Belligerents, to the United States, had never been called in Question, and had been recognised by his Majesty's Supreme Court of Appeal, and the terms upon which such Colonial Produce might be re-exported, from the United States, had been formally arranged in a Treaty." [73]

This Treaty was the Treaty of 1806, which was never ratified; and the Trade, the right to which in time of war, is thus acknowledged, is

---

[71] Secretary Gallatin's opinion, according to Erskine's letter to Secretary Smith, Aug. 14, 1809, *A. S. P., F. R.*, III, 306. Erskine's correspondence with Gallatin and Smith, August 9–15, 1809, was enclosed in his dispatch No. 34, of August 31, 1809, F. O. 5: 63.

[72] F. O. 115: 20.

[73] Erskine made the statement in his letter to Secretary Smith of August 14, 1809, copy of which was enclosed in his dispatch to Canning, August 31, 1809, No. 34, F. O. 5: 63. The letter of August 14, 1809 is printed in *A. S. P., F. R.*, III, 305–306, and the statement in question is identical with that in Erskine's manuscript letter. The above quotation, however, is not exact; it should read: "the Right to carry on a Trade from the Colonies of Belligerents to the United States had never been called in Question, and had been recognized by His Majesty's Supreme Court of Admiralty and the Terms even upon which such Colonial Produce might be reexported from the United States had been formally arranged in a Treaty. . . ."

that, from which the United States were excluded, during the last Peace.

The Notes may be considered as extra-official; yet as the answers were written by Mr. Erskine, while he retained his diplomatic character, it is to be feared, they will have much of the weight, to which a more official communication would have entitled them. You will therefore take the first opportunity, of writing an un-official letter to Mr. Smith, disclaiming this unauthorised admission of a Right, which has never been acknowledged by the British Government from the first moment it was asserted.

I inclose a Copy of the letter which it is thought adviseable that you should write, upon this occasion, and I shall reserve for another Dispatch, the grounds upon which the British Government are justified in disclaiming this acknowledgement.

[*Enclosure: Draft of a Letter to be sent to the Secretary of State*]

Sir,

I have some reason to believe that Mr. Erskine has transmitted to His Majesty's Government, Copies of Letters, which passed between you and him, explanatory of a Communication made to him in Nov'r 1808.

I am fully aware, that this Correspondence, as well as the communication to which it refers, was purely extra-official, and I avail myself of a form equally so, to beg you will understand, that when Mr. Erskine in his letter to you stated, that, "the Right to carry on a Trade from the Colonies of Belligerents to the United States had never been called in question, and had been recognised by His Majesty's Supreme Court of Admiralty," it was a declaration, which he was wholly unauthorised to make.

INSTRUCTIONS OF 1810

MARQUESS WELLESLEY TO JACKSON [1]

No. 1.   FOREIGN OFFICE, April 14, 1810.

Sir,

Your Dispatches to No. 32 of last year, and No. 17 of the present year, have been received and laid before The King. The two papers herewith enclosed, being Mr. Pinkney's letter to me on the 2nd. of January, and my answer to it of the 14 of March contain the whole of what has passed officially between Mr. Pinkney and me, upon the Subject of the differences which have unfortunately arisen between you, and The Government of The United States.[2]

My letter to Mr. Pinkney will sufficiently explain to you the principles, which have dictated the Conduct of His Majesty's Government on this embarrassing occasion.

You will observe in that letter, that His Majesty has commanded me to express his undiminished sense of the Zeal, fidelity, and ability, which you have manifested in a long Course of public Service. Under the present circumstances however, your return to Washington[3] for the purpose of resuming your Diplomatic functions could neither be conducive to His Majesty's honor, nor satisfactory to yourself: and you will therefore be at liberty to return to England, as soon as it may suit with your own convenience.

Mr. J. P. Morier[4] who will be the Bearer of a Duplicate of this Dispatch, has been named His Majesty's Charge des Affaires at

---

[1] Draft, F. O. 5 : 68. Richard Colley Wellesley, Marquess Wellesley (1760–1842), Governor-General of India, 1797–1805, and ambassador-extraordinary to the Spanish Junta at Seville in 1809, had become Foreign Secretary on December 6, 1809.

[2] Pinkney's note of January 2, requesting the recall of Jackson (for having "ascribed to the American Government a knowledge that the propositions submitted to its consideration by Mr. Erskine were indispensable conditions," and for having done so even after that knowledge had been distinctly disclaimed), and Wellesley's reply of March 14, 1810, are printed in *A. S. P., F. R.*, III, 352–356. See, also, for Jackson's correspondence with Secretary Smith, *ibid.*, III, 309–323.

[3] Jackson had left Washington after the rupture of relations in November of 1809, but he did not sail for England until September 16, 1810. Meanwhile he visited the seaboard cities and Canada, published an appeal to the American people in the form of a statement to British consuls, and spent £700 on propaganda. See Josephine Fisher, "Francis James Jackson and Newspaper Propaganda in the United States, 1809–1810," *Maryland Magazine of History*, XXX (June, 1935), 93–113.

[4] John Philip Morier (1776–1853) ; he had begun his career in the foreign service in 1799 as secretary to Lord Elgin, then ambassador at Constantinople, and had been employed on various diplomatic missions in the Near East and in Europe. He was secretary of legation and chargé d'affaires at Washington from August 31, 1810 to July 1, 1811.

Washington, for the purpose of carrying on the ordinary business of the mission, untill the appointment of your Successor; and you will accordingly be pleased to deliver into his Custody the Archives of The Mission, together with The Ciphers and Such other papers, as you may judge useful for his guidance.

WELLESLEY TO JACKSON [5]

[No. 2.] [6]   FOREIGN OFFICE, July 3, 1810.

Sir,

I have received The King's Commands to transmit to you herewith His Majesty's letter to the President of the United States notifying that His Majesty has been pleased to recall you from that Mission, which you will deliver to Mr. Morier, the Bearer of this Dispatch, in order that he may convey it to the President.

In order to prevent any misunderstandings which might arise from Mr. Morier's being charged by you with any direct communication from yourself to the President, I have received His Majesty's Commands to give to that Gentleman a letter to the American Secretary of State,[7] acquainting him that he is to remain in charge of His Majesty's Mission in America untill the appointment of your Successor.

WELLESLEY TO JOHN PHILIP MORIER [8]

No. 1.   FOREIGN OFFICE, June 26, 1810.[9]

Sir,

The King having been pleased to appoint you to be His Majesty's Secretary of Legation to The United States, in order that you might take upon yourself the Charge of His Majesty's Concerns in that Country, on the return of Mr. Jackson to England, I have received His Majesty's Commands to direct you to repair forthwith to Portsmouth, there to embark on board His Majesty's Ship Venus, which has been ordered for your Reception.

The Enclosed Copies of Mr. Pinkney's letter to me, dated the 2nd of last January, and of my Answer to Him under date of the 14th of March, have been already communicated to you.[10] These papers having put you fully in possession of the late Misunderstanding which

---

[5] F. O. 115 : 20.

[6] The draft, F. O. 5 : 68, is marked "No. 2."

[7] The letter to Secretary Robert Smith, dated as of July 17, 1810, and the draft of the above instruction are printed in *Papers Presented to Parliament in 1813*, pp. 214–216.

[8] F. O. 115 : 20. On Morier, see note 4, page 302, *supra*. The draft of this instruction is printed in *Papers Presented to Parliament in 1813*, Section B, "Correspondence between The Marquess Wellesley and Mr. Morier, July 1810 to March 1811," pp. 211–214.

[9] The draft, F. O. 5 : 70, is dated July 17, 1810.

[10] See note 2, p. 302, *supra*.

has arisen from the Correspondence between Mr. Jackson and the American Secretary of State, and which has occasioned Mr. Jackson's Recall, they will at the same time explain to you the manner in which His Majesty has appreciated Mr. Jackson's Conduct, and the Language which it is intended that you shall hold towards the American Government, whenever these Circumstances shall be made the subjects of your Conversation. You will at the same time hold in Mind, that it is the Wish of His Majesty's Government, that all discussion relative to this Misunderstanding should terminate with Mr. Jackson's Recall.

On your Arrival at New York, you will deliver to Mr. Jackson the accompanying Dispatch addressed to that Gentleman [11] enclosing His Re Credentials.

Had Mr. Jackson's Mission terminated in the usual manner, He would of course have been instructed to present these Re Credentials in person to The President of the United States; but under the present Circumstances, It is by no means adviseable that an Attempt should be made to renew any intercourse between Mr. Jackson and The American Government, unless it were previously ascertained that it would not prove the means of renewing the late Discussions. Mr. Jackson will therefore be instructed to return into your Hands His Re Credentials, in order that you may present them to The Secretary of State at the Seat of Government. And Mr. Jackson will at the same time furnish you with the usual letter to the American Secretary of State, notifying to him, that Having received His Majesty's Commands to return to England, He had appointed you to take charge of the Concerns of His Majesty's Mission in America, until the appointment of His Successor.

If, on your arrival in America, you should learn that the Heads of the several Departments of the American Government have already quitted Washington, and do not purpose to return to that City until the usual period in the ensuing Autumn, you will be at liberty to take up your Residence either at Philadelphia or at New York, or in any other Town of The United States, where you may think that your Presence will be most conducive to His Majesty's Interests.

You will in this case take the earliest opportunity of forwarding to the American Secretary of State, Copies of His Majesty's Commission appointing you His Secretary of Legation, as well as of Mr. Jackson's Re Credentials, and of the letter [12] with which that Gentleman is to notify your appointment to the American Government.

---

[11] Wellesley to Jackson, July 3, 1810, [No. 2], *supra*.
[12] The copy in F. O. 115 : 20 of Wellesley's note to Secretary of State Robert Smith is dated July 3, 1810, seven days later than the date of this instruction.

In General Terms, you will at all times assure the American Government, that His Majesty remains cordially disposed to unite with them in forming Either a temporary or permanent Convention for an amicable Arrangement of the several points of difference between the Two Countries: But you will explicitly state to the American Secretary of State, in the first Interview which you will have with him (and your Language in Private Conversation will be of the same Tenor) that you are not authorized by His Majesty's Government to propose to that of The United States any Preliminary or Definitive Arrangement whatever, Either of a Political or Commercial Nature; nor will you invite from them any proposals of the kind; but whatever shall be presented to you, you will readily accept, for the purpose of submitting them to the Consideration of His Majesty's Government.

WELLESLEY TO MORIER [13]

No. 2.   FOREIGN OFFICE, June 27, 1810.[14]

Sir.

I am to recommend to your particular attention the enclosed letter from the Secretary of the Admiralty dated the 10th Ultimo, enclosing a Deposition and Examination of George Hassell, stating the circumstances under which he had seen Jefferey the Seaman, who was landed on the Island of Sombrero, by order of The Honorable Captain Lake.[15]

You will take an early opportunity, after your arrival at Washington, to enquire into the Truth of the Facts related in these papers, and you will report to me, for the Information of His Majesty's Government, whatever particulars shall come to your Knowledge, in pursuance of your Enquiries respecting this Transaction.[16]

---

[13] F. O. 115 : 20.

[14] The draft, F. O. 5 : 70, is dated July 17, 1810.

[15] John Barrow, secretary to the Admiralty, in his letter of May 10, 1810 to Under Secretary Hamilton enclosed the deposition of George Hassell, American seaman of Marblehead, Massachusetts, taken at London, April 25, 1810. Hassell stated that he had seen Robert Jeffery ("Governor of Sombrero"), formerly a sailor on H. M. Brig *Recruit*, at Marblehead in March of 1809. Jeffery told him that, for having stolen some of the officers' spruce beer, Captain Lake of the *Recruit* had punished him by marooning him, without provisions, on the desert island of Sombrero. After managing to live for four days on water from crevices in the rocks and on crabs which had been washed ashore, he had been picked up by the schooner *Betsey*, Captain Francis, and brought to Marblehead.

[16] Morier in his No. 8 of Oct. 4, 1810, F. O. 5 : 70, referred Wellesley to Jackson's No. 40 of July 10, 1810, F. O. 5 : 69, with which was enclosed a deposition obtained on June 17, 1810 from Robert Jeffery, blacksmith, at Wenham, Massachusetts. Jeffery, a British subject, stated that he had been impressed in 1807, at Falmouth, England, and had been taken that year on the *Recruit* to the West Indies. There, because of insufficient drinking water, he had broken into the vessel's supply of beer, and for this had been punished. After being marooned nine days on Sombrero, he had been rescued by the schooner *Adams* of Marblehead, John Dennis, master.

WELLESLEY TO MORIER [17]

No. 3.   FOREIGN OFFICE, June 29, 1810.[18]

Sir,

I herewith enclose to you the Copy of a Memorial from the British North American Merchants, together with its Enclosures respecting the Interests of the Trade and Fisheries of His Majesty's North American Colonies, and recommend the same to your attention, whenever an opportunity may present itself for obtaining information on the subject.[19]

WELLESLEY TO MORIER [20]

No. 4.   DOWNING STREET, July 3, 1810.

Sir,

I herewith inclose to you for your information copies of a correspondence which has taken place between Mr. Pinkney and me since the 15th Feby. 1810 respecting the continuation of Blockades of France and her dependent Territories instituted by this Country previous to the 1st. of January 1807, and I am to direct that, should the American Government put any Questions to you upon this Subject, you will avoid entering into any discussion thereon, engaging only to refer their communications to His Majesty's Government.[21]

WELLESLEY TO MORIER [22]

No. 5.   FOREIGN OFFICE, October 24th, 1810

Sir,

I transmit to you herewith, for your information, the copy of an article extracted from His Majesty's General Instructions to His Ministers employed on Foreign Missions, relative to secret Service Money; and also an Extract from the Act of Parliament therein mentioned; to which His Majesty strictly requires and commands that you punc-

---

[17] F. O. 115 : 20.

[18] The draft, F. O. 5 : 70, was first dated June 26, then changed to July 26, 1810.

[19] The memorial, of April 2, 1810, expressed concern at the plans of American merchants to establish settlements on the Columbia River. Morier in his dispatch No. 8, Oct. 4, 1810, F. O. 5 : 70, informed Wellesley that a group of fur traders headed by John Jacob Astor had recently sent out a vessel to that region. An interesting letter from John Jacob Astor to Secretary John Quincy Adams, dated Jan. 4, 1823, on his sending out of the ship *Tonquin*, with 20 guns and 60 men, in September of 1810 to establish the trading post of Astoria at the mouth of the Columbia River, is printed in *A. S. P., Miscellaneous*, II, 1009–1010.

[20] F. O. 115 : 20.

[21] These notes are printed in *A. S. P., F. R.*, III, 350–360. See also Henry Adams, *Hist. U. S.*, V, chap. xiii.

[22] F. O. 115 : 20.

tually conform yourself upon all occasions which may arise during your employment abroad.[23]

WELLESLEY TO MORIER [24]

No. 6.   FOREIGN OFFICE, October 27, 1810.

Sir,

I enclose to you herewith Copies of a Note and accompanying Memorandum which I transmitted by His Majesty's Command, on the 9th of August last, to the Deputies from the new Government of the Carraccas—And I am to instruct you, in any private or official Communications which you may have upon the subject of the proceedings of the Spanish Colonies in America, to conform your Language to the Principles contained in these Documents.[25]

WELLESLEY TO MORIER [26]

No. 7. Duplicate.   FOREIGN OFFICE, 30th: Oct'r: 1810.

Sir,

I have received His Majesty's Commands to instruct you, on no account to grant Passports or protections to American or other Vessels about to sail from any Port in the United States to any blockaded Port.

I am likewise to direct that you should in no instance grant any such licenses or Passports to Passengers proceeding in any Vessel whatever, to any blockaded or enemy's Port, excepting where you have sufficient Reason to believe, that the granting of such Personal protection may be beneficial to His Majesty's Service.

---

[23] According to the regulations (based on 22nd George III, c. 82), the principal officers of state stood charged at the Exchequer for money issued to them for foreign secret service until they filed, within three years from the time of issuance, receipts for such money from their subordinate officers. The latter obtained their discharge at the Exchequer when, within a year from their arrival in England from foreign service, they either returned the money or made oath that they had disbursed it according to the intent and purpose for which it was given.

[24] F. O. 115 : 20.

[25] To Simón Bolívar and Lopez Mendez, agents of the Venezuelan insurgents, Wellesley, after receiving their assurances of loyalty to Ferdinand VII, promised Venezuela maritime protection against France "for the purpose of enabling that Province to defend the rights of its legitimate Sovereign, and to secure itself against the common Enemy." Wellesley urged a reconciliation between Venezuela and the provisional government in Spain, and promised his good offices to effect it. See W. S. Robertson, "The Beginnings of Spanish-American Diplomacy," *Essays in American History dedicated to Frederick Jackson Turner*, pp. 240–247.

[26] F. O. 115 : 20.

INSTRUCTIONS OF 1811

WELLESLEY TO MORIER [1]

No. 1.   FOREIGN OFFICE, January 8th, 1811.[2]
Sir,

I transmit for your information the enclosed Copies of a Letter from Mr. Pinkney to me, dated the 10th Ultimo, and of my answer to him of the 29th, respecting the demands which he has made, by orders of His Government, for the repeal of the British orders in Council and Blockades, which affect the Trade of the United States with France and Her Allies.[3]

I have no further instructions to give you upon this Subject:— The Language which you are to hold in your communications with The American Secretary of State respecting the conduct of the British Government upon this occasion, will be confined to the Principles expressed in my Letter to Mr. Pinkney; and you will assure him of your disposition to transmit to England whatever proposals he may wish to make through you for the purpose of explaining any parts of the Proclamation issued by the President on the 2d. of November last.[4]

WELLESLEY TO MORIER [5]

No. 2.   FOREIGN OFFICE, January 28th: 1811.
Sir,

For your further Information upon the present State of the Negotiation between His Majesty's Government and Mr. Pinkney, respecting the required Repeal of the Orders in Council in consequence of the alledged Advances made by the French Government, I herewith enclose to you (No. 1) a Copy of Mr. Pinkney's Reply [6] to my Letter to Him of the 29th of December last, Copy of which was forwarded to you in my No. 1 of the present year: and (No. 2) a Copy of my letter to The King's Advocate, Dated the 26th of this Month, directing him to stay all further proceedings of the Admiralty Court in the Cases of the American Ship Fox, captured by one of H. M. Cruizers, and of other Ships captured under similar Circumstances, until His Majesty's Pleasure shall be made known to him.[7]

---

[1] F. O. 115: 23.

[2] The draft, F. O. 5: 74, is dated Jan. 7, 1811.

[3] Pinkney's note of Dec. 10, contending that the revocation of the Berlin and Milan decrees (announced by the Duc de Cadore on Aug. 5, 1810) "turns on no condition precedent, is absolute, precise, and unequivocal," and Wellesley's reply of Dec. 29, 1810, are printed in *A. S. P., F. R.*, III, 376–379, 408–409.

[4] The proclamation of November 2, 1810, restoring commercial intercourse with France; printed in *A. S. P., F. R.*, III, 392.

[5] F. O. 115: 23.

[6] Pinkney's reply of Jan. 14, 1811, is printed in *A. S. P., F. R.*, III, 409–411.

[7] The condemnation of the *Fox* and other American vessels seized for violating the orders-in-council was delayed until June 25, 1811. See note 44, p. 324, *infra.*

WELLESLEY TO MORIER [8]

No. 3.   FOREIGN OFFICE, February 18, 1811.
Sir,
   It has been represented to His Majesty's Government that under the existing circumstances of our Relations with America some difficulties may be experienced in the details of the Transaction which Mr. Stuart [9] announced to you in his Letter of the 2nd of November, for the Supply of Lisbon and His Majesty's Troops in Portugal with Grain and Flour from America.[10]
   I am therefore to instruct you, on application being made to you to that effect, to grant Protection to any number of Vessels not exceeding Fifty (before the 10th Day of August next) proceeding from any Port in the United States of America with Grain and Flour only, and bound to Lisbon, if not in the Occupation of the French—Or, on notice of Lisbon having been taken by the Enemy, then to proceed to Cadiz or to Gibraltar:—provided that the Name of the Vessel, it's Tonnage and Master are stated in the Body of your *Protection*, and that you have reason to believe that the Parties applying are engaged in the Transaction mentioned in the former part of this Dispatch.
   You will of course concert with the Resident Consuls at the Ports from whence the several Ships will take their departure any other Regulations, which may be necessary in order to provide against Frauds, by which these Passports might be made use of to cover other Cargoes; And you will particularly attend to the necessity of not allowing any details of the Transaction to transpire as long as the Object in view can possibly be kept secret.

WELLESLEY TO MORIER [11]

No. 4.   FOREIGN OFFICE, 5th. April 1811.
Sir,
   I am commanded by His Royal Highness the Prince Regent to transmit to you for your information and guidance, the inclosed Copies of my correspondence with Mr. Pinkney since the 29th. of December last [12] according to the accompanying Schedule.

---

   [8] F. O. 115 : 23.
   [9] Charles Stuart (1779–1845), afterwards Baron Stuart de Rothesay, minister to Portugal 1810–1814.
   [10] See W. Freeman Galpin, "The American Grain Trade to the Spanish Peninsula, 1810–1814," *Amer. Hist. Review,* XXVIII (Oct., 1922), 24–44.
   [11] F. O. 115 : 23.
   [12] The notes exchanged by Pinkney and Wellesley are in *A. S. P., F. R.* III, 408–415. On February 28, 1811 Pinkney had taken official, and "inamicable," leave of the Prince of Wales (who on February 6, 1811 had assumed the royal office as Prince Regent). John Spear Smith became the American chargé d'affaires at London.

No. 5.　　　　　　　　　　FOREIGN OFFICE, April 26, 1811.

Sir,

Your dispatches to No. 20 of the 3rd. Ulto. have been received, and laid before His Royal Highness the Prince Regent.

This dispatch will be delivered to you by Mr. Augustus John Foster,[14] whom His Royal Highness has in the name and on the behalf of His Majesty, appointed to be His Majesty's Envoy Extraordinary and Minister Plenipotentiary to the United States of America.

I have received His Royal Highness's Commands to convey to you His Royal Highness's Approbation in the name and on the behalf of His Majesty of the Manner in which you have exercised the duties of your Situation, during the period in which you have acted as His Majesty's Chargé d'Affaires at Washington, and I am to desire that you will, immediately on Mr. Foster's Arrival in America, deliver to him all the public Papers and Cyphers in your possession, belonging to His Majesty's Legation, and that you will resume the duties of His Majesty's Secretary of Legation.

WELLESLEY TO AUGUSTUS JOHN FOSTER [15]

No. 1.　　　　　　　　　　FOREIGN OFFICE, April 10th. 1811.

Sir,

The Correspondence and Documents to which you have had access, respecting the several orders passed in Council, for the Regulation of Commerce, in consequence of the hostile Decrees of France, will have apprized you of the general nature of that System of Defence, to which His Majesty was compelled to resort, for the purpose of protecting the Maritime Rights and Interests of His Dominions, against the new description of Warfare adopted by the Enemy.

But as the Question now at issue between Great Britain, France, and America on this important Point, will require you to enter into the fullest explanations with the Government of the United States, His Royal Highness the Prince Regent, acting in the Name and on the Behalf of His Majesty, has commanded me to direct your attention, in a more particular manner, to the Principles on which the Orders in Council, were originally founded; to the actual state of the Question now depending between this Government and the United States, with relation to the Repeal of the Orders in Council; and to the conduct which you are to observe in your intercourse with the American Governm't on this Subject.

---

[13] F. O. 115 : 23.

[14] Augustus John Foster (1780–1848), late British minister to Sweden; he had been secretary of legation at Washington from 1804 to 1808 (see note 8, p. 231, *supra*).

[15] Draft, F. O. 5 : 75. On Foster, see note immediately preceding. This draft is also printed in *Papers Presented to Parliament in 1813,* Section C, "Correspondence between The Marquess Wellesley and Mr. Foster, April 1811 to December 1811," pp. 273–286.

The Decree of Berlin was directly and expressly an Act of War; by which France prohibited all Nations from Trade or Intercourse with Great Britain, under peril of Confiscation of their Ships and Merchandize, although France had not the means of imposing an actual Blockade in any degree adequate to such a purpose: The immediate and professed object of this hostile Decree, was the destruction of all British Commerce, through means entirely unsanctioned by the Law of Nations, and unauthorized by any received doctrine of Legitimate Blockade.

This violation of the established Law of Civilized Nations in War, would have justified Great Britain in retaliating upon the Enemy, by a similar interdiction of all Commerce with France, and with such other Countries, as might co-operate with France in her System of Commercial Hostility against Great Britain.

The Object of Great Britain was not the destruction of Trade, but it's preservation, under such Regulations as might be compatible with her own Security, at the same time that She extended an indulgence to Foreign Commerce, which, strict principle would have entitled her to withhold. The retaliation of Great Britain was not therefore urged to the full extent of her Right; our prohibition of French Trade was not absolute but modified; and in return for the absolute prohibition of all Trade with Great Britain, we prohibited, not all Commerce with France, but all such Commerce with France, as should not be carried on through Great Britain. It was evident, that this System must prove prejudicial to Neutral Nations: this calamity was foreseen, and deeply regretted. But the injury to Neutral Nations arose from the aggression of France, which had compelled Great Britain in her own defence to resort to adequate retaliatory measures of War: The operation, on the American Commerce, of those precautions, which the Conduct of France had rendered indispensable to our Security, is therefore to be ascribed to the unwarrantable aggression of France, and not to those proceeding on the part of Great Britain which that aggression had rendered necessary and just.

From this view of the Origin of the Orders in Council, you will perceive, that the object of our System was not to crush the Trade of the Continent, but to counteract an attempt to crush the British Trade; that we have endeavoured to permit the continent to receive as large a portion of commerce as might be practicable through Great Britain; and that all our subsequent Regulations, and every modification of the System, by new Orders or modes of granting or withholding Licences, have been calculated for the purpose of encouraging the Trade of Neutrals through Great Britain, whenever such encouragement might appear advantageous to the general interests of commerce, and consistent with the Public safety of the Nation; the preservation of which is the primary object of all National Councils, and the paramount duty of Executive Power.[16]

In every discussion which has taken place, we have rested the justification of our Orders in Council, and the continuance of that System of defence, upon the existence of the Decrees of Berlin and Milan, and upon the perseverance of the Enemy in the System of hostility, which has subverted the Rights of Neutral Commerce on the Continent.

We have therefore uniformly declared, that whenever France shall have effectually repealed the Decrees of Berlin and Milan, and shall have restored neutral commerce to the Condition in which it stood previously to the promulgation of those Decrees, we shall immediately repeal Our Orders in Council.

In contradiction to the Statement on which we have founded the justification of our Orders in Council, France has asserted that the Decree of Berlin was a measure of just retaliation on her part, occasioned by our previous aggression; and the French Government has insisted, that our System of Blockade, as it existed previously to the Decree of Berlin, was a manifest violation of the received Law of Nations.

In order to understand the purport of this allegation, it is necessary to refer to the Articles of the Decree of Berlin,[17] in which are specified the Principles of our System of Blockade, which France considers to be new, and to be contrary to the Law of Nations.

In the 4th. and 8th. articles it is stated, as a justification of the French Decree, that Great Britain "extends to unfortified Towns and commercial Ports, to Harbours and to the Mouths of Rivers, those Rights of Blockade, which by reason, and by the usage of nations, are applicable only to Fortified Places; and that the rights of Blockade ought to be limited to Fortresses, really invested by a sufficient Force."

It is added in the same articles, that Great Britain "has declared Places to be in a state of Blockade, before which She has not a single Ship of War, and even Places, which the whole British Force would be insufficient to Blockade, entire Coasts, and a whole Empire."

Neither the practice of Great Britain, nor the Law of Nations, has ever sanctioned the Rule here laid down by France, "that no Places excepting Fortresses in a complete state of investiture, can be deemed lawfully Blockaded by Sea." If such a Rule were to be admitted, it would become nearly impracticable for Great Britain to attempt the Blockade of any Port of the Continent; and our submission to this perversion of the Law of Nations, while it would destroy one of

---

[16] On the economic warfare between Great Britain and France, and the licensed trade-with-the-enemy carried on by both belligerents, see Frank E. Melvin, *Napoleon's Navigation System*, and Eli F. Heckscher, *The Continental System.*

[17] The Berlin Decree is printed in *A. S. P., F. R.,* III, 289–290.

the principal advantages of our Naval Superiority, would sacrifice the common Rights and Interests of all Maritime States.

In objecting to the practice of Great Britain, in the exercise of the Rights of Blockade, the Decree of Berlin imputes to us principles, which we have never asserted, nor attempted to carry into effect. The Decree does not distinctly specify the particular Blockade, which France deems exceptionable; but it is evident that the Blockade of May 1806, was the principal pretended justification of the Decree of Berlin, although neither the Principles on which that Blockade was founded, nor its practical operation afforded any Colour for the proceedings of France.

In point of Date, the Blockade of May 1806, preceded the Berlin Decree, but it was a just and legal Blockade, according to the established Law of Nations, because it was intended to be maintained, and was actually maintained by an adequate Force, appointed to guard the whole Coast, described in the Notification, and consequently to enforce the Blockade. Great Britain has never attempted to dispute, that in the Ordinary Course of the Law of Nations, no blockade can be justifiable or valid, unless it be supported by an adequate Force, destined to maintain it, and to expose to hazard all Vessels attempting to evade its operation.

The Blockade of May 1806 was notified by Mr. Secretary Fox on this clear principle; nor was that Blockade announced until he had satisfied himself by Communication with the Admiralty that the Admiralty possessed the means, and would employ them, of watching the whole Coast from Brest to the Elbe, and of effectually Enforcing the Blockade.

The Blockade of May 1806 was therefore (according to the Doctrine maintained by Great Britain) just and lawful in its origin, because it was supported, both in intention and fact, by an adequate Naval Force. This was the justification of that Blockade, until the period of time, when the Orders in Council were issued.

The Orders in Council were founded on a distinct principle,—That of defensive Retaliation; France had declared a Blockade of all the Ports and Coasts of Great Britain and Her Dependencies, without assigning, or being able to assign any Force to support that Blockade; Such an Act of the Enemy would have justified a declaration of the Blockade of the whole Coast of France, even without the application of any particular Force to that Service. Since the promulgation of the Orders in Council, the Blockade of May 1806, has been sustained and extended, by the more Comprehensive principle of defensive retaliation, on which those regulations are founded; But if the Orders in Council should be abrogated, the Blockade of May 1806 could not continue, under our construction of the Law of Nations, unless that Blockade should be maintained by a due application of an adequate Naval Force.

America appears to concur with France in asserting, that Great
Britain was the Original Aggressor, in the attack on Neutral Rights,
and has particularly objected to the Blockade of May 1806, as an
obvious Instance of that Aggression, on the part of Great Britain.
Although the Doctrines of the Berlin Decree respecting the Rights
of Blockade are not directly asserted by the American Government,
Mr. Pinkney's Correspondence would appear to countenance the principles on which those Doctrines are founded; The objection directly
stated by America against the Blockade of May 1806 rests on a Supposition, that no Naval Force, which Great Britain possessed, or
could have employed for such a purpose, could have rendered that
Blockade effectual; and that therefore it was necessarily irregular,
and could not possibly be maintained in conformity to the Law of
Nations.

Reviewing the Course of this Statement, it will appear, that the
Blockade of May 1806 can not be deemed contrary to the Law of
Nations, either under the objections urged by the French, or under
those declared or insinuated by the American Government, because
that Blockade was maintained by a sufficient Naval Force; That the
Decree of Berlin was not therefore justified, either under the pretexts
alledged by France, or under those Supported by America; That the
Orders in Council were founded on a just principle of defensive Retaliation against the Violation of the Law of Nations, committed by
France in the Decree of Berlin; That the Blockade of May 1806 is
now included in the more extensive Operation of the Orders in Council; and lastly, that the Orders in Council will not be continued beyond the effectual Duration of the Hostile Decrees of France; nor
will the Blockade of May 1806 continué, after the Repeal of the Orders
in Council, unless we shall think fit to sustain it by the special application of a sufficient Naval Force: This fact will not be suffered to
remain in doubt; and if the Repeal of the Orders in Council should
take place, the Intentions of this Government respecting the Blockade
of May 1806 will be notified at the same time.

Having thus explained the original Foundation of the Orders in
Council, It is now my Duty to direct your attention to the actual
State of the Question, now depending between This Government,
and The United States, with relation to the Repeal of the Orders in
Council.

In the Letter from the French Minister for Foreign Affairs to the
American Minister at Paris dated the 5th: August 1810,[18] France
announced the Repeal of the Decrees of Berlin and Milan, in terms
of studied Ambiguity; which however have since been fully explained
by the conduct and Language of the French Government. The

---

[18] The letter of the Duc de Cadore to John Armstrong, American minister to France, dated
Aug. 5, 1810, is printed in *A. S. P., F. R.*, III, 386–387.

Gov't of the United States appears to have construed the French Letter of the 5th: of August 1810, with reference exclusively to that part of the Letter, which states that "The Hostile Decrees are repealed, and that the repeal is to take effect on the [1st] [19] November 1810," without adverting to the Conditional Terms, which accompany that Declaration.

The American Government has therefore Viewed the Letter as such an unconditional and unqualified Revocation of The Decrees of Berlin and Milan, as required us, under our Uniform Declarations, to revoke our Orders in Council; and has added a demand for the Annulment of the Blockade of May 1806.

But the French letter of the 5th: of August, announced, not an immediate or absolute, but a prospective and Conditional, Repeal of the Decrees of Berlin and Milan, the Operation of which Repeal was to have commenced on the [1st] [20] of November 1810, on condition, either that Great Britain should have repealed by that time Her Orders in Council, and should also have renounced her principles of Blockade; or on condition, (if Great Britain should not have made these Concessions to France) that the Government of the United States should have opened the Trade with France, and should have taken measures for asserting the Rights of America against Great Britain.

This Construction of the Letter of the 5th: of August has been confirmed in the most unequivocal manner, not only by the subsequent conduct of France towards America, but expressly by the formal and Personal Declaration of Buonaparte himself, in his Speech addressed to the Deputies of the Hanse Towns on the [20th][21] March 1811, of which a Copy is annexed to this Dispatch.[22]

It is evident, therefore, that the Repeal of the Decrees of Berlin and Milan was contingent upon the performance of one of two Conditions: The one, required from Great Britain, The other, from America, in the event of our not submitting to the condition exacted from Us.

The Condition exacted from Us required, not merely that we should repeal our Orders in Council, or even that we should annul the Blockade of 1806: But that we should renounce our system and principles of Blockade, which we contend to be just and legitimate, recognized by the Law of Nations, and essential to the Security of our Maritime Rights.

---

[19] A blank space was left here for the date.
[20] A blank space was left here for the date.
[21] A blank space was left here for the date.
[22] In addressing some deputies of the Hanseatic League at the Tuileries, Napoleon declared: "The Decrees of Berlin and Milan are the fundamental laws of my empire. They cease to have effect only for nations that defend their sovereignty and maintain the religion of their flag." Henry Adams, *Hist. U. S.*, V, 397. The enclosure, which gives the date of the address as March 20, 1811, is printed (with an English translation) in *Papers Presented to Parliament in 1813*, pp. 286–291.

To this unwarrantable Exaction, Great Britain cannot consent to submit; and as we cannot comply with the Condition, on which the Revocation of the Berlin and Milan Decrees depends, as far as relates to us, their supposed Revocation becomes nugatory; unless America shall pursue the unjust Course of performing the alternative Condition proposed to her by France, and shall proceed to Enforce the submission of Great Britain to the inordinate demands of France.

The Government of America appears to be disposed to adopt this Course, and to enforce the Non intercourse, or the Non importation Law,[23] against Great Britain, unless we shall repeal our Orders in Council, and shall annul the Blockade of 1806.

In answer to this demand, we have replied, That France has neither actually repealed her hostile Decrees, nor announced any Intention of repealing them, on the terms proposed by America to Us: Nor is it reasonable to suppose, that France would be satisfied with our acquiescence in those terms; unless by the revocation of the Blockade of May 1806, we signified an intention of renouncing also our general system and principles of Blockade: Without a Concession of this extent, on the part of Great Britain, no reason exists to justify any other conclusion, than that France would still maintain her Decrees, without any relaxation.

In addition to this consideration, it is obvious, that even if the Decrees of Berlin and Milan should be repealed by France, the subsequent French Decrees, (prohibiting not only all Commerce in British Articles, in every part of the Continent, but all Colonial and Neutral Trade) would leave the most pernicious and destructive parts of the hostile system of France in full violence.

The pretext of municipal right, under which the Violence of the Enemy is now exercised against neutral Commerce in every part of the Continent, will not be admitted by Great Britain; nor can we ever deem the repeal of the French hostile decrees to be effectual, until neutral Commerce shall be restored to the condition, in which it stood, previously to the Commencement of the French System of comercial warfare, as promulgated in the Decrees, to which this Dispatch refers.

In this state the question rested at the period of time, when Mr. Pinkney stated, that he would not proceed in the discussion, but must refer the result to his own Government.

His Royal Highness the Prince Regent, in the name and on the behalf of His Majesty, commands me to direct you to resume the discussion with the Government of the United States at this point, and to endeavour, by a temperate appeal, to enforce the justice of

---

[23] Congress confirmed Madison's policy by the act of March 2, 1811.

the argument stated in this Dispatch, and in the Correspondence which has passed with Mr. Pinkney.

Events have indisputably proved, that our construction of the nature of the alledged repeal of the Berlin and Milan Decrees was correct; But the American Government appear to have misunderstood the real purport of that transaction; and under this erroneous construction, had induced the subjects of America to commence a Trade with France, in the expectation that Great Britain must have repealed her Orders in Council, before these Commercial adventures could reach France.

Under these circumstances, the Condemnation of Vessels (which have sailed from America with the expectation of finding the Orders in Council actually repealed) has been stayed, until accurate information could be obtained, whether the French regulations had been so effectually and absolutely repealed, as to induce this Government to issue an order for the release of such Vessels.

Although we cannot consent to repeal the Orders in Council in the present state of the question, this Government will not condemn the property of Merchants, which has been exposed to capture by the error of their own Government, as long as any hope can be entertained of prevailing on America to correct that error, and to render justice to Great Britain.

With regard to the Blockade of 1806, the argument on that subject has been already stated in this Dispatch.

That Blockade would not be continued after the repeal of the Orders in Council, unless it should be maintained by an adequate force, actually applied to support it, according to the acknowledged Law of Nations.

But we cannot consent to connect the Revocation of the Blockade of 1806, with the discussion, which has arisen between Great Britain and France, nor to involve Ourselves in any Concession, which shall impair the Maritime Rights of this Country.

Upon the whole matter, you will observe, that if America shall absolutely enforce her Non intercourse, or Non importation Act, against Great Britain, and shall open her Trade with France, Our Orders in Council must remain in force, and must operate to the Interruption of that Trade; until France shall repeal her hostile Decrees absolutely and unconditionally, and shall restore Neutral Commerce to its former State.

Even in this Situation, it is the anxious desire of His Royal Highness The Prince Regent, in the name and on the behalf of His Majesty, to avoid a direct rupture with America.

But no Extremity can induce His Royal Highness to relinquish the ancient and established Rules of Maritime War, the maintenance of which is indispensable, not only to the Commercial Interests, but to the Naval Strength, and to the National Honor of Great Britain, as well as to the rights of all Maritime States, and to the general prosperity of Navigation and Commerce throughout the Civilised World.[24]

WELLESLEY TO FOSTER [25]

No. 2.   FOREIGN OFFICE, April 10, 1811.
Sir,
    In addition to the Instructions contained in My Dispatch No. 1 I am commanded by His Royal Highness The Prince Regent, in the Name and on the behalf of His Majesty, to direct the Manner in which you are to proceed, with regard to the final Adjustment of the Differences, which have arisen between Great Britain and The United States of America, in the Affair of the Chesapeake Frigate.
    You will take an Early opportunity, after your Arrival at Washington, of presenting a Note, acquainting The American Secretary of State, First, That you have been instructed to repeat to The American Government the prompt Disavowal made by His Majesty (and recited in Mr. Erskine's Note of the 17th. of April 1810 [*sic*] to Mr. Smith)[26] on being apprized, of the unauthorized Act of the officer in Command of His Naval Forces on the Coast of America; Whose Recall from a highly important and honorable Command immediately Ensued, as a Mark of His Majesty's Disapprobation.
    Secondly, That you are authorized to offer in addition to that Disavowal, on the part of His Royal Highness, in the Name and on the behalf of His Majesty, the immediate Restoration as far as circumstances will admit, of the men, who in consequence of Admiral Berkley's Orders, were forcibly taken out of The Chesapeake to the Vessel from which they were taken; or if that Ship should be no longer in Commission, to such Sea Port of The United States, as The American Government may name for the purpose.
    Thirdly, That you are also authorized to offer to The American Government a suitable pecuniary Provision for The Sufferers, in consequence of the attack on the Chesapeake, including the Families of those seamen, who unfortunately fell in The Action, and of the wounded Survivors.
    If these Propositions should meet with an amicable Reception from The Government of The United States, you will refer the Answer of

---

[24] Foster was formally presented to President Madison on July 2, 1811 by James Monroe, who on April 2, 1811 had succeeded Robert Smith as Secretary of State. On July 3, 1811 Foster opened the debate with Secretary Monroe over the orders-in-council with a note based closely upon, and in many cases identical, with the above instruction. See *A. S. P.*, *F. R.*, III, 435–437, and ff.
[25] Draft, F. O. 5 : 75. Also printed in *Papers Presented to Parliament in 1813*, pp. 291–292.
[26] Erskine's note to Secretary Smith of April 17, 1809, is printed in *A. S. P., F. R.*, III, 295.

The American Secretary of State to me, together with your Report of the detailed Arrangement requisite for carrying the proposed adjustment into Effect. You will be careful not to receive, as the Answer of The American Government This honorable Conduct on the part of Great Britain, any Expressions in any Manner derogatory to The Honor of The King, or to The Character of the The British Nation.[27]

WELLESLEY TO FOSTER [28]

No. 3.   FOREIGN OFFICE, April 10th 1811.
Sir,

The attention of The British Government has of late been called to the Measures pursued by The United States for the Military Occupation of West Florida. The Language held by The President, at the opening of the present Session of Congress, the hostile Demonstration made by The American Force under Captain Gaines,[29] the actual Summoning of the Fort of Mobille upon The Perdido, and The Bill submitted to the approbation of The American Legislature for the Interior Administration of The Province, are so many direct and positive proofs, That The Government of America is prepared to subject the Province of West Florida to The Authority of The United States.[30]

The Enclosed Copy of the Note, which The Spanish Minister addressed to me upon this Subject on the 19th ulto. expresses in Sufficient Detail the feelings of The Spanish Government on this unprovoked Aggression upon the Integrity of That Monarchy.[31]

Mr. Morier in his Note to Mr. Smith, of the 15th Dec'r 1810 [32] has already reminded The American Government of the intimate alliance subsisting between His Majesty and Spain: and He has desired such Explanations on the Subject, as might convince His Majesty of the pacific Disposition of The United States towards Spain: Mr. Smith in his Reply has stated That it was Evident that no hostile or unfriendly purpose was Entertained by America towards Spain, and that The American Minister at this Court had been enabled to make whatever Explanations might comport with the frank and conciliatory Spirit, which had been invariably manifested on the part of The United States.

---

[27] Upon his arrival at Washington in July of 1811 Foster delayed acting upon this instruction because of the *Little Belt-President* encounter of May 16, 1811. On Nov. 1, 1811 he formally offered reparations for the Chesapeake attack, and on Nov. 12, 1811 Monroe accepted them. *A. S. P., F. R.,* III, 499–500.

[28] Draft, F. O. 5 : 75.

[29] Captain Edmund Pendleton Gaines (1777–1849).

[30] See Isaac J. Cox, *The West Florida Controversy, 1798–1813,* p. 513 and *passim.*

[31] The enclosure is lacking.

[32] Morier's note to Secretary Smith is printed in *A. S. P., F. R.,* III, 399.

Since the date of this Correspondence, Mr. Pinkney has offered no Explanation whatever of the Motives which have actuated the Conduct of The United States in this Transaction, A Bill has been introduced into Congress for the Establishment, Government and Protection of The Territory of Mobille, And The Fortress of that Name has been summoned without Effect.

His Royal Highness The Prince Regent, in the Name and on the behalf of His Majesty is still willing to hope, That The American Government has not been urged to this Step by ambitious Motives, or by a desire of foreign Conquest; and territorial Aggrandizement. It would be satisfactory however to be enabled to ascertain, That no consideration connected with the present State of Spain, has induced America to despoil that Monarchy of a valuable foreign Colony.

The Government of The United States contends, That The Right to The Possession of a certain Part of West Florida will not be less open to Discussion in the occupation of America, than under the Government of Spain.

But The Government of The United States, under this pretext, cannot expect to avoid the Reproach, which must attend the ungenerous and unprovoked Seizure of a foreign Colony, while The Parent State is Engaged in a Noble Conquest for Independence, against a most unjustifiable and Violent Invasion of The Rights both of the Monarch, and People of Spain.

If notwithstanding the Remonstrances of His Majesty's Charge d'affaires at Washington, and the manifest Injustice of The Act, you shall find on your Arrival at Washington, That America still perseveres to claim by Menaces and active demonstrations, the military occupation of West Florida, you will present to The Secretary of State the Solemn Protest of His Royal Highness, in the Name and on the behalf of His Majesty, against an attempt, so contrary to Every principle of public Justice, faith and National Honor, and so injurious to the alliance, subsisting between His Majesty and The Spanish Nation.

You will communicate to me without loss of time, for The Information of His Royal Highness The Prince Regent, a Copy of The Answer which you may receive from The American Secretary of State upon this Subject,[33] and you will regularly inform me of Every Circumstance relating to an Aggression, which may deeply affect The Interest of The Spanish Alliance, and also those of His Majesty's Subjects in the Neighbouring West Indie Islands.

---

[33] Foster's note of July 2, relative to West Florida, and Monroe's reply of July 8, 1811, are printed in *A. S. P., F. R.*, III, 542–543. His note of Sept. 5, respecting the activities of Governor Matthews of Georgia on the East Florida frontier, and Monroe's reply of Nov. 2, 1811, are printed in *ibid.*, III, 543–545.

If any attempt should be made to occupy East Florida on the part of The American Government, you will instantly remonstrate against Such a Proceeding, for which It will not be possible to allege Even the slight pretexts, which have been attempted in justification of the Aggression on West Florida.

In your communications with The American Government on the Subject of Florida, His Royal Highness The Prince Regent, in the Name and on the behalf of His Majesty, particularly Commands Me to direct, That you should abstain from any hostile or menacing language, and That you should confine your Representations within the Limits of a friendly and candid Exposition of the unjust and ungenerous nature of the Proceedings of The Government of The United States against The Foreign Possessions of Spain, in the present Situation of The Spanish Government and Nation.

Great Britain cannot view such Proceedings against Her ally, without regret and Pain; but It is not a necessary Consequence of those Sentiments, That This Government should proceed to vindicate the Rights of Spain by force of Arms.

The Conduct of Great Britain on this point must be determined by future Considerations; and you will be cautious not to use any language, or to adopt any Measure, which may compromise the ultimate Decision of This Government in a matter of such serious Importance.

WELLESLEY TO FOSTER [34]

No. 4.   FOREIGN OFFICE, April 10 1811.
Sir,

Information has been received from various Quarters that Since the date of The President's Proclamation of the 2nd. of November in the last year, interdicting the Entrance of British men of war into American Ports, french Privateers have been permitted to bring or send into American Ports, British Prizes.

I am commanded by His Royal Highness The Prince Regent to direct you to Enquire into the fact of these Statements, and in case you shall ascertain That The American Government has permitted the Neutrality of The American Ports to be violated in this Manner, you will immediately present to The American Secretary a distinct Representation of the facts, and a Remonstrance against the Impropriety of such Conduct: you will state, That Great Britain can never permit the Vessels and property of her Subjects to be brought or sent into a neutral Port, by the Ships of the Enemy, Especially, while Ships of War bearing British Colours are excluded from such neutral Port.

The American Government must be sensible, That a continuance of

---

[34] Draft, F. O. 5 : 75. Also printed in *Papers Presented to Parliament in 1813*, pp. 293–294.

such conduct would be more injurious to British commerce, than a State of open War between America and Great Britain; and It is to be hoped, That if The American Government shall in any case have submitted to this Violation of the neutral Rights of America, the necessity will be felt, of affording to His Majesty's Subjects Every practicable Redress, and of reverting without delay to the established rules of Maritime Law, and common Justice amongst civilized Nations.[35]

WILLIAM HAMILTON TO FOSTER [36]

FOREIGN OFFICE, April 27. 1811.

Sir,

I am directed by The Marquess Wellesley to transmit to you, for your Information, the enclosed Copy of a letter which, by Command of His Royal Highness The Prince Regent, His Lordship has written to the Lords Commissioners of the Admiralty, on the subject of the Instructions which have been given to you, respecting the Differences which have arisen between this Country and America, in the Affair of the Chesapeake.[37]

WELLESLEY TO FOSTER [38]

No. 5.   FOREIGN OFFICE, April 29th 1811.

Sir,

I have received the special commands of His R. H. The Prince Regent acting in the name and on the behalf of His Majesty to communicate to you the sentiments which His Royal Highness was pleased on the part of His Majesty to express to Mr. Pinkney upon the occasion of his audience of leave.

His Royal Highness signified to Mr. Pinkney the deep regret with which he learnt that Mr. Pinkney conceived himself to be bound by the instructions of his Gov't to take his departure from this Country.

His Royal Highness informed Mr. Pinkney that one of the earliest acts of his Gov't in the name and on the behalf of his Majesty was to appoint an Envoy Extraordinary and Minister Plenipotentiary to the Gov't of the United States and added that this appointment had been made in the spirit of amity and with a view of maintaining the subsisting relation of friendship between the two Countries.

---

[35] Foster made "such representations as the nature of the case could warrant," and gave as his opinion that "this Government do not appear to have countenanced infringements of their neutrality in this respect." Foster to Wellesley, Sept. 18, 1811 (extract), enclosing copies of three notes to Monroe, July 23, Aug. 16, and Sept. 1, 1811, in *Papers Presented to Parliament in 1813*, pp. 376–382.

[36] Draft, F. O. 5 : 75. William Richard Hamilton (1777–1859) was under secretary for foreign affairs Oct. 16, 1809 to Jan. 22, 1822.

[37] The enclosure is lacking.

[38] Draft, F. O. 5 : 75. Also printed in *Papers Presented to Parliament in 1813*, pp. 294–295.

H. R. Highness further declared to Mr. Pinkney that he was most sincerely and anxiously desirous on the part of His Majesty to cultivate a good understanding with the United States by every means consistent with the preservation of the Maritime Rights and Interests of the British Empire.

His Royal Highness particularly desired that Mr. Pinkney would communicate these declarations to the President of the United States in the manner which might appear best calculated to satisfy the President of His R. H's. solicitude to facilitate an amicable discussion with the Gov't of the United States upon every point of difference which had arisen between the two Governments.[39]

I am commanded to direct you to notify the substance of this dispatch to the Gov't of the United States at the Earliest period of time after your arrival in America.[40]

WELLESLEY TO FOSTER [41]

No. 6.   FOREIGN OFFICE, April 29, 1811.

Sir,

The last dispatches from Mr. Morier having informed this Gov't that the Gov't of the United States has actually passed an Act of Nonimportation [42] under circumstances of considerable aggravation and injury towards the Commerce of Great Britain, I am commanded to direct you to urge against this unjustifiable proceeding the same course of argument stated in my Dispatch No. 1—of the 10th. inst.

At the time when that dispatch was closed the intelligence of the Actual enactment of the Nonimportation Law in America had not reached this Country, but the general tenor of the reasoning detailed in that Dispatch appears applicable to the present Circumstances of the case without any alteration.

WELLESLEY TO FOSTER [43]

No. 7.   FOREIGN OFFICE, April 29, 1811.

Sir,

Since the close of my Dispatch No. 1 of the 10th inst. (in which you were informed that the condemnation of certain American Vessels, under the Circumstances stated in that Dispatch, had been stayed) the information received from France and America has re-

---

[39] A similar account was given by Pinkney in his note to Secretary Smith, March 1, 1811, *A. S. P., F. R.,* III, 415.

[40] Foster acted upon this instruction immediately upon his arrival at Washington. His note to Monroe of July 2, 1811, is printed in *ibid.,* III, 435.

[41] Draft, F. O. 5 : 75. Also printed in *Papers Presented to Parliament in 1813,* pp. 295–296.

[42] The act was passed March 2, 1811.

[43] Draft, F. O. 5 : 75. Also printed in *Papers Presented to Parliament in 1813,* pp. 296–297.

moved any doubt, which might have been entertained, with respect to the conduct either of the French or American Governments in relation to the System of Commercial Warfare, described in that dispatch.

It is therefore necessary to apprize you, that, as the considerations, which occasioned the condemnation of the American Vessels in question to be stayed, no longer exist, you are not authorized to state to the Gov't of America, that the ordinary proceedings of the Courts in these cases will be further delayed.[44]

WELLESLEY TO FOSTER [45]

No. 8. *Secret.*   FOREIGN OFFICE, April 1811.
Sir,
Altho' it is the anxious desire of H. R. H. The Prince Regent in the name and in the behalf of His Majesty to avoid a rupture with the United States of America, and for this purpose to endeavour to conduct all discussions with the American Gov't in the most conciliatory spirit, it is still necessary to apprize that Gov't, that a perseverance in the course of hostile measures already commenced towards our Maritime and Commercial Rights and Interests, will compel us to resort to adequate means of retaliation.

It is also expedient, that the American Gov't should be made sensible, of the great extent of the means, which this Country possesses, of affecting the Commerce and interests of the United States, without resorting to the extremity of war.

It is unnecessary to enter into any minute Details upon this subject, as you are already fully aware of the advantages possessed by Great Britain in such a Commercial Contest.

You will use your discretion in suggesting these considerations to the American Gov't, at the time, and in the manner, which may appear most convenient and useful.

In enumerating the measures, to which we may eventually resort, you will not fail to advert to the probability of our encreasing the duties on American imports, and of our excluding the American Trade from the East Indies; a Step which will be facilitated by our recent acquisitions, Eastward of the Cape of Good Hope.

It will be desirable that you should inform me as soon as possible of the result of your discussions with the American Gov't, for the purpose of enabling H. R: H: The Prince Regent in the Name and on the

---

[44] On June 25. 1811, in the case of the *Fox* and other vessels, Sir William Scott rendered his final decision that the French decrees were as yet unrevoked, and that American ships were liable to condemnation. *A. S. P., F. R.,* III, 417, 421.
[45] Draft. F. O. 5: 75.

behalf of His Majesty to conform the spirit of the proceedings of this Gov't to the course which may be adopted by the Gov't of the United States after your arrival in America.[46]

WELLESLEY TO FOSTER [47]

No. 9.   FOREIGN OFFICE 2nd: May, 1811.
Sir,
His Royal Highness the Prince Regent having been informed by a letter from Barbadoes dated the 28th: Feb'ry 1811; that several large French Privateers fitted out in American Ports were then cruizing off Guadaloupe, one of them a ship of 24 Guns called the Wagram, I am to desire that immediately upon your arrival at the Seat of the American Government you will make the strongest remonstrances against the conduct of that Government, in permitting the neutrality of their territory to be thus violated, and that you will take the earliest opportunity of informing me of the result of your representations.[48]

WELLESLEY TO FOSTER [49]

No. 10.   [FOREIGN OFFICE] May 11, 1811.
Sir,
I am commanded by His Royal Highness the Prince Regent to transmit to you a Copy of the opinion of the King's advocate respecting the admission of the Cruizers of the Enemy, or their Prizes into the Ports of the United States.
You are hereby directed to make an immediate remonstrance on this subject, according to the principles stated by the King's Advocate, and to require a distinct answer from the American Government, which you will transmit to me without delay.[50]

WELLESLEY TO FOSTER [51]

Separate.   FOREIGN OFFICE, 7th June: 1811.
Sir,
I am commanded by His Royal Highness The Prince Regent, to convey to you His Commands that you from time to time furnish His Exc'y The Commander in Chief of His Majesty's Forces in the

---

[46] Extracts of Foster's dispatches, enclosing copies of the notes exchanged by him and Monroe in their long and futile debate, are printed in Papers Presented to Parliament in 1813, p. 324 ff. See also A. S. P., F. R., III, 435 ff.
[47] Draft, F. O. 5: 75.
[48] See note 35, p. 322, supra.
[49] Draft, F. O. 5: 75.
[50] See note 35, p. 322, supra.
[51] Draft, F. O. 5: 75.

Island of Barbadoes, with such information upon subjects of Public Interest, as you may think it adviseable that His Excellency should be acquainted with; for the advantage of His Majesty's Service.

WELLESLEY TO FOSTER [52]

No. 11.   FOREIGN OFFICE, July 4th, 1811.
Sir,

I am commanded by His Royal Highness The Prince Regent, acting in the Name and on the behalf of His Majesty, to transmit to you by an Express Messenger the papers of which a list is annexed to this Dispatch.

From the official documents communicated to me by the Lords Com'ners of the Admiralty it appears that a violent act of aggression has been committed by a Frigate of the United States upon one of His Majesty's Ships.[53]

On reference to the American Minister at this Court I find that he has not received any instructions from his Government to explain this transaction or to disavow the alleged act of aggression in the Name of the United States.

It might have been expected that the American Gov't would have manifested a prompt disposition to obviate by an early disavowal and by just reparation the necessary tendency of such an event to disturb the friendship subsisting between the two States, and the example afforded by this Gov't in the case of the Chesapeak Frigate entitled us to form such an expectation.

In this situation however it is absolutely requisite that you should not lose a moment in communicating the documents herewith enclosed to the Gov't of the United States and that you should accompany this communication with a demand of the immediate disavowal on the part of the United States of the act of aggression committed against His Majesty's Ship, and also [with a requisition for just reparation of the injury received by His Majesty's Ship in this transaction.] [54]

His R. H. The Prince Regent commands me to direct you to carry these instructions into effect as soon as possible after you shall have received them.

You will transmit the answer of the American Gov't to me by the Messenger who carries this dispatch. The Vessel on which he embarks being ordered to return with him.

---

[52] Draft, F. O. 5: 75.
[53] On May 16, 1811, off the American coast, the American frigate *President*, Commodore John Rodgers, was fired upon (according to the American account, affirmed by all officers and men of the *President*) by the British sloop-of-war *Little Belt*, Captain Arthur Batt Bingham. In the resulting engagement the *Little Belt* was badly damaged and had thirty-two men killed or wounded. See *A. S. P., F. R.*, III, 471–499.
[54] The words enclosed by brackets were written on the margin, for insertion.

It will be expedient that you should communicate to the officer commanding His Majesty's Naval Forces on the Coast of America the substance of the reply which you may receive on this occasion from the American Gov't.

WELLESLEY TO FOSTER [55]

No. 12.   FOREIGN OFFICE, July 4, 1811.
Sir,

In addition to the Documents, Enclosed in My Dispatch No. 11. I am commanded by His Royal Highness The Prince Regent, to transmit to you the Enclosed Copy of a Letter from Admiral Sawyer, just now received by The Admiralty, together with its Enclosures; and to direct you to call the particular attention of The American Gov't to The Instructions of Admiral Sawyer to Capt'n Bingham, which furnish the strongest Evidence of the pacific and friendly intentions of This Government, and a presumptive proof of the Truth of Captain Bingham's Statement.[56]

WELLESLEY TO FOSTER [57]

No. 13.   FOREIGN OFFICE, August 26. 1811.
Sir,

I am commanded by H. R. H. The Prince Regent, in the Name and on the Behalf of H. M'y, to transmit to you the accompanying Copies of a Letter which I have received from the American Chargé d'Affaires at this Court dated the 22d. Ulto. on the subject of the alledged Repeal of the French Decrees of Berlin and Milan; of my answer to Mr. Smith, dated the 8th. Inst. and of a second communication, which I made to him on the 14th: in consequence of the intelligence contained in your private Letter of the 7th: of July, that you had already commenced a Negotiation at Washington on the subject of the British Orders in Council.[58]

I inclose likewise for your information and guidance during the progress of your Negotiation, a Paper marked D. which contains some observations on the state of the actual relations between this Country

---

[55] Draft, F. O. 5 : 75.

[56] Foster's note to Monroe of Sept. 4, 1811, together with its enclosures which included Rear Admiral Herbert Sawyer's letter to the Admiralty of June 11, and Sawyer's instructions to Captain Arthur Batt Bingham of H. M. Sloop *Little Belt,* are printed in *A. S. P., F. R.,* III, 472–476. Bingham's account is printed in *Niles' Register,* I, 34–35, Sept. 21, 1811.

[57] Draft, F. O. 5 : 75. Also printed in *Papers Presented to Parliament in 1813,* pp. 297–298.

[58] The note of John Spear Smith, American chargé at London, of July 23 (not July 22, as above), with its enclosure, and Wellesley's replies of Aug. 8 and Aug. 14, 1811, are printed in *A. S. P., F. R.,* III, 447–448. Smith had enclosed a copy of the letter sent him July 14. 1811 by Jonathan Russell, American chargé at Paris, to the effect that the release by the French government of five American vessels, the *Grace Ann Greene, New Orleans Packet, Two Brothers, Good Intent,* and the *Star,* was to be considered conclusive evidence that the French decrees had been revoked

and America, as affected by the conduct of France towards the Trade and Property of Neutrals.

You will derive such advantage from the considerations stated in this Paper, as they may afford, in explaining to the American Gov't the honourable and just Principles by which Great Britain has been guided throughout this discussion.

[*Enclosure: Draft of Paper marked D*] [59]

Great Britain declined repealing her Orders in Council on two Grounds. First she contended that the Decrees of Berlin and Milan were not absolutely but conditionally revoked by France the condition being either the repeal of the British Orders and Blockades before the first of November 1810; or the exclusion of the British Trade from the American Ports by the act of the United States. Secondly Great Britain contended, that there was no satisfactory proof given of the entire repeal of the French Decrees, even if either of these conditions were complied with. What has since happened has fully justified both these propositions. American vessels were in all instances seized subsequently to the first of November 1810 under the provisions of the Berlin and Milan decrees, and were in no instance released until the Government of France had received intelligence, that one of the conditions on which they professed to be willing to revoke their decrees had been complied with, by the exclusion of British Ships and British Manufactures from the American Ports—in other words, the French Government did not repeal, in any degree, the provisions of those decrees against the United States, until the United States had submitted to the demand of adopting the substance of those very decrees against Great Britain. It now also is notorious, that at the time when the President of the United States issued his proclamation, by which America complied with this demand of the French Government, he had no assurance whatever that France had in any degree revoked those decrees, the revocation of which was the alledged ground of that proclamation. The Non-importation Act passed also subsequently, without any explanation whatever being given on this subject. It was then; and as far as it appears, it was up to the Month of June last, a matter of doubt in America, to what extent these decrees have been repealed, even if any repeal whatever has taken place. The American Government had either not enquired, or had not then been informed whether by this supposed repeal American vessels may proceed from any other ports than the ports of the United States direct to the ports of France: Whether the cargoes although neutral and coming from American ports may consist of any other articles than the produce of the United

---

[59] F. O. 5 : 75. This is also printed in *Papers Presented to Parliament in 1813*, pp. 298–306.

States; nay, whether there are not certain Articles, (the produce of the United States) the importation of which is still to be considered as absolutely prohibited. The American Government also appear to have been ignorant, up to the last advices from thence, whether American Vessels are to be permitted to return from France to the United States with any cargoes; and if with any, under what conditions such cargoes are to be exported; whether this trade, so restricted, as it is allowed to be, is to exist at all except with certain ports in America and France: nay whether even this trade, so circumscribed as to articles, and confined as to particular ports, will be allowed to exist except under a licence given by the Government of France. It is needless to observe that in that last doubt is included a question, whether even now, under all the circumstances of the case the French decrees are in any degree whatever revoked: for if the French decrees are to any extent repealed, to that extent at least no licence is necessary, a licence being given to allow what but for that licence would be prohibited.

Even Mr. Russel so far as can be collected from his communication with Mr. Smith appears, as late as the 14th of July, to be more able to state to what extent these decrees are not repealed, than to what extent they are.[60] They are not repealed it seems so far as to admit British Manufactures in American Ships, although such cargoes should be neutral property. All that he can attempt to state as certain is that the decrees are not to be enforced on the high seas, but this is perfectly consistent with all the provisions of these decrees, being in full power in the ports of France, if they have any Article on board except the produce of the United States; if they have any but the permitted articles of that produce; if they come from any but the enumerated ports; if they attempt to come from those ports, and with the permitted articles without the special sanction of a licence granted by the Government of France: if they have touched at a British port or have been boarded by a British cruiser. Can this be called a revocation of the French Decrees? Is this placing neutral commerce on the footing it was previously to their publication? Is the submission of the United States to these provisions such a resistance to the arbitrary proceedings of France against all neutral rights, as to render the British Orders of Council on that ground no longer necessary? Is Great Britain to repeal her Orders against the trade of France because the United States has adopted the substance of the French decrees against the trade of her own people?

Even if the conduct of the American Government had been different; if they had not issued their proclamation and passed their non-importa-

---

[60] The letter of Jonathan Russell, American chargé at Paris, to John Spear Smith, American chargé at London, dated July 14, 1811. See note 58, p. 327, *supra*.

tion Act against the trade of this Country under the alledged revocation of the French decrees, at a time when the American Government had no assurance that such a revocation had taken place: and are even now uncertain whether they be not partially and in special instances only suspended; still it would have been necessary for the American Government to have made a more precise representation of what has been done by France before they made this out of France the ground for applying to Great Britain for the repeal of her Orders. If the French Decrees have been either in part or in the whole repealed there must exist some instrument by which that repeal has been affected. And if there be any fair dealing on this transaction, no reason can be given for not producing it. The Letter of the French Minister to Gen'l Armstrong so much relied upon by Mr. Pinkney ought never to have been produced as an official record of that revocation: and the American Minister cannot now refer to it, as that letter asserted the entire and absolute repeal of those decrees on the 1st: of November 1810, when it is now admitted by Mr. Russel himself in his last letter that they are only partially repealed, and it is evident that they continued in force after the 1st: of November.

But if these decrees are only partially repealed it is the more necessary to see the instrument by which that repeal is effected; in order to judge to what extent they are repealed. No such instrument has hitherto been produced. There is every reason to believe that the American Government were not in June last in possession of it. It is almost certain that Mr. Russel was not in possession of it on the 14th: of July of this year; for he would otherwise have stated in his communication with Mr. Smith, at least the substance of it. Nay it is doubtful whether the directors of customs at Bordeaux where its provisions are to be observed, have hitherto ever seen it. For if it be true that this repeal goes at least thus far (as is contended both by Mr. Russel and Mr. Smith) that American vessels are not liable to seizure only on the ground of having been boarded by British cruizers or touching at a British port, how could it have happened, that the Grace Ann Green, and New Orleans Packet were seized on their entrance into Bordeaux, since Mr. Smith states expressly they were only seized for these very aggressions of the Berlin and Milan decrees? How came they not to be released until Mr. Russel had made his remonstrances to the French Government in consequence of such seizure?[61] How came these Officers not to have been reprimanded for giving so unauthorised an interruption to a permitted trade; if they were in possession of that instrument

---

[61] On the seizure and subsequent release of the *New Orleans Packet* and the *Grace Ann Greene*, see Russell to the Secretary of State, Dec. 11, 1810, May 8, June 9, 1811, and Russell to J. S. Smith, July 5, 1811, *A. S. P., F. R.,* III, 390–392, 506, 502–503, 447.

which revoked that part of the decrees under which they were seized.

It is essential to remark, that the declaration of the British Government was not an engagement to repeal the orders of Council, on the simple condition, that the Decrees of Berlin and Milan were revoked. It was not difficult to foresee, that other decrees, as injurious to the British Commerce, and the Rights of neutral nations, might be subsequently issued, and that these might remain, and be in force, after the original decrees had been withdrawn. It was therefore expressly added, as another condition, that the neutral ·trade must be restored to the state in which it was previous to the promulgation of those Decrees. Is it possible for any one to contend, that this second Condition has been complied with? Has the first, in truth, been complied with? Have the Berlin and Milan decrees been even partially repealed? Have they not, on the contrary, been declared to be fundamental laws of the Empire, since the 1st of November 1810, the alledged period of their revocation? The Conduct of France towards the American Trade, as far as it has been represented by the American Ministers, and taking it in its most favourable point of view, amounts to no more than this, that, in consequence of the American Congress having, in the Non-importation Acts, adopted the substance of the French decrees, by excluding the British flag from their ports, and by prohibiting the importation of British Produce and manufacture, France has been prevailed upon to suspend the operation of the Rambouillet Decree,[62] in certain special cases, at the intercession of the American Minister, leaving the decrees of Berlin and Milan unrepealed, and the trade of neutral nations subject to the molestations to which, since the promulgation of the decrees, that trade has been exposed.

What is asked, therefore, of the British Government, is this—that because they declared that the Orders of Council should be revoked whenever the Berlin and Milan decrees were repealed, and the trade of neutral nations was placed on the footing on which it was previous to their promulgation, therefore they are now bound to revoke these Orders, because the operations of another decree have been, in some special instances, suspended,[63] although neither of the conditions have been complied with, the fulfilment of both of which was declared to be necessary, previous to the revocation of the Orders of council.

France cannot be justified by America, by the argument that her Decrees are now only enforced upon the Continent, while those of Great Britain are executed upon the high seas. There is less chance of escape from the French Custom Houses in the ports of the Continent,

---

[62] Issued at Rambouillet March 23, 1810, in *A. S. P., F. R.*, III, 384

[63] At this point in the draft there is a space of six and a half lines. There is no space, however, in the printed copy of the draft in *Papers Presented to Parliament in 1813*, p. 304.

than from British cruizers at sea, and France has only been able effectually to execute in this manner her laws against neutral trade.

To none of these usurpations, destructive, as they must have been viewed even in America, of the rights of neutrals have the United States ventured to offer any opposition: no remonstrance, no intercession, no arguments have come from America to plead the cause of neutrals, in the cases of Hamburg, Oldenburg, Sweden, &c. all of which have been incorporated into the French Empire, or forced into a war with England.

It has not indeed, as yet, been satisfactorily proved, that any instructions have been given to the French cruizers, not to molest neutral vessels, which are bound to a British port, or shall be proceeding from one. That instructions were given to capture vessels of that description, is evident, for it can now no longer be denied, that the Berlin and Milan decrees were so executed, and if this manner of executing them is no longer to be practised, some instruction to that effect must exist; but it is worthy of remark, that no copy of such instructions has been produced, nor has any copy of any decree appeared which contained such a provision.

It may further be observed, that the prohibition of British Ships of War to enter the American Ports, at the time when the Ships of the other belligerent are allowed to enter those Ports, might perhaps justify Great Britain in asserting, that whatever reasons she may have for repealing or modifying her Orders in Council, so as to lessen, or intirely remove, the pressure now unavoidably laid on the trade of neutral nations, yet she might refuse to enter into any discussion on that subject with the U. States, until, either by the revocation of this prohibition, or the placing of all the belligerents under the same prohibition, America shall cease to violate the duties of a neutral nation.

WELLESLEY TO FOSTER [64]

No. 14.   DOWNING STREET Oct'r 22, 1811.
Sir,
Your Dispatches to No. 9, have been received and laid before His Royal Highness The Prince Regent.

I am commanded by His Royal Highness, Acting in the Name and on the behalf of His Majesty, to signify His gracious approbation of your Conduct in the discharge of the important trust committed to you.

It does not appear to be necessary, as far as relates to the Discussions, which have arisen respecting the orders in council, to make

---

[64] Draft, F. O. 5 : 75. Also printed in *Papers Presented to Parliament in 1813*, pp. 306–314.

any material alteration at present in The Instructions, which you have received from me, under H. R. H's. Commands.

I am commanded however particularly to direct your attention to the following Considerations.

It appears that British Ships of war are excluded from American Ports, while the Ships of war belonging to France are freely admitted.

It is to be presumed that the reestablishment of certain Parts of The Non-Intercourse Act is directed against Great Britain, in retaliation, on the part of America, of the orders in Council, by which the Entrance of American Ships, among other Neutral Ships, into the French Ports, is prohibited. Without examining the justice of any such retaliatory System on the part of America, It may be observed, that The British Orders of Council, which are purely of a Commercial Character, do not warrant the exclusion of British Ships of War from American Ports.

The Orders of Council do not in any degree affect the Ships of War belonging to The United States: Such Ships may freely enter The Ports of France, directly from America: They may proceed from British Ports to the Ports of France, and from The Ports of france to this Country: Unless some strong ground existed, to prove that these National Ships were employed to convey Tribute to The Government of France, or were actually converted into Trading Ships, Great Britain would not be disposed to molest them on their Voyage.

On a retaliatory System directed against our orders of council, The United States may exclude British Manufactures and Produce, while those of The Enemy are freely admitted: Such Regulations indeed cannot be considered as Acts of Amity; but they are certainly not Violations of Neutrality.

But the Exclusion of British Ships of War rests on a different Principle.

The exclusion by a Neutral Power of all Ships of War belonging to one belligerent Party, while The Ships of War of the other are protected by the Harbours of that Neutral Power, has always been considered as a direct Violation of the principles and duty of Neutrality. This doctrine The United States appeared to acknowledge, when in consequence of the affair of The Chesapeake, British Ships of war were first excluded from the American Ports. The Government of America then distinctly dis-claimed any desire of giving any preference "in favor of the Ships of War of one belligerent to those of another." That Exclusion was declared to be only temporary, as a precautionary Measure, to prevent a recurrence of similar conflicts between our respective Ships of War. If it should be said, that this Exclusion is still precautionary, because no Satisfaction has yet been given on the Subject of The Chesapeake, It may be remarked, that no Event has occurred to justify the renewal of a precaution, which The American Government during the last year deemed it safe and honorable to discontinue. It may further be observed, that The American Government must be apprized, That you are ready to offer the most ample Satisfaction respecting the affair of the Chesapeake.

You will therefore State to The American Government, that before America can justly claim the Rights of a Neutral Nation, She ought to fulfil the established Duties belonging to that Character. Great Britain would be fully justified in declining all Explanation either of her Orders in Council, or Her intentions regarding those Regulations, so long as this part of the Non-Intercourse Act respecting British Ships of War shall remain unrepealed, while French Ships shall be freely admitted into The American Ports. This Point will require your serious and immediate attention; and you will not fail to bring the Subject under the early and distinct Notice of The American Government.

The Instructions with which you have already been furnished by the Command of The Prince Regent, and the whole tenor of My Correspondence with Mr. Pinckney, demonstrate the expediency of requiring an authentic Copy of The Instrument, by which The French Decrees may be stated to have been revoked.

You will therefore require from The American Government a Copy of The Instrument by which the French Decrees are stated to be revoked, before you proceed to any definitive Discussion founded on the Presumption of such a Revocation.

The American Gov't cannot offer any reasonable excuse against the production of such a Copy, if that Document actually exists. Many considerations concur to dissuade Great Britain from adopting any decided Measures, according to the Views of America, untill such a Document shall have been produced. The French Decrees were formally promulgated, Their Revocation should be equally formal; If They are only partially revoked, It becomes more necessary to Examine a Document, which will exhibit the precise extent of the alledged Revocation: The extent of the alledged Revocation cannot by any other means be ascertained with precision. The principal point at issue between the two Governments, is in fact the precise operation and extent of the Act or Acts of the french Gov't by which The Decrees are said to have been repealed; on this question doubts have been stated by Great Britain, and certainly have been entertained in America. The Conduct of Great Britain must be regulated by the Solution of those doubts, and by the real, practical, extent of The Revocation of the French Decrees: It is therefore indispensable, that a copy of The Instrument of Revocation should be formally produced. In addition to these observations, It must be remarked, that The Revocation of These Decrees has already been notified, That The Notification has proved to be false in Substance, and completely fraudulent in practical effect; and yet Great Britain has been required to repeal her Orders of Council, in consequence of a Transaction so imperfect and fallacious in all its circumstances. In such a state of affairs, It is just and reasonable that Great Britain should refuse to become a Party to any arrangement, which shall not rest upon an authentic regular production of a Copy of The Act of the French Government, by which The hostile Decrees have been repealed.

If to these representations The American Government should reply, That Great Britain has been accustomed to notify the Repeal of Blockades by Letters to the Ministers Resident at this Court, and that Such Notification is considered to be sufficient; you will observe, That these notifications are founded on regular and formal orders, the production of which, if required, Great Britain would readily grant, and which in no instance has been refused. These Notifications are addressed from one Nation in Amity to Another, in the same relation: No corresponding abandonment of commercial or other Restrictions is required from that Nation, to whose Minister such a Notification is made; He is on the Spot; He can ascertain the truth of the facts stated; If any doubts should exist, he can obtain explanation, if necessary, directly from The Government, under whose Authority the Notification is made; and he may act upon the Notification, or not, according to his own judgement and Discretion.

On the other hand, The Notifications, now under Discussion, are made by the Enemy. Great Britain is called upon to act in consequence of a Notification from The French Government in a State of war; and is required to forego her Measures of self-defence against the Enemy upon the mere faith of his own Declarations. No Resident Minister in France can ascertain on the part of Great Britain the truth of the alledged Revocation: No satisfactory means exist of obtaining explanations of those Ambiguities, in which The Notification appears to be studiously involved: In this case, It is the peculiar Intent of The Enemy to deceive; and it is well known to be his practice to attempt fraud, whenever fraud promises subsidiary aid to Violence, and Treachery can facilitate the use of Force.

The Admission of some ships into the Ports of France, contrary to the Provisions of the French Decrees, and the release of others are no proofs that the Decrees are revoked. These Vessels may have entered under Special Licences: they may have been released by Special favour: at the utmost it is evidence only of a temporary Suspension of the Decrees. If the Decrees are revoked bonâ fide and are really no longer in existence, some Instrument must exist by which that Revocation has been effected. If the production of such an Instrument be pertinaciously refused, or studiously evaded, the inducements, for requiring this satisfaction on our part, are greatly strengthened by the suspicions, which must arise from the colour of the whole transaction.

Since the preceding part of this Dispatch was written, your Dispatches to No. 14 have been received, and laid before His Royal Highness The Prince Regent.

I am commanded by His Royal Highness to signify to you His Royal Highness's entire approbation of the prompt, able, and energetic manner in which you have replied (in your Note of the 26th. of July to Mr. Munroe)[65] to the unfounded insinuations contained in that Minister's Answer to your former Communications. His Royal Highness fully approves of the terms, in which you have stated the Question of the Blockade of May 1806 (which indeed applied solely to Neutral Vessels passing from one Enemy's Port to another) as well as of your statement of the undue partiality, and injustice of the American Government, in still persisting to consider the Commerce of their Citizens, as affected exclusively by the British Restrictions.

The Letter of the Minister of Justice dated the 25th. of December last, (to which your Note to Mr. Munroe refers) states that "The American Ships detained after the First of November 1810, are to be released," (not in consequence of the Repeal of the French Decrees, but) "in consequence of the American Non-importation Law." The conclusion to be drawn from this Statement is, that the Non-importation Act cannot be justified by America, as in consequence of the Revocation of the French Decrees: The Non-importation Act seems in fact to have been the cause of a partial relaxation of the French Decrees.

Nothing has happened since that period of time in any degree to weaken the argument (as stated by you conformably to your Instructions) demonstrating that the French Decrees do still operate very injuriously against Neutral Trade; The only relief granted to the Trade of America, in mitigation of the most strict and rigorous effect of the French Decrees, still continues to be the arbitrary admission of certain American Vessels directly from America into the Ports of France, on conditions and under regulations, which might be allowed by France, even if America and France were in a positive state of Hostility.

His Royal Highness anxiously hopes that the American Congress will detect the pernicious designs of the Enemy against the Commerce

---

[65] Foster's note of July 26, in reply to Monroe's note of July 23, 1811, is printed in *A. S. P., F. R.,* III, 443–445.

of the World, and against the Rights of all Neutral States, however those designs may be disguised for the purpose of deluding America into the fatal consequences of a War with Great Britain: The Prince Regent also trusts that the moderation and temper, which this Government has manifested towards the United States, throughout the whole progress of this protracted discussion, will be justly appreciated by the American People.

You will assure the American Government, that His Royal Highness The Prince Regent, acting in the Name and on the Behalf of His Majesty, is anxious to interpret all their transactions in the most favorable and amicable sense; But His Royal Highness cannot view with indifference the unmerited restrictions, placed, by the operation of the Non-importation Act, upon the commerce of His Majesty's Subjects; nor the unfriendly preference, manifested towards the Ships of War of His Majesty's Enemy, while His Majesty's Ships of War are excluded from every Port belonging to the United States, although His Majesty's officers have been most carefully instructed to avoid every occasion of disagreement with those of America.

Nor can His Royal Highness consent to resign, at the request of America, or by compromise with the Enemy, any of those great Maritime Rights, which Great Britain has maintained as the Bulwarks of her National Security and Glory, and which she has exercised, not more for her own interests and honor, than for the general protection of Trade, and for the freedom and independence of all Commercial States.

WELLESLEY TO FOSTER [66]

No. 15.   FOREIGN OFFICE, Oct'r 22, 1811.

Sir,

Referring you to His Royal Highness' former commands upon the subject of aid and protection supposed to be given in the Territory of The United States of America to the French privateers which molest the Trade of H: My's: subjects in those seas, I am further commanded by His R. H. to convey to you the enclosed communication from The Sec'y at Lloyd's, respecting the capture of the ship Tottenham by the D. of Dantzig french privateer. You will immediately inquire into the particulars of this transaction and report the same to me for the information of H. R. H. The Prince Regent.[67]

---

[66] Draft. F. O. 5 : 75.

[67] The British ship *Tottenham* had been captured off the Barbadoes by the French privateer *Duke of Dantzig* and sent into New York, where her cargo was permitted to be sold in order to pay for necessary repairs. Foster made representations to Monroe on Sept. 1, and Dec. 13, 1811, and was informed by Monroe on Jan. 18, 1812 that the proceedings as to this vessel had been "such as are pointed out by the long-established regulations of this Government." *Papers Presented to Parliament in 1813*, pp. 379–381, 439–443, 534–537.

WELLESLEY TO FOSTER [68]

Separate and Secret.   FOREIGN OFFICE, October 22d: 1811.

Sir,

In addition to the Instructions, which I have been commanded by His Royal Highness The Prince Regent to transmit to you for the guidance of your conduct, in my Dispatch No. 14. I am further commanded to direct you to avoid, on any occasion, to state prospectively the precise extent of the Revocation of the French Decrees, which Great Britain has a Right to expect: You will carefully abstain from giving an opinion upon any particular Cases, which may be stated to you, (for the purpose of embarrassing your Argument,) as affording a practical proof of the revocation of the Decrees: You may truly state, that you cannot, in such Cases, be in possession of all the circumstances, which mark their Character, and which may give a different colour to the transaction.

The Instrument, by which the alledged revocation shall have been positively effected, can be your only safe guide; and without the production of such a Document, you will not enter into any Engagement for the Repeal of the Orders in Council.

WELLESLEY TO FOSTER [69]

[FOREIGN OFFICE,] Oct. 1811.

Sir,

His Royal Highness The Prince Regent has commanded me to communicate to you the Inclosed official Copy of Mr. Mellish's [70] Patent as H. M. Consul General in Louisiana, and to direct you immediately to notify the same to The American Government, in order that they may issue the necessary Exequatur, to Enable Mr. Mellish to Enter upon his Consular functions immediately on his arrival at New Orleans.

I also Enclose to you for your Information the accompanying copy of The Instructions w'h Mr. Mellish has rec'd for the guidance of his conduct during his residence in the Territory of the United States.

Mr. Mellish will leave England by the first opportunity which shall occur for The Island of Jamaica, and The Commanding officer of His Majesty's Naval Force upon that Station will be instructed to forward him, in the most expeditious manner to New Orleans.

---

[68] Draft, F. O. 5: 75.
[69] Draft, F. O. 5: 75.
[70] Joseph Charles Mellish.

WELLESLEY TO FOSTER [71]

FOREIGN OFFICE, Nov'r 1811.

Sir,

In communicating to you the enclosed Papers, relative to the escape of a British seaman from on board the American Frigate Constitution, now lying at Portsmouth, I am commanded by His Royal Highness the Prince Regent acting in the name and on the behalf of His Majesty to direct that you will lay this case before the American Government, and request they will give the necessary directions to prevent in future the inveigling of British Subjects into the Service of the United States.[72]

---

[71] Draft, F. O. 5 : 75.

[72] The deposition of Charles Davis, to the effect that he was a British seaman who had been impressed into the American navy at Charleston, S. C., Oct. 6, 1810, and had effected his escape from the frigate *Constitution*, Nov. 12, 1811, is printed in *Papers Presented to Parliament in 1813*, pp. 452–459.

INSTRUCTIONS OF 1812

WELLESLEY TO FOSTER [1]

No. 1.   FOREIGN OFFICE, January 28, 1812.

Sir,

Your dispatches to No. 29. of last Year have been submitted to His Royal Highness The Prince Regent.

His Royal Highness has received with considerable regret the communications which they contain, with respect to the conduct of the American Government, and to the tone of the conversation which has passed between you and Mr. Monroe.

The intimation made to you by Mr. Monroe of the intention of the American Government to arm their Merchant Ships, and to send their trade under Convoy, announces a System, which, if carried into practice, must occasion Acts of Hostile Violence.

Although these several modes of arming are represented to be intended merely for defensive purposes, and not with any view to offensive operations, it is impossible to consider this System otherwise than as a plan of defence for the Merchant Traders of America against the search of British Cruizers.

The General right of search cannot be surrendered by Great Britain, consistently with the security of His maritime power; and, as this principle cannot be unknown to the American Government, the intention of pursuing measures, which must compel Great Britain to assert that important right by force cannot be viewed without the most serious concern.

Notwithstanding the appearances of the unfriendly disposition of the American Government, His Royal Highness the Prince Regent feels so sincere a desire for the preservation of peace and amity with America, that He determined not to alter the conciliatory expressions of the Speech delivered by His Royal Highness's Command to both Houses of Parliament: and His Royal Highness now commands, that the discussions with America should be continued in the same spirit of moderation and friendship which has hitherto been observed by Great Britain.

The conversation which has passed between you and Mr. Monroe, afford[s] an opportunity for renewing the most explicit declarations of

---

[1] Draft, F. O. 5 : 83. Also printed in *Papers Presented to Parliament in 1813*, pp. 314–321.

the disposition and sentiments of this Government towards the United States, and the unfounded report stated by Mr. Monroe, respecting the conduct of His Majesty's Ambassador in Spain, requires a distinct repetition of the amicable views of His Royal Highness the Prince Regent.

You will therefore, in the name, and by the authority of His Royal Highness, not only assure the Government of the United States, that the report of Mr. Wellesley's [2] supposed conduct in instigating Spain to a War with America, is utterly unfounded: but that His Royal Highness would consider the event of War with America, a most serious calamity to this Country.

The injury, which this calamity would not fail to inflict upon America would aggravate the regret which this Government would feel for such an occurrence.

Various ancient relations of mutual kindness render the welfare of America, an object of our sincere good wishes: The direct interests of Great Britain are also essentially concerned in the prosperity of that Country; from our intercourse with which important advantages have accrued to our Commerce.

These sentiments are stated for no other purpose, than to prove the sincerity of our desire for the amity of America, in the preservation of which our own interests are materially involved.

With these views we continue to deprecate a War with America, although the conduct of the Government of the United States now exposes us to injuries and losses, nearly as great as we might probably incur by actual War.

The System of Non: intercourse adopted by America; the admission not only of French Merchantmen, but of French Ships of war into the ports of America while British Ships of both descriptions are excluded, approach to measures of actual hostility.

But, even under these provocations, the Prince Regent commands me to repeat the expression of His anxiety to avoid war with America, if it be possible to preserve the relations of amity, without surrendering the national honour of Great Britain, and those principles of maritime Right and national Law, which are essential to the existence of this Empire.

The direct exposure which Mr. Monroe made to You of the determination of the American Government, to resort to the measures, which I have already described, was accompanied by an intimation

---

[2] Henry Wellesley (1773–1847) brother of Lord Wellesley and his successor as envoy to the Spanish Junta. Foster had reported Monroe's remarks in his dispatch of Nov. 21, 1811, and stated: "The only inference which I can draw from this extraordinary language, My Lord, is, that being decided on seizing East Florida, this Government are looking after every kind of pretext, and endeavouring to build on every false and momentary rumour, as a foundation to support them in their ambitious projects." *Papers Presented to Parliament in 1813*, pp. 419–420.

of his apprehension, that such a communication might be construed as a menace by this Government. His Royal Highness the Prince Regent however has received this communication in the spirit in which Mr. Monroe professed it to be intended; and His Royal Highness therefore confidently expects, and claims an equally favorable construction of the declaration, which You are hereby directed to make in His Royal Highness's name.

In this expectation, His Royal Highness commands You to acquaint the Government of the United States, that Great Britain cannot relinquish Her right of search upon the High Seas, and cannot recognize any power in Neutral States, to exempt their Merchantmen from that right of Search, either by arming Trading Vessels, or by affording them the protection of Convoy.

The distinct expression of our opinion on matters of such importance, so far from being an indication of any unfriendly disposition, is necessary for the purpose of preventing a State of affairs which might probably lead to acts of Force.

The Prince Regent views the intention of America to adopt this System of armament, with additional concern, because it bears the appearance of a direct acquiescence on the part of America in the demand of France for war against Great Britain.

In the note of the French Minister, respecting the pretended revocation of the Decrees of Berlin and Milan, it was required of America, that she should cause Her flag to be respected, in order to entitle Herself to the benefit of that conditional repeal, which was not to be made absolute, until America should have fulfilled the condition exacted from her.

It is justly to be apprehended that the proposed armament may be resorted to by America in compliance with this Exaction.

Adverting to the instructions which You have already received You will observe, that the alternative conditions required by the French Government were—From Great Britain the revocation of the Orders in Council, and the renunciation of our principles of Blockade, which were described to be *New*; or, from America the assertion of the independence of Her flag.

With the condition required from Great Britain, it must have been evident to France and to America, that we could not comply: since the principles of blockade which we were required to renounce as *new*, were in fact coeval with the foundation of the British Monarchy, recognized by the established Law of Nations, and inseparable from the security of our naval power.

The alternative condition required from the American Government has been sufficiently explained by the French Government. The French Government has declared that every Ship is to be considered as *denationalized*, (or deprived of the national rights of the State to which it belongs) if it shall submit to be visited or searched by a, Belligerent. This appears to be the true construction of the manner in which America is required to assert the independence of Her Flag: nor can it be supposed, that the French Government will be satisfied with the compliance of America, unless it shall extend to such measures as shall be calculated to prevent, according to the French expression, the Ships of America from being denationalized; or, in other words to preclude the exercise of our right of search on the high Seas.

Under this view of the question, it is evident that the entended revocation of the Decrees of Berlin and Milan was in fact a fresh enactment and confirmation of those Decrees.

The Prince Regent directs me to point Your particular Attention to these considerations, and to desire that, in stating them to Mr. Monroe, You will explain how strongly they serve to illustrate the apprehensions entertained by this Government, that the armament of the American Trade should occasion such acts of Violence as may tend to produce the calamity of war between the two Countries.

In remarking to Mr. Monroe the circumstances of difference between the conduct of the French and British Governments towards America, You will not fail to draw the necessary conclusions from the following circumstances.

The American Non: intercourse Act, was applied equally to Great Britain and to France. The French Government retaliated by the decree of Rambouillet; and You are fully acquainted with the seizures which have been made of American Ships and Property in France, since the enactment of that Decree.

Although the Non: intercourse Act has been reestablished by America against Great Britain (while it is repealed with respect to France, and while French Ships of War are admitted into the Ports of America, and those of Great Britain are excluded) Great Britain has continued to permit without obstruction the entrance of American Vessels into Her Ports.

The general tenor of our conduct indeed sufficiently manifests a real solicitude to avoid the extremity of War, so long as our most essential rights and interests shall remain in security; nor has this Government suffered the repeated provocations which it has received on points of inferior (although considerable) importance, to divert it's attention from the plain and direct course which it has pursued throughout these protracted discussions.

The circumstances of contradiction which You have justly observed in the language of the American Ministers on several occasions, have been particularly noticed by the Prince Regent.

His Royal Highness commands me to direct You to persevere in the same moderate but firm conduct and language, which Your instructions have uniformly prescribed to You; and He trusts, that by this prudent and undeviating course, the variable Councils of the American Government may ultimately be led towards a just sense of the peril to which they will expose their country; if, in compliance with the unjust demands of France, they should involve America in a War with Great Britain.

WELLESLEY TO FOSTER [3]

No. 2.   Secret.   FOREIGN OFFICE, 28th: Jan'ry 1812.

Sir,

Your dispatch (No. 26 secret) has been received and submitted to His Royal Highness the Prince Regent.

His Royal Highness commands me to signify to you, that he cannot perceive any circumstance in your dispatches or in the Correspondence or conversations which have passed between you and Mr. Monroe or Mr. Madison to justify any departure from the principle of the instructions, which you have already received respecting the British Orders in Council and those rules of maritime War on which is founded our system of blockade.

In your Instructions No. 14 you were directed to demand a Copy of the instrument or public Act by which the Berlin and Milan decrees are stated to have been revoked, and the grounds on which that demand is to be made are fully explained in those instructions. You will therefore continue to urge your demand for the production of a copy of that instrument stating that it is absolutely necessary to ascertain precisely the conduct of France before Great Britain can regulate her own.

His Royal Highness is deeply concerned to learn that the Government of the United States can expect to derive any advantage from arming the American Merchant vessels, a proceeding which whatever may be its professed object, must in its necessary operation impede our general right of search.

Although His Royal Highness is extremely anxious by all Means, consistent with the honor and interests of the Country to avoid Hostilities with the American Government; the measure suggested of arming the trading vessels of America must be met by the British Cruizers according to the necessity of the Case.

In such a painful extremity our honor and interests must be maintained; and the Orders in Council must be executed by force. You will take an early opportunity of representing this determination to the American Government, in the most temperate but firm language,

---

[3] Draft, F. O. 5 : 83.

such as may be calculated to convince them, that although this Government is anxious to cultivate the relations of Amity by every reasonable effort of conciliation, the great foundations of the maritime interests of the British Empire must be preserved; and that no menace of hostility can deter this Government from asserting those rights to which Great Britain is entitled by every principle of reason and justice.

The Prince Regent further directs me to acquaint you, that H. R. H. cannot approve the expedient which you have suggested of a partial repeal of the Orders in Council, as far as concerns their operation on the American Coasts.[4]

Such a concession would be subversive of all the rules by which our blockades have hitherto been regulated.

It is one of the fundamental rules of the Court of Adm'y that when a Port is blockaded and the notification of that blockade is considered to have reached the Port of lading, any vessel bound from such Port to the Port blockaded, falls under the restriction of the blockade from the moment of the departure, otherwise it would be impracticable to fix the period, when any such ship could be considered as violating the blockade, and consequently as liable to capture.

The Prince Regent commands me to caution you, against employment of any suggestions of compromise to the American Government, (such as you have stated in your secret dispatch) without previous instructions signified to you under H. R. H's: Orders. Such suggestions may induce the American Gov't to doubt the sincerity or firmness of this Gov't in the determination already announced of maintaining stedfastly the system of defence which we have adopted; until the Enemy shall relinquish his unwarrantable mode of Attack upon our Interests, through the violation of neutral Rights.

The Ground of our proceeding in this course is plain and direct, and the clear justice of our cause must not be embarrassed by any attempts to suggest expedients, inconsistent with the general principles on which the question has been rested throughout the whole tenor of your instructions.

Upon the subject of East Florida, you have already addressed a Remonstrance to the American Gov't: [5]—In this dispatch I shall only direct you to renew that remonstrance without delay, in the name and by the authority of the Prince Regent, and you will declare in the most distinct terms to the Gov't of the United States, that H. R. H. the Prince Regent in the name and on the behalf of H. M. must protest

---

[4] Alarmed by the rising war fever, Foster made this suggestion to Wellesley in his dispatch No. 26, secret, in cipher, of Nov. 23, 1811, F. O. 5 : 77.

[5] Foster's note to Monroe of Sept. 5, 1811, respecting the "revolutionizing" activities in East Florida of George Matthews, formerly governor of Georgia, and Monroe's reply of Nov. 2, 1811, are printed in A. S. P., F. R., III, 543–545.

against any attempt to seize that Province from our Ally, and cannot view with indifference the execution (under any pretence) of such hostile proceedings by a foreign power against a dependency of Spain, at the moment when Spain is engaged in contending for her independence and honor with so great a degree of spirit and perseverance.

P. S.   You may take an opportunity of acquainting Mr. Monroe, that Mr. Pinkney never communicated to this Government the instruction which it appears by your dispatch No. 21, that he received from His Government respecting the proposed aggression against East Florida, a verbal communication on this point was made by Mr. Smith [6] who was informed that you would state the Sentiments of this Government on the question.

WELLESLEY TO FOSTER [7]

No. 3.   Secret.   FOREIGN OFFICE, Jan'y (28th :), 1812.
Sir,
Your Dispatches respecting the final adjustment of the affair of the Chesapeake Frigate have been submitted to H. R. Hs the Prince Regent.[8]

H. R. Hs commands me to acquaint you that although it would have been more conformable to your original Instructions and more advantageous to the general state of the questions depending with the Gov't of America to have proposed the adjustment of this affair immediately upon your arrival the motives which induced you to postpone the execution of that part of your Instructions cannot be disapproved by H. R. Hs.

It is however extremely important that you should observe the utmost degree of caution in separating the affair of the Chesapeake from every other point of discussion which has arisen with the American Gov't.

The terms of the communication proposed to be made to you by Mr. Monro were certainly exceptionable on the ground which you have stated; and although the original objections have been in some degree removed by the alterations to which Mr. Monro agreed, the

---

[6] John Spear Smith, the American chargé at London, had explained the purport of the act of Congress approved by President Madison on Jan. 15, 1811; an act (Monroe wrote Foster) "authorizing the Executive to accept possession of East Florida from the local authorities, or to take it against the attempt of a foreign Power to occupy it, holding it in either case subject to future and friendly negotiation." Monroe to Foster, Nov. 2, 1811, *A. S. P., F. R.,* III, 545. See Julius W. Pratt, *Expansionists of 1812,* chap. ii.

[7] Draft, F. O. 5 : 83.

[8] See note 27, p. 319, *supra.*

Prince Regent cannot consider the expressions ultimately adopted by Mr. Monro with complete satisfaction.[9] I am commanded however to inform you that H. R. Hs does not wish to revive any part of this unpleasant discussion, and therefore directs you to proceed to the final completion of the adjustment as soon as may be practicable upon the conditions stated in your original Instructions.

WELLESLEY TO FOSTER [10]

No. 4.   FOREIGN OFFICE, 1st: Feb'ry 1812.

Sir,

In reply to that part of your dispatch No. 28 of the 26th of last November, which relates to the progress which according to the representations made to you has taken place in the improvement of American Manufactures,[11] I am to direct you to institute such further enquiries into this important Subject, as may enable you to verify upon positive and Correct information the Statements which you have received.

It appears to be not improbable that these communications have been made to you for political purposes, as being judged likely to influence the decision of this Gov't in the Consideration of the Main Question between the two Countries. The repeal of the Orders in Council.

It becomes therefore peculiarly necessary that you should be on your guard against all insinuations of this Kind, and that you should endeavour to learn the real Truth of such Representations by all the Means within your power.

The rejection of the proposal to encrease the duties on the importation of the Articles specified in your dispatch [12] seems to be at

---

[9] In his dispatch No. 23 of Nov. 12, 1811, F. O. 5 : 77, Foster stated that Monroe's draft of a note accepting the offer of reparations for the *Chesapeake* attack (a copy of which Foster enclosed) contained the insinuation that the President received the offer "merely out of consideration for the Personal character of His Royal Highness the Prince Regent, and that it seemed some distinction was meant to be drawn between His Royal Highness and his Cabinet." Monroe had protested against such an inference, but had revised the phrasing of his note of acceptance on this and on other points.

[10] Draft, F. O. 5 : 83.

[11] In his dispatch No. 28 of Nov. 26, 1811, F. O. 5 : 77, Foster had reported : "From every quarter I have accounts of the rapid progress which the Manufactures are making in these States, particularly those of coarse cloth and of cotton. There are frequent arrivals of workmen from the Western parts of England, and it is in serious agitation at Washington to pass laws which shall secure to this Country hereafter the manufacture of many articles of which they are in most need, and which they formerly imported principally from His Majesty's Dominions."

[12] The House of Representatives on Nov. 26, 1811 refused to consider a resolution for additional duties on imported coarse goods manufactured from hemp, flax, and cotton. *Annals of Congress,* 12th., 1st. sess., p. 371.

variance, with the Improvement which you describe to have taken place in the Manufactures of America, and at a time when the importation of any description of British Manufacture into the United States is prohibited, it seems to be a futile menace to declare that it is in contemplation to prohibit the importation of certain Articles of British Manufacture, in consequence of the rapid success of the Manufactories established in America.

VISCOUNT CASTLEREAGH TO FOSTER [13]

No. 1.   FOREIGN OFFICE; Feb'ry 28th. 1812.
Sir,
    I have it in command from His Royal Highness The Prince Regent to desire that you will immediately make the most diligent Enquiries into the actual Military Establishment of the United States, specifying the different arms whether Cavalry, Infantry, or Artillery of the Regular Forces and the Militia; and that you will likewise transmit to me for the information of The Prince Regent, such plans of the Forts, Military Stations and principal towns, within the Country, as you can procure—the former part of this Instruction has in part been met by the regular returns made to Congress by the American Secretary at War, which you have already transmitted to this office. You will however report to me for the information of His Royal Highness such additional explanations and observations as may be necessary to illustrate Them.
    I am likewise to instruct you to transmit to me in a separate Dispatch such further information as you are able to procure respecting the Naval Establishment of the United States.

CASTLEREAGH TO FOSTER [14]

No. 2.   Cipher.   FOREIGN OFFICE, Feby. 29th 1812.
Sir,
    Intelligence has been received [from the Admiralty],[15] that three Persons, whose description is given in the accompanying Enclosure [16] sailed from Brest on the 4th inst. in a Ship called "The General Clifton" bound to a port, unknown, in America, where they are to receive passports as American Subjects, and then to proceed for this Country.

---

[13] Draft, F. O. 5 : 83. Robert Stewart, second Marquis of Londonderry, better known as Viscount Castlereagh (1769–1822), on Feb. 28, 1812, following Wellesley's resignation on Feb. 19, had become Secretary for Foreign Affairs, a post which he held until his death in 1822.
[14] Draft, F. O. 5 : 83.
[15] Phrase in brackets supplied from notation on margin.
[16] The enclosure is lacking.

You will immediately make the most diligent and secret Enquiries as to the real and pretended objects of these Persons, and particularly for the name of The Ship on board of which They may take their passage for England.

CASTLEREAGH TO FOSTER [17]

No. 3.   FOREIGN OFFICE: March 4th. 1812.
Sir,
    In reference to the Marquess Wellesley's dispatch to you of this year marked No. 3. directing you to proceed to the final completion of the adjustment of the affair of the Chesapeake as soon as may be practicable, on the conditions stated in your original Instructions I am now to acquaint you that the two seamen named in the margin [James Strachan, alias Horey; Daniel Martin] formerly belonging to the Chesapeake have been put on board of His Majesty's Schooner Bramble, ordered to join Vice Adm'l Sawyer off the Coast of America and that officer will immediately advise you of their arrival.
    Of the two other persons who were taken from the Chesapeake, John Wilson, alias Jenkin Ratford,[18] who in the memorandum transmitted to you last year from the Admiralty was returned as not having been heard of since he quitted the Leopard, was hanged on board of the Halifax Sloop of War on the 31st. of August 1807, in pursuance of the sentence of a Court Martial, appointed to try him for Desertion.
    The Fourth, William Ware, died in the Hospital at Halifax on the 9th. of January 1809.
    You will immediately communicate these circumstances to the American Secretary of State, and you will arrange with him in the least objectionable way, the manner in which the two surviving persons shall be delivered over to the American Government.

CASTLEREAGH TO FOSTER [19]

No. 4.   FOREIGN OFFICE. March 4th 1812.
Sir,
    I herewith transmit to you the Copy of a Memorial [20] from Messrs. Coats & Burnside Merchants of Glasgow requesting the interference of H. M.'s Govt: to procure the Restitution of Goods sent to New Orleans in the American Ship Aurora in December 1810—and I am to desire that you will lay the same before the American Govt: and take such steps as you may deem most proper for the Recovery

---

[17] Draft, F. O. 5 : 83.
[18] See note 36, p. 240, *supra*.
[19] Draft, F. O. 5 : 83.
[20] The enclosure is lacking.

of this Property, the American Consul at Liverpool having assured the Owners that it would be given up notwithstanding the President's Proclamation under which it was condemned.

CASTLEREAGH TO FOSTER [21]

Private.   FOREIGN OFFICE, March 7, 1812.
My Dear Sir,

I cannot allow the Mail to sail for America without notifying to you my appointment to the Foregn Dept. The very few days that have Elapsed since I received the Seals, have not admitted of my being informed, with any precision of the State, in which the discussions with America now stand; I am desirous of explaining this, that you may not be Surprized at the arrival of a Mail without any official notice of your late Communications—not having received from Lord Wellesley information that any practical point was at this Moment pending, on which Instructions were called for, I must reserve for a future occasion addressing you on the business of your Mission.

CASTLEREAGH TO FOSTER [22]

No. 5.   FOREIGN OFFICE, March 19th. 1812.
Sir,

I have received His Royal Highness the Prince Regent's commands to transmit to you the enclosed Papers, in order that you may lay the same before the American Government, at the time, and in the manner you may judge most expedient.

You will perceive, that they relate to English Seamen who have been detained against their Will on board of certain Ships of War of the United States which have of late visited the Ports of Great Britain.

Under the present circumstances, as affecting the relations between this Country and the United States, His Royal Highness's Government have been most unwilling to press on the United States' Government any fresh subjects of irritation; and His Royal Highness is sincerely disposed to believe, that these several sources of complaint have originated without the concurrence or participation of a state with which He is so anxious to preserve an amicable and friendly intercourse.

You are not therefore to consider yourself instructed to accompany your communication of the facts contained in these papers, to the American Government, with any strong expressions of complaint

---

[21] Draft, F. O. 5: 83.
[22] Draft, F. O. 5: 83. Also printed, with enclosures, in *Papers Presented to Parliament in 1813*, pp. 449–473, 187–191.

or dissatisfaction on the part of His Royal Highness, as the Prince Regent is disposed to believe, that the Government of America has only to be informed of the fact, to take prompt and satisfactory measures for the correction of the practice.

The American Government will likewise perceive, from this amicable communication, that it is not on that side of the water alone, that the inconvenience necessarily resulting from the similarity of habits, language, and manners between the inhabitants of the two Countries is productive of subjects of complaint and regret: These are however at the same time natural and strong inducements for a conformity of interests, and most particularly for a readiness to give and receive mutual explanations upon all subject of difference; and you may repeat to Mr. Monroe, for the information of His Government, that the Government of His Royal Highness the Prince Regent will continue to give the most positive orders against the detention of American citizens on board His Majestys Ships; and that no difficulties beyond what are requisite for clearly ascertaining the national Character of Individuals, whose cases are brought before the Lords Commissioners of the Admiralty, will be interposed to prevent or delay their immediate discharge.

The Earl of Liverpool, whilst he held the Seals of this Department ad interim,[23] was commanded to make known to Mr. Russell, the case of William Bowman, stated, by the affidavit of his Wife, to be forcibly detained on board the United States' Ship "Hornet." The departure of this vessel precluded Mr. Russell from making the necessary representation to the Commanding Officer of the Hornet. You will, however, communicate the circumstance to the American Government; and I have no doubt, that you will obtain his ready release.[24] Of the papers above referred to, those marked No. 1. contain the statement upon oath of Charles Davis, an Irishman by birth, who was lately a Seaman on board the United States Frigate "Constitution." No. 2. contains the Report of English Seamen on board the United States' Ship "Constitution" and "Wasp." No. 3. contains a statement of the real name and birth of W. Smith: No. 4 contains the affidavits of George Warren and Charles Murphy, British Seamen, who left the American Ships "Constitution" and "Hornet," and the affidavit of Elizabeth Bowman above alluded to. No. 5. contains the deposition

---

[23] The Earl of Liverpool, Secretary of state for war and colonies in the Perceval ministry, served as foreign secretary ad interim from Feb. 19 to Feb. 28, 1812.

[24] The note of the Earl of Liverpool to Jonathan Russell (American chargé at London since November of 1811), dated Feb. 20, 1812, enclosing the affidavit of Elizabeth E. Bowman, and stating that a writ of habeas corpus for Bowman, if issued, would be enforced by the British government, together with Russell's reply of Feb. 21, 1812, are printed in A. S. P., F. R., III, 426. On June 10, 1812 Secretary Monroe (in answer to Foster's representations of June 1, 1812) transmitted to Foster the affidavit of William Bowman, alias William Helby, alias William Elby, dated June 1, 1812, to the effect that he had voluntarily enlisted on the Hornet, July 3, 1811, and was perfectly sober at the time. Ibid., III, 468.

upon oath of John Taylor, alias William Smith. No. 6 contains the correspondence between the Earl of Liverpool and Mr. Russell on the subject of Bowman.[25]

CASTLEREAGH TO FOSTER [26]

No. 6.   FOREIGN OFFICE, March 19, 1812.
Sir,

The enclosed extract of a Letter from the late Commander in Chief of the Channel Fleet to the Secretary to the Admiralty,[27] contains all the particulars which have as yet come to the knowledge of this Government, respecting a most unwarrantable outrage committed against an Officer and part of the Crew of His Majesty's Ship Niemen by the Master of the American Ship Purse, detained under the Orders in Council, in a successful attempt on the part of the Master to rescue the Prise from the Captors. You will take an early opportunity of laying before the American Government the mischievous and fatal consequences which must ensue, if they do not immediately, and in the most urgent manner, discountenance amongst their Citizens this species of unjustifiable resistance, which, if systematically resorted to, will in the first instance reduce the captors to the necessity of resorting to measures of unusual rigour, and will expose the participator in these outrages, to that exemplary punishment, which the Laws of all civilized Nations dispense to premeditated murder. The neutral trader cannot be permitted to set himself up as the judge of the legality or justice of orders, under which his Vessel is detained by the Cruizers of a Belligerent: An assumption of this nature would lead to the violation of all neutral rights, would produce the most inextricable confusion in all the relations of neutral and belligerent Powers, and the range of War already so extensive would no longer be circumscribed by any limits.

It becomes then the most sacred duty of the American Government, in preserving their neutral Rights, not unnecessarily to compromise the lives and properties of their fellow Citizens, to put a stop to this practice in limine, and to inculcate amongst the trading part of their population the Importance, and Necessity of leaving the points of law and justice, on which the orders affecting neutral commerce are grounded to be discussed—where alone they can be amicably and rightfully canvassed—in the legal course of judicial proceeding, or between the Executive Governments of the two Countries.

---

[25] Foster made representations to Monroe, June 1, 1812, on the subject of Bowman, and enclosed the above papers with the exception of No. 6. A. S. P., F. R., III, 459–460. All of the enclosures are printed in *Papers Presented to Parliament in 1813*, pp. 452–473, 187–191.

[26] Draft. F. O. 5: 83.

[27] The enclosure is lacking.

CASTLEREAGH TO FOSTER [28]

No. 7.   FOREIGN OFFICE, March 19, 1812.

Sir,

It is desirable, that you should take an early opportunity of laying before the American Government the substance of the information contained in the enclosed communication from the Admiralty, respecting the treatment experienced at Sea by the American Brig, John, bound from Boston to Tonningen, from two French Frigates and a Brig—in order that the Government of the United States may set on foot such enquiries as they may judge expedient, to enable them to appretiate the regard shewn by French Officers to the flag and property of Individuals of the United States.[29]

CASTLEREAGH TO FOSTER [30]

No. 8.   FOREIGN OFFICE, April 10th: 1812.

Sir,

I inclose to you the Moniteur of the 16th. Ultimo, containing a Report made to Bonaparte, and communicated to the Conservative Senate on the 10th. Ulto by the Duke of Bassano, French Minister for Foreign Affairs; [31] which confirms, if any thing were wanting to confirm, the repeated assertions of Great Britain, that the Berlin and Milan Decrees have never been revoked, however some partial and insidious relaxations of them may have been made in a few instances, as an encouragement to America to adopt a System beneficial to France and injurious to Great Britain; and which being accompanied by conditions directly hostile to British Rights, gave to that relaxation the character of being founded in an expectation that America would submit to those obnoxious terms.

I need not bring to your recollection the various attempts, which have been unsuccessfully made, not only to induce the American Government to produce any formal Instrument by which the Decrees of Bonaparte were repealed, but to make an explicit avowal that America did not adopt the conditions upon which the Repeal was offered. The first she was unable to do, the latter she has studiously avoided.

---

[28] Draft, F. O. 5 : 83. Also printed, with its enclosure, in *Papers Presented to Parliament in 1813,* pp. 473–475.

[29] The master of the *John,* according to the Admiralty statement enclosed, reported that the French squadron had recently burnt a Baltimore brig and would have destroyed the *John* had there been room enough in the French vessels for himself and his crew.

[30] F. O. 115 : 23. The draft of this instruction is printed in *Papers Presented to Parliament in 1813,* pp. 475–491.

[31] The report of March 10, 1812 is printed in *ibid.,* pp. 492–505, and in *A. S. P., F. R.,* III, 457–459.

We have therefore a distinct right to complain of America, that She should demand of us, to recognize an *absolute* Repeal of the French Decrees, when she could only produce a conditional offer of repeal on the part of France; which if accepted in it's extent by America, would only form fresh matter of complaint, and a new ground for declining her demands. America must feel, that it is impossible for Great Britain to rescind her Orders in Council, whilst the French Decrees are Officially declared to remain in force against all Nation, not subscribing to the New Maritime Code promulgated in those Decrees; and also whilst America maintains so suspicious a reserve, with regard to the Conditions annexed by France to the repeal of those Decrees. For, after what has passed, unless a full and satisfactory explanation be made on both these Points, Great Britain cannot relinquish her retaliatory System against France without implying her consent to the admissibility of the Conditions in question.

I trust, however, when you have delivered in the inclosed Paper to the American Government, that a new disposition will begin to manifest itself, which may render it unnecessary to return to the late Causes of our just Complaints.

It will be at once acknowledged that this Paper is a Republication of the Berlin and Milan Decrees in a more aggravated form, accompanied as it is with an extension of all the obnoxious doctrines which attend those Decrees, inflamed by a declaration, that Bonaparte has annexed to France every Independent State in his Power, which had eluded them; and that he was proceeding against all other Maritime parts of Europe, on the pretence, that his System could not be permanent and complete, so long as they retained their liberty with regard to it.

The outrageous principle here avowed connects itself obviously with the proposition too much countenanced by America, that the Continental System of Bonaparte, as far as it operates to the Confiscation of Neutral Property on shore, on the ground of such Property being British Produce or Manufacture, is a mere Municipal Regulation, which Neutral or Belligerent Nations have no right to resent, because it does not violate any principle of the Law of Nations. It is unneccessary to recur to the various Arguments by which it has been shewn, that this System does not partake of the Character of Municipal regulation; but that it is a mere War Measure, directed with the most hostile Spirit against this Country;—you will dwell as forcibly as possible upon this Circumstance;—that, in order to extend this System on the principle of municipal regulation, all the Rights of Independent Neutral Nations are to be violated, their Territories are to be seized, without any other Cause of War whatever, but that they may be incorporated with the French Nation, and thence becoming subject to her Rights of Dominion, receive the Continental System as a municipal regulation of France; and thus the mere possibility of non-compliance with the whole of this System is made the ground for the Occupation, or invasion, the incorporation or extinction, of every State on the Continent of Europe.

Great Britain cannot believe that America will not feel a just indignation at the full developement of such a System;—a System which indeed Bonaparte has partially opened before, and has, in the instances of the Hanseatic Towns, of Portugal, and other Countries, carried into complete execution; but which he has never completely unfolded in all it's extent 'till the present moment; and in what an insulting and preposterous Shape does he now attempt to bring forward, and promulgate this Code, which he is to force upon all Nations? He assumes the Treatry of Utrecht to be in force, and to be a Law binding upon all States,—because it suits his convenience at this moment; when the navy of France is driven from the Ocean, to revive the doctrine of "free Ships making free Goods;"—He has recourse to a Treaty, no longer in force, in which such a Stipulation existed;—a Treaty, which, by his own express refusal at Amiens to renew any of the ancient Treaties, was not then revived, even as binding on Great Britain and France, between whom alone, as Parties to it, and only while they were at Peace with each other, could it ever have had any legal effect:—yet even this Treaty is too narrow a Basis for his present pretensions, since he cannot find it in his rule for limiting Maritime Blockades, to Fortresses actually invested, besieged, and likely to be taken;—no provision of any description having been made in that Treaty, either for defining or regulating Blockades.

Surely, at such an instant, America will not urge Great Britain to abandon, or to soften, any precautionary, any retaliatory Rights against such a Power. The British Government not only feels itself imperiously bound to defend them, as they respect Great Britain, with all vigour, but to call upon every Nation to resist such exorbitant pretensions.

If, at such a moment, Great Britain were to relax Her Orders in Council against France, unless America should give an explicit proof of her determination to join the Common Cause of all Civilized Nations, would not those Nations have reason to complain, that the Common Cause was abandoned.

America must feel that Bonaparte is not acting, as indeed he has never acted, with any view of establishing Principles of real freedom with respect to Navigation,—but is merely endeavouring to cloak his determination, if possible, to ruin Great Britain, by novel demands and rejected Theories of Maritime Law. America must see that Bonaparte's object is to exclude British Commerce from every Coast and Port of the Continent, and that in pursuit of this object, trampling on the Rights of Independent States, he insultingly proclaims his determination to effect it by direct invasion of those Independent States, which he as insultingly terms a Guarantee; thus making the most solemn and sacred term in the Law of Nations ignominious [synonimous] [32] with usurpation of Territory and extinction of Independence. America must see that as all the States hitherto in his power have been seized on to *guarantee* his System, he is now proceeding to destroy whatever remains of Independence in other Neutral States to make that *Guarantee* complete. From his want of power to pass the Atlantic with his armies (a want of Power for which the United States are indebted to the Naval Superiority of Great Britain) his System of a Guaranteeing Force may fail as to America; but as he cannot hope to shut American Ports against Great Britain by occupancy and invasion, he hopes to effect his purpose by Management and fraud, and to accomplish that by insidious relaxation which he cannot accomplish by Power:— Great Britain he feels is only to be ruined by excluding her from every Port in the World;—He hopes therefore to shut every Port in Europe by force; and every Port in America by management. He pretends to conciliate America by applause of her Conduct, and a relaxation of his System in her favour. He accompanies that relaxation by Conditions which he trusts America will not disavow, if She does not actually accept, and which he knows Great Britain must reject—knowing at the same time that the relaxation of his Decrees will be of little use to America, without a corresponding relaxation by Great Britain: He throws every obstacle against Concession to America by Great Britain, by making Her perseverance in her retaliatory System more than ever essential to Her honor and existence. And surely it will not escape the notice, or fail to excite the indignation of the American Government, that the Ruler of France by taking this New Ground has retracted the Concession which America supposed him to have made; he has inconsistently and contemptuously withdrawn from Her the ground upon which She has taken an hostile attitude against Great Britain, since the Repeal of Our Orders in Council, and even the renunciation of Our Rights of Blockade would no longer suffice to obtain a Repeal of his Berlin and Milan Decrees.

It is to be hoped, that America, considering all the extravagant pretentions; all the monstrous Doctrines set forth by the Ruler of France, in the Duke of Bassano's Report; and at the same time the Resolution to march his Armies into all States, into the Ports of

---

[32] In the draft, F. O. 5 : 83, the word here is "synonimous."

which the English Flag is admitted, will acknowledge that this doctrine and resolution constitute a complete annihilation of Neutrality; and that She is bound as a Neutral Power to disavow and resist them. Every State that acquiesces in this Report must act upon the Principle, that Neutral and Enemy are to be considered henceforward as the same, in the language of the French Law of Nations;—and Great Britain has a right to consider that every Nation who refuses to admit Her Flag upon the principle assumed, admits and recognizes the doctrine of the Report.

With respect to the Blockade of May 1806, which Bonaparte brings forward so prominently as the foundation and justification of all his violent measures, I do not think it probable that, in the present State of the discussion America is likely to rest much upon that Point. The recent Communications which have taken place between the Two Governments, have, I trust, satisfactorily shewn to America, that that Blockade was not at the first enforced, nor has it at any time been maintained, or defended by Us, upon any New Principles. It rested for it's efficacy, as well as it's legality, upon the Naval force assigned to enforce it: but, if it should be insisted upon [impeached] by America,[33] you will continue to maintain it's justice, as well as the necessity for imposing it (menaced as the Country then was, with an Invasion) and that it was a Blockade, which gave great latitude to the Rights of Neutrals. You will continue, if necessary, to remark, that the execution of this Blockade was previously provided for, and subsequently maintained by a competent Force: You will further observe, that it was a Measure that was not complained of by America at the time, and under which the most friendly Negociations went forward for settling a Commercial Treaty, which was then actually concluded in England with America. Indeed the legality of that Blockade, assuming the Blockading force to have been sufficient to enforce it, Mr. Monroe has latterly not questioned.

You will observe that it was impossible Great Britain should not receive, otherwise than with the utmost jealousy, the unexpected demand made by America for the Repeal of the Blockade, as well as of the Orders in Council, when it appeared to be made subsequent to, if not in consequence of, one of the Conditions in Bonaparte's pretended repeal of his Decrees, which Condition was our renouncing what he calls "Our New Principles of Blockade." That the demand on the part of America was additional and new, is sufficiently proved by reference to the Overture of Mr. Pinkney, as well as from the terms on which Mr. Erskine had arranged the Dispute with America relative to the Orders in Council. In that Arrangement nothing was brought forward with regard to this Blockade. America would have

---

[33] The draft, F. O. 5 : 83, has here : "impeached by America."

been contented at that time without any reference to it.   It certainly
is not more a grievance or an injustice now, than it was then. Why
then is the renunciation of that Blockade insisted upon now, if it was
not necessary to insist upon it then? It is difficult to find any Answer,
but by reference to subsequent Communications between France and
America, and a disposition in America to countenance France in requiring the disavowal of this Blockade, and the principles upon which
it rested, as the *sine quâ non* of the Berlin and Milan Decrees.   It seems
to have become an object with America, only because it was prescribed
as a Condition by France.

On this Blockade, and the Principles and Rights upon which it was
founded, Bonaparte appears to rest the justification of all his Measures
for abolishing Neutrality, and for the invasion of every State, which
is not ready with him to wage a war of extermination against the
Commerce of Great Britain.

America, therefore, no doubt saw the necessity of demanding it's
renunciation; but She will now see, that it is in reality vain, either
for America, of for Great Britain, to expect an actual Repeal of the
French Decrees, untill Great Britain renounces first the basis;—
vizt.—the Blockade of 1806, on which Bonaparte has been pleased to
found them; next, Her Right of retaliation, as subsequently acted
upon in Her Orders in Council:—further, till She is ready to receive the
Treaty of Utrecht, interpreted and applied in the Duke of Bassano's
Report, as the Universal Law of Nations:—and finally, till She ab-
jures all the principles of Maritime Law which support Her established Rights, now more than ever essential to Her existence as a
Nation.

Great Britain feels confident that America never can maintain or
ultimately sanction such pretensions, and His Royal Highness entertains the strongest hope that this last proceeding of France will strip
her measures of every remnant of disguise, and that America in justice
to what She owes to the Law of Nations, and to her own houour
and independence as a Neutral State will instantly withdraw her countenance from the outrageous System of the French Government, and
cease to support by hostile Measures against British Commerce, the
enormous fabrick of usurpation and tyranny which France has endeavoured to exhibit to the world as the Law of Nations.   America
cannot now contend that the Orders in Council, exceed in spirit of
retaliation, what is demanded by the Decrees, the principles, or the
usurpations of Bonaparte.   America must at last be convinced, that
the partial relaxation of those Decrees in her favour has been insid-
iously adopted by France, for the mere purpose of inducing her to
close her Ports against Great Britain, which France cannot herself
effect by force; and She must admit, if Great Britain were now to

repeal her Orders in Council against France, it would be gratuitously giving to France the Commerce of America, and all the benefits
derivable from her Flag, as an additional Instrument for the annoyance
of Great Britain; and that, at the moment when America not only
unites [omits] [34] to assert her own Rights against France, but at the
very time all other States are threatened with destruction, or really
destroyed, for merely supporting their own Rights, [and as incident
to those rights,] [35] the Commerce of Great Britain.

Upon the whole of this important Subject, it is the Prince Regent's
pleasure, that you do declare to the American Government, in a
tone of equal firmness and conciliation, that Great Britain can never
concede, that the Blockade of May 1806 can justly be made the foundation, as it avowedly has been, for the Decrees of Bonaparte; and
further, that the British Government must ever consider the principles
on which that Blockade rested (accompanied as it was by an adequate
Blockading Force) to have been strictly consonant to the Established
Law of Nations, and a legitimate instance of the practice which it
recognizes:—Secondly, that Great Britain must continue to reject the
other spurious doctrines, promulgated by France, in the Duke of
Bassano's Report, as binding upon all Nations. She cannot admit,
as a true declaration of Public Law, that free Ships make free Goods,
nor (the converse of that proposition) that Enemy's Ships destroy
the Character of Neutral Property in the Cargo: She cannot consent
by the adoption of such a principle to deliver absolutely the Commerce of France, from the pressure of the Naval power of Great
Britain and by the abuse of the neutral flag, to allow Her enemy to
obtain without the expense of sustaining a Navy, for the trade and
property of French Subjects, a degree of freedom and security which
even the Commerce of Her own Subjects cannot find under the protection of the British Navy.

She cannot admit as a principle of public law, that maritime blockade can alone be legally applied to Fortresses, actually invested by
land, as well as by Sea, which is the plain meaning, or consequence
of the Duke of Bassano's definition.

She cannot admit, as a principle of Public Law, that arms and
military Stores, are alone contraband of War, and that Ship-timber,
and Naval Stores are excluded from that description. Neither can
She submit without retaliation, that the mere fact of Commercial
Intercourse with British Ports and Subjects, should be made a crime
in all Nations, and that the armies and Decrees of France should be
directed to enforce a principle so new; and unheard of in War.

Great Britain feels, that, to relinquish Her just measures of self

---

[34] The draft, F. O. 5 : 83, has here : "omits."
[35] The draft, F. O. 5 : 83, has the words in brackets.

defense, and retaliation, would be to surrender the best means of Her own preservation, and Rights, and with them the Rights of other Nations, so long as France maintains and acts upon such Principles.

You will represent to the Government of America, that Great Britain feels itself entitled to expect from them an unreserved and candid disclaimer of the right of France to impose on Her and on the World the maritime Code which has been thus promulgated, and to the penalties of which America is Herself declared to be liable, if She fails to submit Herself to it's Enactments. America cannot, for Her own Character, any longer temporize on this Subject, or delay coming to a distinct explanation with France, as well as with Great Britain, if She wishes to clear Herself from the imputation of being an abetter of such Injustice.

America, as the case now stands, has not a pretence for claiming from Great Britain a Repeal of Her Orders in Council. She must recollect that the British Government never for a moment countenanced the idea, that the repeal of those Orders could depend upon any partial or conditional repeal of the Decrees of France. What Great Britain always avowed, was, Her readiness to rescind Her Orders, so soon as France rescinded absolutely and unconditionally Her Decrees:—She never engaged to repeal those Orders, as affecting America alone, leaving them in force against other States, upon condition that France would except singly and specially America from the operation of Her Decrees;[36] She could not do so, without the grossest Injustice to Her Allies, as well as all other neutral Nations: much less could She do so, upon the supposition, that the special exception in favor of America was to be expressly granted by France, as it has been hitherto tacitly accepted by America, upon conditions utterly subversive of the most important and indisputable maritime Rights of the British Empire.[37]

America has now a proceeding forced upon Her on which, without surrendering any of those principles which She may deem it necessary for Her own Honour and Security to maintain, She may separate Herself from the violence and injustice of the Enemy. She owes it not only to Herself to do so, but she is entitled to resent that course of conduct on the part of France, which is the only impediment to Her obtaining what She desires at the hands of Great Britain: namely the repeal of the Orders in Council. You may renew to

---

[36] Compare with Castlereagh to Foster, June 17, 1812, No. 20, *infra*.

[37] Foster communicated this instruction to Monroe, and presented it (with some changes) in writing to the Secretary of State on May 30, 1812, *A. S. P., F. R.*, III, 454–457. The above paragraph was not identically repeated in the note of May 30, and the discrepancy was the subject of an inquiry by Monroe on June 3, 1812, *ibid.*, III, 460–461. See, also, Foster's dispatches, and enclosures, May 28, June 6, June 8, 1812, *Papers Presented to Parliament in 1813*, pp. 576–615.

the American Govt. the assurance of His Royal Highness's anxious desire to meet the wishes of America upon this point whenever the conduct of the Enemy will justify him in doing so.

Whilst America could persuade Herself however erroneously that the Berlin and Milan Decrees had been actually and totally repealed; and that the execution of the engagement made on that condition by the British Government, had been declined, She might deem it justifiable, as a consequence of such a persuasion to treat the interest and Commerce of France with preference and friendship, and those of Great Britain with hostility;—but this delusion is at an end: America now finds the French Decrees not only in full force, but pointed with augmented hostility against Great Britain. Will the American Government declare, that the measure now taken by France is that repeal of the obnoxious decrees, which America expected would lead to the repeal of the British Orders in Council? Will the American Government unless upon the principle of denying our retaliatory Right of Blockade, under any imaginable circumstances, declare that there is at this moment, a ground upon which the Repeal of our Orders in Council can be pressed upon Us; or that the repeal could now be warranted upon any other ground, than an express abdication of the right itself, which America well knows, whatever may be Our desire to conciliate, is a concession which the British Government cannot and will not make. If this be true, for what purpose can She persevere in Her hostile atitude towards Great Britain, and her friendly one towards France? Does America really wish to aid France in Her attempts to subjugate Great Britain? Does America expect that Great Britain, contending against France, will, at the instance of America, disarm Herself and submit to the mercy of Her Opponent? If both these questions are answered in the negative, upon what ground can She for a moment longer continue Her hostile measures against Us? The American Non Intercourse Act was framed upon the express principle of continuing in force against the Power, whether France or Great Britain that should refuse to repeal it's respective Laws of which America thought Herself entitled to complain. But the repeal contemplated by that Act was a bonâ fide repeal, and not a Repeal upon an inadmissible Condition.

The French Government came forward with an insidious offer of repealing Her Decrees: Great Britain professed Her readiness to adopt a corresponding Measure so soon as the offer of France should be notified in a regular Form unaccompanied by inadmissible Conditions. It now appears that America was too credulous and that Great Britain was justified in the Suspicion She entertained of the Enemy's bad Faith. It is impossible America should not feel under these Circumstances that She has not only an Act of Justice to perform by Great Britain, but perceive that France has deliberately attached Conditions to the Repeal of Her Decrees which She knew Great Britain never could accept, hoping thereby to foment Disunion between Great Britain and America. America can never be justified, in continuing to resent against Us that failure of Relief, which is alone attributable to the insidious Policy of the Enemy.

It is not for the British Government to dictate to that of America what ought to be the Measure of it's just indignation against the Ruler of France for having originated and persevered in a System of lawless Violence to the Subversion of Neutral Rights, which being necessarily retaliated by Great Britain, has exposed America, with other Neutral States to losses which the British Government has never ceased most sincerely to deplore. America must judge for Herself, how much the Original Injustice of France towards Her has been aggravated by the fraudulent Professions of relinquishing Her Decrees by the Steps adopted to mislead America in order to embark Her in Measures which we trust She never would have taken, if She could have foreseen what has now happened; and, ultimately, by threatening America with Her Vengeance as a denationalized State, if She does not submit to be the Instrument of Her designs against Great Britain.

These are Considerations for America to weigh; but what we are entitled to claim at Her Hands, as an act not less of Policy, than Justice, is, that She should cease to treat Great Britain as an Enemy. The Prince Regent does not desire retrospect, where the Interests of two Countries, so naturally connected by innumerable Ties, are concerned. It is more Consonant to His Royal Highness's Sentiments to contribute to the restoration of harmony and friendly Intercourse, than to enquire why it has been interrupted. Feeling that nothing has been omitted on his part to relieve America from the Inconveniences, to which a novel System of warfare on the part of France, unfortunately continues to expose Her: and that the present unfriendly Relations which to their mutual prejudice, subsist between the two Countries, have grown out of a misconception on the part of America, both of the conduct and purpose of France: His Royal Highness considers himself entitled to call upon America to resume her Relations of Amity, with this Country:—In doing so She will best provide for the Interests of her own People; and you are authorized to assure the American Government that altho' His Royal Highness, acting in the Name and on behalf of His Majesty, can never suffer the fundamental Maxims of the British Monarchy in Matters of maritime Right, as consonant to the recognized Law of Nations, to be prejudiced in his hands; His Royal Highness will be ready at all times to concert with America, as to their exercise; and so to regulate their application, as to combine, as far as may be, the Interests of America, with the Object of effectually retaliating upon France the measure of her own Injustice.

You are at liberty to communicate the whole, or any part of this Dispatch to the American Government [38] trusting, that they will trace in it, the sincere desire, which animates the Councils of Great Britain, to conciliate America as far as may be consistent with the principles, which the Preservation of the Power and Independence of the British Monarchy is held essentially to depend.

CASTLEREAGH TO FOSTER [39]

No. 9.   FOREIGN OFFICE, April 10th: 1812.

Sir,

The communication which you are authorized by my dispatch No. 8 to make to the American Government, cannot fail to prove a touchstone of their policy and intentions. It is impossible they should not deeply feel the embarrassments, in which the insidious policy of the enemy and their own weakness, have placed them. Under ordinary circumstances it might be expected, that the conduct of a Government, determined to prove to the World, that they would neither submit to be deceived, nor be involved by France in such disgraceful transactions, would be to resent in the most decided manner, the imposition practised upon them; but the internal Politicks of America have so much connected the interests of the Party in power with the French Alliance, that I cannot encourage much expectation, whatever they may in their hearts feel, that they will be induced to assume any authoritative Tone against France.

It is more probable, that the new aspect the question has now assumed, may awaken them to a Sense of the folly [40] of attempting either to force, or intimidate Great Britain; and that, alarmed at the danger even to themselves of the former attempt, and the hopelessness of the latter, they may with more prudence than has lately marked their Councils, see, in this new posture of affairs, an opportunity of receding without disgrace from the precipice of War, to which they have been so inconsiderately approached.

To assist their retreat without any unnecessary sacrifice of national dignity, is the sincere desire and the best policy of Great Britain:— To rescue America from the influence of France, is of more importance, than committing Her in War with that Power;—and to revive the relations of amity and commerce between Great Britain

[38] See note immediately preceding.
[39] F. O. 115 : 23. The draft of this instruction is printed in *Papers Presented to Parliament in 1813*, pp. 505–513.
[40] In the draft. F. O. 5 : 83, the word "desperate" precedes "folly."

and America, are more to be aimed at (whilst none of our essential rights are compromised) than protracted discussions or controversial questions of maritime Law. It is on these grounds the desire of the Prince Regent, if you should perceive a becoming temper in the Councils of America, that it should be met by a marked disposition on your part to conciliate. In the close of the former dispatch I was commanded by His Royal Highness to declare, that, whilst He never could compromise the maritime Rights of Great Britain, His Royal Highness would be ready at all times to concert with America as to their exercise, and so to regulate their application, as to combine as far as possible the interests of America with the object of effectually retaliating upon France the measure of Her own injustice.

It is with reference to this principle that I am now directed to call your attention to the question of Licences to trade with the blockaded Ports, in relaxation of the Orders of April 1809.[41] You will not fail to recollect, that the complaints of America have never yet been urged very distinctly upon this ground;—The Government of The United States having been in the habit of standing upon higher grounds of objection:—but it nevertheless has been occasionally urged by them, that although these Licenses have been uniformly granted to neutral as well as to British Trade, the neutral Merchant cannot profit by such relaxation, (especially the American Merchant from his remote situation) in the same degree as the British Merchant can, regulating his transactions on the Spot where the Licenses are issued.

The extent to which this intercourse under Licenses has been carried, and the disposition evinced on the part of the French Government to give greater extension to it, will probably attract the notice of the American Government, and lead them to instance the magnitude of this particular trade, as an additional proof of the alledged injustice of Our System; but, if it should not occasion any formal representation on their part, there can be no objection to your reverting to it as a circumstance strongly indicative, that, whatever the Duke of Bassano may think fit to assert, of the efficacy of the French Decrees against British Commerce, and however France may be desirous to cloak Her present projects in the North of Europe, under the pretext of enforcing by Her arms the Continental System, She is Herself at this moment obliged to yield at home, in breach of Her own System, to the pressure of our retaliating measures, a very extensive direct trade with this Country.[42]

In adverting to this subject, you will observe that if, instead of impeaching the fundamental principles of our Retaliatory Rights, the Government of America had represented against the partial effects

---

[41] See note 32, p. 270, *supra*.
[42] See note 16, p. 312, *supra*.

of any particular relaxation of those Rights which We had adopted, the British Government would not have been indisposed to listen to such representations. It would have been ready on the contrary to have sustained much of national inconvenience, to remove such grounds of complaint, provided there had been reason at the same time to believe, that such a Concession on It's part, would have led to a return of amity and Commercial intercourse between the two States.

You may represent to the American Government, that the Order of April 1809, was in a great measure intended to meet the wishes of America, as well as to consult the interest of Our Allies, by the removal of certain inconveniences, to which they were subjected, but which were not considered essential to the efficacy of our Retaliatory System.

If America at the time had expressed any satisfaction with that modification of our Orders in Council, which, whilst it confined their Sphere of action within narrower limits, applied the principle of the blockade itself within those limits, without any modification or exception;—the British Government would not have broken in upon the strict rule of that order by Licenses:—But when We found it received by America, in as hostile a Spirit, as the original Orders in Council, there remained no reason, as far as the question of concilia- tion was concerned, why We should not accompany that Order with some of the same regulations, relative to trade to and from the block- aded Coast, and the Ports of Great Britain (not only for ourselves but for neutrals) by means of Licenses, as were, without any Licenses, introduced into the original Orders, and formed a material part of the system on which they proceeded.

It has been urged against these partial relaxations of the blockade, that they tend to prevent or retard the attainment of it's alledged object, namely, the abandonment of the hostile decrees on the part of the enemy, in which Neutral Powers, who suffer from the effects of the blockade, have an interest as large as our own.

The objection would be just, if urged by a neutral who had acquiesced in the blockade, consented to await it's effect, and done nothing to obstruct it's operation. But the United States on the con- trary have opposed our exercise of this retaliatory right, and per- mitted, not to say, encouraged, the breach of the blockade, by the American Merchants. The consequence has been, that very con- siderable numbers of American Ships have been able, either by avoid- ing the notice of our Cruizers, or by the mask of a false destination, to enter the Ports of blockaded Countries, and to sail from thence; thus relieving the necessities of the enemy, and delivering him in no small degree from the pressure of our retaliatory measures. They have also cooperated with France, by prohibiting, in concurrence with Her, the importation of British produce and manufactures into the Ports of America.

Under such circumstances, America cannot fairly object to our accepting from the enemy such partial and progressive practical retractions of his own rigorous system, as his necessities, arising out of the pressure of these very measures, may constrain him to yield, nor to our enabling Our Merchants by Licenses to avail themselves of those reluctant concessions, without being exposed to capture, by Ships of War of their own Country, for engaging in a prohibited trade.

To relieve our commerce and manufacture from the oppressive effects of the hostile decrees, by imposing upon the enemy such a measure of distress, as might oblige him to recall them, was the main object of our retaliatory system. To reject the exceptions, therefore, which He is driven to admit, would be in some degree to sacrifice the end for the sake of the means. The only adequate motives for such a Sacrifice, would be either, that, by refusing the exception, and maintaining the blockade with undeviating strictness, the general end might be sooner and more entirely attained; or that our retaliatory System might by such strictness be reconciled more easily to the views of neutral Powers. But both these motives have been hitherto precluded by the conduct of the United States. While they are found irreconcileably adverse to the rule itself, it matters not, in a view to harmony with them, whether the rule itself be more strictly or loosely applied; nor can it be material to the ultimate effect on the enemy, whether exceptions to the rule by British Licenses, or Contraventions of it by American Merchants, with the approbation of their own Government, alleviate the enemy's distress. At least America has no right to exact from Us an abstinence from the one, while She refuses to desist from the other.

If, however, the views of the American Government are altered on this subject;—and if, without raising any further question on the principles in dispute, they are disposed to open the intercourse with Us, upon condition, that We shall again resort to the principle of rigorous blockade against the French Dominions, to the exclusion of our trade equally with that of neutral Nations, an arrangement upon such a basis you are hereby authorized to conclude;—In which arrangement you may undertake, that, upon an assurance being received through you, that the Government of America had actually determined to re: open Her intercourse with Great Britain, from a period to be named, when it might be presumed, that such a notification had been received here;—no fresh Licenses in defeasance of such blockade will be issued by this Government.

You will understand, that these Acts must be made contemporaneous as far as possible in their effects, as the British Government could not stand justified to it's own Merchants and manufacturers, were they to relinquish the trade to France, at a moment when it promises to become so considerable, and affords so decisive a proof of the efficacy of our Orders in Council: unless the immediate reopening of the markets of America should afford some sufficient compensation for the loss of that Trade.

If you are right in supposing, that the American Government only wants some new Step on the part of this Government, on which to found a change of policy; and if the new and extravagant pretensions of the French Government should strangely fail to furnish a satisfactory ground for such conduct; the proposition you are hereby authorized to make will afford them the fairest Opportunity. If it fails of success, it will at least have served, as a test of the principles on which America stands. It will remove the whole argument of grievance on our part, so far as it rests upon the collateral ground of the relaxations our Orders in Council have undergone, and bring the question at once back to the broad principles of our rights of blockade and retaliation.

If, however, America persists in requiring Us to abandon Our maritime Rights, either as resting on the ordinary Laws of maritime blockade, or the particular right We now insist on of retaliating upon the Enemy, as claimed under the Orders in Council, You will not express yourself in such a manner as to encourage the most distant hope of our being induced to make such a sacrifice.

If, on the other hand, She complains only of the mode in which these rights are exercised, in the intercourse permitted under Licenses with the blockaded Ports, the British Government is ready, either to concert with America as to the mode in which they shall be hereafter exercised upon principles of mutual Convenience; or it is ready, as above proposed, to wave all relaxations whatever, and to stand in future on the rigorous execution of the blockade.

Should, however, America refuse either of these Alternatives;— and, notwithstanding the evidence She has lately obtained of the real designs of France, continue to exclude British Commerce and British Ships of War from Her Ports, whilst they are open to those of the enemy, it is then clear, that we are at Issue with America upon principles, which, upon the part of this Government, You are not at liberty to compromise.

CASTLEREAGH TO FOSTER [43]

No. 10.   Private.   FOREIGN OFFICE, April 10: 1812.
Sir,

In the management of the Negociation, with which you are entrusted, you will continue to conduct yourself with the utmost conciliation towards America; You will firmly adhere to the principles, on which this Government considers itself bound to act, but you are to avoid pressing them upon America, in such a manner as might expose the Negociation to an abrupt termination. Whilst no injurious concession is made to the United States, nor any necessary exertion against the Enemy relaxed, it is not essential to the interest of Great Britain, that America should be urged to an immediate decision. In proportion as a Rupture can be delayed, the insidious designs of France must become apparent; the chances of Peace being preserved with America be improved, and it will become more and more difficult for the American Government to embark that Country in a War with Great Britain.

Should the Councils of America reject every pacific suggestion, it will be your object, to regulate the discussion in such a manner, as to throw distinctly upon the United States the option of War: Much must depend hereafter on the impression made in this respect on the feelings, and understandings, of the American People.

Your forbearance must not however lead you to withdraw from the temperate discussion and refutation of the pretences, upon which the American Government will attempt to justify their conduct; and I am particularly to recommend to you, whenever the Arguments, against which you have to contend, may lead you for a time from the main points in dispute, that you do upon all occasions endeavour to bring back the discussions to the broad features of the Case; and never allow the American Government to escape from the Position, that if they are determined upon War, it is a War undertaken to compel Great Britain to submit to France, her inveterate Enemy, her Maritime Rights and Power: That the demand upon Great Britain from the outset, has been to surrender her Rights, of ordinary Blockade, to France, and her Rights of Retaliation, to America; and that she is now called upon for the additional sacrifice to France, of every remaining principle, upon which her safety or greatness as a Maritime Power depends. You must never suffer it to be lost sight of, that the Blockade of 1806 is the true hinge, upon which the whole Contest turns: whatever may have been supposed to be the State of the Question before, it is now plain from the manner in which France brings forward her pretensions, that the abandonment of the principles, on which that Measure was founded;—vizt.—the established principles of Maritime Blockade, as distinguished from those now pro-

---
[43] F. O. 115 : 23.

mulgated by France, has been throughout the invariable and indispensable condition, on the part of France, of the Repeal of the Berlin and Milan Decrees. Unless Great Britain was prepared to relinquish these principles, She might surrender her System of Retaliation to America, but she could not deliver herself thereby from the interdict of France.

It is not therefore merely a Contest with respect to the Orders in Council. It is a contest for the most antient, undoubted and essential maxims of Maritime Law; and America must never be allowed to state, that Great Britain has had any option of complying with her demands, but at the Expence of surrendering her most vital and essential Rights to France, and standing helpless and disarmed in the presence of her adversary.

To what purpose begin by rescinding the Orders in Council, in order to conciliate America, when it has been avowed that the Decrees of France, would continue in force, not only against Great Britain, but against America herself, if America acted in contravention of her new Code? Why should America if she means to resist, and not to submit to France, wish us to retract them? Can she in the former case find so cheap and so effective an Instrument of coercion against that Power?

You may put the whole upon this issue: Will America join France in an attempt to impose a System upon the World, which, under the mask of Municipal Regulations, aided by the overwhelming principles of incorporating or invading all States, reluctant, or disobedient to her Will, is to give to that Nation absolute Dominion over the Land, whilst the Cover of a Neutral Flag is to render her Power as unassailable by Sea?

Great Britain, you may declare, has other views and duties to perform, and from the performance of those duties she cannot shrink.

The Instructions you now receive will enable you to represent, that nothing has been omitted to conciliate America. Every minor Question has been conceded; and nothing remains but fundamental Rights, which can admit of no compromise. The decision therefore rests with America, and it is to be hoped her determination will be founded on a fair review of the Claims and Interests of both States.

CASTLEREAGH TO FOSTER [44]

No. 11. Duplicate.   FOREIGN OFFICE, April 10th. 1812.

Sir,

I am to acquaint you, that your dispatches, as numbered in the margin [to No. 35 of 1811, and to No. 10 of 1812], have been received and laid before the Prince Regent.

---

[44] F. O. 115 : 23.

In reply to your dispatch No. 30 an answer, bearing date the 18th February was prepared by the Marquess Wellesley, but not having been forwarded at the time, it is only necessary for me now shortly to call your attention to that dispatch, for the purpose of cautioning you against giving any countenance hereafter to reports or expectations of a change of policy on the part of this Country, altogether unwarranted by the tenor of your Instructions. Altho' you made no direct declaration to that effect, it is a hazardous expedient to give indirect encouragement to false hopes.[45] The Line pursued by Great Britain upon all the leading principles of the Controversy with America, has been clear and uniform. These have been distinctly laid down in all your Instructions and I am to desire you will not encourage the expectation, that, under any Circumstances, it can be departed from.

P. S.

In case the question of alledged British Interference in the hostilities between the United States of America, and the Indian Nations should be revived, I send you the enclosed Copies and Extracts of Correspondence between General Sir James Craig and the Earl of Liverpool, which may enable you to give an official refutation of so unjust an imputation on the character of Great Britain.[46]

CASTLEREAGH TO FOSTER [47]

No. 12.   FOREIGN OFFICE, 17th: April, 1812.

Sir,

I enclose the copy of a communication made sometime since to the Marquess Wellesley by Mr. Russell, American Charge d'Affaires at this Court.[48]

You will observe, that this comunication established nothing beyond the mere fact, that certain American Vessels, visited at Sea by British Cruizers, or touching at British Ports, have recently been released by the Prize Courts at Paris, under circumstances not explained, and at a period prior to the date of the Duke of Bassano's report.[49] It does not alledge, that they have been released upon any alledged repeal of the obnoxious Decrees replacing neutral Rights generally, upon the footing, on which they stood, prior to the enactment of those Decrees.

---

[45] In his dispatch No. 30, to Wellesley, Dec. 11, 1811, F. O. 5 : 77, Foster stated that to offset the clamor for war he had "allowed from hints and inuendos inferences to be drawn that possibly a modification or change in the Orders in Council may soon be effected."

[46] See Foster to Monroe, June 7, 1812, with enclosures, *A. S. P., F. R.,* III, 462–464.

[47] Draft, F. O. 5 : 83.

[48] Russell's letter to Wellesley of Feb. 8, 1812, enclosing a letter from Joel Barlow, American Minister to France, of Jan. 29, 1812, is printed in *A. S. P., F. R.,* III, 425.

[49] The report communicated to the Conservative Senate, March 10, 1812. See note 81, p. 353, *supra.*

The most, then, that can be inferred from this Statement, is, that there has been a partial relaxation of these decrees in favor of the United States, in acknowledgement probably of the hostile measures adopted by America against our Commerce and in the hope of thereby encouraging her to measures of more decisive hostility against this Country.

The report in question clearly shews, that, if these Cases were decided, upon any general principle incompatible with the Provisions of the Berlin and Milan decrees, the Enemy has already abandoned that principle, and reverted to the full rigour of his prohibitory Rules. If such a proposition can now be disputed, the important State paper above alluded to renders it more than ever incumbent on you to maintain, that the actual Instrument must be produced, by which the Repeal is alledged to have been effected, before the British Government can be justly called upon to admit, that it has taken place.

CASTLEREAGH TO FOSTER [50]

No. 13.   FOREIGN OFFICE, April 17th. 1812.
Sir,

The Result of the Instructions which I have transmitted to you by Command of His Royal Highness The Prince Regent, on the subject of the pretended Repeal of the French Decrees, will shew you, that it is His Royal Highness's Pleasure, that, in all the discussions which you may hold with the American Secretary of State, upon the Conduct of His Government; You will constantly maintain the necessity of the Production of the Document, by which those Decrees are absolutely and unconditionally repealed, before His Majesty's Government can think the moment is arrived, when they may justly be called upon to act upon the supposition of such Repeal; And in case the American Government shall attempt to quit this, the real point at issue, and shall advert to the Position that, assuming the Fact of the Repeal, quo ad America, America is in that supposition entitled to demand, that the British Orders in Council should be rescinded, as far as they affect America; in answer to this hypothetical case, you will always reply, that Great Britain can never allow, that any such partial Repeal of the French Decrees (even supposing that it had taken place) can be pleaded in defeasance of Her Natural Rights: [51] An Acquiescence in such a Principle on the part of Great Britain, would be to give to France the power, not only of delivering herself from the pressure of the War, as may best suit her own pur-

---

[50] Draft, F. O. 5 : 83. Also printed in *Papers Presented to Parliament in 1813*, pp. 519-520.

[51] This was stoutly maintained by Foster to the end : see his note to Monroe of June 14, 1812 (ten days after the House had passed the war bill, and three days before the Senate concurred in it), *A. S. P., F. R.*, III, 470.

poses, but of choosing which Neutral shall be favored, and in what degree, by both Belligerents, is a doctrine so monstrous that it cannot possibly be assented to on the part of this Country.

CASTLEREAGH TO FOSTER [52]

FOREIGN OFFICE, April 21, 1812.

Sir,

I transmit to you herewith the Copy of a Declaration and of an Order in Council, which His Royal Highness the Prince Regent has this day been pleased, in the Name and on the Behalf of His Majesty, to issue, in consequence of the official Declaration on the part of the French Government of the 10th of last Month, respecting the Berlin and Milan Decrees [53]—and I am to desire that you will lose no time in communicating the same to the American Government.

CASTLEREAGH TO FOSTER [54]

No. 14.   FOREIGN OFFICE, 22 April 1812.

Sir,

I herewith enclose to you a copy of the official note [55] with which I transmitted to Mr. Russell the American Chargé des Affaires at this Court, the declaration and order in Council, which were issued by H. R. H. The Prince Regent on the 21st. instant.

Nothing has occurred since the date of my last dispatch to make it necessary for me to add any thing to the Instructions you have already received.

CASTLEREAGH TO FOSTER [56]

Private.   FOREIGN OFFICE, April 27. 1812.

Sir,

I deem it proper to apprize you, "unofficially" of an overture for Peace received on the 20th. inst. from Paris. As far as the Separate Interests of Great Britain are concerned, It may be considered highly liberal, as the basis Imposed would leave His Majesty in possession of *all his Conquests* in all parts of the World, but the demands of france with respect to Spain are such, as afford little reason to expect that an arrangement, consistent with good faith, and general policy

---

[52] F. O. 115 : 23.

[53] The declaration and order of April 21, 1812 were to the effect that if the Berlin and Milan decrees were, by some authentic act of the French government, absolutely and unconditionally revoked, Great Britain without any further order would revoke absolutely and wholly her orders-in-council of Jan. 7, 1807 and April 26, 1809. They are printed, together with Castlereagh's covering note to Jonathan Russell of April 21, 1812, in *A. S. P., F. R.*, III, 429–432.

[54] Draft, F. O. 5 : 83.

[55] See note 53 above.

[56] Draft, F. O. 5 : 83.

is likely at present to be effected. I mention this, in case a Knowledge of the fact might be of use in the Course of your Discussions, in which case it may be stated Confidentially.

Mr. Russell has replied to my note accompanying the order and Declaration, assigning some bad reasons why the Measure now adopted by this Gov't should not be satisfactory to America.[57] I did not inform him of the Propositions relative to the Licence Trade; which you were authorized to make to His Gov't.

You will be able now to press, that no further act on the part of this State is wanting, to effect the actual Revocation of the orders in Council; the Act of france will be sufficient in itself to perfect that measure, and the fact established in a Court of Law will secure to the Americans the full benefits of such revocation.

P. S. I have directed a Copy of Mr. Russell's Answer to be sent for your Information.

CASTLEREAGH TO FOSTER [58]

No. 15.   FOREIGN OFFICE, May 7th 1812.
Sir,
Your Dispatches to No. 16 have been received and laid before The Prince Regent.

The Intelligence communicated in your Dispatch No. 13, of the disclosure made by Mr. John Henry,[59] of his Correspondence with Sir James Craig, and with His Majesty's Government, had reached this Country, through the American Newspapers, a few days previous to the receipt of your Dispatches; and I have only waited for the Arrival of your Official Communications, in order to convey to you the Commands of His Royal Highness The Prince Regent, with respect to the Language which you are to hold to the Government of the United States upon this subject.

Immediately on the Receipt of this Dispatch, you will deliver to Mr. Monroe an Official Note,[60] by Command of His Royal Highness The Prince Regent, in which you will, in the strongest and most direct Terms, disclaim, on the part of this Government, any knowledge of the nature of the Mission upon which Mr. Henry was sent by Sir James Craig, until several Months after the whole was terminated,

[57] Russell's reply of April 25, 1812, is printed in *A. S. P., F. R.*, III, 427–429, and in *Papers Presented to Parliament in 1813*, pp. 192–201.
[58] F. O. 115 : 23.
[59] On the disclosures of John Henry, British secret agent employed in New England during the Embargo discontent of 1809 by Governor General Craig of Canada, see *A. S. P., F. R.*, III, 545–557; *Report on Canadian Archives*, 1896, pp. 38–69; and E. A. Cruikshank, *The Political Adventures of John Henry*.
[60] The disavowal was made orally to Monroe by Anthony St. John Baker, the British chargé. See Baker to Castlereagh, Aug. 24, 1812, *Papers Presented to Parliament in 1813*, pp. 717–719.

and after Mr. Henry had been specially recalled from the Territory of the United States;—You will add that no Authority, or Instructions, were ever given by this Government to Sir James Craig, to send into The United States any Mission of the description alluded to.

You will acquaint the American Government, that, upon the receipt of Sir James Craig's Dispatch of the 9th. of June 1809, by which the Instructions upon which Mr. Henry acted, were first made known to His Majesty's Government, it appeared to them that this Person was sent into the United States for the purpose of procuring Information at a period of menaced Hostilities, when Military Preparations for the Invasion of Canada, were actually making, and when the Secretary of State of America had recently declared to Mr. Erskine, His Majesty's Minister in America, (who, as his Duty required, had reported that declaration to Sir James Craig)—that, under the Conduct which had been pursued, both by Great Britain and France, towards America, his Government would feel itself justified in commencing Hostilities against either Belligerent without further Notice.

It was under these circumstances, and at a period when the Military Defence of the Government committed to his Charge, was considered by that Officer as likely to be materially affected by the Temper and the Disposition of the Neighbouring States to act against Canada, that the Instructions in question were framed by him, without the Authority or Knowledge of the Government at Home;—It never was, however, intended in any manner to approve, nor is it now proposed to justify the Clause in those Instructions, which, even under the Menace of Attack, authorized the Agent to receive, in Sir James Craig's Name, Communications from leading Men in those States, of the course they were likely to adopt in the event of War taking place between Great Britain and America.

When this subject was first brought under the observation of His Majesty's Government, the Transaction was some Months gone by;—the Intentions of the Governor of Canada were proved, by the recal[1] of the Agent, to have been dependent on the Expectation of approaching Hostilities; the part of the Instructions which appeared objectionable had never been acted upon; and the pacific Intentions of His Majesty's Government towards America, had been so recently, pointedly, and expressly conveyed to that Officer, in a Dispatch bearing date the 9th. of April, as to preclude any apprehensions on their part with respect to the future.

With regard to the recommendation which Mr. Henry received on leaving England last Year, (Two Years after the Termination of the whole Transaction) you will explain to the American Government that there was no intention whatever, in taking this Step, to convey, either to Mr. Henry or to Sir George Prevost,[61] any direct or indirect Approbation of the Instructions under which Mr Henry acted. The recommendation given to him with a view to his receiving Remuneration, was considered merely as the fulfilment of a Promise made to him by Sir James Craig.

You will, on the same occasion, intimate to the American Government,—but in terms as little calculated as possible to augment the Irritation which this Disclosure appears to have occasioned,—that His Royal Highness The Prince Regent has felt an equal degree of surprize and concern, that the American Government, upon receiving the Communication from Mr. Henry (by whatever motives and means that Communication had been drawn from him) did not, in compliance with the course of all Diplomatic Usage between Nations at Peace, require an Explanation of the Transaction through you, or through their own accredited Agent at this Court, before they resorted to the extraordinary measure of bringing forward a Charge of this Nature against the British Government, upon an ex parte Statement, and upon Documents the Fidelity of which they had not the means of verifying.

This Act, however, on the part of the American Government, cannot be suffered to impede the frank and explicit Explanation which the British Government deems it due to its own Character to make upon this Subject; and His Royal Highness The Prince Regent confidently hopes and expects, that the Declaration and Explanations, which you are directed by this Dispatch to address to the American Government, will be received by them in the same Disposition to remove every existing Cause of Difference between the Two Countries, with which I have been commanded by the Prince Regent to address them to you.

CASTLEREAGH TO FOSTER [62]

Private.   FOREIGN OFFICE, May 7, 1812.

Sir,

I am unwilling to add to the voluminous Instructions with which I have furnished you by the Prince Regent's Commands on the Subject of the existing discussions with America, until your Receipt of my earliest Communications, and your Report of the manner in which they were received by the American Government, shall enable this Government to come to some more accurate decision, upon what may be the probable line of conduct which America will adopt towards England and France under existing Circumstances. I have

[61] Sir George Prevost in 1811 had succeeded Sir James Craig as Governor General of Canada.
[62] F. O. 115 : 23.

not therefore sent you Mr. Russell's Note [63] in an Official form, nor am I to direct you officially to make any representation to the American Government upon its contents. I have however thought proper to furnish you with the inclosed Draft Copy of this Document, accompanied with a few Marginal Notes, from which you will be able to judge of the manner in which it has been received by His Majesty's Government and you will know how to regulate your language on the subject, should it ever be introduced in your conversations with the President or with Mr. Monroe. It is not however intended that you should make any official use of these notes, except in as far as they coincide with the letter and spirit of your Instructions.

CASTLEREAGH TO FOSTER [64]

No. 16.   FOREIGN OFFICE, 7th May 1812.

Sir,

In reply to your separate dispatch of the 12th Ultimo, enclosing the detailed Cases of Three American Citizens, supposed to be now on board British Ships of War, I am able to acquaint you, for the Information of the Persons interested in the Situation of these Three Individuals, That from a Report received yesterday from The Lords of the Admiralty, it appears that the first named in the Margin [Richd. M. Sydnor] [65] was ordered to be discharged from the Narcissus on the 29th day of January last, and that the Cases of the others are now under Enquiry; the Result of which will be communicated without Loss of Time.

CASTLEREAGH TO FOSTER [66]

Private.   FOREIGN OFFICE, May 9, 1812.

Sir,

In addition to the Instructions which are contained in my Dispatch No. 15, of this date, directing you to make a formal and direct Disavowal of any intention on the part of this Government, to create Dissentions amongst the Citizens of the United States, during a State of Amity and Peace between the two Countries, I have thought it expedient to furnish You with the enclosed Copies and Extracts from the private and official Correspondence between Sir James Craig and the Colonial Department in the years 1808–1809.

A List of these Papers is subjoined to this Letter.

---

[63] Russell's note of April 25, 1812. See note 57, p. 373, *supra.*
[64] F. O. 115 : 23.
[65] The other two impressed Americans were Alexander McPherson and Philip Read Copper.
[66] F. O. 115 : 23.

You will not fail to perceive from an attentive perusal of these Documents, that all the communications received from Sir James Craig respecting Mr. Henry, previous to that dated the 9th. of June 1809, represented him merely in the Light of a person in the first instance volunteering, and afterwards employed to procure, *intelligence* on the existing State of Parties in the Eastern States of America. You will see that, in the whole of this Transaction, Sir James Craig was actuated by no other feeling than a desire to possess himself of such information from the neighbouring States, as might enable him in the event of War the better to defend the British Dominions in North America; for which purpose it was material he should ascertain the probable means the American Govt. had, from the disposition of their Subjects, for assembling an army to invade Canada. It was not less important to the Arrangement of his System of Defence, and especially to the distribution of his Army, to be informed, what part the Eastern States, upon the Commencement of Hostilities, were likely to take. The particular instruction given to Mr. Henry cannot be justified, but that such was the sole purpose for which this Agent was employed, is proved by his being recalled the moment the menace of Invasion was at an End.

In all communications from the Government to Sir James Craig upon this subject, You will observe nothing more was in Contemplation than the procuring of Intelligence, and from no part of the Correspondence can it be possible to draw the Conclusion, that this Government ever entertained a Wish to bring about a Dissolution of the American Confederacy. On the contrary, my Letter of the 8th. of April, 1809 [67] demonstrates, that their sincere and anxious purpose was to conciliate America, and so conduct their Measures of Precaution in Canada, as to avoid every Circumstance that was likely to irritate or to lead to War.

I have also furnished You with the annexed Copies and Extracts of four Despatches from Mr. Erskine dated 4th December 1808 and Jany. 1st and 3d, and 16th March 1809 which go distinctly to prove, First, that Sir James Craig had ample and sufficient Cause for the Alarm of Invasion under which he acted upon this occasion, and, Secondly, That the fact referred to in Sir James Craig's Instruction to Mr. Henry, namely, the probable Dissolution of the American Confederacy in the Event of a War with this Country pressing upon the prosperity and Resources of a particular part of the Union, was one of general Notoriety—that it was, at the time, reported to his Govt. by Mr. Erskine in a Despatch since given to Parliament, which

---

[67] Castlereagh was then Secretary of State for War and Colonies; his instructions to Craig in 1808 and 1809 are calendared in the Canadian *Report of the Public Archives*, 1930, pp. 15–24.

Despatch has laid upon the Table of both Houses since the Month of February, 1810,[68] without being supposed by the Government of America to afford any Indication, that the Policy of this Country was directed to foment that disposition in the Eastern States, however necessary and justifiable it might be, in the Event of actual War, to take advantage of it in our own Defence.

I hope that the Explanation afforded to You in this Despatch, will effectually relieve You from the Embarrassments in which you were placed by the extraordinary Disclosure of Mr. Henry's Papers; and will enable You, in your official and private Conversations to deny in the strictest and most direct Terms, any intent whatever in the minds of His Majesty's Govt., either in 1809 or 1811, to countenance or encourage a Dissolution of the American Union; as well as to correct any Misconceptions that may arise, from the very loose and inaccurate manner in which Statements made in both Houses of Parliament on this subject have been reported in the Newspapers.

P. S.   I think it proper to add to the above for your information that there is every reason to believe that all the Documents published under the name of Mr. Henry's letters to Sir James Craig in the year 1809, have been prepared for the purpose in America, as upon comparing them with the original letters, in the War Department, they not only differ in the dates of time and place, but there are scarcely ten Sentences in the whole collection, which correspond exactly with the originals—so that it is more than probable that Mr. Henry had only Memoranda and notes with him, of the general purport of his letters, but was not in possession of Drafts or Copies of any of them.[69] You are at liberty to acquaint Mr. Munroe with this fact; but you need not lay any stress upon this circumstance.

In order to remind the American Government of the pacific disposition of this Country towards America in 1809, you will state to them the circumstance of the amicable Manner in which the affair which took place at Niagara, when several British boats were destroyed,[70] was terminated by negotiation between The Agents of the two Governments.

---

[68] Reference is made to Erskine's dispatch to Canning, Dec. 4, 1808, ordered to be printed with other material Feb. 5, 1810, and printed in *Correspondence Relating to America, Presented to Parliament in 1810* (A. Strahan, London, 1811), pp. 31–37. Erskine stated (p. 37) that a war with Great Britain would endanger the popularity of the Republican administration and, perhaps, the safety of the American Union.

[69] E. A. Cruikshank, *The Political Adventures of John Henry*, pp. 194–197, prints in parallel columns Henry's original letter to Sir James Craig, from Burlington, Vt., Feb. 14, 1809, and the garbled copy of it which Henry gave to the American government.

[70] See Canning to Erskine, Aug. 4, 1808, No. 8, Jan. 5, 1809, No. 2, *supra.*

WILLIAM HAMILTON TO FOSTER [71]

FOREIGN OFFICE, May 11th. 1812.

My dear Sir,

A circumstance of the most melancholy and unexpected Nature has taken place this afternoon, which is the cause of my addressing you at the moment of dispatching the Messenger, Shawe, with Lord Castlereagh's Dispatches to You of the 7th and 9th inst.

Mr. Perceval [72] was assassinated this afternoon about 5 o'clock, on Entering the lobby of the House of Commons.

An Event of this Description will of course create great alarm throughout this Country and abroad—and is not unlikely to be misinterpreted.

I have however the Satisfaction, amidst the universal gloom which this horrid transaction has thrown over this whole Town, to assure you, that as far as the Enquiries have as yet been made into the causes which have influenced it, It does not appear that It was occasioned by any feeling of a public Nature. It has been, as far as is yet known, the act of an Individual, who has fancied himself to be aggrieved by not receiving from this Govt. the redress which he conceived himself to be Entitled to, for some losses which he experienced several years ago in a Commercial Transaction at Petersburgh. The Name of the assassin is Bellingham [73] and He has long petitioned at the public offices. His case has received in all quarters the most attentive Examination, and it was found totally undeserving the compensation he claimed.

Our latest Intelligence from Lisbon left Lord Wellington's Head Quarters at Alfayates on the road from Badajoz to Cuidad Rodrigo, the investment of which place His Lordship would relieve in a few days' March.

Nothing positive is known of the Movements of the french troops in the North—but It was supposed they were advancing from the Oder to the Vistula.

CASTLEREAGH TO FOSTER [74]

No. 17.   FOREIGN OFFICE, 13 May 1812.

Sir,

In further reference to your dispatch of the 12th of March last and to mine of the 7th Instant I am to state to you for the information of the relatives of Philip Read Copper that by a communication from The Lords Comm'rs. of the Admiralty to this Department I learn

---

[71] F. O. 115 : 23. Hamilton was under secretary for foreign affairs, 1809–1822.

[72] Spencer Perceval (1762–1812), prime minister since October of 1809. The Earl of Liverpool became prime minister in June of 1812; Viscount Castlereagh continued as foreign secretary.

[73] John Bellingham.

[74] Draft, F. O. 5 : 83.

that no such person as P. R. Copper, an American, is on board H. M. Frigate Bacchante to which Ship the Crew of the Eurydice were turned over.

CASTLEREAGH TO FOSTER [75]

No. 18.   FOREIGN OFFICE, June 6. 1812.

Sir,

In reply to your separate dispatch of the 5th of May last, containing Mr. Pitkin's application for the discharge from His Majesty's Service of James Brown, a Citizen of the U. S. of America,[76] I have the satisfaction to inform you that the Lords Comm'rs. of the Admiralty have given orders for his immediate discharge.

The Crew of the Conqueror on board of which ship he lately was, were turned over, on that vessel being paid off to the Barham and Chatham.[77]

CASTLEREAGH TO FOSTER [78]

No. 19.   FOREIGN OFFICE, June 13, 1812,

Sir,

In reference to Your dispatch No. 17. of the 18th: of September, 1811, relating to the conduct of Captain Pasco of His Majesty's Ship Tartarus, in anchoring in Hampton Roads, (as it was affirmed, without having gone through the necessary formalities in reporting his Vessel) and in sending prisoners on shore while lying in those Roads, and thereby occasioning some Irritation at Norfolk, I am commanded by H. R. H. the Prince Regent to instruct You to state to the Government of the United States, that this Government, anxious to pay attention to every circumstance affecting the good Understanding between the two Nations, immediately caused Enquiry to be made into the circumstances alluded to; and You will acquaint them, that, from the result of such Enquiry it has appeared, that Captain Pasco arrived on the 24th: July in Hampton Roads charged with Dispatches to Yourself: and That on the 3rd August, in pursuance of his Instructions, He left those Roads to cruize at a distance from the Coast, having first regularly apprized His Majesty's Vice Consul at Norfolk, that on or about the 20th: August, he should again call there for any Dispatches which might be ready from him or from You for the Admiral at Halifax.

---

[75] Draft. F. O. 5 : 83.

[76] In his separate dispatch of May 5, 1812, F. O. 5 : 85, Foster had enclosed a copy of a letter from Timothy Pitkin, Federalist member of the House of Representatives from Connecticut, requesting the release of James Brown, a native of Connecticut, impressed in 1808–09. Foster believed that the request deserved attention because Pitkin's friendly disposition had been shown by his addressing the letter to the British Minister and not to the State Department, and because Pitkin forebore to state in his letter instances of severe treatment accorded Brown.

[77] In a note to Foster of June 18, 1812, F. O. 115 : 23, Under Secretary Wm. Hamilton informed him that the Admiralty had further reported that James Brown was not to be found on board either the *Barham* or the *Chatham*.

[78] Draft, F. O. 5 : 83.

On the short Interval between his departure and his return he detained two American Vessels, which Vessels have since been condemned as Prize at Halifax.

On Captain Pasco's Arrival off the Capes of Virginia, he sent his first Lieutenant on Shore for his dispatches, without intending to anchor; but on the following day, when expecting to be joined by the Lieutenant, for which purpose he had kept close in with Cape Henry, it came on to blow a heavy Gale with thick weather, and he was obliged to take Shelter in Hampton Roads. Captain Pasco allowed no communication with the Shore until after the arrival on board of his Lieutenant, and then, at the request of the American Seamen, whom he had taken out of the detained Vessels, not as prisoners, but for the better securing of the Vessels, He allowed them to proceed, where they' thought proper, in a Passage Boat. There might have been subject of Complaint, had Captain P: acted otherwise.

On the same day, his dispatches being now on board, and a favorable Breeze having sprung up, he determined to proceed to Sea, and with that view endeavoured, but in vain, to purchase his Anchor; finding his efforts fruitless, (the Anchor he supposed having hooked something) and the Ebb Tide having nearly done, Captain Pasco, anxious to execute his orders, ordered the cable to be cut, leaving however a Buoy upon it, giving notice of the circumstance to the Consul at Norfolk, and requesting him to use other means for raising the Anchor and recovering it for His Majesty.

This circumstance accounts for the misrepresentation in the American Newspapers alluded to In Your dispatch, in which it is said that "Captain Pasco was aware of his imprudence early enough to make his Escape, but, as it would seem, by cutting his Cable."

I am to desire that, in making the United States' Government acquainted with the details of this Transaction, You will express the Gratification which H R: H: the Prince Regent feels that there does not appear in Capt. P's Conduct Any thing hostile to the Rights of the United States, but on the contrary an Obedience to the Orders of H: R: H: to conciliate the Exercise of His own duties with the strictest Respect to the Rights of other Nations.

CASTLEREAGH TO FOSTER [79]

Most Secret.
Duplicate.
No. 20.   FOREIGN OFFICE, June 17, 1812.
Sir,

As it is desirable that you should be apprized of the Intentions of this Government respecting the Orders in Council as early as pos-

---

[79] F. O. 115 : 23. The draft of this instruction is printed in *Papers Presented to Parliament in 1813*, pp. 760–762.

sible, I enclose a Memorandum of the Declaration, which has been made by His Majesty's Ministers in general terms, in both Houses of Parliament.

The Step taken by the French Government by the publication (so repeatedly called for in vain) of a Decree for the Repeal of the Berlin and Milan Decrees, as far as they relate to American Vessels,[80] appears to have afforded an opportunity of putting to the Trial the real disposition of that Government, to proceed towards a restoration of the usual Intercourse of Nations during War; and at the same time of putting equally to the test the disposition of the American Government to terminate its differences with Great Britain, and to concur with us in Some Amicable Arrangement, by which the Invasions of France upon Neutral Rights may, if She perseveres in them, be satisfactorily resisted.

In a few days you will receive some formal Document upon this Subject, with Instructions as to your conduct towards the American Government. In the mean time I only intend this communication to enable you to open in conversation the general nature of the Measure, about to be taken: but you will not present any Note to the American Government, nor even allow to be read the enclosed Memorandum, nor permit any Minute to be taken of your conversation upon this Subject, as the Arrangement in its details must be considered as yet open to discussion.[81]

[Memorandum enclosed in No. 20.]

Duplicate.

Memorandum

The Revocation of the Orders in Council, as far as regards America, to take effect on the 1st day of August next, but the Orders to revive on the 1st of May 1813, unless the Conduct of the French Government, and the Result of the Communication with the Government of the United States should be such, as to enable His Majesty to declare their Revival at that time unnecessary.

---

[80] The Decree of St. Cloud, bearing the date of April 28, 1811, printed in *A. S. P., F. R.*, III, 603. Enclosed with the above instruction was a copy of Jonathan Russell's letter to Castlereagh of May 18, 1812 (printed in *ibid.*, III, 432), transmitting a copy of the Decree of St. Cloud. In a note accompanying the above instruction, Under Secretary Hamilton, at the request of Castlereagh, told Foster that the Ministry had not acted sooner upon Russell's communication because of the political uncertainty caused by Perceval's death, which lasted until Lord Liverpool became prime minister on June 8. Hamilton to Foster, June 17, 1812, F. O. 115 : 23.

[81] This instruction of June 17, 1812 was not received at Washington until Aug. 5, 1812 (by Anthony St. John Baker, British agent, to whom Foster had sent it upon receiving it at Halifax, July 22, 1812, as he was about to depart for England. *Papers Presented to Parliament in 1813*, pp. 775–784). Meanwhile at Washington, on June 18, 1812, President Madison had approved the act of Congress declaring that a state of war existed between Great Britain and the United States.

If, however, within 14 days after the Declaration, to be hereafter transmitted, shall have been duly notified to the Government of the United States, the exclusion of His Majesty's Ships of War from the Ports of the United States, and the restrictive Measures on the Trade and Navigation of His Majesty's Subjects shall not have been revoked for the same period, in that case the Orders in Council shall immediately revive.

CASTLEREAGH TO FOSTER [82]

Circular.   FOREIGN OFFICE, June 23, 1812.
Sir,
I transmit to you for your information, a printed Copy of an Order in Council which His Royal Highness the Prince Regent acting in the Name and on the Behalf of His Majesty, was this day pleased to issue for the Revocation (on the conditions therein specified) of the Orders in Council of the 7th of January 1807, and of the 26th of April 1809, so far as may regard American Vessels and their Cargoes being American property, from the 1st of August next.[83]

CASTLEREAGH TO FOSTER [84]

No. 21.   Duplicate.   FOREIGN OFFICE, 25th June 1812.
Sir,
You will lose no time in communicating officially to the Govt. of the United States the enclosed copy of an order passed by H. R. H. the Prince Regent in Council on the 23d. Inst: and you will call upon The President to exercise without delay the Powers which he possesses, to annul by proclamation, all those restrictive Laws which either interdict the Commerce of His Majesty's Subjects, or exclude the Ships of War of Great Britain from the harbours of the U. S.

Should any acts of Congress be in force of a like nature over which the President has no immediate Jurisdiction, you will claim on the part of your Govt. the repeal of such Laws at as early a period as circumstances will permit, and if you should deem it necessary, either from the injurious nature of the particular Laws, or from the interval that is likely to elapse before the ordinary meeting of Congress, you will represent to the American Government the importance of assembling that Body at an earlier period, with a view to this Special object.

---

[82] F. O. 115 : 23.
[83] Enclosed was a copy of a Supplement to *The London Gazette* of Tuesday, June 23, 1812, containing the order of that date. The order is printed in *A. S. P., F. R.*, III, 433.
[84] F. O. 115 : 23. The draft of this instruction, and its enclosures, are printed in *Papers Presented to Parliament in 1813*, pp. 763–770, 738–741.

I enclose herewith the form of an Instrument (No. 1) to be communicated by you to the American Secretary of State, notifying the above mentioned order in Council, and the conditions, on the observance of which the revocation of the former Orders in Council with respect to America, is declared to depend; and I am to desire that in presenting this Instrument, you will declare the period within which (upon conference with the American Govt.) you may deem it proper to require the President to perform the Acts requisite on his part, to annul the restrictive Laws in question.

The Instrument (No. 2) is to be used, in case the Govt. of the U. S., contrary to our just expectations, should refuse to abrogate the above Laws.[85] Should you unfortunately have ocasion to make use of this power, whereby the revocation of the Orders in Council will be rendered null and of no effect, you will lose no time in making the Same Public, transmitting immediate intelligence to His Majesty's Naval Commanders, on the American Station, desiring the same may be forthwith notified to the Naval Officers commanding at Jamaica, and in the West Indies.

You will observe that the present order upon the face of it contains an absolute and unqualified Revocation of the orders of Janry 1807 and of April 1809. It was at first in contemplation to make it only a suspensive Order for a fixed period, as was proposed by the American Govt. in 1809 to Mr. Jackson, with a view to a Negotiation in the interval upon all subsisting difficulties, Doubts however having been suggested whether the Powers given, by "The supplement to the non Intercourse Act["] would authorize the President to issue his proclamation upon a mere Suspension of the orders, It was deemed expedient to revoke the Orders, reserving the power to restore or modify them upon due notice.

This measure has been adopted by the Prince Regent in the earnest wish and hope, either that the Government of France, by further Relaxations of it's System, may render a perseverance, on the part of Great Britain, in retaliatory measures unnecessary, or if this hope should prove delusive, that H. M. Govt. may be enabled in the Absense of all irritating and restrictive Regulations on either side, to enter with the Govt. of the U. S. into amicable Explanations for the purpose of ascertaining whether if the necessity of retaliatory measures should unfortunately continue to operate, the particular measures to be acted upon by Great Britain can be rendered more acceptable to the American Government than those hitherto pursued.

---

[85] On the margin of the draft of this instruction, in F. O. 5 : 83, opposite this sentence, there was written the following observation, which does not appear in the instruction or in the printed copy of the draft: "The Amer: Gov't will probably accept from ye abrogation such Sections of the N. I. Act as might be necessary for the preservation of particular Manufactures already pretty far advanced. 'Q' would such exceptions be admitted?"

The revocation of the Orders in Council has been made to commence from the 1st. of Augt. next; when it is presumed the measure may be tendered for the acceptance of the American Govt. You will however observe that a retrospective effect is given to the order from the date of Mr. Russell's communication, so that America, if she entitles herself to the benefit of this revocation, will not sustain any disadvantage from the delay which has necessarily occurred, in bringing the french Decree under the consideration of His Majty's Govt.

You will not fail to observe that the present order in Council revokes the orders in Council of Janry 1807 and April 1809 only so far as relates to American Vessels, and their Cargoes being American Property: In any discussion upon this Subject you will be careful not to admit, that this alledged Repeal of the French Decrees, in favor of a particular State, can give that State a claim of right to a Corresponding Revocation of the British Orders in Council. The reasons for this distinction have been fully detailed in former Dispatches; and it is only necessary now to remark that the course adopted towards America upon the present occasion rests on a principle, of conciliation, and not of obligation.

Should any question be put to you, with respect to the existence of the Blockade of 1806, adhering to your former Language in maintaining of the lawfulness of that Blockade, you may acquaint the American Government, that in point of fact, this particular Blockade has been discontinued for a length of time, having been merged in the general retaliatory Blockade of the Enemy's Ports under the orders in Council, and that H. M. Govt. have no Intention of recurring to this, or to any other of the Blockades of the Enemy's Ports, founded upon the ordinary and accustomed principles of Maritime Law, which were in force previous to the Orders in Council without a new notice to neutral Powers in the usual form.

As the British Govt cannot doubt, that the present measure will immediately lead to an amicable Understanding, and a restoration of Intercourse between the two States, It is presumed the American Govt will lose no time in sending a Minister to this Country, possessed of their entire confidence.

The remoteness of America from the events passing in Europe making it of the utmost importance to the cultivation of a good understanding, that an accredited Minister, fully authorized to act for them in the many delicate cases that necessarily grow out of the present state of Europe, and the measures adopted by the Belligerents Should be resident at this Court.

The requisition contained in the order with respect to the immediate admission of British Ships of War into the Harbours and

Waters of the United States, rests upon the fact, that the Ships of war of the Enemy are at this moment admitted, those of His Majesty being excluded; and upon the undoubted claim the respective Belligerents have, to be placed in this respect upon the same footing, Should french Ships of War be excluded, you are not [to] consider a corresponding exclusion as applied to ours, as necessarily invalidating the effects of the present order, the Grounds on which the measure is taken remaining to be subsequently discussed between the two Governments.[86]

[*Enclosure No. 1, in No. 21.*]

In obedience to directions received from his Court The Undersigned H. Bnic. Majty's Minister in America has the honor to transmit to Mr. Monroe the inclosed Document being an Order of H. R. H. The Prince Regent in Council in the name and on the behalf of His Majty, bearing date the 23d day of June last, revoking from the 1st day of Augt 1812 so much of the Orders in Council of the 7th of Janry 1807 and of the 26th of April 1809, as may regard American Vessels and their Cargoes being American Property.

The Undersigned solicits the attention of the Govt of the U S of America, to that part of the *Order* which relates to the time, when it may be expected that the Govt of the said U. S., will conformable to it's repeated declarations revoke or cause to be revoked the Act or Acts by which H. B. Majty's Ships of War, are excluded from entering the Ports and Waters of the U. S. on the same terms on which French Ships are admitted therein, and by which the Commercial intercourse between Great Britain and the U. S. is interdicted.

The Undersigned begs leave at the same time to signify to Mr. Monro[e] that he is ready and desirous to receive from Mr. Monroe such Communications on the subject of those Acts as may prevent the friendly provisions of the Order of the 23d. day of June from becoming Null and of no effect.[87]

---

[86] In the draft of this instruction, in F. O. 5 : 83, the following postscript (which does not appear in the instruction or in the printed copy of the draft) was written in pencil: "The American Gov't must be satisfied with the Concession of the orders in Council[:] they may nevertheless, be disposed, Confiding in the general sentiments in favor of conciliating The U. States prevalent in England, to meet their demands on the Question of Impressment— indeed they have pledged themselves in a great Measure to require some explanation respecting it. it might therefore be necessary to know how far H. M. G[ovt.] are disposed to concede on this point. a generall Inquiry into the cases of the 10,000 Seamen of the U. S. now said to be on board H. M. Ships would no doubt go a great way in allaying the ferment that prevails respecting them—but it would be necessary to know precisely whether the Question of Impressment could be conceded or not. It does not seem probable that the U. S. Gov't would venture to continue the war until they should be perfectly satisfied respecting it, but they would scarcely be consistent in not requiring some Explanation."

[87] On the draft of this enclosure, in F. O. 5 : 83, at this point, and with reference to this paragraph, there was written in pencil the following observation : "perhaps the latter paragraph might be better reserved for a second note if necessary."

[*Enclosure No. 2, in No. 21.*]

In pursuance of the Provisions of the Order of H. R. H. the Prince Regent in Council in the Name and on the behalf of His B. Majty bearing date the 23d day of June 1812, and communicated by the Undersigned to Mr. Monroe Secretary of State to the Govt of the United States of America on the   day of   by which it is ordered and declared that,

"Whereas by certain Acts of the Govt of the U. S. all British Armed Vessels are excluded from the Harbours and Waters of the said U. S., the armed Vessels of France being permitted to enter therein and the Commercial intercourse between Great Britain and the said U. S. is interdicted, the commercial Intercourse between France and the said U. S. having been restored, H. R. H. the Prince Regent is pleased hereby further to declare, in the name and on the behalf of H. M., that if the Govt of the said U. S. shall not as soon as may be after the order shall have been duly notified by H. Mty's Minister in America, to the said Govt, revoke, or cause to be revoked the said Acts, The present Order shall in that Case after due notice signified by H. M. Minister in America to the said Govt be thenceforth null and of no Effect.["]

The Undersigned H. B. Mty's Minister in America does by virtue of the Powers with which he is invested hereby signify to Mr. Monroe that the Government of the U. S. of America has not as soon as might be revoked, or caused to be revoked the said Acts, But that the Govt of the said U. S. having (refused) [(] or declined) (or delayed) within a reasonable time to revoke the same, or cause the same to be revoked:—The aforesaid Order of the 23d June 1812 is thereby according to the Provisions thereof rendered, and is henceforth to be considered null and have no effect.

CASTLEREAGH TO FOSTER [88]

No. 22.   FOREIGN OFFICE, June 29. 1812.

Sir,

I transmit to you for your information and guidance the enclosed copies, of my note to Mr. Russell of the 23rd. inst. communicating to him the Order in Council of that date, Mr. Russell's answer of the 26th and of the observations which by His Royal Highness' commands I have addressed to him on the points alluded to in his letter.[89]

---

[88] F. O. 115 : 23.
[89] Castlereagh's two notes to Russell of June 23, 1812, the order-in-council of that date which he transmitted, Russell's note of June 26, and Castlereagh's reply of June 29, 1812, are printed in *A. S. P., F. R.*, III, 433–434. Castlereagh assured Russell that the blockade of May, 1806 had been discontinued.

CASTLEREAGH TO FOSTER [90]

No. 23. FOREIGN OFFICE, July 3. 1812.

Sir,

If the return of a good Understanding between the two Countries should appear to you to offer a favorable opportunity for bringing again before the notice of the American Government the Claims of the Original Grantees of Land in the Mississippi Territory, which have been frequently recommended to the attention of your Predecessors, and the latest Documents relating to which were transmitted in Mr. Canning's dispatch No. 10—of the 10th. July 1809, to Mr. Jackson; you will not omit to represent to that Government the Justice of their proposing some fixed Sum as a remuneration to these Persons for the Losses which they have sustained, not withstanding the legality of their Claims has never been disputed.[91]

These Claimants are aware that they must forego all hopes of regaining the possession of the Soil; and repeated References to the Courts of Justice in America would only create additional Sources of Irritation and Expense. They are still however entitled to a liberal Consideration on the part of the United States' Government, and it may fairly be expected from that Government that they should engage to propose to Congress, early in the ensuing Session, some general Measure for a liberal adjustment of these Claims. Such an Engagement Could not fail to present to the People of this Country a satisfactory proof that the Government of the United States are disposed cordially to unite with this Government in all such Measures as may be deemed proper and just, for a final and amicable settlement of all subsisting differences between the two Countries.

CASTLEREAGH TO FOSTER [92]

No. 24. FOREIGN OFFICE, July 8th: 1812.

Sir,

Official information has been received, by the Lords Commissioners of the Admiralty, that, when His Majesty's Brig "Castor" was lately at Lisbon, an apprentice of the name of Thomas Hepton was kidnapped from her Crew, by the Master of the American Brig "Industry" named Russell Bassett: I am to desire that you will acquaint the American Government with this fact, and request that they will take the most effectual means in their power to reprimand the said Master, and that they will make him duly sensible of the impropriety of his Conduct.

---

[90] F. O. 115 : 23.
[91] See note 7, p. 203 ; note 3, p. 247 ; note 63, p. 295, *supra*.
[92] F. O. 115 : 23.

Thomas Hepton having since made his escape from the American Ship, no further steps will be necessary, on the part of this Government, or on that of America, than what is above provided for.

CASTLEREAGH TO FOSTER [93]

No. 25.   FOREIGN OFFICE, July 8: 1812.
Sir,
Your dispatches to No. 40 of the 28th. May have been received and laid before The Prince Regent.

Altho' from the tenor of your dispatch No. 38 it appeared to be then probable that the Congress might recommend to the American Government the immediate issue of Letters of marque and reprisal against both Belligerents, this Government is willing to hope that a more mature consideration of the manner in which the Government of France have treated the proposals of the American Minister at Paris, may have so far opened the Eyes of the American people to the real state of their respective relations with Great Britain and France, as to induce them to pause before they resort to a measure of such direct hostility against this Country:—At the same time His Royal Highness The Prince Regent has judged it expedient that you should be furnished with Instructions for your conduct in such an Emergency.

The instructions which were forwarded to the commanding Officers of His Majesty's Ships and Vessels on the American Stations early in May last will have already pointed out to them the line of conduct, which they were to pursue, in the event of the Government of the United States having issued letters of Marque and reprisal against the Ships and Vessels of His Majesty or of His Subjects; in which event they were directed to proceed immediately to acts of hostility against the ships and vessels belonging to the Government and citizens of the United States. If this be unfortunately the state of the relations between the Two Countries at the period of time, when my dispatch arrives, announcing to you the repeal of the Orders in Council, by the Order in Council passed on the 23rd. Ultimo, You will immediately propose to the American Government, that if they will without delay recall their letters of marque and reprisal against the British Ships, you will instantly require the Commanders of His Majesty's Ships and Vessels on the American Stations to desist from corresponding measures of War, in order that not a moment may be lost in suspending, in every part of the World where the former Instructions may be eventually in force, the hostilities between His Majesty's Subjects and the citizens of the United States.

[93] F. O. 115 : 23.   The draft of this instruction is printed in *Papers Presented to Parliament in 1813*, pp. 771–772.

His Royal Highness's Commands have been signified to the Lords Commissioners of the Admiralty, that their Lordships do frame their Instructions to the commanding officers on the American Stations in conformity with the tenor of this dispatch. A copy of my letter to their Lordships upon this subject is herewith enclosed.[94]

CASTLEREAGH TO FOSTER [95]

No. 26.   FOREIGN OFFICE, July 17, 1812.

Sir,

I herewith enclose to you for your information and guidance copies of a note from Mr. Russell, of a letter from The Proctor on behalf of the Claimants in the case of the American Ship Snipe, and of the answers which have been severally returned to those papers relative to the Subject of the alledged Revocation of the Decrees of Berlin and Milan, prior to the promulgation of the Decree of the french Government, bearing date the 28th day of April 1811.[96]

---

[94] A copy of this letter, Viscount Castlereagh to the Lords of the Admiralty, May 9, 1812, is printed in *Papers Presented to Parliament in 1813*, pp. 773–775.

[95] Draft, F. O. 5 : 83.

[96] The enclosures are lacking. The dates of these letters on the margin of the draft are: Russell's of July 9, the Proctor's of July 15, and the answers of July 13, July 17, 1812.

INDEX

[Bibliographical references are entered but once usually; they refer to the first mention of the work or collection cited.]

391